BOHN'S ANTIQUARIAN LIBRARY.

MALLET'S
NORTHERN ANTIQUITIES.

YGGDRASILL,

The Mundane Tree

see p. 492.

NORTHERN ANTIQUITIES;

OR,

AN HISTORICAL ACCOUNT OF THE MANNERS, CUSTOMS, RELIGION
AND LAWS, MARITIME EXPEDITIONS AND DISCOVERIES,
LANGUAGE AND LITERATURE

OF THE

ANCIENT SCANDINAVIANS,

(DANES, SWEDES, NORWEGIANS AND ICELANDERS.)

WITH INCIDENTAL NOTICES RESPECTING OUR SAXON ANCESTORS.

TRANSLATED FROM THE FRENCH OF M. MALLET,

BY BISHOP PERCY.

NEW EDITION,

REVISED THROUGHOUT, AND CONSIDERABLY ENLARGED; WITH A TRANSLATION
OF THE PROSE EDDA FROM THE ORIGINAL OLD NORSE TEXT;
AND NOTES CRITICAL AND EXPLANATORY,

BY I. A. BLACKWELL, ESQ

TO WHICH IS ADDED,

AN ABSTRACT OF THE EYRBYGGJA SAGA,

By Sir Walter Scott.

LONDON:
HENRY G. BOHN, YORK STREET, COVENT GARDEN.

1847.

Reprinted from the edition of 1847, London
First AMS EDITION published 1968
Manufactured in the United States of America

Library of Congress Catalogue Card Number: 68-57868

AMS PRESS, INC.
New York, N.Y. 10003

THE EDITOR'S PREFACE.

BISHOP PERCY's Edition of M. Mallet's "Northern Antiquities" having been published at a period when the most important documents bearing on the subject were but imperfectly known, the present Editor has necessarily been obliged to revise the work throughout, and omit such portions as were founded on views obviously erroneous, or on authorities which the historical researches of the present age have shown to be fallacious; while he has sought to render the whole more in accordance with these researches, by insertions in the body of the text*, and notes critical and explanatory†. Supplementary chapters have also been added, in which, as well as in the remarks on the Prose Edda, several questions that have given rise to learned discussions and conflicting theories have been carefully investigated, and, perhaps, in some instances, placed under a novel point of view.

In the prosecution of his laborious task, the Editor has made it an invariable rule to test the statements even of writers who are generally regarded as authoritative on the subject, by referring to the Eddas, the Sagas, and the Grágás, from which almost all the information we possess respecting Scandinavia in the olden time has been, either mediately or immediately, derived. In short, he has endeavoured, by unremitting attention and diligent research, to make this one of the most complete works on Northern Antiquities hitherto published. How far he may have succeeded will be for the reader to judge; who, he trusts, will bear in mind the quaint admonition "of old Dan Geffry" that—

> " For every word men may not chide or pleine
> For in this world certain ne wight ther is
> That he ne doth or sayth sometime amis."

I. A. B.

London; August 16th, 1847.

---

* Distinguished by being placed within brackets.
† These notes, when they do not refer to his own text, are distinguished by the letters ED.

v

CONTENTS.

BISHOP PERCY'S PREFACE.

THE Author of the following work had a share in the education of that amiable Prince, Christian VII., king of Denmark. During his residence in the North, Mons. Mallet (who has all the talents of a fine writer) was engaged by the late king, Frederick V., to write a history of Denmark in the French language. By way of introduction to that history, he drew up these two prefatory volumes *, the merit of which has long been acknowledged in most parts of Europe.

Though intended only as a preliminary piece, it has all the merit of a complete independent work; and, except to the natives of Denmark, is much more interesting and entertaining than the history itself, which it was intended to precede. It very early engaged the attention of the present translator : whose reading having run somewhat in the same track with that of the author, made him fond of the subject, and tempted him to give in an English dress a work in which it was displayed with so much advantage. As he happened also to have many of the original books from which the French author had taken his materials, he flattered himself they would supply some illustrations, which might give an additional value to the version.

For this reason, as also to afford himself an agreeable amusement, the Translator some time ago undertook this work; but a series of unexpected avocations intervened, and it was thrown aside for several years. At length he was

* Bishop Percy's Translation of M. Mallet's work was published in 1770, in 2 vols. 8vo.

B

prevailed upon to resume it; and as many of his friends were so obliging as to share among them different parts of the translation, he had little more to do but to compare their performances with the original, and to superadd such remarks as occurred to him. These are distinguished from those of the author by the letter P.

He was the rather invited to undertake this task, as he perceived the author had been drawn in to adopt an opinion that has been a great source of mistake and confusion to many learned writers of the ancient history of Europe; viz., that of supposing the ancient Gauls and Germans, the Britons and Saxons, to have been all originally one and the same people; thus confounding the antiquities of the Gothic and Celtic nations. This crude opinion, which perhaps was first taken up by Cluverius*, and maintained by him with uncommon erudition, has been since incautiously adopted by Keysler† and Pelloutier‡, the latter of whom has, with great diligence and skill, endeavoured to confirm it. In short, so much learning and ingenuity have scarcely ever been more perversely and erroneously applied, or brought to adorn and support a more groundless hypothesis. This mistake the translator thought might be easily corrected in the present work; and by weeding out this one error, he hoped he should obtain the author's pardon, and acquire some merit with the English reader.

And that it is an error he thinks will appear from the attentive consideration of a few particulars, which can here be only mentioned in brief: for to give the subject a thorough discussion, and to handle it in its full extent, would far exceed the limits of this short preface.

The ancient and original inhabitants of Europe, according to Cluverius and Pelloutier, consisted only of two distinct races of men, viz., the Celts and Sarmatians; and that from

* Philippi Cluveri Germaniæ Antiquæ Libri Tres, &c. Lugduni Batav. Apud Elzev. 1616, folio.

† Antiquitates Selectæ Septentrionales et Celticæ, &c. Auctore Joh. Georgio Keysler, &c. Hannoveræ, 1720. 8vo.

‡ Histoire des Celtes, et particulièrement des Gaulois et des Germains, &c., par M. Simon Pelloutier. Haye, 1750. 2 tom. 12mo. This learned writer, who is a Protestant minister, counsellor of the Consistory, and librarian to the Academy at Berlin, is descended from a family originally of Languedoc, and was born at Leipsic, 27th October, 1694, O.S.

one or other of these, but chiefly from the former, all the ancient nations of Europe are descended. The Sarmatians or Sauromatæ, were the ancestors of the Sclavonian tribes, viz., the Poles, Russians, Bohemians, &c., who continue to this day a distinct and separate people, extremely different in their character, manners, laws and language, from the other race, which was that of the Celts, from whom (they will have it) were uniformly descended the old inhabitants of Gaul, Germany, Scandinavia, Britain and Spain, who were all included by the ancients under the general name of Hyperboreans, Scythians, and Celts, being all originally of one race and nation, and having all the same common language, religion, laws, customs and manners.

This is the position which these writers have adopted and maintained, with an uncommon display of deep erudition, and a great variety of specious arguments. But that their position, so far as relates to the Celts, is erroneous, and the arguments that support it inconclusive, will appear, if it can be shown, that ancient Germany, Scandinavia, Gaul and Britain, were not inhabited by the descendants of one single race; but on the contrary, divided between two very different people; the one of whom we shall call, with most of the Roman authors, Celtic, who were the ancestors of the Gauls, Britons, and Irish; the other Gothic or Teutonic, from whom the Germans, Belgians, Saxons and Scandinavians, derived their origin; and that these were *ab origine* two distinct people, very unlike in their manners, customs, religion, and laws.

As to the arguments by which Cluverius and Pelloutier support their hypothesis that the Gothic and Celtic nations were the same, they may all be reduced to two heads; viz., either to Quotations from the ancient Greek and Roman writers; or to Etymologies of the names of persons or places, &c.

With regard to the latter (viz., Etymologies), these two writers lay it down that the present high German is a genuine daughter of the ancient Celtic or Gaulish language[*], because from it they can explain the etymology of innumerable names that were well known to be Gaulish or Celtic[†];

[*] Pelloutier, vol. i. p. 165, &c.
[†] Vid. Cluv. lib. 1, cap. vi. vii. viii. &c. Pellout. liv. 1, chap. xv.

B 2

and this being admitted, it must follow that the Germans
are a branch of the Celts, and consequently, that the Celtic
and Teutonic nations were the same. In prosecuting this
argument it must be acknowledged that they have produced
many instances that appear at first sight very plausible. But
whoever considers how little we can depend upon the etymology of obsolete words, derived from barbarous dead languages, in which there are no books extant, will not build
very securely on proofs of this sort. No one will assert that
the present German bears any resemblance now to the
modern Welsh and Irish languages; and yet there are writers
in abundance who will undertake to account for the name of
almost every place, person or office, in ancient Europe, from
one or other of these two living tongues, and will produce
instances fully as plausible and conclusive, as any adduced by
Cluverius or his followers *. After all, there is probably a
good deal of truth on both sides; I can readily believe that
all the names of places and persons in ancient Germany, or
such other countries as any of the Teutonic nations at any
time penetrated into, will be reducible to the language now
spoken by their descendants : and that in like manner, from
the Irish and Welsh languages, which may be allowed to be
genuine daughters of the ancient Gallic or Celtic tongue, it
will be easy to explain such names as were imposed by any
of the ancient Celtic or Gallic tribes. Indeed in the very
remote ages, prior to history, one cannot pretend to say what
were the distinct bounds or limits of each people. They
were, like all other barbarous nations, roving and unsettled;
and often varied their situation; being sometimes spread
over a country; at other times driven out by some stronger
tribe of barbarians, or forsaking it themselves in search of
new settlements. Cæsar informs us, that some of the Gallic
tribes forced their way into Germany, and there established
themselves †. It is equally probable, that before his time,
bands of Germans might at different periods penetrate into

---

* See that excellent antiquary Lluyd, in Archæologia Britannica, &c.,
not to mention many late writers of a different stamp, viz., Jones, Parsons,
&c. &c.

† *Fuit antea tempus cum Germanos Galli virtute superarent et ultrò bella
inferrent, ac . . . trans Rhenum colonias mitterent, &c.* Vid. plura
apud. Cæs. de Bell. Gall. lib. vi.

Gaul*; where, although their numbers might be too small to preserve them a distinct nation, yet these emigrants might import many names of persons and places that would outlive the remembrance of their founders. This will sufficiently account for the dispersion of words derived from both languages, and inform us why Celtic derivations may be found in Germany, and German names discovered in Gaul. So much for arguments derived from etymology; which are so very uncertain and precarious, that they can only amount to presumptions at best, and can never be opposed to solid positive proofs.

With regard to the other source of arguments, by which these learned writers support their opinion of the identity of the Gauls and Germans, viz., quotations from the ancient Greek and Roman authors; these they have produced in great abundance. But even if it should be granted that the Greeks and Romans applied sometimes the names of Celtic, Scythian or Hyperborean indiscriminately to the ancient inhabitants of Germany and Gaul, of Britain and Scandinavia, the inference will still be doubted by those that consider how little known all these nations were to the early writers of Greece and Rome; who, giving them all the general name of Barbarians, inquired little farther about them, and took very little pains to be accurately informed about their peculiar differences and distinctions. Even a long time after these rude nations had begun to press upon the empire, and had made the Romans dread their valour, still their writers continued to have so confused and indistinct a knowledge of their different descent and character, as to confound both the Celts and Goths with the Sarmatians, whom all writers allow to have been a distinct nation from them both †: thus Zosimus, an historian of the third century, includes them all under the common name of Scythians ‡; and this, at a time when, after their long and frequent intercourse with the Romans, their historians ought to have been taught to distinguish them better.

---

* This Cæsar expressly tells us of the Belgæ, who were settled to the north of the Seine and the Marne. *Plerosque Belgas esse ortos à Germania; Rhenumque antiquitus transductos, propter loci fertilitatem ibi consedisse; Gallosque qui ea loca incollerent, expulisse.* De Bell. Gall. lib. ii.

† See Pelloutier, vol. i. liv. i. chap. ii. passim.

‡ See Pelloutier, vol. i. p. 17.

However, the Greek and Roman authors were not all equally indistinct and confused on this subject. It will be shown below, that some of their best and most discerning writers, when they had an opportunity of being well informed, knew how to distingush them accurately enough: so that both Cluverius and Pelloutier have found themselves much puzzled how to reconcile such stubborn passages with their own favourite hypotheses, and have been entangled in great difficulties in endeavouring to get over the objections these occasion. Even with regard to the more early historians, they appear to have been sometimes more precise and accurate in their descriptions. There is a remarkable passage of this kind in Strabo [*]; in which he informs us that, although the old Greek authors gave all the northern nations the common name of Scythians or Celtoscythians, yet that writers still more ancient [†], divided all " the nations who lived beyond the Euxine, the Danube, and the Adriatic Sea, into the Hyperboreans, the Sauromatæ, and Arimaspians ; as they did those beyond the Caspian Sea into the Sacæ and Messagetæ." The Sacæ and Messagetæ might possibly be the ancestors of the Saxons and Goths, who, in the time of those very remote Greek writers, possibly had not penetrated so far westward as they did afterwards : as it is well known that the Germanii are mentioned by Herodotus [‡] as a Persian people. Now the most authentic historians and poets of the Teutonic nations all agree that their ancestors came at different emigrations from the more eastern countries [§]. But with regard to the three other nations, the Hyperboreans, the Sauromatæ and the Arimaspians ; if we agree with Pel-

---

[*] Strabo, lib. xi. ῎Απαντας μὲν δὴ τοὺς προσβόρρους κοινῶς οἱ παλαιὰ τῶν ῾Ελλήνων συγγραφεῖς, Σκύθαι καὶ Κελτοσκύθαι ἐκαλοῦν, &c. Vid. Cluv. lib. i. p. 22. Pellout. vol. i. p. 2.

[†] Οἱ δὲ ΕΤΙ ΠΡΟΤΕΡΟΝ διέλοντες, &c.

[‡] Herod. in Clio. Edit. R. Steph. 1570, p. 34.

[§] All the old northern Skalds and historians agree that their ancestors came thither from the East, but then some of them, to do the greater honour to their country, and to its antiquities, pretend that they first made an emigration into the East from Scandinavia. See Sheringham *De Anglorum Gentis origine*. *Cantabrigiæ* 1670, 8vo. passim. It is the great fault of Sheringham not to know how to distinguish what is true and credible from what is improbable and fabulous in the old northern Chronicles : because some parts are true, he receives all for authentic ; as a late ingenious writer, because some parts are fabulous, is for rejecting all as false. (See Clarke, in his learned treatise on the connection between the Roman, Saxon, and Eng-

loutier *, that under the two former the Celts and Sarmatians are plainly designed; when he contends † that the Arimaspians are a mere fabulous people, which never existed, who does not see that he is blinded by hypothesis? Why may not the ancient Finns or Laplanders have been intended by this term, which he himself interprets from Herodotus to signify One-eyed, and supposes it descriptive of some nation that excelled in archery, as alluding to their practice of winking with one eye in order to take aim ‡. Tacitus expressly assures us that the Fenni were great archers §; and, it is highly probable that at some early period of time, both the Finns and Laplanders were possessed of much larger and better tracts of country than the northern deserts to which they are now confined.

But whether this interpretation be admitted or not, and whatever the more early Greek and Roman writers knew concerning the Celtic and Teutonic nations, it is very certain that in latter times, such of them as had most discernment, and the best opportunities of being informed, have plainly and clearly delivered that the Germans and Gauls were two distinct people, of different origin, manners, laws, religion and language, and have accurately pointed out the difference between them.

Before we descend to particulars, it may be premised, that these two races of men were in many things alike, as would necessarily happen to two savage nations who lived nearly in the same climate, who were exposed to the same wants, and were obliged to relieve them by the same means. The more men approach to a state of wild and uncivilized life, the greater resemblance they will have in manners, because savage nature, reduced almost to mere brutal instinct, is simple and uniform; whereas art and refinement are infinitely various: thus one of the rude natives of Nova Zembla will bear a strong resemblance in his manner of life to a savage of New Holland:

lish coins, &c. Lond. 1767, 4to.) By the same rule we might reject the whole Grecian history: for that of the north has, like it, its fabulous, its doubtful, and more certain periods; which acute and judicious critics will easily distinguish.

* Liv. i. chap. i.   † Vol. i. p. 9, 10.
‡ Pelloutier, ibid. Herod p. 129, 145.
§ *Sola in sagittis spes.* Tac. de Mor. Germ. cap. ult.

they will both live upon fish and sea fowls, because their
desert shores afford no other food; they will both be clad in
the skins of seals and other sea animals, because their country
affords no other clothing; and they will both live by fishing
in little boats, and be armed with lances pointed, for want of
metal, either with sharp flints or the bones of fishes: but will
it therefore be inferred that the inhabitants of these two opposite poles of the globe were originally one and the same
people? The ancient Britons in the time of Cæsar painted
their bodies, as do the present Cherokees of North America,
because it would naturally enough occur to the wild people of
every country, that by this practice they might render them
selves terrible to their enemies: nor will this prove that the
Cherokees are descended from the ancient Britons. When
therefore Cluverius and Pelloutier solemnly inform us that
the Germans and Gauls lived both of them in small huts or
caverns; that they subsisted either on venison slain in hunting, or on the milk and cheese procured from their flocks:
that both people led a wandering roving life, and equally
disliked to live in cities, or follow agriculture, and of course
ate little or no bread: that they both of them drank out of
the horns of animals *, and either went naked, or threw a
rude skin over their shoulders: when they collect a long series
of such resemblances as these, and bring innumerable quotations from ancient authors to prove that all these descriptions
are equally given of both people, who does not see that all
these traits are found in every savage nation upon earth, and
that by the same rule they might prove all the people that
ever existed to be of one race and nation?

But notwithstanding these general resemblances, we have
sufficient testimony from some of the most discerning ancient
authors, that the Germans and Gauls, or in other words, the
Celtic and Teutonic nations were sufficiently distinguished
from each other, and differed considerably in person, manners,
laws, religion and language.

Cæsar, whose judgment and penetration will be disputed

* Some of the ancient German tribes drank beer and ale, as did the old
inhabitants of Gaul. (See Pelloutier, vol. i. lib. 2. ch. ii. p. 216, 217, &c.)
This, however, proves them not to be the same people, any more than our
drinking tea and coffee, proves us to be descended from the Chinese and
Arabians.

by none but a person blinded by hypothesis*, and whose long residence in Gaul gave him better means of being informed than almost any of his countrymen; Cæsar expressly assures us that the Celts or common inhabitants of Gaul "differed in language, customs and laws" from the Belgæ. on the one hand, who were chiefly a Teutonic people, and from the inhabitants of Aquitain on the other, who, from their vicinity to Spain, were probably of Iberian race. Cæsar positively affirms that the nations of Gaul differed from those of Germany in their manners, and in many other particulars, which he has enumerated at length. And this assertion is not thrown out at random, like the passages brought by Cluverius against it; but is coolly and cautiously made, when he is going to draw the characters of both nations at length in an exact and well finished portrait, which shows him to have studied the genius and manners of both people with great attention, and to have been completely master of his subject †.

It is true, the Gauls and Germans resembled each other in complexion, and perhaps in some other respects, as might be expected from their living under the same climate, and nearly in the same manner; yet that they differed sufficiently in their persons, appears from Tacitus, who says that the inhabitants of Caledonia resembled the Germans in features, whereas the Silures were rather like the Spaniards, as the inhabitants of South Britain bore a great resemblance to the Gauls ‡. This plainly proves that the Spaniards, Germans, and Gauls, were universally known to differ in their persons.

They differed also in manners and customs. To instance only in one point, among the Germans, the wife did not give a dowry to her husband, but the husband to the wife, as Tacitus expressly assures us §. Whereas we learn from

* Cæsar is so much more precise and positive against the hypothesis espoused by Cluverius, Keysler, Pelloutier, &c., than the common Roman authors, who were generally inattentive to the differences of the barbarous nations; that all the writers above mentioned set out with accusing Cæsar of being for ever mistaken; whereas he and Tacitus were probably the only Romans that were generally exact.

† See the passage in Cæsar, lib. 6, at large, it was too long to be inserted here.

‡ Tacit. in Vit. Agricolæ, c. ii.

§ *Dotem non uxor marito, sed uxori maritus offert.* De Mor. Germ. c. 18.

Cæsar, that among the Gauls, the husband received a portion in money with his wife, for which he made her a suitable
settlement of his goods *, &c.

They differed no less in their institutions and laws. The
Celtic nations do not appear to have had that equal plan of
liberty, which was the peculiar honour of all the Gothic
tribes, and which they carried with them, and planted
wherever they formed settlements.   On the contrary, in
Gaul, all the freedom and power chiefly centered among the
Druids and the chief men, whom Cæsar calls *Equites*, or
knights; but the inferior people were little better than in a
state of slavery †; whereas every the meanest German was independent and free ‡.

But if none of these proofs of difference of person, manners, institutions or laws, could have been produced, or should
be explained away, still the difference was so great and essential between the Celtic and Teutonic nations, in regard to
religion and language, as can never be got over, and plainly
evince them to have been two distinct and different people.
These two points are so strong and conclusive, that the whole
proof might be left to rest upon them.

In comparing the religious establishment and institutions
of the Celtic tribes, with those of the Teutonic nations, the
most observable difference, and what strikes us at first sight,
is that peculiar hierarchy or sacred college among the Celts,
which had the entire conduct of all their religious and even
civil affairs, and served them both for magistrates and priests,
viz., that of the Druids; which has nothing to resemble it
among any of the Gothic or Teutonic nations. This difference appeared to Cæsar so striking, that he sets out with this,
at his entrance on his description of the Germans, as a fundamental and primary distinction §. I do not here enter into
a minute description of the nature of the Druids' establishment, or an enumeration of their privileges, because these
may be found in Cæsar and Pliny among the ancients, and

---

* *Viri quantas pecunias ab uxoribus dotis nomine acceperunt, tanta ; ex
suis bonis, æstimatione facta ; cum dotibus communicant.* De Bello Gall.
iib. 6.

† De Bell. Gall. lib. 6.

‡ Tacitus de Mor. Germ., passim.

§ De Bell. Gall. lib. 6.

in so many authors among the moderns * : it will be sufficient to say that, although the Teutonic nations had priests, they bore no more resemblance to the Druids, than the pontiffs of the Greeks and Romans, or of any other Pagan people. The learned and ingenious Dr. Borlace has left nothing to be desired on the subject of the Druids and their institutions. He has however been drawn in by Keysler to adopt this hypothesis, that the religion of the ancient Germans was, in fundamentals, the same with that of the Gauls and Britons (vid. p. 71). As nothing that falls from so excellent a writer ought to be disregarded, I shall consider his arguments with attention. He proves the identity of the German and Gaulish religion from the conformity of the Germans and Gauls in the following points; viz., " 1, the principal Deity of both nations was Mercury; 2, they sacrificed human victims; 3, they had open temples; and, 4, no idols of human shape; 5, they had consecrated groves; 6, worshipped oaks; 7, were fond of auspicial rites; and 8, computed by nights and not by days."

I shall consider each of these proofs in their order; and as for the first, that " both nations worshipped Mercury." This amounts to no more than this, that the Gauls and Britons worshipped for their chief Deity, some Celtic god, which Cæsar finding to resemble in some of his attributes the Roman Mercury, scrupled not to call by that Roman name; so again the Germans worshipped for their supreme God, a Divinity of their own, whom Tacitus likewise called Mercury, from a fancied resemblance to that Roman Deity, perhaps in other of his attributes. We know very well that the Supreme Deity of all the Teutonic nations was Odin or Woden, called by the ancient Germans Votam and Gotam, or Godam, (vid. not. in Tac. Varior. p. 602), who seems chiefly to have resembled the Roman Mercury, in having a particular power over the ghosts of the departed. (Vide Bartholin, lib. 2, c. 7 *Odinus Manium fuit Dominus; Mercurio comparandus.*) In

---

* Vid. Cæsar. De Bello Gall. Comment. lib. 6. Plinii Nat. Hist. lib. 16, c. 44.

Of the moderns, see Toland's Specimen of a Hist. of the Druids, in Miscel. Works, vol. i. 1747, 8vo. Stukely's Stonehenge, and Abury, 2 vols. 1740, &c., folio. But especially Dr. Borlace's Antiquities of Cornwall, 2nd edit. 1769, folio.

other respects, how much they differed will appear at first sight in the Edda. Now if the Celtic Mercury resembled the Roman nó more than Odin did; we see how unlike they might be to each other. We are not even sure that these two Mercuries of the Gauls and Germans agreed with the Mercury of the Romans in the same points of resemblance.

But, 2, "both nations sacrificed human victims; 3, had open temples; 5, consecrated groves; and 7, were fond of auspicial rites." These descriptions I believe may be applied to all the Pagan nations in the world, during their early barbarous state. For 2, all Pagan nations have offered human victims; have had 3, open temples before they got covered ones; and, previous to their erecting magnificent domes for their religious rites, have either set up circles of rude stones, or retired under the natural shelter of 5, solemn groves, which, upon that account, they consecrated: and 7, all pagan people have dealt in omens, auspices, and all the other idle superstitions of that sort. There is not one of the above circumstances but what is mentioned in Scripture, as practised by the idolatrous nations which surrounded the Jewish people, and was equally observed by some or other of the inhabitants of Italy and Greece; so that the Germans resembled the Gauls with regard to these particulars no more than they did the old idolatrous inhabitants of Canaan, Assyria, Greece, and Italy. As for the Teutonic nations, they very soon got covered temples, and also idols of human shape, as had indeed the Celtic nations also in the time of Cæsar; for so Dr. Borlace himself (p. 107) interprets that passage of his concerning the Gauls (lib. 6): *Deum maximé Mercurium colunt: Hujus sunt* PLURIMA SIMULACRA. If these *simulacra* had not been images, but only rude unformed stones, Cæsar would doubtless have expressed himself with more reserve. When, therefore, Dr. Borlace says that the Gauls and Germans resembled each other in having (4) "no idols of human shape," he must only mean in their more early state of idolatry, which I suppose may also be predicated of every savage nation, before they have attained any skill in sculpture.

But he says, 6, that both nations "worshipped oaks." His proof, however, that the Germans had this superstition only, is, that "the Sclavonians worshipped oaks, inclosed

them with a court, and fenced them in, to keep off all un-
hallowed access;" and for this he refers to the note in Tacit.
Variorum ad c. 9, where Helmoldus has said, that the Russians held their groves and fountains sacred, and that the
Sclavi worshipped oaks. This proves nothing with regard to
the Teutonic nations, but plainly shows that many of the
Druidic superstitions had been caught up and adopted by
nations in no way allied to the Celts; and therefore suggests
an easy answer to the last proof that is urged of the resemblance of the Germans and Gauls in their religious rites and
opinions; viz., that,

8, Both people "computed by nights, and not by days."
This is in reality the only solid argument that has been produced. But to this the answer is very obvious. The Teutonic nations, it is allowed, had this very peculiar arbitrary
custom, which they probably borrowed from their Celtic
neighbours, although of a very different race, and professing,
in the main, a very different religion : for if the Sclavonian
tribes, whose situation lay so much more remote from the
Celts, had adopted their superstitious veneration for the oak,
which seems in no degree to have infected the Germans, it
would have been wonderful indeed, if the latter, who lay con-
tiguous to the Celts, had picked up none of their opinions or
practices.

Not only in the peculiar nature of their priesthood, but
in their internal doctrines as well as outward rites, they
differed.

The Druids taught, and the Celtic nations believed, the
metempsychosis, or a transmigration of the soul out of one
body into another. This is so positively asserted of them by
Cæsar [*], who had been long conversant among them, and
knew them well, that it is not in the power of any of the
modern system-makers to argue and explain his words away,
as they have attempted to do in every other point relating to
the Celtic antiquities. However, they attempt to qualify it,
by asserting that the Celtic nations believed only that the
soul passed out of one human body into another, and never
into that of brutes [†]: which distinction I shall not now stay

[*] Lib. vi.—Vid. Diodor. Sicul. lib. v. c. 2, & Val. Max. lib. ii. c. 6.
Ammian. Marcel. lib. xv.

[†] Vid. Keysler Antiq. Sept. p. 117. Borlace, p. 98, 99, &c.

to examine, but proceed to observe, that all the Teutonic nations held, on the contrary, a fixed Elysium, and a Hell, where the valiant and the just were rewarded, and where the cowardly and the wicked suffered punishment. The description of these forms a great part of the Edda.

In innumerable other instances, the institutions of the Druids among the Celts were extremely different from those of the Teutonic nations. To mention a few: the former frequently burnt a great number of human victims alive, in large wicker images, as an offering to their Gods *. The Gothic nations, though like all other pagans they occasionally defiled their altars with human blood, appear never to have had any custom like this.

The Druids venerated the oak and the mistletoe, which latter was regarded by them as the most divine and salutary of plants, and gathered with very particular ceremonies. In the Teutonic mythology, if any tree seems to have been regarded with more particular attention than others, it is the ash: and as for the mistletoe, it is represented in the Edda rather as a contemptible and mischievous shrub.

But what particularly distinguishes the Celtic institutions from those of the Teutonic nations, is that remarkable air of secrecy and mystery with which the Druids concealed their doctrines from the laity; forbidding that they should ever be committed to writing, and upon that account, not having so much as an alphabet of their own †. In this, the institutions of Odin and the Skalds was the very reverse. No barbarous people were so addicted to writing, as appears from the innumerable quantity of Runic inscriptions scattered all over the north; no barbarous people ever held letters in higher reverence, ascribing the invention of them to their chief deity, and attributing to the letters themselves supernatural virtues. Nor is there the least room to believe that any of their doctrines were locked up or concealed from any part of the community. On the contrary, their mythology is for ever displayed in all the songs of their Skalds, just as that of the Greeks and Romans is in the odes of Pindar and Horace. There never existed any institution in which there appears

---

* Vid. Cæsar de Bell. Gall. lib. vi.   Borlace, p. 127.
† Cæsar, lib. vi

less of reserve and mystery than in that of the Scandinavian people.

After all, it may possibly be true that the Teutonic nations borrowed some opinions and practices from the Celts, without being at all descended from them, or having any pretensions to be considered as the same people. The Celtic tribes were probably the first that travelled westward, and it is not impossible but that several of the Druidic observances might be caught up and imitated by the other nations that came after them. Some relics of the Druidic superstitions, we have seen, prevailed among the Sclavonians: and still more might be expected to be found among those of Teutonic race, both from their nearer vicinage and greater intercourse with the Celtic nations; from whom the Sarmatians lay more remote. Nothing is more contagious than superstition; and therefore we must not wonder, if in ages of ignorance one wild people catch up from another, though of very different race, the most arbitrary and groundless opinions, or endeavour to imitate them in such rites and practices as they are told will recommend them to the gods, or avert their anger.

Before I quit this subject of the religion of the Celtic and Teutonic nations, I must beg leave to observe, that the mythology of the latter was probably in the time of Cæsar and Tacitus a very crude and naked thing, compared to what it was afterwards, when the northern Skalds had had time to flourish and adorn it. From a very few rude and simple tenets, these wild fablers had, in the course of eight or nine centuries, invented and raised an amazing superstructure of fiction. We must not therefore suppose that all the fables of the Edda were equally known to the Teutonic nations of every age and tribe. As truth is uniform and simple, so error is most irregular and various; and it is very possible, that different fables and different observances might prevail among the same people in different times and countries. From their imperfect knowledge of the divine attributes, all pagan nations are extremely apt to intermix something local with their idea of the Divinity, to suppose peculiar Deities presiding over certain districts, and to worship this or that God with particular rites, which were only to be observed in one certain spot. Hence, to inattentive foreigners, there might appear a difference of religion among nations who all maintained, at the bottom, one common creed; and this will account for whatever disagreement is remarked between Cæsar and Tacitus in their descriptions of the Gods of the ancient Germans. It will also account for whatever difference may appear between the imperfect relations of the Roman writers, and the full display of the Teutonic mythology held forth in the Edda. It is indeed very probable that only the mere first rudiments of the Teutonic religion had begun to be formed, when the Germans were first known to the Romans. And even when the Saxons made their irruptions into Britain, though they had the same general belief concerning Odin or Woden, Thor and Frigga, &c., yet probably the complete system had not arrived to the full maturity it afterwards attained under the inventive hands of the Skalds.

The essential difference remarked above, between the religion of the Celtic and Teutonic nations, in their tenets, institutions, and worship, affords a strong proof that they were two races of men *ab origine* distinct. The same truth is proved still more strongly, if possible, by their difference in language; this is an argument of fact, that amounts in questions of this nature almost to demonstration.

Tacitus assures us, that the ancient British language was very little different from that spoken in Gaul; *Sermo haud multum diversus;* there was probably no more than a small difference in dialect. But that the Gaulish language widely differed from that of the Germans, appears from the whole current of history. Thus Cæsar plainly shows that the German and Gaulish languages were very different, when he tells us that Ariovistus, a German prince, only learnt to speak the latter by his long residence in Gaul[*]. Again, Suetonius tells us, that Caligula, returning from his fruitless expedition against the Germans, in order to grace his triumph with an appearance of prisoners of that nation, for want of real Germans, chose from among the Gauls such as were of very tall stature, whom he caused to let their hair grow long, and to colour it red, to learn the German language, and to adopt German names; and thus he passed them off for prisoners from Germany[†]. These, and other proofs from Tacitus, are

---

[*] De Bell. Gall. lib. i. c. 47.   [†] Sueton. Caligula, c. 47.

produced by Pelloutier himself, though he afterwards endeavours to obviate their force, by pretending that the languages
of Gaul and Germany differed only in dialect *, &c.   But that
they were radically and essentially different, will appear beyond contradiction, to any one that will but use his eyes and
compare any of the living languages which are descended
from these two ancient tongues.   This question receives
so clear, so full, and so easy a solution, by barely inspecting
such of the languages of Celtic and Gothic origin as are now
extant, that to conclude the inquiry, I shall only lay before
the reader specimens of them both.

That the languages now spoken in Germany, Sweden, Denmark, Holland, and England, are all allied to the ancient
German no one can deny, because the words are visibly the
same in them all, only differing in dialect.   On the other
hand, that the ancient British was a language very little different from that of the Gauls, we have the express testimony
of Tacitus above mentioned.   Let us now compare the several dialects of the ancient British; viz. the Welsh, the
Armoric, and the Cornish, and see whether they contain the
most distant resemblance to any of the Teutonic dialects above
mentioned.

Whoever looks into the following specimens, will observe
that the modern English and German are two languages evidently derived from one common source; almost all the words
in both being radically the same; and yet it is near 1200
years since the English language was transplanted out
of Germany, and cut off from all intercourse with the mother
tongue.   In the mean time, the people who have spoken
it have undergone amazing revolutions and changes in their
government, religion, laws and manners, and their language
in particular has been subject to more than common innovations.   On the other hand, let him compare the same English
specimen with that of the Welsh language, and see if he can
discover the most distant resemblance between them; and yet
both these are spoken upon the same island, and that by fellow-citizens, who for many hundred years have been subjects
to the same prince, governed by the same laws, have professed
the same religion, and adopted nearly the same system

---

* Pellout, vol. i. liv. i. ch. xv.

of manners. And now at last, after all this intercourse, what two languages can be more unlike? Can this radical dissimilitude be called only a difference in dialect? During the rude ages prior to history, before the Britons or Germans were invaded by other nations, or had adopted any foreign refinements, while both people were under the uninterrupted influence of their original institutions, customs, and manners, no reason can be assigned why their language should undergo any material alterations. A savage people, wholly occupied by their present animal wants, aim at no mental or moral improvements, and are subject to no considerable changes. In this state, their language being affected by none of the causes that commonly introduce very great innovations, will continue for many ages nearly the same. The great causes that introduce the most considerable changes in language, are invasions of foreigners, violent alterations in religion and laws, great improvements in literature, or refinements in manners. None of these, so far as we know, had happened either to the Germans or Britons before the time of Cæsar, and yet even then there appeared no resemblance between the languages of these two people. On the other hand, all these causes have been operating with combined force ever since, and yet no considerable resemblance has obtained between the languages of England and Wales; nor has the radical affinity between those of England and Germany been effaced or destroyed. Upon what grounds then can it be pretended that the ancient languages of Gaul and Germany flowed from one common source? Or who will believe so improbable a fact?

M. Pelloutier tells us *, that "it having been pretended that the ancient Celtic is preserved to this day in the languages of Wales and Brittany in France, he had looked into a few glossaries of the Welsh and Armoric tongues †, and

---

* Hist. des Celtes, vol. i. p. 155.

† The Armoric language, now spoken in Brittany in France, is a dialect of the Welsh; that province being peopled with a colony from Britain in the fourth century; and though the two people have been separated so many ages, and have been subject to two nations so different in their laws, religion, and manners, still the two languages contain so strong a resemblance, that in our late conquest of Belleisle, such of our soldiers as came out of Wales were easily understood by the country people, and with their Welsh language, served for interpreters to the other soldiers who only spoke Eng-

had indeed discovered "that several words of the ancient Celtic were, in effect, preserved in those tongues." But he plainly hints, that he could not consider the bulk of the language as there perpetuated; and, indeed, considering how thick a film the prejudice of system had drawn over his eyes, it is a wonder he could discover any Celtic words at all; for he, taking it for granted that the High Dutch language was the genuine Celtic, only looked for such words as bore any resemblance to that tongue; and there being, as indeed there are, very few that have any similitude, no wonder that he found so few Celtic words in a genuine Celtic language *.

I shall now proceed to lay before the reader specimens of the Teutonic and Celtic languages, properly classed †, which,

lish. This is a fact related to me by a person who was there. Perhaps, upon comparing the specimens subjoined, the two dialects may appear to the eye more remote from each other than the above relation supposes; but, it may be observed, that their orthography not having been settled in concert, the same sound may have been expressed by very different combinations of letters, and the other differences may be only those of idiom; so that the two languages, when spoken, may have a much greater resemblance than appears upon paper to a person ignorant of them both. To give one instance; the Welsh word *Drwg*, and the Armoric *Drouc* (Eng. Evil), though so differently written, are in sound no further distant than *Droog* and *Drook*, the vowels in both being pronounced exactly alike.

* It is much to be lamented that a writer of so much learning, sagacity, and diligence, as Mons. Pelloutier, should have spoiled, by one unfortunate hypothesis, so excellent a work as his 'History of the Celts,' after all, certainly is. Had he not been drawn into this fundamental error, which infects his whole book; but on the contrary, had been apprised of the radical distinction between the Gothic and Celtic antiquities; had he assigned to each people the several descriptions which occur of them in ancient history; had he pointed out the distinct features of their respective characters, and shown in what particulars they both agreed, and wherein they differed; had he endeavoured to ascertain the limits of each people in ancient Europe, and shown by which of them the several countries were formerly inhabited, and from which of them the modern nations are chiefly descended; he would then have performed a noble task, and have deserved equally well of the past and future ages; his book, instead of being a perpetual source of mistake and confusion, would then have served as a clue to guide us through the labyrinth of ancient history, and he would have raised a noble monument to the memory alike of the Celts and Goths, from one or other of which ancient people so many great nations are descended.

† Specimens of these languages, taken from more correct sources than were available in Bishop Percy's time, and classed in conformity with the present state of the science of glossology, will be given after the remarks we shall have to make on the learned Bishop's admirable preface.—ED.

it is apprehended, will decide this question better than any conjectural or moral reasoning. The great and uniform similitude, discoverable at first sight between all the specimens of the Gothic or Teutonic languages, must indeed be very striking, even to foreigners unacquainted with these tongues. But to those that know them intimately the affinity must appear much nearer and stronger, because many words that were originally the same are disguised by the variations of pronunciation and orthography, as well as by the difference of idiom : thus, the German *Geheiliget*, and the English *Hallowed*, are both equally derived from the Teutonic *Helig, Holy.*

It may further be observed, that time has introduced a change, not only in the form, but in the meaning of many words, so that, though they are equally preserved in the different dialects, they no longer retain the same uniform appearance, nor can be used with propriety to express the same exact meaning. Thus, the Latin word *Panis* is translated in the Gothic and Anglo-Saxon *Hlaf*, or *Hlaif*, which word is still current among us in its derivative *Loaf*, but with a variation of sense that made it less proper to be used in the Paternoster than the other Teutonic word *Bread*, which is preserved in all the other dialects, but in a great variety of forms. Thus in the old Frankic, *Brot;* German, *Brod;* Dutch, *Brood;* Old Norse, *Braud;* Swedish and Danish, *Bröd.*

Again, it is possible that in many of these languages there was more than one word to express the same idea; and if there was a variety, then the different translators, by using some of them one word, and the rest another, have introduced a greater difference into their versions than really subsisted in their several languages. Of this kind I esteem the word *Atta (Pater)*, used by Ulphilas, whose countrymen had probably another word of the same origin as *Fæder* or *Father*, as well as all the other Gothic nations. So again, the Anglo-Saxons (besides their word *Hlaf*) had probably another term, whence we derived our present word *Bread.*

As the strong resemblance of the several Teutonic specimens to each other, so their radical dissimilitude to those of Celtic origin, must appear decisive of the great question discussed in the foregoing preface, not but here and there a word may have been accidentally caught up on either side : viz., borrowed by the Goths from the Celtic language, and *vice versâ*; or perhaps adopted by each of them from some third language radically different from them both. Thus, from the Welsh *Tâd*, our vulgar have got the common English word *Dad* and *Daddy*. And, from the French *Delivre*, are derived both the English *Deliver*, and the Armoric *Diluir*, whence the Cornish *Dilver*.

Before I conclude these slight remarks, I must beg leave to observe, that as the great subject of this present book is Gothic antiquities, which I apprehend to be totally distinct from the Celtic, I do not take upon me to decide on any of the points which relate either to the Celtic antiquities or Celtic tongues. For this reason I avoid entering into the dispute, which has of late so much interested our countrymen in North Britain: viz. whether the Erse language was first spoken in Scotland or Ireland. Before the inquisitive reader adopts either opinion, he would do well to consider many curious hints, which are scattered up and down in Lluyd's most excellent Archæologia Britannica, 1707, fol., and especially in his Welsh and Irish prefaces, translated in the appendix to Nicholson's Irish Historical Library, &c., 1736, folio.

In reply to those who contend that the true name of the Erse language is *Gaelic* or *Galic*, and that this word is the same with *Gallic*, the name of the ancient language of Gaul, I will merely observe, without deciding the question as to the origin of the Erse language itself, that the ancient name of *Gallic* does not seem to have been used by the natives of Gaul themselves, but to have been given them by foreigners. They called themselves Celtæ, and their language Celtic *; in like manner as the inhabitants of Wales, though called Welsh by us, term themselves Cymru, and their own language Cymraeg; who at the same time call us Saissons, and our tongue Saissonaeg, thus reminding us of our Saxon origin.

---

* Qui ipsorum lingua Celtæ, nostra Galli appellantur. Cæsar de Bell. Gal. L. 1.——"Celtæ, the *Gauls*, Cædil, Cadil, or Keill, and in the plural, according to our dialect, Keiliet, or Keilt, (now Guidhelod) *Irishmen*. The word Keilt could not be otherwise written by the Romans, than Ceilte or Celtæ." See Lluyd's Irish Preface, p. 107, in Nicholson's Irish Historian.

In the same place the reader will find many of the ancient names of offices, persons, &c., mentioned by Cæsar as prevailing in Gaul, explained from the modern Irish language, as, *Allobrox, Divitiacus, Vercingetorix, Vergasillaunus, Vergobretus,* &c.

REMARKS ON BISHOP PERCY'S PREFACE.

BY THE EDITOR.

Professor Rask, in the Introduction to his Icelandic Grammar*, observes that, " after Bishop Percy's most excellent Preface to Mallet's Northern Antiquities, the Teutonic and Celtic languages can no longer be confounded, nor comprised under the vague and unmeaning appellation of Scythian, Sarmatian," &c. Since the publication of the learned Danish Professor's work thirty-five years have elapsed, during which period the study of glossology, or comparative philology, has made as rapid a progress as that of biology, or comparative anatomy and physiology. By the latter we have become acquainted with the organization and affinities of animals; by the former, with the construction and relationship of languages. At the present day a zoologist, by the mere inspection of a few fossil bones, will seldom be at a loss in ascertaining to what description of animal they belonged, and, if the animal be of an unknown species, what place he ought to assign it in the reticulated chain of organic existence. A glossologist, in like manner, by subjecting to a critical examination the few literary remains of some ancient idiom, which a lucky accident may have preserved from oblivion, will not fail to reconstruct them into a language more or less perfect in all its parts, and point out its near or remote affinity to well-known cognate tongues. When a writer of the 17th or 18th century attempted to do any thing of the kind, he was sure to be led astray by some vague theory or other which we should now deem unworthy of serious consideration, or, like a person threading the mazes of a sylvan labyrinth, would frequently turn aside when on the point of entering the right path and wind

* Published at Copenhagen in 1811.

round the object he was in quest of without ever being able to attain it *. Cluverius and his followers thus perceived that there was a certain affinity between the Celtic and Teutonic languages, but, in order to account for this affinity, had recourse to a gratuitous assumption on which they founded arguments that were necessarily erroneous and inconclusive. No one could have refuted these arguments with greater perspicuity and force of reasoning than Bishop Percy has done in the preceding admirable dissertation; but, while he completely demolishes the crude theory of Pelloutier, he falls himself into the error of denying that any, " even the most distant, resemblance" exists between the languages of the Celtic and Teutonic nations. "Upon what grounds then," he adds, " can it be retended that the ancient languages of Gaul and Germany flowed from one common source? or who will believe so improbable a fact?" †

Now this fact, improbable as it appeared to Bishop Percy, has been admitted by the greatest philologists of the present age. No one certainly will any longer hesitate to regard the Celtic and Teutonic languages as forming two distinct linguistic families; but we think sufficient evidence has been adduced by those who have thoroughly investigated the subject, to warrant the conclusion that these families are remotely cognate, and, with six other linguistic families, do really

---

* These writers could manage well enough to draw up a tolerable grammar from the remains of an ancient tongue, but they generally thrust the language thus reconstructed into a wrong place. This was the case with the Mœso-Gothic. The reader will find, by referring to one of Bishop Percy's notes to chap. xi., that the fragments of a translation of the Gospels made by the Gothic Bishop Ulphilas in the fourth century, were discovered in the sixteenth century, in the library of a Westphalian convent. Now Hickes, Lye, and other celebrated English philologists of the last century, confounded this Gothic idiom with the Anglo-Saxon. The first part of Hickes's " Thesaurus," published in 1705, consists of an Anglo-Saxon and Mœso-Gothic Grammar, " a work," as Rask observes, (see the Preface to his " Anglo-Saxon Grammar," Cop. 1830,) "far from faultless, as well by reason of the unfortunate idea of treating the two most dissimilar of the Teutonic tongues together, as in the execution of its respective parts." In 1772 Lye published his " Dictionarium Saxonico et Gothico-Latinum," in 2 vols. fol., in which we observe, to use Rask's words, " the same unfortunate blending of Anglo-Saxon and Mœso-Gothic, languages which no more admit of being treated together than Hebrew and Arabic, or Greek and Latin."

† See page 18.

" flow from one common source." We shall not reproduce
the arguments brought forward in support of this opinion, as
we should be obliged to enter into a philological discussion,
which for most of our readers would be totally devoid of interest; but as frequent mention will be made in this work of
Scandinavians, Saxons, Goths, and other Teutonic nations,
we shall attempt to point out, as briefly as possible, the precise relationship they stand in to each other, and conjointly,
to other nations or races sprung from the same " common
source," referring the reader to the works of Rask, Schlegel,
Grimm, Klaproth, Bopp, Arndt, and other eminent writers of
the German school of philology, for more ample information
on the subject, which he will find, on closer examination, to
be well deserving of his attention.

Among the numerous sciences which the researches of the
present age have given rise to, is one which, for want of a
better name, has been called ethnology. This science falls
into two branches—a physiological branch, which might appropriately be termed anthropology; and a philological branch,
which forms the science of glossology. Anthropology shows
the organic distinctions that constitute the varieties of the
human species, inquires how these varieties have originated,
whether they be reducible to one common type, or to several
distinct types, strives to trace the affinities that connect
them, and form a systematic classification of the various races
that have hitherto appeared on the face of the globe. Glossology, on the other hand, investigates the construction and
affinities of the various languages spoken by mankind, from
the earliest that have left any vestiges of their existence down
to those of the present day, assumes that a certain number
may be regarded as primitive, from which all the others are
derived, points out clearly this derivation, and then strives to
connect the primitive languages themselves by tracing any
philological affinities that may exist between them, with a
view both of co-ordinating them into a systematic arrangement,
and of ascertaining whether they have all sprung from a common source—from a primordial tongue—or constitute a number of glottic groups totally unconnected. It will thus be seen,
that although each of these sciences establishes a separate
class of facts, they have essentially the same object in view, and
may therefore be subordinated to a higher science, which by

investigating and comparing the facts they respectively furnish, will ascertain how far physiological and philological affinities may be made to coincide—whether, for instance, several nations speaking cognate languages, but remotely connected with any other known tongue, are also distinguished by physiological traits sufficiently prominent to constitute a distinct race. A higher class of facts will thus be elicited, from which we may obtain by induction all the truths ethnological science can make us acquainted with.

It is obvious, however, that this science cannot be cultivated with success until the subordinate sciences of anthropology and glossology have attained a certain degree of perfection. Anthropology, unfortunately, is still in its infancy. Man has certainly been made the object of a special study in every quarter of the globe, but it is only since a very recent period that this study has been conducted on scientific principles. The facts elicited are therefore not sufficiently numerous to form the groundwork of a well constructed system or warrant any general conclusion that might be drawn from them. We may, however, take for granted that man—the genus homo—has only one species—which zoologists have been pleased to designate by the somewhat equivocal appellation of *homo sapiens;* or, in other words, that no specific difference exists among mankind. But this fact, even if it were established with a more rigorous certainty than it is at present, does not by any means solve the problem of the origin of the human race; for similar causes operating on two or more points of the globe, under similar circumstances, would necessarily produce similar results. Be this as it may, the varieties of the human species are endless, a circumstance which renders an accurate classification of them as difficult a task as a scientific arrangement of the animal kingdom itself.

When zoologists fancied that the scale of being ascended in a straight line from the lowest radiary animals to man, classifications were comparatively easy, but when they at length discovered that instead of a chain it formed a most intricate network, in some places ravelled, in others rent, the task became much more difficult. They found that their classes and orders were connected by intermediate links, often too imperceptible to be seized, and that nature disregarded these artificial distinctions invented to assist the memory and enable our limited faculties to embrace the multifarious ramifications of organic life, diverging from a common trunk, and again uniting in the highest class of beings that has hitherto appeared on the face of the globe. They found, for instance, that the cyclostoma * are a connecting link between fish and worms, that the cirrhopoda, or malentozoa, form a complete transition from molluscous to articulated animals, and that the animal and vegetable kingdoms themselves, which had been supposed so distinct, were intimately connected by the psychodiaria. Now, when we attempt to classify the varieties of the human species, we are placed in the same predicament as the zoologists. We might certainly, like the writers of a bygone age, leave the ark with Noah, and make Shem, Ham, and Japhet the progenitors of mankind †; but when we confine ourselves within the domain of science, we must necessarily proceed on principles more in accordance with physiological researches and historical facts; and then, whatever varieties may be taken as types for our classification, we find, when we

* The lowest class of cartilaginous fish, comprising the lampril, the lamprey, &c.

† When we say of a bygone age, we fear that we must except some of our own writers who, somehow or other, generally manage to lag half a century behind their continental brethren; for we find in Jamieson's " Hermes Scythicus," a work of some pretension, published not in the seventeenth but in the nineteenth century, in the year of grace 1814, that the Thracians were the descendants of " Tiras, or rather Thiras, the son of Japhet." !! " And it seems beyond dispute," says this learned Scotch philologist with imperturbable gravity, " that the Cimmerii were the posterity of Gomer, the eldest son of Japhet, the Japetus of the Greeks, and that they were the first race that peopled Europe. The name is obviously retained by the descendants of the ancient Britons, who still denominate themselves Cumri." !!! This is much on a par with the raving of Dr. Parsons, who, in his " Remains of Japhet," published however in 1747, and consequently at a more pardonable epoch, maintains that the blood of Gomer still flows unsullied by any extraneous admixture in the veins of the Welsh and Irish, and that king George III. might claim descent from a long line of Scythian kings that can be traced up to Magog. In juxtaposition with the passage from Jamieson's work, published in 1814, we might place the following observations from Schlözer's " Allgemeine Nordische Geschichte," published in 1771. " The Gomerites and Magogites should no longer be suffered to disfigure our oldest northern history. Such names or such unlearned plictriplactri should be left to the English authors of the universal history, and to their German mechanical compilators." A passage which shows, more especially as Schlözer was by no means free from the erroneous ideas of the period, that the Germans are generally half a century in advance of us.

group the other varieties around them, such a many odd fish like the cyclostoma in our way, that we soon become puzzled what to do with them.

If a person saw before him a German, a Chinese, a Malay, an American Indian, and a Negro, he would not hesitate a moment to recognise five distinct varieties of the human species. But when these are taken for the types* of a scientific classification, we are obliged to group the Jew with the German, the Finn with the Chinese, and the Caffre of the Cape with the Negro of Senegal. This, however, is the classification generally adopted, but it is so obviously defective that, in order to render it somewhat more in accordance with nature, we shall modify it as follows:—

VARIETIES OF THE HUMAN SPECIES.

1. The WEST ASIATIC, or Caucasian Variety.

Comprising the natives of India, Afghanistan, Persia, Mesopotamia, Syria, Arabia, the Caucasus, Tartary, and Northern Africa, and, with the exception of those belonging to the Tshudic (Finnic) Race and a few Samojedes, all the Europeans and their descendants in America and the colonies.

2. The EAST ASIATIC, or Mongol Variety.

The Mongols, Kalmucks, Manshus, Thibetans, Chinese, Japanese, Siamese, &c.

3. The NORTH ASIATIC, or Arctic Variety.

Most of the natives of the boreal regions of the globe. The Tshuds, (Finns, Lapps, Permians, &c.,) extending from the White Sea, along the Oural mountains, down to the Caspian. The Samojedes, Youkagirs, and various

---

* As the subject may be novel to many of our readers, we subjoin a definition of a type from Professor Whewell's " Philosophy of the Inductive Sciences."

" Natural groups are best described, not by any definition which marks their boundaries, but by a *type* which marks their centre. The type of any natural group is an example which possesses, in a marked degree, all the leading characters of the class.

" A natural group is steadily fixed, though not precisely limited; it is given in position, though not circumscribed; it is determined, not by a boundary without, but by a central point within; not by what it strictly excludes, but by what it eminently includes; by a type, not by a definition." —92nd and 93rd *Aphorisms concerning Ideas.*

other tribes in Siberia, and the Esquimaux in America
and Greenland.

4. The OCEANIC, or Malay Variety.
    The natives of Java, Sumatra, Borneo, the Moluccas,
    Philippines, &c., and the islands of the Pacific and
    Madagascar.

5. The AMERICAN, or Copper-coloured Variety.
    Excepting the Esquimaux, all the aboriginal inhabitants
    of America.

6. The EASTERN AFRICAN, or Demi-Negro Variety.
    The Gallas of Abysinnia, the natives of the eastern
    coast of Africa, the Caffres and Hottentots of the Cape,
    the Congoese, &c.

7. The CENTRAL AFRICAN, or Negro Variety.
    The type being the Negro of Senegal.

8. The AUSTRALIAN Variety.
    The natives of Australia, and the Papous and Alfouras
    of some of the Malaisian Isles.

In the present state of the science, all such classifications as the above will necessarily be more artificial than
natural. A natural arrangement of the varieties of the human
race ought, in fact, to be reticular and not vertical, and the
main groups connected by intermediate links, which, in these
artificial vertical arrangements, are entirely omitted *.

---

* We have given the vertical arrangement as it is generally followed,
though it is equally as defective as a vertical arrangement of the animal
kingdom. The absurdity of placing the four great divisions of this kingdom,
the radiata, mollusca, articulata, and vertebrata, in a straight line became
apparent when, according to this artificial arrangement, the cephalopoda or
highest class of molluscous animals—which includes the sepia, or cuttle-fish
as it is improperly termed—was immediately preceded, in the ascending scale,
by the enthelmintha or lowest class of articulated animals, that of intestinal
worms. By placing the mollusca and articulata on collateral lines, and connecting them with each other, as well as with the radiata and vertebrata, by
intermediate groups, this absurdity was avoided. In the above classification
the American Indian is placed between the Malay and the Demi-Negro
Varieties, which is obviously an anomaly. This is avoided, in other vertical
arrangements, by making the American Variety the second instead of the
fifth; but the red man of the forest then treads on the heel of the European, and is followed by the Chinese, which is almost as bad as the sepia
following the tape-worm. The Caucasian Variety is unquestionably the
highest, and the Australian the lowest in the scale; but we might probably
ascend, from the Australian to the Caucasian, by two or three collateral lines,
placing on one the American, and on the other the Mongol Variety, and con-

Glossology has been cultivated with much greater success than anthropology, though another century will probably elapse before it attains its full development. Human speech presents, in fact, the same endless varieties as the human species. A person travelling through England, for instance, would find in every county a different form of speech; but, although some would be as unintelligible as an unknown tongue, he would not hesitate to regard them as *dialects* of one *language.* Now we might take the most prominent of these dialects for *types*, around which the others might be arranged, and thus form a certain number of glottic groups, which we might term *idioms.* The dialects of the six northern counties, for instance, might be termed the Northumbrian Idiom; the dialects of Scotland, the Caledonian Idiom*, **&c.** The result of this process would be one *language*—the English—possessing six or seven *idioms*, and each idiom, probably, from ten to twenty *dialects.* By subjecting the dialects of North Germany, Friesland, and Holland, to a similar process, we should obtain the Low German (Platt deutsch), the Frisic, and the Dutch languages. On comparing the four languages thus obtained, we should find that, as distinct *languages*, they stood much in the same relationship to each other as the seven English idioms, and as *dialectic* affinities constituted an *idiom*, and *idiomatic* affinities a *language*, these *linguistic*

necting them by the Malay Variety, which would also form a transition to the West Asiatic.

* The dialects of Scotland and the North of England are owing to the influence of the Old Norse—the common language of all the ancient Scandinavians ; those of the midland and eastern counties to the language spoken by the Angles, the language of the Saxons prevailing more in the southern counties, though both these languages soon coalesced into one common tongue —the Anglo-Saxon. The English *dialects* might probably be arranged, so as to form six or seven *idioms*, as follows :—

1. The Standard Idiom, or language of the educated classes.
2. The Saxonic Idiom . .   the southern counties of England.
3. The Anglic or Mercian Idiom. . . . . .   the eastern and midland counties.
4. The Northumbrian Idiom   the six northern counties.
5. The Hibernian Idiom .   Ireland.
6. The American Idiom .   the United States.
7. The Caledonian Idiom .   Scotland.

(Comprising the dialects of)

We place the Caledonian Idiom, or Scotch dialect as it is generally called, the last, because it differs the most from the Standard Idiom, and is, in fact, regarded by some glossologists as a distinct language.

affinities would entitle us to comprehend the languages in question under the general denomination of Saxonic. The dialects of Central and Southern Germany would furnish us with the High German language, which, with three ancient tongues, would be found to differ from the Saxonic group of languages sufficiently to constitute a separate group, which we might term the Alemannic; but the affinity existing between these two glottic groups would entitle us to comprehend them under the denomination of Germanic. The Scandinavian languages would form another group, radically allied to the Germanic, though differing too much to be rendered subordinate to it; we might, therefore, comprehend both under the appellation of Teutonic, and should thus form all the languages, we had subjected to a critical examination, into a distinct linguistic family.

Having thus shown how a linguistic family may be synthetically formed from provincial dialects, we shall proceed to lay before the reader the ordinary classification of the Teutonic and Celtic languages, which constitute two distinct linguistic families; but, as glossologists have not as yet adopted the reticular arrangement, we must regard our glottic groups as the branches and sub-branches of a family stem, and arrange them as follows :—

TEUTONIC LANGUAGES.

		Extinct languages, remains of which have been preserved.	Living languages derived from them.
Germanic Branch.	Alemannic, or High German Sub-branch *.	Mœso-Gothic, Alemannic, Frankic,	German.
	Saxonic, or Low German Sub-branch †.	Old Saxon, Old Frisic, Anglo-Saxon,	Low German, Dutch ‡, Frisic, English.

* To this sub-branch belong the totally extinct languages (languages of which no literary remains have been preserved) of the ancient Suevi, Taurisci, Quadi, Marcomanni, Hermaduri, Longobardi, Goths, Ostro-Goths, Visi-Goths, Vandals, Burgundians, &c.

† The totally extinct languages belonging to this sub-branch are those of the ancient Angli, Cherusci, Chauci, Menapii, Batavi, &c.

‡ We have not inserted Flemish, as it is generally regarded as an idiom

	Extinct languages, remains of which have been preserved.	Living languages derived from them.
Scandinavian Branch . .	Old Norse (*Norræna Túnga*).	Icelandic (*Islenzka*), Færœic *, Norwegian †, Swedish, Danish.

CELTIC LANGUAGES.

	Extinct languages with literary remains.	Living languages derived from them.
Gaelic Branch.	Ancient Irish.	Erse, spoken in Ireland Gaelic, spoken in the Highlands. Manks, spoken in the Isle of Man.
Kymric Branch.	Ancient British.	Welsh ‡ Armorican (*Breyzad*), spoken in Bas-Bretagne.

Glossologists have grouped the various languages, spoken by mankind, into upwards of five hundred families, each with its branches, idioms, and dialects. Of such linguistic families, the West Asiatic Variety possesses twenty-four; the East Asiatic, ten or twelve; the North Asiatic, eight or ten; the Oceanic only one, divided into four main branches; the American, upwards of three hundred; the Eastern African, from ten to twenty; the Central African, upwards of fifty; and the Australian, probably as many. Besides these, there are from fifty to a hundred languages of small tribes and isolated people, belonging to the West and East Asiatic Varieties, too little known to be classed, so that, on further investigation,

of the Dutch language; in the same manner as the "Scotch dialects" form an English idiom.

* Spoken in the Færöe, or, as they are commonly, though improperly, termed, the Ferroe Isles.

† Norwegian ceased to be a literary language in the middle of the sixteenth century; since which period, Danish has been the language of the educated classes in Norway, Norwegian only continuing to be spoken by the peasantry in the rural districts, and consequently remaining without a standard idiom. Since the union with Sweden, the Norwegian patriots have been trying to revive the language of their forefathers. The Norse, formerly spoken in the Orkney and Shetland Isles, was a Norwegian *idiom.*

‡ Cornish, which became extinct in the middle of the last century, was also a Celtic language of the Kymric branch.

the number of linguistic families will probably be found to
exceed six hundred, a circumstance which has been adduced
by several writers in support of the autochthonic theory of
the origin of the human race. It will be seen, however, from
the above statement, that there are not more than fifty well-
known linguistic families in the civilized parts of the globe,
only twenty-three of which possess a literature. These twenty-three families contain about eighty distinct languages; but,
if the different periods of a literature be taken into account,
a person, in order to become acquainted with the literature of
all nations and ages, would probably have to learn upwards of
a hundred different tongues.

When glossologists had succeeded in grouping languages
into families, their next step was to ascertain whether any of
these families might be regarded as cognate. Now, if we
compare the Teutonic and Semitic families, for instance *, we
shall find that not the slightest analogy exists between them,
or at least no further analogy than all forms of human speech
must necessarily possess; whereas a comparison of the Teutonic and Celtic families will show them to be remotely allied.
A radical affinity will, on further investigation, probably be
found to exist between several linguistic families of Eastern
Asia, but, at present, glossologists only admit seven such
families to be sufficiently cognate to constitute what we shall
not hesitate to call, for want of a better name, a linguistic
tribe †. These families—generally comprised under the

---

* The Semitic family comprises the Hebrew, Syriac, Arabic, and other
cognate languages.

† Glossology is still in want of a scientific nomenclature, the word language being indiscriminately used, in the plural, to designate a linguistic
tribe, family, branch, and sub-branch, as in the phrases, " Indo-European
languages," " Teutonic languages," " Germanic languages," " Saxonic languages," &c., phrases which convey no precise meaning, and from which it
would be impossible to surmise that the Saxonic languages were included
under the term Germanic, the Germanic under Teutonic, and the Teutonic
under the general term of Indo-European. If it were laid down as a rule,
that dialects constitute an idiom; idioms a language; languages a tongue,
corresponding to a branch; tongues, a linguistic family which might appropriately be termed a glott; and families or glotts, a tribe or panglott; we
might express ourselves in much clearer terms. It might then be said, for
instance, that the Indo-European panglott comprises seven glotts, and the
Celtic glott two tongues, one of them having three, and the other two, living
languages; and that each of these languages has a certain number of idioms
and dialects.

vague denomination of "Indo-Germanic or Indo-European *languages*—are the Hindostanic, Iranic, Hellenic, Romanic, Slavonic, Teutonic, and Celtic." We should far exceed our prescribed limits were we to point out the affinities that connect these families, or enter into any details concerning the languages they respectively comprise; suffice it to say, that the Hindostanic family possesses three ancient languages, the Sanskrit, Bali, and Kavi, from which most of the living languages of Northern and Central India are derived; the Iranic family has also three extinct languages, the Zend, Pehlvi, and Parsi, the latter being the parent of modern Persian; the Hellenic family has ancient and modern Greek; the Romanic family, Latin, from which are derived Italian, Spanish, Portuguese, Occitannic (La Langue d'oc), French, Rumansch (spoken in the Canton of Grisons), and Rumenic, a language spoken by 3,400,000 Valachs, in Hungary, Transylvania, Moldavia, Walachia, and Bulgaria. The Slavonic family comprises the Illyrian, Servian, Croatian, Russian, Polish, Bohemian, and other cognate languages. The Teutonic and Celtic families have already been described. The most ancient languages of this tribe are the Sanskrit and Zend, to which, it would appear, the Celtic languages have but a remote affinity. The Celtic may, in fact, be regarded as the family the most distantly related to its tribe. The families that offer the greatest resemblance are the Hindostanic, Iranic, Hellenic, Romanic, and Teutonic.

Returning to the anthropological branch of ethnology, we must remark that each variety of the human species may be divided into races—each race offering certain physiological and psychological traits that distinguish it from all others. Thus, among the numerous races that constitute the West Asiatic Variety, the two that are the immediate object of the present inquiry may be thus characterized.

TEUTONIC RACE.	CELTIC RACE.
Physiological Character.—Fair complexion, fair, often flaxen, reddish, golden-coloured smooth hair, commonly not curled; large blue eyes, ruddy cheeks, broad high brow, skull larger and	*Physiological Character.*—Dark (sallow) complexion, dark brown eyes, and black hair, with a disposition to turn grey at an early age, and to fall out (bald-head), commonly not curled; stature of middle

rounder than in the Celtic variety, bones thicker, chest broader, so the hips, legs straight, heels and ankles strong, feet often large, even clumsy when compared with the Celtic variety; greater strength of muscle, tallness of figure, above what is called the middle size; skull and face of a form that approaches nearer to a half circle, to which the thinner end of the oval is added; disposition to become corpulent. Temperament :—Sanguine, nervous, and phlegmatic prevailing.

Psychological Character.—Slowness, but accuracy of perception; general slowness, but depth and penetration of mind; not brilliant for witticism like the Celtic variety, but distinguished by acuteness; fondness of independence, it being valued more highly than equality of condition or rank; provident, cautious, reserved, hospitable, but not sociable on a large scale with aristocratic conservative tendencies; respect for women, without assuming the Celtic character of frivolous flippancy; sincerity, forgetfulness of received injuries, adventurous, distinguished for cleanliness.

size, slender make, legs curved somewhat inwards, as in females; comparatively narrow chest, narrow hips, face and upper part of the skull the exact form of an oval, heels and ankles slender, feet small. Temperament :—Bilious and bilious-nervous prevailing.

Psychological Character.—Quickness of perception, great powers of combination, application, love of equality, of society, of amusement, of glory, want of caution and providence, prevalent disposition for sexual intercourse, gallantry, national vanity, fine blandishing manners, great external politeness, without inward sympathy; irascible, not forgetful of injuries, little disposition for hard work*.

* We have taken this description from the remarks Dr. Gustaf Kombst has appended to his Ethnographic Map of Great Britain and Ireland, published in Johnstone's splendid edition of Berghaus's Physical Atlas, omitting, however, such of his moral and intellectual (psychological) characteristics as

We may remark that physiological characteristics are, in a great measure, indelible; but the original psychological quali-

we deemed inapplicable, either on account of their savouring too much of a preconceived theory, or of their being more attributable to the influence of social institutions than to idiosyncrasy of race. We subjoin these passages as we should regret giving a gentleman of Dr. Kombst's learning and abilities any reason to complain of their omission. They are, for the Teutonic race, "Want of concentrativeness; self-government in all spheres of life. Fond of titles and social distinctions" (a trait quite as applicable, we should imagine, to mankind in general as to the Teutonic race). "No foundling hospitals; spirit for benevolent foundations. Recklessness regarding other nations' rights, overbearing, haughty spirit. Musical talent in most Teutonic tribes great. Skilful seamen. On the whole, fond of spirituous liquors." And, for the Celtic race, "Disposition for concentrating political and administrative power. Want of respect for human life—want of penetration, and desire for personal independence and political freedom. Disposition to superstition and hierarchy. Foundling hospitals. In most Celtic countries, no laws regarding paternity, or for the sustenance of, so-called, natural children by the father. Bad seamen. Not fit for colonising."

"Recklessness regarding other nations' rights, overbearing, haughty spirit," is much the same kind of phrase as a Parisian journalist would make use of to designate "la perfide Albion." Now admitting, for the sake of argument, that, as a nation, we do possess this character, and we will admit that we are somewhat too haughty and overbearing—very unenviable qualities certainly, but which are the necessary consequences of our unexampled maritime power and commercial prosperity—still Dr. Kombst would not be justified in attributing such psychological traits to the Teutonic race, for our good-natured brethren the Germans, who form the mass of this race, are unquestionably the least haughty and overbearing people in existence. We presume that, when Dr. Kombst attributed "want of respect for human life" to the Celtic race, he had the Irish in view, and forgot for the moment that the Scandinavians of the olden time showed less "respect for human life" than any people whose sanguinary deeds ever stained the pages of history. And as to the agrarian outrages of Ireland, they are the necessary result of the wretched system pursued for centuries in that unhappy country. Place any people on the face of the earth, no matter of what race or of what religion, in the same deplorable situation as the Irish peasantry, and the same consequences will inevitably ensue. The inhabitants of Cornwall, who are regarded by Dr. Kombst as "the purest Celtic race of any in Great Britain and Ireland," do not figure in our criminal records more frequently than their Saxon neighbours of the adjacent counties; neither have we heard of their being "bad seamen," a quality which Dr. Kombst also ascribes to their race. The rude Styrian boor, as prone to superstition as the Irish Celt, and uniting low cunning with an obtuseness of intellect almost unparalleled; the lively, jovial Rheinlander and the intellectual Saxonian present the same physiological traits, and belong to the same branch (the High Germanic) of the Teutonic race; yet we think Dr. Kombst, who, we presume, is also a German, would be somewhat puzzled to draw up "a moral and intellectual character" equally applicable to them.

D 2

ties, due to physical conformation and temperament, are so modified and changed by the influence of civil and religious institutions, that we ought to be extremely cautious in applying them to characterize a race. There are, however, certain psychological traits, which may be regarded as inherent, susceptible of undergoing a slight modification—of assuming a greater or lesser degree of intensity ; but, so long as the race remains unmixed, totally ineradicable, these ought to be carefully distinguished from *adventitious* qualities, which may be applied to a particular tribe or nation, and ascribed to the influence of its peculiar institutions, but never made use of to designate a race. Among the psychological characteristics which ethnological writers have applied to the Teutonic and Celtic races, we have selected, though with some slight hesitation, such as we deem *inherent*, discarding others which, for the reasons stated in the note, we must consider as entirely *adventitious.*

Anthropology having established the existence of distinct races, and glossology the existence of distinct linguistic families, it remained for the higher science of ethnology to ascertain whether the races of the one coincide with the families of the other. In the two races and families we have especially in view, this is strictly the case. All nations that belong physiologically to the Teutonic race, either speak, or have originally spoken, one or other of the Teutonic languages, and those belonging to the Celtic race one or other of the Celtic languages. The physiological character of a nation lasts, however, much longer than its language. Hence when two nations present the same physiological traits, we may take for granted that they are of a common origin, although the languages they speak may not possess the slightest affinity. The inhabitants of Cornwall, for instance, speak English, but present all the characteristics of the Celtic race, and we know that their Celtic language only became extinct in the last century *.

* For the "distribution of races" in the British Isles, we refer the reader to Dr. Kombst's map before mentioned, and subjoin the following extract from the remarks which accompany it.

"If we were," he says, "to make an *average* calculation as to the ethnographic quality of the blood in the population inhabiting Great Britain, (for an accurate calculation will for the present at least be out of the question,) we would most probably arrive at the following result."

In the British islands the Teutonic and Celtic races have remained tolerably distinct; but it is obvious that centuries of war and conquests have frequently blended into one nation tribes of different races, though the effects which such a fusion produces are, generally speaking, not so great as might be expected. The conquerors of a country have generally been a much less numerous body than the people they conquered, which will account for the slight modification that the physiological character of several subjugated nations has undergone. Thus, although France has been successively conquered by the Romans, by the Franks, Burgundians, and other Germanic tribes, and at a more recent period by the Normanno-Saxons of England, we find that the French of the present day retain in a marked degree all the physiological and psychological traits that characterize the Celtic race. On closer examination we may certainly perceive the traces of these conquests in the shades of character and physiognomy that distinguish the inhabitants of the various provinces. The people of Normandy, for instance, still retain some of the characteristic traits of the Scandinavians; the

I. Pure Blood.

1. Teutonic, in England, Scotland, and the east and north-east of Ireland 10,000,000
2. Celtic, in Cornwall, Wales, the Scottish Highlands, and Ireland 6,000,000

_____

16,000,000

II. Mixed Blood.

1. Teutonic (that is, with prevalent Teutonic character), in England, Scotland, and the east and north-east of Ireland 6,000,000
2. Celtic (that is, with prevalent Celtic character), in Cornwall, Wales, the Scottish Highlands, and Ireland . . . 4,000,000

_____

10,000,000

Total of Teutonic pure and mixed 16,000,000
Total of Celtic pure and mixed 10,000,000

_____

26,000,000

We must observe, that in our acceptation of the terms, Dr. Kombst's map is not an ethnographic but an anthropographic map, as it merely distinguishes _races_ and not _languages_. A map indicating languages would be a glossographic map, and one indicating both races and languages, a real ethnographic map.

Germanic traits are still perceptible in the other provinces north of the Loire, and the Romanic in several of those situated on the south of that river; but the Celtic character every where predominates, and the account which Cæsar gives of the character of the ancient Gauls might be literally applied to their descendants—our volatile neighbours across the Channel. Whenever a fusion of nations speaking different languages takes place by conquest, the language of superior intellectual development soon becomes the common tongue of the conquerors and the conquered. It was thus that the Celtic language of the ancient Gauls was replaced by the Latin, whereas the Franks and the other Germanic tribes soon lost their Teutonic idioms, and adopted the language of the Romanized Gauls they subjugated.

We will not attempt to give even a sketch of the state of Europe before the dawn of authentic history, as we should be obliged to examine a number of hypotheses, and after all should arrive at no satisfactory result. From the high lands of Central Asia races of men seem to have been propelled like waves one after another from the remotest period, comparatively speaking, down to the present time, and we may take for granted that the Celtic race preceded the Slavonic, and the latter the Teutonic, for we find at the earliest period to which even conjectural reasoning can safely ascend, that the Celts occupied the greater part of western and south-western Europe, the northern and north-eastern parts being in possession of the Tshuds—a race belonging to the Arctic variety of the human species—and the south-eastern parts, comprising the present countries of Turkey in Europe, Greece, and Southern Italy, peopled by various tribes, whose origin it is impossible to ascertain. Among these were the Thracians and Pelasgi—or we should perhaps say the Thracians *or* Pelasgi—for whether these people were of the same race, and whether this was a mixed or a pure race, whether the Thracians, as some writers assert, were a powerful tribe of the Teutonic, or as others maintain, of the Slavonic race, we will not pretend to decide, the arguments respectively brought forward in support of these opinions being more or less hypothetical. All that can be said with any degree of historical certainty is, that the people, who at a somewhat later period spoke the Greek language, were a mixed race, and those we find established in ancient Latium, and speaking the Latin language, a race still more mixed. But as these languages have the greatest affinity with Sanskrit, it is evident that the mixed races in question which we have denominated the Hellenic and Romanic, were chiefly composed of tribes from Central Asia, and the former, as well as the latter, may probably have had for its nucleus a Thracian or Pelasgian tribe, which by amalgamating with Semitic (Phenician) and other tribes, formed the Hellenic, and with Celtic and various Italic tribes of an unknown origin, the Romanic race. At a still later period the Slavonic and Teutonic races entered Europe. The Slavonians, after driving the Tshuds further north, occupying the parts now known under the names of Russia, Poland, Hungary, Bohemia, &c., and the whole of north Germany. The hardy Teutons drove Tshuds, Slavonians, and Celts, before them; the Scandinavian branch of this race expelling the Tshuds from the southern parts of Sweden and Norway, and the Germanic branch conquering and amalgamating with the Slavonic tribes settled in Germany, traces of this fusion being still perceptible in the dark eyes and hair, and comparatively darker complexions, of several of the northern Germans. If we had an authentic history of the migrations of these various races, we should probably find that none of them are unmixed; however, comparatively speaking, the Celtic, Slavonic, and Teutonic, may be regarded as pure, and the Hellenic and Romanic as mixed races.

As frequent mention will be made in this work of the Finns, it may not be irrelevant to say a few words respecting the Tshudic* race, to which they belong. The languages spoken by the various tribes of this race may be classed as follows:—

---

* As the English sh corresponds to the German sch, we do not see the utility of retaining the c in words not of German origin. We might also notice here the error which most of our geographical writers fall into of retaining the German w, which corresponds to the English v, in the proper names of other languages than German. Why not, for instance, write Valachia, as the natives of that country, and the Germans themselves, pronounce the word, instead of Walachia.

TSHUDIC LANGUAGES (3,200,000) *.

Suomic Branch (2,075,000).

1. Finnic (1,500,000), spoken in Finnland and the Governments of St. Petersburg, Novgorod, and Olonetz.
2. Esthonic (500,000), in Esthonia and Livonia.
3. Livic the ancient language of Livonia, now almost extinct.
4. Lappic (75,000), spoken by the Laplanders in Russia, Sweden, and Norway.

Permic Branch (1,125,000).

Northern Sub-Branch (375,000).

5. Komic or Permic Proper (35,000), in the Government of Perm.
6. Sürænic (40,000), in the Gov. of Perm, Viatka, Vologda, Archangel, and Tobolsk.
7. Votækic (100,000), in the Governments of Viatka and Kasan.
8. Vogulic (100,000), in the Governments of Perm, Tobolsk, and Tomsk.
9. Asjach (100,000), on the rivers Obi and Jertush.

Southern Sub-Branch (750,000).

10. Tshervassic (400,000), in the Governments of Kasan, Nijnii Novgorod, Simbirsk, Saratov, and Astrakhan.
11. Tsheremissic (220,000), in the Governments of Kasan, N. Novgorod, Simbirsk, and Astrakhan.
12. Mordvinic (130,000), in the Governments of N. Novgorod, Simbirsk, Tambov, Penza, and Saratov.

* The figures denote the number of persons speaking the respective languages, or, in other words, the population of each tribe and branch; the

That the tribes speaking these languages belong to the
Arctic variety of the human species is unquestionable; but
whether they are all of the same *race* we will not pretend to
decide. We should, in fact, be inclined to regard the Finns
and Lapps as belonging to distinct races, their physiological
and psychological characteristics differing materially. The
Lapp is distinguished for his obstinacy, suspicion, and child-
ishness of feeling; the Finn for his energy and gloomy
earnestness. "The man by his word, the ox by his horn," is
a Finnic proverb. The Lapps consider it an honour to belong to the Finns, and both people call themselves Suomi *,
but the Finn regards the Lapp with the same contemptuous
disdain as the Magyar looks down on the Slovak, or as the
Norman regarded the Saxon, a feeling which would imply
that at some remote period the Finns conquered the Lapps,
who were probably the aborigines of Finnland and Esthonia.
Ptolemy places the Fenni south-west of the Lithuanians;
Tacitus more north; Strabo describes them under the name
of Zoumi (Suomi), and according to the classic writers, they
were very savage and dirty, and much in the same state as the
Australians of the present day†.

whole Tshudic race being estimated at 3,200,000. We have calculated the
population from the data given by Berghaus in his "Grundriss der Geographie. Breslaw, 1842."

* Suomi is an abbreviation of Suomenmaa, and this of Suomiehenmaa,
literally, "Morass-man's-land," from suo, morass; mies, gen. michen, man;
and maa, land.

† Several writers place the Magyar language in the Tshudic family, but
we think on very inconclusive grounds. See, for instance, Gyarmath's
"Affinitas Linguæ Hungaricæ cum linguis Fennicæ originis grammaticæ
demonstrata," Gotting. 1799. That a certain affinity exists we will not
deny; but the Magyar is probably an original Asiatic idiom, amalgamated
with various Tshudic and Turkish dialects into one of the most energetic
and copious languages we are acquainted with. We have heard of Hungarian patriots taking it for granted that Magyar was the language spoken
by Adam and Eve—and we presume also by the serpent—in Paradise, and
it is certainly *séduisante* enough in the mouth of a fair lady to tempt a man
somewhat beyond the bounds of discretion. The origin of the Magyars
themselves is a *quæstio vexata* we will not attempt to solve. Horváth—the
Hungarian Rudbeck, makes them the descendants of the Parthians ! ! The
Magyars of the tenth century, according to the description given of them by
contemporary writers presented all the physiological characteristics of the
Mongol variety. If this was really the case, they must have been crossed
by other races, for at the present day they are as fine a race of men as any

We have already mentioned the close relationship of the Hindostanic, Iranic, Hellenic, Romanic, and Teutonic linguistic families, and we may conclude these observations on Bishop Percy's Preface, which have led us somewhat further than we intended, by calling the attention of the reader to the most remarkable fact which the annals of mankind can produce, and which future historians, when ethnological truths have become more popular, will no longer pass over in silence. It is the striking, we should say the main, the fundamental fact of human history, that from the earliest period of recorded time, down to the present day, a powerful people speaking a language belonging to one or other of these five families, should have, in a great measure, swayed the destinies of the human race.

When we strive to pierce the mysterious gloom that shrouds an infant world, it is the heaven-aspiring peaks of Central Asia* that we first discern, illumined by those primeval myths, which, like the dazzling coruscations of a polar winter, play fantastically amidst the night of ages, ere history's dawn has yet streaked time's hoary horizon with its earliest ray. And when at length the opening morn dispels these visionary splendours, we behold the luxuriant plains of the Ganges already occupied by an intelligent people, with its sages and philosophers attempting, by rendering matter the shadowy phenomenal of mind, to idealize the metempsychosis of nature into an eternal self-emanating and self-absorbing unity. It is to these Hindoo sages that we are indebted for most of the philosophical and theological ideas that we still strive to weave into a system that shall finally explain what we ought, ere this, to be aware will, for beings endowed with our limited faculties, for ever remain inexplicable. It would, in fact, be easy to show—were it not foreign to our purpose—how the metaphysical speculations of these

in Europe, the higher classes especially are distinguished for their noble and expressive physiognomy, but they have probably as much German and Italian as Magyar blood in their veins, and on a closer examination the Magyar peasantry will be found to offer physiological traits that would indicate a mixture of the Caucasian and Arctic—not to say Mongol—varieties; the Caucasian, however, generally predominating.

* The Himalaya, or Heavenly mountains, the Sanskrit, himala, corresponding to the M. Gothic, himins; Alem., himil; Germ., Swed. and Dan., himmel; Old Norse, himin; Dutch, hemel; Ang. Sax., heofon; Engl., heaven.

sages, after being recast in a classic mould by Plato, were engrafted by the first fathers of the Church on the primitive doctrines of Christianity, through which they still exercise a powerful influence over the most civilized nations of the globe.

Proceeding westward, we find, as the morn of time expands into day, the Iranic race, founding one of the mightiest monarchies the world ever witnessed, and in conformity with the precepts of Zoroaster's dualistic monotheism,

> " Make
> Their altars the high places and the peak
> Of earth-o'ergazing mountains, and thus take
> A fit and unwalled temple, there to seek
> The spirit, in whose honour shrines are weak
> Upreared of human hands."

Led on by Cyrus and by Cambyses we find these Iranites, or early Persians, subjugating all the neighbouring nations, and finally ruling with uncontrolled dominion from the Indus to the Nile; the Egyptians, who were probably an offshoot from the same parent stem, being, for near two centuries, their tributaries. But while they were thus proceeding in their career of glory, various small tribes of a mixed race, located on the isles and coasts of Greece and Asia Minor, and bound together by the ties of a common language, were essaying every form of self-government which the unshackled spirit of freedom suggests to the mind of man. Thus nerved for heroic deeds, their Hellenic idioms moulded into a classic tongue by the inspired strains of their immortal bards, the metaphysical speculations of their earliest sages and the forensic eloquence of their patriot statesmen, they fearlessly encountered the all-conquering Iranic race, and wrested from its trembling grasp the destinies of the world, on the ever-memorable plains of Marathon. The part assigned to this intellectual people in the great drama of life, was to emancipate the human mind from the hierarchial thraldom in which it had so long lingered; to render man conscious of his own dignity, to show what marvels self-government and free inquiry can accomplish, and thus hand down a glorious heritage of imperishable principles for the guidance of future generations.

It would be needless to point out how the Hellenic race had, in its turn, to cede the destinies of mankind to a cognate and more energetic, though less intellectual people; and how Roman valour and discipline, in acquiring the dominion of the then known world, diffused among the Celtic nations of western Europe the germs of a civilization grounded on municipal freedom, making them at the same time acquainted, by means of the Latin language, with that Hellenic intellectuality which they had themselves approoriated as the most glorious prize of their conquest.

The time at length arrived when, by the inevitable laws of nature, Roman freedom had degenerated into imperial despotism. Humanity was stagnating into a lethargic slumber; the world was in its wane. But the hardy tribes of the Teutonic race then issued from the forests of Germania, and after a long period of desolation and slaughter, regenerated the Romanized nations of Europe, by infusing into them, along with their Teutonic blood, a portion of that spirit of personal independence which appears to be the peculiar characteristic of the Teutonic race. The meridional European nations were thus blended into a mixed Teuto-Romano-Celtic race, speaking various languages derived from Latin, which, as the language of superior intellectual development, had predominated over the unpolished idioms of the barbarous Teutons and Celts.

Since this eventful epoch, one or other of the nations belonging either to this mixed race, or to the pure Teutonic race located in Germany, Holland, England and Scandinavia, has swayed, singly or conjointly with a cognate nation, the destinies of mankind. And at the present day we find the Germans arrived at the highest point of intellectuality the human mind has hitherto attained, recasting in a Teutonic mould those ancient systems of Hindostanic and Hellenic philosophy, which have become so intimately inwoven with our whole social existence, that without them, modern civilization would be but a sensual refinement doomed to inevitable decay. And when we turn our attention to a small island on the north western coast of Europe, we behold a nation, formed by the genial blending of Saxonic and Scandinavian tribes, arrived at a height of commercial prosperity and maritime greatness hitherto unparalleled. Ay, 'tis a pardonable vanity to record the fact; England, matchless in the mechanical arts, irresistible in arms, sweeping from the surface of the ocean the fleets of every rival nation that dares dispute her maritime supremacy, is now in possession of that heritage, whose succession we have traced through cognate races, and will, we trust, long retain it by virtue of the law which appears to have regulated its transmission; that it should be held for the time being, by the most energetic tribe of the race to which it had devolved, by the tribe that [physiological and psychological qualities rendered the most adapted to make use of it for the development of humanity.

We have thus seen how five cognate races have successively been the rulers, if not always physically, at least intellectually, and the civilizers of mankind, and how the civilization that germinated on the plains of the Ganges some forty centuries ago, has been transmitted westward from race to race, until we now find it in the north-west of Europe, with the Germans in possession of the more intellectual, and the English of the more practical, elements that constitute its essence. But the most singular fact connected with this social metempsychosis is, that the Saxon should now rule with uncontrolled sway over that antique land, whence the heritage he so gloriously holds was originally transmitted to him, and should there impart to his Hindostanic brethren a civilization whose germs had been planted by their common ancestors, at a period when the vast mountain barrier that bounds that luxuriant realm still gleamed with mythic radiancy athwart the gloom of hoar antiquity.

The day, however, must necessarily arrive when the Teutonic race, after running its destined career from barbarism to civilization, from civilization to decay, will have, either to cede this heritage to a more primitive and vigorous race, or to be regenerated by that fusion of nations which a century of war and devastation has at different epochs invariably produced. May this day be still far distant; but when German philosophy shall degenerate into Hellenic sophistry, and British refinement into Roman luxury, we may safely conclude that the Teutonic race has reached its point of culmination, and must necessarily fall before the race destined, by the inscrutable designs of an Allwise Providence, to carry on the development of humanity on earth, and render it more fit for a higher intellectuality hereafter.

> " Sic rerum summa novatur
> Semper, et inter se mortales mutua vivunt.
> Augescunt aliæ gentes, aliæ minuuntur :
> Inque brevi spatio mutantur sæcla animantum ;
> Et, quasi cursores, vitaï lampada tradunt."

SPECIMENS OF LANGUAGES.

TEUTONIC LANGUAGES.

GERMANIC BRANCH.—ALEMANNIC SUB-BRANCH.

MŒSO-GOTHIC, FOURTH CENTURY.

[1]ATTA unsar, thu ïn himinam, veihnai namo thein; [2]qimai thiudinassus theins; [3]vairthai vilja theins, sve ïn himina, jah ana airthai; [4]hlaif unsarana thana sinteinan gif uns himma daga; [5]jah aflet uns thatei skulans sijaima, svasve jah veis afletam thaim skulam unsaraim; [6]jah ni briggais uns ïn fraistubnjai, [7]ak lausei uns af thamma ubilin; [8]Unte theina ïst thiudangardi, jah mahts, jah vulthus, ïn aivins.—*From Gabelentz and Lœbe's edition of Ulphilas, Altenb. and Leipsig,* 1836.

ALEMANNIC, A.D. 720.

[1]Fatter unseer, thu pist in himele, wihi namun dinan; [2]chweme rihi din; [3]werde willo din, so in himile, sosa in erdu; [4]proath unseer emezhic kip uns hiutu; [5]oblaz uns sculdi unseero, so wir oblazen uns skuldikem; [6]enti ni unsih firletti in khorunka, [7]uzz erlosi unsih fona ubile.—*From Adelung's Mithridates,* ed. 1809, vol. ii. spec. 124.

FRANKIC, NINTH CENTURY.

[1]Fater unser, thu thar bist in himile, si giheilagot thin namo; [2]queme thin rihhi; [3]si thin uuillo, so her in himile ist, so si her in erdu; [4]unsar brot tagalihhaz gib uns hiutu; [5]inti furlaz uns unsara sculdi, so uuir furlazemes unsaren sculdigon; [6]inti ni gileites unsih in costunga, [7]uzouh arlosi unsih fon ubile. — *From Schmeller's Evangelii secundum, Matthæum versio Francica,* sæculi ix. *Stuttg.* 1827.

GERMAN, THIRTEENTH CENTURY.

[1]Fater ynser, tu in Hümele, din Name urde geheiliget; [2]din Ricke kome; [3]din Uile gskehe in Erdo alz Hümele; [4]ynser tagolicko Brod kib ynss hiuto; [5]undto ynsere Sculdo blaze yns, als wij belatzen ynser Sculdige; [6]unde in Corunga nit leitest du unsich, [7]nun belose unsich fone Ubele.—*From Adelung's Mithridates*, vol. ii. spec. 130.

GERMAN, A.D. 1462.

[1]Vatter unser, du do bist in den Himeln, geheyliget werd dein Nam; [2] zuo kum dein Reich; [3]dein Wil der werd, als im Himeln vnd in der Erd; [4]unser teglich Brot gib uns heut; [5]und vergib uns unser Schuld, als und wir vergeben unsern Schuldigern; [6]und für uns nit in Versüchung, [7]sunder erlöss uns von den Ubeln. *From Adelung's Mithridates*, vol. ii. spec. 137, taken from the first printed Bible.

GERMAN, NINETEENTH CENTURY.

[1]Unser Vater, der du bist im Himmel, geheiliget werde dein Name; [2]dein Reich komme; [3]dein Wille geschehe, wie im Himmel, also auch auf Erden; [4]unser tagliches Brodt gieb uns heute; [5]und vergieb uns unsere Schulden wie wir vergeben unsern Schuldigern; [6]und führe uns nicht in Versuchung [7]sondern erlöse uns von dem Uebel. [8]Denn dein ist das Reich, und die Kraft, und die Herrlichkeit, in Ewigkeit. —*From " Das Allgemeine Gebetbuch," Lond.* 1845.

SAXONIC SUB-BRANCH,

OLD SAXON

The earliest specimen of this language extant, is a poetical Paraphrase of the Gospels, made in the ninth century; an edition of which has been published by Schmeller from a MS. in the British Museum.

The Paraphrase of the Lord's Prayer is as follows :—

Fadar is usa· firiho barno. the is an them hohon· himi— larikea. Geuuihid si thin namo· uuordo gehuuilico. Cuma thin craftag riki. Uuerda thin uuilleo· obar thesa uuerold. al so sama an erdo. so thar uppa ist an them hohon· himilri- kea. Gef us dago gehuuilikes rad· drohtin the godo. thina

helaga helpa. Endi alat us hebenes uuard· managoro men-
sculdio. al so uue odrum mannum doan. Ne lat us farledean·
letha uuihti so ford an iro uuilleon· so uui uuirdige sind. Ac
help us uuidar allun· ubilon dadiun. — *Heliand. Poema
Saxonicum seculi noni. edit. J. A. Schmeller,* 1 v. 4°. *Monachii*
1830, p. 48, 8–16.

OLD FRISIC.

The oldest specimen extant of this language is the Asega-
bók, a Code of Laws of the Rustringian Friesians, of the
thirteenth century, from which we subjoin an extract, taken
from Wiarda's edition, 1 v. 4to. Berlin, 1805, page 1, with a
literal translation, though for the English reader a translation
is scarcely necessary.

Thit riuht skref God selva,
use hera, tha thet was thet
Moyses latte thet israheliska
folk thruoh thene rada se and
of there wilda wostene, and se
komon tho tha berge ther 'is
beheten Synay. Tha festade
Moyses twia fiuwerth dega
and nachta; ther efter ief
God him twa stenena tefla
ther hi on eskrivin hede tha
tian boda ; tha skolde hi lera
tha israheliska folke.

This law (right) wrote God
himself, our Lord, when (that
was, that) Moses led the
Israelite folk through the Red
Sea and the wild waste, and
they came to the mount that
is called (hight) Sinai. Then
fasted Moses twice forty days
and nights; thereafter gave
God him two stone tables on
which he written had the ten
commandments; these should
he teach the Israelite folk.

LOW GERMAN.

[1] Unse Vader, in dem hemmel, dyn name werde gehilliget;
[2] dyn rike kame; [3] dyn wille geschae up erden, alse im
hemmel; [4] unse dachlike brod gif uns hüden; [5] und vorgyf
uns unse schülde, alse wy unsen schüldeners vorgeven; [6] und
vöre uns nicht in versökinge, [7] sunder vorlöse uns van dem
övel. [8] Wente dyn ys dat rike, unn de kraft, unde de her-
licheit, in ewicheit. — *From Adelung's Mithridates,* vol. ii.
spec. 168.

FRISIC (MOLKWERIC IDIOM).

[1] Uhs Fader, der y binne ynne himmelen; jen namme
worde heilige; [2] jen kenningryk komme; [3] jen wille geschae,

allyk ynne hymmel, soa aeak op jerde ; [4] uhs dägs brae jouw
uhs joed; [5] in forjauw uhs unzze schielden, allyk aek wy
forjouwe uhs schieldeners ; [6] in lied uhs naet yn forsieking,
[7] mar forlos uhs fen den quaeden.   [8] Want jens ist kenningryk, in de kräft, in de haerlykheit, ynne jewigheid.—
From Adelung's Mithridates, vol. ii. spec. 150.

FRISIC (DIALECT OF HELIGOLAND).

[1] Ohsem Baabe, de dö beest öhne hemmel, hallig waarde
dann nahme ; [2] thokamme dinn kenning-rik ; [3] dann walle
schien öfh dä eerde, allick ös öhn dä hemmel ; [4] dühn ös
delling ös daaglicks bruud ; [5] en verjeef ös öse schöll, allick
ös wie verjeefe öse schellers ; [6] en fehr ös eech hanninn öhn
verseeking, [7] men help ös vohnt eävel en eerg.   [8] Dirram datt
dat kenning-rick dinn is, en dä krafft, en dä hucheit, öhn
iwigkeit.—*From Adelung's Mithridates*, vol. ii. spec. 152.

DUTCH.

[1] Onze Vader, die in de hemelen zijt, uw naam worde
geheiligd ; [2] uw koningrijk kome ; [3] uw wil geschiede, gelijk
in den hemel, alzoo ook op de aarde ; [4] geef ons heden ons
dagelijksch brood ; [5] en vergeef ons onze schulden, gelijk ook
wij vergeven onzen schuldenaren ; [6] en leid ons niet in
verzoeking, [7] maar verlos ons van den booze.   [8] Want uw is
het koningrijk, en de kracht, en de heerlijkheid in eeuwigheid.
—*From the Dutch State Bible, edit. Leyden*, 1842.

ANGLO-SAXON.

[1] Fæder úre, thú the eart on heofenum, sí thín nama ge-
hálgod ; [2] tó-becume thín ríce ; [3] gewurðe thín willa on
eorthan, swá swá on heofenum ; [4] úrne dæghwamlican hláf
syle us tó dæg ; [5] and forgyf us úre gyltas, swá swá we for-
gifað úrum gyltendum ; [6] and ne gelæd thú us on costnunge,
[7] ac alýs us of yfele.—*From Rask's Anglo-Saxon Grammar,
Copenhagen*, 1830.

ENGLISH, THIRTEENTH CENTURY.

[1] Oure Fader, that art in hevenes, halewid be thi name ;
[2] thy kingdom come ; [3] to be thi wille do as in hevene, and in
erthe ; [4] gyff to us this day oure brede over other substance ;
[5] and forgyve to us oure dettis, as forgyven to oure dettours;

E

[6]and lede us not into temptatioun, [7] but delyve us fro yvel.—
From Chamberlayne's Oratio Dominica. Amst. 1715, p. 72.

ENGLISH, SIXTEENTH CENTURY.

[1] Oure Father which arte in heven, halowed be thy name;
[2] let thy kingdome come; [3] thy will be fulfylled, as well in
erth as it is in heven; [4] geve us this daye oure dayly bred;
[5] and forgeve us oure treaspases, even as we forgeve oure tres-
pacers; [6] and leade us not into temptacion, [7] but delyver us
from evyll. [8] For thyne is the kyngedome, and the power,
and the glorye for ever.—*From Tyndal and Coverdale's Bible.
Black letter.* 1537.

SCANDINAVIAN BRANCH.

OLD NORSE (NORRÆNA TUNGA).

Not being aware of any work that contains the Our Father
in Old Norse, we shall give, as a specimen of this language,
part of the long argument made use of by King Olaf Tryggvason to persuade Sigmund Bresterson to embrace Christianity,
extracted from Rafn's edition of the Færeyinga Saga, ch. 29.

OLD NORSE.	TRANSLATION.
Nú allra helzt fyrir thá skyld, er ek hefi spurt, at thú hafir aldri blótat skúrgoð eptir hætti annarra heiðinna manna, thá hefi ek góða von á, at hinn háleiti himnako-núngr, skapari allra hluta, muni thik leiða til kynníngar síns helga nafns ok heilagrar trúar af mínum fortölum; ok gera thik mér samfèlaga i rèttum átrúnaði, svà sem jafnan at afli ok allri atgervi, ok öðrum sínum miskunnargjöfum, er hann hefir thèr veitt sem mèr, löngum tíma fyrr enn ek hafði nokkura vissu af dýrð hans.	Now it is chiefly on this account, because I have learned that thou hast never sacrificed to idols after the custom of other heathen men, that I have good hope, that the most high heavenly king, the creator of all things, may lead thee to the knowledge of his hallowed name and holy faith through my supplication; and make thee my fellow companion in the right worship, as thou art like to me in strength and skill, and in other gifts of his grace, that he hath bestowed upon thee as upon me, a long time before I had any knowledge of his glory.

ICELANDIC (ISLENZKA).

[1]Fader vor, thú sem ert á himnum, helgest thitt nafn ; [2]til-kome thitt ríke ; [2]verde thinn vile, so á jördu, sem á himne ; [4]gef thu oss í dag vort daglegt braud ; [5]og fyrergef oss vorar skullder, so sem ver fyrergefum vorum skulldunautum ; [6]og innleid oss eige í freistne, [7]helldur frelsa thú oss fra illu. [8]Thvíad thitt er ríked, og máttur, og dyrd, um allder allda.— *From the Icelandic Bible, published at Copenhagen,* 1813.

FÆRŒIC.

We shall give as a specimen of this language, the pre-ceding passage of the Færeyinga Saga, from the Færœic translation made by two clergymen of the Færoe Isles, for Rafn's edition of the Saga.

Nú allarhelst firi tan Skjild, at e hävi spurt, at tú hevir aldri ofra til Afgudar sum ärir hajdnir Men häva til Si, tå hävi e gowa Vown til tes, at tan höji Himnakongur, skäpari äf ödlun Lutin, man laja te til at kunnast vi sujt hajlia Navn og til hajlia Trygv äf hesari mujni Tälu, og gjera te lujka so sam-sintan vi me um tä rattu Trúna, sum han hevir gjört te javnan vi me uj Stirka og adlari Kviklihajd ; og örun sujnun Mis-kunargåvun, sum han vajt tär sum mär, lenga Tuj firin e heji näka Vitniskji um Harlihajt hansara.

NORWEGIAN*.

[1]Faer vaar, du som er i himlen, helket vaarde dit namn ; [2]tilkome os dit rike ; [3]sje di völlie her aa jera, sem den sjer i hiimlen ; [4]giv os höer dak vaart daklike brö ; [5]og forlat os vaar sjuld, som vi forlate vaare sjulner ; [6]leet os ikkie uti früstelse, [7]men frals os fra det one. [8]Ty riket er dit, aa makten, aa aran, i evikhet.—*From Adelung's Mithridates,* vol. ii. spec. 181.

SWEDISH.

[1]Fader vår, som äst i himlom, helgadt varde ditt namn ; [2]tilkomme ditt rike ; [3]ske din vilje såsom i himmelen, så ock på jordene ; [4]gif oss i dag vårt dageliga bröd ; [5]och förlåt oss våra skulder, såsom ock vi förlåte dem oss skyldige äro ; [6]och inled oss icke i frestelse ; [7]utan fräls oss ifrån ondo. [8]Ty riket är ditt, och magten, och härligheten, i evighet.—*From the Bible Society's edit. of the Bible, Stocholm,* 1837.

* That is to say, a Norwegian dialect, see note 5, page 15.

134139

DANISH.

[1]Vor Fader, du som er i himlene, helliget vorde dit navn; [2]komme dit rige; [3]skee din villie, som i himmelen, saa og paa jorden; [4]giv os i dag vort daglige bröd; [5]og forlad os vor skyld, saa som vi og forlade vore skyldnere; [6]og leed os ikke ind i fristelse, [7]men frie os fra det onde. [8]Thi dit er riget, og kraften, og herligheden, i evighed.— *From the Bible Society's edition of the Bible, Christiana,* 1835.

CELTIC LANGUAGES.

GAELIC BRANCH.

ERSE.

[1]Ar na thaír atá ar neamh, náomhthar hainm; [2]tigeadh do rioghachd; [3]deúntar do thoil ar an ttalamh, mar do nithear ar neamh; [4]ar narán laéathamhail tabhair dhúinn a niu; [5]agus maith dhúinn ar bhfíacha, mar mhaithmídne dar bhféitheamh-nuibh féin; [6]agus na léig sinn a ccathughadh, [7]achd sáor inn ó olc. [8]Oir is leachd féin an ríoghachd, agus an cumhachd, agus an ghloír, go síorruighe.—*From the Bible Society's New Test., Lond.,* 1824.

GAELIC.

[1]Ar n-Athair a ta air nèamh, gu naomhaichear t'ainm; [2]thigeadh do rioghachd; [3]deanar do thoil air an talamh, mar a nithear air nèamh; [4]tabhair dhuinn an diugh ar n-aran laitheil; [5]agus maith dhuinn ar fiacha, amhuil mar a mhaitheas sinne d'ar luchd-fiach; [6]agus na leig am buaireadh sinn; [7]ach saor sinn o olc. [8]Oir is leatsa an rioghachd, agus an cumhachd, agus a' ghloìr, gu siorruidh.—*From the Gaelic New Testament, Edinburgh,* 1813.

MANKS.

[1]Ayr ain t'ayns niau, casherick dy row dty ennym; [2]dy jig dty reeriaght; [3]dty aigney dy row jeant ery thalloo, myr te ayns niau; [4]cur dooin nyn arran jiu as gagh laa; [5]as leih dooin nyn loghtyn, myr ta shin leih dauesyn ta jannoo loghtyn nyn 'oï; [6]as ny leeid shin ayns miolagh, [7]agh livrey shin veih

olk. [8]Son lhiat's y reeriaght, as y phooar, as y ghloyr, son dy bragh.—*From the Bible Society's Manks New Testament, London*, 1815.

KYMRIC BRANCH.

WELSH.

[1]Ein Tad, yr hwn wyt yn y nefoedd, sancteiddier dy enw; [2]deled dy deyrnas; [3]gwneler dy ewyllys, megis yn y nef. felly ar y ddaear hefyd; [4]dyro i ni heddyw ein bara beunyddiol; [5]a maddeu i ni ein dyledion, fel y maddeuwn ninnau i'n dyledwyr; [6]ac nac arwain ni i brofedigaeth, [7]eithr gwared ni rhag drwg. [8]Canys eiddo ti yw y deyrnas, a'r nerth, a'r gogoniant, yn oes oesoedd.—*From the Welsh New Testament, Wyddgrug*, 1835.

ARMORICAN (BREYZAD).

[1]Hon Tad, pehini a so en eon, hoch ano bezet sanctifiet; [2]roet deomp ho ruanteles; [3]ho bolonte bezet gret en duar, evel en eon; [4]roet deomp hon bara pebdeziec; [5]a pardonet deomp hon offansu, evel ma pardonomp dar re pere ho devus hon offanset; [6]ne bermettet ket e cuessemp e tentation ebet; [7]oguen hon delivret a zruc.—*From Adelung's Mithridates*, vol. ii. spec. 118.

TSHUDIC LANGUAGES.

SUOMIC BRANCH.

FINNIC.

[1]Isä meidän, joka olet taiwaisa, pyhitetty olkon sinum nimes; [2]lähestykön sinun waldakundas; [3]olkon sinun tahtos niin maasa, kuin taiwasa; [4]anna meille tänäpänä meidän jokapäiwäinen leipämme; [5]ja anna meille meidän welkamme andexi, niinkuin mekin andexi annamme meidän welwollistemme; [6]ja älä johdata meitä kiusauxeen; [7]mutta päästä meitä pahasta. [8]Sillä sinun on waldakunda, ja woima, ja kunnia, ijankaikkisesti.—*From the Bible Society's N. Test., pub. at Turusa*, 1815.

ESTHONIC (DORPAT DIALECT)

[1]Meije Issa, taiwan, pühhändatus sago sinno nimmi; [2]sinno rikkus tulgo; [3]sinno tahtminne sündko, kui taiwan

nida ka ma pääl; [4]meije päiwalikko leiba anna meile täämba; [5]nink anna meile andis meije süda, nida kui ka meije andis-anname ommille süüdleisille; [6]nink ärrasaatko meid kiu-satusse sisse; [7]enge pästa meid ärra kurjast. [8]Sest sinno perralt om rikkus, nink wäggi, nink auwustus, iggawetsel ajal.—*From the Bible Society's Esthonic N. Test., pub. Mitau,* 1815.

LAPPIC.

[1]Attje mijen, jukko leh almesne, ailesen sjaddes to namma; [2]pätes to rik; [3]sjaddes to wiljo ko almesn, nau ai üdnamen naln; [4]mijen färten peiwen laipeb wadde miji udne; [5]ja luoite miji mijen laikoit andagas, nau ko ai mije luoitebe mijen welkolatjita; [6]ja ale sislaide mijeb kättjeleb-mai; [7]walla warjele mijeb pahast. [8]Jutte to le rik, ja faomo, ja härlogwuot, ekewen aikai.—*From the Lappic Bible, pub. at Hernösandesne,* 1811.

PERMIC BRANCH.

TSHEREMISSIC.

[1]Atjà memnàn, ílscha kjuschnasótaschta, ljum tünin swjatoi lísha; [2]i tólsha tünin schmàk; [3]lisha tünin wolja, kusè tün-jaschtá, tugè rokaschta; [4]kíndam memnánam kashdakétschel-scham pu malanà tagátscha; [5]kodà malanà sulukwlajam memnanam, kusè i me kodalnà menàp parmawljanam; [6]it púrta memnàm oltalmáschka; [7]siorlaja memnàm schoitan getschen. [8]Tùnin úla ischmak, koàt, tschelja, ikschta nin.—*From Adelung's Mithridates, vol. iv. spec.* 60.

M. MALLET'S PREFACE.

HISTORY has not recorded the annals of a people who have occasioned greater, more sudden, or more numerous revolutions in Europe than the Scandinavians *, or whose antiquities, at the same time, are so little known. Had, indeed, their emigrations been only like those sudden torrents of which all traces and remembrance are soon effaced, the indifference that has been shown to them would have been sufficiently justified by the barbarism they have been reproached with. But, during those general inundations, the face of Europe underwent so total a change, and during the confusion they occasioned, such different establishments took place; new societies were formed, animated so entirely with a new spirit, that the history of our own manners and institutions ought necessarily to ascend back, and even dwell a considerable time upon a period, which discovers to us their chief origin and source.

But I ought not barely to assert this. Permit me to support the assertion by proofs. For this purpose, let us briefly run over all the different revolutions which this part of the world underwent, during the long course of ages which its history comprehends, in order to see what share the nations of the north have had in producing them. If we recur back to the remotest times, we observe a nation issuing step by step from the forests of Scythia †, incessantly increasing

---

* Than the Teutons, or people of the Teutonic race, would have been a more appropriate expression ; the tribes belonging to the Germanic branch of this race having unquestionably "caused more numerous revolutions in Europe" than those belonging to the Scandinavian branch.—ED.

† There is not a vaguer term in ancient geography than that of Scythia. Taken in its most extensive signification, it would embrace all the countries lying between the present river Don in the west, the great desert of Gobi in the East, the Hindoo Kosh mountains on the south, and the plains of

and dividing to take possession of the uncultivated countries
which it met with in its progress. Very soon after, we see
the same people, like a tree full of vigour, extending long
branches over all Europe; we see them also carrying with
them, wherever they came, from the borders of the Black Sea
to the extremities of Spain, of Sicily, and Greece, a religion
simple and martial as themselves, a form of government dictated by good sense and liberty, a restless unconquered spirit,
apt to take fire at the very mention of subjection and constraint, and a ferocious courage, nourished by a savage and
vagabond life. While the gentleness of the climate softened
imperceptibly the ferocity of those who settled in the south,
colonies of Egyptians and Phenicians mixing with them upon
the coasts of Greece, and thence passing over to those of
Italy, taught them at last to live in cities, to cultivate letters,
arts and commerce. Thus their opinions, their customs and
genius, were blended together, and new states were formed
upon new plans. Rome, in the mean time arose, and at
length carried all before her. In proportion as she increased
in grandeur, she forgot her ancient manners, and destroyed,
among the nations whom she overpowered, the original spirit
with which they were animated. But this spirit continued

Siberia on the north, in which direction the boundaries might be limited or
extended to suit any particular theory, this region being for the ancients
terra incognita. We would also venture to say that there is scarcely a
nation or tribe known in European history that has not, by one writer or
other, been called Scythian. We could cite works in which Pelasgi, Thracians, Celts, Goths, Saxons, Finns, Huns, Magyars, Turks, Tatars, and
various other nations are respectively designated as Scythians, or of Scythian
origin. Jamieson in his "Hermes Scythicus" gravely informs us that " with
respect to their (the Scythians) origin, the most general opinion is, that they
were the descendants of Magog, the second son of Japhet ! ! !" The confusion of ideas that long prevailed on this subject arose from writers applying
the term "Scythians" ethnographically instead of geographically, applying it
to designate a distinct race like the terms Teutons, Slavonians, Celts, &c.,
and not an assemblage of nations of various origin, such as we comprehend
under the terms Europeans, Africans, Asiatics, &c. It is only in the latter
signification that the word can be tolerated at the present day. When our
author, therefore, talks of "*a nation* issuing from the forests of Scythia" he
must be understood to mean the various races of Asiatic origin, some of
them, as we have shown in our preceding remarks, remotely cognate, that
spread themselves over Europe at an epoch far beyond the bounds of authentic
history, as well as others who may have "trod upon the heels of their fathers"
at a more recent period.—ED.

unaltered in the colder countries of Europe, and maintained itself there like the independency of the inhabitants. Scarce could fifteen or sixteen centuries produce there any change in that spirit. There it renewed itself incessantly; for, during the whole of that long interval, new adventurers issuing continually from the original inexhaustible country, trod upon the heels of their fathers towards the north, and, being in their turn succeeded by new troops of followers, they pushed one another forward, like the waves of the sea. The northern countries, thus overstocked, and unable any longer to contain such restless inhabitants, equally greedy of glory and plunder, discharged at length, upon the Roman empire, the weight that oppressed them. The barriers of the empire, ill defended by a people whom prosperity had enervated, were borne down on all sides by torrents of victorious armies. We then see the conquerors introducing, among the nations they vanquished, viz. into the very bosom of slavery and sloth, that spirit of independence and equality, that elevation of soul, that taste for rural and military life, which both the one and the other had originally derived from the same common source, but which were then among the Romans breathing their last. Dispositions and principles so opposite, struggled long with forces sufficiently equal, but they united in the end, they coalesced together, and from their coalition sprung those principles and that spirit which governed, afterwards, almost all the states of Europe, and which, notwithstanding the differences of climate, of religion, and particular accidents, do still visibly reign in them, and retain, to this day, more or less the traces of their first common origin.

It is easy to see, from this short sketch, how greatly the nations of the north have influenced the different fates of Europe; and if it be worth while to trace its revolutions to their causes, if the illustration of its institutions, of its police, of its customs, of its manners, of its laws, be a subject of useful and interesting inquiry; it must be allowed, that the antiquities of the north, that is to say, every thing which tends to make us acquainted with its ancient inhabitants, merits a share in the attention of thinking men. But to render this obvious by a particular example; is it not well known that the most flourishing and celebrated states of Europe owe originally to the northern nations, whatever

liberty they now enjoy, either in their constitution, or in the
spirit of their government? For although the Gothic form
of government has been almost every where altered or abolished, have we not retained, in most things, the opinions, the
customs, the manners which that government had a tendency
to produce? Is not this, in fact, the principal source of that
courage, of that aversion to slavery, of that empire of honour
which characterize in general the European nations; and of
that moderation, of that easiness of access, and peculiar attention to the rights of humanity, which so happily distinguish
our sovereigns from the inaccessible and superb tyrants
of Asia? The immense extent of the Roman empire had
rendered its constitution so despotic and military, many
of its emperors were such ferocious monsters, its senate was
become so mean-spirited and vile, that all elevation of sentiment, every thing that was noble and manly, seems to have
been for ever banished from their hearts and minds; insomuch that if all Europe had received the yoke of Rome in
this her state of debasement, this fine part of the world, reduced to the inglorious condition of the rest, could not have
avoided falling into that kind of barbarity, which is of all
others the most incurable; as, by making as many slaves as
there are men, it degrades them so low as not to leave them
even a thought or desire of bettering their condition. But
nature had long prepared a remedy for such great evils,
in that unsubmitting, unconquerable spirit, with which she
had inspired the people of the north; and thus she made
amends to the human race, for all the calamities which,
in other respects, the inroads of these nations, and the over-
throw of the Roman empire produced.

"The great prerogative of Scandinavia (says the admirable
author of the Spirit of Laws), and what ought to recommend
its inhabitants beyond every people upon earth, is, that they
afforded the great resource to the liberty of Europe, that is,
to almost all the liberty that is among men. The Goth Jornandes (adds he) calls the north of Europe the forge of mankind. I should rather call it, the forge of those instruments
which broke the fetters manufactured in the south. It was
there those valiant nations were bred, who left their native
climes to destroy tyrants and slaves, and to teach men that
nature having made them equal, no reason could be assigned
for their becoming dependent, but their mutual happiness."

If these considerations be of any weight, I shall easily be excused for having treated at so much length the antiquities of the north. The judicious public will see and decide whether I have conceived a just idea of my subject, or whether, from an illusion too common with authors, I have not ascribed to it more importance than it deserves. I should not be without some apprehensions of this kind, if that were always true which is commonly said, that we grow fond of our labours in proportion as they are difficult. Many tedious and unentertaining volumes I have been obliged to peruse: I have had more than one language to learn; my materials were widely scattered, ill digested, and often little known. It was not easy to collect them, or to accommodate them to my purpose. These are all circumstances ill calculated, it must be owned, to give me much assurance. But I have likewise met with very considerable assistances; several learned men have treated particular points of the antiquities of the north with that deep erudition which characterizes the studies of the last age. I cannot mention, without acknowledgment and praise, Bartholinus, Wormius, Stephanius, Arngrim Jonas, Torfæus, &c.

Is it necessary that I should take notice, before I conclude, that I am about to delineate a nation in its infancy, and that the greatest part of the other Europeans were neither less savage, nor less uncivilized, during the same period? I shall give sufficient proofs of this in other places, being persuaded that there is among nations an emulation of glory, which often degenerates into jealousy, and puts them upon assuming a pre-eminence upon the most chimerical advantages; that there glows in their bosoms a patriotic zeal, which is often so blind and ill informed, as to take alarm at the most slender and indifferent declarations made in favour of others.

NORTHERN ANTIQUITIES.

CHAPTER I.

OF THE FIRST INHABITANTS OF DENMARK, AND PARTICULARLY OF THE CIMBRI.

It is useless to inquire at what period of time Denmark began to be inhabited. Such a research would doubtless lead us up to an age when all Europe was plunged in ignorance and barbarity. These two words include in them almost all we know of the history of the first ages. It is very probable, that the first Danes were like all the other Teutonic nations, a colony of Scythians *, who spread themselves at different times over the countries which lay towards the west. The resemblance of name might induce us to believe that it was from among the Cimmerian Scythians (whom the ancients placed to the north of the Euxine Sea) that the first colonies were sent into Denmark; and that from this people they inherited the name of Cimbri, which they bore so long before they assumed that of Danes. But this resemblance of name, which many historians produce as a solid proof, is liable to so many different explanations, that it is better to acknowledge once for all, that this subject is as incapable of certainty, as it is unworthy of research.

Whatever was the origin of the Cimbri, they for a long time before the birth of Christ inhabited the country, which received from them the name of the Cimbrica Chersonesus, or Cimbric Peninsula, and probably comprehended Jutland, Sleswic, and Holstein, and perhaps some of the neighbouring provinces. The ancients considered this people as a branch of the Germans, and never distinguished the one from the other in the descriptions they have left us of the manners

* See the note page 55.

and customs of that nation. The historical monuments of the north give us still less information about them, and go no farther back than the arrival of Odin; the epoch of which I am inclined to place, with the celebrated Torfæus, about seventy years before the birth of Christ. All that passed in Denmark before that period would be entirely unknown to us, if the famous expedition of the Cimbri into Italy had not drawn upon them the attention of a people who enjoyed the advantage of having historians. It is a single gleam, which for a moment throws light upon the ages of obscurity; short and transient as it is, let us nevertheless catch it, in order to discover, if possible, a feature or two of the character of this people.

The history of Rome * informs us, that in the consulship of Cæcilius Metellus and Papirius Carbo, about one hundred and eleven years before the Chistian era †, the republic was agitated by intestine divisions which already began to threaten its liberty, when the intrigues of the several factions were all at once suspended by the sudden news of an irruption of barbarians. More than three hundred thousand men, known by the names of Cimbri and Teutones, who chiefly issued from the Cimbric Chersonese and the neighbouring islands, had forsaken their country to go in search of a more favourable climate, of plunder and glory. They attacked and subdued at once whatever people they found in their passage, and as they met with no resistance, resolved to push their conquests farther. The Gauls where overwhelmed with this torrent, whose course was for a long time marked by the most horrible desolation. Terror every where went before them, and when it was reported at Rome, that they were disposed to pass into Italy, the consternation there became general. The senate despatched Papirius Carbo with an army to guard the passage of the Alps, deeming it a sufficient degree of good fortune, if they could but preserve Italy from these formidable guests. But as they took a different route, and stopped some time on the banks of the Danube, the Romans resumed courage, and condemning their former fears, sent in a menacing tone to the Cimbri, to bid them take care not to

* See Plutarch in Mario.—Oros. l. 5.—Vel. Patercul. l. 2.—T. Liv. epit. l. 68.—Flor. l. 3. chap. 30.
† Anno Urb. Cond. 640.

disturb the Norici their allies. At the same time the **Cimbri**, being informed that a Roman army approached them, and respecting the character of the Republic, sent ambassadors to the Consul Papirius, "to excuse themselves, forasmuch as having come from the remote parts of the north, they could not possibly know that the Norici were the allies of the Romans:" adding, "that they only knew it to be a received law among all nations, that the conqueror hath a right to whatever he can acquire; and that the Romans themselves had no other pretensions to most of the countries they had subdued, than what was founded on the sword. That they had, however, a great veneration for the Roman people on account of their virtue and bravery; in consideration of which, although they knew not what it was to fear, they consented to leave the Norici in peace, and to employ their valour in some other quarter, where they could do it without incurring the displeasure of the commonwealth." Satisfied with so moderate an answer, the consul suffered them quietly to remove; but when the Cimbri were retired into Dalmatia, and expected nothing less than hostilities from the Romans, a party of these commanded by Carbo surprised them by night asleep and unarmed. These brave warriors full of indignation flew to their arms, and defended themselves with so much intrepidity, that they wrested the victory out of their enemies' hands, and forced them to seek their safety by flight. But although the Romans almost all escaped the vengeance of their enemies, this defeat was not the less fatal to the republic; for the splendour and reputation which it added to the arms of the Cimbri, drew on all sides under their banners such nations as were either impatient of the Roman yoke, or jealous of their encroachments; particularly the Tigurini and Ambrones, two people originally of Helvetia. With these new auxiliaries, they overwhelmed Gaul a second time, and advancing to the foot of the Pyrenees, endeavoured to establish themselves in Spain; but meeting with a vigorous repulse from the Celtiberians, and tired of so many unprofitable invasions, they sent a new embassy to the Romans, to offer them their services, upon condition they would give them lands to cultivate. The Senate, too prudent to enter into any kind of accommodation with such dangerous enemies, and already divided among themselves about the distribution of lands, returned a direct refusal to their demand. Upon which the Cimbri resolved to seize by force what they could not gain by entreaty, and immediately fell with so much fury upon the new consul Silanus, who had received orders to march against them, that they forced his intrenchments, pillaged his camp, and cut all his army in pieces. This victory was soon after followed by another, which their allies the Ambrones gained over Cassius Longinus at the mouth of the Rhone; and to complete the misfortune, a third army of Romans, more considerable than the two former, was soon after entirely defeated. Scaurus, who commanded it, was made prisoner, and afterwards put to death; his two sons were slain, and more than fourscore thousand of the Romans and their allies were left dead in the field. Last of all, two other generals, the consul Manlius, and the proconsul Cæpio, to whom had been intrusted a fourth army already half vanquished with fear, and who were disunited and jealous of each other, were attacked near the Rhone, each of them in his camp, and entirely defeated.

Such repeated losses filled Rome with grief and terror; and many began to despair even of the safety of the state. In this melancholy conjuncture, minds less firm than those of these spirited republicans would, doubtless, have suggested the imprudent measure of granting to the conquerors conditions capable of softening them : they would have given them at once the lands they had required, or perhaps have purchased their friendship with a sum of money. This dangerous policy would probably have ruined Rome in this exigence, as it did some ages after. The Gauls, the Germans, and the Scythians, poor and greedy nations, who grasped after nothing but slaughter and booty, roving and warlike, as well by inclination as necessity, would have harassed, by continual inroads, a people which had let them see that they were at once richer and weaker than themselves. The prudent firmness of the Senate, and the valour of Marius, saved Rome for this time from the danger under which it afterwards sunk. All the citizens now turned their eyes towards the conqueror of Jugurtha, as their last and only support. They decreed him consular honours for the fourth time, and associated with him Catulus Luctatius, a person scarcely inferior to him in

military skill, and who far exceeded him in all the other qualities which make a great statesman.

Marius having quickly discovered that the ill success of his
predecessors was the effect of their imprudence, formed to
himself a very different plan of conduct. In particular, he
resolved not to join battle with the enemy till their furious
ardour was abated, and till his soldiers familiarized to the
sight of them, should no longer consider themselves as conquered before they came to blows. Their former victories,
their tallness of stature, rendered still more terrible by their
dress, their ferocious air, their barbarous shouts, and unusual
manner of fighting, had all contributed to strike the Romans
with the greatest terror; and this terror was the first enemy he
had to encounter; an enemy which time alone could subdue.
With this view, Marius judged it necessary to encamp on the
banks of the Rhone, in a situation naturally advantageous,
where he laid in all sorts of provisions in great abundance,
that he might not be compelled to engage before he saw a
convenient opportunity. This coolness of the general was regarded by those barbarians as a mark of cowardice. They
resolved, therefore, to divide themselves into different bodies,
and so penetrate into Italy. The Cimbri and Tigurini went
to meet Catulus; the Ambrones and Teutones, hoping to provoke the Romans to fight, came and encamped in a plain full
in their front. But nothing could induce Marius to change
his resolution.

Nevertheless, these barbarians insulted the Romans incessantly by every means they could devise: they advanced as
far as the very intrenchments of their camp to reproach and
deride them; they challenged the officers and the general
himself to single combat. The Roman soldiers were by degrees accustomed to look their enemies in the face, while the
provocations they received every day more and more whetted
their resentment. Many of them even broke out into reproaches against Marius for appearing so much to distrust
their courage; and this dexterous general to appease them,
had recourse to a Syrian prophetess in his camp, who assured
them that the gods did not yet approve of their fighting

At length the patience of the Teutones was exhausted, and
they endeavoured to force the Roman intrenchments; but

here they were repulsed with loss: upon which, they resolved to abandon their camp, and attempt an irruption into Italy. They filed off for six days together in the presence of Marius's army, insulting his soldiers with the most provoking language, and asking them if they had any message to send to their wives whom they hoped soon to see. Marius heard all these bravados with his accustomed coolness; but when their whole army was passed by, he followed them as far as Aix in Provence, harassing their rear-guard without intermission. When he was arrived at this place, he halted, in order to let his soldiers enjoy what they had ardently desired so long—a pitched battle. They began with skirmishing on both sides, till the fight insensibly growing more serious, at length both armies made the most furious attacks. Thirty thousand Ambrones advanced first, marching in a kind of measure to the sound of their instruments. A body of Ligurians, supported by the Romans, repulsed them with great loss; but as they betook themselves to flight, their wives came forth to meet them with swords and hatchets in their hands, and bitterly reproaching them, and striking indiscriminately friend and foe, endeavoured to snatch with their naked hands the enemies' weapons, maintaining an invincible firmness even till death. This first action raised the courage of the Romans, and was the prelude to a victory still more decisive.

After the greatest part of the Ambrones had perished in that day's action, Marius caused his army to retire back to his camp, ordering them to keep strict watch, and to lie close without making any movement; as if they were affrighted at their own victory. On the other hand, in the camp of the Teutones were heard continual howlings, like to those of savage beasts; so hideous, that the Romans, and even their general himself could not help testifying their horror. They, notwithstanding, lay quiet that night, and the day following, being busily employed in preparing all things for a second engagement. Marius, on his part, took all necessary precautions; he placed in an ambuscade three thousand men commanded by Marcellus, with orders to attack the enemy in the rear, as soon as they should perceive the battle was begun. When both armies were come within sight of each other, Marius commanded his cavalry to dismount; but the Teutones, hurried on by that blind impetuosity which distinguishes all

F

barbarous nations, instead of waiting till the Romans were come down into the plain, attacked them on an eminence where they were advantageously posted. At the same instant, Marcellus appeared suddenly behind with his troops, and hemming them in, threw their ranks into disorder, so that they were quickly forced to fly. Then the victory declared itself entirely in favour of the Romans, and a most horrible carnage ensued. If we may take literally what some of the Roman historians have related*, there perished more than a hundred thousand Teutones, including the prisoners. Others content themselves with saying, that the number of the slain was incredible; that the inhabitants of Marseilles for a long time after, made inclosures for their gardens and vineyards with the bones; and that the earth thereabouts was so much fattened, that its increase of produce was prodigious. Marius loaded with glory, after a victory so illustrious in itself, and so important in its consequences, was a fifth time honoured with the consular fasces; but he would not triumph till he had secured the repose of Italy, by the entire defeat of all the barbarians. The Cimbri, who had separated themselves from the Teutones, still threatened its safety. They had penetrated as far as the banks of the Adige; which Catulus Luctatius was not strong enough to prevent them from crossing. The progress they made still caused violent alarms in Rome; Marius was charged to raise a new army with the utmost speed, and to go and engage them. The Cimbri had halted near the Po, in hopes that the Teutones, of whose fate they were ignorant, would quickly join them. Wondering at the delay of these their associates, they sent to Marius a second time to demand an allotment of land, sufficient to maintain themselves and the Teutones their brethren. Marius answered them, that " their brethren already possessed more than they desired, and that they would not easily quit what he had assigned them." The Cimbri, irritated by this raillery, instantly resolved to take ample vengeance.

They prepared immediately for battle, and their king, or general, named Bojorix, approached the Roman camp with a small party of horse to challenge Marius, and to agree with him on a day and place of action. Marius answered, that although it was not the custom of the Romans to consult their

* See Plutarch's Life of Marius.

enemies on this subject, he would notwithstanding for once oblige them, and therefore appointed the next day but one, and the plain of Verceil for their meeting. At the time appointed, the two armies marched thither; the Romans ranged themselves into two wings: Catulus commanded a body of twenty thousand men, and Sylla was in the number of his officers. The Cimbri formed with their infantry an immense square battalion: their cavalry, consisting of fifteen thousand men, was magnificently mounted; each soldier bore upon his helmet the head of some savage beast, with its mouth gaping wide; an iron cuirass covered his body, and he carried a long halberd in his hand. The extreme heat of the weather was very favourable to the Romans. They had been careful to get the sun on their backs; while the Cimbri little accustomed to its violence, had it in their faces *. Besides this, the dust hid from the eyes of the Romans the astonishing multitude of their enemies, so that they fought with the more confidence, and of course more courage. The Cimbri, exhausted and dispirited, were quickly routed A precaution, which they had taken to prevent their being dispersed, only served to forward their ruin; they had linked the soldiers of the foremost ranks to one another with chains; in these they were entangled, and thereby exposed the more to the blows of the Romans. Such as could fly, met with new dangers in their camp; for their women who sat upon their chariots, clothed in black, received them as enemies, and massacred without distinction their fathers, brothers, and husbands; they even carried their rage to such a height, as to dash out the brains of their children; and completed the tragedy, by throwing themselves under their chariot wheels. After their example, their husbands in despair turned their arms against one another, and seemed to join with the Romans in promoting their own defeat. In the dreadful slaughter of that day, a hundred and twenty thousand are said to have perished; and if we except a few families of the Cimbri, which remained in their own country, and a small

---

* We are told that the Cimbri were on the point of gaining the victory, when the sun, breaking through the clouds, blinded them. If this story be true, the fate of the world hung upon a sunbeam! It *apparently* often does hang upon a very slender thread. " Si le nez de Cléopatre eût été plus court, toute la face de la terre auroit changé," says Pascal, 1 P. A. 9, s. 56.—ED.

number who escaped, one may say, that this fierce and valiant
nation was all mowed down at one single stroke. This last
victory procured Marius the honours of a triumph, and the
services he thereby rendered the commonwealth appeared so
great, that he received the glorious title of Third Founder of
Rome.

Thus have we given, in a few words, what historians relate
of the expedition of the Cimbri; it drew upon them for a
moment the attention of all Europe. But as literature, and
the fine arts, can alone give lasting fame to a nation, and as
we easily lose the remembrance of those evils we no longer
fear, this torrent was no sooner withdrawn within its ancient
bounds, but the Romans themselves lost sight of it, so that
we scarcely find any farther mention of the Cimbri in any of
their writers. Strabo only informs us, that they afterwards
sought the friendship of Augustus, and sent for a present a
vase, which they made use of in their sacrifices; and Tacitus
tells us, in one word, that the Cimbri had nothing left but a
celebrated name, and a reputation as ancient as it was extensive.

I do not pretend to decide whether the first inhabitants of
these countries were all of them, without any mixture, of
Germanic origin, Cimbri and Teutones *. For although to

* Whether the ancient Cimbri, and their confederates the Teutones, who
made the irruption into the Roman empire in the time of Marius, were a
Celtic or a Gothic people may perhaps admit of some disquisition. They
who contend that they were Celts, may urge the resemblance of the name of
Cimbri to that of *Cymri*, by which the Britons have always called themselves in their own language : they may also produce the authority of Ap-
pian, who expressly calls the *Cimbri* Celts; as well as of several of the Roman authors, who scruple not to name them Gauls [a]. It may further be observed in favour of this opinion, that the emigration of so large a body of the
old Celtic inhabitants, would facilitate the invasion of the Gothic tribes who
succeeded them in these northern settlements, and will account for the rapid
conquests of Odin and his Asiatic followers : it might also be conjectured,
that the small scattered remains of these old Celtic Cimbri, were the savage
men who lurked up and down in the forests and mountains, as described by

[a] " Appianus *in Illyricis* Cimbros *Celtas,* addito *quos Cimbros vocant,* ap-
pellavit. Et evolve Florum, lib. iii. cap. 3. Salustium *Bell. Jugurth. in
fine.* Rufum *Brev.* cap. vi. qui omnes *Cimbros* diserté *Gallos* et *ab extremis
Galliæ* profugos, nominarunt." Speneri Notitia Germaniæ Antiquæ. Hal.
Magd. 1717, 4to. p. 123.

me this appears very probable, with regard to Denmark, it cannot be denied that the Finns and Laplanders anciently

the ancient Icelandic historians, and who, in their size and ferocity, so well correspond with the descriptions given us of their countrymen that invaded the Roman empire. Thus far such an opinion is equally consistent both with the Roman and northern historians. On the other hand, that the *Cimbri* of Marius were not a Celtic, but a German or a Gothic people, is an opinion that may be supported with no slight arguments. On this head it may be observed, with our author, Mons. Mallet, " that the ancients generally considered this people as a branch of the Germans," and that their tall stature and general character rather corresponds with the description of the Germans than of the Celts : that as for the name of *Cimbri* or *Cimber*, it is resolvable into a word in the German language, which signifies warrior or warlike [a] : and that the authorities of the Roman historians cannot much be depended on, because (as has been before observed) they were seldom exact in the names they gave to the barbarous nations. It may further be urged, that the facility with which the Cimbri made their way through Germany into Gaul, renders it probable that they were rather a branch of the German people, than of a race in constant enmity with them, like the Celts, and who, upon that account, would have been opposed in their passage ; especially as the Germans appear in these countries rather to have prevailed over the Celts, and to have forced them westward, driving them out of many of their settlements. But lastly, if the Cimbri had been a Celtic people, then such of them as were left behind in their own country, and were afterwards swal-

---

[a] *Germanis quidem* Camp *exercitum aut locum ubi exercitus castra metatur, significat ; inde ipsis vir castrensis et militaris* Kemffer *et* Kempher *et* Kemper *et* Kimber *et* Kamper, *pro varietate dialectorum vocatur ; vocabulum hoc nostro* (sc. Anglico) *Sermone nondum penitus exolevit ; Norfolciences enim plebeio et proletario sermone dicunt* " He is a Kemper Old Man." *i. e. Senex vegetus est.* Sheringham, p. 57. See also, Kemperye Man, in the " Reliques of Ancient English Poetry," vol. i. p. 70. Sheringham afterwards adds, *Illud autem hoc loco omittendum non est,* Cimbros *quoque à proceritate corporis hoc nomen habere potuisse* . . . . Kimber *enim aliâ significatione hominem giganteâ corporis mole præditum designat.* " *Danico hodie idiomate,* (inquit Pontanus, in additam. ad Hist. Dan. lib. 1). Kimber *sive* Kempe *et* Kemper *non bellatorum tantùm sed proprie Gigantem notat.*" Sheringham, p. 58. From hence it should seem, that a gigantic person was called *Kimber*, from his resemblance to the ancient *Cimbri ;* rather than that this people were called *Cimbri*, from their gigantic size ; so that this favours the opinion that the Cimbri were a different race from the ancient Danes, &c., because no nation would think of calling themselves giants ; for if they were all uniformly gigantic, there would appear to themselves nothing remarkable in their size ; whereas this would strike another people as a primary and leading distinction.

possessed a much more considerable part of Scandinavia than they do at present. This was the opinion of Grotius and Leibnitz. According to them, these people were formerly spread over the southern parts of Norway and Sweden, whence, in process of time, they have been driven out by new colonies of Scythians and Germans, and banished among the northern rocks; in like manner as the ancient inhabitants of Britain have been dispossessed by the Saxons of the greatest and most pleasant part of their island, and constrained to conceal themselves among the mountains in Wales, where, to this day, they retain their language, and preserve some traces of their ancient manners. But whether the Finns were formerly the entire possessors of Scandinavia, or were only somewhat more numerous than they are at present, it is very certain that this nation has been established there from the earliest ages, and has always differed from the other inhabitants of the north, by features so strong and remarkable, that we must acknowledge their origin to be as different from that of the others, as it is utterly unknown to us. The language of the Finns has nothing in common with that of any neighbouring people, neither does it resemble any dialect of the ancient Teutonic or Celtic tongues. The learned, who have taken the pains to compare the great Finland Bible printed at Abo, with a multitude of others, could never find the least resemblance between this and any other known language, so that after all their researches on this head, they have been obliged to propose mere conjectures, among which

lowed up among the succeeding Gothic tribes who invaded Scandinavia, would have given a tincture of their Celtic language to that branch of the Teutonic, which was spoke in these countries: or, at least, we should have found more Celtic names of mountains, rivers, &c., in the Cimbric Chersonese than in other Gothic settlements: but I do not find that either of these is the case; the old Icelandic seems to be as free from any Celtic mixture, as any other Gothic dialect; nor is there any remarkable prevalence of Celtic names in the peninsula of Jutland, more than in any part of Germany; where I believe its former Celtic inhabitants have up and down left behind them a few names of places, chiefly of natural situations, as of rivers, mountains, &c. This at least is the case in England, where, although the Britons were so entirely extirpated, that scarce a single word of the Welsh language was admitted by the Saxons; and although the names of towns and villages are almost universally of Anglo-Saxon derivation, yet the hills, forests, rivers, &c., have generally retained their old Celtic names.—P.

mankind are divided according to the particular light in which every one views the subject *.

CHAPTER II.

THE GROUNDS OF THE ANCIENT HISTORY OF DENMARK, AND OF THE DIFFERENT OPINIONS CONCERNING IT

On whatever side we direct our inquiries concerning the first inhabitants of Denmark, I believe nothing certain can be added to the account given of them above. It is true, if we will take for our guides certain modern authors, our knowledge will not be confined within such scanty limits. They will lead us step by step through an uninterrupted succession of kings and judges, up to the first ages of the world, or at least to the deluge : and there, receiving the descendants of Noah, as soon as they set foot out of the ark, will conduct them across the vast extent of deserts into Scandinavia, in order to found those states and kingdoms, which subist at present. Such is the scheme of Petreius, Lyschander, and other authors, who have followed what is called, among Danish historians, the Gothlandic hypothesis †, because it is built upon some pretended monuments found in the isle of Gothland, on the coast of Sweden : monuments which bear so many marks of imposition, that at present they are by common consent thrown aside among the most ill-concerted impostures.

The celebrated Rudbeck, a learned Swede, zealous for the glory of his countrymen, has endeavoured no less to procure

---

* The reader will find, by referring to page 40, that at the present day, the Finnic language is no longer a mystery, and that so far from having " nothing in common with that of any neighbouring people," it has every thing in common with the languages of the neighbouring Lapps, Esthonians, Permians, &c.—Ed.

† Petreius is a Danish author of the sixteenth century : Lyschander was historiographer to King Christian IV. His work, printed in Denmark at Copenhagen in 1669, bears this title : " An Abridgment of the Danish Histories from the beginning of the world to our own times." The arguments on which these authors found their accounts did not merit the pains which Torfæus and others have taken to refute them. The reader may consult, on this subject, the last-cited writer, in his " Series of Kings of Denmark," lib. i. c. 8.

them the honour of a very remote origin; as if, after all, it were of any consequence, whether a people, who lived before us so many ages, and of whom we retain only a vain resemblance of name, were possessed sooner or later of those countries, which we quietly enjoy at present. As this author joined to the most extensive learning an imagination eminently fruitful, he wanted none of the materials for erecting plausible and frivolous systems. He has found the art to apply to his own country a multitude of passages in ancient authors, who probably had never so much as heard of its name. According to him Sweden is the Atlantis of which Plato speaks, and for this reason he assumed that word for the title of his book. He makes no doubt but Japhet himself came thither with his family, and he undertakes to prove the antiquity of the Scandinavians by the expeditions, which according to him they have undertaken in the remotest ages [*]. The first of these he places in the time of Serug, in the year of the world 1900: the second under the direction of Hercules in the interval between the years 2200, and 2500. He lays great stress upon the conformity which is found between the names, manners, and customs of certain nations of the South and those of the North, to prove that the former had been subdued by the latter; which he affirms could never have been done, if Scandinavia had not been for a long time back overcharged, as it were, with the number of its inhabitants. It doubtless cannot be expected that I should go out of my way to encounter such an hypothesis as this: it is very evident that Rudbeck and his followers have falsely attributed to the Goths of Scandinavia, whatever the Greek or Latin historians have said of the Getae, or Goths, who dwelt near the Euxine. And as to the arguments brought from a resemblance of names, we know how little these can be depended on. Proofs of this kind are easily found wherever they are sought for, and never fail to offer themselves in support of any system our heads are full of.

Having thus set aside these two pretended guides, there only remains to choose between Saxo Grammaticus [†] and

[*] See Ol. Rudbeck. Atlantica, cap. xxxv.

[†] Saxo, surnamed, on account of his learning, Grammaticus, or the Grammarian, wrote about the middle of the twelfth century, under the reigns of Valdemar the First, and Canute his son. He was provost of the cathedral

Thermod Torfæus. The first of these supposes that a certain person, named Dan, of whom we know nothing but that his father was named Humble, and his brother Angul, was the founder of the Danish monarchy, in the year of the world 2910 : that from him Cimbria assumed the name of Denmark ; and that it hath been ever since governed by his posterity. Saxo himself takes care to give us, in his preface, the grounds on which his account is founded. These are, first, the ancient hymns or songs, by which the Danes formerly preserved the memory of the great exploits of their heroes, the wars and most remarkable events of each reign, and even sometimes the genealogies of princes and famous men. Secondly, the inscriptions which are found up and down in the north, engraven on rocks and other durable materials. He also lays great stress on the Icelandic chronicles; and on the relations which he received from archbishop Absalon. It cannot be denied but Saxo's work is written with great elegance for the time in which it was composed, but the rhetorician and the patriot are every where so apparent, as to make us distrust the fidelity of the historian. In short, to be convinced that this high antiquity, which he attributes to the Danish monarchy, is extremely uncertain, we need only examine the authorities on which he builds his hypothesis. Torfæus *, a native of Iceland, and historiographer of Norway, has shown this at large in his learned "Series of Kings of Denmark." He there proves that those songs, from which Saxo pretends to have extracted part of what he advanced, are in very small number; that he can

church of Roschild, then the capital of the kingdom. It was the celebrated Absalon, archbishop of Lund, one of the greatest men of his time, who engaged him to write the history of Denmark ; for which he furnished him with various helps. Sweno, the son of Aggo, contemporary with Saxo, wrote also, at the same time, and by the command of the same prelate, a history of Denmark, which is still extant. But this author seems rather to lean to the Icelandic hypothesis ; for he differs from Saxo in many essential points, and in particular concerning the founder of the monarchy, who, according to him, was Skiold the son of Odin, the same who, according to the Icelandic chronicles, was the first King of Denmark.

* Thermodius Torfæus, who was born in Iceland in the last century, and died about the beginning of the present, had received his education at Copenhagen, and passed the greatest part of his life in Norway. He was a man of great integrity and diligence, and extremely conversant in the antiquities of the north.

quote none of them for many entire books of his history ; and that they cannot exhibit a chronological series of kings, nor ascertain the date of any one event. Nor could the inscriptions, adds he, afford greater assistance to that historian; they contain very few matters of importance, they are for the most part eaten away with time, and are very difficult to understand *. With regard to the Icelandic chronicles, Torfæus thinks that they might have been of great use to Saxo, had he often consulted them ; but this, notwithstanding his assertions, does not sufficiently appear, since they rarely agree with his relations. Finally, the recitals of archbishop Absalon are doubtless of great weight for the times near to those in which that learned prelate lived ; but we do not see from whence he could have drawn any information of what passed a long time before him. Upon the whole, therefore, Torfæus concludes, with reason, that Saxo's first books, that is to say, nearly half his history, scarce deserve any credit so far as regards the succession of the kings, and the dates of the principal events, although they abound with various passages, which contribute to throw light on the antiquities of the North. Having thus overturned the hypothesis of that ancient historian, let us now see whether Torfæus is equally successful in erecting a new one in its stead.

The knowledge which this learned man had of the old Icelandic language, enabled him to read a considerable number of ancient manuscripts, which have been found in Iceland at different times, and of which the greatest part relate to the history of that island and the neighbouring countries. After having carefully distinguished those which appeared to him most worthy of credit, from a multitude of others which strongly savoured of fiction and romance, he though the had found in the former materials for drawing up a complete

---

* Wormius had read almost all those which are found in Denmark and Norway, as Verelius had also done the greatest part of those which subsisted in his time, in Sweden. Both of them agree that they scarce throw any light upon ancient history. To be convinced of this, one need only to examine the copies and explanations they have given of them. See " Olai Wormii Monumenta Runica," lib. iv., and " Olai Verelii Runagraphia Scandica Antiqua," &c. Since Verelius's work there has been published a complete collection of all the inscriptions found in Sweden, by John Goransson; at Solm, 1750, folio.

series of Danish kings, beginning with Skjöld the son of Odin, who, according to him, began his reign a short time before the birth of Christ.   Thus he not only cuts off from history all the reigns which, according to Saxo, preceded that era ; but he changes also the order of the kings, which succeeded it; affirming that Saxo had one while inserted foreign princes, another while lords or powerful vassals ; that he had represented as living long before Christ some who did not reign till many years after; and that, in short, he has visibly enlarged his list of monarchs, whether with design to flatter his own nation by making the Danish monarchy one of the most ancient in the world, or whether he only too credulously followed the guides who seduced him.

It will appear pretty extraordinary to hear a historian of Denmark cite, for his authorities, the writers of Iceland; a country cut off, as it were, from the rest of the world, and lying almost under the northern pole.   But this wonder, adds Torfæus, will cease, when the reader shall be informed, that from the earliest times the inhabitants of that island have had a particular fondness for history, and that from among them have sprung those poets, who, under the name of Skalds, rendered themselves so famous throughout the north for their songs, and for the credit they enjoyed with kings and people. In effect, the Icelanders have always taken great care to preserve the remembrance of every remarkable event that happened not only at home, but among their neighbours the Norwegians, the Danes, the Swedes, the Scots, the English, the Greenlanders, &c.   The first inhabitants of Iceland were a colony of Norwegians, who, to withdraw themselves from the tyranny of Harold Hárfagra, retired thither in the year 874 ; and these might carry with them the verses and other historical monuments of former times.   Besides, they kept up such a constant intercourse with the other people of the north, that they could readily learn from them whatever passed abroad.   We must add, that the odes of these Icelandic Skalds were continually in every body's mouth, containing the genealogies and exploits of kings, princes, and heroes : and as the poets did not forget to arrange them according to the order of time, it was not difficult for the Icelandic historians to compose afterwards, from such memoirs, the chronicles they have left us.

These are the grounds of Torfæus's system : and one cannot help highly applauding the diligence and sagacity of an author, who has thrown more light on the first ages of Danish history than any of his predecessors. At the same time we must confess, that there still remains much darkness and uncertainty upon this subject. For, although the annals of the Icelanders are, without contradiction, a much purer source than those which Saxo had recourse to ; and although the reasons alleged by Torfæus in their favour are of some weight ; many persons, after all, will hardly be persuaded that we can thence draw such exact and full information, as to form a complete and firm thread of history. For, in the first place, the Icelandic writers have left us a great number of pieces which evidently show that their taste inclined them to deal in the marvellous, in allegory, and even in that kind of narrations, in which truth is designedly blended with fable. Torfæus himself confesses * that there are many of their books, in which it is difficult to distinguish truth from falsehood, and that there are scarce any of them, but what contain some degree of fiction. In following such guides there is great danger of being sometimes misled. In the second place, these annals are of no great antiquity : we have none that were written before Christianity was established in the north . therefore the compilers of the Icelandic annals found no written memoirs earlier than their own : as we have great reason to believe, then, their narratives are only founded on traditions, inscriptions, or relics of poetry.

But can one give much credit to traditions, which must have taken in so many ages, and have been preserved by a people so ignorant ? Do not we see that among the common class of men, a son remembers his father, knows something of his grandfather, but never bestows a thought on his more remote progenitors ? With regard to inscriptions, we have already seen what assistance they were likely to afford : we may add that there are very few of them, which were written before the introduction of Christianity into the north ; and, indeed, as we shall prove in the sequel, before that time very little use was made of letters. Lastly, as for the verses or songs which were learnt by rote, it cannot be denied, but the

* See his Series Dynast. et Reg. lib. i. cap. 6.

Icelandic historians might receive great information from them, concerning times not very remote from their own. But was a rough and illiterate people likely to bestow much care in preserving a great number of poems, through a succession of eight or nine centuries? Or can one expect to find in such compositions much clearness and precision? Did the poets of those rude ages observe that exactness and methodical order, which history demands? In the third place, if the Icelandic annalists could not know with certainty, what passed a long time before them in Iceland and Norway, must not their authority be still weaker in what relates to a distant state like that of Denmark; which doubtless in those times had not such intimate connections with the other countries of the north, as it hath had since? We must be sensible that almost all that could be then known in Iceland of what passed in other nations, consisted in popular rumours, and in a few songs, which were handed about by means of some Icelandic Skald who returned from thence into his own country *.

What course, then, ought an historian to pursue, amid such a wide field of contrary opinions, where the momentary gleams of light do not enable him to discover or trace out any certain truth? In the first place, I think he ought not to engage himself and his readers in a labyrinth of entangled and useless researches; the result of which, he is pretty sure, can be only doubt. In the next place, he is to pass rapidly over all those ages which are but little known, and all such facts as cannot be set clear from fiction. The interest we take in past events is weakened in proportion as they are remote and distant. But when, besides being remote, they are also doubtful, unconnected, uncircumstantial and confused, they vanish into such obscurity, that they neither can, nor ought to engage our attention. In those distant periods, if any events occur, which ought not wholly to be passed over in silence, great care should be taken to mark the degree of probability which appears to be due to them, lest we debase history by

---

* There is much truth in these remarks though they are too indiscriminately applied, which necessarily renders them inconclusive. Saga literature has been subjected, since our author's time, to a critical examination, and a due distinction is now made betwen the mythic, the romantic, and the historical Sagas. Some of the latter, though they cannot claim to be ranked with authentic history, may at least be relied on as much as the monkish chronicles of the middle ages, to which, in every other respect, they are infinitely superior.—ED.

reducing it to one undistinguished mass of truth and fable. It is true, by conforming to this rule, an historian will leave great chasms in his work, and the annals of eight or nine centuries which, in some hands, fill up several volumes, will by this means be reduced within very few pages. But this chasm if it be one, may be usefully filled up. Instead of discussing the doubtful facts which are supposed to have happened among the northern nations, during the dark ages of paganism, let us study the religion, the character, the manners and customs of the ancient inhabitants during those ages. Such a subject, I should think, may interest the learned, and even the philosopher. It will have to most readers the charm of novelty, having been but imperfectly treated of in any modern language : and so far from being foreign to the History of Denmark, it makes a very essential part of it. For why should history be only a recital of battles, sieges, intrigues, and negotiations ? And why should it contain merely a heap of petty facts and dates, rather than a just picture of the opinions, customs, and even inclinations of a people ? By confining our inquiries to this subject, we may with confidence consult those ancient annals, whose authority is too weak to ascertain events. It is needless to observe that great light may be thrown on the character and sentiments of a nation, by those very books, whence we can learn nothing exact or connected of their history. The most credulous writer, he that has the greatest passion for the marvellous, while he falsifies the history of his contemporaries, paints their manners of life and modes of thinking without perceiving it. His simplicity, his ignorance, are at once pledges of the artless truth of his drawing, and a warning to distrust that of his relations. This is doubtless the best, if not the only use, we can make of those old relics of poetry, which have escaped the shipwreck of time. The authors of those fragments, erected into historians by succeeding ages, have caused ancient history to degenerate into a mere tissue of fables. To avoid this mistake, let us consider them only on the footing of poets, for they were in effect nothing else; let us principally attend to and copy those strokes, which, without their intending it, point out to us the notions, and mark the character of the ages in which they lived. These are the most certain truths we can find in their works, for they could not help delivering them whether they would or not.

CHAPTER III.

OF ODIN, HIS SUPPOSED ARRIVAL IN THE NORTH, AND THE
CHANGES WHICH HE IS SAID TO HAVE EFFECTED.

BEFORE I describe the state of ancient Scandinavia, I must
stop one moment. A celebrated tradition, confirmed by
the poems of all the northern nations, by their chronicles, by
institutions and customs, some of which subsist to this day, informs us, that an extraordinary person named Odin, formerly
reigned in the north : that he made great changes in the government, manners, and religion of those countries; that he
enjoyed there great authority, and had even divine honours
paid him. As to what regards the origin of this man, the
country whence he came, the time in which he lived, and the
other circumstances of his life and death, they are so uncertain, that the most profound researches, the most ingenious
conjectures about them, discover nothing to us but our own
ignorance. Thus previously disposed to doubt, let those ancient authors I have mentioned relate the story : all their
testimonies are comprised in that of Snorri, the ancient historian of Norway, and in the commentaries and explications
which Torfæus added to his narrative.

The Roman Commonwealth was arrived to the highest pitch
of power, and saw all the then known world subject to its
laws, when an unforeseen event raised up enemies against it,
from the very bosom of the forests of Scythia, and on the
banks of the Tanäis. Mithridates by flying, had drawn Pompey after him into those deserts. The king of Pontus sought
there for refuge, and new means of vengeance. He hoped to
arm against the ambition of Rome, all the barbarous nations
his neighbours, whose liberty she threatened. He succeeded
in this at first; but all those people, ill united as allies, ill
armed as soldiers, and still worse disciplined, were forced to
yield to the genius of Pompey. Odin is said to have been of
this number. He was obliged to withdraw himself by flight
from the vengeance of the Romans; and to go and seek in countries unknown to his enemies that safety which he could no
longer find in his own. His true name was Sigge, son of Fri-
dulph; but he assumed that of Odin, who was the Supreme

God among the Teutonic nations: either in order to pass among his followers for a man inspired by the Gods, or because he was chief priest, and presided over the worship paid to that deity. We know that it was usual with many nations to give their pontiffs the name of the God they worshipped. Sigge, full of his ambitious projects, we may be assured, took care to avail himself of a title so proper to procure him respect among the people he meant to subject.

Odin, for so we shall hereafter call him, commanded the Æsir, whose country must have been situated between the Pontus Euxinus, and the Caspian Sea. Their principal city was Asgard. The worship there paid to their supreme God was famous throughout the circumjacent countries. Odin having united under his banners the youth of the neighbouring nations, marched towards the north and west of Europe, subduing, we are told, all the people he found in his passage, and giving them to one or other of his sons for subjects. Many sovereign families of the north are said to be descended from these princes. Thus Horsa and Hengist, the chiefs of those Saxons, who conquered Britain in the fifth century, counted Odin, or Wodin in the number of their ancestors; it was the same with the other Anglo-Saxon princes; as well as the greatest part of those of Lower Germany and the north. But there is reason to suspect that all these genealogies, which have given birth to so many insipid panegyrics and frivolous researches, are founded upon a mere equivoque, or double meaning of the word Odin. This word signified, as we have seen above, the Supreme God of the Teutonic nations; we know also that it was customary with all the heroes of these nations to speak of themselves as sprung from their divinities, especially their god of war. The historians of those times, that is to say the poets, never failed to bestow the same honour on all those whose praises they sung: and thus they multiplied the descendants of Odin, or the Supreme God, as much as ever they found convenient.

After having disposed of so many countries, and confirmed and settled his new governments, Odin directed his course towards Scandinavia, passing through Cimbria, at present Holstein and Jutland. These provinces, exhausted of inhabitants, made him no resistance; and shortly after he passed into Fünen, which submitted as soon as ever he appeared.

He is said to have staid a long time in this agreeable island, where he built the city of Odensee, which still preserves in its name the memory of its founder. Hence he extended his arms over all the north. He subdued the rest of Denmark, and made his son Skjöld be received there as king; a title, which according to the Icelandic annals, no person had ever borne before, and which passed to his descendants, called after his name Skjöldungians; if this name was not rather given them on account of the shield, which they were accustomed to bear, for this is called Skjold in the Danish language to this day. Odin, who was apparently better pleased to give crowns to his children, than to wear them himself, afterwards passed into Sweden, where at that time reigned a prince named Gylfi, who persuaded that the author of a new worship consecrated by conquests so brilliant, could not be of the ordinary race of mortals, paid him great honours, and even worshipped him as a divinity. By favour of this opinion, which the ignorance of that age led men easily to embrace, Odin quickly acquired in Sweden the same authority he had obtained in Denmark. The Swedes came in crowds to do him homage, and by common consent bestowed the regal title and office upon his son Yngvi and his posterity. Hence sprung the Ynglingians, a name by which the kings of Sweden were for a long time distinguished. Gylfi died, or was forgotten. Odin governed with absolute dominion. He enacted new laws, introduced the customs of his own country; and established at Sigtuna (a city at present destroyed, situate in the same province with Stockholm) a supreme council or tribunal, composed of twelve pontiffs or judges. Their business was to watch over the public weal, to distribute justice to the people, to preside over the new worship, which Odin brought with him into the north, and to preserve faithfully the religious and magical secrets which that prince deposited with them. He was quickly acknowledged as a sovereign and a god, by all the petty kings among whom Sweden was then divided; and he levied an impost or poll-tax upon every head through the whole country. He engaged on his part to defend the inhabitants against all their enemies, and to defray the expense of the worship rendered to the gods at Sigtuna.

These great acquisitions seem not, however, to have satisfied his ambition. The desire of extending farther his religion,

G

his authority and his glory, caused him to undertake the conquest of Norway. His good fortune or address followed him thither, and this kingdom quickly obeyed a son of Odin named Sæming, whom they have taken care to make head of a family, the different branches of which reigned for a long time in that country.

After he had finished these glorious achievements, Odin retired into Sweden; where perceiving his end to draw near, he would not wait till the consequences of a lingering disease should put a period to that life, which he had so often bravely hazarded in the field; but assembling the friends and companions of his fortune, he gave himself nine wounds in the form of a circle with the point of a lance, and many other cuts in his skin with his sword. As he was dying, he declared he was going back to Asgard to take his seat among the other gods at an eternal banquet, where he would receive with great honours all who should expose themselves intrepidly in battle, and die bravely with their swords in their hands. As soon as he had breathed his last, they carried his body to Sigtuna, where, conformably to a custom introduced by him into the north, his body was burnt with much pomp and magnificence.

Such was the end of this man, whose death was as extraordinary as his life. The loose sketches which we have here given of his character, might afford room for many curious conjectures, if they could be depended on as well founded. Among those which have been proposed, there is nevertheless one which deserves some attention. Several learned men have supposed that a desire of being revenged on the Romans was the ruling principle of his whole conduct. Driven from his country by those enemies of universal liberty; his resentment, say they, was so much the more violent, as the Teutonic tribes esteemed it a sacred duty to revenge all injuries, especially those offered to their relations and country. He had no other view, according to them, in running through so many distant kingdoms, and in establishing with so much zeal his sanguinary doctrines, but to spirit up all nations against so formidable and odious a power. This leaven, which he left in the bosoms of the northern people, fermented a long time in secret; but the signal, they add, once given, they all fell as it were by common consent upon this unhappy empire; and after many repeated shocks, entirely overturned it; thereby revenging the affront offered so many ages before to their founder.

I cannot prevail on myself to raise objections against so ingenious a supposition. It gives so much importance to the history of the north, it renders that of all Europe so interesting, and, if I may use the expression, so poetical, that I cannot but admit these advantages as so many proofs in its favour. It must after all be confessed, that we cannot discover anything very certain concerning Odin, but only this, that he was the founder of a new religion. I will not answer for the truth of the account given of his origin. I only suspect that at some period of time more or less early, either he, or his fathers, or the authors of his religion, came from some country of Scythia, or from the borders of Persia. I may add, that the god, whose prophet or priest he pretended to be, was named Odin, and that the ignorance of succeeding ages confounded the Deity with his priest, composing out of the attributes of the one and the history of the other, a gross medley, in which we can at present distinguish nothing very certain. New proofs of this confusion will occur in all we shall hereafter produce on this subject; and it will behove the reader never to lose sight of this observation. I shall now mention some farther particulars recorded of Odin, which will not only confirm what I have been saying, but give us some insight into his character.

The Icelandic chronicles paint out Odin as the most persuasive of men. They tell us that nothing could resist the force of his words, that he sometimes enlivened his harangues with verses, which he composed extempore, and that he was not only a great poet, but that it was he who first taught the art of poesy to the Scandinavians. He was also the inventor of the Runic characters, which so long prevailed among that people. But what most contributed to make him pass for a god was his skill in magic. He persuaded his followers that he could run over the world in the twinkling of an eye, that he had the direction of the air and tempests, that he could transform himself into all sorts of shapes, could raise the dead, could foretel things to come, could by enchantments deprive his enemies of health and vigour, and discover all the treasures concealed in the earth. The same authors add, that he also knew how to sing airs so tender and melodious, that the very plains and mountains would open and expand with delight; and that the ghosts attracted by the sweetness of his songs, would leave their infernal caverns, and stand motion-less about him.

But if his eloquence, together with his august and vener-able deportment, procured him love and respect in a calm and peaceable assembly, he was no less dreadful and furious in battle. He inspired his enemies with such terror, that they thought they could not describe it better, than by saying he rendered them blind and deaf; that he would appear like a wolf all desperate, and biting his very shield for rage, would throw himself amidst the opposing ranks, making around him the most horrible carnage, without receiving any wound himself*.

[The legend of "the historical Odin" is founded on the authority of the Ynglinga Saga, which forms the first book of Snorri's "Heimskringla," or "Chronicles of the Kings of Nor-way." The first of these kings, whose existence cannot be called in question, is Halfdan the Black, who reigned over Westfold and some other petty states in the south of Norway towards the middle of the ninth century, and with his reign Snorri begins his second book, entitled "Saga Halfdanar Svarta," Rögnvalld, the son of Halfdan's brother Olaf, being the last king mentioned in the Ynglinga Saga. Now, we think that notwithstanding all that has been written on this Saga, a suffi-cient distinction has not been drawn between that part which may be regarded as semi-historical, and that which is purely fictitious. We shall therefore venture to make this distinc-tion, and regard the Ynglinga Saga as composed of a chronicle of the kings of Sweden—or, more properly speaking, of the Upsal district—and a chronicle of the kings of Westfold and Raumariki in Norway. The chronicle of the Swedish kings commences by giving an account of a people established on the east of the river Tanaquisl. who were governed by a pontiff-king called Odin, residing in the city of As-

---

* As there are several writers who still believe that a personage called "the historical Odin" actually conquered Scandinavia at the head of an army of Asiatics, we deemed it advisable to retain this chapter, omitting a few passages obviously erroneous, and adding our own opinions on the sub-ject, though it is by no means entitled to the consideration that the learned men of the north have thought proper to bestow upon it.—ED.

gard *. The manner in which Odin invaded Scandinavia—an event which, according to Schöning, took place 40 years before the Christian era—has been already related. The successor of Odin, we are told, was Njörd, of the race of the Vanir, who was succeeded by his son Frey, called Yngvi-Frey†, the founder of the Yngling dynasty, the last king of which, being the 21st in descent from Frey, was Ingialld Illradi, whose reign is placed in the beginning of the seventh century. At his death the kingdom of Upsal or Svithiod came into possession of Ivar Vidfami, a lineal descendant from Odin's son Skjöld, the founder of the Skjöldungian dynasty of Denmark. Now that such men as Ingialld and Ivar may have existed, and the latter acquired possession of a petty state in Sweden in the seventh century, we will not pretend to deny; but the account given of Ingialld's ancestors in the Ynglinga Saga, and of Ivar's, by Saxo-Grammaticus, are obviously fictitious, or at all events their veracity may be said gradually to diminish as we ascend from these semi-historical personages to the supposed founders of their dynasties, who are evidently no other than the deities worshipped by the ancient Scandinavians, anthropomorphized to flatter the vanity of their earliest rulers; these deities themselves being but the symbolical representations of the inscrutable phenomena elicited by the elemental strife of nature. We shall therefore, whenever we have occasion to allude to the subject in our subsequent remarks, regard this part of the Ynglinga Saga—chap. 1 to 45 inclusive—as a document of little or no historical value, and any theories or arguments founded on it as undeserving of serious attention.

The second part of the Saga, or chronicle of the Norwegian kings—chap. 46 to 55 inclusive—begins by stating that at the death of Ingialld, his son Olaf, perceiving that the Swedes were determined to rid themselves of the Yngling dynasty, went with his followers into the uninhabited district westward of the Vænir lake, and having cleared the forests settled there, and gave it the name of Vermaland (Warmland). Olaf

---

* This river is supposed to be the Tanais or Don, and the learned northern antiquaries have not hesitated to identify Asgard with the Aspurg of Strabo, the Tana of the middle ages, and the Azof of the present day!!!

† The reader will find an account of these deities, transformed by the Saga-man into kings, in the prose Edda, chap. 23 and 24.

was soon joined by all who were discontented with the change
of dynasty, and although his enemies tried to ridicule his proceedings by calling him "The Woodcutter" (Tretelgia), his
colony grew into a petty state of some importance. A scarcity
however ensued, which the people attributed to the king
having been remiss in his religious duties, meaning probably
that he had not given them a sufficient number of sacrificial
banquets. They accordingly surrounded Olaf's house, and
burnt him in it, offering him as a sacrifice to Odin for a good
harvest. The most enlightened amongst them saw, however,
that the real cause of the famine was a surplus population,
and that it would be a much wiser plan for them to rely on
their own exertions, than to sit down and die of starvation in
the vain expectation that Odin would supply their wants with
crops of superabundant fertility. They therefore crossed the
mountains to Norway, and having made Olaf's son, Halfdan
Whitebone, their king, conquered Raumariki, Westfold, and
other petty states in the southern part of that country. Halfdan was succeeded by his son Eystein, who was drowned at
sea. His son and successor, Halfdan, enriched himself
by successful Viking expeditions, and obtained the singular
surname of "The Munificent and Food-sparing," because he
gave his followers plenty of money, but nearly starved them
to death. The son and successor of this sea-roving king was
Gudreyd the Magnificent, at whose death, which is said to
have taken place in the year 841, the kingdom of Westfold was divided between his two sons, Olaf and Halfdan the
Black.

That Halfdan was a real historical personage, and the
father of the celebrated Harald Hárfagra, of whom frequent
mention will be made in this work, is unquestionable ; and
although the evidence is by no means conclusive, we should
be inclined to admit that his ancestors, up to the Woodcutter,
were also men of real thews and sinews, who played their
parts, with more or less success, in the ever-varying drama of
human existence. We have devoted more attention to the
Ynglinga Saga than it probably deserves, as it will be frequently alluded to in the following chapters, and must
remark in conclusion, that to throw discredit on the whole of
Snorri's Heimskringla merely because the first book is little
better than a legendary fiction, would be equally as absurd as

to impeach the veracity of Livy because he begins his Roman history by the legend of Romulus, which Niebuhr has shown to be equally as devoid of foundation as that of the historical Odin.]

CHAPTER IV.

A GENERAL IDEA OF THE PRIMITIVE WORSHIP OF THE NORTHERN NATIONS.

It is not easy to form an exact notion of the religion formerly professed in the north of Europe. What the Latin and Greek authors have written on this subject is commonly deficient in point of exactness. They had for many ages little or no intercourse with the inhabitants of these countries, whom they styled barbarians; they were ignorant of their language, and, as most of these nations made a scruple of unfolding the grounds of their religious doctrines to strangers, the latter, who were thereby reduced to be mere spectators of their outward forms of worship, could not easily enter into the spirit of it. And yet, if we bring together the few short sketches which these different writers have preserved of it, if we correct them by one another, if we compare their accounts with those of the ancient poets and historians of these nations themselves, I flatter myself, we shall throw light enough upon this subject to be able to distinguish the most important objects in it.

A few plain easy doctrines seem to have comprised the whole of religion known to the first inhabitants of Europe. The farther back we ascend to the era of the creation, the more plainly we discover traces of this conformity among the several nations of the earth; but in proportion as we see them dispersed to form distant settlements and colonies, they seem to swerve from their original ideas, and to assume new forms of religion. The nations, who settled in the southern countries, were they who altered it the first, and afterwards disfigured it the most. These people derive from their climate a lively, fruitful, and restless imagination, which makes them greedy of novelties and wonders: they have also ardent passions, which rarely suffer them to preserve a rational freedom of mind, or to see things coolly and impartially. Hence the wild frenzies of the Egyptians, Syrians and Greeks in religious matters; and hence that chaos of extravagances, in some respects ingenious, known by the name of mythology; through which we can hardly discover any traces of the ancient doctrines. And yet we do discover them, and can make it appear, that those first doctrines, which the southern nations so much disguised, were the very same that were preserved in the north without any material alteration. There the rigour of the climate necessarily locks up the capricious desires, confines the imagination, lessens the number of the passions, as well as abates their violence, and by yielding only to painful and unremitted labour, wholly confines to material objects that activity of mind which produces among men levity and disquiet.

But whether these causes have not always operated with the same efficacy, or whether others more powerful have prevailed over them; the greatest part of these nations, after having, for some time, continued inviolably attached to the religion of their first fathers, suffered it at length to be corrupted by an intermixture of ceremonies, some of them ridiculous, others cruel; in which, by little and little, as it commonly happens, they came to place the whole essence of religion. It is not easy to mark the precise time when this alteration happened, as well for want of ancient monuments, as because it was introduced by imperceptible degrees, and at different times among different nations: but it is not therefore the less certain, that we ought to distinguish two different epochs or ages in this religion, and in each of these we should be careful not to confound the opinions of the sages with the fables or mythology of the poets. Without these distinctions it is difficult to reconcile the different accounts, often in appearance contradictory, which we find in ancient authors. Yet I cannot promise to mark out precisely, what belongs to each of these classes in particular. The lights which guide us at intervals through these dark ages, are barely sufficient to show us some of the more striking objects; but the finer links which connect and join them together will generally escape us.

Let us first of all examine this religion in its purity. It taught the being of a " supreme God, master of the universe, to whom all things were submissive and obedient." Such, according to Tacitus, was the supreme God of the Germans. The ancient Icelandic mythology calls him "the author of every thing that existeth; the eternal, the ancient, the living and awful Being, the searcher into concealed things, the Being that never changeth." This religion attributed to the Supreme Deity "an infinite power, a boundless knowledge, an incorruptible justice," and forbade its followers to represent him under any corporeal form. They were not even to think of confining him within the enclosure of walls, but were taught that it was only within woods and consecrated forests that they could serve him properly. There he seemed to reign in silence, and to make himself felt by the respect which he inspired. It was an injurious extravagance to attribute to this deity a human figure, to erect statues to him, to suppose him of any sex, or to represent him by images. From this supreme God were sprung (as it were emanations of his divinity) an infinite number of subaltern deities and genii, of which every part of the visible world was the seat and temple. These intelligences did not barely reside in each part of nature; they directed its operations, it was the organ or instrument of their love or liberality to mankind. Each element was under the guidance of some being peculiar to it. The earth, the water, the fire, the air, the sun, moon, and stars had each their respective divinity. The trees, forests, rivers, mountains, rocks, winds, thunder and tempests had the same; and merited on that score a religious worship, which, at first, could not be directed to the visible object, but to the intelligence with which it was animated. The motive of this worship was the fear of a deity irritated by the sins of men, but who, at the same time, was merciful, and capable of being appeased by prayer and repentance. They looked up to him as to the active principle, which, by uniting with the earth or passive principle, had produced men, animals, plants, and all visible beings; they even believed that he was the only agent in nature, who preserves the several beings, and disposes of all events. To serve this divinity with sacrifices and prayers, to do no wrong to others, and to be brave and intrepid in themselves, were all the moral consequences they derived from these doctrines. Lastly, the belief of a future state cemented and completed the whole building. Cruel tortures were there reserved for such as despised these three fundamental precepts of morality, and joys without number and without end awaited every religious, just, and valiant man.

These are the principal heads of that ancient religion which probably prevailed for many ages through the greatest part of the north of Europe, and doubtless among several nations of Asia. When it began to lose the most beautiful features of its original purity, and whether this change must be attributed to the natural inconstancy of mankind and their invincible proneness to whatever is marvellous, and strikes the senses, or was brought about by violence and conquest, is difficult to decide. The eye is lost and bewildered, when it endeavours to trace out events so remote and obscure. To unravel and distinguish the several causes, and to mark exactly the distinct influence of each, is what we can hardly do in the history of such ages as are the most enlightened and best known to us. Let us then confine ourselves within more narrow limits, and endeavour to sketch out a new picture of this same religion, as it was afterwards altered, and like a piece of cloth so profusely overcharged with false ornaments, as hardly to show the least glimpse of the original groundwork. This picture will take in a space of seven or eight centuries, which intervened between the time of Odin and the conversion of Denmark to the Christian faith. The Icelandic Edda, and some ancient pieces of poetry, wherein the same mythology is taught, are the sources whence I shall draw my information

CHAPTER V.

OF THE RELIGION WHICH PREVAILED IN THE NORTH, AND PARTICULARLY IN SCANDINAVIA, AFTER THE PRIMITIVE WORSHIP HAD BEEN ALTERED.

THE most striking alteration in the doctrines of the primitive religion, was in the number of the gods who were to be worshipped. A capital point in the ancient dogmas, was that preeminence, I have been describing, of one only all-powerful and perfect being over all the other intelligences with which universal nature was peopled. But men becoming in all appearance weary of this simplicity of religion, associated to the supreme God many of those genii or subaltern divinities who had been always subordinate to him. As these differed rather in degree of power, than in essence, the transition was very easy to a people who were not very refined and subtle. To this another reason also contributed. As each of these inferior divinities governed with absolute power every thing within his respective sphere; fear, desire, all their wants and passions, inclined a rude people to have recourse to them, as to a more present, speedy and more accessible help in time of need, rather than to the supreme God, whose name alone imprinted so much respect and terror. It is an inevitable mistake of the human mind to carry the imperfections of its own nature into the idea it forms of the Deity. The deep conviction we have every moment of our own weakness, prevents us from conceiving how it is possible for one single being to move and support all parts of the universe. This is, especially, inconceivable to an ignorant people who have never suspected that there is any connection between the several parts of nature, and that a general mechanism can produce so many different phenomena. Accordingly, all barbarous nations have ever substituted, instead of the simple and uniform laws of nature, which were unknown to them, the operation of spirits, genii and divinities of all kinds, and have given them as assistants to the Supreme Being in the moral and physical government of the world. If they have paid to any of them greater honours than to others, it has usually been to those whose dominion extended over such things as were most dear to them, or appeared most worthy of admiration. This was what happened in Scandinavia. In process of time that Supreme Being, the idea of whom takes in all existence, was restrained to one particular province, and passed among the generality of the inhabitants for the God of War. No object, in their opinion, could be more worthy his attention, nor more proper to show forth his power. Hence those pictures which are left us of him in the Icelandic mythology, where he is always meant under the name of Odin. He is there called " The terrible and severe God ; the father of slaughter; he who giveth victory, and reviveth courage in the conflict; who nameth those that are to be slain." The warriors who went to battle made a vow to send him a certain number of souls, which they consecrated to him; these souls were Odin's right, he received them in Valhalla, his ordinary place of residence, where he rewarded all such as died sword in hand. There it was that he distributed to them praises and delight; there he received them at his table, where in a continual feast, as we shall see hereafter, the pleasure of these heroes consisted. The assistance of this Deity was implored in every war that was undertaken; to him the vows of both parties were addressed; and it was believed that he often descended to intermix in the conflict himself, to inflame the fury of the combatants, to strike those who were to perish, and to carry their souls to his celestial abodes.

This terrible deity, who took such pleasure in shedding the blood of men, was at the same time, according to the Icelandic mythology, their father and creator. So easily do gross and prejudiced minds reconcile the most glaring contradictions: this same god, according to the Edda, "liveth and governeth during the ages, he directeth every thing which is high, and every thing which is low, whatever is great and whatever is small; he hath made the heaven, the air, and man, who is to live for ever; and before the heaven and the earth existed, this god lived already with the giants." The principal strokes of this picture are found many times repeated in the same work. They have been frequently used by other northern poets. Nor were they peculiar to the inhabitants of Scandinavia. Many ancient people, the Germans for example, attributed in like manner to the supreme God a superintendence over war. They drew their gods by their own character, who loved nothing so much themselves as to display their strength and power in battle, and to signalize their vengeance upon their enemies by slaughter and desolation. There remains to this day some traces of the worship paid to Odin in the name given by almost all the people of the north to the fourth day of the week, which was formerly consecrated to him. It is called by a name which signifies Odin's day *.

* Old Norse, Odinsdagr; Swe. and Danish, Onsdag.; Ang. Sax. Wodenesdæg, Wodnesdæg; Eng .Wednesday; Dutch, Woensdag. As Odin or Wodan was supposed to correspond to the Mercury of the Greeks and Romans, the name of this day was expressed in Latin Dies Mercurii.

The principal goddess among the ancient Scandinavians was Frigga, the wife of Odin. It was the opinion of many ancient nations, as well as of the first inhabitants of Greece, that the supreme Being or celestial God had united with the earth to produce the inferior divinities, man, and all other creatures. Upon this was founded that veneration they had for the earth, which they considered as a goddess, and the honours which were paid her. They called her Mother Earth, and Mother of the Gods. The Phenicians adored both these two principles under the name of Tautes and Astarte. They were called by some nations Jupiter and Apia; by the Thracians, Cotis and Bendis; by the inhabitants of Greece and Italy, Saturn and Ops. All antiquity is full of traces of this worship, which was formerly universal. We know that the Scythians adored the earth as a goddess, wife of the supreme God; the Turks celebrated her in their hymns; the Persians offered sacrifices to her. Tacitus attributes the same worship to the Germans, particularly to the inhabitants of the north of Germany. He says, "They adore the goddess Herthus*, (meaning the earth,") and gives a circumstantial description of the ceremonies which were observed in honour of her in an island, which he does not name, but which could not have been far from Denmark†. We cannot doubt but this same goddess was the Frigga of the Scandinavians. Another celebrated goddess was Freyja, the Goddess of Love. It was she that was addressed in order to obtain happy marriages and easy childbirths. She dispensed pleasures, enjoyments, and delights of all kinds. The Edda styles her the most favourable of the goddesses; but she went to war as well as Odin, and divided with him the souls of the slain:

* The name which Tacitus gives to this goddess signifies the earth in all the Teutonic languages. Thus it is in the ancient Gothic, Airtha; in the Anglo-Saxon, Eorthe, Ertha, Hertha; English, Earth; in Danish, Jord, &c.—P.

† Cluverius pretends that it is the isle of Rugen, which is in the Baltic Sea, on the coast of Pomerania (Germ. Antiq., p. 134). Yet as Tacitus places it in the ocean, it is more likely to have been the isle of Heligoland, which is not far from the mouth of the Elbe. The Angles (Angli, from whom our English ancestors derived their name) were seated on this coast; and Arnkiel hath shown in his Cimbric Antiquities, that the ancient Germans held this island in great veneration. The word Heligoland signifies "Holy Land."—P.

and indeed it would have been very hard if the goddess of pleasure had been deprived of an amusement which her votaries were so fond of. It appears to have been the general opinion that she was the same with the Venus of the Greeks and Romans, since the sixth day of the week, which was consecrated to her under the name of Freytag, Friday, or Freyja's day, was rendered into Latin, *Dies Veneris*, or Venus's day *.

The second principal god of the ancient Scandinavians was named Thor, and was no less known than Odin among the Teutonic nations. In the system of the primitive religion, the God Thor was probably only one of those genii or subaltern divinities sprung from the union of Odin, or the supreme being, and the earth. The Edda calls him expressly the most valiant of the sons of Odin. He was considered as the defender and avenger of the gods. He always carried a mallet, which, as often as he discharged it, returned back to his hand of itself; he grasped it with gauntlets of iron, and was further possessed of a girdle which had the virtue to renew his strength as often as was needful. It was with these formidable arms that he overthrew to the ground the monsters and giants, when the gods sent him to oppose their enemies †.

The deities whom we have mentioned were the principal objects of the worship and veneration of all the Scandinavians; but they were not all agreed among themselves about the preference which was due to each of them in particular. The Danes seem to have paid the highest honours to Odin; the inhabitants of Norway and Iceland appear to have been under the immediate protection of Thor; and the Swedes had chosen for their tutelar deity Freyja, or rather Frey, her brother, who, according to the Edda, presided over the seasons of the year, and bestowed peace, fertility, and riches. The number and employment of these deities of the second order it is not very easy to determine; and the matter besides being of no great

---

* Old Norse, Freydagr, Fríadagr; Sw. and Danish, Fredag; Ang. Sax., Frigedæg; Dutch, Vrijdag; Germ., Freytag.

† The fifth day of the week was consecrated to Thor. Old Norse, Thórsdagr; Sw. and Dan., Torsdag; Ang. Sax., Thuresdæg, Thursdæg; Eng. Thursday; Germ. Donnerstag; Dutch, Donderdag (the Thunderers day). The name of this day was rendered into Latin by Dies Jovis, Jupiter, according to the ideas of the Romans, being also the God of Thunder.

consequence, I shall point out some of the most material. The prose Edda reckons up twelve gods and as many goddesses, to whom divine honours were due, and who, though they had all a certain power, were nevertheless obliged to obey Odin, the most ancient of the gods, and the great principle of all things. Such was Njörd, the Neptune of the northern nations, who reigned over the sea and winds. The extent of his empire rendered him very respectable ; and we find in the north, to this day, traces of the veneration which was there paid him. The Edda exhorts men to worship him with great devotion.

Baldur was another son of Odin, wise, eloquent, and endowed with such great majesty that his very glances were bright and shining. Tyr, who must be distinguished from Thor, was also a warrior deity, and the protector of champions and brave men *. Bragi presided over eloquence and poetry. His wife, named Iduna, had the care of certain apples, which the gods tasted when they found themselves grow old, and which had the power of instantly restoring them to youth. Heimdall was their porter. The gods had made a bridge between heaven and earth ; this bridge is the rainbow. Heimdall was employed to watch at one of the extremities of this bridge, for fear the giants should make use of it to get into heaven. It was a difficult matter to surprise him ; for the gods had given him the faculty of sleeping more lightly than a bird, and of discovering objects by day or night farther than the distance of a hundred leagues. He had also an ear so fine that he could hear the very grass grow in the meadows and the wool on the backs of the sheep. He carried in the one hand a sword, and in the other a trumpet, the sound of which could be heard through all the worlds. I suppress here the names of the other gods, who made up the number of twelve ; but I ought to bestow a word upon Loki whom the ancient Scandinavians seem to have regarded as their evil principle, and whom, notwithstanding, they ranked among the gods. The Edda calls him " the calumniator of the gods, the

---

* From Tyr is derived the name given to the third day of the week in most of the Teutonic languages, and which has been rendered into Latin by Dies Martis. O. Norse, Tirsdagr, Tisdagr ; Sw., Tisdag ; Dan., Tirsdag; Germ., Dienstag ; Dutch, Dingsdag ; Ang. Sax., Tyrsdæg, Tyvesdæg, Tivesdæg; Eng., Tuesday.

grand contriver of deceit and frauds, the reproach of gods and men. He is beautiful in his figure, but his mind is evil, and his inclinations inconstant. Nobody renders him divine honours. He surpasses all mortals in the arts of perfidy and craft." He has had many children, besides three monsters, who owe their birth to him; the wolf Fenrir, the Midgard serpent, and Hela or Death. All three are enemies to the gods, who after various struggles have chained this wolf till the last day, when he shall break loose and rush against them. The serpent has been cast into the sea, where he shall remain till he is conquered by the God Thor. And Hela or Death has been banished into the lower regions, where she has the government of nine worlds, into which she distributes those who are sent to her. We find here and there in the Edda several other strokes concerning Loki, his stratagems against the gods, their resentment, and the vengeance they took of him, when he was seized and shut up in a cavern formed of three keen-edged stones, where he rages with such violence that he causes all the earthquakes that happen. He will remain there captive, adds the same mythology, till the end of the ages; but then he shall be slain by Heimdall, the door-keeper of the gods.

We have seen above that the Icelandic mythology reckons up twelve goddesses, including Frigga, the spouse of Odin, and the chief of them all. Their names and respective functions will be found specified in the prose Edda, c. 35. Besides these twelve goddesses there are numerous virgins in Valhalla, or the paradise of the heroes. Their business is to wait upon them, and they are called Valkyrior. Odin also employs them to choose in battles those who are to perish, and to make the victory incline to whatever side he pleases. The court of the gods is ordinarily kept under a great ash tree, and there they distribute justice*. This ash is the greatest of all trees; its branches cover the surface of the earth, its top reaches to the highest heaven, it is supported by three vast roots, one of which extends to the ninth world. An eagle, whose piercing eye discovers all things, perches upon its branches. A squirrel is continually running up and down it to bring news; while a parcel of serpents, fastened to the

* See the Edda, c. 15.

trunk, endeavour to destroy him.   From under one of the roots runs a fountain wherein Wisdom lies concealed.   From a neighbouring spring (the fountain of past things) three virgins are continually drawing a precious water, with which they water the ash tree: this water keeps up the beauty of its foliage, and after having refreshed its leaves, falls back again to the earth, where it forms the dew of which the bees make their honey.   These three virgins always keep under the ash; and it is they who dispense the days and ages of men. Every man hath a destiny appropriated to himself, who determines the duration and events of his life.   But the three destinies of more especial note are Urd (the past), Verdandi (the present), and Skuld (the future).

Such were the principal deities, formerly worshipped in the north of Europe ; or rather these were the ideas which the poets gave of them to the credulous people.   It is easy to discover their handywork in these fictions, sometimes ingenious, but more frequently puerile, with which they thought to set off the simplicity of the ancient religion ; and we ought not to believe that such of them as were men of sense and discernment ever considered them in any other light.   But after having shown the names and attributes of their principal deities, let us proceed to set forth, after the Edda and the poem named Völuspá, the other doctrines of their religion.

We have seen that among the qualities of which they supposed Odin or the Supreme God to be possessed, that of the creator of heaven and earth is expressly attributed to him. What the Icelandic mythology has preserved to us on this head, merits so much the more attention, as it discovers to us the sentiments that prevailed at a very early period on this important point, and at the same time expresses them frequently with a greatness and sublimity equal to the finest strokes of classical antiquity on the same subject.   The Völuspá begins by a description of Chaos.   " In the day-spring of the ages," says the prophetess, " there was neither sea, nor shore, nor refreshing breezes.   There was neither earth below, nor heaven above, to be distinguished.   The whole was only one vast abyss, without herb, and without seeds.   The sun had then no palace : the stars knew not their dwelling-places, the moon was ignorant of her power."   After this we are told that " there was a luminous, burning, flaming world

H

towards the south; and another, nebulous and dark, toward the north. From the latter world flowed out incessantly into the abyss that lay between the two, torrents of venom, which in proportion as they removed far away from their source, congealed in their falling into the abyss, and so filled it with scum and ice. Thus was the abyss by little and little filled quite full : but there remained within it a·light and immoveable air, and thence exhaled icy vapours. Then a warm breath coming from the south, melted those vapours, and formed of them living drops, whence was born the giant Ymir. It is reported that whilst he slept an extraordinary sweat under his arm-pits produced a male and female, whence is sprung the race of the giants ; a race evil and corrupt, as well as Ymir their author. Another race was brought forth *, which formed alliances with that of the giant Ymir : this was called the family of Bor, so named from the second of that family, who was the father of Odin. The sons of Bor slew the giant Ymir, and the blood ran from his wounds in such abundance, that it caused a general inundation, wherein perished all the giants, except only one, who saving himself in a bark, escaped with all his family. Then a new world was formed. The sons of Bor, or the gods, dragged the body of the giant in the abyss, and of it made the earth: the sea and rivers were composed of his blood ; the earth of his flesh; the great mountains of his bones ; the rocks of his teeth and of splinters of his bones broken. They made of his skull the vault of heaven, which is supported by four dwarfs named North, South, East, and West. They fixed there tapers to enlighten it, and assigned to other fires certain spaces which they were to run through, some of them in heaven, others under the heaven : the days were distinguished, and the years were numbered. They made the earth round, and surrounded it with the deep ocean, upon the outward banks of which they placed the giants. One day, as the sons of Bor, or the gods, were taking a walk, they found two pieces of wood floating upon the water ; these they took, and out of them made a man and a woman. The eldest of the gods gave them life and souls ; the second motion and knowledge ; the third the gift of speech, hearing and sight, to which he added beauty and raiment. From this man and this woman, named Ask and

* See the Edda, c. 6.

Embla, is descended the race of men who are permitted to inhabit the earth."

It is easy to trace out in this narration vestiges of an ancient and general tradition, of which every sect of paganism has altered, adorned or suppressed many circumstances, according to their own fancy, and which is now only to be found entire in the books of Moses. Let the strokes we have here produced be compared with the beginning of Hesiod's Theogony, with the mythology of some Asiatic nations, and with the book of Genesis, and we shall instantly be convinced that the conformity which is found between many circumstances of their recitals, cannot be the mere work of chance. Thus in the Edda the description of the Chaos; that vivifying breath which produces the giant Ymir; that sleep during which a male and female spring from his sides; that race of the sons of the gods; that deluge which only one man escapes, with his family, by means of a bark; that renewal of the world which succeeds; that first man and first woman created by the gods, and who receive from them life and motion : all this seems to be only remains of a more ancient and more general belief, which was carried into the north, and altered there more slowly than in other countries. One may discover also in the very nature of these alterations the same spirit of allegory, the same desire of accounting for all the phenomena of nature by fictions, which has suggested to other nations the greatest part of the fables with which their theology is infected. To conclude, the style itself, in which the expressions, one while sublime, one while extravagant and gigantic, are thrown together without art, the littlenesses that accompany the most magnificent descriptions, the disorder of the narrative, the uniform turn of the phrases, confirms to all who read this work an idea of a very remote antiquity, and a mode of thinking and writing peculiar to a simple and gross people, who were unacquainted with any rules of composition, and whose vigorous imagination, despising or not knowing any rules of art, displays itself in all the liberty and energy of nature.

It was thus the world was created; or to express it in a manner more conformable to Scandinavian notions, it was thus that the matter already existing, but without order and without life, was animated and disposed by the gods in the

present state in which we behold it.   I have already remarked, that they were far from supposing that after it had
received the first motion from the hands of the gods, the
world continued to subsist, and to move independent of its
first movers.   Perhaps no religion ever attributed so much to
a Divine Providence as that of the northern nations.   This
doctrine served them for a key, as commodious as it was universal, to unlock all the phenomena of nature without exception.   The intelligences united to different bodies penetrated
and moved them, and men needed not to look any farther
than to them, to find the cause of everything they observed in
them.   Thus entire nature, animated and always moved immediately by one or more intelligent causes, was in their system nothing more than the organ or instrument of the
divinity, and became a kind of book in which they thought
they could read his will, inclinations, and designs.   Hence
that weakness formerly common to so many nations, and of
which the traces still subsist in many places, that makes
them regard a thousand indifferent phenomena, such as the
quivering of leaves, the crackling and colour of flames, the
fall of thunderbolts, the flight or singing of a bird, men's
involuntary motions, their dreams and visions, the movements
of the pulse, &c., as intimations which God gives to wise men,
of his will.   Hence came oracles, divinations, auspices, presages, and lots; in a word, all that rubbish of dark superstitions called at one time religion, at another magic, a science
absurd to the eyes of reason, but suitable to the impatience
and restlessness of our desires, and which only betrays the
weakness of human nature, in promising to relieve it.   Such,
notwithstanding, was the principal consequence which the
Teutonic nations drew from the doctrine of a Divine Providence.   The ancient Scandinavians carried it to as extravagant a pitch as the rest, as will appear from what I shall
say of their sacrifices and presages, when I come to treat of
their exterior worship.   With respect to the moral precepts,
we know very well that it has ever been the failing of mankind to regard these as the least essential part of religion.
When they admitted that continual and immediate action of
the Divinity on all creatures, the Scandinavians had thence
concluded that it was impossible for men to effect any change
in the course of things, or to resist the destinies.   The Stoics

themselves did not understand this term in a more rigorous sense than the people of the north. Nothing is more common in the ancient chronicles than to hear their warriors complaining that the destinies are inflexible, that they are unalterable and cannot be surmounted. We have seen above that they reckoned the Parcæ or goddesses of destiny to be three in number, as well as the Greeks; and like them attributed to them the determination of all events. Every man had also his own destiny, who assisted at the moment of his birth, and marked beforehand the period of his days. It is yet probable that they considered Odin, or the supreme God, as the author and arbiter of the destinies. This the Edda insinuates pretty clearly, when it tells us that he has established from the beginning governors to regulate the destinies of mortals. One may conceive what impression this doctrine must have made upon men who were naturally warlike. Recent examples have shown us, that it never fails among men to add strength to their ruling passion, and to produce, particularly in such as love war, a blind temerity which knows neither measure nor danger *. But to this unlucky prejudice the ancient inhabitants of the north added another, the effects of which were no less barbarous; which was, that the term of a man's life might be prolonged, if any one would put himself in his place and die in his stead. This was often practised when a prince or illustrious warrior was ready to perish by some accident; Odin, appeased by such a sacrifice, and content to have a victim, revoked, they said, the decree of the destinies, and lengthened the thread of his life whom they were so desirous to save

The other precepts of this religion probably extended no farther than to be brave and intrepid in war, to serve the gods, and to appease them by sacrifices, not to be unjust, to show hospitality to strangers, to keep their words inviolably, and to be faithful to the marriage bed †. There are many

* The author (I suppose) alludes to Charles XII. of Sweden. See his History by Voltaire.—P.

† Carlyle, in the work he has devoted to " Heroes and Hero-worship," remarks in his peculiar manner, that " Among these shadowy Edda matters, amid all that fantastic congeries of assertions and traditions, in their musical mythologies, the main practical belief a man could have was probably not much more than this : of the Valkyrs and the Hall of Odin ; of an inflexible

remarks to be made upon the sense in which these precepts were taken, and upon the manner in which they were observed; but to avoid repetitions, I shall reserve them for the article in which I shall treat of the manners of the ancient Scandinavians. There we shall be best able to judge what influence their religion had upon these people, and by a natural circle thence form the most exact idea of the spirit of the religion itself. It is now time to discuss another of its doctrines, that of the state of man after death, and the final destiny of the world he now inhabits.

"There will come a time, says the Edda, a barbarous age, an age of the sword, when iniquity shall infest the earth, when brothers shall stain themselves with brothers' blood, when sons shall be the murderers of their fathers, and fathers of their sons, when incest and adultery shall be common, when no man shall spare his friend. Immediately shall succeed a desolating winter; the snow shall fall from the four corners of the world, the winds shall blow with fury, the whole earth shall be hard bound in ice. Three such winters shall pass away without being softened by one summer. Then shall succeed astonishing prodigies; then shall the monsters break their chains and escape; the great serpent shall roll himself in the ocean, and with his motions the earth shall be overflowed; the earth shall be shaken, the trees shall be torn up by the roots, the rocks shall be dashed against each other. The wolf Fenrir, broke loose from his chains, shall open his enormous mouth which reaches from heaven to earth; the fire shall flash out from his eyes and nostrils ; he shall devour the sun; and the great serpent who follows him shall vomit forth upon the waters, and into the air, great torrents of venom. In this confusion the stars shall fly from their places, the heaven shall cleave asunder, and the army of Surtur shall break in. But Heimdall, the door-keeper of the gods, rises up, he sounds his clanging trumpet; the gods

destiny; and that the one thing needful for a man was to be brave; the Valkyrs or Choosers of the Slain ; a destiny inexorable, which it is useless trying to bend or soften, has appointed who is to be slain ; this was a fundamental point for the Norse believer ; as indeed it is for all earnest men everywhere, for a Mahomet, a Luther, for a Napoleon too. It lies at the basis this for every such man, it is the woof out of which his whole system of thought is woven."

awake and assemble; the great ash-tree shakes its branches; heaven and earth are full of horror and affright. The gods fly to arms; the heroes place themselves in battle array. Odin appears armed in his golden casque and his resplendent cuirass; his vast scimitar is in his hands. He attacks the wolf Fenrir; he is devoured by him, and Fenrir perishes at the same instant. Thor is suffocated in the floods of venom which the serpent breathes forth as he expires. Loki and Heimdall mutually kill each other. The fire consumes everything, and the flame reaches up to heaven. But presently after a new earth springs forth from the bosom of the waves, adorned with green meadows; the fields there bring forth without culture, calamities are there unknown, a palace is there raised more shining than the sun, all covered with gold. This is the place that the just will inhabit, and enjoy delights for evermore. Then the powerful, the valiant, he who governs all things, comes forth from his lofty abodes, to render divine justice. He pronounces decrees. He establishes the sacred destinies which shall endure for ever. There is an abode remote from the sun, the gates of which face the north; poison rains there through a thousand openings: this place is all composed of the carcasses of serpents: there run certain torrents, in which are plunged perjurers and assassins."*

Notwithstanding the obscurities which are found in these descriptions, we see that it was a doctrine rendered sacred by the religion of the ancient Scandinavians, that the soul was immortal, and that there was a future state reserved for men, either happy or miserable, according to their behaviour here below. All the Teutonic nations held the same opinions, and it was upon these they founded the obligation of serving the gods, and of being valiant in battle: but although the Greek and Latin historians who have spoke of this people, agree in attributing these notions to them, yet none of them have given any particular account of the nature of these doctrines; and one ought to regard in this respect the Icelandic mythology as a precious monument, without which we can know but very imperfectly this important part of the religion of our fathers. I must here sacrifice to brevity many reflections, which the

* See the Prose Edda, ch. 51.

picture I have here copied from thence naturally presents to the mind. Many in particular would arise on the surprising conformity that there is between several of the foregoing strokes, and those employed in the gospel to describe the same thing. A conformity so remarkable that one should be tempted to attribute it to the indiscreet zeal of the Christian writer who compiled this mythology, if the Edda alone had transmitted to us this prophecy concerning the last ages of the world, and if we did not find it with the same circumstances in the Völuspá, a poem of greater antiquity, and in which nothing can be discovered that has an air of interpolation, or forgery.

One remark, however, ought not to be omitted, which is, that this mythology expressly distinguishes two different abodes for the happy, and as many for the culpable; which is what several authors who have written of the ancient religion of Europe have not sufficiently attended to. The first of these abodes was the palace of Odin named Valhalla, where that god received all such as died in a violent manner, from the beginning to the end of the world, that is, to the time of that universal desolation of nature which was to be followed by a new creation, and what they called Ragnarök, or the twilight of the gods. The second, which after the renovation of all things was to be their eternal abode, was named Gimli, that is, the palace covered with gold, the description of which we have seen above, where the just were to enjoy delights for ever. It was the same as to the place of punishments; they distinguished two of those, of which the first, named Niflheim, was only to continue to the renovation of the world, and the second that succeeded it was to endure for ever. This last was named Nåströnd, the shore of the dead; and we have seen in the description of the end of the world, what idea was entertained of it by the ancient Scandinavians. With regard to the two first places, the Valhalla and Niflheim, they are not only distinguished from the others in being only to endure till the conflagration of the world, but also in respect to rewards and punishments. Those only whose blood had been shed in battle, might aspire to the pleasures which Odin prepared for them in Valhalla. The pleasures which they expected after death show us plainly enough what they relished during life. " The heroes, says the Edda, who are received into the palace of Odin, have every day the pleasure of arming themselves, of passing in review, of ranging themselves in order of battle, and of cutting one another in pieces; but as soon as the hour of repast approaches, they return on horseback all safe and sound back to the hall of Odin, and fall to eating and drinking. Though the number of them cannot be counted, the flesh of the boar Sæhrimnir is sufficient for them all; every day it is served up at table, and every day it is renewed again entire: their beverage is ale and mead; one single goat, whose milk is excellent mead, furnishes enough of that liquor to intoxicate all the heroes. Odin alone drinks wine for his entire liquor. A crowd of virgins wait upon the heroes at table, and fill their cups as fast as they empty them." Such was that happy state, the bare hope of which rendered all the inhabitants of the north of Europe intrepid, and which made them not only to defy, but even seek with ardour the most cruel deaths. Accordingly King Ragnar Lodbrok, when he was going to die, far from uttering groans, or forming complaints, expressed his joy by these verses. "We are cut to pieces with swords; but this fills me with joy, when I think of the feast that is preparing for me in Odin's palace. Quickly, quickly seated in the splendid habitation of the gods, we shall drink beer out of curved horns*. A brave man fears not to die. I shall utter no timorous words as I

---

* We have substituted "curved horns" for "the skulls of our enemies;" Finn Magnusen, and Professor Rask having shown that this is the true meaning of the original passage, literally " soon shall we drink ale out of the curved branches of the skull," i. e. of an animal, a figurative expression employed by the Skald to indicate the usual drinking horns, and that Olaus Wormius, Bartholin and other writers of that period, whom our author has followed, were totally mistaken in rendering it " ex concavis crateribus craniorum," and " ex concavis craniorum poculis," or as one of them gives it, " confestim, ex cranibus hostium capacitate conspicuis, cerevisiam bibemus." It is this mistake that has given rise to the erroneous notion, that the heroes of Valhalla drank their ale out of the skulls of those they had slain in battle.

> " They thought
> One day from Ella's skull to quaff the mead,
> Their valour's guerdon,"

says Southey. We think that a daily dinner consisting solely of boiled pork, washed down with ale and an occasional draught of mead, was bad enough in all conscience, without making skulls serve for drinking cups.—Ed.

enter the Hall of Odin." This fanatic hope derived additional force from the ignominy affixed to every kind of death
but such as was of a violent nature, and from the fear of being
sent after such an exit into Niflheim. This was a place consisting of nine worlds, reserved for those that died of disease
or old age, Hela or Death, there exercised her despotic
power; her palace was Anguish; her table Famine; her waiters
were Slowness and Delay; the threshold of her door was
Precipice; her bed Care; she was livid and ghastly pale; and
her very looks inspired horror.

After this description of the religion of the Scandinavians,
can we be surprised that they should make war their only
business, and carry their valour to the utmost excesses of
fanaticism. Such also will be the features which I shall most
frequently have occasion to present, when I come to give a
picture of their manners : there the influence of a doctrine
so pernicious will be felt in its utmost extent. But justice
obliges me to observe here, that the reproach arising from
it does not affect the ancient inhabitants of the north more,
than those of all Europe in general, unless it be that they
continued to deserve it longer. However strange to a man
who reasons coolly may appear the madness of making war
habitually, for the sake of war itself, it must notwithstanding be allowed, that this has been for a succession of ages the
favourite passion of all those nations at present so polite;
and it is but, as it were, of yesterday that they began to be
sensible of the value of peace, of the cultivation of arts, and
of a government favourable to industry. The farther we look
back towards their infancy, the more we see them occupied in
war, divided among themselves, cruelly bent on the destruction
of each other, by a spirit of revenge, idleness and fanaticism.
There was a time when the whole face of Europe presented
the same spectacle as the forests of America; viz. a thousand
little wandering nations, without cities or towns, or agriculture,
or arts; having nothing to subsist on but a few herds, wild
fruits and pillage, harassing themselves incessantly by inroads and attacks, sometimes conquering, sometimes conquered, often totally overthrown and destroyed. The same
causes everywhere produce the same effects : a savage life
necessarily produces cruelty and injustice; disquiet, idleness
and envy naturally lead to violence, and the desire of rapine

and mischief. The fear of death is no restraint when life has no comfort. What evidently proves the unhappiness of those nations who live in such a state as this, is the facility with which they throw their lives away. The pleasure arising from property, from sentiment and knowledge, the fruits of industry, laws and arts, by softening life and 'endearing it to us, can alone give us a relish for peace and justice.

CHAPTER VI.

OF THE EXTERIOR WORSHIP AND RELIGIOUS CEREMONIES OF THE NORTHERN NATIONS.

In laying open the principal doctrines of the ancient Scandinavians, I have already had frequent occasion to remark their conformity with those of the other Teutonic nations of Europe. The same conformity is observable in the worship which they paid the Deity; and one may presume that it would appear still greater if it were easy to pursue with exactness the history of that religion through its several stages of purity and alteration. Thus, for instance, it is easy to comprehend why the ancient Scandinavians made use of temples; although, on the other hand, it would appear that the use of them was proscribed by the primitive religion, which taught that it was offensive to the gods to pretend to inclose them within the circuit of walls; and that men thereby checked and restrained their action, which is to penetrate all creatures freely in order to support them in being. There was doubtless a time, when the Scandinavians, admitting the same doctrine, worshipped their divinities only in the open air, and either knew not or approved not of the use of temples. Although we want the greatest part of the monuments which might instruct us concerning that stage of their religion, the traces of it are not yet entirely destroyed. We find at this day here and there, in Denmark, Sweden, and Norway, in the middle of a plain, or upon some little hill, altars, around which they assembled to offer sacrifices and to assist at other religious ceremonies. The greatest part of these altars are raised upon a little hill, either natural or artificial. Three long pieces of rock set upright serve for a basis to a great flat stone, which forms the

table of the altar *. There is commonly a pretty large cavity
under this altar, which might be intended to receive the
blood of the victims; and they never fail to find stones for
striking fire scattered round it; for no other fire, but such as
was struck forth with a flint, was pure enough for so holy a
purpose. Sometimes these rural altars are constructed in a
more magnificent manner; a double range of enormous stones
surround the altar and the little hill on which it is erected.
In Zealand we see one of this kind †; which is formed of
stones of a prodigious magnitude. Men would even now be
afraid to undertake such a work, notwithstanding all the
assistance of the mechanical powers which in those times they
wanted. What redoubles the astonishment is, that stones of
that size are rarely to be seen throughout the island, and that
they must have been brought from a great distance. What
labour and time then must have been bestowed upon these
vast rude monuments, which are unhappily more durable than
those of the fine arts! But men in all ages have been persuaded that they could not pay greater honour to the Deity,
than by making for him (if I may so express it) a kind of
strong bulwarks; in executing prodigies of labour; in consecrating to him immense riches. The sacrifice of whatever is
vicious in our passions, which he only requires of us for our
own happiness, is always the last thing that is thought of to
offer to him, because it is perhaps what is after all the most
difficult. At Ephesus they displayed their devotion by laying out upon one single temple all the treasures of Greece
and Asia. The Goths, whose bodily strength was all their
riches, showed their zeal by rolling enormous rocks to the
summits of hills.

In some places of Norway are found grottoes, which have
also been employed for religious uses. Some of them have

Our author who, throughout his work, places too great a value on the
somewhat Utopian account which Tacitus has left us of the ancient Germans, fancies that these rude monuments were the altars that served for what
he is pleased to term "the primitive worship of mankind." (See Chap. IV.)
Without entering into a discussion of an hypothesis which we deem to be
perfectly gratuitous, we will merely observe that places where such circles of
upright stones are found, were, generally speaking, *Thingsteads*, that is to
say, the places where the *Things* or legislative and judicial assemblies were
held, and where the kings were also elected.— Ed.

† Vide Olai Wormii Monum. Danic.

been cut with incredible pains in the hardest rocks; others are formed of prodigious stones brought near and combined together with a force no less surprising *.

By degrees, as the Scandinavians formed new intercourses and connections with the other nations of Europe, whether by the expeditions they undertook, or by the foreign colonies which came to establish themselves among them, their religion, changing by degrees, tolerated insensibly temples and idols, and at length adopted them without reserve. The three principal nations of Scandinavia † vied with each other in erecting temples, but none were more famous than that of Upsal in Sweden. It glittered on all sides with gold. A chain of the same metal (or at least gilded) ran round the roof, although the circumference was not less than nine hundred ells. Hakon, earl of Norway, had built one near Drontheim, which was not inferior to that of Upsal. When Olaf Tryggvason, king of Norway, introduced the Christian faith into that country, he caused this temple to be razed to the ground, and broke to pieces the idols it contained. They found there great riches, and particularly a ring of gold of great value. Iceland had also its temples, and the chronicles of that country speak with admiration of two especially, one situate in the north of the island, the other in the south. In each of these temples "there was," says an author of that country ‡, " a private chapel, which was regarded as a holy place : there they placed the idols upon a kind of altar, around which they ranged the victims that were to be offered up. Another altar stood opposite to it, plated with iron, in order that the fire which was to burn there perpetually should not damage it. Upon this altar was placed a vase of brass, in which they received the blood of the victims. Beside it stood a brush which they made use of to sprinkle the blood upon the bystanders. There hung up likewise a great silver ring, which they stained with blood, and which whoever took an oath on any occasion was required to hold in his hand. In one of these temples, there was also near the chapel a deep pit or well, into which they cast the victims."

* Worm. Monum. Danic. lib. i. p. 6.
† Sweden, Denmark, and Norway.
‡ Vid. Arngrim. Jon. Crymogæa.

When Denmark had embraced the Christian faith, they applied themselves with as much zeal to destroy these temples, as they had a little before to serve their false gods in them. In a short time they were all razed to the ground, and the very remembrance of the places where they stood was totally lost. But the altars that are very often found scattered upon the mountains and in the woods, testify at this day that the ancient Danes were not less attached to this mode of worship than the other northern nations. All the gods whose names I have enumerated, and many others of inferior note, were worshipped and invoked by the ancient Scandinavians, but not all in the same manner, nor on the same account. The great temple of Upsal seemed to be particularly consecrated to the three superior deities, and each of them was characterized by some particular symbol. Odin was represented holding a sword in his hand : Thor stood at the left hand of Odin, with a crown upon his head, a sceptre in one hand, and his mallet in the other. Sometimes they painted him on a chariot, drawn by two he-goats of wood, with a silver bridle, and his head surrounded with stars. Frey stood at the left hand of Thor, and was represented of both sexes, (as an hermaphrodite,) and with divers other attributes which characterized productiveness. I do not here enter into a minute account of the worship rendered to the other gods : that which was paid to the three superior deities consisted principally in sacrifices, and deserves to be described more at large.

There were three great religious festivals in the year. The first was celebrated at the winter solstice. They called the night on which it was observed the Mother-night, as that which produced all the rest; and this epoch was rendered the more remarkable as they dated from thence the beginning of the year, which among the northern nations was computed from one winter solstice to another, as the month was from one new moon to the next. This feast, which was very considerable, was named Jul*, and was celebrated in honour of Frey, or the sun, in order to obtain a propitious year and fruitful seasons. Sacrifices, feasting, nocturnal assemblies, and all the demonstrations of a most dissolute joy, were then authorized by the general usage. These answered to the

---

* Hence is derived the word Yeol or Yule, the old name for Christmas. P.

Saturnalia of the Romans, and were in a great measure renewed afterwards among the people on occasion of the feast of Christmas. The second festival was instituted in honour of the earth, or of the goddess Goa, to request of her pleasures, fruitfulness, and victory; and it was fixed at the first quarter of the second moon of the year *. The third, which seems to have been the most considerable in ancient times, was instituted in honour of Odin; it was celebrated at the beginning of the spring, in order to welcome in that pleasant season, and especially to obtain of the god of battles happy success in their projected expeditions. There were also some feasts in honour of the other gods, and they were often multiplied on occasion of particular events.

In the earliest ages the offerings were simple, and such as shepherds and rustics could present. They loaded the altars of the gods with the first fruits of their crops, and the choicest products of the earth. Afterwards they sacrificed animals. When they had once laid it down as a principle that the effusion of the blood of these animals appeased the anger of the gods, and that their justice turned aside upon the victims those strokes which were destined for men, their great care then was for nothing more than to conciliate their favour by so easy a method. It is the nature of violent desires and excessive fear to know no bounds, and therefore when they would ask for any favour which they ardently wished for, or would deprecate some public calamity which they feared, the blood of animals was not deemed a price sufficient, but they began to shed that of men. It is probable that this barbarous practice was formerly almost universal, and that it is of a very remote antiquity. It was not entirely abolished among the northern nations till towards the ninth century, because before that time they had not received the light of the gospel, and

---

* This was the chief festival of the Swedes, during which they held their Al-thing. Goa is not mentioned in the Edda, but is supposed to correspond to the nymph or goddess Saga, and the festival to have been in honour of all the Disir—beings, though of a different sex, corresponding in their attributes to the Roman genii loci. In other parts of Scandinavia a festival took place at this period in honour of Freyja. It seems probable, in fact, that all the female deities, Asynior, Norns, Valkyrior, and Disir, were invoked at these vernal festivities.—See *Finn Magnusen's Eddalæren*, IV. 144.—ED.

were ignorant of those arts which had softened the ferocity of the Romans and Greeks whilst they were still pagans.

The appointed time for these sacrifices was always deter mined by another superstitious opinion which made the northern nations regard the number three as sacred and particularly dear to the gods. Thus in every ninth month they renewed this bloody ceremony, which was to last nine days, and every day they offered up nine living victims, whether men or animals. But the most solemn sacrifices were those which were offered at Upsal in Sweden every ninth year. Then the king and all the citizens of any distinction were obliged to appear in person, and to bring offerings, which were placed in the great temple described above. Those who could not come themselves sent their presents by others, or paid the value in money to those whose business it was to receive the offerings. Strangers flocked there in crowds from all parts: and none were excluded except those whose honour had suffered some stain, and especially such as had been accused of cowardice. Then they chose among the captives in time of war, and among the slaves in time of peace, nine persons to be sacrificed. The choice was partly regulated by the opinion of the bystanders, and partly by lot. But they did not always sacrifice such mean persons. In great calamities, in a press-ing famine for example, if the people thought they had some pretext to impute the cause of it to their king, they even sa-crificed him without hesitation, as the highest price with which they could purchase the Divine favour. In this manner the first king * of Vermaland was burnt in honour of Odin to put an end to a great dearth; as we read in the history of Nor-way. The kings, in their turn, did not spare the blood of their subjects; and many of them even shed that of their children. Earl Hakon, of Norway, offered his son in sacrifice, to obtain of Odin the victory over the Jomsburg pirates. Aun, king of Sweden, devoted to Odin the blood of his nine sons, to prevail on that god to prolong his life †. The ancient history of the north abounds in similar examples. These

---

* This was a petty king of a province of Sweden. See Wormius, in Mo-num. Dan. p. 25, 26. See also page 86.—ED.

† Worm. Monum. Danic. lib. i. p. 28.

abominable sacrifices were accompanied with various ceremonies. When the victim was chosen, they conducted him
towards the altar where the sacred fire was kept burning
night and day; it was surrounded with all sorts of iron and
brazen vessels. Among them one was distinguished from the
rest by its superior size; in this they received the blood of
the victims. When they offered up animals, they speedily
killed them at the foot of the altar; then they opened their
entrails to draw auguries from them, as among the Romans;
afterwards they dressed the flesh to be served up in a feast
prepared for the assembly. Even horse-flesh was not rejected,
and the chiefs often eat of it as well as the people. But when
they were disposed to sacrifice men, those whom they pitched
upon were laid upon a great stone, where they were instantly
either strangled or knocked on the head. The bodies were
afterwards burnt, or suspended in a sacred grove near the
temple. Part of the blood was sprinkled upon the people,
part of it upon the sacred grove; with the same they also
bedewed the images of the gods, the altars, the benches and
walls of the temple, both within and without.

Near the temple of Upsal there was a grove of this sort, of
which every tree and every leaf was regarded as the most
sacred thing in the world. This, which was named Odin's
Grove, was full of the bodies of men and animals who had
been sacrificed. In whatever manner they immolated men,
the priest always took care in consecrating the victim to pronounce certain words, as, "I devote thee to Odin." "I send
thee to Odin." Or, "I devote thee for a good harvest; for
the return of a fruitful season." The ceremony concluded
with feastings, in which they displayed all the magnificence
known in those times. They drank immoderately; the kings
and chief lords drank first, healths in honour of the gods;
every one drank afterwards, making some vow or prayer to
the god whom they named. Hence came that custom among
the first Christians in Germany and the North, of drinking to
the health of our Saviour, the apostles, and the saints;
a custom which the church was often obliged to tolerate. The
licentiousness of these feasts at length increased to such
a pitch as to become mere bacchanalian meetings, where,
to the sound of barbarous music, amidst shouts, dancing, and

I

indecent gestures, so many unseemly actions were committed, that the wisest men refused to assist at them.

The same kinds of sacrifices were offered, though perhaps with less splendour, in Denmark, Norway and Iceland. Let us hear on this subject an historian of the eleventh century, Dithmar, bishop of Merseburg *. "There is," says he, "in Zealand a place which is the capital of Denmark, named Lederun (this is now Lethra or Leyre, of which I shall speak hereafter). At this place, every nine years, in the month of January, the Danes flock together in crowds, and offer to their gods ninety-nine men, as many horses, dogs and cocks, with the certain hope of appeasing the gods by these victims." Dudo of St. Quentin, a French historian, attributes the same practice to the Normans or Norwegians †; but he informs us that it was in honour of Thor that these sacrifices were made. Arngrim Jonas, an Icelandic author, who has written with great learning upon the antiquities of his nation ‡, remarks that there were formerly in Iceland two temples in which they offered up human victims, and a famous pit or well in which they were thrown headlong. There are still in Friesland, and in several places of Germany, altars composed of such large stones that they could neither be destroyed by the ravages of time, nor by the zeal of the first converts to Christianity. These altars, according to the tradition of the inhabitants, and the reports of credible historians, have served for the same horrid purposes. The Gauls for a long time offered men to their supreme god Esus. The first inhabitants of Italy, and Sicily, the Britons, the Phœnicians, the Carthaginians, and all the nations we know of in Europe and Asia, have been covered with the same reproach. And can we wonder at it? Every nation buried in ignorance must inevitably fall into error, and from thence into fanaticism and cruelty. Men are born surrounded with dangers and evils, at the same time that they are weak and naked. If, as they grow up to manhood, the arts of civil life and the security of laws do not disperse their fears, soften their dispositions, and diffuse through their minds calmness, moderation, and the social affections, they become a prey to a thousand gloomy

* Dithm. Merseburg. Chronic. lib. i. p. 12.
† Dudo Quint. sub init.
‡ J. Arngr. Crymog. lib. i. c. 7.

terrors, which paint out all nature to them as full of dangers and enemies, and keep them perpetually armed with ferocity and distrust. Hence that thirst of revenge and destruction which barbarous nations cannot lay aside : hence that impious prejudice which makes them imagine the gods to be as sanguinary as themselves. It is the unhappiness of our nature, that ignorance suggests fear, and fear cruelty. They must therefore be very little acquainted with human nature, and still less so with history, who place the golden age of any people in the age of its poverty and ignorance. It is so true that men are everywhere alike in this respect, that nations who have never had any commerce with those of Europe, have run into the same excesses with equal fury. The Peruvians anciently offered human sacrifices. The Mexicans once offered up to their gods, upon one single occasion, five thousand prisoners of war. Multitudes of people, half unknown and wandering in the deserts of Africa or forests of America, do to this day destroy each other, from the same principles and with the same blind fury.

Tacitus informs us that, among the Germans, the power of inflicting pains and penalties, of striking, and binding a criminal, was vested in the priests alone. And these men, so haughty, who thought themselves dishonoured if they did not revenge the slightest offence, would tremblingly submit to blows and even death itself from the hand of the pontiff, whom they took for the instrument of an angry deity. In short, the credulity of the people, and the craft and presumption of the priest went so far, that these pretended interpreters of the Divine will dared even to demand, in the name of Heaven, the blood of kings themselves; and they obtained it. To succeed in this, it was only requisite for them to avail themselves of those times of calamity, when the people, distracted with sorrow and fear, lay their minds open to the most horrid impressions. At those times, while the prince was slaughtered at one of the altars of the gods, the others were covered with offerings, which were heaped up on all sides for their ministers.

I have already observed, that the ancient religion of the northern nations made the deity to interpose in the most indifferent events, as well as the most considerable ; and they only considered the elements as so many organs by which he

manifested his will and his resolves.   This opinion once admitted, interest or superstition quickly drew from thence a
consequence natural enough: namely, that by studying with
care the phenomena of nature, or, to speak in the spirit of
that religion, the visible actions of that unseen deity, men
might come to know his will, inclinations, and desires: in
one word, they entered into a kind of commerce with him;
oracles, auguries, divinations, and a thousand practices of that
kind, quickly sprung up in crowds, from this erroneous principle.   Accordingly, in all our ancient fables and chronicles,
we see the northern nations extremely attached to this vain
science.   They had oracles, like the people of Italy and
Greece, and these oracles were not less revered, nor less
famous, than theirs.   It was generally believed, either that
the gods and goddesses, or, more commonly, that the three
destinies, whose names I have given elsewhere, delivered out
these oracles in their temples.   That of Upsal was as famous
for its oracles as its sacrifices.   There were also celebrated
ones in Dalia, a province of Sweden; in Norway and Denmark.   " It was," says Saxo the Grammarian, " a custom
with the ancient Danes to consult the oracles of the Parcæ,
concerning the future destiny of children newly born.   Accordingly Fridleif, being desirous to know that of his son
Olaus, entered into the temple of the gods to pray; and,
being introduced into the sanctuary, he saw three goddesses
upon so many seats.   The first, who was of a beneficent nature, granted the infant beauty and the gift of pleasing.   The
second gave him a noble heart.   But the third, who was envious and spiteful, to spoil the work of her sisters, imprinted
on him the stain of covetousness."   It should seem that the
idols or statues, themselves, of the gods and goddesses delivered these oracles *vivâ voce*.   In an ancient Icelandic chronicle we read of one Indrid, who went from home to wait for
Thorstein, his enemy.   " Thorstein," says the author, " upon
his arrival, entered into the temple.   In it was a stone (cut
probably into a statue) which he had been accustomed to wor·
ship; he prostrated himself before it, and prayed to it (to inform him of his destiny).   Indrid, who stood without, heard
the stone chaunt forth these verses:—' It is for the last time,
it is with feet drawing near to the grave, that thou art come
to this place: for it is most certain, that, before the sun

ariseth, the valiant Indrid shall make thee feel his hatred."[*]
The people persuaded themselves, sometimes, that these idols
answered by a gesture or a nod of the head, which signified
that they hearkened to the prayers of their supplicants.

I shall not enter into a description of the other kinds of
oracles. Enough has been said to convince the discerning
reader, that here was the same credulity on the one side, and
the same imposture on the other, as had formerly procured
credit to the oracles of Greece and Asia. There is no essential difference between those of the two countries, though so
far distant from each other. If the luxury of the southern
nations set theirs off with more pomp and magnificence than
comported with the simplicity of the rude inhabitants of the
North, the latter had no less veneration and attachment to
their own oracles than they. It has been thought to be no
less for the interest of religion to attribute these of the North
to the artifices of the devil than the others, as well as the
pretended science of magic, of which the North has passed so
long for the most celebrated school and peculiar country. It
is true that men have not advanced on the subject of the
northern oracles, as they have done with respect to those of
the south, that they ceased at the birth of Christ, although
the assertion is as true of the one as the other: but for want
of this proof, an ill-grounded zeal hath found plenty of others;
as if the advantages resulting from true religion were less important, or our gratitude less due, because the evils, from
which it has delivered mankind, did not proceed from supernatural causes.

Oracles were not the only efforts made by the curiosity of
the Scandinavians to penetrate into futurity, nor the only relief imposture afforded them. They had diviners, both male
and female, honoured with the name of prophets, and revered
as if they had been such. Some of them were said to have
familiar spirits, who never left them, and whom they consulted
under the form of little idols; others dragged the ghosts of
the departed from their tombs, and forced the dead to tell
them what would happen. Poetry was often employed for the
like absurd purposes, and those same Skalds or bards, who, as
we shall see hereafter, enjoyed such credit among the living,

---

[*] Holmveria saga apud Bartholin. lib. iii. c. 11

boasted a power of disturbing the repose of the dead, and of dragging them out of their gloomy abodes by force of certain songs which they knew how to compose. The same ignorance, which made poetry be regarded as something supernatural, persuaded them also that the letters or Runic characters, which were then used by the few who were able to write and read, included in them certain mysterious and magical properties. Impostors then easily persuaded a credulous people that these letters, disposed and combined after a certain manner, were able to work wonders, and, in particular, to presage future events. There were letters, or Runes, to procure victory—to preserve from poison—to relieve women in labour—to cure bodily diseases—to dispel evil thoughts from the mind—to dissipate melancholy—and to soften the severity of a cruel mistress. They employed pretty nearly the same characters for all these different purposes, but they varied the order and combination of the letters; they wrote them either from right to left, or from top to bottom, or in form of a circle, or contrary to the course of the sun, &c. In this principally consisted that puerile and ridiculous art, as little understood, probably, by those who professed it, as it was distrusted by those who had recourse to it.

I have already remarked that they had often no other end, in sacrificing human victims, than to know what was to happen by inspection of their entrails, by the effusion of their blood, and by the greater or less degree of celerity with which they sunk to the bottom of the water. The same motive engaged them to lend an attentive ear to the singing of birds, which some diviners boasted a power of interpreting. The ancient history of Scandinavia is as full of these superstitious practices as that of Rome itself. We see in Saxo Grammaticus, as in Livy, auguries which forebode the success of an expedition, warriors who are struck by unexpected presages, lots consulted, days regarded as favourable or unlucky, female diviners who follow the armies, showers of blood, forebodings, wonderful dreams which the event never fails to justify, and the slightest circumstances of the most important actions taken for good or bad omens. This has been, we well know, a general and inveterate disease in human nature, of which it has only begun to be cured in Europe. To recall to view a spectacle, which tends so much to mortify and humble us, would be a labour as useless as discouraging to an historian, if the knowledge of all these practices did not make an essential part of that of manners and of the causes of events, without which there could be no history; and also if the sketch of the errors and mistakes of human reason did not convincingly prove to us the necessity of cultivating it.   A person endued with natural good sense will also find, by this means, remedies proper to cure whatever remains of such weakness and credulity hang about him.   It is true, one cannot always refute the marvellous and supernatural stories of ancient historians, by the bare circumstances of their relations; because, besides that it would be endless to enter continually upon such discussions, we often want the pieces necessary to enable us to make all the researches such an examination would require.   But what needs there more to convince us that we have a right to reject, without exception, all facts of this kind, than to consider, on the one hand, how ignorant the vulgar are even in our days—how credulous—how easy to be imposed on; and to be even the dupes of their own fancy, greedy of the marvellous, inclined to exaggeration, and precipitant in their judgments: and, on the other hand, that among those nations, whose history appears so astonishing at present, for a long time all were vulgar, except, perhaps, a few obscure sages, whose voice was too feeble to be heard amid the clamours of so many blind and prejudiced persons? Is it not sufficient to consider further, that the age of the greatest ignorance of such nations is precisely that which has been most fruitful of oracles, divinations, prophetic dreams, apparitions, and other prodigies of that kind?—that they appear more seldom in proportion as they are less believed?—and, finally, that the experience of our own times shows us, that wherever reason is brought to the greatest perfection, all things fall into the order of natural and simple events, insomuch that the lowest and meanest class of men accustom themselves to believe nothing which is not agreeable to good sense and accompanied with some probability?

But I repeat it once more, that superstition did not blind all the ancient Scandinavians without exception; and history testifies, that there were, after all, among them men wise enough to discover the folly of the received opinions, and courageous enough to condemn them without reserve.   In the history of Olaf Tryggvason a warrior fears not to say

publicly, that he relies much more on his own strength and on
his arms, than upon Thor or Odin. Another, in the same book,
speaks thus to his friend:—" I would have thee know, that I
believe neither in idols nor spirits. I have travelled in
many places; I have met with giants and monstrous men:
they could never overcome me; thus to this present hour
my own force and courage are the sole objects of my belief."
Unluckily there seems too much room to suspect that this
contempt of superstition did but throw them for the most
part into the opposite extreme. So true is it that we seldom
are able to observe a just medium. At least, many of the
northern warriors seem to have been so intoxicated with
their courage as to esteem themselves independent beings,
who had nothing to ask or fear from the gods. In an Icelandic chronicle, a vain-glorious person makes his boast to a
Christian missionary, that he had never yet acknowledged
any religion, and that his own strength and abilities were
every thing to him. For the same reason, others refused to
sacrifice to the gods of whom they had no need. St. Olaf,
king of Norway, demanding of a warrior, who offered him his
services, what religion he professed; the warrior answered,
"I am neither Christian nor Pagan; my companions and I
have no other religion, than the confidence in our own
strength, and in the good success which always attends us
in war; and we are of opinion it is all that is necessary."
The same thing is related of Rolf, surnamed Kraki, king of
Denmark: one day, when one of his companions proposed
to offer a sacrifice to Odin, he said that he feared nothing
from that blustering spirit, and that he should never stand
in awe of him. But as it was not always kings who durst
manifest sentiments so bold and hardy, the followers of the
prevailing religion sometimes punished these irreligious persons. In the life of King Olaf Tryggvason, mention is made
of a man who was condemned to exile for having sung in a
public place, verses, the sense of which was to this purpose,
" I will not insult or affront the gods; nevertheless, the goddess Freyja inspires me with no respect: it must certainly
be that either she or Odin are chimerical deities." It is easy
to conceive how much natural good sense, supported by that
confidence which bodily strength inspires, could excite in those
ancient warriors contempt for their mute and feeble deities,
and for the childish or troublesome rites in their worship.

But besides this, the primitive religion, as I have already observed, in its original purity admitted only a simple and reasonable worship, and one sole, principal deity, who was invisible and almighty.   One may then suppose, with a good deal of likelihood, that this religion was not by length of time so much defaced, but that some traces of it still remained in the memory of sensible persons, and in the soundest part of the nation.   Indeed we see appear at intervals in ancient Scandinavia, some men of this stamp endued with a real strength of mind, who not only trampled under foot all the objects of the credulity and idle superstition of the multitude, (an effort which pride renders easy, and sometimes alone produces,) but who even raised their minds to the invisible master of every thing we see ; " the father of the sun, and of all nature."   In an Icelandic saga, a person named Giest says to his nephew, who is just ready to embark for Greenland * : " I beseech and conjure him who made the sun to give success to thy undertaking."   A celebrated Norwegian warrior, named Thorstein, says, speaking of his father, " He will receive upon this account a recompense from him who made the heaven and the universe, whoever he be : " and, upon another occasion, he makes a vow to the same being, " who made the sun," for, adds he, " his power must needs have been excessive to produce such a work." All his family entertained the same sentiments, and it is expressly noted in many places of the same saga, that it was their religion to believe in him, " who was creator of the sun."   Torkill, a supreme judge of Iceland, a man of unblemished life, and distinguished among the wisest magistrates of that island during the time that it was governed in form of a republic, seeing his end draw near, ordered himself to be set in the open air, with his face turned towards the sun, and having rested there some moments in a kind of ecstasy, expired, recommending his soul to him among the gods who had created the sun and the stars †.   But of all the strokes of this kind, none is more remarkable than what a modern Icelandic historian relates in his manuscript supplement to the history of Norway.   Harold Hárfagra, the first

* Vatzdæla. apud Barthol. c. 6, lib. i. p. 83.
† Arn. Jon. Crymog. lib. i. c. 6.

king of all Norway, says this author, being yet but young, held the following discourse in a popular assembly :—" I swear and protest in the most sacred manner, that I will never offer sacrifice to any of the gods adored by the people, but to him only who hath formed this world, and every thing we behold in it." Harold lived in the middle of the ninth century, at a time when the Christian religion had not yet penetrated into Norway.

CHAPTER VII.

OF THE FORM OF GOVERNMENT WHICH FORMERLY PREVAILED IN THE NORTH.

THE character of the ancient northern nations is, in some measure, laid open in the former book. It is the nature of every religion which is the handiwork of men, always to carry marks of the weakness of its authors, and to breathe forth the same spirit with which they themselves were animated. Their government and laws are another faithful mirror wherein that spirit may be seen with no less advantage. It is obvious that the laws cannot long be contrary to the genius of a nation. Sooner or later they will be impressed with its character, or they will give it theirs. These are two streams very different in their sources, but which as soon as they unite in the same channel, have but one force and one direction. The importance of this subject makes it incumbent on me to treat it with some extent, and to bring together with the utmost care all the feeble and scattered rays which throw any light upon it amid the obscurity of so many dark ages.

In the first place, let us consult Tacitus, that excellent historian of ancient Germany, who in his little compendious narrative has given in a few pages a most striking picture of the inhabitants of this vast country. His words ought to be given here entire, and weighed with care. Among this people, he says, " the chiefs, or princes *, determine some affairs of less importance; all the rest are reserved for the

---

* *De minoribus rebus* Principes *consultant; de majoribus* Omnes. Tacit. Germ. c. 11, 12, 13, 14, &c.

general assembly : yet even these, the decision of which is vested in the people, are beforehand discussed by the chiefs.... At these assemblies they take their seats all of them armed. Silence is commanded by the priests, whose business it is at such times to maintain order. Then the king or chief speaks first ; afterwards the great men are heard in their turns with that attention which is due to their age, to their nobility, their reputation in war, their eloquence ; greater deference being paid to their power of persuasion, than to their personal authority. If their advice displeases, the people reject it with a general murmur ; if it is approved of, they clash their lances. It is the most honourable way of expressing their assent, or of conferring praise, to do it by their arms. .... Criminal causes may also be brought before this great council of the nation. .... In the same assemblies are elected the chiefs or princes, whose business it is to distribute justice through the towns and villages. To each of these are joined a hundred assessors chosen out of the people, who assist the chief with their advice and authority *. .... The kings are chosen for their noble birth ; the leaders or generals for their personal valour. The power of the kings is not arbitrary, but limited. The leaders are not so much to give orders as examples : they must signalize themselves by their courage and activity, and their authority must be founded on esteem and admiration. .... Extreme youth does not exclude from the rank of prince or chief, those whom their noble birth, or the distinguished merit of their fathers, entitle to this dignity. As they advance in age and acquire esteem, other young warriors attach themselves to them and swell their retinue. Nor does any one blush to be seen among these attendants or followers. Yet they have different degrees of rank, which are regulated by the chief's own judgment. Among the followers is great emulation who shall stand highest in the chief's or prince's favour ; among the princes who shall have the most numerous and valiant attendants. This is their dignity, their strength, to be always surrounded with a body of chosen youths. This is their glory in peace, their security in war. And not only in their own nation, but among neighbouring states, they acquire a name and reputation, in

---

* Reges *ex nobilitate ;* Duces *ex virtute sumunt.* Tacit. c. 7.

proportion to the number and valour of their attendants. Then
is their friendship sought after by embassies, and cultivated
by presents. . . . . In battle, it would be a disgrace to the
chief to be excelled in courage by any of his followers ; a disgrace to his followers not to equal their chief. Should he
perish, they would be exposed to the highest infamy through
life if they should survive him, and escape from battle. . . . .
The chiefs fight for victory—they for their chief. . . . . To
retain their followers in their service, no prince or chief has
any other resource but war. They require of him one while
a horse trained for war ; one while a victorious and bloody
lance. His table rudely served, but with great abundance,
serves them instead of pay."

All the most distinguished circumstances which characterize
the ancient Teutonic form of government are contained in
this remarkable passage. Here we see kings, who owe their
advancement to an illustrious extraction, presiding, rather
than ruling, over a free people. Here we see the nation assembling at certain stated times, and making resolutions in
their own persons on all affairs of importance, as to enact
laws, to choose peace or war, to conclude alliances, to distribute justice in the last resort, and to elect magistrates. Here
also we distinguish a body of the chiefs of the nation, who
prepare and propose the important matters, the decision of
which is reserved for the general assembly of all the free
men : that is, we trace here the first lineaments, if I may so
say, of what was afterwards named in different countries,
" the council of the nation," " the senate," " the house of
peers," &c. Here we discover the origin of that singular
custom, of having an elective general, under an hereditary
king ; a custom received among most of the nations of German extraction, who had either mayors of the palace, or
grand marshals, or constables, or counts : for all these different
names only expressed the same thing in different countries.
Lastly, if we examine with attention the words of Tacitus, we
cannot doubt but vassalage and the feudal tenure had already
taken footing among this people before ever they left their
native forests. For although perhaps they did not in those
early times give lands in fee, and although their fees or fiefs
were then perhaps nothing but arms, war-horses, and banquets ;
what we read of the reciprocal engagements between the

princes or chiefs and their followers evidently contains whatever was essential to the nature of vassalage, and all the changes which were afterwards made in it were only slight and accidental, occasioned by the conquests and new establishments which followed from it.

If we consider after this the character of these nations, as it is sketched out by Tacitus, we shall not be surprised to see them wedded to institutions which they found so suitable to their situation and temper; for being the most free and warlike people upon earth, they must have had a natural aversion to the authority of a single person; and if they placed themselves under leaders, it was only because war cannot be conducted in any other form. As free men they would only obey from choice, and be less influenced by personal authority than by reason; as warriors they conceived no other duty to be owing to a prince than to be ready to shed their blood for his cause.

But how came these men to preserve themselves in so great a degree of liberty? This was owing to their climate and manner of life, which gave them such strength of body and mind as rendered them capable of long and painful labours, of great and daring exploits. "Accordingly we have since found liberty to prevail in North America, but not in the south;"* for the bodily strength of the northern warriors kept up in them that courage, that opinion of their own valour, that impatience of affronts and injuries, which makes men hate all arbitrary government and despise those who submit to it. Being less sensible of pain than the more southern nations, less easily moved by the bait of pleasure, less susceptible of those passions which shake the soul too violently, and weaken it by making it dependent on another's will, they were the less a prey to ambition, which flatters and intimidates by turns in order to gain the ascendant. Their imagination more constant and lively, their conception more steady than quick, naturally resisting novelties, kept them from falling into those snares out of which they would not have known how to escape.

They were free because they inhabited an uncultivated

* Montesquieu, L'Esprit des Lois, tom. 2.

country, rude forests and mountains; and liberty is the sole
treasure of an indigent people; for a poor country excites no
avidity, and he who possesses little defends it easily. They
were free because they were ignorant of those pleasures, often
so dearly bought, which render the protection of a powerful
master necessary. They were free because hunters and
shepherds, who wander about in woods through inclination or
necessity, are not so easily oppressed as the timorous inhabitants of inclosed towns, who are there chained down to the
fate of their houses; and because a wandering people, if
deprived of their liberty in one place, easily find it in
another, as well as their subsistence. Lastly, they were free
because, knowing not the use of money, there could not be
employed against them that instrument of slavery and corruption, which enables the ambitious to collect and distribute
at will the signs of riches.

Further, that spirit of liberty, arising from their climate,
and from their rustic and military life, had received new
strength from the opinions it had produced, as a sucker which
shoots forth from the root of a tree strengthens by embracing
it. In effect these people, esteeming beyond all things the
right of revenging an affront, the glory of despising death and
perishing sword in hand, were always ready to attack tyranny
in the first who dared to attempt it, and in whatever formidable shape it appeared.

By these means was liberty preserved among the inhabitants of Germany and the north, as it were in the bud, ready
to blossom and expand through all Europe, there to flourish
in their several colonies. This powerful principle exerted
the more strength in proportion as it was the more pressed;
and the whole power of Rome having been unable to destroy
it, it made that yield in its turn from the time it began to be
enfeebled till it was entirely overturned. Indeed there was
scarce a moment wherein these two opposite powers preserved
an even balance. As soon as ever that of Rome ceased to be
superior, it was destroyed: its celebrated name, that name
which had been so long its support, was only a signal of vengeance, which served as it were to rally and assemble at the
same instant all the northern nations; and immediately all
these people, breaking forth as it were by agreement, over-

turned this unhappy empire, and formed out of its ruins limited monarchies—states not less known before by name than by their form of government

In effect we every where see in those swarms of Germans and Scandinavians, a troop of savage warriors, who seem only born for ravage and destruction, changed into a sensible and free people as soon as ever they had confirmed their conquests; impregnating (if I may so say) their institutions with a spirit of order and equality; electing for their kings such of their princes of the blood royal as they judged most worthy to wear the crown; dividing between those kings and the whole nation the exercise of the sovereign power; reserving to the general assemblies the right of making laws and deciding important matters; and lastly, to give a solid support to the powers immediately essential to monarchy, distributing fiefs to the principal warriors, and assigning certain privileges proper to the several orders of the state.

Such for a long time was the constitution of all the governments which these people founded in Italy, in Spain, in Gaul, in Britain, at that memorable era which changed the fate and place of abode of so many nations—an era for ever memorable, since here we trace the first link (as it were) of a new chain of events; and hence we see spring forth the laws, the manners and principles, which have ever since governed so many celebrated nations, whose superiority of genius seems to have called them forth to determine one day the fate of almost all the rest of the world.

One cannot without difficulty quit an object so pleasing. It is time, however, to confine myself to what more particularly relates to my subject. All that we learn from the historical monuments of the north perfectly confirms the testimony of Tacitus, and either gives or receives new light from the annals of the other Teutonic nations. This remarkable agreement made M. de Montesquieu say that, "in reading Tacitus we every where see the codes of the barbarous nations; and in reading the codes of the barbarous nations, we are continually reminded of Tacitus." Notwithstanding this, we must not flatter ourselves that we can discover exactly the extent of power which the ancient kings of Scandinavia enjoyed, nor the particular rights and privileges of each order of the state If these were never very precisely determined among a rude people, who had no other laws but

custom, how can we distinguish them exactly at the present
great distance of time? All that we can obscurely discover,
is, that the Danes, who before the arrival of Odin were divided into many nations, and lived in great independence,
were by force of arms subjected to kings more absolute, whom
this conqueror placed over them*.

They were not long, however, before they recovered their
right of electing their kings, and consequently all the other
rights less essential to liberty. It is true, the people seem
always to have made it a law to choose the nearest relation of
the deceased king, or at least some one of the royal family,
which they respected as issued from the gods. They still
show the places where these elections were made: and as
Denmark was for a long time divided into three kingdoms, we
find accordingly three principal monuments of this custom;
the one near Lunden in Scania, the other at Leyra or Lethra
in Zealand, and the third near Viburg in Jutland. These
monuments, whose rude bulk has preserved them from the
ravages of time, are only vast unhewn stones, commonly
twelve in number, set upright and placed in form of a circle.
In the middle is erected a stone much larger than the rest, on
which they made a seat for their king†. The other stones
served as a barrier to keep off the populace, and marked the
place of those whom the people had appointed to make the
election. They treated also in the same place of the most
important affairs ‡. But if the king chanced to die in war or
at a distance from home, they formed upon the spot a place
after the same model by bringing together the largest stones
they could find. The principal chiefs got upon these stones,
and with a loud voice delivered their opinions; then the soldiers who stood in crowds about them signified their approbation or assent by clashing their shields together in a kind
of cadence, or by raising certain shouts. We know that this
custom of electing their kings in the open field prevailed
among all the northern nations, and was for a long time
necessary, because they had no cities. The emperors of Germany were for many ages elected after the same manner.

In Sweden, they joined to the other ceremonies which I

* This is an assumption founded on the Ynglinga-saga. See page 84.—
ED.

† Worm. Monum. Danic.

‡ The places indicated were in fact Thing-steads. See Note, page 108.—ED.

have been describing, an oath reciprocally taken between the king and his subjects *. One of the judges of the provinces convoked an assembly to make a new election immediately after the death of the king, and demanded with a loud voice of the people, if they would accept for king the person he named, who was always one of the royal family. When they had all given their consent, the new king was lifted up on the shoulders of the chiefs, in order that all the people might see and know him. Then he took Odin to witness, that he would observe the laws, defend his country, extend its boundaries, revenge whatever injuries his predecessors had received from their enemies, and would strike some signal stroke which should render him and his people famous. This oath he renewed at the funeral of his predecessor, which was usually celebrated with great pomp; and also on occasion of the progress which he was obliged to make through the chief provinces of the kingdom, in order to receive the homage of his subjects. I relate here all the particulars of this ceremony, because the exact conformity which we find between the manners of the Danes and Swedes during the ages of paganism, will not suffer us to doubt but that the kings of Denmark were elected after the same manner. This supposition is confirmed by what we can discover of the ancient constitution of the kingdom of Norway. But it is sufficient just to mention here this identity of government in the three principal kingdoms of the North. To describe it minutely in them all would occasion tiresome repetitions.

The ancient inhabitants of Germany and Scandinavia emerged but slowly from a state of nature. The ties which linked different families together were for a long time nothing but a confederacy to exercise violence or to repel it. They possessed a great extent of lands, of which they cultivated but little, and resided on less: in short, they lived too separate from each other to have any great need of civil laws; and their chiefs had too little authority to make them observed, if they had. Hence so many little societies and confederacies. Men banded together to revenge an injury; and the sentiment of honour, as well as interest, made them faithful to each other in an association so necessary to their wel-

---

* Dalin. Suea Rikes. Hist. tom. i. chap. 7.

K

fare. A man's relations and friends who had not revenged his death, would instantly have lost that reputation which constituted their principal security. The inhabitants of Friesland lived for a long time in a state of this kind. Most of the other German nations had already advanced a step beyond this in the time of Tacitus. Endless disorders, the unavoidable consequences of the right of self-revenge, had suggested to the wiser sort among them the necessity of magistrates, who should interpose their authority in private quarrels, and oblige the offended person or his relations to receive a present from the aggressor; that so a compensation being made for an injury, might prevent the consequences of an eternal resentment, which from private persons might extend to the public. And for fear that this manner of terminating differences should become a new source of them, the compensation was determined by an invariable rule, and commonly limited to a certain value in cattle, the only money known in those rude ages. A mark of submission of this sort satisfied men's pride as to the point of honour, gratified their avarice, and sufficiently secured them from a repetition of the offence. The Danes, in this respect, followed the steps of the neighbouring nations. Mere parity of reason might give one a right to suppose this, even if we had not more positive proofs; but without accumulating these unnecessarily, we need only cast our eyes on the ancient laws of the conquerors of Great Britain, most of which are still extant; and whoever will run over the collections published by Lambard, Wilkins, and Leibnitz, will not doubt but they were all dictated by the same spirit, and were really the same at the bottom. It will be sufficient to quote a few particulars, to enable us to judge of their general spirit; for this is all I undertake to show of them. As to their more particular minute circumstances, they have doubtless varied a thousand times, in different ages and countries; but these we shall not descend to at present.

The laws of the Saxons, as regulated by Charlemagne, and published by Leibnitz *, established a composition in money for most sorts of crimes; and for want of money this was to be paid in the flesh of cattle, every limb and joint of which had its known value regulated by law. They carefully distin-

* Leibnitz, Rer. Brunswic. tom. i.

guished the different degrees of offence, as well as those of the rank which the offended person bore in the state. Accordingly for the murder of a noble or a prince the composition was 1440 *sous* *, and the same for every wound that deprived him of his hearing, sight, or use of his limbs. But if this injury was done to a free man, and not to a noble †, the composition was only 120 *sous* ‡; at the same time the murder of a slave was rated but 30; which was precisely the price of a simple blow, that produced neither swelling nor blackness, if given to a prince or noble. Much the same proportions were observed by the law of the Angles. Wounds given to a maiden were estimated at double the rate they would have been, if given to a man of the same rank of life. It was not the same with a woman who had borne children. Outrages against modesty were also valued with a degree of exactness of which one would not have thought matters of that nature susceptible. " The laws of these people," says M. de Montesquieu, " judged of insults offered to men by the size of the wounds, nor did they show more refinement as to the offences committed against women; so that they seem to have measured injuries as one measures figures in geometry."

These laws vary more in what relates to theft. By the law of the Saxons, it was in most cases punished with death. By that of the Angles, which doubtless approaches nearer to the laws of the Danish nations, the robber compounded by paying triple the value of what he had stolen. But when government had acquired a little more stability, and when the manners were a little more civilized, men were not satisfied with opposing to the disorder a barrier so often ineffectual. The magistrates appointed to watch over the public peace pretended that THEY were insulted as often as that peace was broken, and therefore, over and above the composition which was to atone for the offence, they exacted a fine, either as a satisfaction due to the public, or as a recompense for the trouble given themselves in making up the difference and in protecting the offender. These fines were for a long time all, or almost all

* If the author computes by modern money, it is 720 pence English, or about 3*l*. sterling.—P.

† The original is *Roda*, whence comes the word *Roturier*, by which the French express at present one who is not a gentleman.

‡ Sixty pence, or five shillings sterling.—P.

the punishment which could possibly prevail among a valiant and free people, who esteemed their blood too precious to be shed any other way than in battle. Their kings had for many ages no other revenue than what arose from these fines, and from their own private demesnes: all other kinds of imposition were not known till long after that period of time to which we at present confine our researches.

If this way of punishing crimes may justly pass for singular, that of establishing proofs in the administration of justice may be esteemed no less so. Here all the ignorance, all the barbarity of our ancestors manifest themselves so plainly, that it is not in the power of our reflections to add to them. Their embarrassment was so great when they endeavoured to distinguish truth from falsehood, that they were obliged to have recourse to the most strange expedients and most ridiculous practices. Thus they sometimes obliged the accused to produce a certain number of persons called Compurgators; not that these men had, or were supposed to have any knowledge of the affair in question, but they were simply to swear they were persuaded the accused spoke true. Besides this, they often appointed what was called the judiciary combat, and how absurd soever this custom was, it was so intimately connected with their opinions concerning destiny and providence, that it triumphed for a long time over religion, popes, and councils; and though a hundred times proscribed, as often revived and appeared again under different shapes. Lastly, when the discovery of truth appeared to them to exceed all human powers, they had recourse to supernatural means, and what they called divine judgments. They had many ways of consulting that oracle. For as, according to their notions, all the elements were animated by an intelligence as incorruptible in its justice as the deity whence it sprung, they thought they had nothing to do but to unite the accused person to one of these divinities, and so oblige it to declare by the manner of its acting upon him, what judgment it entertained of his innocence. Thus sometimes they cast him into a deep water, tied about with cords: if he sunk, that is, if the genius of the water received him into its bosom, it declared him to be innocent; if it rejected him, if he swam upon the surface, he was looked upon as convicted of the crime. This was called the watery ordeal and was more dangerous than it appears to have been at first sight; for though a man thrown into the water commonly sinks at first to the bottom, yet as they tied him about with large cords, " and withs," he sometimes swam on the surface spite of his teeth. This kind of proof indeed, as well as that of boiling water, was only for persons of inferior rank. Others handled hot iron, or put their hands into a red-hot gauntlet, or walked blindfold over burning ploughshares. If at the end of certain days there remained any marks of the fire on the hands or feet, the accused were judged guilty; if not, he was acquitted. There is reason to think that, notwithstanding they took all possible precaution, they also had recourse to certain preservatives against the effects of fire, and perhaps the same that mountebanks in our times make use of as oft as they amuse the people with spectacles of the same kind. Besides this, men who were accustomed to hard labour, to the toils of hunting, and constant handling of arms, had rendered their skins so thick and callous, that they could not easily be hurt; and as for the ladies, they were generally allowed champions to undergo the trial for them. The proof by fire, or fiery-ordeal, seems to have been more in use afterwards, and founded upon a different train of reasoning; for in things of this nature, we must not expect such rude minds to act very consistently.

As for the ceremonies which accompanied these kinds of proof, the cases in which they were appointed, and the other minute circumstances, they varied in different times and places: and as imitation and habit perpetuate customs long after the causes of them have ceased, the ordeal was practised during many ages by men, who doubtless believed nothing about the genii presiding over the several elements, or the other doctrines of the ancient religion *. I shall not enter on the minute history of the ordeal, &c., which was not peculiar to the ancient Danes, and may be found described in other books †. I thought proper only to mark the connection be-

* Thus long after Christianity was established among the Anglo-Saxons, king Edward the Confessor (a reputed saint) is said to have put his mother to the proof of the burning ploughshares. And even down to our own times, the watery ordeal, or proof by swimming, has been employed by the vulgar for the trial of witchcraft, whenever they could find means to put it in practice.—P.

† Vid. Wormius in Monum. Danic. lib. i. c. 2, and Steph. Stephanius in his Notes on Saxo Grammaticus.

tween them and the doctrines of that religion, which I described in the preceding chapters: a connection which has
been seldom attended to, and which shows that it is only for
want of studying mankind that they appear to act wholly without motives or principles of conduct.   It was king Valdemar
the Second * to whom the glory belongs of having abolished
this absurd and inhuman practice in Denmark †.

CHAPTER VIII.

THE PASSION OF THE ANCIENT SCANDINAVIANS FOR ARMS : THEIR
VALOUR : THE MANNER IN WHICH THEY MADE WAR.

" Rome had reckoned from its foundation six hundred and
forty years, when the arms of the Cimbri were first heard of
among us.   From that time to the present have elapsed two
hundred and six years more.   So long have we been in conquering Germany.   And in the course of so tedious a war,
what various losses have been sustained by each party?   No
nation has given us more frequent alarms; neither the Sam-
nites, the Carthaginians, the Spaniards, the Gauls, nor even
the Parthians : so much less vigour has the despotic power
of Arsaces had, than the liberty of the Germans.   For, except
the defeat of Crassus, what has the conquered and prostrate
East to object to the current of our success?   Whereas the

---

* He reigned from the year 1202 to 1241.—P.

† I cannot conclude this subject without observing that we find some
traces of the ordeal among the ancient Greeks and Romans.   Thus in the
Antigone of Sophocles, (Act II. Sc. II.) we have the following remarkable
passage, which shows it was not unknown in Greece :—
          " The guards accused each other ; nought was proved,
              But each suspected each, and all denied,
              Offering in proof of innocence to grasp
              The burning steel, to walk thro' fire, and take
              Their solemn oath they knew not of the deed."
See Franklin's Sophocles and note on the above passage.   See also Stiernhök
de Jur. Vet. Suec. lib. i. c. 8, apud Dalin, Sue. Rik. Hist. tom. i. ch. 7.

Pliny, speaking of a feast, which the ancient Romans celebrated every year
in honour of the Sun, observes that the priests, who were to be of the family
of the Hirpians, danced on this occasion barefoot on burning coals without
burning themselves : this was apparently a relic of the fiery ordeal.   Plin.
Hist. Nat. lib. vii. 2.

Germans have taken or defeated five generals of the republic who commanded so many consular armies. They cut off Varus and three legions from Augustus himself. Nor was that advantage obtained with impunity, which Marius gained over them in Italy, the divine Julius in Gaul, and Drusus, Tiberius and Germanicus in their own country. And even presently after this, the tremendous threats of Caligula became the object of their sport. A respite followed, till profiting by our discord and civil wars, they attacked our legions in their winter quarters, and even undertook the conquest of Gaul. We have since driven them back beyond the Rhine: but in these latter times, our victories over them have been less real, than the pomp of our triumphs. . . . . If this people cannot be brought to love us, at least may they always hate each other! since in the present declining fates of the empire, fortune can grant us no greater favour, than the dissensions of our enemies." *

Such was the opinion entertained of the German and northern nations by the people who conquered the rest of the world. Such, according to the confession of Tacitus, was that martial courage, that ardour, that constancy in defending and avenging their liberty, which so early threatened the power of Rome, and in a few ages after overturned it. It is not my present business to write the history of that great revolution, which changed the face of Europe, but my subject leads me to disclose its causes, since they are contained in the opinions and manners which I am describing. We only want here that penetrating eye, that deep sense and energy of style, which distinguished the author I have been translating. The sources whence issued those torrents of people, which from the north overwhelmed all Europe, the principles which put them in motion, and gave them so much activity and force, these objects, so grand and interesting, have been but slightly and weakly treated of. The more enlightened people, who were the victims of these ravages, were too much pressed with the weight of their calamity to have leisure to trace its remote causes. Like the thunder which remains unseen in the clouds till the moment it bursts forth, and whose nature we have no time to study while it is

* Tacit. Germ. c. 37, et c. 33.

striking us; these unexpected irruptions would hardly become the objects of research till after their effects were forgotten. Hence the relations that have been given us of them are so uninteresting, confused, and obscure; faults to which every history will be liable which only gives us a heap of facts, without being able to develop their causes. The greatest part then of the historical phenomena of the middle ages can only be explained by a deep insight into the manners of the northern nations. It is only from thence we can ever be able to comprehend what could induce whole nations to transport themselves from one extremity of Europe to the other; could break through the ties of country, which so strongly attach men to the places of their birth; could render them unanimous in such strange projects, and make them thus spread themselves beyond their own boundaries with such exuberance and impetuosity.

I have already hinted that the ancient Teutonic nations breathed nothing but war, which was at once with them the source of honour, riches, and safety. Their education, laws, prejudices, morality and religion, all concurred to make that their ruling passion and only object. From their most tender age they applied themselves to learn the military art; they hardened their bodies, and accustomed themselves to cold, fatigue, and hunger. They exercised themselves in running, in the chace, in swimming across the greatest rivers, and in handling their arms. The very sports of childhood itself, and of early youth, were directed all towards this end: dangers were always intermingled with their play; for it consisted in taking frightful leaps, in climbing up the steepest rocks, in fighting naked with offensive weapons, in wrestling with the utmost fury: it was therefore common to see them at the age of fifteen years already grown robust men, and able to make themselves feared in combat. It was also at this age that their young men became their own masters, which they did by receiving a sword, a buckler, and a lance. This ceremony was performed in some public meeting. One of the principal persons of the assembly armed the youth in public. "This, we are told by Tacitus, was his *Toga Virilis*, his entrance upon dignities; before this he made only part of a family, now he became a member of the state." After this he was obliged to provide for his own subsistence, and was either now to live by hunting, or by joining in some incursion against an enemy. Particular care was taken to prevent these young soldiers from enjoying too early an acquaintance with the opposite sex, till their limbs had acquired all the vigour of which they were capable. Indeed they could have no hope to be acceptable to the women but in proportion to the courage and address they had shown in war and in their military exercises. Accordingly we see in an ancient song, preserved by Bartholin, a king of Norway extremely surprised that, as he could perform eight different exercises, his mistress should presume to reject his suit. I shall frequently have occasion to produce new instances of this manner of thinking among their women: it is sufficient at present to observe, that they were not likely to soften their children by too much delicacy or indulgence. These tender creatures were generally born in the midst of camps and armies. Their eyes, from the moment they were first opened, saw nothing but military spectacles, arms, effusion of blood, and combats either real or in sport: thus as they grew up from their infancy, their souls were early disposed to imbibe the cruel prejudices of their fathers.

Their laws, for the most part like those of the ancient Lacedemonians, seemed to know no other virtues than those of a military nature, and no other crimes but cowardice. They inflicted the greatest penalties on such as fled the first in battle. The laws of the ancient Danes, according to Saxo, excluded them from society, and declared them infamous. Among the Germans this was sometimes carried so far as to suffocate cowards in mud; after which they covered them over with hurdles; to show, says Tacitus, that though the punishment of crimes should be public, there are certain degrees of cowardice and infamy which ought to be buried in eternal silence. The most flattering distinctions were reserved for such as had performed some signal exploit, and the laws themselves distributed men into different ranks according to their different degrees of courage. Frotho, king of Denmark, had ordained, according to Saxo, that whoever solicited an eminent post in the army, ought upon all occasions to attack one enemy; to face two; to retire only one step back from three; and not to make an actual retreat till assaulted by four. Hence was formed that prejudice so deeply rooted among these people, that there was no other way to acquire glory but by the profession of arms and a fanatic valour: a prejudice the force of which displayed itself without obstruction at a time when luxury was unknown, when that desire, so natural, and so active among men, of drawing upon themselves the attention of their equals, had but one single object and support; and when their country and their fellow-citizens had no other treasure but the fame of their exploits, and the terror thereby excited in their neighbours.

The rules of justice, far from checking these prejudices, had been themselves warped and adapted to their bias.   It is no exaggeration to say, that all the Teutonic nations entertained opinions on this subject quite opposite to the theory of our times.   They looked upon war as a real act of justice, and esteemed force an incontestable title over the weak, a visible mark that God had intended to subject them to the strong.   They had no doubt but the intentions of this divinity had been to establish the same dependence among men which there is among animals, and setting out from the principle of the inequality of men, as our modern civilians do from that of their equality, they inferred thence that the weak had no right to what they could not defend.   This maxim, which formed the basis of the law of nations among the ancient inhabitants of Europe, being dictated by their most darling passion, we cannot wonder that they should so steadily act up to it in practice.   And which, after all, is worst; to act and think as they did, or like the moderns, with better principles to act as ill ?   As to the ancient nations, we attribute nothing to them here but what is justified by a thousand facts.   They adopted the above maxim in all its rigour, and gave the name of Divine Judgment not only to the Judiciary Combat, but to conflicts and battles of all sorts: victory being in their opinion the only certain mark by which Providence enables us to distinguish those whom it has appointed to command others.   "Valour," says a German warrior in Tacitus, "is the only proper goods of men.   The gods range themselves on the side of the strongest." *

Lastly, religion, by annexing eternal happiness to the

* Tacit. Hist. lib. iv. c. 17.

military virtues, had given the last degree of activity to the ardour and propensity these people had for war. There were no fatigues, no dangers nor torments capable of damping a passion so well countenanced, and the desire of meriting so great a reward.

[The story of the celebrated Jomsburg sea-rovers will corroborate what is here advanced, and offer, moreover, some very curious traits respecting the customs and superstitions of the Northmen. Antiquarian researches have given rise to various conjectures respecting the first establishment and exact situation of Jomsburg. At a very early period the Vends—a Slavonic tribe occupying the whole of the southern coast of the Baltic from the Elbe to Esthonia—had a seaport called Julin, situated in that part of the delta of the Oder that forms the present island of Wollin. Adam of Bremen, mentions Julin as being the largest and most flourishing commercial city of Europe in the eleventh century; but it was destroyed in 1176 by Valdemar I., King of Denmark, and the renown of its former splendour and prosperity only survived in the legendary accounts which the romantic writers of the fourteenth and fifteenth centuries gave of a town they called Vineta, which they represented as having been swallowed up by the sea, its ruins, they contended, being still discernible at a short distance from the coast, near the island of Usedom. Modern criticism has, however, shown that these legends originated in mistaking a reef of basaltic columns for the ruins of a city, and in some blundering scribe writing Vineta for Jumneta (Julin) in a manuscript. Whether Harald Bluetooth, who reigned in Denmark A.D. 941-91, in one of his numerous expeditions against the Vends, erected a stronghold called Jomsburg, in or near Julin, and placed a Danish garrison in it, is uncertain. It is, however, a well authenticated fact that during the reign of that monarch, Palnatoki, a celebrated sea-rover, established himself in a stronghold bearing that name, situated somewhere near Julin, and had probably the whole island of Wollin ceded to him by the Vendic prince Borislav.

Palnatoki, who appears to have possessed in an eminent degree all the good and bad qualities of a Scandinavian freebooter, is said to have made of Jomsburg a second Sparta; and some writers even go so far as to compare his legislation with that of Lycurgus!! When the facts, however, are divested of that romance which the undiscriminating admirers of Saga literature are too apt to indulge in, we shall find that this pretended legislation merely consisted in Palnatoki rendering more stringent the regulations observed on board a pirate vessel in that age, as well as in most succeeding ones. No one, for instance, under 15 or above 50, was to be admitted into the community. No one who had not shown that he did not fear to face two men equally as strong and well armed as himself. The associates were to regard each other as brethren. Any feud that might unavoidably arise, as, for instance, when a person previous to entering the association had killed any one whose death another member was bound by the ties of consanguinity or sworn friendship to avenge, was to be referred to Palnatoki, and the parties were to abide by his decision. All booty was to be brought together, and divided according to established usage. All tidings were to be first communicated to Palnatoki, and no one, without his permission, was to be absent for more than one night from Jomsburg, into which no females were to be admitted *.

Palnatoki's band soon became famous for its exploits throughout the North, and it was esteemed an honour to

---

* The writers alluded to, taking for granted that whenever men and women come together some mishap or other is sure to be the consequence, award great praise to their piratical Lycurgus for this exclusion of females from his community. No one in Jomsburg, they gravely assure us, was allowed to marry. Palnatoki's object was to form a band of invincible warriors, hence he very wisely eschewed female charms, and, like St. Senanus, might have exclaimed to any stray dame who attempted to allure his followers—

> " Oh haste and leave this *pirate* isle
> *Unwelcome* bark ere morning smile,
> For on thy deck, though dark it be,
> A female form I see;
> And I have sworn this *Spartan* sod
> Shall ne'er by woman's foot be trod."

Professor Müller has shown, however, that only ladies of a certain class were refused admittance into Jomsburg, and that Palnatoki's followers were not only allowed to marry, but obtained permission to introduce their wives, *de temps en temps*, into the stronghold. So that after all, this old sea-rover was not quite such an ungallant gentleman as his admirers would make him.

belong to it. We are told that amongst other distinguished persons, Sigvald and Thorkell the Tall, the sons of the Sealand Jarl Strut-Harald, were admitted as members of the association. These chieftains on their way to Jomsburg had supplied themselves with provisions by making a cattle foray* in the island of Bornholm; and although this was regarded as a very trifling offence in these predatory times, Jarl Viseti, to whom the island belonged, demanded compensation from Strut-Harald, and as the latter felt no great inclination to pay for the freaks of his roving offspring, Viseti ravaged three of the Jarl's estates in Sealand, a proceeding which Strut-Harald retaliated by doing equal mischief in Bornholm. Previous to this Bui the Thick, one of Viseti's sons, had plundered Strut-Harald's treasury, and taken away among other things, 20 lbs. weight of silver, and the splendid cap by which Harald had acquired his surname†. Svend, the son of Harald Bluetooth‡, now interfered between the two powerful chieftains, and proposed that Bui should keep the silver but return the cap, and that Sigurd, another of Jarl Viseti's sons, should marry Strut-Harald's daughter. The parties having agreed to these conditions, the marriage was celebrated with great pomp, after which Bui and Sigurd went to Jomsburg, and were admitted as members of the piratical community§.

This honour was shortly afterwards solicited by Vagn, the grandson of Palnatoki, but the old sea-rover would not listen to his request for two very cogent reasons; first, because Vagn was only twelve years old; and, secondly, because he

---

* Called a Strandhögg, or Strand-hewing, because the cattle were generally slaughtered on the strand.

† Struts-fugl is the Old Norse for Ostrich (Struthio). Harald probably acquired his surname from possessing a cap ornamented with an ostrich feather, which in those days must have been a great rarity.

‡ A writer is often puzzled whether he ought to adopt the Old Norse, the modern Danish, or the current English orthography for the names of Scandinavians mentioned in English history. Thus the names of the conqueror of England, and his son and successor, are in Old Norse, Sveinn and Knútr, and in modern Danish, Svend and Knud, names which have been changed by our historians into Sweyne, Sweno, and Canute.

§ We are not told whether Sigurd's fair Countess or Jarless accompanied him. If she did, we presume that Palnatoki, notwithstanding his Spartan predilections, would hardly have been so ungallant as to refuse admittance to a lady during her honeymoon.

had already acquired the reputation of being the most unruly and turbulent youngster who ever sailed on a viking cruise. Vagn very coolly replied, that as to his age he was ready to show, by fighting with Jarl Sigvald, that he possessed the strength of a youth of eighteen. The challenge was of course accepted, but when the combatants had belaboured each other for some time with their battle axes, Palnatoki, perceiving that Sigvald was losing ground, separated them, and Vagn was received by general acclamation into the community. Four years after this event Palnatoki fell sick, and, strange to say, died very quietly in his bed, after having appointed Jarl Sigvald his successor*.

Sigvald, who appears to have been more impressionable to female charms than Palnatoki, was not, we are told, over-strict in requiring the due observance of the Jomsburg Spartan code. He, in fact, set his followers a very good example in this respect, by soliciting the hand of Borislav's daughter, the lovely Astrida. The young lady was, however, patriotic enough to require that her lover, ere he obtained her consent, should free the Vends from the tribute they had to pay to Denmark. Sigvald, in order to accomplish this task, managed to take Svend, who had succeeded his father to the throne, prisoner, and convey him to Jomsburg, where he dictated the terms of his ransom. These terms were that the tribute should no longer be paid, that Svend should give his sister Thyra in marriage to Borislav, and marry himself the Vendic Prince's daughter Gunhilda, Sigvald at the same time to espouse Astrida. These marriages took place the same evening, the brides being veiled, a circumstance that prevented Svend from remarking, until it was too late, that Astrida was far more lovely and amiable than her sister. He was obliged however to stifle his resentment, and return home with Gunhilda, though he inwardly vowed to take ample revenge on Sigvald for his perfidy.

It was the custom of the Scandinavians that when a person of note died, his heir should at the first convenient opportunity give a sumptuous banquet to his friends and dependents, during which he should drink to the memory of the defunct, and then place himself in the high-seat always

* Œhlenschlæger has made Palnatoki the hero of one of his tragedies.

occupied by the master of the house, and generally placed between two carved columns, which was regarded as a sign of his having taken possession of the heritage. King Svend, shortly after his marriage, summoned all the chief persons in his dominions to such a succession-banquet, and as the Jarls Strut-Harald and Viseti had died a short time before, he invited Sigvald and Bui the Thick to come with their brothers to the feast, assuring them that horns should also be emptied to the memory of their fathers. The Jomsburg chiefs accepted the invitation, but repaired to the festival with thirty—some accounts say with eighty—large ships, manned with their bravest followers, Sigvald being no doubt of opinion that a retinue could not be too numerous when he visited a king whom he had forced to marry an ugly woman while he at the same time espoused her handsome sister. On the first day of the feast, King Svend before he placed himself in the high-seat of his ancestors, filled a horn and drank to his father's memory, making at the same time, according to custom, a solemn vow that before three winters had passed he would go with a large army to England, and either kill King Ethelred, or drive him out of the country. After all the guests had drunk to King Harald's memory, the horns were again filled, and emptied in honour of Christ†, the Jomsburg chieftains being supplied with the largest horns and the strongest liquor. The third toast was given to Michael the Archangel, after which Jarl Sigvald filled a large horn and drank to his father's memory, making a solemn vow

---

† The first missionaries, as M. Mallet has observed, page 113, were obliged to substitute the names of Christ and the Saints for those of Odin and the gods on these festive occasions.

Though several Danish kings were baptized Christianity had made very little progress in Denmark in the tenth century. The Danes and the Jomsburg sea-rovers were, however, at this period regarded by the Norwegians as Christians. Svend although he is said to have died a Christian, did not cease to persecute Christianity during his lifetime. He seems, in fact, to have been as fanatical a worshipper of Thor and Odin as any of his predecessors. Canute, in the beginning of his reign, was in this respect not much better than his father, but afterwards, owing probably to the influence of his Norman wife Emma (the widow of Ethelred), he became, outwardly at least, a very zealous Christian, and it was during his reign that Christianity became firmly established in Denmark, though worshippers of Odin were still to be found there so late as the twelfth century.

that before three winters were over he would go to Norway, and either kill Jarl Hakon or drive him out of the country. Thorkell the Tall and Bui the Thick then made solemn vows that they would accompany Sigvald and stand by him to the last, and Vagn, when it came to his turn, took the drinking horn, and vowed that he would also go with Sigvald and not return from Norway before he had slain Thorkell Leire, and taken to him that Jarl's daughter, the fair Ingjibjörg, without the consent of her friends and relations. The next morning, when they came to their sober senses, the Jomsburg chieftains regretted having made such rash vows; as they however could not retract them, they began without delay to make preparations for the contemplated expedition. Sigvald; by the advice of Astrida, tried to induce Svend to join them, but could only obtain his promise to furnish them with forty vessels duly manned and armed, a promise, however, which he seems to have had no intention of performing.

The expedition of the Jomsburg sea-rovers is said to have taken place in the year 994. Sailing along the coast of Norway with a powerful fleet they signalized their approach by plundering, burning, killing all the men capable of bearing arms, and by the perpetration of all those other revolting and remorseless deeds which in those ages invariably marked the progress of a band of Scandinavian freebooters. The crafty Norwegian Jarl, Hakon, having in the meantime collected his forces, sailed with a fleet of 150 vessels, and fell in with the Jomsburg fleet at a place called Hjörungavag (now Lievog), and at break of day a combat began, which was maintained by the sea-rovers with their accustomed valour, though they were greatly inferior in numbers to the Norwegians. Hakon, in fact, after trying in vain to break through the line of his opponents, found it prudent to retire with his fleet to the coast, and we are told that he then went into a forest to consult a famous sorceress, or prophetess, called Thorgerd Hördabrud, in whom he put all his trust in any great emergency. She was, however, for a long time deaf to his supplications for assistance, although Hakon prostrated himself on the earth before her and offered to perform any bloody sacrifice she might require. She at length told him that the victory could only be obtained by the sacrifice of his son Erling, a very handsome boy then in his seventh year. Hakon did not hesitate to offer up his son, and then returned to his fleet and renewed the engagement. Towards evening a dreadful thunderstorm arose, during which hailstones of an unusual size fell on board the Jomsburg vessels. The sea-rovers also fancied that they saw Thorgerd Hördabrud herself at the prow of Hakon's ship, with whole volleys of arrows flying from her fingers, each arrow bringing to one of them his death-wound. Twenty-five of the Jomsburg ships had already fallen into the hands of the Norwegians, when Sigvald cut the cable by which the remainder were fastened together, and bidding the other chieftains follow him, sailed away from the combat, saying that he had made a vow to fight against men and not against witches. Meanwhile Hakon and his son Eirek boarded the vessel of Bui the Thick, and when that chieftain saw that further resistance was fruitless, he took two chests full of gold, and calling out "Overboard all Bui's men," plunged with his treasure in the sea and perished. Thorkell and Sigurd then took to flight and arrived in Denmark with 30 vessels. Vagn, however, continued to fight valiantly with his division against the combined forces of the Norwegians, but was at length overpowered and taken prisoner with 30 of his followers.

The next morning, when Hakon and his sons had breakfasted, they ordered the prisoners to be led out to execution. The proceedings on this occasion show at the same time the barbarity of the age, and the kind of heroism which was more the result of this barbarity than of the pretended legislation of Palnatoki. The prisoners being seated on a log of wood with their legs bound together by a rope, withies or osier twigs were twisted in their hair. A slave was then placed behind each to keep his head steady by holding fast the withies twisted into a band for that purpose. The executioner was no less a personage than Thorkell Leire, one of the most renowned Norwegian chieftains, whose daughter Vagn had vowed to gain possession of without the consent of her relations.

Thorkell began his sanguinary task by striking off the head of him who sat outmost on the log. After he had beheaded the next two he asked the prisoners what they thought of death.

"What happened to my father," replied one, "must happen to me. He died, so must I."

Another said that he remembered too well the laws of Jomsburg to fear dying: a third declared that a glorious death was ever welcome to him, and that such a death was far more preferable to an infamous life like that of Thorkell's.

"I only beg of thee," said a fourth, "to be quick over thy work; for thou must know that it is a question often discussed at Jomsburg, whether or not a man feels anything after losing his head. I will therefore grasp this knife in my hand; if, after my head is cut off, I throw it at thee, it will show that I still retain some feeling; if I let it fall, it will prove just the contrary. Strike therefore and decide the question without further delay."

Thorkell, says the Saga-man, struck off the man's head with a stroke of his battle-axe, but the knife instantly fell to the ground.

"Strike the blow in my face," said the next, "I will sit still without flinching, and take notice whether I even wink my eyes; for we Jomsburg people know how to meet the stroke of death without betraying an emotion."

He kept his promise, and received the blow without showing the least sign of fear, or so much as winking his eyes. Sigurd, the son of Bui the Thick, a fine young man in the flower of his age, with long fair hair, as fine as silk, flowing in ringlets over his shoulders, said, in answer to Thorkell's question, "I fear not death, since I have fulfilled the greatest duty of life, but I must pray thee not to let my hair be touched by a slave or stained with my blood."

One of Hakon's followers then stepped forward and held his hair instead of the slave, but when Thorkell struck the blow Sigurd twitched his head forward so strongly that the warrior who was holding his hair had both his hands cut off. Eirek, the son of Jarl Hakon, who seems to have relished this practical joke, then came up and asked Sigurd whether he would have his life spared.

"That depends," replied the youth, "upon who it is that makes me the offer."

"He who has the power to do it, Jarl Eirek," said the son of the Norwegian chieftain.

"From his hand will I accept it," said Sigurd, and he was immediately loosed from the rope. Thorkell enraged at Eirek's clemency, exclaimed, "If thou spare the lives of all these men, Jarl, at least Vagn Akason shall not escape me." So saying he ran at Vagn with uplifted axe, but the crafty sea-rover threw himself on the ground, so that Thorkell fell over him and cut the rope with his axe, seeing which Vagn sprung up, and seizing the weapon, gave Thorkell his death-wound. Jarl Eirek, notwithstanding his father's remonstrances, then asked Vagn if he would accept life from his hands.

"Willingly," replied Vagn, "provided thou wilt give it to all of us."

"Loose the rope," said Eirek, and it was done: eighteen had been beheaded, and twelve were spared by Eirek thus interfering, among whom was a Welshman named Björn.

After this the army dispersed: Jarl Hakon went to Drontheim highly dissatisfied with his son's proceedings. Jarl Eirek, however, does not seem to have cared much for his father's displeasure, for we are told that he shortly afterward married Vagn to Thorkell Leire's daughter Ingjibjörg, the young lady, be it remembered, whom the sea-rover had vowed to gain possession of without her friends' consent, and whose father he had actually killed. However, such events were of frequent occurrence in those turbulent ages, and would not be regarded as singular. Vagn after his marriage returned to Denmark with three ships which Eirek had made him a present of, and became a renowned chieftain and the founder of a powerful family. Sigvald on his arrival at Jomsburg was received very coolly by his fair lady Astrida, who jeered him ever afterwards for returning from a battle without a single wound, an action which in her eyes was quite unpardonable.

Such is the account transmitted to us of this celebrated expedition of the Jomsburg sea-rovers*, and whatever may be thought of some of the incidents related, they serve at least to show the manners and customs of that rude period, while the main features of the story, corroborated as they are by collateral evidence, may be regarded as strictly historical.

* See Jomsvikinga-Saga. The Heimskringla, vi. 38–47; and Müller's Sagabib. iii. p. 39.

It is even not at all improbable that Jarl Hakon sacrificed his son at the suggestion, or rather command of Thorgerd Hördabrud, for we know from other sources that he placed implicit reliance in the oracular responses of this woman. We thus read in the Færeyinga Saga that when Sigmund Brestisson was ready to sail on his expedition to the Færoe isles, he went to Jarl Hakon, who asked him in whom he put his trust.

"I trust in my own might and main," replied Sigmund—a phrase of much the same import as "I trust in my own good sword," which a modern hero might make use of under similar circumstances. Hakon told him that he was wrong in doing this, and that he should rather put his trust in Thorgerd Hördabrud. "In her," he added, "I have always placed my faith, and I will now lead thee to her." The Jarl then took Sigmund into a forest, in which they had not proceeded far before they came to a house with glass windows, and Sigmund remarked that the interior was ornamented with gold and silver, and a number of images of the Scandinavian divinities. At the entrance stood a woman attired in very costly apparel, before whose feet Hakon instantly prostrated himself, and remained for some time in that attitude. On rising he told Sigmund that they must gain the favour of this woman, who was no other than Thorgerd Hördabrud herself, by placing silver on a stool that stood before her, a kind of offering which was no doubt the most likely of all others to render her propitious.

"It will be a sign," added the Jarl, "that she listens to my prayer when she lets go the ring she holds in her hand, and that ring will bring thee good fortune, Sigmund."

Hakon then began to pull at the ring, but the more he pulled the faster she held it. He then prostrated himself at her feet a second time and burst into tears. On rising he again pulled at the ring with all his force, and Thorgerd at length quitting her hold, he obtained possession of it, and returned home highly pleased that he was able thus to give Sigmund a charm that would preserve him from danger and insure his future welfare, and for which, we presume, he had left the sylvan lady hard cash to treble the amount of its intrinsic value *.]

* See Færeyinga-Saga, ch. 23.

Constancy in the last moments was not, however, the peculiar effect of the laws and education of the Jomsburg sea-rovers.   The other Danes have often given the same proofs of intrepidity; or rather this was the general character of all the inhabitants of Scandinavia.   It was with them an instance of shameful pusillanimity to utter upon such occasions the least groan, or to change countenance, but especially to shed tears.   The Danes, says Adam of Bremen *, " are remarkable for this, that if they have committed any crime, they had rather suffer death than blows.   There is no other punishment for them but either the axe or servitude.   As for groans, complaints and other bemoanings of that kind, in which we find relief, they are so detested by the Danes, that they think it mean to weep for their sins, or for the death of their dearest relations."   But if a private soldier looked upon tears as peculiar to weakness or slavery, their great warriors, the chiefs, all who aspired to fame and glory, carried the contempt of death much further.   King Ragnar, who, as I have once before observed, died singing the pleasure of receiving death in the field of battle, cries out at the end of a stanza, "The hours of my life have passed away, I shall die laughing:" † and many passages in ancient history plainly show that this was not a poetical hyperbole.   Saxo, speaking of a single combat, says, that one of the champions fell, laughed, and died, an epitaph as short as energetic ‡.   An officer belonging to a king of Norway, celebrating in verse the death of his master, concludes his eulogium with these words, " It shall hereafter be recorded in histories, that King Halfer died laughing." § A warrior having been thrown upon his back, in wrestling with his enemy, and the latter finding himself without his arms, the vanquished person promised to wait without changing his posture while he fetched a sword to kill kim; and he faithfully kept his word.   To die with his arms in his hand was the vow of every free man; and the pleasing idea they had of this kind of death would naturally lead them to dread such as proceeded from disease and old age.   In the joy therefore which they testified at the approach of a violent death, they

* Adam Bremen. de situ Daniæ, c. 213.
† That is to say, the Skald who composed Ragnar's famous death-song puts these words in the mouth of his dying hero.—Ed.
‡ Saxe Gram. lib. ii.   § Barthol. p. 6.

might frequently express no more than their real sentiments, though doubtless it was sometimes intermixed with ostentation. The general tenor of their conduct proves that they were most commonly sincere in this; and such as know the power which education, example and prejudice have over men, will find no difficulty in receiving the multitude of testimonies which antiquity hath left us of their extraordinary valour. " The philosophy of the Cimbri," says Valerius Maximus, " is gay and courageous: they leap for joy in a battle, that they are going to quit life in so glorious a manner: in sickness they lament for fear of a shameful and miserable end."* Cicero remarks, that in proportion as men are intrepid in war, they are weak and impatient under bodily pains. " Happy in their mistake," says Lucan, " are the people who live beneath the pole! persuaded that death is only a passage to a long life, they are undisturbed by the most grievous of all fears, that of dying. Hence they eagerly run to arms, and their minds are capable of meeting death: hence they esteem it cowardice to spare a life which they shall so soon recover." The history of ancient Scandinavia is full of passages expressive of this manner of thinking. The illustrious warriors, who found themselves wasting by some lingering illness, were not always content barely to accuse their fate. They often availed themselves of the few moments that were yet remaining, to shake off life by a way more glorious. Some of them would be carried into a field of battle, that they might die in the engagement; others slew themselves; many procured this melancholy service to be performed them by their friends, who considered this as a most sacred duty. " There is on a mountain in Iceland," says the author of an old Icelandic romance †, " a rock so high that no animal can fall from the top and live. Here men betake themselves when they are afflicted and unhappy. From this place all our ancestors, even without waiting for sickness,

---

* Val. Max. lib. ii. cap. 6, p. 11. Cicero Tusc. Quæst. lib. ii. cap. ult.

† The old Saga, or history here quoted, contains a mixture of truth and fiction, but shows us plainly what opinion was held of suicide, and how commonly it was practised heretofore in the north. Procopius attributes the same thing to the Heruli, a Gothic people. " Apud Herulos," says he, "nec senibus, nec ægrotis fas erat vitam producere: et si quem senium occupasset, aut morbus, rogare is cogebatur propinquos, ut quamprimum hominum numero eum tollerent." Procop. Goth. lib. ii. c. 14.

have departed unto Odin. It is useless, therefore, to give ourselves up to groans and complaints, or to put our relations to needless expenses, since we can easily follow the example of our fathers, who have all gone by the way of this rock." There was such another in Sweden *, appropriated to the same use, which was figuratively called the Hall of Odin, because it was a kind of vestibule or entry to the palace of that god†. Lastly, if none of these reliefs were afforded, and especially when Christianity had banished these cruel practices, the heroes consoled themselves at least by putting on complete armour as soon as they found their end approaching; thus making (as it were) a solemn protest against the kind of death to which they were forced involuntarily to submit. After this it will not be thought wonderful that those who followed a great chieftain in some expedition, should make a vow not to survive their commander; or that this vow should always be performed in all its rigour. Neither will it

* There are several of these rocks in Sweden, called Ättestupor (stem or family rocks). One situated on the borders of a lake in the province of Bleking, and two others in West Gothland, bear the name of Valhalla. To another of these rocks, called Stafva Hall, is attached the remarkable local tradition, that at an annual festival held there in pagan times, a number of people, after dancing and singing, and partaking in the general amusement, threw themselves from it into the lake below, in the same manner as the classic writers tell us was practised by the Scythians and Hyperboreans. See Geijer. G. Sch. I. 103.—Ed.

† We have a particular description of this place by Sir William Temple; which it will be worth while to produce at large.

" I will not," he says, " trouble myself with more passages out of the Runic poems concerning this superstitious principle [of preferring a violent death, &c.], but will add a testimony of it, which was given me at Nimeguen, by count Oxenstern, the first of the Swedish ambassadors in that assembly. In discourse upon this subject, and in confirmation of this opinion having been general among the Goths of those countries, he told me there was still in Sweden a place which was a memorial of it, and was called Odin's Hall. That it was a great bay in the sea, encompassed on three sides with steep and ragged rocks; and that in the time of the Gothic paganism, men that were either sick of diseases they esteemed mortal or incurable, or else grown invalid with age, and thereby past all military action, and fearing to die meanly and basely (as they esteemed it) in their beds, they usually caused themselves to be brought to the nearest part of these rocks, and from thence threw themselves down into the sea, hoping by the boldness of such a violent death to renew the pretence of admission into the Hall of Odin, which they had lost, by failing to die in combat, and with their arms."—Miscellanea, part II. essay 3, part 4.—P.

be surprising that private soldiers should sometimes form among themselves a kind of society or confraternity, in which the several members engaged, at the expense of their own lives, to avenge the death of their associates, provided it were honourable and violent. All these dangers were, in their opinion, so many favourable and precious occasions of meriting glory and eternal happiness. Accordingly, we never find any among these people guilty of cowardice, and the bare sus-picion of that vice was always attended with universal con-tempt. A man who had lost his buckler, or who had received a wound behind, durst never more appear in public. In the history of England*, we see a famous Danish captain named Siward, who had sent his son to attack a province in Scotland, ask with great coolness those who brought the news of his death, whether he had received his wounds behind or before? The messengers telling him he was wounded before, the father cries out, " Then I have only cause to rejoice: for any other death would have been unworthy of me and my son." A con-queror could not exercise a more terrible vengeance upon his captives, than to condemn them to slavery. " There is," says Saxo, " in the heart of the Danes, an insurmountable aver-sion to servitude, which makes them esteem it the most dreadful of all conditions."† The same historian describes to us a king of Denmark, named Frotho, taken in battle by a king his enemy, and obstinately refusing all offers of life which that prince could make him. " To what end," says he, " should I reserve myself for so great a disgrace? What good can the remainder of my life afford me, that can counterba-lance the remembrance of my misfortunes, and the regret which my misery would cause me? And even if you should restore me my kingdom, if you should bring me back my sister, if you should repair all the loss of my treasure, would all this recover my honour? All these benefits would never replace me in my former state, but future ages would always say, Frotho hath been taken by his enemy." In all combats, and the number of them is prodigious in the ancient histo-ries of the north, we always find both parties continually re-peating the words glory, honour, and contempt of death, and

* Brompton. Ubb. Jom. Chronic. p. 946.
† Saxo Gramm. lib. xii.

by this means raising one another to that pitch of enthusiasm which produces extraordinary actions. A general never forgot to remind his troops of these motives when he was going to give battle; and not infrequently they prevented him, and flew to the engagement of themselves, chanting songs of war, marching in cadence, and raising shouts of joy.

Lastly, like the heroes of Homer, those of ancient Scandinavia, in the excess of their over-boiling courage, dared to defy the gods themselves. " Though they should be stronger than the gods," says a boastful warrior speaking of his enemies, " I would absolutely fight them." * And in Saxo Grammaticus we hear another wishing ardently that he could but meet with Odin, that he might attack him: expressing his mind by verses to this effect :—" Where at present is he whom they call Odin, that warrior so completely armed, who hath but one eye to guide him? Ah, if I could but see him, this redoubted spouse of Frigga; in vain should he be covered with his snow-white buckler, in vain mounted upon his lofty steed, he should not leave his abode of Lethra without a wound. It is lawful to encounter a warrior god." The same author relates that a Danish prince, named Hother, resisted the united forces of Odin, Thor, and the squadrons of the gods. " And the victory," he adds, " would have remained with the gods, if Hother, breaking through their thickest ranks, and assailing them with such fury as a mortal can superior beings, had not rendered the mallet of the god Thor useless, by cutting it off at the handle. Weakened by this sudden and unexpected stroke, the gods were forced to betake themselves to flight." It was a received opinion among them, that a man might attack and fight the gods; and it is needless to remark with Saxo, that these were only imaginary deities. No one is tempted to take such relations literally, and they only deserve to be mentioned because they show us what manner of thinking prevailed among the people who invented stories of this sort. From them we may at least infer that the confidence with which their bodily strength and courage inspired these ancient Danes must have been excessive to make them brave and defy whatever was most formidable in their system of religion. But Diomedes's wounding Venus concealed in a

* Bartholin, lib. i. c. 6.

cloud, his defying Jupiter, as well as the other combats of men with the gods described in the Iliad, have already shown us to what a degree of intoxication and madness men may arrive, who think themselves above all fear.

A passion so strong, so general and so blind, could not but give a tincture of its character to whatever it could possibly extend to; and therefore we must not be surprised that they should take it into their heads almost to deify the instruments of war, without which that passion could not have been gratified. The respect they had for their arms made them also swear by instruments so valuable and so useful, as being the most sacred things they knew. Accordingly, in an ancient Icelandic poem, a Scandinavian, to assure himself of a person's good faith, requires him to swear "by the shoulder of a horse, and the edge of a sword."* This oath was usual more especially on the eve of some great engagement: the soldiers engaged themselves, by an oath of this kind, not to flee though their enemies should be never so superior in number.

From the same source proceeded that propensity to duels and single combats, so remarkable among all the Teutonic nations, and which of all their barbarous customs has been most religiously kept up by their present descendants. In Denmark, and through all the north, they provoked a man to fight a duel, by publicly calling him Niding or "infamous:"† for he who had received so deep a stain, without

---

* It is therefore with peculiar propriety and decorum (as is well observed by his commentators) that Shakspeare makes his Prince of Denmark call upon his companions to swear upon his sword.

> ———— Come hither, gentlemen, ·
> And lay your hands again upon my sword,
> Never to speak of this that you have heard
> Swear by my sword. ———— ————
>
> *Hamlet*, A. 1, sc. ult.—P.

† In the same manner as giving the lie is the highest provocation in modern times, because it implies a charge of meanness, falsehood and cowardice; so the word Niding or Nithing anciently included in it the ideas of extreme wickedness, meanness and infamy. It signified a villanous base wretch, a dastardly coward, a sordid stingy worthless creature. No wonder that an imputation of this kind should be so reproachful among an open and brave people, or that they would rather do anything than incur it. We have a remarkable proof in English history how much this name was dreaded and abhorred by our ancestors. King William Rufus having occa-

endeavouring to wash it out with the blood of his adversary, would have lost much more than the life he was so desirous to save. Banished by public indignation from the society of men, degraded from his quality of citizen, and scarce regarded as a human creature, he had nothing left for it but a shameful and insecure flight.

[Nithing * was unquestionably the most insulting epithet that a Northman could apply to an adversary. There was, moreover, a peculiar way of applying it that greatly increased its virulence, although it gave the aggrieved party the right to seek redress by an action at law. This was by setting up what was called a Nithing-post or Nithing-stake [Nidstaung]. A mere hazel twig stuck in the ground by a person who at the same time made use of some opprobrious epithet, either against an individual or a community, was quite sufficient to come under the legal definition of a Nithing-post. Several super- stitious practices were, however, commonly observed on the occasion which were supposed to impart to the Nithing-post the power of working evil on the party it was directed against, and more especially to make any injuries done to the person

sion to draw together a sudden body of forces, only sent word to all such as held of him in fee, that those who did not repair to his assistance should be deemed Nithing; and without further summons they all flocked to his stand- ard. *Rex irâ inflammatus,* says Matthew Paris, *stipendiarios milites suos Anglos congregat, et absque morâ, ut ad obsidionem veniant, jubet, nisi velint sub nomine* Nithing, *quod Latine* nequam *sonat, recenseri. Angli (qui nihil contumeliosius et vilius estimant quam hujusmodi ignominioso vocabulo notari) catervatim ad regem confluentes, ingentes copias conficiunt.* (M. Par. sub ann. 1089.) The word Nithing for some ages after continued in use in this kingdom, but chiefly in the sense of stingy, niggardly, &c. The translator has seen an ancient MS. poem, that was written between the reigns of Edward III. and Edward IV. in which a person is thus exhorted,

> Looke thou be kind and curteous aye,
> Of meate and drinke be never Nithing.

which sense of the word still obtains in Denmark, as we learn from Bartho- lin. *Denotat* Niding *modernis Danis virum sordide parcum atque tenacem.* Lib. i. c. 7, p. 98.—P.

* There are three old Norse words, naud, need, German noth; nithr, downward; and nid, contumely, infamy, disgrace, from which etymologists respectively derive the word Nithing. The derivation from nid is at least the most significant, and the word seems to correspond with the Greek ὄνιδος, which has the same meaning, and with the German neid, Mœso-Goth neiths, envy.

erecting it recoil on those by whom they had been perpe
trated. A pole with a horse's head, recently cut off, stuck on
it, was considered to form a Nithing-post of peculiar efficacy *.
Thus when Eigil, a celebrated Icelandic skald of the ninth
century, was banished from Norway, we are told that he took
a stake, fixed a horse's head on it, and as he drove it in the
ground said, "I here set up a Nithing-stake, and turn this
my banishment against King Eirek and Queen Gunhilda." He
then turned the horse's head towards the land, saying, "I
turn this my banishment against the protecting deities of this
country, in order that they may, all of them, roam wildly
about and never find a resting-place until they have driven out
King Eirek and Queen Gunhilda." He then set sail for
Iceland, with the firm persuasion that the injuries he had received by his banishment, would by the efficacy of his charmed
Nithing-post recoil on the royal couple they had, in his opinion,
proceeded from †.

Mention is frequently made in the Sagas and the Icelandic
laws of this singular custom. We are told for instance, in
the Vatsndæla Saga, that Jökul and Thorstein having accepted a challenge from Finbogi and Björg, went to the place
of meeting on the day and hour appointed. Their opponents,
however, remained quietly at home, deeming that a violent
storm, which happened to be raging, would be a sufficient excuse for their non-appearance. Jökul, after waiting for some
time on the ground, thought that he would be justified in
setting up a Nithing-post against Finbogi, or as would now be
said, in posting him for a coward. He accordingly fashioned
out a block of wood into the rude figure of a human head, and
fixed it on a post in which he cut magical runes. He then
killed a mare, opened her breast, and stuck the post in it with
the carved head turned towards Finbogi's dwelling ‡.

* Some curious details respecting superstitious practices with horses' heads
are given by Grimm in his "Deutsche Mythologie," p. 42 and 426. Several
Teutonic tribes, for instance, killed the horses taken from the Romans in
battle, and eat their flesh, but dedicated their heads, which they stuck on poles
round their encampment, to the gods they worshipped ; and Pliny tells us that
a pole with the skeleton of a horse's head stuck on it and placed in a garden,
was reckoned a good remedy against caterpillars.

† Müller's Sagabib. I. 116.

‡ This anecdote will, we trust, serve to convince the most incredulous of
the rapid strides civilization has made since the time of the Northmen. A

In an old Swedish code of laws cited by Wachsmuth*, some very precise rules are given respecting the manner of proceeding on such occasions; for instance, " when a man makes use of ill words to another, and says, ' Thou art nothing like a man, hast nothing manly in thee;' and the other answers, ' I am as much a man as thou art,' they shall encounter each other at a place where three roads meet. If he who made use of the ill words comes to the place of meeting, and he to whom they were given comes not, then shall he (the latter) be held for worse than he was called, and shall be declared incompetent to have an oath administered to him, or to give evidence either for man or woman. If he to whom the ill words were applied comes, and he who applied them comes not, then shall the former call out three times Nithing, and make a mark on the ground. If they both meet properly armed, and he to whom the ill words were given be killed, only half mulct shall be demanded. But if the giver of the ill words fall, then will his tongue have justly forfeited him his life, and he shall be left lying on the earth without atonement," that is to say, the other would have no mulct to pay for killing him.]

The dreadful consequences of their sensibility with regard to what we falsely call honour, extended often from private persons to a whole people; and nations, blind to their true welfare, waged long and cruel wars for such chimerical interests as really ought not to have armed one single individual against another. Under the reign of Harald Blaatand, king of Denmark, the Icelanders provoked by his having detained

---

duellist of the ninth century, after waiting for some time, in the vain expectation either of killing or getting killed, has at length recourse to the expedient of posting his adversary for a coward. A duellist of the nineteenth century, in similar untoward circumstances, also posts his opponent, not exactly on a Nithing-post, but in the columns of the Morning Post, which is much the same thing. The substitution of hair-trigger pistols for battle axes, typographic characters for Runic ones, and above all the saving in horse-flesh, will therefore indicate the progress civilization has made during the last ten centuries. Something, however, may always be learned from our barbarous ancestors, and we should suggest the expediency of reviving the old custom of killing a horse on such occasions, for horse-flesh having become rather an expensive article, its use, being thus rendered as imperative by the modern as it was by the ancient code of honour, might deter many of our modern Jökuls and Finbogis from indulging too freely in their pugnacious propensities.

Europ. Sitteng. 2 Th. p. 161.

one of their ships laden with merchandise, flew for revenge to
a species of arms that were familiar to them, and made verses
upon him so very satirical, that Harald, stung to the quick,
sent out a fleet to ravage the island.   This obliged the inhabitants to make a law, which is still extant in their ancient
code, forbidding any person, under capital punishment, to
compose satirical verses upon the kings of Denmark, Sweden,
or Norway*.

After so many efforts to acquire glory, it was very natural
to think how to perpetuate it.   To this end the ancient Scandinavians employed various means suitable to the grossness
and rudeness of the times; which if they have deceived the
expectation of those who hoped for fame and immortality from
them, have done them no great injustice.   The most common
method consisted in burying the heroes under little hills which
they raised in the middle of some plain, and in giving to
these hillocks. and sometimes to the plains themselves, the
name of the person who was there interred.   This rude monument kept up at the same time the memory of the hero,
and the emulation of the neighbouring inhabitants.   We
find in Denmark at this day a great number of such artificial
hills, which bear the name of some warrior or king of ancient
times.

They commonly pitched upon some public place, some great
road, some fountain, or other well-frequented spot, as the
most proper to raise these tombs in.   They adorned them
frequently with one or more large stones and epitaphs, as will
be explained when I come to speak of the funerals of this
people.   But above all, they had recourse to·the art of poetry,
when they were disposed to immortalize their kings or great
captains.   The skalds, or bards, were employed to compose
odes or songs, which related all their most shining exploits,
and sometimes the whole history of their lives.   These songs
were propagated from one reciter to another; and there was
no public solemnity in which they were not sung or chaunted.
The praises which these poets gave to valour, the warlike enthusiasm which animated their verses, the great care men took
to learn them from their infancy, being all of them the natural effects of the ruling passion of this people, served in

* Grágás, ix. 15.

their turn to strengthen and extend it. Lastly, the common
objects which they usually had before their eyes, the rocks
scattered all over the country, the bucklers, the trophies
raised in the field of battle, the walls and hangings of their
houses, all contributed to preserve the memory of great actions and intrepid warriors, by means of the Runic characters,
the hieroglyphics, and the symbols, which were engraven or
inscribed upon them.

A people who nourished so strong a passion for war, could
seldom be at loss for occasions of it. Accordingly the ancient
Scandinavians were continually involved in one hostile dispute or other, and their whole history would have consisted of
nothing else but melancholy and disgusting details of these
wars, if they had been at the needless pains to write it. But
the little that is left of their history is more than sufficient to
satisfy the curiosity of those who admire courage, no matter
with what spirit it is animated; and who are astonished that
men should be so prodigal of their lives, when they were ignorant of the art how to render them agreeable. We have
already observed, that the inhabitants of Germany and the
north were accustomed every spring to hold a general assembly, at which every free man appeared completely armed, and
ready to go upon any expedition. At this meeting they considered in what quarter they should make war: they examined
what causes of complaint had been received from the several
neighbouring nations, their power or their riches, the easiness
with which they might be overcome, the prospect of booty, or
the necessity of avenging some injury. When they had determined on the war, and settled the plan of the campaign,
they immediately began their march, furnished each of them
with a proper quantity of provisions; and almost every grown
man in the country made haste to join the army thus tumultuously assembled. We are not to wonder after this, that
there should issue from the north swarms of soldiers, as
formidable for their numbers as their valour; and we ought
not hastily to conclude from hence, that Scandinavia formerly
contained more people than it does at present. I know what
is related of the incredible multitudes of men which that
country is said to have poured forth; but on the other hand,
who does not know how much nations and historians have
been, in all ages, inclined to exaggeration in this respect; some

being desirous to enhance the power of their country, and
others, when it has been conquered, being willing to save its
credit by making it yield only to superior numbers; but the
greatest part have been guilty of enlargement from no other
motive than a blind love of the marvellous, authorized by the
difficulty of pronouncing with certainty on a subject, in which
men often commit great mistakes even after long researches.
Besides this, it is very probable that many particular circumstances of those famous expeditions made by the Scandinavians, have contributed to countenance that name of *Vagina
gentium*, which an historian gives their country *.   For when
these emigrations were made by sea, the promptitude and
celerity with which they could carry their ravages from one
coast to another, might easily multiply armies in the eyes of
the people they attacked, and who heard many different irruptions spoken of almost at the same time.   If, on the contrary,
they issued forth by land, they found everywhere on their
march nations as greedy of fame and plunder as themselves,
who joining with them, afterwards passed for people of the
same origin with the first swarm which put itself in motion.
It should also be considered, that these emigrations did not
all of them take place at the same time; and that after a
nation was thus exhausted, it probably remained inactive
until it had been able to recruit its numbers.   The vast extent of Scandinavia being in those times divided among many
different people who were little known and only described by
some one general name, as that of Goths, for instance, or
Normans, (that is " Northern men,") it could not exactly be
ascertained from what country each troop originally came, and
still less to what degree of depopulation each country was reduced after losing so great a quantity of its inhabitants.   But
what, in my opinion, best accounts for those numerous and
frequent inundations of northern people, is that we have rea-

---

* Jornandes de rebus Geticis.—Sir William Temple calls it the Northern
Hive : and Milton has taken a comparison from thence to express exuberant
multitudes.
      " A multitude like which the populous North
        Pour'd never from her frozen loins, to pass
        Rhene or the Danaw, when her barbarous sons
        Came like a deluge on the South, and spread
        Beneath Gibraltar to the Lybian sands.
                    Par. Lost, B. I. 351.—P.

son to believe entire nations often engaged in enterprizes of this sort: even the women and children sometimes marched in the rear of the armies, when a whole people, either by inconstancy, by indigence, or the attraction of a milder climate, resolved to change their place of abode. Projects of this kind, it is true, appear very strange to us at present; but it is no less true that our ancestors often engaged in them. In the time of Cæsar, the Helvetians, that is, the ancient inhabitants of Switzerland, desirous to establish themselves in Gaul, burnt their houses with their own hands, together with such of their effects as were not portable, and, followed by their wives and children, set out with a resolution of never more returning home. What a multitude might not one expect such a nation to form? And yet Cæsar remarks * that according to the musters of the Helvetians themselves, found in their camp, they did not exceed three hundred and sixty thousand in all, including old men, women and children : a number, without dispute, small compared with that of the inhabitants of the same country at present. The expedition of the Cimbri had also been an entire transplantation of that people; for it appears, by the request they made to the Romans, that their view was to obtain new lands to settle in. They, as well as the Helvetians, took with them their wives and children; and accordingly Cimbria (at present Sleswick and Jutland) continued after this emigration so depopulated, that at the end of two whole centuries, viz. in the time of Tacitus, it had not been able to recover itself, as we have already remarked from this historian, who had been himself in Germany.

The expedition of the Anglo-Saxons furnishes us with proofs no less convincing than those I have mentioned. The first Angles, who passed into Britain under the conduct of Hengist and Horsa, were a mere handful of men. The ancient Saxon chronicle † informs us, that they had only three vessels, and it should seem that their number could not well exceed a thousand. Some other swarms having afterwards followed their example, their country was reduced to a mere desert, and continued destitute of inhabitants for more than two centuries; being still in this state in the time of

* De bello Gallic. lib. i. c. 11.
† Chronic. Anglo-Sax. à Gibson, edit. p. 13.

M

Bede, from whom the author of the Saxon chronicle borrowed this fact. Let any one judge after this, whether it was always out of the superfluity of its inhabitants, as has been frequently asserted, that the North poured forth its torrents on the countries they overwhelmed. For my part I have not been able to discover any proofs that their emigrations ever proceeded from want of room at home: on the contrary, I find enough to convince me that their country could easily have received an additional number of inhabitants, When Alboin formed the project of leading the Lombards into Italy, he demanded auxiliaries from the Saxons, his allies. Twenty thousand Saxons, with their wives and children, accompanied the Lombards into Italy: and the kings of France sent colonies of Swabians to occupy the country which the Saxons had left desert. Thus we see the Saxons, who are thought to have been one of the most numerous people of Germany, could not send forth this feeble swarm without depopulating their own country: but this is not all. The twenty thousand Saxons, disagreeing with the Lombards, quitted Italy, and returned back (undiminished in number) into their own country, which they found possessed by the Swabians above mentioned. This presently gave rise to a war, notwithstanding all the remonstrances of the Swabians, who, as an ancient historian * assures us, demonstrated to the Saxons, that both nations might easily share the country among them, and live all of them in it very commodiously. I make no doubt but there were throughout all Saxony, as well as Scandinavia, vast tracts of land which lay in their original uncultivated state, having never been grubbed up and cleared. Let any one read the description which Adam of Bremen † gives of Denmark in the eleventh century, and he will be convinced that the coasts alone were peopled, but that the interior parts formed only one vast forest.

From what has been said, therefore, I think one may safely conclude, that as all were soldiers among the ancient Scandinavians, they could easily fill all Europe with the noise of their arms, and ravage for a long time different parts of it, although the sum total of the inhabitants should have been much less than it is at present. If it was otherwise, we must

---

* Paul. Diacon. de Gest. Longobard. lib. ii. c. 6.
† Adam Brem. Hist. Eccles. Cap. de Situ Daniæ.

acknowledge, that this extreme population can be very ill reconciled, either with what history informs of the manners, customs, and principles of the ancient Scandinavians, or with the soundest notions of policy with respect to what makes the true prosperity of a people. For we cannot allow them such a superiority over us in the number of inhabitants, without granting them at the same time a proportionable excellence in their customs, manners, civil regulations, and constitution of government, as so many efficacious causes of the good or bad state of all societies, and consequently of their greater or less degree of population. But who can persuade himself, that those savage times, when men sowed and reaped but little; when they had no other choice but that of the destructive profession of arms, or of a drowsy indolence no less destructive; when every petty nation was torn to pieces either by private revenge and factions within, or by war with their neighbours from without; when they had no other subsistence but rapine, and no other ramparts but wide frontiers laid waste; who, I say, can believe such a state as this to be more favourable to the propagation of the human species, than that wherein men's goods and persons are in full security; wherein the fields are covered with labourers, and their cities, rich and numerous, flourish in tranquillity; wherein the people are left to breathe during long intervals of peace, and there is never more than a small part of the inhabitants to whom war is destructive; and lastly, wherein commerce, manufactures, and the arts offer so many resources, and second so well that natural propensity to increase and multiply, which nothing but the fear of indigence can check and restrain.

Let us now consider in what manner the ancient nations of of the North made war. When an army was upon the march, the whole body, as well generals as private soldiers, equally desired to terminate the campaign by some speedy and decisive action. Their numbers, their poverty, the want of provisions, and of the other precautions observed at present, did not permit these people to wait leisurely the favourable occasions of giving battle. The plunder, as it was their principal object, so it was generally their greatest resource; and they were not of a character to brook either long delays, or severe discipline, without which all military knowledge is useless.

Naturally impetuous and ardent, they only fought with courage so long as the first heat of their passion continued, and while they were encouraged by the hope of speedy success. Whenever they attacked a civilized and warlike people they were always sure to be defeated sooner or later, provided the operations were slow and cautious. It was thus Marius repaired the repeated losses which Rome had suffered from the imprudence of the former generals, by only opposing to the Cimbri a studied slackness, which blunted the edge of their impetuosity, and threw them into dejection and decay by reducing them to inaction. One need only read the account which the English historians give of the irruptions made by the Danes in England, to be convinced that it was rather by surprise and sudden excursions than by a regular war, that they made a conquest of that country. The northern kings, as well as those of the other parts of Europe, had not then any regular troops, excepting perhaps a small number of armed cavalry which served them for guards. When they would raise an army, they convoked, as we have said above, a general assembly of the freemen of the nation: in this assembly they levied soldiers, and fixed the number which each farm, village or town was to furnish. There is room to believe that in Denmark, as in other kingdoms, the soldiers received no regular pay; but every one returned home as soon as the expedition was finished and the booty divided. Nevertheless the more valiant among them, unable to lie inactive, till their own country should offer them new occasions to enrich and signalize themselves, entered into the service of such other nations as were at war. This was a general custom among all the Teutonic nations, and ancient history affords us a thousand examples of it. We have seen the Cimbri ask the Romans to assign them lands, promising in return to be always ready to arm themselves in their quarrels. A long time after we frequently see the Goths and Danes in the pay of the Roman emperors. Saxo informs us that in succeeding ages the emperors of Constantinople intrusted to them the guard of their persons, and gave them the first ranks in their armies.

It is very difficult to say any thing more particular of the tactics or military art of these ancient nations. It appears to have been the custom of the Scandinavians to dispose their troops in the form of a triangle or pyramid, the point of which was directed against the centre of the enemy's army. This body was only composed of infantry, the cavalry being generally upon a very inconsiderable footing in the North, whether because the country is so divided there by mountains and arms of the sea, or whether because their principal forces were reserved for the marine*. They had only some soldiers who served both on foot and horseback, and who were commonly placed in the flanks of their armies. When they were going to join battle, they raised great shouts, they clashed their arms together, they invoked with a great noise the name of Odin, and sometimes sung hymns in his praise. They made an intrenchment with their baggage round the camp, where the women and children remained during the engagement. The conquered in vain fled there for refuge if they happened to be routed. Most commonly the women only waited their coming back to cut them in pieces, and if they could not oblige them to return to battle, they chose to bury themselves and their children in one common carnage with their husbands rather than fall into the hands of a merciless conqueror†. Such were the dreadful effects of that inhumanity with which war was then carried on. An act of rigour occasioned an act of cruelty, and this again produced a degree of barbarity still greater. The chains and punishments which were reserved for the vanquished, only served to render the victory the more bloody, and to make it cost the dearer to those who purchased the honour of destroying their fellow-creatures without necessity.

Their offensive weapons were commonly the bow and arrows, the battle-axe, and the sword. The sword was short, most frequently crooked in the manner of a scimitar, and hung to a little belt which passed over the right shoulder. Yet they sometimes made use of very long swords which went by a different name, and these were what the Cimbri employed, according to Plutarch. Their champions or heroes took particular care to procure very keen swords, which they inscribed with mysterious characters, and called by such

---

* .Dalin. Suea, Rike's Hist. tom. i. ch. 8.

† This account, derived from a classic source, even if it could be implicitly relied on, which is far from being the case, would only be applicable to the early migratory expeditions of the Germanic and Celtic tribes.—ED.

names as might inspire terror. The battle-axe had two edges; when it had a long handle it went by the name of an halberd, and was particularly affected by the Trabants, or those who stood upon guard in the castles of their kings*. The Scandinavians were reckoned very skilful at shooting, and accordingly made great use of the bow, as we learn from all the ancient chronicles. But besides these arms, some warriors employed whatever others they judged most proper to second their valour. Thus we sometimes read of javelins, slings, clubs stuck round with points, lances, and a sort of daggers. There was no less variety in their defensive arms. Of these the shield or buckler was the chief. This most commonly was of wood, bark, or leather. The shields belonging to warriors of distinction were of iron or brass, ornamented with painting and sculpture, often finely gilt, and sometimes plated over with gold or silver. We have seen what great account the ancient Danes made of their shields, and what penalties were reserved for such as lost them in battle. Their shape and size varied much in different countries: the Scandinavians generally had them of a long oval form, just the height of the bearer, in order to protect him from arrows, darts, and stones. They besides made use of them to carry the dead to the grave, to terrify the enemy by clashing their arms against them, to form upon occasion a kind of shelter or tent when they were obliged to encamp in the open field, or when the weather was bad. Nor was the shield less useful in naval encounters; for if the fear of falling into their enemies' hands obliged one of their warriors to cast himself into the sea, he could easily escape by swimming upon his buckler†. Lastly, they sometimes made a rampart of their shields, by locking them one into another,

---

* The word halbard is, I believe, of later date, though it is of Gothic origin, being compounded of the Teutonic, barde an axe, and halle a court; halberds being the common weapons of guards. The weapon itself, however, was probably in use from the earliest times. Trabants (or rather drabants) is the name given to the yeomen of the guard in the Northern courts.—P.

† Vid. Holberg's Dannem. og Norg. Beskrivelse, chap. xiii.

Plutarch, in his Life of Marius, tells us, that the Cimbri, when they were passing the Alps, took great delight in climbing up to the tops of the mountains over the ice and snow, and there placing their broad shields under their bodies, would slide down those vast slippery descents.—P.

in the form of a circle; and at the end of a campaign they suspended them against the walls of their houses, as the finest decoration with which they could adorn them.

All these uses which they made of their shields could not but inspire the Scandinavians with a high respect for this part of their armour. It was the most noble manner in which a hero could employ his leisure, to polish his shield to the utmost brightness, and to represent upon it either some gallant feat, or some emblematical figure expressive of his own inclinations or exploits; and this served to distinguish him when, being armed at all points, his helmet hid his face. But then every one could not carry these painted or carved shields indifferently. When a young warrior was at first enlisted, they gave him a white and smooth buckler, which was called the "Shield of expectation." This he carried till, by some signal exploit, he had obtained leave to have proofs of his valour engraven on it. For this reason none but princes, or persons distinguished by their services, presumed to carry shields adorned with any symbol; the common soldiers could not obtain a distinction of which the chieftains were so jealous. Even so early as the expedition of the Cimbri, the greatest part of the army, according to Plutarch, had only white bucklers. In following times, but not till long after, these symbols which illustrious warriors had adopted, passing from father to son, produced in the North, as well as all over Europe, hereditary coats of arms.

The casque or helmet was known to the Scandinavians from the most early ages. The private soldiers had their helmets frequently of leather; those of the officers were of iron, and, if their rank or wealth permitted, of gilded brass. The coat of mail, the breast-plate and back-piece, the armour for the thighs, and other less essential pieces, were only for such as were able to procure them.

They did not carry to much perfection the art of fortifying or attacking places of defence. Their fortresses were only rude castles situate on the summits of rocks, and rendered inaccessible by thick misshapen walls. These rude forts were seldom taken by the enemy, unless by surprise or after a long blockade: however, when these were of great importance, they raised terraces and artificial banks on that side of the fort which was lowest; and by this means annoyed the besieged by throwing in arrows, stones, boiling water, and melted pitch; offensive arms, which the besieged, on their part, were not negligent in returning.

[Although the military art of these rude ages cannot be compared with the tactics of the Greeks and Romans, or even with the improved methods of warfare which the crusades gave rise to, there can be little doubt but that such as it was, the Scandinavians understood it as well, and probably better, than any people with whom they came in contact. They were not only unrivalled at sea, but, what is very remarkable, also excellent horsemen. They fought, in fact, equally well on foot, on horseback, and on board a vessel. In their naval engagements they generally lashed their vessels together, so as to form a floating rampart, with a row of shields placed along the sides of the ships for the protection of the combatants. Harald Hardráda, at the battle of Stamford Bridge, drew up his army much in the same manner as a general of the present day would do against an enemy superior in cavalry. With both wings bent backwards until they met, the army formed an irregular square, in which Harald, with his chief officers, placed himself, beside his famous banner, called—very appropriately—the Land Ravager. The men stood close together, shield against shield, the first rank setting their spears on the ground, and the second holding theirs forward, thus forming a bristling rampart which the Anglo-Saxon cavalry tried in vain to break through *. The Scandinavians were probably also as well acquainted with the art of besieging towns as their contemporaries, although in their marauding expeditions they were generally unprovided with the engines necessary for carrying on a regular siege. We find, however, that when they invested Paris, in 886, they constructed a moveable platform, three stories high, on which they placed sixty men at arms, and brought it to bear against the tower of the bridge over the Seine, in which they attempted on the day following to make a breach with three battering rams †.

Harald Hardráda, who commanded more disciplined troops than the leaders of these piratical bands, is said to have fought, during the ten years he was in the service of the Byzantine emperors, eighteen regular battles, and to have taken

---

* Heimsk. ix. 92.   † Depping, Liv. iii. ch. 1.

eighty fortified places from the Saracens in Africa, besides several others in Sicily. He took one of these Sicilian towns by having recourse to a very singular expedient. The walls were so strong that he began to doubt whether it would be possible to make a breach in them, and the inhabitants had plenty of provisions and every thing that they required for their defence. Under these circumstances, Snorri informs us that "Harald ordered his fowlers to catch the small birds that nested in the town, and flew to the forest during the day in quest of food for their young. He then caused splinters of inflammable wood, smeared with wax and sulphur, to be fastened on their backs and enkindled. The birds, when set at liberty, flew immediately to their nests, under the roofs of the houses in the town, which were thatched with reeds and straw. The fire from the birds soon caught the thatch, and although each bird bore but a small quantity, their number was so great that one house after another began to burn until the whole town was in flames."* The inhabitants then came out and implored mercy, and Harald thus gained possession of the place, and increased his treasures by its plunder.

During the siege of another of these Sicilian towns, Harald fell sick, and his sickness increased so rapidly that his life was despaired of. His men, knowing that the besieged had been informed by their spies of the dangerous state in which their commander lay, thought they might turn the circumstance to advantage, and gain possession of the town by a well-contrived stratagem. Demanding, therefore, a parley, they made known to the besieged that Harald was dead, and trusted that the clergy would allow his body to be brought into the town and buried with due solemnity. No proposal could have been more favourably listened to than this was by the churchmen. The burial of a wealthy and renowned prince was not an event of everyday occurrence, and large would be the sums, and costly the presents, they would receive for the due performance of their pious offices. Out accordingly they went, with cross and banner, shrine and reliquary, and found the Varangians ready to accompany them with a splendid coffin. Preceded by the monks and priests, chaunting their hymns and litanies, a chosen band of Varangians bore the coffin under a canopy of

---

* Heimsk. ix. 6. Olga, the widow of the Russian Scandinavian Czar Igor, is said to have set fire to a town by a similar expedient.

the finest linen, and marched in solemn procession toward the town, but no sooner were they within the gateway than they set down the coffin right across the entrance, placed a bar to keep the gate open, drew their swords, and sounded to arms with their trumpets. The whole army, at this signal, rushed to the assault, soon made themselves masters of the town, and with the usual Scandinavian barbarity, massacred all the male inhabitants. The priests and monks, who had been so eager to offer their services, were in the worst plight, for the Varangians, says Snorri, " cut down every one around them, priest and layman, without distinction." *

A somewhat similar story, though not mentioned in any of the Icelandic sagas, is told by the Norman chroniclers of the famous sea-king Hastings. This adventurer having heard of the wealth and splendour of the capital of the Christian world, entered the Mediterranean, about the year 857, with a fleet of one hundred vessels, and after plundering the coasts of Spain and Africa, and the Balearic Isles, appeared before the ancient Etruscan city of Luna †, which he mistook for Rome, when the inhabitants were celebrating the festival of Christmas. Finding the town well prepared for defence, Hastings had recourse to that perfidy which a Northman never scrupled to employ against an adversary. He accordingly sent some of his followers to inform the count and bishop that he had merely entered the port to repair his shattered fleet; and that being also weary of a sea-roving life, he was desirous of becoming a Christian, in order to find that repose in the bosom of the church which he had so long sighed for. Deceived by these fair words, the worthy bishop went to the camp of the Northmen and baptized Hastings. But although the Italians furnished their unwelcome visitors with provisions and other necessaries, they took care not to let them enter the city. Hastings, ever fertile in expedients, therefore pretended to be dangerously ill, and whilst his camp resounded with the lamentations of his followers, he made known his intention of leaving the rich booty he had acquired to the church, provided the bishop would allow him to be interred in one of the sacred edifices in the city. This was con-

* Heimsk. ix. 10.
† Some traces of this ancient city are still discernible on the left bank of the Magra, near Carrara.

ceded without much difficulty, and shortly afterward a chosen band of Northmen bore a coffin into the cathedral, supposed to contain the lifeless body of their chieftain. But no sooner had they set it down than Hastings started up, sword in hand, and killed without hesitation the poor bishop who had baptised him, whilst he was celebrating the sacred office at the altar for the repose of the soul of the remorseless sea-rover *. His followers then drew forth their concealed weapons, massacred all who were assembled in the cathedral, and made themselves masters of the city, which they set fire to, after committing their usual acts of ferocity †. Hastings, we are told, then loaded his vessels with a rich booty, and set sail on his return home, not forgetting to take with him the handsomest women of Luna ‡.

Although these stories of Harald and Hastings have no historical value, the events narrated are quite in accordance with the character of the Northmen, and may perhaps have actually taken place. All that we know with certainty, however, is, that Harald took several towns in Sicily, and that the city of Luna was destroyed in the middle of the ninth century, by a band of Norman sea-rovers; a fact which is attested by several Italian writers as well as by the Norman chroniclers.]

---

* The Norman Trouvère Benoit, in his rhymed Chronicle of the Dukes of Normandy, says—

" E Hastenc est en pez sailli,
Enz en sun poin s'espée nue
Cum male deserte a rendue
A saint euesque sun parein
Tut le fendi de ci qu'al sein
Mort l'a e le conte ensement
S'a il des meillors plus de cent."

† " Braient dames, plorent puceles
Aqui l'em coupe braz e mameles.
Suz les auters les escruient,
Tut detrenchent et tut occient,"
says Benoit.

‡ Depping, Liv. ii. ch. 3.

CHAPTER IX.

OF THE MARITIME EXPEDITIONS OF THE ANCIENT
SCANDINAVIANS.

How formidable soever the ancient Scandinavians were by
land to most of the inhabitants of Europe, it must yet be
allowed that their maritime expeditions occasioned still more
destructive ravages and greater terror. We cannot read the
history of the eighth, the ninth and the tenth centuries, without observing with surprise the sea covered with their vessels,
and from one end of Europe to the other, the coasts of those
countries, now the most powerful, a prey to their depredations.

During the space of two hundred years, they almost incessantly ravaged England, and frequently subdued it. They
often invaded Scotland and Ireland, and made incursions on
the coasts of Livonia, Courland and Pomerania. Already
feared, before the time of Charlemagne, they became still
more terrible as soon as this great monarch's eyes were
closed. He is known to have shed tears on hearing that
these barbarians had, on some occasion, defied his name, and
all the precautions he had made to oppose them. He foresaw what his people would suffer from their courage under
his feeble successors. And never was presage better grounded.
They soon spread, like a devouring flame, over Lower Saxony,
Friesland, Holland, Flanders, and the banks of the Rhine as
far as Mentz. They penetrated into the heart of France,
having long before ravaged the coasts; they everywhere
found their way up the Somme, the Seine, the Loire, the
Garonne and the Rhone. Within the space of thirty years,
they frequently pillaged and burnt Paris, Amiens, Orleans,
Poitiers, Bourdeaux, Toulouse, Saintes, Angoulême, Nantes,
and Tours. They settled themselves in Camargue, at the
mouth of the Rhone, from whence they wasted Provence and
Dauphiny as far as Valence. In short, they ruined France,
levied immense tribute on its monarchs, burnt the palace of
Charlemagne at Aix-la-Chapelle, and, in conclusion, caused
one of the finest provinces of the kingdom to be ceded to

them. They often carried their arms into Spain *, and even made themselves dreaded in Italy and Greece. In fine, they no less infested the north than the south with their incursions, spreading everywhere desolation and terror: sometimes as furiously bent on their mutual destruction, as on the ruin of other nations; sometimes animated by a more pacific spirit, they transported colonies to unknown or uninhabited countries, as if they were willing to repair in one place the horrid destruction of human kind occasioned by their furious ravages in others.

A people, who are ignorant of manual arts and professions, of justice, and of all means of providing for their own security or subsistence except by war, never fail to betake themselves to piracy, if they inhabit a country surrounded by the sea. The Pelasgi or first Greeks were generally pirates and robbers. "Some of them," says Thucydides †, "attacked un-

---

* In September, 844, a band of these sea-rovers, after plundering the coasts from the Tagus to the Guadalquiver, sailed up the latter river and attacked Seville, which they soon made themselves masters of, the inhabitants having fled, on their approach, to Carmona, and the Moorish troops making but a feeble resistance. On learning this unexpected event, Abderahman II. sent a flotilla with fresh troops down the river, from Cordova, and a sanguinary conflict took place between the sectaries of Odin and Mahomet, presenting, no doubt, one of the most singular scenes recorded in history. On one side the fair-haired sons of the north, on the other the swarthy warriors of Mauritania; both possessing indomitable courage, and both excited by the spirit of religious fanaticism. The Northman beholding the shadowy forms of the Valkyrior hovering over the field of battle, ready to conduct him in triumph, when he fell, to participate in the boisterous joys of Valhalla; the Moor, amidst the clash of arms, equally convinced that dark-eyed Houris were waving their green kerchiefs to welcome those who braved death for Allah and his prophet, to an eternity of blissful voluptuousness. No decided advantage appears to have been gained by either party, we only know that the sea-rovers redescended the Guadalquiver unmolested, carrying with them the spoil of the city and a great number of captives, among whom we may picture many a weeping damsel, who, amidst the frozen regions of the north would long sigh in vain for the sunny plains and vine-covered hills of Andalusia. The Northmen continued cruising for some time after this along the coast, but Abderahman, by stationing vessels at the mouths of the rivers, and troops on the sea-shore, effectually prevented them from committing any further depredations. This seems to have been the first time that the Moors came into contact with the Northmen, whom they took for a people of magicians. See Depping, Histoire des Expéd. Maritimes des Normands, Liv. II. chap. 2.—ED.

† See Thucyd. lib. i. cap. 5.

fortified cities; others, such as the Carians and Cretans, who dwelt along the coasts, fitted out fleets to scour the seas." But whereas the Greeks are represented to us as pirates in the first periods of their history, it is to be observed, that the Scandinavians did not become so till late. Sidonius Apollinarius, a writer of the fifth century, is, I think, the first who mentions the piracy of the Northern nations. He attributes this practice to the Saxons, of whom he draws a frightful picture *. The Danes and Norwegians had not as yet ventured far from their coasts. I imagine that their nearest neighbours had not allurements sufficient to tempt them. The inhabitants of those countries, as poor and warlike as themselves, were likely to return them blow for blow. Britain and Gaul were too distant and too well defended to become the first attempt of the Scandinavian ravagers. They began then by arming a few vessels, with which they plundered the states nearest to them, and overpowered such few merchant ships as

---

* The Saxons are first noticed by the ancient writers as occupying, towards the close of the second century, the islands lying near the mouth of the Elbe. Ptol. Geogr. II. 2. A century later they had become so troublesome by their predatory expeditions, that the Emperors Diocletian and Maximian deemed it advisable to place the coasts under the special command of an officer, afterwards dignified with the title of Count of the Saxon Shore. Carausius, a Menapian, who first held this office, instead of warring with the pirates, entered into an alliance with them, and by their assistance, and that of his German (Frankic) soldiers was proclaimed emperor, and reigned in Britain from 287 to 294. "Under his command," says Gibbon, "Britain, destined in future ages to obtain the empire of the sea, already assumed its natural and respectable station of a maritime power. His fleets rode triumphant in the Channel, commanded the mouths of the Seine and of the Rhine, ravaged the coasts of the ocean, and diffused beyond the columns of Hercules the terror of his name."

The coasts of France continued to be infested by Saxon sea-rovers during the fourth, fifth, sixth and seventh centuries. Their expeditions were conducted precisely in the same manner as that of their Scandinavian brethren of the eighth, ninth and tenth centuries. They ascended the rivers in their light barks, pillaged the towns on their banks, and retired with their booty to an island or other naturally strong position on the coast, where they generally passed the winter. A band of these Saxon pirates even succeeded in acquiring a permanent settlement in Neustria, and like their Norman successors, left off their predatory habits for the peaceful pursuits of commerce and agriculture. The district they occupied is called in a charter of Charles-le-Chauve, Otlingia Saxonica. They had also permanent establishments at Caen, Bayeux, St. Omer, and at the mouth of the Loire. See Depping, Hist. des Expéd. Marit. des Normands, Lib. II. ch. 1.—ED.

traversed the Baltic. Insensibly enriched by their success in little enterprizes, and encouraged to attempt greater, they were at length in a condition to become formidable to distant nations, such as the Anglo-Saxons, the French, or the Flemings, who all of them possessed wealth enough to tempt freebooters, and lived under a government too defective and weak to repel them. From that time this people conceived an amazing fondness for maritime expeditions, and towards the beginning of the ninth century we find these adventurers vastly increased, who, by a strange association of ideas, imagined they acquired eternal glory by committing everywhere, without any pretext, the most horrible violence.

In proportion as the divisions, incapacity and imprudence of Charlemagne's successors weakened their governments, the Scandinavians, encouraged by their growing wealth, constantly fitted out still more numerous fleets. "The French monarchy," says an author of that age[*], "labouring under the weight of a bad interior policy, hath been obliged to leave the seas exposed to the barbarous fury of the Normans." The mal-administration of the Saxon kings of England produced the same effect in that island. Both the one and the other had the dangerous imprudence to purchase peace from these pirates; which was not only putting arms into the hands of the enemy, but was also attended with this further inconvenience, that the commanders in these expeditions, who had no authority over each other, only considered themselves bound by their own separate engagements; so that those harassed nations were no sooner freed, by dint of money, from one set of ravagers, than another succeeded, ready to attack them with the same impetuosity, if they were not appeased by the same means. The better to account for that strange facility with which the Scandinavians so long plundered, and so frequently conquered the Anglo-Saxons and the French, we must remark, that their cruelty, which gave no quarter, and which occasioned those sad lamentations so well known[†], had impressed these nations

---

[*] Auctor Vitæ Sti. Genulfi, lib. xi.

[†] The monks inserted it as a petition in the Litany, *A furore Normannorum, libera nos, Domine.*—The French called these adventurers in general Normans, i. e. Northern-men; which afterwards became the proper name of the colony that settled in Neustria, whose history is given below.—P.

with such terror, that they were half vanquished at their very appearance. Besides, there was no contending with an enemy who did not make war, like regular forces, on any direct and consistent plan, but by sudden irruptions in a hundred places at once, as expeditious in retreating to their ships where they met with resistance, as in darting down upon the coasts where they found them quiet and defenceless. It is, nevertheless, probable that a wise and well-ordered government might have remedied all these evils: and in fact that it did so, we have an incontestable proof in the conduct of the great Alfred, under whose reign the Danes were obliged to leave England unmolested. But what appears an easy matter to us at this time, required in those ages of ignorance and confusion the uncommon genius of an Alfred to accomplish *.

If we reflect on the interior state of Scandinavia during the times that its inhabitants were so unfortunately famous, we shall soon see the cause of that amazing exterior power which they possessed. I have before observed that they neglected agriculture, which, among a thousand other good effects, extinguishes in a rising people the relish for savage life, and inspires them with the love of peace and justice, without which the cultivation of their lands is useless. Their flocks being almost their only income, they were neither obliged to a constant abode on the same spot, nor to wait for the time of harvest, and consequently such a people, though in fact but few, were able, on short notice, to levy numerous armies. Most of them brought up in a maritime country, and inured to the sea from their childhood, had no fear of the dangers, or rather knew not that there were dangers of any kind attend-

* Alfred, as is well known, translated the works of several Latin writers into Anglo-Saxon for the instruction of his countrymen. To his translation of Orosius's "Epitome of Ancient History," he subjoined a geographical treatise which he had drawn up partly from communications made to him by travellers and navigators. In this treatise he has inserted the narratives which Otter or Ohter, a Norwegian, and Vulfstan (Ulfstein) a Dane, gave him of their discoveries in the northern seas, and has thus transmitted to us the earliest account we have of a voyage round Cape North. This was made by Otter, who proceeded as far as the White Sea, on the eastern coasts of which he found the Beormas (Permians), a people who spoke nearly the same language as the Finns of Scandinavia. Ulfstein's voyages were confined to the Baltic, the shores of which were no doubt at that period accurately known to his countrymen.—Ed.

ing such a life. What a boundless field for conquests was here opened by the sole advantage of navigation! What a free scope was here afforded a warlike people to spread universally the terror of their arms! The profession of piracy was so far from appearing disgraceful to them, that it was in their eyes the certain road to honours and to fortune: for it was wisely contrived that the word honour, to which so many different ideas are annexed, was among them solely confined to a disregard of dangers. Hence it is that in the ancient chronicles, more than one hero boasts of being the most renowned pirate in the north; and that often the sons of the great lords and kings made cruising voyages in their youth, in order to render themselves illustrious, and to become one day worthy of command. This is what we see happen very frequently after Harald Hárfagra had once made himself master of all Norway, which before his time was divided into several petty states *. Many chieftains, seeing themselves thus stripped of their possessions, retired into Iceland, the Orkneys, the isles of Faro and Shetland, and thence covering the sea with their vessels, infested all the coasts of Scandinavia; where for many ages there was no sailing with any safety. Adam of Bremen, who travelled through Denmark some time after Christianity was received there, gives a very affecting description of the desolations they made in that kingdom †. Nor were they in reality less formidable in the north, than to France or England. The coasts of Denmark, Sweden and Norway were obliged to be under constant guard. They increased so much, that on some occasions, and particularly under King Ragnar Lodbrok,

---

* Harald made a vow neither to comb nor cut his hair until he had subdued the whole of Norway, and as it took him several years to do this, it grew so long and thick that he was called *Haralld hinn Lúfa*, Harald the Hirsute. Having finally accomplished the object of his wishes, and being on a visit at Jarl Ragnvald's in Möre, he took a bath, which he no doubt stood very much in need of, and afterwards combed his hair, and got Ragnvald to trim it for him. His appearance was so much changed for the better by these cleansing operations that Ragnvald gave him the surname of Hárfagra, by which he is known in history; *Haralld hinn Hárfagra*, Harald the Fair-haired, or as he might be termed in English, Harold Fairfax. See Heimsk. iii. c. 23.—ED.

† Vid. Adam Brem. de situ Dan. passim.

the Danes were perhaps more numerous on sea than on land.

As soon as a prince had attained his eighteenth or twentieth year, he commonly requested of his father a small fleet completely fitted out, in order to achieve with his followers some adventure that might be productive of glory and spoil. The father applauded such an inclination in his son, as indicating a rising courage and heroic mind. He gave him ships, the commander and crew of which mutually engaged not to return, unless adorned with laurels and loaded with plunder. That nation became the first object of their resentment from whom they had received any injury; and frequently their principal aim was to make reprisals on some province which served for the retreat of other corsairs. If the fleets of two different nations met by chance in their voyage, this was also an occasion of fighting which they never neglected.

The vanquished party was commonly put to death, though sometimes the conquerors were contented to make them slaves; and often, by a singular strain of generosity, which the love of glory was able to produce in minds in other respects so ferocious, if the enemy that fell in their way had fewer ships than themselves, they set aside part of their own vessels, that so, engaging upon equal terms, the victory might not be attributed to superiority of numbers. Many of them also regarded it as dishonourable to surprise the enemy by night. Sometimes the chiefs thought it best to decide the dispute by single combat; in this case they landed on the nearest shore: if one of them happened to be disarmed or thrown down, he frequently refused to receive quarter, and was killed on the spot; but if he had defended himself gallantly, the victor granted him his life, demanded his friendship, adopted him for a kind of foster-brother, and they mutually swore to preserve an eternal friendship. In token of this alliance the two heroes made incisions in their hands or arms, and besmeared their weapons with the blood, or mixing it in a cup, each of them covering their heads with a sod, drank of it, swearing that the death of the first of them who fell in battle should not pass unrevenged. Many of these piratical princes, whom success and custom had attached and habituated to this profession, never quitted it, but gloried

in passing the remainder of their lives on board their ships.
We meet with them sometimes, in their ancient histories,
boasting that they never reposed under an immoveable roof,
nor drank beer in peace by their fireside.

The vessels of these corsairs were always well provided
with offensive arms, such as stones, arrows, cables, with
which they overset small vessels, and grappling irons to
board them, &c. Every individual was skilful in swimming,
and as their engagements were seldom far distant from the
shore, the vanquished party often saved themselves by swimming to land. Each band had its own peculiar stations,
ports, places of rendezvous, and magazines: and many cities
in the north owe their present prosperity to the advantage
they had of affording them retreats. Such was Lunden in
Scania, which, according to Adam of Bremen*, contained
great riches laid up there by the pirates: and for a long time
the kings themselves countenanced and shared their plunder,
by selling them the liberty of retiring into their harbours.

The manner in which the lands were parcelled out in
Denmark and Norway evidently shows that every thing there
was directed towards this one end of having a powerful maritime force. Each division, whether more or less considerable, derived its name from the number of vessels it was
capable of fitting out, and these names still subsist in some
places. In the history of Denmark may be seen the particular taxes imposed on each province for that purpose, and
the number of ships of which their fleets were composed. At
first they were inconsiderable, but in proportion as the chiefs
who followed this piratical profession were enriched by it, the
northern seas were seen covered with one or two hundred
vessels, or still more numerous squadrons. We read in history of a fleet of seven hundred ships, commanded by Harald,
surnamed Bluetooth, king of Denmark, and a Norwegian
earl named Hakon. This number is no greater than what
we often find in the fleets under the following reigns, and
besides it is certain that the vessels of which it consisted
were but small. The first we hear of were only a kind
of twelve-oared barks; they were afterwards built capable of
containing one hundred or a hundred and twenty men, and

---

* Vid. Adam Brem. de sit. Dan. cap. ccxiii.

these were very common in the eleventh and twelfth centuries. The northern kings also sometimes constructed vessels of an extraordinary size, but these were rather for show
than defence. Such was that of Harald Hárfagra, a long
ship which the chronicles mention with admiration, under the
name of the Dragon. King Olaf Tryggvason had one of the
same kind, named the Long Serpent: the chronicles say it
was very long, large and high, and of a most durable construction; a serpent or dragon was carved on its prow, and
both that and its poop were gilded. It carried thirty-four
banks of rowers, and was, they add, the finest and largest
ship that had been ever seen in Norway*.

These piratical expeditions were not always confined to the
devastation of some province, or to a few naval engagements;
events which, producing no farther consequence than the immediate misfortune of the people who then suffered by them,
were soon forgot by posterity. I should digress from my subject were I to relate all the conquests made by the inhabitants
of the north in their cruising voyages. I will only take
notice of the emigration of the Angles, who along with the
Saxons, invaded Britain in the fifth century, and gave it their
name. As for the rest, I shall only borrow from the old
chronicles some facts and relations little known to strangers,
but which will afford the best idea of the maritime power of
these ancient Northmen, formerly dreaded by so many nations.

It is well known that the Britons, unable to defend themselves from the northern inhabitants of their isle, sought for
assistance from the Danes and Saxons, their allies†. The

* Olaf Tryggvason captured this vessel from Raud, a Norwegian chieftain, whom he put to death in the most cruel and barbarous manner for his
refusing to embrace Christianity.—See the Heimsk. vi. 87.—ED.

† Modern historical criticism, which has dissipated some of our most
cherished classical illusions, will no longer listen to the old story of Vortigern
seeking assistance from Saxon chieftains bearing such very equivocal names
as those of Hengist and Horsa[a]. It is, in fact, obvious, that swarms of
hardy sea-rovers who had long infested the coasts of Britain, and only been
prevented from establishing themselves in the country by the disciplined troops
of imperial Rome, would require no invitation from British princes to cross

[a] Hengist—A. Sax. Hengest; Old Norse, Heingéstr; Sw. and Dan.
Hingst; Germ. Hengst, a stallion.
Horsa—An. Sax. hors; Dan. hors; Germ. Ross, a horse; Old Norse, hros
and hors, a mare.

ancient Saxon chronicle, published by Gibson, informs us, that those people who went over and settled in Britain were originally of three different countries. One party of them were the ancient Saxons, that is to say, the people of Lower Saxony; another were the Angles or English, who inhabited that part of the duchy of Sleswic in the neighbourhood of Flensbourg, still called Angelen, and were consequently Danes. Lastly, there passed over into Britain also a considerable number of Jutes, which is the name given at this day to the inhabitants of Jutland. "From the Jutes," says the chronicler, "came the Kentish-men and the Wightwarians, that is, the tribe which now dwells in Wight, and that race among the West-Saxons which is still called the race of Jutes. From the Old-Saxons came the men of Essex and Sussex and Wessex. From Anglia, which has ever since remained waste betwixt the Jutes and Saxons, came the men of East Anglia, Middle Anglia, Mercia, and all North-humbria: " * and adds, that the Angles wholly abandoned their own country, situated between the territories of the Jutes and Saxons, and that it had ever since stood waste. Thus although this people were not yet known by the name of Danes, it is evident that at least two-thirds of the conquerors of Great Britain came from Denmark; so that when the Danes again infested England about three or four hundred years after, and finally conquered it toward the latter end of the tenth century, they waged war with the descendants of their own ancestors †.

the sea, when they became aware that these troops had finally abandoned the island. It is indeed highly probable, that the Saxons had fixed themselves, according to the invariable custom of the northern pirates, on several strong points on the coast, even during the dominion of the Romans. Be this as it may, their leaders would easily perceive that by taking part in the quarrels of British princes, and opposing their hardy bands to a people long unaccustomed to warfare, much more was to be gained than by mere sea-roving.

Higden, in his Polycronicon, i. 26, gives an odd etymology of the word Saxon. " Men of that cowntree, he says, ben more lyghter and stronger on the sea than other scommers and theeves of the sea, and pursue theyr enemyes full harde both by water and by londe, and ben called Saxones of Saxum, that is a stone, for they ben as harde as stones, and uneasy to fare with."—ED.

* Anglo-Saxon Chronicle, Bohn's Stand. Lib. Edit.

† That two-thirds of the conquerors—not of Great Britain—but of England, came from Denmark, if by Denmark our author meant the territories composing the Danish monarchy in his time, is unquestionable, for the Jutes came from Jutland, the Angles from the duchy of Sleswick, and the greater part of the Saxons from Holstein; but it does not by any means follow that

A particular event served to rekindle that spirit of rapine and conquest which had already been so fatal to this island. Harald Hárfagra having (as I said above) completed the con-

because these tribes came from districts that fell under the Danish sceptre at a later period, they were of Danish, that is to say, of Scandinavian origin. The fact is, ethnology as a science was too little known in the last century for a writer to make a proper distinction even between races, much less between the different branches of the same race. Having elsewhere discussed this subject[a], we will merely observe, that the Teutonic race has two main branches, the Scandinavian and the Germanic, the latter of which presents two distinct sub-branches, the Alemannic or Upper Germanic, and the Saxonic or Lower Germanic. Except by a few of our own writers, who, if we may judge by an article in a recent number of one of our most esteemed periodicals, seem still to cling pertinaciously to the crude notions of a bygone age on such subjects, it is no longer disputed that the Saxon invaders of England belonged to the Lower Germanic, and the Jutes to the Scandinavian branch of the great Teutonic family. But under which of these branches are we to class the Angles? Placed geographically between the two, they might have belonged either to the one or the other, and as no remnant of their language has been handed down to us, we are unable to decide the question by direct philological evidence. Professor Rask, however, very justly observes, in the Preface to his excellent Anglo-Saxon Grammar, that "it is reasonable to infer that the Angles were a Germanic and not a Scandinavian tribe, from the circumstance of their being so closely connected with the Saxons, that the whole of them accompanied the latter in their emigration, and this conjecture becomes almost a certainty from the fact, that the dialects of these invaders so soon coalesced into one common tongue, and assumed a character so decidedly Germanic, that, with the exception of a few Normanisms, introduced in later times, there is scarcely a vestige deserving of notice of the old Scandinavian structure to be found in Anglo-Saxon; so that in this respect even the old Saxon bears a closer resemblance to the Scandinavian tongue." We think the reasons thus adduced by one of the greatest philologists of the present age, are quite sufficient to warrant the conclusion, that the Angles were a Germanic tribe speaking a language very similar to Old Saxon and Frisic. They were also probably a more numerous body than the Saxons, for they finally acquired a greater extent of territory, and gave their name to the whole nation, though to the present day we are called by the Welsh and the Scotch Highlanders, in their respective idioms, not *Angles* or *Englishmen*, but *Saxons*. However, whether the Angles or the Saxons were the more numerous, it is certain that the Jutes formed but a mere fraction of the invaders, so that instead of "two-thirds of the conquerors" being of Scandinavian origin, as M. Mallet would seem to infer, we may safely assume that at least three-fourths of them were Germanic, the more so as it is highly probable that a considerable number of Frisians took an active part in the enterprize. It would, therefore, appear that the invaders of England belonged to three Germanic tribes, speaking respectively Anglic, Old Saxon, and Frisic, and to a Scandinavian tribe speaking Jutic ; and that Anglo-Saxon, which soon became the common lan-

---

[a] See the Remarks on Bishop Percy's Preface.

quest of Norway about the year 880, and being desirous of procuring that repose for such of his subjects as dwelt along the coasts, which they themselves would not grant to their neighbours, prohibited all pirates of Norway, under the severest penalties, from exercising any hostilities against their own country. But notwithstanding this prohibition, a Norwegian earl named Rolf or Rollo*, sprung, as it is said, from the ancient kings of Norway, made a descent on the province of Viken, nor retired thence till laden with a great booty of cattle. Harald, who was in the neighbourhood, was enraged at Rollo to the last degree, for thus daring to disobey him almost in his very presence, and instantly condemned him to perpetual banishment from Norway. In vain Hilda, the mother of this unfortunate youth, threw herself at the king's

guage of the conquerors, and which differs as much from Old Saxon as Italian does from Spanish, was formed by the rude mixture of their respective idioms, the Anglic and Old Saxonic elements being unquestionably the predominant.—ED.

* Rollo was the son of the Jarl Ragnvald mentioned in the note, page 177, and from his earliest youth a celebrated sea-rover. He was, however, of such a great bulk or stoutness of growth, that no horse could carry him, and hence was obliged in all his journeys to go on foot, from which circumstance he was called *Gaungo-Rolf*, i. e. Rolf the Walker, or Ganging Ralph. See Heimsk. iii. 24. We should imagine, however, that Rollo was not a very bulky, but an unusually tall man, and that he obtained his surname from his legs appearing to touch the ground when he was on horseback. When Rollo became Duke of Normandy and his descendants kings of England, genealogists had no difficulty in making out a suitable pedigree for him, tracing his ancestors, in the maternal line, up to Sigurd Ring, and in the paternal, to the Finnish family of the Fornjótr, which they supposed had been established from time immemorial in Norway. Several of our modern writers have given this genealogy as they found it in the works which furnished the materials for their respective compilations; but the reader may judge of its value, when we state that Sigurd Ring was a king of Denmark of the ante-historical or heroic period, and that the word Fornjótr means the oldest or primordial giant, and was used to designate a mythological personage, who had three sons called *Fire, Wind,* and *Ocean!!* These, it must be confessed, are very good progenitors, and what is more very appropriate ones, for the royal descendants of the Norman sea-rover have generally possessed a good portion of fire, and we all know that her present most gracious Majesty as fearlessly braves the wind as she gloriously rules the ocean. We are sorry to say, however, that modern criticism, instead of remounting to the elements, stops short at Rollo's grandfather. All that can be ascertained, in fact, with any degree of historical certainty, is that Jarl Ragnvald was the son of Eystein Glumru, one of the chiefs or petty kings of the Drontheim district.— ED.

feet, imploring pardon for her son, and chanting, according
to the custom of those times, these verses, which the chronicles have preserved to us: " Is the very name of our race
become hateful to you? You drive from his country one of
the greatest men it has ever produced, the honour of the Norwegian nobility. Ah! why will you provoke the wolf to devour the flocks who wander defenceless through the woods?
Fear, lest becoming outrageous, he should one day occasion
great misfortunes." The king remained inflexible, and Rollo,
perceiving that he was for ever cut off from all hopes of return
to his own country, retired with his fleet among the islands of
the Hebrides to the north-west of Scotland, whither the
flower of the Norwegian nobility had fled for refuge ever since
Harald had become master of the whole kingdom. He was
there received with open arms by those warriors, who, eager
for conquest and revenge, waited only for a chief to undertake
some glorious enterprize. Rollo setting himself at their head,
and seeing his power formidable, sailed towards England,
which had been long as it were a field open on all sides to the
violences of the northern nations. But the great Alfred had
some years before established such order in his part of the
island, that Rollo, after several fruitless attempts, despaired of
forming there such a settlement as should make him amends
for the loss of his own country. He pretended, therefore, to
have had a supernatural dream, which promised him a glorious
fortune in France, and which served at least to support the
ardour of his followers. The weakness of the government in
that kingdom, and the confusion in which it was involved,
were still more persuasive reasons to assure them of success
Having therefore sailed up the Seine to Rouen, he imme
diately took that capital of the province, then called Neustria,
and making it his magazine of arms, he advanced up to Paris,
to which he laid siege in form. The events of this war
properly belong to the history of France, and all the world
knows that it at length ended in the entire cession of Neustria, which Charles the Simple was obliged to give up to Rollo
and his Normans, in order to purchase a peace. Rollo received it in perpetuity to himself and his posterity, as a feudal
duchy dependent on the crown of France. This famous treaty,
by which Charles agreed to give his daughter Gisele in marriage
to Rollo, together with that part of Neustria since called

Normandy, upon condition that he would do homage for it, and would embrace the Christian religion, was concluded at Saint Clair, A.D. 912. A description of the interview between Charles and this new duke, gives us a curious picture of the manners of the Normans, for Rollo would not take the oath of fealty to his sovereign lord any other way than by placing his hands within those of the king, and absolutely refused to kiss his feet, as custom then required. It was with great difficulty he was prevailed on to let one of his warriors perform this ceremony in his stead; but the officer to whom Rollo deputed this service suddenly raised the king's foot so high that he overturned him on his back; a piece of rudeness which was only laughed at, to such a degree were the Normans feared and Charles despised *.

Soon after, Rollo was persuaded to embrace Christianity, and he was baptized with much ceremony by the Archbishop of Rouen in the cathedral of that city. As soon as he saw himself in full possession of Normandy, he exhibited such virtues as rendered the province happy, and deserved to make his former outrages forgotten. Religious, wise, and liberal, this captain of pirates became, after Alfred, the greatest and most humane prince of his time. Far from treating Normandy as a conquered province, his whole attention was employed to re-establish it. This country was, by the frequent devastations of the Scandinavians, rendered so desert and uncultivated, that Rollo could not at first reside in it; but Charles was obliged to yield up Brittany to him for awhile, till Normandy was in a condition to furnish subsistence to its new masters †. Nevertheless, the fertility of the soil seconding the industry of the people, it became, in a few years, one of the finest provinces of Europe. Thus it was that this prince, afterwards known under the name of Rollo or Raoul I., secured to his

* " Le roi enversa tut arière
    De ce fu ris à grant manière,"
says Robert Wace in his Roman de Rou.

† So say the old Norman chroniclers, but the French historians of the present day have shown this yielding up of Brittany to be a mere fiction. The territory ceded to Rollo in the year 912 was only that part of the ancient province of Neustria that corresponds to the present *Département de la Seine Inférieure*, and a portion of the *Département de l'Eure*, and this can scarcely be called a cession, for no mention is made of any legal document having been drawn up on the occasion. The plain story, when divested of romance, seems to be this: Rollo went to Saint Clair, and gave his hand to the king as a sign that he wished to live in peace with the Franks, provided

children this noble possession, which they, two hundred years afterwards, augmented by the conquest of England; as if it were destined that this island should at all times receive its sovereigns from among the northern nations*.   As to the French historians, they agree with the Icelandic chronicles, in describing Rolla as a man of uncommon wisdom and capacity; generous, eloquent, indefatigable, intrepid, of a noble figure and majestic size.   Many other Scandinavian princes and chieftains are drawn in the same colours.   Such were Harald

they would leave him in quiet possession of the territory he had conquered, and which he then held in virtue of the only right that a worshipper of Thor and Odin would be inclined to recognize, that of the sword; and Charles the Simple was no doubt too glad to accept these conditions; and although he may have stipulated for the observance of the usual ceremonies of investiture, it seems very unlikely that Rollo would even have deigned to listen to the proposal; at all events there is not the slightest evidence to show that he took the feudal oath of fealty.   It would also appear, that so far from the new duchy being "desert and uncultivated," it was probably as populous and flourishing a district as any other in Charles's dominions, for during the ten years preceding this so-called treaty, it had been so well governed as to afford, both to heathens and Christians, a much greater security for person and property than could be found in any of the adjacent territories, a circumstance which had induced a considerable number of Charles's subjects to settle in the country.   See Depping, liv. iii. c. 2.—Ed.

* The passion of the Normans for a wild adventurous life seems by no means to have abated after their conversion to Christianity.   As pagans they had been the most zealous sectaries of Thor, the god of battles, the combater of giants, monsters, demons, and every other typified evil principle. As Christians they became the enthusiastic devotees of Michael the archangel, whom they were taught to believe was equally as renowned in demoniacal warfare as the Scandinavian deity.   We therefore find them in the beginning of the eleventh century making pilgrimages to Mount Gargano in Apulia in honour of their new protector, and shortly afterwards taking an active part in the incessant warfare carried on by Lombards, Germans, Byzantines and Saracens, for the possession of Southern Italy.   In 1029 the Byzantines deemed it advisable to cede Aversa to one of their leaders, and ten years later three of the gallant sons of Tancred de Hauteville had made themselves masters of Apulia, and parcelled out the land among their followers as Rollo had done in Normandy, and William the Conqueror subsequently did in England.   These conquests were completed by the celebrated Robert Guiscard, the craftiest politician of his age, who drove the Saracens from Sicily, and transmitted to his brother Roger a dominion corresponding to the limits of the present kingdom of Naples.   The latter half of the eleventh century, in which these stirring events took place, forms a conspicuous epoch in history.   We find a William the Conqueror in England, a Henry IV. in Germany, a St. Ladislaus in Hungary, a Malek Schah in Persia, the Cid in Spain, Robert Guiscard in Italy, and a Hildebrand in the chair of St. Peter; and the century closes by Godfrey de Bouillon planting the chivalric banner of the crusaders on the walls of Jerusalem.—Ed.

Hárfagra, Olaf Tryggvason, Magnus, king of Norway, Canute the Great, &c., men born with truly heroic qualities, which they, alas! degraded by injustice and inhumanity; but who wanted only another age and another education to render them most accomplished persons.

It was not by this expedition alone, important as it might be, that the Norwegians were distinguished under the reign of Harald Hárfagra. The ambition of that prince gave birth to a conquest of a more peaceable kind, which though little known to the rest of the world, had yet very interesting consequences in the history of the north. For, not satisfied with having happily subdued the little tyrants who had for a long time weakened and distressed Norway, he was disposed to exercise such absolute authority over his subjects, as, far from submitting to, they had not even a name for it. The greatest part of the Norwegian nobility perceiving that it was in vain to oppose their strength to his, determined to abandon a country where they were obliged to live depressed, impoverished and obscure.

[It fortunately happened that at this period Iceland began to be known. The Landnámabók informs us that the first Northman who landed on the shores of that island was Naddod, a celebrated sea-rover, who being driven by a violent storm on the eastern coast about the year 860, entered one of the friths and ascended a high mountain that commanded an extensive prospect, but discovering no traces of the country being inhabited, set sail again, after giving it the name of *Snæland*, Snowland. Four years afterwards Gardar Svafarson, a Swede, was also driven by a storm to Iceland, which by circumnavigating he ascertained to be an island, and called it *Gardarhólm*, Gardar's Isle. The favourable account Gardar gave of it on his return having excited the spirit of adventure among the Northmen, Floki, another famous sea-rover, went out with the intention of settling there, but all the cattle he had taken with him having perished during the winter, and the spring being unusually cold, and the bays and friths covered with ice, he returned in the summer to Norway, and bestowed the name of *Island*, Iceland, on the island in which he had passed such a gloomy season, and which he declared was uninhabitable either for man or beast. We are told that Floki, previous to setting out on his expedition, performed a great sacrifice, and having consecrated three ravens to the gods, took them with him to guide him on his voyage. After touching at the Shetland and Færoe islands, he steered N.W., and when he was fairly out at sea, let loose one of his ravens, which after rising to a considerable elevation, directed its flight to the land they had quitted, whence Floki very sagely concluded that it was nearer to him than any other. Onward, therefore, went Floki. The second bird, after being some time on the wing, returned to the ship, a sign that land was too far distant to be descried even by a raven hovering in the sky. Floki therefore continued his course, and shortly afterwards let loose his third raven, which he followed in its flight until he reached the eastern coast of Iceland*.

In the year 870 Ingolf, a Norwegian chieftain, wintered in Iceland, and was so pleased with the appearance of the country, that on his return to Norway, he being discontented like the other chieftains with Harald's proceedings, began to make preparations for emigrating there.]

It is, indeed, said, that the apprehension of being punished for a murder he had committed, was, equally with the tyranny of Harald, a motive for his flight; but this latter inducement was certainly what engaged a multitude of noble families of Norway to join him†. These illustrious fugitives being embarked, Ingolf, whom they had chosen for their leader, conducted them, in the year 874, to Iceland. As soon as they discovered it at a distance, Ingolf, according to an ancient and superstitious custom, threw a wooden door‡ into the sea, determining to land where the gods should seem to point out, by the direction of this floating guide; but the waves carrying it out of sight, after a fruitless search, they were obliged to disembark in a gulf toward the south part of the island, which still bears Ingolf's name. Hjörleif, his brother-in-law, settled in another part. They both found the island uninhabited and

* Floki was probably not the only sea-rover who, in those days, made ravens serve him for a compass. There may have been a particular brood of these birds trained and consecrated by religious rites for the purpose, which would account for the custom falling into disuse on the introduction of Christianity; the more so as the raven was the bird of Odin, the Raven-god—*Hrafnagud*, as he is called in Skaldic poesy.

† Arngrim. Jon. Crymogæa, sive de reb. Island. lib. iii. Hamb. 1593.

‡ It was not a wooden door that Ingolf threw into the sea, but the sacred columns of his temple—the öndvegissulur.—ED.

SCANDINAVIAN MARITIME EXPEDITIONS. 189

uncultivated, but covered with thick forests of birch trees, through which they could not penetrate but by cutting their way before them. There are now no forests in Iceland, nor any birch trees, except here and there a few short and slender shrubs: but the trees that are still found deep buried in the earth, and frequently among the rocks, should prevent our too hastily rejecting the evidence of the ancient chronicles, when they describe the country as different from what it is at present* Torfæus remarks the same thing. " Should any one object (says he) that modern Iceland does not answer the ancient descriptions of it, it may be justly answered, that this country has greatly degenerated. This I can affirm, from what I have been an eye-witness of myself: I have seen in my youth great alterations in the face of this country; shores swallowed, and others thrown up by the violence of the waves; meadows formerly fruitful now buried under vast heaps of sand; plains all covered and valleys filled up with stones and sand brought down by the torrents of melted snow."†. The Norwegian adventurers imagined that this island had been formerly inhabited, or at least that people had landed on the shore, as Ingolf found there wooden crosses, and other little pieces of workmanship, after the manner of the Irish and Britons. These people had embraced Christianity before that time, and very possibly some of their fishermen, thrown upon the coasts, might have left a few of their effects behind them‡.

---

* Vid. Arngrim. Jon. Crymogæa, lib. i. c. 2, p. 21.
† Vide Torfæi, Hist. Norveg. tom. i. c. 5, p. 12.
‡ The Landnámabók and other ancient Icelandic documents merely state that " before Iceland was settled by the Northmen, there were men there called by the Northmen Papæ. These men were Christians and are thought to have come from the west, for there were found Irish books and bells and various other things, whence it is thought that they were Westmen," and that these things were found in Papey, a small island, *the isle of the Papæ,* on the eastern coast which still bears the same name, and at Papylio in the interior, and that " the Christians left the country when the Northmen settled there." These people were probably fishermen from the north of Ireland and the Western Isles of Scotland, and may have annually frequented the northern seas and made Papey one of their winter stations; for Dicuil, an Irish monk of the ninth century, expressly states in his geographical treatise de mensura orbis terræ, that Iceland and the Færoe Isles had been discovered by his countrymen.—ED.

The success of Ingolf's expedition being much talked of in
Norway, other families were eager to fly to this place of refuge
from the ambitious encroachments of their king.   The Icelandic annals are very exact in relating the names of these
adventurers, the several numbers of which they consisted,
together with the names of the places where they settled,
which, for the most part, are still retained.   All the other
circumstances of these voyages are handed down with equal
precision, and we may confidently assert, that the ancient history of Iceland is more complete than that of any other
country in Europe.   The several particulars and the sequel of
the event are foreign to this work; we need only observe, that
this Icelandic colony carried with them a violent hatred for
arbitrary power, and bravely preserved their liberty and independence against every attempt to deprive them of those
blessings.   This was endeavoured by several Norwegian princes
in vain; so that it was full four hundred years before this republic became subject to Norway, along with which it was
afterwards united to the crown of Denmark.

The Scandinavians, now masters of the northern ocean, and
flushed with success, became possessed, at different times, of
all the islands in those seas.   Thus, while the Danes were reducing England, the Norwegians conquered a considerable
part of Scotland, together with the Orkneys, the Hebrides,
and the Shetland Isles.   Towards the end of the eleventh
century, Magnus Barefoot, the son of Olaf, one of their
princes, filled that part of the world with the renown of his
arms.   Ordericus Vitalis, whose acknowledged veracity in the
histories of France and England may serve to establish that
of our old Icelandic chronicles, with which he perfectly agrees,
relates, that " in the fifth year of the reign of William Rufus,
king of England, Magnus, king of Norway, visited the Orkneys, and made a tour through part of Scotland, and all the
islands in those seas that belonged to him, as far as Anglesey.
He settled colonies in the Isle of Man, which was then a
desert, commanded them to build houses, and took care they
should be provided with necessaries of every kind.   He afterwards made a progress through several other islands in the
great ocean, which are, in a manner, beyond the limits of the
world; and, exerting his royal authority, obliged several

people to go and inhabit them. With the same earnestness did this prince apply himself for many years to increase his subjects and enlarge his empire."*

[In the year 1266 King Magnus Lagabätter sold the Hebrides and the Isle of Man to Alexander III. of Scotland for 4000 marks sterling, but the Norwegian sovereignty over the Orkney and Shetland islands continued until the year 1468, when it was mortgaged to James III., by Christian I., king of Norway, Denmark and Sweden, for 50,000 Rhenish florins, this sum being part of the dowry he had stipulated to give his daughter Margaret on her marriage with the Scottish monarch. In 1549 an assessment was levied in Norway to redeem the mortgaged sovereignty, and after that period several Danish kings asserted their right to redeem it; but it is needless to observe that the Scotch were unwilling to listen to any proposals that tended to deprive them of these important dependencies. The islands continued to be governed by the laws and customs of Norway, and their inhabitants to speak the Norse language, until the seventeenth century; and the substitution of the Scotch weights and measures for the Norwegian, together with the augmentation of the public burdens, formed a subject of complaint down to a much later period.

The Scandinavian sea-rovers began very early to ravage the coast of Ireland. In the annals of Ulster they are termed Lochlanach, and the country they came from Lochlin, and we find them in the ninth century in possession of Dublin, Limerick and Waterford, and other towns of minor importance, which became the capitals of petty maritime states, governed by the laws and customs of Norway.

The eastern coasts of the Baltic were as much infested by Swedish, as those of the British Isles and France were by Danish and Norwegian marauders. In the ninth century, Oskold, the leader of one of these piratical bands, established himself at Kiew, on the Dneiper, and Rurik, the

* The expedition alluded to by Odericus Vitalis took place in 1096, and it was after fighting a battle with two earls of Norman descent, who had established themselves in Anglesey, that Magnus gained possession of that island. In 1102 Magnus, in conjunction with a king of Connaught, overran Leinster and Ulster, but as he was preparing to embark on St. Bartholomew's Day in the following year, to return to Norway, was treacherously attacked by his Irish allies, and lost his life in the conflict.—See Heimsk. xi. 27.—ED.

leader of another band, took possession of Novgorod, and became the founder of the Russian empire, and the ancestor of
a long line of princes, Feodor I., the last czar of his dynasty, dying in 1598 *. When the Scandinavians had obtained
a footing in Russia, they began to infest the shores of the
Black Sea, and in the year 866 appeared before Constantinople, which was, however, too strongly fortified for them to
think of attacking with any chance of success, though their
retreat was ascribed by the Byzantines to the sacred homo-
phorion, or *chemise* of the Virgin, which the priests carried in
solemn procession and dipped in the sea†. This, however,
did not prevent the pagans from returning, and although the
Byzantines were protected not only by the Virgin's chemise,
but also by their celebrated Greek fire, the hardy sea-rovers
seldom failed in extracting considerable sums from the degenerate emperors. An obscure account of one of their expeditions to the Caspian Sea, during the reign of Rurik's son

* Rurik and his followers are said to have come from a district in Sweden
called Roslagen, Rodeslagen, Roden, whence, according to the supposition of
several eminent northern writers, they were called by the Slavonic tribes
they subdued *Russians*, a name which was afterwards applied to the inhabitants of the country, who had previously been called *Slavonians*. Be this
as it may, for we have no great confidence in such etymological disquisitions,
it is certain that Constantine Porphyrogenitus designated by these names
(ῥωσιστι and σκλαβινιστι), the two races and languages in the middle of the
tenth century, and it would appear that to this day the Finns have continued
to call the Swedes *Ruotsolaiset*. See Geijer's Ges. Schw. i. 36, and a note
to the Preface of Rask s Icelandic Grammar.

† The Virgin's chemises appear to have been regarded in those ages as
the most efficacious arm that could be employed against the worshippers of
Odin. The inhabitants of Chartres, for instance, ascribed the somewhat dubious victory which they gained over Rollo, in the year 911, to the wonder-
working properties of one of these chemises, which had long been the chief
object of veneration in their cathedral, and which they had borne before
them, suspended on a lance like a banner, when they sallied forth, with their
bishop, to attack the Northmen : —

> " Quant Rou si grant gent vei, si s'en est esbahi,
> De la procession ki de Chartres issi,
> Des relikes k'ils portent, è des cants k'il oï.
> De la Sainte Kemise ke la Dame vesti,
> Ki mere è virge fu quant de lié Dex naski,
> Ont Rou si grant poor, è tant s'en esbahi,
> N'i osa arester, verz sis nés tost s'enfui ;"

says old Wace in his Roman de Rou. See Depping, lib. iii. c. 3.

Igor (Ingvar) *, has also been transmitted to us   In this expedition they carried their light barks from one river to another—from the Don to the Volga—as was frequently done by the Normans and Danes in France and England.

The Scandinavian sea-rovers in the Baltic were known under the name of *Varæger*, which corresponds to the *Væringjar* of the Icelandic Sagas and the *Varangi* (Βαραγγοι) of the Byzantine writers. In the year 902 the Emperor Alexis took seven hundred of these Varæger from Kiew in his pay, and from that period down to the fall of Constantinople the Byzantine emperors committed the care of their persons to a body-guard chiefly, if not wholly, composed of Scandinavian adventurers, at first of Russian Varæger, and, at a later period, of Danes, Norwegians and Icelanders. The Codex Flatoyensis gives the number of men in this guard, in the eleventh century, at three hundred, and distinguishes it from another corps of Franks and Flemings, also in the imperial service †. This celebrated Varangian body-guard, to use the words of Gibbon, "with their broad and double-edged battle-axes on their shoulders, attended the Greek emperor to the temple, the senate, and the hippodrome; he slept and feasted under their trusty guard; and the keys of the palace, the treasury, and the capital, were held by the firm and faithful hands of the Varangians." ‡ Our great historian might have added that

* The widow of this Czar, Olga, who was distinguished for what we are sorry to say appear to have been the two principal traits of the old Scandinavian character—craft and cruelty—was baptized at Constantinople in 957, and introduced Christianity into Russia, which about thirty years later was firmly established by Vladimir, surnamed, like Canute, and with equal propriety, the Great. Vladimir, on his marriage with the Byzantine princess, Anna, caused the image of Perun—the Slavonic god of thunder—to be tied to a horse's tail, and after being dragged through the town to be thrown into the Dnieper. Shortly afterward, when another image of the same deity was thrown into the Volga at Novgorod, we are told—every superstition has had its speaking images—that it began to complain bitterly of the ingratitude of the people it had so long protected. See Grimm. Deut. Mythol. 733.

† Cod. Flat. col. 507, quoted by Müller in his Sagabib. ii. 149.

‡ Gibbon. Dec. and Fall, ch. 55. When Gibbon further says that the Varangians "preserved till the last age of the empire the inheritance of spotless loyalty, and the use of the Danish *or* English language," he can only mean the Old Norse *and* Anglo-Saxon, two distinct languages, which the writers of the last century were too apt to confound. (See note, page 181). And we presume that "the inheritance of spotless loyalty" is merely one of those

these adventurers also plundered the palaces as well as guarded them, for it would appear that at the death of an emperor the Varangians were allowed to go through all the imperial palaces and take whatever they could lay their hands on.   It was thus that the celebrated Harald Hardráda, who commanded the Varangians in the time of the Empress Zoe, was fortunate enough to be at Constantinople at the deaths of three of the nominal emperors whom that ambitious woman had placed on the throne ; and what with the plunder of the palaces and the booty he acquired in his campaign against the Saracens, he amassed a treasure that enabled him to marry the daughter of the Russian czar, and gain possession of the throne of Norway *.]

CHAPTER X.

OF THE CUSTOMS AND MANNERS OF THE ANCIENT NORTHERN NATIONS †.

WHOEVER attempts to delineate the manners of the ancient inhabitants of the north, will find their love of war and passion for arms amongst the most characteristic and express-sive lines of the portrait.   Their prejudices, their customs,

stereotype phrases which historians frequently make use of to give due weight to a sentence.

* Snorri tells us some strange stories respecting the adventurous life Harald led when he was in the service of the Byzantine emperors, which, although they cannot be regarded as historical facts, have at least furnished Œhlenschläger with excellent materials for his tragedy entitled " The Varangians in Con-stantinople ;" Væringerne i Miklagord."   See Heimsk. ix. 1—17.   Harald, as is well known, lost his life in the battle of Stamford Bridge, but it has not, we think, been sufficiently remarked that his alliance with Tostig, by draw-ing off the forces of our last Anglo-Saxon monarch to the north, greatly facili-tated the Norman conquest.

† We have omitted a chapter in which Mr. Mallet gave an account of the discovery of Greenland and America by the Scandinavians, the sources which were available when his work was published (in the year 1755) being too meagre and defective to furnish him with correct information on the sub-ject.   The reader will find an account of this discovery, taken from the most recent and authentic works that have been published relating to it, in our first supplementary chapter.—ED.

their daily occupations, their amusements, in short, every action of their lives, were all impressed with this passion. They passed the greatest part of their time either in camps or on board their fleets, employed in real engagements, in preparations for them, or in sham fights; for whenever they were constrained to live in peace, the resemblance of war furnished out their highest entertainment. They then had reviews, mock battles, which frequently ended in real ones, tournaments, the bodily exercises of wrestling, boxing, racing, &c. The rest of their time was commonly spent in hunting, public business, drinking and sleeping. "The Germans," says Tacitus, "when not engaged in war, pass their time in indolence, feasting and sleep. The bravest and most warlike among them do nothing themselves; but transfer the whole care of the house, family and possessions to the females, the old men and such as are infirm among them: and the same people, by a strange contradiction of nature, both love inaction and hate peace." All the Celtic nations lie under the same reproach from the Greek and Roman authors; and it is easy to conceive, that a people who affixed ideas of contempt to all labour of body and mind, had for the most part nothing else to do but to carouse and sleep, whenever the state did not call them to arms. This was the badge and noblest privilege of their liberty; every free man placed his glory and happiness in being often invited to solemn entertainments; and the hopes of partaking of eternal feasts filled, as we have seen, the north with heroes. Other pleasures and other rewards have been conceived under the influence of other climes: all nations have in their infancy been governed by the force of climate; and their first legislators, far from endeavouring to stem this torrent, but borne away with it themselves, have ever by their laws and institutions enlarged and increased its natural prevalence. We find remarkable instances in the Icelandic Sagas of frequent and excessive feastings. Tacitus observes, that the plentiful tables of the chiefs, were, among the Germans, the wages of their dependents. Nor could a great lord or chieftain take a readier way to attract a numerous train of followers, than by often making magnificent entertainments. It was at table that the Germans consulted together on their most important concerns, such as the electing of their princes,

the entering into war, or the concluding of peace, &c. On
the morrow they re-considered the resolutions of the preceding
night, supposing, adds the same historian, "that the proper
time to take each other's opinions was when the soul was too
open for disguise; and to determine, when it was too cautious
to err."* The common liquors at these carousals were either
beer, mead, or wine, when they could get it: these they drank
out of earthen or wooden pitchers, or else out of the horns of
wild bulls, with which their forests abounded. The principal
person at the table took the cup first, and rising up, saluted
by name either him who sat next him, or him who was nearest in rank; then he drank it off, and causing it to be filled
up again to the brim, presented it to the man whom he had
saluted †. Hence came the custom of drinking to the health
of the guests: but I know not whether that of drinking to
the honour of the gods was generally practised among all the
Teutonic people, or only among the Scandinavians. Snorri
Sturlason says, "that in the solemn festivals, such as usually
followed the sacrifices, they emptied what was called the cup
of Odin, to obtain victory and a glorious reign; then the cups
of Njörd and of Frey, for a plentiful season; after which
several used to take off another to Bragi, the God of Eloquence
and Poetry." The Scandinavians were so much addicted to
this custom, that the first missionaries, unable to abolish it,
were forced instead of these false deities to substitute the
true God, Jesus Christ, and the saints; to whose honour they
devoutly drank for many ages. In the pagan times, they
also drank to the heroes, and to such of their friends as had
fallen bravely in battle. Lastly, it was at these feasts, for the
most part, that those associations were formed and confirmed
which the old chronicles so often mention. There was
scarcely a valiant man who was not a member of one or more
of these societies; the chief tie of which was a solemn obligation entered into, to defend and protect their companions on
all occasions, and to revenge their deaths at the hazard of

* Tac. de mor. Germ. c. 14.
† This ancient ceremony is still kept up, at solemn feasts, in some of the
Colleges in our Universities.—In like manner our custom of drinking to
the memory of departed persons, is evidently a relic of the ancient superstition of drinking to the manes of their heroes, kings and friends.—P.

their own lives *. This oath was taken and renewed at their festivals, which had also their respective laws. Fraternities of this sort still subsisted after the Christian religion was received in the north, but by degrees the object was changed. When the harbouring projects of enmity and revenge were forbidden at them, these meetings had no other object or support but drunkenness and intemperance †. More than two

---

* In the early state of society, when the laws were too weak to afford protection, individuals had no other means of securing their lives and property, but by entering into these associations, in which a number of men engaged to vindicate and avenge each other. These confederacies, which were at first necessary for self-preservation, and might originally be confined to self-defence, often proceeded afterwards to act offensively, and so were productive of great mischiefs.

Confraternities of the same kind prevailed in this kingdom, not only during the Anglo-Saxon times, but for some ages after the conquest. They were called Bandships, and were often under the patronage of some great man; they had public badges by which each band or confederacy was distinguished, and at length grew to such a pass as to support each other in all quarrels, robberies, murders and other outrages : this occasioned a particular act of parliament for their suppression, 1 Rich. II. ch. 7.—Dr. Hickes has preserved a very curious bond of this kind, which he calls *Sodalitium ;* it was drawn up in the Anglo-Saxon times, and contains many particulars which strongly mark the manners and character of those rude ages. See his *Dissertatio Epistolaris,* p. 21.—P.

† Were it not foreign to our subject, a chapter might be written to show the influence which Guilds had in working out the municipal franchises of the middle ages. We cannot however refrain from remarking, that before the introduction of Christianity the Scandinavians used to meet in select parties for the purpose of feasting and drinking—used in fact to have regular *drinking-bouts,* at which he who drank the deepest, or emptied the largest horn at a single draught, was regarded as the hero of the festival. They were too fond of guzzling their ale and mead, to abandon this custom when they became Christians ; but as drinking gave rise to quarrels which generally ended in bloodshed, these private meetings were, through the influence of the clergy, gradually changed into public confraternities or *Guilds,* the members of which, or Guild-brethren as they were called, pledged themselves to keep the peace and to check intemperance. The Guilds established by the Norwegian king Olaf, the Quiet, in the latter half of the eleventh century, appear to have been of this description—convivial clubs in fact, whose members were pledged to keep good order and behave like gentlemen ; and as such a club or guild was placed under the patronage of a saint, some worthy bishop or other high dignitary of the Church could preside at the social board and empty his cup—for cups were in this century substituted for drinking horns—in honour of the sainted patron, without in any way infringing the decorum of his sacred office. In the latter half of the twelfth century we find these convivial guilds had become powerful and influential corporate bodies, and that the guild-

hundred years after the Scandinavians had embraced Christianity there were still confraternities of which the first nobility
were members.   But the disorders committed at these meetings increasing, the Councils were at last obliged to suppress
them *.

While the attention of these people was thus engrossed by
their passion for arms and the pleasures of the table, we may
conclude that love held no violent dominion over them.   It
is besides well known that the inhabitants of the north are
not of very quick sensibility.   The ideas and modes of thinking of the Scandinavians were in this respect very different
from those of the Asiatics and more southern nations; who
by a contrast as remarkable as it is common, have ever felt
for the female sex the warm passion of love, devoid of any
real esteem.   Being at the same time tyrants and slaves;
laying aside their own reason, and requiring none in the ob-

brethren were pledged to afford each other mutual aid and protection, especially
in judicial affairs.   And although conviviality frequently outstepped the
bounds of reason and good order, the statutes of these protective associations
show that the members devoted their attention to the amelioration of the
laws for the security of person and property.

It would lead us too far to follow the changes which gradually took place in
these protective guilds until they became trades-guilds or companies.   Neither
will it be necessary for us to inform the guild-brethren of the city of London that their worshipful companies are the lineal descendants of the old
Scandinavian *drinking-bouts*, for they seldom fail to show the public that
this is a fact which they are perfectly aware of.

The word Guild—Ang. Sax. Gylda ; Dan. and Germ. Gilde ; Swed. Gilde,
Gille ; is probably derived from the Old Norse verb gjalda, to pay, to contribute to.—Ed.

* The reader will find many curious particulars relating to the above-
mentioned confraternities (or Gilds, as they called them in the north) in
Bartholin, who has given some of the laws or statutes observed by them,
particularly those found in a MS. of the thirteenth century.—One of these
statutes will give us an idea of the sobriety of those times : *Si quis pro ebrietate
ceciderit in ipsa domo convivii, vel antequam propriam curiam intraverit,
Oram* (a small piece of money) *persolvat.*   Not less remarkable are the
statutes of another confraternity instituted in honour of S. Olave, king of
Norway ; among which we find these : *Quicunque potum suum effundit latius
quam pede velare poterit,* VI *Denarios persolvat.   Quicunque dormierit in
banco convivii in conspectu fratrum, Oram persolvat.   Quicunque ebrietatis
causâ in domo convivii vomitum fecerit, Dimidiam Marcam persolvat, &c*
(Barthol. caus. contempt. mort. &c., p. 133.)

Our modern clubs are evidently the offspring of the ancient gilds or
guilds of our northern ancestors.—P.

ject, they have ever made a quick transition from adoration to contempt, and from sentiments of the most extravagant and violent love, to those of the most cruel jealousy, or of an indifference still more insulting. We find the reverse of all this among the northern nations, who did not so much consider the other sex as made for their pleasure, as to be their equals and companions, whose esteem, as valuable as their other favours, could only be obtained by constant attentions, by generous services, and by a proper exertion of virtue and courage. I conceive that this will at first sight be deemed a paradox, and that it will not be an easy matter to reconcile a manner of thinking which supposes so much delicacy, with the rough, unpolished character of this people. Yet I believe the observation is so well grounded that one may venture to assert that it is this same people who have contributed to diffuse through all Europe that spirit of equity, of moderation, and generosity shown by the stronger to the weaker sex, which is at this day the distinguishing characteristic of European manners; nay, that we even owe to them that spirit of gallantry which was so little known to the Greeks and Romans, how polite soever in other respects.

That there should in the north be a communication of liberty and equality between the two sexes, is what one might expect to find there in those ancient times, when men's property was small and almost upon an equality; when their manners were simple; when their passions disclosed themselves but slowly, and then under the dominion of reason; being moderated by a rigorous climate and their hard way of living; and, lastly, when the sole aim of government was to preserve and extend liberty. But the Scandinavians went still farther; and these same men, who on other occasions were too high-spirited to yield to any earthly power, yet in whatever related to the fair sex seem to have been no longer tenacious of their rights or independence. I have often asserted that the immediate intervention of the Deity, even in the slightest things, was one of their most established doctrines, and that every, even the most minute, appearance of nature was a manifestation of the will of Heaven to those who understood its language. Thus men's involuntary motions, their dreams, their sudden and unforeseen inclinations, being considered as the salutary admonitions of Heaven, became the objects of serious attention; and a universal respect could not but be paid to those who were considered as the organs or instruments of a beneficent Deity. Now women must appear much more proper than men for so noble a purpose, who being commonly more subject than we to the unknown laws of temperament and constitution, seem less to be governed by reflection, than by sensation and natural instinct. Hence it was that the Germans admitted them into their councils, and consulted with them on the business of the state. Hence it was that among them, as also among the Gauls, there were ten prophetesses for one prophet; whereas in the East we find the contrary proportion, if, indeed, there was ever known an instance in those countries of a female worker of miracles. Hence also it was, that nothing was formerly more common in the north than to meet with women who delivered oracular informations, cured the most inveterate maladies, assumed whatever shape they pleased, raised storms, chained up the winds, travelled through the air, and, in one word, performed every function of the fairy art. Thus endowed with supernatural powers, these prophetesses being converted as it were into fairies or demons, influenced the events they had predicted, and all nature became subject to their command. Tacitus puts this beyond a dispute when he says, " The Germans suppose some divine and prophetic quality resident in their women, and are careful neither to disregard their admonitions, nor to neglect their answers." * Nor can it be doubted but that the same notions prevailed among the Scandinavians. Strabo relates that the Cimbri were accompanied by venerable and hoary-headed prophetesses, apparelled in long linen robes most splendidly white. We also find this people always attended by their wives even in their most distant expeditions, hearing them with respect, and after a defeat, more afraid of their reproaches than the blows of the enemy. To this we may add, that the men being constantly employed either in war or hunting, left to the women the care of acquiring those useful branches of knowledge which made them regarded by their husbands as prophetesses and oracles. Thus to them belonged the study of simples and the art of healing wounds, an art as mysterious in those times, as the occasions of it

* Tacit. de Mor. Ger. c. 8.

were frequent. In the ancient chronicles of the north, we find the matrons and the young women always employed in dressing the wounds of their husbands or lovers. It was the same with dreams; which the women alone were versed in the art of interpreting; probably because they paid more attention to them than the men, and gave more credit to them.

But this is not all. At a time when piracy and a fondness for seeking adventures exposed weakness to continual and unexpected attacks, the women, especially those of celebrated beauty, stood in want sometimes of deliverers, and almost always of defenders. Every young warrior, eager after glory (and this was often the character of whole nations), must have been glad then to take upon him an office which promised such just returns of fame, which flattered the most agreeable of all passions, and at the same time gratified another almost as strong, that for a wandering and rambling life. We are apt to value what we acquire, in proportion to the labour and trouble it costs us. Accordingly the hero looked upon himself as sufficiently rewarded for all his pains, if he could at length obtain the fair hand of her he had delivered; and it is obvious how honourable such marriages must have been among the people who thought in this manner. This emulation would quickly increase the number of those gallant knights; and the women, on their parts, would not fail to acquire a kind of stateliness, considering themselves as no less necessary to the glory of their lovers, than to their happiness and pleasure. That fair one who had stood in need of several champions, yielded only to the most courageous; and she who had never been in a situation that required protectors, was still desirous of the lover who had proved himself capable of encountering all kind of dangers for her sake. This was more than enough to inflame such spirits as these with an emulation of surpassing each other, and of displaying their courage and intrepidity. Besides, the character of the northern women themselves left the men no other less glorious means of gaining their hearts. Naturally chaste and proud, there was no other way but this to come at them. Educated under the influence of the same prejudices concerning honour as the men, they were early taught to despise those who spent their youth in a peaceful obscurity. All the historical records of ancient Scandinavia prove what I advance. We see there the

turn for chivalry as it were in the bud.   The history of other
nations shows it afterwards as it were opening and expanding
in Spain, France, Italy, and England, being carried there by
the swarms that issued from the North.   It is in reality this
same spirit, reduced afterwards within juster bounds, that has
been productive of that polite gallantry so peculiarly observable in our manners, which adds a double relish to the most
pleasing of all social bands, which unites the lasting charms
of· sentiment, regard, and friendship·with the fleeting fire of
love, which tempers and animates one by the other, adds to
their number, power, and duration, and which cherishes and
unfolds sensibility, that most choice gift of nature, without
which neither decorum, propriety, chaste friendship nor true
generosity, can exist among men.   It would be needless to
prove, that we are not indebted for this manner of thinking
to the ancient Romans.   We may appeal for this to all who
know any thing of their character, and safely conclude that
the respect we show to the fair sex is derived from that superstitious reverence which our ancestors had for them, and
is only a relic of that ancient authority, which the women enjoyed among the northern nations.

As few young men of any rank were able to obtain an
advantageous or honourable alliance until they had distinguished themselves in war, we may naturally conclude they
could not marry till late in life.   This is also confirmed by
other proofs.   Cæsar says, that "among the Germans, the
greatest praise is allowed to those who remain the longest unmarried; and that it is reckoned very shameful for young men
to be acquainted with women before they are twenty years of
age."*   Tacitus adds, that "the Germans retain the vigour
of youth the longer, by deferring their union with the other
sex; nor are they in haste to have their daughters married." †
That age once past, it was common for the people of the north
to marry two wives or more, and this was a very ancient custom ‡.   Men of wealth and power considered a number of

---

* Cæs. de Bell. Gall. lib. vi. 19.
† Tacit. Germ. c. 20.
‡ In Scandinavia monogamy was the rule, polygamy the exception.   In
Iceland a man had frequently a concubine, but never more than one legiti-
mate wife.   Priests in Iceland were not prohibited from marrying before the

wives as a mark of grandeur. And according to Tacitus *, political reasons also sometimes brought about these matches, since the great were often obliged to yield to the importunity of families which sought their alliance. The Christian religion, not without great difficulty, got the better of this custom; which still prevailed in the north so late as the tenth century. Nevertheless, one of the wives seems to have possessed a superior rank, and to have been considered as the chief and most legitimate.

The matrimonial ceremonies were very simple, and chiefly consisted in feasting. The bridegroom having obtained the maiden's consent, together with that of her parents and guardians, appointed the day; and having assembled his own relations and friends, sent some of them to receive in his name the bride and her portion from her father. The friends were answerable for the charge that was committed to them, and if they abused their trust, the law amerced them in a sum treble to what was paid for murder. The father or guardian of the young woman attended her also to the husband's house, and there gave her into his hands. After this the new married pair sat down to table with their guests, who drank to their healths along with those of the gods and heroes. The bride's friends then took her up and bore her on their shoulders, which was a mark of esteem among the Goths; her father afterwards led her to the nuptial bed, a great number of lights being carried before her; a custom known to the Greeks and Romans, and still in use in some parts of the North The marriage being consummated, the husband made his wife several presents, such as a pair of oxen for the plough, an harnessed horse, a buckler, together with a lance and a sword. "This was to signify," says Tacitus †, "that she ought not to lead an idle and luxurious life, but that she was to be a partaker with him in his labours, and a companion in dangers, which they were to share together in peace and war." He adds that "the women, on their parts gave some arms;

year 1178, and then the prohibition does not appear to have had much effect, for we read of married priests exercising their sacerdotal functions at a still later period.—ED.

* He says, the Germans in his time were for the most part content with one wife, *Exceptis admodum paucis*, adds he, *qui non libidine, sed ob nobilitatem plurimis nuptiis ambiuntur.* De mor. Ger. c. 18.—P.

† Tac. de mor. Germ. c. 18.

this was the sacred band of their union, these their mystic rites, and these the deities who presided over their marriage." The yoked oxen, the caparisoned horse, and the arms, all served to instruct the women how they were to lead their life, and how perhaps it might be terminated. The arms were to be carefully preserved, and being ennobled by the use the husband made of them, were to be consigned as portions for their daughters, and to be handed down to posterity.

The German women have been justly noted for fidelity to the marriage-bed; and indeed chastity seems to have been the general character of this nation *. Let us see what that most excellent writer Tacitus says on this subject: " A strict regard for the sanctity of the matrimonial state characterizes the Germans, and deserves our highest applause. . . . . Among them female virtue runs no hazard of being debauched by the outward objects which are presented to the senses, or of being corrupted by such social gaieties as inflame the passions. The art of corresponding by letters is equally unknown to both sexes. Very few adulteries happen in that populous nation: where the power of instantly inflicting punishment is granted to the injured husband; who, after having cut off her hair in the presence of her relations, drives her naked out of his house, and whips her through the village. Chastity once prostituted is never forgiven; nor to such a one can the attractions of beauty, youth or riches procure a husband. Vice is not there made the object of wit and mirth; nor can the fashion of the age be pleaded in excuse either for being corrupt, or for en-

---

* M. Mallet has fallen into his usual error of placing implicit reliance on the statements of Tacitus. It will, we presume, be scarcely necessary at the present day to remark that the Latin historian exaggerated the few virtues common to most barbarous nations, in order to form a greater contrast with the corruption that prevailed amongst his own countrymen. The passage quoted by our author, for instance, would be far more truthful if applied *negatively* to the Romans, than *affirmatively* to the Germans.

If Tacitus, in describing the manners of his countrymen had said, " Among them female virtue runs a great hazard of being debauched. Vice is there made the object of wit and mirth," &c., &c., his observations would have been entitled to much greater consideration. Nothing, however, can be more natural than that female chastity should be more prevalent in a northern than in a southern climate; and when this is not the case, we may safely conclude that the laws and institutions are either remarkably vicious and defective in the former, or in the latter of surpassing excellence.—ED.

deavouring to corrupt others. . . . . Good customs and manners avail more among these barbarians, than good laws among
a more refined people."*

Our own historical monuments confirm these testimonies.
I have before observed, that their religion threatened the
seducers of women with the severest torments of the next
world. Adam of Bremen, in his Voyage to Denmark, observes,
that adultery was there most strictly punished; and that the
woman who was detected in it was sold on the spot. The
law in Iceland was equally remarkable; for it not only denounced very severe punishments against rapes and adulteries, but proceeded farther; expressly prohibiting even
kissing or secret embraces †. If a man abused a free woman
he was punished with exile; if a slave, he was amerced three
marks. Among the Swedes and Danes, the husband who
caught his wife in the act of adultery, might immediately
kill her, and render her lover incapable of again infringing
the laws of conjugal morality.

When the people of the north migrated into the southern
parts of Europe, they carried along with their laws a chastity
and reserve which excited universal surprise. Salvian, a
priest of Marseilles in the fifth century, exclaims, " Let us
blush," says he, " and be covered with a confusion which
ought to produce salutary effects. Wherever the Goths become masters, we see no longer any disorders, except among
the old inhabitants. Our manners are reformed under the
dominion of Vandals. Behold an incredible event ! an un-
heard-of prodigy ! Barbarians have, by the severity of their
discipline, rendered chaste the Romans themselves; and the
Goths have purified those places which the others had defiled
by their debaucheries. A cruel nation," adds he, "but worthy
to be admired for their continence." ‡ These virtues were
not there of long continuance; the climate soon warmed their
frozen imaginations; their laws by degrees relaxed, and their
manners still more than their laws.

A numerous offspring was commonly produced from these

* Tacit. Germ. c. 18, 19.

† By referring to the supplementary chapter III., the reader will find
that, notwithstanding this prohibition, both kissing and secret embraces
were as common in Iceland as in any other country.—ED.

‡ Salvian. lib. vii. de Gubern. Dei.

marriages; but neither the rich nor the poor scrupled to expose such of their children as they did not choose to bring up. Both the Greeks and Romans were guilty of this barbarous practice, long before they can be said to have been corrupted by prosperity, luxury, and the arts. So true is it that ignorance is no security from vice, and that men always know enough to invent crimes. It is no less remarkable, that a kind of infant baptism was practised in the north, long before the first dawning of Christianity had reached those parts. Snorri Sturlason, in his chronicle, speaking of a Norwegian nobleman who lived in the reign of Harald Hárfagra, relates, that he poured water on the head of a new-born child, and called him Hakon, from the name of his father *. Harald himself had been baptized in the same manner, and it is noted of king Olaf Tryggvason, that his mother Astrida had him thus baptized and named as soon as he was born †. The Livonians observed the same ceremony; which also prevailed among the Germans, as appears from a letter which the famous pope Gregory the Third sent to their apostle Boniface, directing him expressly how to act in this respect ‡. It is probable that all these people might intend by such a rite to preserve their children from the sorceries and evil charms which wicked spirits might employ against them at the instant of their birth. Several nations of Asia and America have attributed such a power to ablutions of this kind; nor were the Romans without such a custom, though they did not wholly confine it to new-born infants §.

I shall not here repeat what I have said above concerning

---

* Vid. Snor. Sturles. c. lxx.

† Baptism is expressly mentioned in the Háva-mál and Rígs-mál, and alluded to in other Eddaic poems. It is possible that the water used in this ceremony was regarded as a symbol of the water of the Urdar-fount; but we cannot go so far as some of the German mythologists, who suppose that the stream flowing from this fountain of ever-enduring time was regarded as the type of etherial light and life, as the animating and sentient spirit of the universe. Such metaphysical notions presuppose a refinement of ideas, which we should willingly attribute to the priests of ancient India, Persia, and Egypt; but certainly not to the pontiff-chieftains of Scandinavia.—ED.

‡ Vid. Epist. 122. apud Nic. Serar in Epist. Sti Bonifacii martyris.

§ Vid. Keysler. Antiq. Select. p. 313, who has a very learned note on this subject, where he has collected together a number of curious passages from authors ancient and modern, classic and barbarous writers, relating to this practice.

the hardy way of bringing up children in the north. But I cannot omit mentioning the great advantages gained from it in respect to their health and bodily force. The Greek and Latin authors speak with surprise of the size and strength of the northern men. Cæsar observes of the Suevi, that they feed chiefly on milk, and exercise themselves much in hunting, which, together with the free unrestrained life they lead, never being from their childhood impelled against their inclinations to any discipline or duty, he assigns as effective causes of their very large and robust make *. Vegetius expressly affirms, that the tallness of the Germans gave them great advantage in combat over the lesser Romans. The lances, swords and other arms which have been preserved to this time, and may yet continue to more remote ages, are objects of curiosity and astonishment to those whose ancestors were able to wield them. But the greatest proof of their prodigious strength arises from the rude enormous monuments of architecture which were raised by these northern people. We have all heard of that monument on Salisbury plain in England, where we see a multitude of vast stones of monstrous weight set up endwise, and serving as bases to other stones, many of which are in length sixteen feet. Nor are the monuments of this kind less astonishing which we meet with in Iceland, in Westphalia, and particularly in East Friezeland, Brunswick, Mecklenburg, and many parts of the north. The dark ignorance of succeeding ages not being able to comprehend how such stupendous edifices could be constructed by mortals, have attributed them to demons and giants. But although the founders of these had not probably all the assistance we derive from the mechanic powers, yet great things might be accomplished by men of such mighty force co-operating together. The Americans, unaided by the engines we apply to these purposes, have raised up such vast stones in building their temples, as we dare not undertake to remove †. One may, however, conceive that patience united

---

* Bell Gall. lib. iv. c. 1.

† See Acosta's Hist. of the Indies, lib. vi. cap. 14. This author, speaking of the buildings and fortresses which the Incas had erected in Cusco and other places of Peru, says, " they used no mortar nor cement, neither had iron nor steel to cut the stones with ; no engines or other instruments to carry them ; and yet they were so artificially wrought that in many places

with strength, might, by taking time, be able to move such vast bodies from one place to another, and afterwards to set them up on end, by means of artificial banks, down the slopes of which they made them slide. It is without dispute from such proofs of the great size and strength of the first inhabitants of the earth, that ancient history has generally painted them as giants. The atmosphere, which was formerly more cold and bracing in Europe than it is now, the continual exercises which men then persisted in, together with their continence, their avoiding an early commerce with the other sex, their simple diet and savage life, in the fatigues of which the mind bore no part, were, without doubt, the causes which produced such enormous strength; and will convince us, whenever the like circumstances again occur, that nature, ever young and inexhaustible, will always produce the like effects.

To that wonderful constitutional vigour, the Scandinavians were indebted for such a long and healthy old age as many of them enjoyed: an advantage which they for the most part only regarded with indifference, and even with disdain, though so highly valued by mankind since the acquisition of arts, and the refinements of pleasure, have shortened the date, but rendered the journey of life more agreeable. In truth, few of them awaited the distant period allotted by nature; single combats or general engagements, the dangers and fatigues of the sea, together with the frequent practice of suicide, were so many passages ever open to conduct them to that glorious path which they thought led to a happy futurity. The influence which this doctrine had upon their minds, cannot be more particularly seen, than in the customs observed in their last scene of life and funeral ceremonies. In the most early ages these were very simple; the Scandinavians doing nothing more than lay the dead body, together with his arms, under a little heap of earth and stones *.

---

the joints are hardly seen:" and as for their size, he assures us he measured one of the stones himself, which was 38 feet long, 18 feet broad, and 6 feet thick. And in the wall of the fortress of Cusco there are stones of a still greater bigness."—P.

* There is room to believe that this custom of burying the dead under little hills or mounts of earth prevailed among many of the ancient inhabitants of Europe. Isidore speaks of it as a general custom. *Apud majores*, he says, *potentes aut sub montibus, aut in montibus sepeliuntur.* (Orig. lib. xv. c.

[Odin is said to have introduced the custom of burning the dead; but as the arrival of the so-called historical Odin is a mere legendary fiction, all that we know with certainty is, that burning the dead on funeral piles seems to have prevailed in the north at a very early period, and to have been super- seded by burial, which may, perhaps, have been but the revival of a former custom. Be this as it may, when the body was burnt, the ashes were generally collected in an urn, or small stone chest, over which a low mound not above a yard high was raised. Burial took place in various ways; sometimes the body was merely covered with a rude heap of stones, but was more frequently placed in a kind of vault formed of loose stones, the outside ones being in regular layers. Such kinds

11.) And Virgil and Servius expressly attribute it to the ancient Italians: See Servius on that verse of Æn. II.

——— *Fuit ingens monte sub alto*
Regis Dercenni terreno ex aggere bustum.

This custom Bartholin thinks Odin brought with him into the north out of Scythia; where it anciently prevailed, as we learn from Herodotus, lib. iv. c. 71. And Mallet assures us that some travellers "have seen in Crim Tartary (part of the ancient Scythia), and in the neighbouring countries, arti- ficial hills like those which are found in Denmark and throughout all the north." Mallet 1st Edit. See also Bell's Travels, vol. i. This traveller found these sepulchral hills in his journey to China.

We have in England many ancient monuments of this kind, which are of such remote antiquity that it is not easy to decide whether they ought to be ascribed to our Teutonic ancestors the Saxons and Danes, or to the more ancient inhabitants of Celtic race, viz., the Britons, &c. Some antiquaries are for referring every vestige of this sort to the times of the Druids; but it is very certain that the ancient Scandinavians buried in the same manner: indeed this sort of monument is so simple and obvious, that it has doubtless prevailed among many nations of very different origin.

Monuments of this kind particularly abound in the south-west parts of this island. "There are many in Wiltshire, round and copped, which are called burrows or barrows; perhaps raised in memory of the soldiers slain there: for bones are found in them; and I have read that it was a custom among the northern people, that every soldier who survived a battle should bring a helmet full of earth towards raising of monuments for their slain fellows." So far from Camden: to which Gibson adds, that "upon these downs (in Wiltshire) are several sorts of barrows. 1. Small circular trenches with very little elevation in the middle. 2. Ordinary barrows. 3. Barrows with ditches round them. 4. Large oblong barrows, some with trenches round them, others without. 5. Oblong barrows with stones set up all round them." Of this last sort "that large oblong barrow, called Milbarrow, is more especially remarkable, as being environed with great stones about 6 or 7 feet high." Which was doubtless "the sepulchre of some Danish com- mander."—P.

of vaults, though found occasionally in Denmark, are more frequently to be met with in Norway, and do not appear to have ever been covered with earth. When the deceased was a person of distinction, a high mound, or barrow, was generally raised over his remains. Most Scandinavian barrows are either round or oblong, and some of them have rows of upright stones set round them. Some oblong barrows have been found to contain two cinerary stone chests, one at each end, and occasionally one in the middle. Round barrows were commonly raised over stone vaults or mortuary chambers in which the dead body was deposited, either buried in sand or laid out on a flat stone, and sometimes placed in a sitting posture. Barrows of this description have frequently two or more vaults, and there is generally a passage in the eastern or southern side, leading to, and on a level with, the mortuary chambers. Barrows with wooden chambers would appear to be the most recent of all, and to have been raised not long before the introduction of Christianity, and are, therefore, likely to offer the most tempting spoil for antiquaries. Barrows in considerable numbers were often raised on a field of battle, high, stone encircled barrows over the fallen chieftains, and lower mounds over those of their followers. Mention is also frequently made of boats and even large ships being drawn on shore, turned keel uppermost, the bodies of the slain deposited under them, and stones and earth superimposed, thus forming what may appropriately be termed *ship-barrows*. A long, square-shaped stone standing two or three yards out of the ground, and called a *Bautastein* was also frequently erected in memory of a fallen warrior. These rude cenotaphs are very common in Norway and Sweden, but we believe none have yet been found bearing inscriptions.

Snorri, in his preface to the Ynglinga-Saga, makes a distinction between the age of burning—*Bruna-ölld*, and the age of burial—*Haugs-ölld*. But as this distinction is founded on the authority of the Ynglinga-Saga itself, the greater part of which is a mere legend undeserving the notice which the learned have bestowed on it, the reasons assigned for such a distinction are without any historical value *. The northern antiquaries, in the classification of the weapons, uten-

* See p. 84, and our remarks on the Heimskringla in the 4th supplementary chapter.

sils and other objects of the olden time, distinguish three epochs, which they term respectively the Stone, Bronze, and Iron age. Stone weapons were no doubt the first in use, and were probably replaced by bronze, and these again by weapons of iron and steel; so that, in this respect, the classification appears to be well founded. Whether it be applicable or not to distinguish the relative age of barrows is another question, which we should be inclined to answer in the negative. We are told, for instance, that the barrows with stone vaults in which the dead were deposited without burning, belong to the Stone Age, because the objects found in those that have been opened are generally of stone, and very seldom of metal; at most only a few bronze or gold ornaments, and never any thing of silver, having been discovered. It is further assumed that in the next, or Bronze Age, burning on funeral piles prevailed, the weapons found in cinerary chests in the mounds and barrows containing them being generally of bronze, and the other objects either of bronze, gold, or amber, and never of silver. The barrows with wooden mortuary chambers, are placed by the learned antiquaries in the Iron Age, when they suppose that burial again prevailed, although burning on funeral piles continued to be practised *. The opening of a dozen barrows would probably upset this specious theory, which, as it seems to be founded on the fictions of the Ynglinga-Saga, we can place no confidence in, even admitting that the statements respecting the objects found in the different kinds of barrows were quite unobjectionable, which however is far from being the case.

The learned Skulius Thorlacius was of opinion that the stone weapons found in barrows were mere *simulacra armorum*, meant to typify the power of Thor over the elves and spirits of darkness, and protect the dead from their machinations †. Thor killed his demoniacal adversaries by launching his mallet at them; that is to say, an evil principle, typified under the form of a giant, was destroyed by the lightning of heaven. Now, according to Thorlacius, the cuneiform stone axe was

* See a work entitled "Leitfaden zur Nordischen Alterthumskunde," published—so at least it is stated in the title page, otherwise we should have doubted the fact—by the Royal Society of Northern Antiquaries.

† Om Thor og hans Hammer. Skand. Mus. 1802. Nos. 3 and 4.

emblematic of the splitting, the arrow head of the piercing, and the malleiform axe of the shattering force of the thunderbolt hurled by the renowned Scandinavian deity, and these are the stone weapons generally found in barrows. Whether this hypothesis of the learned Dane be well founded or not, we will not pretend to decide ; it is at all events sufficiently ingenious to make us hesitate in assuming that a barrow in which only stone weapons are found must *necessarily* have been raised at a period when bronze and iron were unknown, or not in general usage. William Grimm, in the supplement to his work on German runes, in which he cites this hypothesis of Thorlacius, has given some very interesting statements respecting the barrows of the ancient Germans. In a barrow near Maden in Hesse-Cassel *, three cinerary urns were found, and also three skeletons lying with the face to the ground. A barrow at Eichstätt contained three skeletons, the middle one lying with the face upwards and turned towards the east, the two others with the face downwards and turned to the south. In one of the Braunfels barrows a single skeleton was found ; in another, a skeleton and an urn filled with incinerated human bones. On one side of the mortuary chamber of a barrow near Warnstadt, in Saxony, was found an urn containing the burnt bones of a child, on the opposite side lay a mouldering skeleton, and in the middle a perfect skeleton of a man with a spear. Grimm supposes that a skeleton found lying with the face downwards must be that of a slave ; and, admitting this to be the case, we should be justified in concluding from the facts stated, that the Maden barrow was raised at a period when the Germans burnt the body of the master and buried that of the slave, and the Eichstätt barrow when it was the custom to bury both slave and freeman ; care, however, being taken to indicate by the position in which the bodies were laid that death itself did not put an end to servitude. If the errors into which the northern antiquaries have fallen did not warn us to be exceedingly cautious in drawing conclusions from vague assumptions and dubious facts, we might, perhaps, infer from the respective positions of these skeletons, that our Teutonic forefathers were of opinion that the soul of a slave

* The ancient inhabitants of Hesse Cassel were the Chatti, a tribe belonging to the upper Germanic branch of the Teutonic race.

would descend to the abodes of darkness, while that of his master soared to the regions of ethereal light and everlasting bliss. Be this as it may, we may safely conclude that burning and burying the dead were contemporaneous usages, both cinerary urns and skeletons, face upwards, having been found in barrows near Wisbaden, in others, near Darnburg in the Duchy of Weimar, as well as in several barrows raised by the ancient Slavonic inhabitants of Pomerania. Barrow burial, or barrowing—if the term be admissible—was practised not only by the Scandinavians and Germans, but also by several Slavonic and Celtic tribes, as well as by the ancient Greeks and Etruscans, and may probably have originally been founded on some religious dogma, held at a very remote period by the common ancestors of all these nations. From the eastern shores of the Black Sea we may follow lines of barrows in a north-easterly direction through the steppes of Tartary to the wilds of Siberia, and in a north-westerly course through Russia and northern Germany, to Scandinavia and the British Islands. It is somewhat singular that although there are a considerable number of barrows in Silesia, Saxony, Prussia, and the whole of northern Germany, none are to be seen, with the exception of those near Eichstätt, in Austria, Bavaria, Wurtemberg and Baden *. In Iceland and Norway there are very few of these rude monuments; Denmark has a considerable number of them, but in no country are they so abundant as in Sweden.]

When a hero or chief fell gloriously in battle, his funeral obsequies were honoured with all possible magnificence. His arms, his gold and silver, his war-horse, and whatever else he held most dear, were placed with him on the pile. His dependants and friends frequently made it a point of honour to die with their leader, in order to attend on his shade in the palace of Odin.

Nothing, in fact, seemed to them more grand and noble than to enter Valhalla with a numerous retinue, all in their finest armour and richest apparel. The princes and nobles never failed of such attendants. His arms, and the bones of the horse on which Chilperic I. supposed he should be presented to this warrior god, have been found in his tomb. They did

* See Grimm Über deutsche Runen, p. 265.

in reality firmly believe, and Odin himself had assured them, that whatever was buried or consumed with the dead, accompanied them to his palace. The poorer people, from the same persuasion, carried at least their most necessary utensils and a little money, not to be entirely destitute in the other world. From a like motive, the Greeks and Romans put a piece of silver into the dead man's mouth, to pay his passage over the Styx. The Laplanders to this day provide their dead with a flint and every thing necessary for lighting them along the dark passage they have to traverse after death. In whatever degree civilized nations resemble the savage part of mankind, their strongest features are those which respect religion, death, and a future state. Men cannot contemplate these interesting objects coolly, nor uninfluenced by such hopes and fears as shackle and impede the proper exertion of their reasoning faculties. Accordingly all that the theology of the Egyptians, the Greeks and Romans, those people in other respects so wise, taught them on many points, was only one great delirium, and was (if we consider it impartially) in no respect superior to that of the ancient Scandinavians; if indeed it was not more indecent and extravagant still than theirs.

Odin was supposed to guard these rich deposits from the sacrilegious attempts of rapine by means of certain sacred and wandering fires which played round the tombs. And for their better security the law promulged its severest edicts against all offences of this kind. The nineteenth chapter of the Salic law is full of the different punishments decreed against such as shall carry off the boards or carpeting with which the sepulchres were covered; and interdicts them from fire and water. This law appears to have been well observed in the north during the times of paganism, since, in digging into old burial grounds, there are now frequently found arms, spurs, rings, and different kinds of vases. Such were the contents of the tomb that was opened near Guben in Germany. The person who had been interred there seems to have been a lover of good cheer; for he had carried with him several utensils of cookery, together with flagons and drinking vessels of all sizes. In the British isles, in Germany, in Scandinavia, and in many countries in the northern and eastern parts of Asia, are found monuments of the ancient inhabitants, in the form of little round hills and often surrounded with stones, on open plains or near some road.   It is the received opinion that these are the burying places of giants, and indeed bones larger than the human size are often found in them ; but we must remember that as the ancients durst not approach the palace of Odin on foot, and for that reason had their horses buried with them, it is very probable that the bones of these animals are often mistaken for those of men.

CHAPTER XI.

SEQUEL OF THE CUSTOMS, ARTS AND SCIENCES OF THE ANCIENT SCANDINAVIANS.

THE arts, which are necessary to the convenience of life, are but indifferently cultivated among a people who neglect the more pleasing and refined ones.   The Scandinavians held them all equally in contempt: what little attention they bestowed on any, was chiefly on such as were subservient to their darling passion.   This contempt for the arts, which men's desire of justifying their own sloth inspires, received additional strength from their sanguinary religion, from their extravagant fondness for liberty, which could not brook a long confinement in the same place, and especially from their rough, fiery, and quarrelsome temper, which taught them to place all the happiness and glory of man in being able to brave his equals and to repel insults.

As long as this inclination had its full sway among a people who were perpetually migrating from one forest to another, and entirely maintained from the produce of their flocks and herds, they never thought of cultivating the soil.   In the time of Tacitus, the Germans were little used to agriculture. " They cultivate," says that historian, " sometimes one part of the country, and sometimes another; and then make a new division of the lands.   They will much easier be persuaded to attack and reap wounds from an enemy, than to till the ground and wait the produce.   They consider it as an indication of effeminacy and want of courage to gain by the sweat of their brow, what they may acquire at the price of their blood." * This prejudice gradually wore out, and they applied themselves more to agriculture. The great consumption of grain in a country, where the principal part of their food and their ordinary liquor was chiefly made of nothing else, could not but produce this effect. In the ninth and tenth centuries we see the freemen, the nobility and the men of great property, directing the operations of husbandry themselves †. At length Christianity having entirely extinguished the' taste for piracy, and thus restored to the land one half of its inhabitants, laid them under a necessity of deriving from thence all their subsistence.

But the other arts were still depressed under the influence of this prejudice, and were for a long time considered as abject occupations befitting none but slaves; which not only dishonoured the present professors, but even fixed a stain on all their posterity. The Gauls, the Germans, and the Scandinavians never employed in any of their domestic and handicraft trades other than slaves, freedmen, women, or such miserable old men as preferred a dishonourable life to death. They were of course ignorant of all the pleasing conveniences and ornaments of life, excepting such as they either acquired by violence in their piratical excursions, or gained to themselves by foreign service. Their wives spun themselves the wool which made one part of their clothing, and skins supplied the rest. Their habits sat close to their bodies, and were short and neat like those of all the Teutonic ‡ nations: not wide, long and flowing, like those of the Sarmatians and eastern people. They were perhaps still less luxurious in their manner of lodging.

In the time of Tacitus, the Germans had not yet built themselves cities, or even towns: "Every one," says that author, "places his house on whatever spot he chooses, near

---

* Tac. Germ. c. 14, &c.

† Vid. Arng. Jon. Crymog. lib. i. p. 52.

‡ In the habits of the ancient Teutonic nations we see evidently the rudiments of the modern European dress. They consisted of a kind of waistcoat, and breeches, or rather a kind of trowsers which came down to the feet, and were connected with the shoes; whereas the ancient Romans were naked at the knee. Upon the pillars of Trajan and Antonine the dresses of such nations as were of Teutonic race bear a great resemblance to those of our common sailors and peasants.—P.

a spring. a wood, or open field, at a distance from any neighbour, either from ignorance in the art of building, or for fear
of fire."* When religion permitted temples to be erected
to the gods, the concourse of those who came to offer oblations,
engaged them to build round about them, and towns insensibly arose. The same thing happened near the castles of
their kings, princes, and great men; and lastly, the markets,
whither the peasants repaired for the mutual exchange of
those few commodities in which the trade of these days consisted, gave birth to a third kind of towns, which still in their
names bear evident traces of their origin†. The houses of
which these towns consisted were nothing better, for the most
part, than cottages supported by thick heavy posts joined together by boards and covered with turf. The very lowest
rank of people were not even so well off; having no other defence from the severity of the winter, but only miserable huts.
But I again repeat it, that it was only a small part of this
people who lived so totally ignorant of the conveniences of
life. Their chiefs were early distinguished by edifices sumptuous for those times. Their chief ambition was to have them
of vast extent, and the wooden columns that supported them
adorned with carved images and runic characters. Fragments
of these are still found in Iceland, nor is the sculpture so bad
as might be expected. The mountaineers of Norway and
Sweden have to this day a remarkable dexterity at carving
with the knife, and in the cabinets of the curious are preserved many pieces which surprisingly show how far genius
can advance unassisted by art. Such of the Scandinavians as
settled in richer countries, soon adopted the luxury of their
new fellow-citizens, and were as desirous as they of distinguishing themselves by sumptuous buildings.

We may judge from the foregoing pages of the state of
commerce in ancient Scandinavia. It is true, the fondness of
the inhabitants for navigation ought to have been favourable
to it; but we know that piracy, which is the result of idleness
in those who practise it, reduces to idleness those who suffer
by it, as it renders all industry useless. We must not, however, suppose that this people carried on no kind of traffic.

* Tac. Germ. c. 16.
† The general termination of these is *koping*, i. e. market.

I think one may discover some views of this sort in those
maritime expeditions of the Norwegians which have been related above : and this conjecture seems to be confirmed by
the great quantity of foreign money which is still found in
different parts of the north; if indeed this is not rather
relics of the plunder collected by these ravagers *. It is probable that for a long time commerce was carried on by means
of this foreign coin, in those parts where they had a sufficient
quantity of it, and in other places by an exchange of commodities. We do not find that there was any money coined
in the three northern kingdoms before the tenth or at most
the ninth century; and there is reason to believe it was
Canute the Great who first brought over Englishmen for the
purpose of coining those little pieces of copper money which
are still shown, and are generally impressed with the figure
of a cross, the sun, or a star, without any letters or inscription.
Under the pagan princes money was also much in use as the
common medium of value, but it seems to have only passed
by weight.

[A great trade appears to have been carried on at this
period, probably from the seventh to the eleventh century, by
the Tshuds of Bjarmaland, the centre of which was Tsherdün,
on the confluence of the Kolva and Kama in the present government of Perm. The Bjarmaland of the Scandinavians
comprised the present Russian Governments of Archangel,
Vologda, Perm, and Viatka, and was almost exclusively
peopled by tribes of the Permic branch of the Tshudic race †.
The produce of India, after a tedious overland conveyance,
was shipped on the eastern shores of the Caspian, and carried
up the Volga and Kama to Tsherdün, whence it was forwarded
by the Tshuds to the Baltic. Tsherdün was also frequented
by caravans from Bokhara, and all accounts concur in repre-

* A great quantity of Arabic coins of the ninth and tenth centuries, and of
countries situated to the south-east of the Caspian Sea, has been found in
Sweden ; and the museum of the Academy of Sciences, at St. Petersburg, is
rich in Arabic coins found in Russia, and which are supposed to have been
part of the plunder of Hastings and other sea-rovers, in the Mediterranean ;
for they are coins of the Ommiades of Spain, the Edressites of Mauritania,
and the Abisside Emirs of Lybia, and all of them prior to the year 815. See
Depping L. II. 9. and Geijer. Gescht. Schw.—ED.
† See page 40.

senting the Permian Tshuds as a wealthy and prosperous people. They appear to have had a considerable establishment on the White Sea at the mouth of the Dvina, where, in the midst of a thick forest, was the temple of their chief deity, Jumala, with a celebrated image, richly apparelled, adorned with pearls and precious stones, and holding on its lap a large silver bowl filled with coins. Near the temple was a cemetery, and the whole was inclosed with palisades, and guarded by six men night and day *. If the account which Tacitus gives of the Tshuds may be relied on †, we must either restrict his description to the Finns, (to the Suomic branch of the race,) or conclude that five or six centuries had wrought a great change in their social condition.]

We may readily suppose that the Scandinavians studied astronomy. A science so requisite for sailors could not but make a great part of the education of a people who aspired to fame by maritime enterprizes. The ancient chronicles frequently present us with young warriors endeavouring to acquire the good opinion of their mistresses by boasting of their accomplishments, such as their skill at chess, their dexterity in swimming and skating, their talents in poetry, and their knowing all the stars by their names. These names had nothing in common with those adopted by the Greeks and Romans; and were often founded on reasons as fantastical as theirs. Thus they called Ursa Major, the *Great Dog*, and the lesser Bear, *Charles's Wain;* the three stars in the belt of Orion, *Frigga's Distaff;* the Swan, the *Cross;* the Milky-way, the *Road of Winter*, &c. It is remarkable that the Scandinavians numbered the unities up to twelve, without stopping at ten like all other nations. This manner of counting is preferable to ours, as twelve is a more perfect number, and more easily broken into fractions, than ten. The Icelanders, and the peasants of certain provinces in Sweden, retain to this day a method of reckoning by great hundreds and little hundreds, great thousands and little thousands: but

* See Schlözer's Nord. Geschichte, p. 439. Geijer Gesch. Schw. p. 85. Grimm. Deutsche Mythol. XXVIII., and Berghaus' Grundriss. der Geographie. Breslau, 1842.
† See page 41.

they seem to have confounded their ancient manner of computation with the modern, since they make their great hundred to consist of 20 times 12 or 120, and their great thousand of 1200, instead of multiplying regularly 12 by 12 *. Their year commonly commenced at the winter-solstice, and they divided it into two half years, or intervals between the two solstices †, which were again divided into quarters and months. There was great variety in the names of these months, which were borrowed generally from the rural occupations to be performed in each of them, or from the religious ceremonies which were then to be observed; these names are still in use in many places of the north. The months were divided into weeks of seven days, a division which hath prevailed among almost all the nations we have any knowledge of, from the extremity of Asia to that of Europe. The day was divided into twelve parts, to each of which they assigned a distinct name; but in their computation of time, they made use of the word night instead of day. Tacitus observes the same thing of the Germans ‡; and the English have still, on some occasions, the same mode of speaking §. The longest night of winter was considered in the north, as that which had produced all the rest, as well as the days; hence they termed it the mother-night, and were persuaded that on such a night the world was created. This notion certainly gave birth to the mode of expression above related.

The necessity of assisting the memory, led them early to invent a kind of calendars, which they called runic staffs. These were a sort of compendious almanacks marked out by lines upon short pieces of board, or smooth sticks ‖. Some of them bear the appearance of great antiquity, but I believe

---

* The same method of reckoning by the great and little hundred still prevails among our English farmers, in their sale of cheese, &c. Their great hundred is 120 lbs., their little hundred 112 lbs.—P.

† That is, by summer and winter, as we in our ordinary conversation do in England.—P.

‡ Tacit. Germ. c. 11.

§ Thus we say sevennight (not seven days), and fortnight, *i. e.* fourteen nights (not fourteen days).—P.

‖ They were called in the north *rim-stocks* and *prim-staffs ;* they exhibited, by different lines and marks, the fasts and festivals, the golden number, dominical letter, epact, &c.—P.

there are none which do not carry evident marks that their owners were Christians. The Pagans, however, may have had instruments of this kind; which the first princes converted to Christianity might alter and adapt to the Christian rites. The runic characters with which they are always inscribed, together with some other marks of paganism, seem to prove this; but the question cannot positively be decided till we have examined whether the Scandinavians were acquainted with the use of letters before they had embraced Christianity. This is a fruitful question which deserves particular discussion.

One cannot travel far in Denmark, Norway or Sweden, without meeting with great stones of different forms, engraven with those ancient characters called runic *, which appear at first sight extremely different from all we know. Several of them were undoubtedly written in pagan times; but as a great part of them bear evident marks of Christianity, some learned men of distinction have thought that the German and Scandinavian missionaries first instructed their converts in the art of writing. The favourers of this opinion allege several proofs in support of it, which deserve some attention.

They produce the testimony of several Greek and Latin authors to invalidate what the northern literati have asserted concerning the great antiquity of the runic character. Androtion, quoted by Elian †, assures us. that " neither the Thracians, nor any other of the barbarous people settled in Europe, make use of letters; looking upon it as somewhat dishonourable to employ them : whereas the use of them is common among the barbarians of Asia." Tacitus is more explicit on this head. " Both the men and the women," says he, speaking of the Germans, " are equally ignorant of the

---

* Runic inscriptions are also found in this island. See a description of a very curious one in Cumberland, and of another in Scotland, in Hicks's Thesaur. Ling. Sept. (*Gram. Island.* Tab. vi. and p. 5.) See also Gordon's Itinerarium Septentrionale, p. 168. There is even extant a coin of King Offa with a runic inscription; whence it should seem that this character had been originally used by the Saxons, as well as their Scandinavian brethren.—P.

† Ælian. Var. Hist. lib. viii. c. 6. Vid. Pelloutier, Hist. des Celtes, tom. i. ch. 10.

secret of writing letters."* Almost all the ancients, who
speak of the Celts, affirm the same thing. They assure us,
that these people held in contempt every occupation, except
that of arms ; that learning to read and write degraded a person in their eyes ; that their Druids or priests, induced either
by interest or superstition, and probably by both, utterly forbade them the use of letters, and encouraged them in the
aversion they entertained for this admirable secret; and that
these Druids pretended their doctrines ought to be reserved
for the initiated only, and concealed from all others, which
could not have been had they committed them to an indiscreet paper. These statements, in respect to the Teutonic
nations, are corroborated by divers facts. Thus Theodoric,
king of Italy, could not so much as sign the first letters of his
name, though he had spent his youth among the Romans.
Eginhard, in his life of Charlemagne, says. that this emperor,
though in other respects not unlearned, could not write, and
that there were entire nations in Germany subject to him,
whose laws were not yet committed to writing. The Saxons
under Louis le Débonnaire, persisting in their resolution of
not learning to read, he was obliged to have the Old and New
Testament turned into verse, which they willingly learned by
heart, and sung after their own manner. Lastly, the literati,
whose sentiments we here give, think they can unravel all the
difficulty arising from the particular form of the runic characters, and prove that these were not known in the north
before Chrisianity, by reducing them to the Roman letters;
from which, say they, these do not differ any farther than this,
that the people of the north having been obliged at first to
engrave them in wood and stone, found it convenient to draw
their letters chiefly in straight lines, and to avoid as much as
possible all round strokes and turnings.

These arguments are specious, but are they equally solid ?
It is true the ancients denied that the northern nations had
the knowledge, or at least the use of letters among them ;
but our present inquiry only regards the Scandinavians, and
such of the Germans as lived nearest them. These are the
only people among whom the runic characters are found, and

---

* " Literarum secreta viri pariter ac fœminæ ignorant." Tac. Germ. c. 19.

with them the ancients were least acquainted. As for Tacitus, he has probably been misunderstood; those who are acquainted with his style and manner, if they reconsider the passage, wlil not doubt but this is his meaning; that " both the German men and women were ignorant of the secret of writing letters or epistles;" that is, with a view to carry on an intrigue *. We may easily suppose there were among them many warriors and illustrious men who could not write, without concluding from thence that the whole nation was equally ignorant. As for the last argument, which attributes to the first missionaries the honour of introducing letters into the north, it does not appear to me to carry much weight. The Runic characters might possibly be borrowed from the Roman alphabet, without any necessary ·conclusion that the Scandinavians had waited for the secret till the introduction of Christianity among them. The Runic letters might even have a great resemblance to the Roman without being copied from them, since both may have been derived from one common original. But the strongest argument of all is, that this resemblance has been nothing less than proved; for that the difference between the runic and Roman letters is all owing to the necessity of writing on wood or stone, and of tracing the letters iu perpendicular lines, leaves such a latitude for changing, adding, or diminishing, that there are few alphabets in the world, which, by means of such a commodious hypothesis, might not easily be reduced to the Roman character. Accordingly, the learned Wormius found the Runic letters as easily reducible to the Greek and Hebrew alphabets as to the Roman †.

The Roman history tells us, that under the reign of the emperor Valens, Ulphilas ‡, bishop of those Goths who were settled in Mœsia and Thrace, translated the Bible into the

---

* So the best translators of Tacitus, and so the Abbé Bletterie has rendered this passage in his celebrated French version.

† Vid. Ol. Worm. Literatur. Runic, passim. It was that great master of northern literature, Dr. Hickes, who first started the notion that the Runic character was borrowed from the Roman: see his *Thesaurus Linguar. Septentrion.*, &c. But this opinion is now generally given up as insupportable.—P.

‡ In the year 369. Vid. Socrat. Hist. Eccles. lib. iv., and Sozomen. lib. vi. 36.

Gothic language. Several authors say, that Ulphilas invented the character in which this version was written; but is it probable that any man should form a new alphabet for a nation which had one already? If the Goths of Mœsia and Thrace had not before his time had any knowledge of letters, would it not have been better to have taught them the use of the Greek character, already understood? Besides, Ulphilas neither wrote the Gospels on wood nor on stone, but on parchment; he would not therefore be under the necessity of disfiguring the alphabet of other nations for the sake of straight lines, which it is alleged gave birth to the Runic letters. At most it could not be the Roman alphabet that was altered; but if any it must have been the Greek, for Ulphilas was at that time in a country where the Greek language was spoken. Nor is it difficult to discover what it was that led historians into the mistake of supposing Ulphilas to have been the inventor of these characters. The Greeks had probably never heard any mention of them before he came among them: the introducer of a novelty easily passes for the author of it; and when we compare the Runic letters taken from the inscriptions scattered up and down on the rocks in the north with the alphabet of Ulphilas, it is easy to see that the bishop has added divers characters unknown to the ancient Scandinavians. It was doubtless the translation of the Bible which obliged him to make these additions. The ancient alphabet, being composed only of sixteen letters, could not express the many sounds foreign to the Gothic language that necessarily occurred in that work. These additional letters might easily confer on Ulphilas the credit of inventing the whole. This is one of those inaccuracies which every day happen. It is no less probable that before Ulphilas, the Goths, even while they were involved in the thickest darkness of paganism, had some knowledge of letters *

* In the sixteenth century there was found in the abbey of Werden, in Westphalia, a very curious fragment of what is believed to have been the identical version of Ulphilas, written in the language of the Mœso-Goths, and exhibiting the characters which that prelate made use of : these are so very remote from the runic, that we may now safely allow the Gothic bishop the honour of their invention, without in the least derogating from the antiquity of the Runic letters. This fragment is now preserved in the library at Up-

What are we to think of those inscriptions in the Runic character, which travellers assure us they have seen in the deserts of Tartary * ?   Tartary has never yet been converted to Christianity; from this and the circumjacent countries issued those swarms which peopled Scandinavia; nor have the Scandinavians ever made any expeditions into their mother

sal, in Sweden, and is famous among all the northern literati, under the name of the *Codex Argenteus*, or Silver Book : for which reason a short account of it may not be unacceptable.

The *Codex Argenteus* contains at present only the four Gospels, though somewhat mutilated ; and is believed to be a relic of the Gothic Bible, all or the greater part of which Ulphilas had translated.   The leaves are of vellum of a violet colour ; all the letters are of silver, except the initials, which are of gold.   These letters (which are all capitals) appear not to have been written with the pen, but stamped or imprinted on the vellum with hot metal types [a], in the same manner as the bookbinders at present letter the backs of books.   This copy is judged to be nearly as ancient as the time of Ulphilas, or at least not later than a century or two after ; yet so near was the copyist to the discovery of printing, that if he had but thought of combining three or four of these letters together he must have hit upon that admirable invention ; whereas he only imprinted each letter singly.   This curious fragment has been several times printed in 4to, first by Junius in 1665 ; and lately in a very elegant manner at Oxford by the learned Mr. Lye in 1750.   Another fragment of this curious version (containing part of the Epistle to the Romans) has been since discovered in the library at Wolfenbüttel, and was published a few years ago in a very splendid volume in 4to by the Rev. F. A. Knitell, Archdeacon of Wolfenbüttel [b].

To conclude, the letters used in the Gothic Gospels, being twenty-five in number, are formed with slight variations from the capitals of the Greek and Latin alphabet, and are extremely different from the Runic.   The invention of them may therefore be very safely attributed to Bishop Ulphilas (as the ancients expressly assert) ; who might not choose to employ in so sacred a work as the translation of the Bible the Runic characters, which the Goths had rendered infamous by their superstitious use of them.—P.

* Consult Strahlemberg's Description of the northern and eastern parts of Europe and Asia (quoted by Er. Benzel. Jun. in Pericul. Runic. Diss. Upsal. 1724).   See also in the same book the map of Tartary.

---

[a] See this fully proved in some late curious tracts written by the learned Dom. Johan Ihre, and other Swedish literati.

[b] Since Bishop Percy's time, several editions of Ulphilas have appeared. The most complete edition is that published at Leipsic, in 1836, edited by H. v. Gabelenz and Dr. Lœbe, which contains the fragments discovered in Palimpsest MSS. by Cardinal Mai.—ED.

Q

country since they embraced the Christian faith.   If, then, the account given us by these travellers is true, we must neces sarily conclude that the Runic writing was an art which had its rise in Asia, and was carried into Europe by the colonies who came to settle in the north.   This is also confirmed by all the old chronicles and poems which I have so often quoted. They universally agree in assigning to the Runic characters a very remote antiquity, and an origin entirely pagan.   They attribute the invention of them to Odin himself; who, they add, was eminently skilled in the art of writing, as well for the common purposes of life, as for the operations of magic.   In a very ancient ode, quoted by Bartholin, the poet thus speaks of the Runic characters.   " The letters which the great an cient traced out; which the gods composed ; which Odin, the sovereign of the gods, engraved."   Had it been otherwise, how could the pagans have so soon forgotten that these letters were introduced among them by the ministers of a religion that was foreign, unknown, and must have been hateful to them, since they were often compelled by violent means to profess it? how could all their poets (who were at the same time their theologians) so expressly call Odin "the inventor of the runes?"

This would be the place to say something of those supersti tious practices, if we had not already given sufficient instances of the weakness of the human mind, and of the strange errors and extravagances to which ignorant nations are subject. Let it suffice, then, just to observe, that the Runic characters were distinguished into various kinds *.   The *noxious*, or, as they called them, the *bitter runes*, were employed to bring va rious evils on their enemies ; the *favourable* averted misfor tunes ; the *victorious* procured conquest to those who used them ; the *medicinal* were inscribed on the leaves of trees for healing ; others served to dispel melancholy thoughts ; to prevent shipwreck ; were antidotes against poison ; preserva tives against the resentment of their enemies, and efficacious to render a mistress favourable : these last were to be used with great caution.   If an ignorant person had chanced to write one letter for another, or had but erred in the minutest stroke, he would have exposed his mistress to some dangerous

* Vid. Worm. Litterat. Runic. p. 33, et Barthol. de Caus., &c., p. 650.

illness; which was only to be cured by writing other runes with the greatest niceness. All these various kinds differed only in the ceremonies observed in writing them, in the materials on which they were written, in the place where they were exposed, in the manner in which the lines were drawn, whether in the form of a circle, of a serpent, or a triangle, &c. In the strict observance of these childish particulars consisted that obscure and ridiculous art, which acquired to so many weak and wicked persons the respectable name of priests and prophetesses, merely for filling rude minds with so much jealousy, fear, and hatred. It is by mischievous errors of the same kind that all nations have been distinguished in their first ages of simplicity and ignorance; those first ages which prejudice makes us regret, and wish that the arts had never corrupted their primeval innocence. Whereas in proportion as the empire of the sciences has prevailed in the north, that of superstition has faded and vanished before its growing light. But the extremity of Scandinavia, where that light has not yet penetrated, still remains faithfully subject to all its ancient errors. Allowing for the difference of their climate and poverty, the Laplanders at present are in this respect what the Scandinavians were formerly. With the same ignorance, they are equally subject to superstition and credulity; for it is a certain rule that magic never fails to work prodigies in all such nations as believe in it. The Ostiacs and other savages of Asia are no less given to sorcery and witchcraft than the Laplanders, and we have all heard of the Jongleurs, those magicians so revered among the barbarians of America.

However, the use of runic letters for more rational purposes became by degrees more common in the north. In the latter ages of paganism they were frequently used for inscriptions. The older these inscriptions are the better they are engraved. We rarely find them written from the right hand to the left *; but it is not uncommon to meet with the line running from the top to the bottom, after the manner of the Chinese and several nations of India; or from the top to the bottom, and then turning round to the left, and so up again to the place it begins at; or else from the left to the right,

---

* Vid. Worm. Litterar. Run. cap. xxv.

and so back to the left again, which was the manner of the early Greeks, and had its name from the resemblance to a furrow traced by the plough *. The greater part of the ancient monuments written in the Runic character, which are still preserved, are inscriptions dispersed here and there in the fields, and cut out on large stones or pieces of rock. The Scandinavians wróte also on wood and on the bark of the birch-tree. As for the manuscripts in the Runic character, the most ancient we can find appear to have been written some time after Christianity took place in the north, as is judged from several proofs, particularly from the frequent intermixture of Roman letters in them. In the tenth and eleventh centuries the runic gave way still more and more to the other; till at length the missionaries succeeded in totally abolishing the use of them, as tending to retain the people in their ancient superstitions. But this reformation did not speedily take place, and there remained traces of this character for many succeeding ages; nor, as we are assured †, is it yet wholly laid aside among the mountaineers of one province in Sweden.

[Upwards of a thousand Runic inscriptions have been discovered in Sweden, and three or four hundred in Denmark and Norway, but few of them are of a date prior to the eleventh century, and there is scarcely one of undoubted authenticity that throws the least light on history. They are, in fact, singularly devoid of interest, and by no means repay the trouble taken by the learned men of the north to decipher them. By far the greater number of these inscriptions are short epitaphs on tombstones, raised after the introduction of Christianity by obscure individuals, in memory of their friends and relations. N. N. set (raised) this stone after (in memory of) N. N. his father, mother, brother, sister, or friend, would be, by the insertion of two ordinary Scandinavian proper names, such as Suti, Steinar, Olaf, &c., a literal translation of the greater part of them. The most interesting Runic inscription we have yet seen is that on the Kingiktorsoak stone which we shall give an account of in the next chapter.

* Βουστροφηδὸν.
† See Dalin. Su. Rik. hist. tom. i. p. 237, and Benzel. collect. hist. p. 1, cap. 1.

The Runic, like the ancient Greek alphabet, originally contained only sixteen letters, arranged as follows :—

Name . .	fe	úr	thurs	ós	reið
Signification	money	a ure-ox	a giant	an estuary	a ride
Figure . .	ᚠ	ᚢ	ᚦ	ᚭ	ᚱ
Power . .	F	U	D.TH	O	R

Name . .	Kön	hagl	nauð	ís	ár	sól
Signification	an ulcer	hail	need	ice	year	the sun
Figure . .	ᚴ	ᚼ	ᚾ	ᛁ	ᛅ	ᛋ
Power . .	K	H	N	I	A	S

Name . .	Týr	björk	lögr	maðr	ýr
Signification	the God Tyr	a birch tree	a lake	a man	a bow
Figure . .	ᛏ	ᛒ	ᛚ	ᛘ	ᛦ
Power . .	T	B	L	M	Y

We will not fatigue the reader by entering into a critical examination of the conflicting theories that have been brought forward to account for the origin of these characters, for notwithstanding the antiquarian lore by which many of them are supported, they have only served to involve the question they were intended to elucidate in still greater obscurity. Leaving, therefore, these erudite lucubrations to those who may have the curiosity to investigate them *, we shall give, as briefly as possible, a few well authenticated *facts* on the subject. It may, in the first place, be taken for granted that the Scandinavian Runic alphabet was in use in the ninth century. It is, moreover, highly probable that the Saxons also possessed a Runic alphabet previous to their invasion of England, for it has been clearly ascertained that the Anglo-Saxons were acquainted with Runic letters when they adopted the Roman

* Schlözer, in his Allg. Nord. Geschichte, edit. 1771, has collected a great deal of literary rubbish on the subject.

alphabet on their conversion to Christianity in the sixth century, as they retained two of them—Þ th and ƿ w—that expressed sounds in their language which could only have been inadequately rendered by a combination of two or more of the Roman characters *. Hrabanus Maurus, an archbishop of Mainz, in the ninth century, has given in his work, " De Inventione Linguarum," a Runic alphabet, which he says was used by the Marcomanni for magical purposes; and another German Runic alphabet has been found in a vellum MS., of the tenth century, in the convent of St. Gallen, in Switzerland; but William Grimm has shown † that these are only modifications of the Anglo-Saxon Runes, though he is of opinion that the alphabet of Hrabanus Maurus may probably be that used by the Nordalbingian Saxons prior to their invasion of England, as well as by several other Germanic tribes. That the Germans were accustomed to write on wooden tablets in Runic characters, is proved by the authority of Venantius Fortunatus, a bishop of Poictiers of the sixth century, who, in one of his epistles to his friend Flavius, tells him that when he is tired of the Latin, he can make use of the Hebrew, Greek, or even of the Runic letters.

> " Barbara fraxineis pingatur runa tabellis ;
> Quodque papyrus agit, virgula plana valet,"

are the words which the poetical bishop makes use of, and by which he meant to designate the German, and not the Scandi-

---

* The so-called Anglo-Saxon characters, except the two mentioned in the text, are a mere corruption of the Roman, and ought to be abandoned. Rask very properly made use of Roman letters for his excellent Anglo-Saxon grammar, observing that he did so, "after mature deliberation, the written Anglo-Saxon characters as they appear in MSS. being themselves a barbarous, monkish corruption of the Roman, and the printed ones a very imperfect imitation of the MSS. To persist, therefore, in the use of them, (however venerable their appearance,) seems to be without good reason; for though called Anglo-Saxon, they are no other than those employed at the same time in the writing of Latin; if, therefore, we should be consistent, we ought to employ types to represent every variation of the monkish characters throughout the middle ages; as the handwriting underwent many changes before the discovery of printing, and the restoration of the Roman alphabet." —Preface, page 55.

† In his compendious work, entitled " Ueber Deutsche Runen," Gotting. 1821.

navian Runes, as is evident from several other passages in which allusion is made to his travels in Germany. Grimm has further shown, in the most clear and satisfactory manner, that the Anglo-Saxon Runic alphabet was derived from the Scandinavian at a period when it had only sixteen letters, the complementary letters of the two alphabets having been formed on principles that offer not the slightest analogy. Hence we may safely infer that the Scandinavians were acquainted with Runic letters in the sixth century, and, in all probability, at a much earlier period, though it is certainly very extraordinary that they should have made so little use of them. Grimm, after having established by the most conclusive arguments the facts above stated, attempts to trace the sixteen original Runes * to a remote Asiatic source, founding his conjectures on their inadequacy to express all the sounds of the Old Norse language, and therefore assuming that they must necessarily have been borrowed from a more primitive tongue. Into this inquiry we will not follow him, as we deem the assumption to be somewhat gratuitous †, but leave the reader to draw his own conclusions from a comparison of the three Runic alphabets which we give in the next page, together with the characters said to have been invented by Ulphilus, but which Grimm supposes were known to the Mœso-Goths long before their learned bishop's translation of the Gospels, their original form having been somewhat changed when the Goths became acquainted with the Greek alphabet, and further modified by Ulphilus rendering them more adaptable for writing.

* Not having as yet met with a satisfactory etymology of the word Rune, we will not give that generally adopted, as it is probably the most erroneous of all, but merely observe that the Norse *ú* corresponds to the German *au*, and that the famous root *mandragora* or rather the demon conjured out of it, is designated in old German by the word *alraun*. See Will. Grimm's Deutsche Runen, p. 67, and Jacob Grimm's Deutsche Mythologie, p. 376.

† In modern German, for instance, the sounds represented by B and P are equally as distinct as in English, yet these sounds are so confounded in some of the provincial dialects, that we much question whether an Austrian village schoolmaster, if called upon to form an alphabet for the jargon he teaches his scholars, would not discard one of them as superfluous.

	Scandinavian Runes.	Anglo-Saxon Runes.	German Runes of Hrabanus Maurus.	Gothic Characters of Ulphilas.		Scandinavian Runes.	Anglo-Saxon Runes.	German Runes of Hrabanus Maurus.	Gothic Characters of Ulphilas.
I	ǀ	ǀ	J	ïï	P	ß	ᛞᚻ	ᛝᚷ	Π
E	ᛁ	M	M	G	V	ᚠ	ᚠ		Υ
A	ᛏᛏ	ᚪ	ᛗᛖ	ᚹ	F	ᚠ	ᚡ	ᚥ	ᚠ
Æ		ᚾ		ᚹ	D	ᚦ	ᚺ	ᚼ	ᛚᚦ
O	ᛏᛏᛏ	ᚾ	ᚴ	X	TH	ᚦ	ᚦ		Ψ
Œ		ᚸ			T	ᛏᛏ	↑	ᛏ	T
U	ᚢ	ᚢ	ᚻ	ᚢ	G		ᛪ		
Y	ᛣ	ᚤ	ΨΦ		G	ᚠ	Χ	ᚪ	Γ
J		φ		ᚷ	K	Υ	ᛏᚤ	ᚪᚪ	Κ
W		ᚦ			Q		ᚤᚢ	ᛃ	ᛰ
H	ᚼ	Η	ᚷᚷ	ᚻ	C		ᚻ		
M	Υ	ᛗ	ᛗ	ᛘ	CH			ᚡᛃ	
N	ᛏᛏ	ᚿ	ᚴ	Ν	S	ᛋ	ᛋ	ᚡᛃ	S
L	ᚱ	ᚱ	ᚠ	ᛚ	TS			ᚤᚤ	Z
R	ᚱ	R	R	ᚱ	X		ᚤ	ᚤᚤ	
B	ᛒ	B	B	ᛒ	ing		ᚶ		

. C, K, and Q represent the same sound in Anglo-Saxon, two of these letters are consequently superfluous. Rask only uses twenty-four characters in his Anglo-Saxon grammar.

We may remark, in conclusion, that no Runic lapidary inscriptions in any of the ancient Upper Germanic languages
have hitherto been discovered, and we believe not more than
two or three in Anglo-Saxon *.]

Mankind, every where essentially the same, have been always led to poetical composition prior to that of prose. This
seems at present the reverse of the natural order; but we
think so either through our prejudices or for want of putting
ourselves in the place of a people who are ignorant of the art
of writing. Pleasing sounds and the attractions of harmony
would strike at first every ear; but song could not long subsist without poetry. No sooner was it observed how these
two united powers fixed and impressed those images on the
mind, which the memory was desirous of retaining, than they
acquired a new degree of esteem, especially among such as
aspired to a lasting fame. Verse was made use of to preserve
the memory of remarkable events and great actions. The
laws of a people, their religious ceremonies and rural labours
were also recorded in numbers, because these are subjects which,
consisting of a great variety of particulars, might easily fall
into oblivion. Hence it was that Greece could already boast
of an Homer, an Hesiod, and of many other poets, several ages
before Pherecydes had written in prose. Hence among the
Gauls and other Celtic nations there were poems composed on

* One of these, cut on a stone cross, was found in Nottinghamshire, and a
copy of it sent by Spelman, in 1618, to the famous northern antiquary,
Olaus Wormius, who has given it in his Monum. Dan. page 161. The inscription consists of thirteen very legible Anglo-Saxon Runes. Wormius, however, taking for granted that the inscription was in the old Norse language,
and not being able to extract any meaning from the letters as they stood, did
not hesitate to transpose some and add others, by dint of which legerdemain,
he at length brought out " *Rino satu Runa stina,* Rino set this Runic stone.
Another erudite northern antiquary, Helverschov, tortured them into " *vilos
eros ateos,*" the barbarous Latin for *vilis ero atheis,* but William Grimm reads,
without changing a letter, the Anglo-Saxon phrase, *Rices dryhtnes,* the
dominion of the kingdom, which may mean the dominion of the kingdom of
heaven over that of earth, or the dominion of a civil jurisdiction, the cross
being probably placed to mark the boundary of a parish or a hundred. This
anecdote will serve to show the reader that the present generation of northern
antiquaries, in having recourse to the Jonathan Oldbuck manner of decipher-
ing lapidary inscriptions—an amusing instance of which will be found in the
next chapter—merely tread in the footsteps of their illustrious predecessors.

all subjects from the earliest ages, which the Druids, who were appointed to educate the youth, frequently employed twenty years in teaching them to repeat *. This custom, rendered sacred by its high antiquity, which ever commands respect from the people, was in force many ages after the art of writing had pointed out a more perfect method of preserving the memorials of human knowledge. In like manner the Scandinavians for a long time applied their Runic letters only to the senseless purposes above mentioned; nor did they, during so many years, ever think of committing to writing those verses with which their memories were loaded; and it is probable that they only wrote down a small quantity of them at last. The idea of making a book never entered into the heads of those fierce warriors, who knew no medium between the violent exercises and fatigues of war or hunting and a stupid lethargic state of inaction. Among the innumerable advantages which accrued to the northern nations from the introduction of the Christian religion, that of teaching them to apply the knowledge of letters to useful purposes, is not the least valuable. Nor could a motive less sacred have eradicated that habitual and barbarous prejudice which caused them to neglect so admirable a secret. The churches and monasteries were at least so many asylums where this secret was preserved, while the ferocity of manners which prevailed in the dark ages tended again to consign it to oblivion.

So long as paganism prevailed in the north, the use of letters being very limited, it is no paradox to say that verse was a necessary medium of knowledge, and the poet an essential officer of the state. And if it requires a peculiar and uncommon genius to excel in this art, the professors of it would of course acquire a very high degree of esteem and respect. All the historical monuments of the north are full of the honours paid this order of men both by princes and people; nor can the annals of poetry produce any age or country which reflects more glory and lustre upon it. The ancient chronicles constantly represent the kings of Denmark, Norway, and Sweden as attended by one or more Skalds; for this was the name they gave their poets. They were more especially honoured and caressed at the courts of those princes, who

---

* Cæsar, Comment. lib. vi. 14.

distinguished themselves by their great actions and passion for glory. Harald Hárfagra, for instance, placed them at his feasts above all the other officers of his court. Many princes entrusted them both in peace and war with commissions of the utmost importance. They never set out on any considerable expedition without some of them in their train. Hakon, Earl of Norway, had five celebrated Skalds along with him in that famous battle, when the warriors of Jomsburg were defeated ; and history records that they sung each an ode to animate the soldiers before they engaged. But they enjoyed another advantage, which would be more the envy of the poets of these days. They were rewarded for the poems they composed in honour of the kings and heroes with magnificent presents ; we never find the Skald singing his verses at the courts of princes without being recompensed with golden rings, glittering arms, and rich apparel. Their respect for this order of men often extended so far as to remit the punishment of crimes they had committed, on condition they sued out their pardon in verse. In a word, the poetic art was held in such high estimation, that great lords and even kings did not disdain to cultivate it with the utmost pains themselves. Ragnvald, Earl of the Orkney islands, passed for a very able poet; he boasts himself, in a song of his which is still extant, that he knew how to compose verses on all subjects. Ragnar Lodbrok was no less distinguished for his skill in poetry, than in war and navigation. Many of his poems were long preserved in the north, and may be found inserted in the history of his life : and it is well known that he died no less like a poet than a hero.

The respect, however, which the northern nations paid to their Skalds was not owing to the nobility of their extraction. A people whose object was glory, could not fail of showing a great deference to those who both published it abroad and consigned it to futurity, let their origin be what it would. A prince or illustrious warrior oftentimes exposed his life with so much intrepidity only to be praised by his Skald, who was both the witness and judge of his bravery. It is affirmed that this kind of men, although poets, were never guilty of flattery, and never lavished their praises on heroes and kings themselves unless their gallant exploits were quite incontestable *

* Vid. Bartholin. p. 154, et cap. 10. lib. i. passim.—P.

Hence arose the custom of always bringing them into the
scene of action: Olaf, king of Norway, placing three of them
one day around him in battle, cried out with spirit, "You
shall not relate what you have only heard, but what you are
eye witnesses of yourselves!" The same poets usually recited
their verses themselves at solemn festivals and in great assemblies. But the subject of these poems was not confined to one
single event, such as a victory or some generous action; it
was frequently a genealogical history of all the kings of the
country, deduced down from the gods to the reigning prince,
who always derived his origin from them. These poems were,
according to Tacitus, the only annals of the Germans. They
had great numbers of them, which were not wholly forgotten
in the eighth century; since Eginhard relates, that Charlemagne caused them to be committed to writing. "And even
learnt himself," adds the historian, "the rude and ancient
songs in which the exploits and the wars of the first princes
were celebrated." In poems of the same kind consisted for
many ages all the history of the Scandinavians. A bard named
Thiodolf celebrated in his verses the exploits of Harald and
thirty of his predecessors; another called Eyvind, composed
an historical poem which went back as far as Odin. Such
are the sources whence Saxo drew his materials for the first
six or seven books of his history, and he might doubtless have
derived great assistance from them, if he had not happened
to live in an age wholly destitute of that exact skill in criticism
which knows how to separate facts from the fictions with which
they are blended.

The necessity there was for poets, the natural attractions of
the art itself, and those it derived from the manners of the
age, greatly multiplied the number of Skalds. An ancient
Icelandic manuscript has preserved a list of all such as distinguished themselves in the three northern kingdoms, from
the reign of Ragnar Lodbrok to that of Valdemar II. * They
are in number two hundred and thirty, among whom we find
more than one crowned head. But what is not less remarkable is, that the greatest part of them are natives of Iceland.
The reader has doubtless by this time observed that we are
indebted to that island for almost all the historical monu-

* Vide Skaldatal in Append. ad Lit. Run. Ol. Worm. p. 242.

ments of the northern nations now remaining. It cannot easily be accounted for how it came to pass that a people, disjoined from the rest of the world, few in number, depressed by poverty, and situated in so unfavourable a climate, should be capable, in those dark ages, of manifesting such a taste for literature, and should even rise to the perception of the more refined mental pleasures. While they were heathens, the Icelandic annalists were always deemed the best in the north. After they had embraced the Christian faith, they were the first who thought of unravelling the chaos of ancient history, who collected the old poems, digested the chronicles into a regular form, and applied themselves to rescue from oblivion the traditions of their pagan theology. Were we better informed of certain particulars relating to the state of the north during those remote ages, we might possibly find the cause of this phenomenon either in the poverty of the inhabitants of Iceland, which drove them to seek their fortunes at the neighbouring courts, or in the success of their first bards, which excited their emulation, and at the same time prepossessed strangers in their favour; or lastly in the nature of their republican government, in which the talent of oratory and the reputation of superior sense and capacity are the direct roads to respect and preferment.

The style of these ancient poems is very enigmatical and figurative, very remote from the common language, and for that reason, grand, but tumid; sublime, but obscure *. If it be the character of poetry to have nothing in common with prose, if the language of the gods ought to be quite different from that of men, if every thing should be expressed by imagery, figures, hyperboles, and allegories, the Scandinavians may rank in the highest class of poets; nor is this unaccountable. The soaring flights of fancy may possibly more peculiarly belong to a rude and uncultivated, than to a civilized people. The great objects of nature strike more forcibly on rude imaginations. Their passions are not impaired by the constraint of laws and education. The paucity of their ideas and the barrenness of their language oblige them to borrow

* If we make a distinction between Eddaic and Skaldic poetry, " grand and sublime " are epithets quite inapplicable to the latter, by far the greater part of which is mere bombast; " tumid and obscure," enough to be utterly worthless.—ED.

from all nature, images fit to clothe their conceptions in. How should abstract terms and reflex ideas, which so much enervate our poetry, be found in theirs? They could seldom have been met with in their most familiar conversations. The moment the soul, reflecting on its own operations recurs inwards, and detaches itself from exterior objects, the imagination loses its energy, the passions their activity, the mind becomes severe, and requires ideas rather than sensations: language then becomes precise and cautious, and poetry, being no longer the child of pure passion, is able to affect but feebly. If it be asked, what is become of that magic power which the ancients attributed to this art, it may be well said to exist no more. The poetry of the modern languages is nothing more than reasoning in rhyme, addressed to the understanding, but very little to the heart. No longer essentially connected with religion, politics, or morality, it is at present, if I may so say, a mere private art, an amusement that attains its end when it has gained the cold approbation of a few select judges.

The most affecting and most striking passages in the ancient northern poetry, were such as now seem to us the most whimsical, unintelligible, and overstrained; so different are our modes of thinking from theirs. We can admit of nothing but what is accurate and perspicuous. They only required bold and astonishing images, which appear to us hyperbolical and gigantic. What also contributes to render their poetry very obscure at present is, that the language of it is borrowed from their mythology; a mythology not so familiar to us as that of the Greeks and Romans. When they did not allude to their own fables, they took their metaphors from other subjects, which were commonly very far-fetched and remote; thus a poet seldom expressed heaven by any other term than " the skull of the giant Ymir," alluding to a fable on that subject. The rainbow was called " the bridge of the gods;" gold was " the tears of Freyja;" poetry, " the present, or the drink of Odin." The earth was either indifferently " the spouse of Odin, the flesh of Ymir, the daughter of the night, the vessel which floats on the ages, or the foundation of the air;" herbs and plants were called " the hair or the fleece of the earth." A combat was termed " a bath of blood, the hail of Odin, the shock of bucklers;" the sea was " the field of pirates and the girdle of the earth;" ice, "the greatest of all bridges;" a ship, "the horse of the waves;" the tongue, "the sword of words," &c. Each of their deities might be expressed by an infinite variety of phrases. In short, a peculiar study of this kind of language was necessary to constitute a poet; for which reason they early composed a dictionary of it for the use of the Skalds, as well as their readers. The same Ragnvald, Earl of the Orkneys, before spoken of, is said to have composed a work of this sort, which, according to Wormius, is still extant, under the name of the "Poetical Key." Another is found at the end of the prose Edda, and is entitled "Skalda, or the Art of Poetry." This is a collection of epithets and synonymous words selected from their best poets, very like those which are put into the hands of young people when they first apply themselves to Latin poetry. It was also usual with the Skalds to interlard their discourse with extemporary verses. Thus it is reported of an Icelandic bard, named Sivard, that when he spoke in prose his tongue seemed embarrassed and to deliver his thoughts with difficulty, but that he expressed himself in verse with the greatest fluency and ease. The historians frequently and positively assure us that these verses were spoken off-hand. This is what is remarked in the life of the poet Egill, for instance, who purchased his pardon from the king of Norway by singing an extemporary ode which still remains, and is entitled the "Ransom of Egill."[*] The same eulogium is often given to another more ancient Skald, called Eyvind. All the chronicles mention his great facility in composing verses, as a matter well known throughout the north.

The taste which the Skalds had for the abstruse and complicated could not fail of running them into allegories and enigmas of every kind: we often meet with princes and great warriors, in the ancient chronicles, proposing riddles, and affixing penalties on such as could not unravel them. But excepting some few which are tolerably ingenious, they are either totally unintelligible, or built on verbal equivocations. The poets were not limited to this kind only. There is mention made from the earliest ages of Logogryphs[†], and other

[*] Vid. Torf. H. N. tom. ii. p. 188, et seq.

[†] A Logogryph is a kind of enigma, which consists of taking, in different senses, the different parts of the same word.—See instances of this species of false wit, in Ol. Wormii Literat. Runic. p. 183, 185, &c.—P.

still more trifling species of wit, for which we happily want
even names. Some of them must have cost much labour, and
all imply such an acuteness and patience in the inventors, as
would hardly be expected from a nation of warriors.

There remains now but one word to add by way of conclusion. When the truth of facts is once solidly established, we
may safely reason concerning their causes. From a representation of such facts, (which are here only brought together
and left to speak for themselves,) a picture has been given of
the ancient northern nations. But having thus informed ourselves concerning the manners of this people, why may we
not proceed a step farther, to consider the general causes of
their character? It does not seem impossible here to discover
and pursue the path which nature has taken. A great abundance of blood and humours, strong and rigid fibres, together
with an inexhaustible vigour, formed the constitutional temperament of the Scandinavians and Germans, as they do indeed of all savage people who live under a like climate.

Hence proceeded that impetuosity and violence of their
passions when they were once roused; and hence, in their
calmer moments, that serious, phlegmatic, and indolent turn.
The exercises of war and the chase which are great fatigues
to a less robust people, were to them only amusements, the
means of shaking off their lethargy, and of giving an agreeable
and even necessary motion to the body. Their relish for this
kind of life, the effect of constitution, strengthened in its turn
the cause that produced it. Thus strongly moulded by the
hand of nature, and rendered hardy by education, the opinion
they entertained of their own courage and strength must have
given the peculiar turn to their character. A man who thinks
he has nothing to fear, cannot endure any sort of constraint;
much less will he submit to any arbitrary authority, which he
sees only supported by human power, or such as he can brave
with impunity. As he thinks himself not obliged to court any
one's favour or deprecate his resentment, he scorns dissimula-
tion, artifice, or falsehood. He regards these faults, the effects
of fear, as the most degrading of all others. He is always
ready to repel force by force; hence he is neither suspicious
nor distrustful. A declared enemy to his enemy, he attacks
openly; he confides in, and is true to others; generous, and
sometimes in the highest degree magnanimous, because he

places his dearest interest in the idea he entertains and would excite of his courage. He does not willingly confine himself to such occupations as require more assiduity than action, more application of mind than body; because moderate exercise is not sufficient to put his blood and fibres into such a degree of motion as is necessary to his own ease. Hence that distaste for the arts; and, as the passions always endeavour to justify themselves, hence also that contempt and prejudice which represent the profession of the arts as dishonourable. War then becomes the only employment he can exercise with pleasure. The frequent and extreme vicissitudes, the fatigues and dangers attendant on this way of life, are alone able to throw him into those violent and continual agitations his habit of body requires. Now if we suppose after this a whole society composed of such men, to what a degree of emulation must their courage arise? The love of distinction, so natural to all men, having here no other object than personal valour, with what ardour must that quality have been cultivated and cherished! The love of arms becoming thus their ruling and universal passion, would soon characterize their religion, dictate their laws, and, in short, form their prejudices and opinions, which decide every thing among mankind.

But it may be objected, that if the manners and character of the ancient northern people proceeded so much from the climate, as the same cause still operates, why is the effect altered? This is only a specious difficulty. A nation is never solely influenced by climate, except in its infancy; while it is uncultivated and barbarous, it is only guided by instinct; the objects of sense and the modes of living being as yet simple and uniform. When, after some ages, reason has been expanded by experience and reflection, when legislators have arisen, who, either by the native force of genius, or by observing the manners of other nations, have so enlarged their understandings as to perceive the necessity of a change of manners, it is then that a new system of principles combat, and either divide the empire with, or totally triumph over, the first physical causes. Such was the immediate effect of Christianity in the north, an event which, considered only in a philosophical light, should be ever regarded as the dawn of those happy days which were afterwards to shine out with superior splendour. In effect, this religion, which tended to

R

correct the abuse of licentious liberty, to banish bloody dissensions from among individuals, to restrain robberies and piracy, softening the ferocity of manners, requiring a certain knowledge of letters and history, re-establishing a part of mankind, who groaned under a miserable slavery, in their natural rights, introducing a relish for a life of peace, and an idea of happiness independent of sensual gratifications, sowed the seeds, if I may so speak, of that new spirit which grew to maturity in the succeeding ages, and to which the arts and sciences, springing up along with it, added still more strength and vigour.

But, after all, is it very certain, as the objection supposes, that the climate of Europe has not undergone a change since the times we speak of? Those who have read the ancients with attention, think differently, and conclude, that the degrees of cold are at this time much less severe than they were formerly. This is not a place to enlarge on a subject which might appear foreign to the work. Let it suffice to observe, that the rivers in Gaul, namely, the Loire and the Rhone, were regularly frozen over every year, so that frequently whole armies with their carriages and baggage could march over them. Even the Tiber froze at Rome, and Juvenal says positively that it was requisite to break the ice in winter, in order to come at the water of that river. Many passages in Horace suppose the streets of Rome to be full of ice and snow. Ovid assures us, that the Black Sea was frozen annually, and appeals for the truth of this to the governor of the province, whose name he mentions: he also relates several circumstances concerning that climate, which at present agree only with Norway or Sweden. The forests of Thrace and Pannonia were full of bears and wild boars, in like manner as now the forests of the north. The northern part of Spain was little inhabited for the same cause. In short, all the ancients who mention the climate of Gaul, Germany, Pannonia and Thrace, speak of it as insupportable, and agree that the ground was covered with snow the greatest part of the year, being incapable of producing olives, grapes, and most other fruits. It is easy to conceive that the forests being cleared away, the face of the country better cultivated, and the marshy places drained, the moist exhalations which generate cold, must be considerably lessened, and that the rays of the sun must have a freer access to warm the earth. The same thing has happened in North America since the Europeans have carried there their accustomed industry. The history of the north leaves us no room to doubt that there have been vast forests cut down, and, by this single means, extensive marshes have been dried up and converted into land fit for cultivation. Without mentioning the general causes which insensibly effect the destruction of forests, it was common to set these on fire in order to procure fertile fields. A king of Sweden was surnamed the wood-cutter, for having grubbed up and cleared vast provinces, and felled the trees with which it was all covered *. Nor were they less cleared away in Norway and Denmark. Thus a change in the climate must long have preceded that in the manners.

What conclusion ought we to draw from all this? If for these fifteen or sixteen centuries, the arts, sciences, industry and politeness have been incessantly advancing in the north of Europe, we cannot but evidently discover three causes of this, which, though different in their natures, have yet been productive of the same effect. The first, is that restlessness natural to the people of all nations, but which acts more forcibly on the inhabitants of Europe, and is ever urging them to exchange their present condition in hopes of a better : the second, slower but equally sure, is the change of climate : the third, more sensible, more expeditious, but more accidental, is that communication formed between mankind by commerce and religion, and cemented by a thousand new relations ; which has, in a short time, transported from the south into the north new arts, manners, and opinions. These three causes have continually operated, and the face of Scandinavia changes daily. It already shines with somewhat more than borrowed lights. Time produces strange revolutions ! Who knows whether the sun will not one day rise in the north?

---

* M. Mallet alludes to the Olaf Tretelgia of the Ynglinga-saga, and the reader will find by referring to page 86, that this so-called king, even if the statement may be relied on, merely cleared a small district, and not " vast provinces," and that the surname of wood-cutter was given him by his enemies, in order to throw ridicule on his proceedings.—ED.

SUPPLEMENTARY CHAPTERS

BY

THE EDITOR.

CHAPTER I.

COLONIZATION OF GREENLAND, AND DISCOVERY OF THE
AMERICAN CONTINENT BY THE SCANDINAVIANS.

ABOUT a century after the discovery of Iceland, of which an account has been previously given *, a Norwegian chieftain named Thorvald, having been banished for homicide, retired thither with his son Eirek, surnamed the Red. Some years afterwards, probably in 982, Eirek was sentenced to three years' exile for a similar offence, and set sail towards the west in quest of a coast that had recently been descried by a Norwegian navigator. His search proved successful, and he landed on a small island, west of Cape Farewell, where he passed the first winter. In the spring he went to survey the mainland, and finding it covered with a pleasing verdure, gave it the name of *Grænland*, Greenland, saying, that a good name would induce people to settle there. Eirek, when the term of his banishment was expired, returned to Iceland, and, in the year 986, again set sail for Greenland with a number of settlers, and established himself in a place he named Bratta-hlid, on a creek called after him, Eireksfjörd (Eric's Frith), which soon became a very considerable colony †. Some years

---

* See page 187.
* Eireksfjörd is supposed to be the modern Tunnulliorbik in the Julianes-haab district on the eastern coast of Baffin's Bay, in lat. 60° 55′. Brattahlid

afterwards, probably in 997, Leif, the son of Eirek, having made a voyage to Norway, met with a favourable reception from King Olaf Tryggvason, who persuaded him to embrace the doctrines of Christianity, or, more properly speaking, to be baptized, and then sent him back, accompanied by a priest, to convert the new colony. Eirek was at first offended at his son for deserting the faith of his forefathers, but was at length obliged to give his tacit consent to the propagation of the new religion, which was soon embraced by all the settlers, though it would appear that Eirek himself remained to the day of his death a worshipper of Thor and Odin. The settlements in Greenland continued to increase and flourish. They were divided into the East and the West *Bygd*, or inhabited districts, the intervening tract being termed the *Ubygd*, or uninhabited country. The West Bygd, at a later period, contained ninety farms, with four churches ; the East Bygd, one hundred and ninety farms and two towns, with one cathedral, eleven churches, and three monasteries. The cathedral was in Garda. The first bishop was ordained in 1121, the seventeenth and last in 1404 ; and documentary proofs of his having officiated in 1409 at a marriage in Garda have lately been discovered by the learned Finn Magnusen, who derives his pedigree from the marriage in question. After this nothing more was heard of the Greenland colonies. How they perished we know not.

The learned men of the seventeenth century, when they recalled to mind that a Christian community had existed on these remote shores for upwards of four centuries, could only account for its extinction by a sudden catastrophe. Some supposed that the settlements had been ravaged by the pirates who infested the north seas at the close of the fourteenth century ; others, that the great pestilence of 1348, called the Black Death, had swept off the greater part of the population, and that the survivors had been massacred by the Esquimaux. But it seems very unlikely that pirates would have directed their marauding expeditions to such a poor country as Greenland, and although the colony may probably have been visited

---

was long the residence of Eirek's descendants, and afterwards of the chief magistrate of Greenland. The word may be rendered by Steepslope ; from *Bratt*, steep, and *hlid*, a slope or acclivity.

by the terrible scourge so graphically described by Boccaccio
in the introduction to his Decameron, we believe there is no
documentary evidence to show that this was actually the case.
We know at least that upwards of half a century later there
was still a bishop at Garda, and may therefore conclude that
the colonists were able to resist the attacks of the Esquimaux,
with whom they appear to have been in constant hostility.
The real cause of the gradual decay and final extinction of
these settlements was, no doubt, the pernicious system of
commercial policy pursued by the mother country. Previous to
the Calmar Union, Queen Margaret had made the trade with
Iceland, Greenland, and the Færoe islands a royal monopoly,
only to be carried on in vessels belonging to, or licensed by,
the sovereign; and this monopoly was kept up by her successors, and, after the dissolution of the union, by the kings
of Denmark, to a very late period, being only abolished for
Iceland in 1776.   Finn Magnusen, in a very able paper
on the trade between England and Iceland during the Middle Ages, published in the *Nordisk Tidskrift for Oldkyndighed*, very justly observes that "Iceland would probably
have shared the same fate as Greenland, had not British merchants, in spite of opposition, supplied it with articles absolutely necessary for the existence of its inhabitants."

A few fruitless attempts were made in the sixteenth century
to rediscover the lost colonies; but as it was not known at
that period that Greenland had a west coast, the two Bygds
were naturally supposed to have been situated on the eastern
one.   Subsequently to the voyages of Davis, Frobisher, and
Baffin, it became the general opinion of northern antiquaries that the East and West Bygds were situated respectively
on the east and west coasts of the peninsula.   In 1721, Hans
Egede, a zealous Norwegian clergyman, prevailed on the king
of Denmark to form a new settlement on the west coast,
Egede himself going out as missionary.   Since the establishment of this colony numerous vestiges of the ancient one have
been discovered; urns, implements, fragments of church bells,
Runic inscriptions, and ruined edifices—especially in the district of Julianeshaab.   We know by several very accurate
topographical descriptions of the ancient settlements that the
West Bygd only contained four churches, and as the ruins
of seven have been discovered in the southern part of West

Greenland, the opinion gradually gained ground that both Bygds were situated on the west coast; the supporters of this hypothesis contending that the current, which sets south-westward from the Polar Seas, accumulates the ice on the east coast of Greenland to an extent which must, in all ages, have rendered the climate much more rigorous than that of the west coast, and formed an insurmountable barrier to colonization. This question was finally set at rest in 1829 by Captain Graah, who, by order of the Danish government, explored the east coast in umiaks—the larger kind of Esquimaux boats—from Cape Farewell to the sixty-fourth parallel of latitude, without finding a single trace of the ancient colonies *

The prevailing opinion of the northern antiquaries at present is, that the East Bygd extended from Cape Farewell to Immartinek, in lat. 60° 50′, and the West Bygd from Arksut Creek, lat. 61° 40′, to lat. 67°. The coast beyond the West Bygd, was called Nordrsetur †, and was much frequented in the summer season by the colonists for fishing. They also appear to have had some permanent settlements on this coast, both to the south and north of Disco Island.

In 1824, a stone was found in the island of Kingiktorsoak, in lat. 72° 54′, long. 56°. west of Greenwich, bearing a Runic inscription, which was submitted to Finn Magnusen, Professor Rask, and Dr. Brynjulfvson of Iceland; and these celebrated Runologists, without any communication on the subject having passed between them, respectively arrived at the same interpretation of the characters, except the last six, which Professor Rask and Finn Magnusen at length agreed meant the numerals MCXXXV; Dr. Brynjulvson contenting himself with expressing an opinion that they might be mere ornaments, but that, from the form of the other characters, he should deem the inscription to be of the twelfth century. These gentlemen gave the inscription as follows:—

---

* See Narrative of an Expedition to the East Coast of Greenland by Capt. W. A. Graah, of the Danish Royal Navy. Translated by the late E. Gordon Macdougall.

† From seta, a seat. The northern seats; or, possessions.

ELLIGR · SIGVATHS · SON : R · OK · BJANNE : TORTARSON :
OK : ENRITHI · ODDSSON : LAUKARDAK · IN : FYRIR GAKNDAG
HLOTHV · VARDATE · OK RYDU : MCXXXV.

which, in correct Norse, would be

" Erlingr Sighvatssonr, ok Bjarni Thórðarson, ok Eindriði
Oddsson, laugardaginn fyrir gagndag, hlóðu varða thessa (*vel*
thenna,) ok ruddu; MCXXXV.

In English:

Erling Sighvatsson, and Bjarni Thordasson, and Eindrid
Oddsson, on Saturday before *Gangday*, raised these marks and
cleared the ground, 1135.

We subjoin a woodcut of the Kingiktorsoak stone, copied
from the *Antiquitates Americanæ*.

Professor Rafn derives *gagndagr*, from *gagn*, victory, and
dagr a day—*the day of victory;* and observes that the Icelanders gave this appellation to two festivals of the church,
one falling on the 14th of May, the other on the 25th of
April, or Ascension Day, which was popularly termed
gagndagrinn eini, and *hinn mikli;* the *unique* and *the great
day of* (spiritual) *victory.* Ascension week was celebrated in
Catholic times with peculiar solemnity ; the priests, accompanied by the people, going in procession with lighted torches,
and sprinkling holy water round the churches. It was no
doubt from this going, or *ganging*, in procession, that the three

days before Ascension Day were called, in Anglo Saxon, *gang dagas*, and in old Scotch, *gang dayis*. Björn Haldorson in his Icelandic dictionary, renders them by *gagndagar*, vel *gángdagar*, the latter being, no doubt, the more popular appellation. Be this as it may, the meaning of the inscription is, that in the twelfth century—and if we admit Professor Rask's interpretation of the last six Runic characters—in 1135, on the Saturday, either before April 25th or May 14th—in all probability the former—three Northmen cleared the ground, and set up marks or mounds, some vestiges of which were observed on the spot where the stone was found, to show that they had taken possession of the land—probably of the whole island. This would indicate an intention of settling there, and they must at all events have passed the winter in this high latitude, Baffin's Bay being unnavigable at so early a season. The discovery of this Runic stone has thus made us acquainted with the singular fact that Northmen explored the Polar Seas, and wintered in these icebound regions, seven centuries previous to the expeditions of Captains Parry and Ross, and that, too, without being furnished with any of the numerous comforts and conveniences of a modern outfit.

Other Runic stones have been discovered in the district of Julianeshaab, but they offer nothing of interest. One of these, a tombstone, with the epitaph " Vigdis rests here, God glad her soul "—was found on the shores of a creek called Igaliko, supposed to be Einarsfjörd, near the foundations of a church 96 feet in length, and 48 in breadth. Some dilapidated walls at the bottom of the same creek, inclosing an area of 120 feet by 100, are supposed to be the remains of the cathedral of Garda; but the most remarkable ruin yet discovered is at Kakortok, situated on a branch of this creek. It is an edifice, evidently a church, 51 feet in length, and 25 in breadth, having a round-headed window at each gable, and four square windows in each of the. lateral walls, which are from 4 to 8 feet thick, and of massive stone *.

We have thus seen that the old Icelandic Sagas state explicitly that colonies of Northmen existed on the shores of

---

* Two views of this ruin are given in the Antiq. Amer. Plate IX.

Greenland from the close of the tenth to the beginning of the fifteenth century. From that period, to the middle of the last century, nothing more was heard of them, and those who had not read the original documents, and been convinced from the internal evidence afforded by the simplicity and truthfulness of the narrative that they dealt with facts, and not with fiction, might reasonably doubt their testimony, and, by analogical reasoning, that of the Sagas in general. The Runic inscriptions, and the numerous vestiges of the former colonies, scattered along the east coast of Baffin's Bay, are therefore doubly interesting and important; for they not only confirm, in the most striking manner, the authenticity of the Sagas relating to Greenland, but warrant the conclusion that those which tell us, in the same artless manner, of the discovery of the American continent are equally trustworthy, though their statements have not as yet been confirmed by the same kind of palpable evidence.

The Sagas, relating to America, were made use of by Torfæus for his "*Historia Vinlandiæ Antiquæ*," published in 1705, which contains a correct account of the discoveries of the Northmen in the western hemisphere. More or less ample information on the subject was also furnished by several eminent writers of the last century; notwithstanding which, the literary world seemed unwilling to admit the startling fact, that a people, who were erroneously supposed to have been without the pale of European civilization, should have crossed the wild waves of the Atlantic, and trod the shores of a mighty continent ages before its name became associated with that of Columbus. In order to remove any further doubts on this point, Professor Rafn undertook the laborious task of publishing the original narratives of the voyages, and we believe that no impartial person who has examined the documentary evidence given in the "*Antiquitates Americanæ* " * will any longer hesitate to acknowledge the claims of the Scandinavians to priority of discovery, though he may differ, as we do, very

---

* Antiquitates Americanæ; sive Scriptores Septentrionales rerum ante Columbianarum in Americâ, 1 vol. fol. Copenh. 1837, published by the Royal Society of Northern Antiquarians. Mr. Rafn, who was assisted in his task by Finn Magnusen, has given the Icelandic (Old Norse) text, with the various readings of the MSS., accompanied by translations in Danish and Latin.

materially from the learned antiquarians of Copenhagen respecting the light in which such a discovery ought to be regarded.

The two most important documents published by Mr. Rafn are the Sagas of Eirek the Red, and of Thorfinn Karlsefni, which were probably first committed to writing in the twelfth century, or about four generations after the events recorded took place. The manuscript of the latter Saga, made use of by Mr. Rafn as the basis of his text, is on vellum, and bears internal evidence of having been written at the close of the thirteenth, or beginning of the fourteenth century. The Saga of Eirek the Red forms a part of the beautiful vellum manuscript called the "Codex Flatoiensis," which is a collection of Sagas transcribed from older manuscripts between the years 1387, and 1395 ; that is to say, a century before the discovery of America by Columbus. Begging the reader to bear in mind this significant fact, we shall proceed, without entering into further details, to give an abstract of these Sagas, with such explanations as may be called for in the course of the narrative, especially on points that have furnished matter for discussion, or further investigation.

Among those who accompanied Eirek the Red to Greenland was Herjúlf, whose son Bjarni was at that time on a trading voyage to Norway. Returning to Iceland in the course of the summer *, and finding that his family had left the island, Bjarni resolved to follow them, and pass the winter, as he had been used to do, at his father's fireside. He accordingly set sail, though neither he nor any of his men had ever navigated the Greenland seas, and for many days was driven by tempestuous north winds, accompanied by dense fogs, he knew not whither. When the weather cleared up, he descried land, which, on approaching, he found to be moderately elevated and overgrown with wood. Being convinced that it could not be Greenland, which had been represented to him as distinguishable at a distance by its snow-capped mountains, he left it to larboard, and, standing out to sea, after sailing two days again descried land, lower than the former, but also overgrown with wood. Continuing his course with a south-west wind, he came in three days to a lofty island, the shore of which

* This must have been in the year 986. See page 244.

presented numerous icebergs and glaciers. The country not appearing to Bjarni very attractive, he again stood out to sea, and after sailing four days, with fresh gales, reached Herjúlfnes *, in Greenland, where his father was settled.

Some years after this Bjarni, being again in Norway, visited Eirek, one of the principal jarls of the country, and was much blamed, when he related his adventures, for not having examined the land he had discovered more accurately. On his return to Greenland, the chief topic of conversation during the long winter evenings was the newly discovered country to the south-west, and the spirit of enterprise being thus kept awake, Leif, son of Eirek the Red, purchased Bjarni's vessel, which he fitted out, about the year 1000, with every requisite for a long voyage, and prevailed on his father to accompany him. Old Eirek happening, however, to fall from his horse, on his way to the place of embarkation, regarded it as a sign that he was not destined to make any further discoveries, and therefore returned home, leaving Leif, with a crew of thirty-five men, to set sail without him.

The first land they made was that which Bjarni had seen last. Going on shore they found no herbage of any kind, but a *bare rugged plain of broad flat rocks*, extending from the foot of a chain of ice and snow-clad mountains to the sea-side. Having given the name of Helluland (1) †, *Shistland, or the land of large flat broad stones*, to this country, Leif continued his voyage, and arrived at *a low level coast, with numerous white sandy cliffs, and thickly covered with wood*, from which circumstance he called it Markland ‡, *Woodland* (2). After sailing two days more, with a north-east wind, they came to an island, and entered a channel between it and a point projecting northwards from the mainland. Holding their course westwards, along the shores of the latter, they remarked that a great extent of ground was left dry at ebb-tide. They afterwards went on shore where a river, issuing from a lake, fell into the sea, and being pleased with the appearance of the country, brought their vessel up the river with the flood-tide, and moored her in the lake. Having made up their minds to winter in this place, they constructed some large and commodious dwellings

---

* Supposed to be the modern Ikigeit, near Cape Farewell.
† The figures refer to the Explanatory Remarks at the end of the chapter.
‡ From mörk, a wood, or thicket.

or booths, known afterwards under the appellation of *Leifs-búdir*, or Leifsbooths (3). Both the lake and the river afforded them an abundant supply of the finest salmon. The soil appeared to be fruitful, and the pasturage excellent. The climate was temperate, there being no severe cold during the winter, and the grass never losing its freshness.

When they had finished building, Leif divided his people into two companies, to be employed alternately in exploring the country and keeping watch at the booths. It happened one day that they missed a German, named Tyrker, who was a great favourite of Leif's, having been for years in his father's service. Leif instantly set out with twelve men in search of him, but they had not gone far when they saw him coming towards them with an air of extraordinary gaiety. He at first, to their great surprise, accosted them in German, but at length told them in Norse that he had been feasting on grapes, having found at a short distance up the country a place covered with wild vines. On Leif appearing to doubt this statement, he added, that he surely ought to know what grapes were, having been born in a country where there was no lack of them (4). They soon ascertained, in fact, that grapes grew in abundance in most parts of the country around them, a circumstance which induced Leif to give it the appropriate name of Vinland, *Wineland* (5). After passing the winter in this place, and loading their vessel with timber, and their long boat with grapes, they set sail in the spring for Greenland (6). On approaching the coast, they descried on a rock a party of shipwrecked people, fifteen in all, including their chief Thorir, and his wife Gudrida. Leif rescued them from their perilous position and took them home with him, and from this circumstance obtained the surname of the Lucky.

On hearing the favourable account that Leif gave of Vinland, his brother Thorvald, deeming that the country had not been sufficiently explored, set out in 1002, in Leif's vessel, with thirty men, and arrived without accident at Leifsbooths. The following spring Thorvald sent a party out in the boat to explore the coast to the south. The party, on their return in autumn, reported that they had found the country everywhere very beautiful and well wooded, the woods extending to within a short distance of the beach, which was in general of a fine white sand; that there were numerous shoals and islands along the coast, but, with the exception of a wooden shed on one of the islands, they had nowhere found any trace either of man or beast (7). The following summer, 1004, Thorvald sailed eastward from Leifsbooths, and then northward, past a remarkable headland, which, with an opposite headland, inclosed a bay. Here they were driven by a violent gale into shoal water, and were obliged to remain a considerable time to make a new keel for their vessel; Thorvald setting up the old one on the headland, which he named, from this circumstance, *Kjalarnes*, Keelness or Cape Keel (8). He then sailed along the coast eastward, and coming to a finely wooded headland, went on shore with all his followers, and was so struck with the beauty of the scenery, that he exclaimed, "Here should I like to fix my dwelling!" As they were preparing to go on board, they observed three canoes or sealskin boats drawn up on the beach, under each of which were three Esquimaux or Skrællings, as they were called by the Northmen. Of the nine natives they killed eight, one escaping in his canoe. They were then, continues the Saga, so weary that they all fell into a profound sleep, but were awakened by a voice crying out, "Arise, Thorvald! if thou wilt save thy life hasten to thy vessel with all thy followers, and set sail without delay." Shortly afterwards they saw a number of canoes, filled with Skrællings, coming from the interior of the bay against them. They endeavoured to protect themselves by raising battle-screens on the ships' sides, but the Skrællings, after discharging a volley of arrows, and shouting for a while, betook themselves to a precipitate flight. Thorvald had been wounded by an arrow, under the arm, and finding that the wound was mortal, turned to his followers, and said:—

"I now advise ye to prepare, as speedily as ye may, for your departure. But me shall ye bear to the headland, which I thought was the most fitting for a dwelling place. It may be that the word which fell from my mouth about abiding there was prophetic. There shall ye bury me, and set up two crosses, one at my head, and the other at my feet, and shall call the place *Krossanes* (9)—Crossness, or Cape Cross—in all times to come."

They did as he had ordered, and then returned to their companions at Leifsbooths, where they passed the winter, and early in the spring of 1005 set sail for Greenland, with a cargo of timber, grapes, and vine sets. Christianity, as before stated, had been introduced into Greenland by Leif, a few years previous to Thorvald's expedition.

Not long after this Thorstein, the third son of Eirek the Red, set sail in the same ship, accompanied by Gudrida his wife, and twenty-five able-bodied men, with the intention of bringing home his brother's body, but after being tossed about the whole summer by adverse winds, they were driven at the beginning of winter into Lysufjörd *, where Thorstein and most of his followers were carried off by a contagious disease, and Gudrida returned in the following spring to Brattahlid with her husband's body.

In the autumn of '1006, two ships came to Greenland from Iceland, the one commanded by Thorfinn, who bore the significant surname of Karlsefni; i. e. possessing manly abilities; the other by Bjarni Grimolfsson and Thorhall Gamlason. Thorfinn was a wealthy and powerful man, of a very distinguished family, tracing his descent from Danish, Swedish, Norwegian, Irish and Scotch ancestors, some of whom were kings or of royal lineage, and he appears to have been one of the most enterprising trading-rovers of that period. He was accompanied by Snorri Thorbrandsson, also of good extraction. Thorfinn and his companions passed the winter with old Eirek the Red, and the festivities of Yule or Christmas were kept up with a splendour never before witnessed in Greenland, owing in a great measure to Thorfinn having stowed his ship with plenty of malt and corn, which he told Eirek to make a free use of. During this festal season, and the long winter nights that followed, Thorfinn having heard a great deal about the fine salmon and wild grapes of Vinland, came to the resolution of founding a colony there. Meanwhile, however, he fell in love with Thorstein's handsome widow, Gudrida, who is represented as possessing every quality that in that age could render a lady attractive, and having obtained the consent of her brother-in law, Leif, married her.

In the spring of 1007 the vessel belonging to Thorfinn and his friend, and it would appear trading partner, Snorri, and that which was the joint property of Bjarni and Thorhall Gamlason, were fitted out for the projected voyage to Vin-

* Supposed to be Issortok Creek, on the east coast of Baffin's Bay, in lat. 65°.

land. A third vessel was commanded by Thorvard, who had married Freydisa, a natural daughter of Eirek the Red. He was accompanied by a dark ill-looking man, of gigantic stature, called Thorhall, who had long served Eirek as huntsman in summer and house-steward in winter, but who is represented as a very bad Christian; a circumstance which might probably have contributed to raise him in the estimation of old Eirek. There were in all one hundred and sixty individuals, furnished with cattle and other live stock in abundance.

They first sailed to the western district of Old Greenland and to Bjarney (10), and then, for two days, in a southerly direction to Helluland, where they found a great many foxes, and describe the *large flat stones or rocks*—several of them twelve ells broad—peculiar to the country. Two days more brought them to the woody shores of Markland, where they killed a bear on an island near the coast, which was named from that circumstance Bjarney, *Bear's Island* (11). Leaving this place, they continued sailing for some time south-west, having the land to starboard, until at length they arrived at Kjalarnes, where there were *trackless coasts and white sandy beaches* of such length as to obtain the name of Furðustrandir *, or *Marvellous Strands* (12). The coast afterwards became more indented with inlets and bays, into one of which they entered. Here Thorfinn landed a Scotch man and woman, called Haki and Hekja, whom Leif had formerly received as a present from Olaf Tryggvason, and who were remarkably swift of foot †, with orders to run across the country and explore it to the southwest for three days, when they were taken on board, bringing with them some wild corn and some grapes. Continuing their course they entered a bay, off the mouth of which was an island so crowded with eider ducks that they could scarcely walk without treading on their eggs. *A strong current* ran past this island, and also further up the bay, from which circumstance they named the former Straumey, *Stream Isle,*

---

* From furða, Gen. furðu, a marvellous or wonderful thing, and strönd, pl. strandir, strands.

† This anecdote has a mythic tinge, which renders it somewhat suspicious ; Thor also taking with him a boy and girl, Thjalfi and Röska, who were remarkably swift of foot, on his expedition to Jötunheim.—See the Prose Edda, ch. 44.

and the atter Straumfjörd, *Stream Frith* (13). Here they un-
loaded their ships and passed the first winter, and it was probably here that Gudrida gave birth to a son called Snorri *.
In the spring they began to experience a scarcity of provisions, the weather having been for a long time too stormy for
fishing. Under these circumstances, they prayed God to send
them food, but the old Sagaman quaintly observes that food
did not come so soon as they thought it might have done.

Thorhall, the huntsman, had meanwhile disappeared, and
after looking for him for three days, they found him sitting
on a rock gazing vacantly around and muttering verses.
Shortly after this, a whale of a species unknown to the Northmen being stranded, they cut it up for food, but we are told
that all who ate of it became sick, owing probably to Thorhall
exclaiming while they were eating it: " The redbeard Thor
has been more helpsome to us than your Christ. I have got
this (the whale) for my verses. Seldom has my protector refused me any thing that I have asked of him;" on hearing
which they threw all that remained of the whale into the
sea, quite horror-stricken at the idea of being indebted to
Thor for their sustenance. The Sagaman piously adds, that
after this the weather became milder, and they were no longer
in want of provisions, being able to hunt, fish, and collect
eggs in the island.

Shortly afterwards Thorhall the huntsman, with eight men,
left Thorfinn and sailed northward in search of Vinland ; but
after passing Kjalarnes was driven out to sea by westerly
gales and thrown on the coast of Ireland, where, according to
the account of traders, he and his party were made slaves.
Thorfinn and his people sailed south, and came to *a river
that flowed through a lake on its way to the sea, and the
mouth of which was so beset with sandbanks as to be only accessible at high water.* To this place he gave the name of
Hóp, *Estuary* (14); and finding the country very beautiful,
with good pasturage for the cattle which they had still with them,
and every thing in great abundance, *corn growing wild on the
low grounds, and vines on the hills,* with the woods well stocked

* Snorri Thorfinnsson was, consequently, the first European on record
born in America. The celebrated sculptor Thorvaldsen, and the no less celebrated northern antiquary Finn Magnuson, claim descent from him by a female line. See the Ninth Genealogical Table in the Ant. Amer.

S

with game, and the rivers and creeks actually teeming with
fish, they resolved to make it their winter quarters, and accordingly set up booths at a short distance from the lake or
bay. No snow fell during the winter, and their cattle remained out in the fields (15).

One morning, soon after their arrival, they saw a number of
natives coming in skin canoes up the bay, brandishing their
poles and making a great noise, which the Northmen responded to by holding up a white shield in token of peace.
The natives then landed, and after gazing for some time at
the strangers in mute astonishment, rowed away again round
the headland. They are described as being of a sallow and
swarthy appearance, with uncouth hair, large eyes, and high
cheek-bones (16). The winter passed without any incident
worthy of notice, but early in spring the natives came again
in such numbers that the bay appeared actually covered with
their canoes. A white shield being again held out by the
Northmen, the Skrællings landed, and eagerly began to barter
their fine grey furs and squirrel skins for bits of red cloth
and milk porridge, which they seem to have highly relished.
What they coveted most were swords and spears, but these
Thorfinn prudently forbade his people to sell them. Whilst
this lucrative traffic was going on, and the Northmen were
dealing out their cloth in smaller shreds, a bull, which Thorfinn had brought with him, issued unexpectedly from the
wood and began to bellow, which so terrified the Skrællings
that they rushed to their canoes and rowed off in the greatest
trepidation. Three weeks after this they again appeared in
still greater numbers, brandishing their poles and setting up
a shout of defiance. Thorfinn, on their landing, caused a red
shield to be borne against them, and a hot skirmish took
place, the Skrællings using their slings with great dexterity.
The Northmen, fancying themselves surrounded, were seized
with a panic, and fled along the river. In this conjuncture
Fredisa rushed out, exclaiming—

" How can such valiant men as ye are run away from these
wretched caitiffs, whom I thought you would have knocked
down like cattle ! Had I a weapon, methinks I could wield
it better than any of you."

They, however, continued their flight into the forest, Freydisa, though far advanced in pregnancy, following them as well

as she was able. At length, picking up the sword of Thor-brand Snorrason, who had been killed with a stone, she turned round on the Skrællings and prepared to defend herself; but her frantic gestures so terrified or bewildered them, that they ran off to their canoes pursued by the Northmen, who killed great numbers of them, only losing two of their own party. Such is the account transmitted to us of the first battle fought by Europeans on the American continent, and it is a curious coincidence that its successful issue should have been owing to the courage of a woman! We are told that the va-liant Northmen could only account for their sudden fear by supposing that they had not only to combat with real men of flesh and blood, but also with a whole legion of phantoms.

After this Thorfinn and his companions felt convinced that although the country held out many advantages, they would be constantly exposed to the attacks of the natives. They, therefore, returned to Straumfjörd, where they passed the third winter; but the number of females being very dis-proportionate to that of the males, violent quarrels arose, " those who had no wives," as the old chronicler quaintly ob-serves, " wishing to take them from those who had."

In the ensuing spring they sailed homewards, and touching at Markland, met with a Skrælling and his two wives and two children. The adults escaped, but the Northmen carried off the children, whom they baptized and taught Norse, and who told them that their people had no houses, but lived in holes and caverns. Bjarni Grimolfsson was driven westward into a sea so infested with worms that his vessel was soon reduced to a sinking state. They therefore had no alternative than to cast lots who should leave the vessel, and try to escape in a small boat, preserved from the attacks of the worms by being smeared with seal blubber. Bjarni himself was among the fortunate; but when he got into the boat a man from the ship called out, " Wilt thou leave me, Bjarni? Didst thou not promise my father, when I left Iceland with thee, that we should share the same lot?" " And that we won't do," re-plied Bjarni; "get thou into the boat and I will return to the ship, for I see thou hast a hankering after life;" so saying, he gave the young man his place in the boat and mounted the vessel, which was never heard of afterwards. Those in the boat made their way to Dublin, where they related what had taken place. Thorfinn and his companions reached Greenland in safety in 1011.

In the same year there arrived in Greenland a ship from Norway, commanded by two brothers, Helgi and Finnbogi, whom Freydisa persuaded to undertake a voyage to Vinland with her. Each party was to fit out a vessel with thirty able-bodied men, and to have an equal share in the profits of the expedition. Freydisa, however, contrived to take five men more than the number stipulated. They arrived at Vinland without any accident, and passed the winter at Leifsbooths, which Freydisa had wished to purchase from Leif, but could only obtain his permission to make use of them. The Norwegian brothers devised all sorts of games and recreations for the people during the winter *, but coolness soon arose between them and Freydisa, who, by her subtle arts, at length persuaded her husband Thorvard to fall on the two brothers, when they were asleep, and murder them and all their followers. As she could not, however, prevail either on her husband or any of his men to lay their hands on the five women of the Norwegian party, she seized a hatchet and butchered them herself. After the perpetration of this base deed, they returned to Greenland in 1013, when the rumour of the crime having reached the ear of Leif, he put three of Freydisa's followers to the torture, and obtained a full account of the sanguinary transaction. Freydisa was left unpunished, but became an object of general abhorrence.

At the time of Freydisa's return Thorfinn was waiting for a favourable wind to sail to Norway with the most valuable cargo that had ever left the shores of Greenland, consisting chiefly of the hard-grained wood and fine furs of the newly discovered country. He disposed of his goods to great advantage in Norway, and we are told that a Bremen merchant gave him as much as half a mark of gold—equivalent to £16 of modern money—for a small piece of Vinland *massur* wood†. In 1014 Thorfinn returned to Iceland, where he purchased the estate of Glaumbæ, in the northern district, and became the founder of a wealthy and powerful family. After his

---

* Captain Parry, placed in similar circumstances, acted in a similar manner, and got up theatrical representations for the amusement of his sailors.

† Probably the variegated, or bird's-eye maple, common in Massachusetts.

death his widow Gudrida went on a pilgrimage to Rome, and afterwards returned to Glaumbæ, where her American-born son Snorri had built a church, and passed the remainder of her days as a religious recluse. Runolf, the son of Snorri's daughter Hallfrida, was the father of the learned Bishop Thorlak Runolfsson, to whom we are principally indebted for the oldest ecclesiastical code of Iceland, published in the year 1123, and it is also probable that the narrative of Thorfinn's voyage was originally compiled by him.

Such is the account transmitted to us of the discovery of Vinland, which, as we have attempted to show in the explanatory remarks, there is every reason to suppose was that part of the American continent that, six centuries later, became known under the appellation of New England. Mr. Rafn has given numerous extracts from the Icelandic Geographical Treatises of the Middle Ages, in which the three American districts Helluland, Markland and Vinland are spoken of. But the most conclusive collateral evidence he adduces is that of Adam of Bremen, who informs us that he heard of the discovery from Sveyn Ethrithson, King of Denmark *, who had entertained him during his mission in the north for the propagation of Christianity. "The king," says the learned ecclesiastic, "also made mention of another region discovered in the northern ocean, which had been visited by many people, and was called Wineland, *because grapes that produce a very good wine grow there spontaneously;* corn also grows there, without sowing, in great abundance;" and emphatically adds, "We know this not by fabulous hearsay, but from *authentic accounts furnished by Danes.*" †

We think Professor Rafn ought to have been satisfied with this evidence, without attempting to fix the latitude of Thorfinn's winter quarters by an astronomical calculation founded on a mere conjectural interpretation of a vague expression in the original text, respecting the time the sun remained above the horizon. He might also have spared us a great deal of learned trifling by omitting his, "*Descriptio vetusti monumenti in regione Massachusetts reperti;*" for these *monumenta vetusta* are, to say the least, of a very dubious character, and the

* A nephew of Canute. He reigned from 1047 to 1076.
† Adam Brem. de situ Dan. c. 246, and Antiq. Amer. p. 338.

dissertation in question affords rich materials for any one who might feel inclined to place the lapidary lore of the Royal Society of Northern Antiquaries on a par with that of the renowned Jonathan Oldbuck. The principal *monumentum vetustum* which has given rise to these erudite lucubrations, is a rock, or boulder, commonly called the Dighton-writing Rock, lying on the banks of the Taunton river a few miles above Mount Hope Bay. Its flat surface is covered with rude designs pecked in the stone, and probably meant for the figures of men and animals, together with some unconnected scrawls which, if we may judge from the series of drawings made at various times between the years 1680 and 1830, and now published by Mr. Rafn, would appear to have gradually grown under the pencil of each successive draughtsman, into something resembling runic characters *. On the faith of these drawings—such as they are—and especially of the last one of the series, which the *docti Insulæ Rhodensis viri* assure Mr. Rafn was made by "the Committee on the Antiquities and Aboriginal History of America † in proper person expressly"—*no doubt expressly*—for the work he had in preparation, the learned Finn Magnusen has not hesitated to transmute the scrawl in question into a very readable Old Norse inscription, purporting that Thorfinn, with 151 followers, took possession of the country around the said Dighton Rock; an interpretation which has no doubt been duly appreciated by the *docti viri* of Massachusetts. We beg the reader not to conclude, from this manner of interpreting lapidary inscriptions, or rather lapidary scrawls, that the characters on the Kingiktorsoak stone were deciphered by a similar process, for we can assure him that there is not the slightest analogy between the two monuments. The Kingiktorsoak stone bears an undoubted runic inscription, offering, with the exception of the last six characters, no great difficulty of interpretation. The Dighton Rock is covered with tortuous lines which may be made to mean any thing or nothing, and which after all the noise that has been made about them may probably be

---

* See Ant. Amer. Plates xi. and xii.

† We have heard of the aborigines and the aboriginal inhabitants of a country, but what the *learned men* of Rhode Island may mean by an "*aboriginal history*" we will not pretend to divine.

the handiwork of one of old Sachem Philip's Wampanoug Indians.

Although the Sagas, of which we have given an abstract, furnish us with a very circumstantial account of the *discovery* of Vinland, Mr. Rafn has not been able to produce any evidence to show that it was ever *colonized* by the Northmen. Trading voyages for the purpose of felling timber and carrying on a lucrative traffic with the natives for their furs and skins were, no doubt, sometimes made both from Greenland and Iceland, and probably also from Norway and Denmark; but no record of such voyages has been preserved. The Icelandic annals only give the following brief memoranda on the subject.

1121. Bishop Eirek sailed from Greenland in quest of Vinland *.

1285. Athalbrand and Thorvald, sons of Helgi, discovered a new land west of Iceland.

1290. Rolf was sent by king Eirek in search of the new land, and took several men with him from Iceland for that purpose.

1295. Death of Rolf, surnamed The Discoverer.

1347. A Greenland bark, of less size than the common Icelandic vessels, ran into Straumfjörd, having lost her anchors. There were seventeen men on board, who had sailed to Markland, and on their return had been tossed about on the ocean.

Athalbrand and Thorvald, mentioned in these annals, were two priests, and we think all that can be said respecting their voyage, is, that they accidently discovered some part of the American continent. This, however, is not enough for Mr. Rafn's *amor patriæ*. John Cabot was sent to Denmark by the Bristol merchants to negotiate concerning their trade with Iceland, which had, as usual, been interrupted by the arbitrary proceedings of the Danish government. And the very next year after the negotiations were concluded, Cabot obtained his patent from Henry VII., and the year following, namely in 1497, set out on his voyage, and discovered Newfoundland.

---

* This is the year in which Eirek was ordained Bishop, and his sailing to Vinland has been adduced as a proof that there was at that period a settlement there. It certainly does seem strange—if we may rely on the Icelandic annals for the record of events occurring in Greenland—that a bishop should undertake such a voyage from a mere motive of curiosity.

What a happy concatenation of events for a northern antiquary to build an hypothesis on! Mr. Rafn accordingly sets to work and tells us that Cabot, from the nature of the negotiations he was entrusted with, would necessarily be led to make inquiries respecting Iceland and its dependencies, and may have received, among other information, some account of this voyage of the Scandinavian priests. The name given to the country he discovered tends, according to Mr. Rafn, to confirm this hypothesis. "Huic hypothesi ipsum nomen favere videtur, verbis Islandicorum Annalium *fundu nyia land* (*Nyia fundu land*,) literatim consonum," are the words he makes use of *. Now, with all due deference to Mr. Rafn, whose philological learning no one will pretend to dispute, we must say that this is a mere quibble. The phrases in the Icelandic annals are, "*fundu* Helgasynir *nyja land* Adalbrandr ok Thorvaldr," and, "Adalbrand ok Thorvardr Helgasynir *fundu nyja land* vestr undan Islandi," which mean literally, "Athalbrand and Thorvald or Thorvard found new land west of Iceland;" that is to say, discovered a country before unknown, and not that they gave the name of Newfoundland to the land—whatever it might be—which they probably did find. Neither would Mr. Rafn venture to say this, but he adroitly transposes the words, *found new land*, into *new found land*, and this philological *hocus pocus* settles all difficulties. The two priests came to *a* new found land, so did, according to Mr. Rafn, John Cabot, therefore *the* new found land of the sacerdotal voyagers must necessarily have been *the* new found land of the Venetian navigator; that is to say, the present island of Newfoundland! A most logical conclusion, truly! quite on a par with the interpretation of the scrawl on the *monumentum vetustum* of Massachusetts! Mr. Rafn is no doubt aware that the voyages of the Cabots, father and son, are involved in great obscurity. We only know that either John or Sebastian Cabot, or both of them, sailed along the east coast of North America, in the vain attempt to find a north-west passage to Cathay, as China was then called; but it is highly probable that the *land they found* was *not Newfoundland* †. Be this as it may, *it is certain* that

---

* Ant. Amer. p. 451.
† See a very interesting work entitled, "A Memoir on Sebastian Cabot." Lond. 1831.

neither they nor any of their men, as it was popularly supposed, gave the American Island the name it now bears. In
the maps of that period, all the newly discovered land in the
northern Atlantic is designated under the term *Terra Nova;*
and a Bristol merchant, in a memorial to Henry VIII. on the
practicability of a north-west passage, says: "After they be
past the pole, they should go on the back of the *new found
land* which of late was discovered by your grace's subjects;"
and again, " if between our *new found land* and Norway the sea
be practicable." The fact is, the name was applied at first to
the whole coast, and afterwards became restricted to the island
that bears it at present, and which was previously called
Bacallaos on account of its cod fisheries. We thus find that
Mr. Rafn's theory rests on no foundation, and we fear this
may be said of several other theories which the northern
antiquaries are too apt to indulge in, and which renders their
opinions, even on subjects more exclusively within the range
of their studies, liable to be received with a certain diffidence;
a circumstance very much to be regretted; for men possessing
a greater amount of solid learning and erudition are no where to
be met with.

In an old Icelandic geographical treatise there is the following passage. "To the south of inhabited Greenland are
wild and desert tracts and ice-covered mountains; then comes
the land of the Skrællings, beyond this Markland, and then
Vinland the Good. Next to this, and somewhat behind it, lies
Albania, that is to say, Hvitramannaland, *Whitemansland*,
whither vessels formerly sailed from Ireland. It was there
that several Irishmen and Icelanders recognised Ari, the son
of Mar and Katla of Reykjanes, whom there had not for a
long time been any tidings of, and whom the natives of the
country had made their chief." The Landnámabók also states
that Ari Marsson was driven by a tempest to Hvitramannaland,
and detained and baptized there *; and we are told in Thorfinn's Saga that the Esquimaux children taken in Markland †
declared that beyond their country lay another, the inhabitants
of which wore *white* dresses and bore flags on long poles, a

---

* Ari Marsson is incidentally mentioned in several of the best authenticated
Sagas, and it would appear that Finn Magnusen claims a lineal descent from
him. See the seventh Genealogical Table in the Antiq. Americanæ, which
begins with Ari Marsson, and ends with Finnr Magnusson.

† See page 259.

statement obviously of no value in itself, but remarkable for the conclusion drawn from it by the Northmen, that the country thus described must necessarily be Hvitramannaland, which shows, at all events *that at the period the Saga was written* the existence of such a country was a fact generally admitted. Mr. Rafn has given us two Sagas * relating to Hvitramannaland, but they are of a totally different character from those which narrate the voyages of Leif and Thorfinn, and by no means entitled to the same degree of credibility †.

It would appear that the Northmen received their account of Hvitramannaland, which was also called *Irland it Mikla*— Great Ireland—from Limerick traders, and that vessels had sailed there previous to the discovery of Vinland. These circumstances, and the mention made of Ari's baptism, have led some writers to suppose that there was an Irish colony established on the coast of America, south of Massachusets, in the ninth or tenth century; but the statements transmitted to us are obviously too vague to possess any historical value; and any opinions they may give rise to must, therefore, be purely conjectural.

All that can be said with *certainty* is, that the Northmen were *tolerably well acquainted* with the coast of America from Labrador to Massachusetts, and had *a vague tradition* that it extended much farther south, and that this southern region was peopled by a race of men differing in many respects from the Esquimaux. We may also admit, when we take into consideration the swarms of freebooters constantly cruizing in the northern seas and along the whole western coast of Europe, that during a violent gale from the north-east several vessels may have been driven across the Atlantic as far south as Florida. Neither is it at all improbable that trading voyages may have occasionally been made from Limerick to some part of the American continent. That the Northmen possessed sufficient seamanship to attempt a voyage across the Atlantic is unquestionable, for we know that, during their piratical ex-

* The Saga of Björn Asbrandson, surnamed Breidvikingakappi; *i. e.* the Champion of Breidavik, or the hero of Bradwick, as he is not inappropriately termed by our great Novelist—a surname he obtained when he belonged to the piratical band of the famous Palnatoki.

† Sir Walter Scott has given the substance of these Sagas in a note to the Eyrbyggja Saga, to which we refer the reader.

peditions, they frequently remained for weeks together at sea; and that trading voyages from Iceland to Ireland and from Norway to Greenland were of common occurrence. The part of America they were acquainted with offered, however, no inducement to freebooters, whose sole object was plunder, and but very few even to traders, to undertake such a voyage, which, under the most favourable circumstances, must always have been attended with considerable risk and danger. Had the sea-kings and their hardy followers been aware that beyond the region of vines and forests there lay another abounding in gold and silver and costly commodities, we should probably have seen at the present day a Norman dynasty reigning in Mexico. It is, in fact, obvious that the merest accident might in that age have led some enterprising adventurer a few degrees further south, and given rise to a series of events resulting in the final conquest of the tropical regions of America by the seafaring Scandinavians. It is useless, however, to speculate on what might have happened, or on the influence which such an event as the one contemplated might have exercised on the social condition of Europe at a period when the principal elements of its future civilization were still in violent conflict. The discovery of America by the Northmen produced no such results, and it was reserved for Columbus and the navigators and adventurers of the sixteenth century to withdraw that mysterious veil which, by some inscrutable design of Providence, had for so many ages shrouded an unknown world.

Finn Magnusen, in a very able dissertation published in one of the early numbers of the " *Nordisk Tidsskrift for Oldkyndighed,*" has fully established the fact of Columbus having visited Iceland in the year 1477, and on this fact, which can no longer be called in question, has constructed, as usual, a very brilliant theory, which we give in his own words :—

" The English trade with Iceland certainly merits the consideration of historians, if it furnished Columbus with the opportunity of visiting that island, there to be informed of the historical evidence respecting the existence of important lands, and a large continent in the west."

" If Columbus should have acquired a knowledge of the accounts transmitted to us of the discoveries of the Northmen, in conversations held in Latin with the Bishop of Skalholt and the learned men of Iceland, we may the more readily conceive his firm belief in the possibility of rediscovering a western continent, and his unwearied zeal in putting his plans in execution. The discovery of America, so momentous in its results, may therefore be regarded as the mediate consequence of its previous discovery by the Scandinavians, which may be thus placed among the most important events of former ages. It has long been known that the fate of the world, and of mankind, frequently hangs on the finest threads, the direction of which it is often very difficult for historians to follow, though it is seldom that this direction should only first be clearly perceived after a lapse of three centuries. This, however, appears to me to have happened in the present case, as we have now, for the first time, a well-founded reason to suppose that the small and barren Iceland not only produced the men who were the first discoverers of the New World, but that it also pointed out to the immortal hero, whom it was long believed ought alone to enjoy that honour, the way by which he could prosecute and terminate the discovery in such a manner, that through it the earth should assume a new form, and mankind acquire, both in a material and intellectual point of view, a new state of existence."

It would be a very easy task to show that this theory is equally as groundless as that of Mr. Rafn respecting Cabot. We will, however, merely observe that it rests on the erroneous supposition that Columbus had formed the idea of discovering or rediscovering a western continent. Now this was so far from being the case, that, until the day of his death, he imagined that the West India Islands and Terra Firma were the easternmost parts of Asia. The relation of Marco Polo's travels and adventures in the East had extended the geographical knowledge of the learned men of the fourteenth and fifteenth centuries far beyond the regions known to the ancients. In the chart made use of by Columbus in his first voyage, constructed for him by Paolo Toscanelli, one of the most scientific men of that age, the eastern shores of Asia are laid down in front of the western coasts of Europe and Africa, the distance from Lisbon to Quisay, since determined to be a part of China, being computed at 6500 nautical miles. Toscanelli, in a letter to the Canon Martinez, describes Quisay to be in a country " where great profits may be made, and many valuable things found, *gold, and silver, and precious stones, and all sorts of spices*, in great abundance;" and speaking of Cipango, which is supposed to have been Japan, he says: "This island greatly abounds in *gold, and pearls, and precious stones*, and, you must know, that the temples and royal palaces are *covered with plates of pure gold.* So, that on account of the way not being known, all these things lie hidden and concealed, and yet they may be gone to in safety." And in one of his letters to Columbus, he tells him that he sees the great and noble desire which he has to go " to those countries where the spices grow," and remarks that the voyage is not only practicable, "but would also be productive of *inestimable profit*, and great power and fame among all Christians." Now, admitting that Columbus received the most ample information respecting the discoveries of the Northmen during his stay in Iceland, he could only have become aware of the existence of a *wild uncultivated country* to the south-west of Greenland, producing nothing but *timber, sour grapes, and salmon*, and peopled by wandering tribes of miserable savages; whereas Toscanelli pointed out the way to the civilized and populous dominions of the great Khan, with their *gold*-covered palaces and temples. The choice could not be doubtful. We accordingly find that the course invariably pursued by Columbus in his first voyage was not in the direction of Vinland, but in that of " the countries where the spices grow," which countries he would have reached had not America existed to bar his passage. His discovery of America was, in fact, *quite accidental*. Marco Polo first made Europe acquainted with China. Paolo Toscanelli pointed out the route to it by sea, and Columbus, in following this route, stumbled on America, and thus was revealed the existence of a vast continent which neither Columbus himself nor any one else in that age, if we except the worthy Bishop of Skalholt, and a few learned Icelanders, had the remotest idea of *.

* As these opinions fully coincide with the views taken in an article in the "Athenæum," No. 514, on Finn Magnusen's Dissertation, it may not be irrelevant to state that that article was written by the editor of this volume.

EXPLANATORY REMARKS ON THE PRECEDING CHAPTER.

(1.) HELLULAND.—This was probably the south-eastern extremity of Newfoundland, which is nearly separated from the
main by two deep bays, so as easily to be mistaken for an
island.   The distance from Cape Broil, on this coast, to Cape
Farewell, in Greenland, is 600 nautical miles, which, with a
fair wind, might easily be run in four days.   The description
given by modern travellers of the coast of Newfoundland fully
corresponds with that of the Sagas ; and Anspach, a modern
German writer, speaks of *" the bare and large flat rocks without a tree or shrub."* *   In the old Icelandic geographical
treatises, Newfoundland is called Little (*Litla*) Helluland, and
the name of Helluland, *hit Mikla*, or Great Helluland, is
given to Labrador and the whole coast of the American continent west of Baffin's Bay.   The Helluland of Thorfinn was
probably the south-eastern extremity of Labrador.   A writer
in the " Philosophical Transactions," † speaking of Labrador,
says : " The surface is every where uneven and *covered with
large stones, some of which are of amazing dimension.*   The
mountains are almost devoid of every sort of herbage, a
blighted shrub and a little moss is sometimes to be seen
upon them, but in general the *bare rock* is all you behold.
In a word, the whole country is nothing more than a *prodigious heap of barren rocks.*" This writer also notices the
great number of foxes that are found in the country.

(2.) Markland can be no other than Nova Scotia.   The
following descriptions of this part of the coast from modern
works on navigation correspond to the letter with those of the
Northmen.   "The land *is low in general,* and not visible
twenty miles off.   Aspotogon hills have a long *level* appearance.   Between Cape Le Have and Port Medway, the coast
to the seaward is *level* and *low,* and the shores marked with
white rocks, with *low* barren points ; from thence to Shel-
bourne and Port Roseway are woods.   From Port Haldimand
to Cape Sable the land is *low, with white sandy cliffs,* particularly visible at sea.   Cape Sable is a *low woody island* at
the south-eastern extremity of a range of *sand cliffs,* which are

---

* Geschichte und Beschreibung von Newfoundland, p. 103.
† Vol. lxiv. pp. 374 and 377, quoted in Antiq. Am. p. 419.

very remarkable at a considerable distance in the offing." *
"From Port Haldimand to Cape Sable the land appears *level
and low*, and on the shore are some *cliffs of exceedingly white
sand*, particularly in the entrance of Port Haldimand and on
Cape Sable, where they are very conspicuous from sea." †

(3.) Mr. Rafn supposes that the course here described was
through Nantucket Bay and Vineyard Sound, and thence up
the Seaconnet Reach and Pocasset River to Mount Hope Bay,
where Leif fixed his booths on the Taunton River; but we
think the indications given in the Saga are too vague to fix
the precise localities. The account of Thorfinn's voyage is
more satisfactory in this respect.

(4.) The anecdote of Tyrker, which, if rightly understood,
will be found to furnish strong evidence of the genuineness of
the narrative, has been treated with ridicule by some writers,
on the erroneous supposition that the Saga describes the old
German as being intoxicated by eating a few fresh grapes.
Even Mr. Laing, who, as the translator of the Heimskringla,
must certainly be aware that there is nothing in the original
Old Norse text of the Saga to warrant such an interpretation,
cannot refrain from remarking, that "All the grapes in Germany, and Vinland to boot, would not make a man drunk,
without their juice undergoing the vinous fermentation. This
is clearly the fiction of some Saga-maker, who knew no more
of wine than that it was the juice of the grape." ‡ Now the
Saga-maker, as Mr. Laing terms him, merely tells us that when
Leif met Tyrker he soon perceived that he was *skapfátt*, or
a little out of his wits. Another manuscript has *skapgott*,
i. e in a merry mood ; and that whilst he was talking German
he twisted his mouth, and turned his eyes many ways. There is
certainly nothing very extraordinary in this. On the contrary,
we may readily conceive that a German who had passed the last
twenty years of his life in the frozen regions of the north,
would be elated somewhat beyond the bounds of reason, on
finding in a strange land the same fruit he had so often relished in his childhood, and, as the recollections of that happy

* The New American Pilot, by J. W. Norie, Lond. 1815, P. ii. pp.
1. 3. 6.

† Laurie and Whittle's New Sailing Directions for the Coasts of North
America, Lond. 1816, p. 7; Antiq. Am. p. 423.

‡ Laing s Heimskringla, vol. i. p. 168.

period rushed on his mind, would give vent to his feelings in his mother tongue. Mr. Laing makes Tyrker speak *Turkish,* such being, in his opinion, the signification of the Icelandic adjective *thyrskr.*—See Laing's "Heimskringla," vol. iii. p. 349. The learned Schöning, who first conceived this notion, gives it as a *mere conjecture:* "Incertus sum," he says, "quomodo illud *á thyrsku,* Latine reddam, linguane Theutonica, an Turcica?"—See Schöning's edit. of the Heimskringla, Copenh. 1777, vol. i. p. 310, note c. Mr. Rafn has satisfactorily shown that *thyrskr* means *German.*—See Antiq. Am. p. 35, note a, and p. 28, note a.

(5.) We shall find that Helluland, Markland, and Vinland, or the three lands of stone, of wood, and of the vine, always occur in succession to the Northmen holding a south-west course from Greenland. This circumstance alone, even if unsupported by collateral evidence, would be sufficient to show that the countries so designated were respectively the projecting lands of Newfoundland, Nova Scotia, and New England, about Massachusetts. Mr. Laing finds, however, that "in the account of the details upon which so much has been built up by modern antiquaries, we find no such consistency, credibility, or external evidence of truthfulness. Leif and his successors, Karlsefne and others, arrive in Vinland in spring—say, in May, June, or July. In what climate or part of the world are grapes to be found in those months? Do vines, or wheat, or corn of any kind grow spontaneously in those countries? This is a question by no means satisfactorily ascertained." "All the geographical speculations upon the sites and localities of the Vinland of the Northmen, built upon the natural products of the land, fall to the ground."* This, at first view, appears to be marvellously conclusive; but Mr. Laing will find by referring to the Saga, that although Leif and his companions may probably have arrived in the country some time in May, June, or July, the incident of Tyrker finding grapes is related as having occurred *after* they had erected their booths, or dwelling-houses, and settled themselves for the winter. Tyrker, therefore, found his grapes precisely in the season when grapes are to be found, viz., in autumn. That vines and corn grow spontaneously in New England is a fact too well attested to be called in question. The island of Martha's Vineyard ob-

* Heimskringla. vol. i. p. 168.

tained its name, from the first English settlers, on account of their finding wild grapes growing there in great abundance.— See also Remark 15.

·(6.) Timber was a very requisite article both in Greenland and Iceland, which produced no wood, or at least none fit for either ship-building or for the construction of the large banquetting halls of the rich landed proprietors. A good deal of drift-wood was, and is still, occasionally found on the coasts, but generally too worm-eaten to be serviceable. Leif, therefore, took out a cargo of timber, and probably some specimens of the fine hard-grained wood of the country, and stowed his long-boat with packages of raisins.

(7.) The account is too scanty to fix the localities visited by the party, but, as they were absent the whole summer, they probably sailed along the coast as far south as the Carolinas.

(8.) It will appear more fully in the narrative of Thorfinn's voyage, that Kjalarnes can be no other than Cape Cod, and the opposite headland, Gurnet Point, which form the entrance of Cape Cod Bay.

(9.) This locality is not so easy to determine, but it may perhaps have been "the bluff head of Alderton," at the south-east of Boston Bay.

(10.) Disco Island, in Baffin's Bay, was called Bjarney, or Bear Island, by the Northmen, but they seem to have applied this name indifferently to several islands. The Bjarney here mentioned was probably one of the numerous islands on the coast of Labrador, from which a vessel might sail with ease in two days to Newfoundland. It is, at all events, quite obvious that Thorfinn, who knew that the country he was in search of lay to the south-west, would not have sailed due north to Disco Island.

(11.) This Bjarney was probably Cape Sable Island.

(12.) The Furðustrandir of the Northmen correspond exactly with the coast of the Nauset Peninsula, and the Chatham and Monomoy beaches. Hitchcock, in his "Report on the Geology of Massachusetts," p. 94, says, in speaking of this coast, "The dunes, or sand hills, which are often nearly or quite barren of vegetation, and of snowy whiteness, *forcibly attract the attention on account of their peculiarity.* As we approach the extremity of the Cape the sand and the barrenness increase; and, in not a few places, it would need only a

T

party of Bedouin Arabs to cross the traveller's path to make
him feel that he was in the depths of an Arabian or Lybian
desert." Mr. Rafn observes, that the name of "*Marvellous
Strands*" may have been given, not so much on account of
their dreary length, as from the Northmen having, perhaps,
witnessed the phenomenon of the *mirage* which frequently
occurs on this coast, and which they would justly have deemed
most marvellous. Hitchcock, in the work above quoted, p. 97,
remarks, "In crossing the sands of the Cape, I noticed a singular *mirage*, or deception. In Orleans, for instance, we
seemed to be ascending at an angle of 3 or 4 degrees; nor
was I convinced that such was not the case, until, turning
about, I perceived that a similar ascent appeared on the road
just passed over."*

(13.) Straumfjörd is supposed to be Buzzard's Bay, and
Straumey, either Martha's Vineyard or the islands of Cutty-
hunk and Nashawenna, which, in the eleventh century, were
probably connected. The Gulf Stream will sufficiently account
for the *strong currents* noticed in the narrative. Lyell remarks,
in his Geology, vol. i. p. 384, "That it is the beach of Nantucket which turns the current of the Gulf Stream at the depth
of from two to three hundred feet below the surface of the
water. "Mr. Laing, who carries his scepticism somewhat too far,
observes, that "The eyder duck, on our side of the world, is
very rarely seen in lower latitudes than 60'. It may be different on the American coast."† And that it is different we
have among other authorities cited by Mr. Rafn, that of Ebe-
ling, a German writer, who says, that "on the numerous isles
on this coast there are an extraordinary quantity of wild
geese and ducks, among which the *eyder duck is very common*."‡

(14.) If it be admitted that Thorfinn passed the first winter
at Buzzard's Bay, Hóp may possibly be the present Mount
Hope Bay. This locality, in fact, perfectly corresponds to the
description given in the narrative. There is *a river*—the
Taunton River—*flowing through a lake*—Mount Hope Bay
might almost be termed a lake—*on its way to the sea*—by the
Pocasset River and Seaconnet Reach, which, owing to their
sandy shoals, are only navigable at high water. It would appear

* See Antiq. Am. p. 427.
† Heimskringla. vol i. p. 169.
‡ See Antiq. Am. p. 444.

that this Mount Hope is merely a corruption of the Indian name *haup*, (pronounced like the Icelandic *hóp*,) which the place bore when the first English settlers arrived there. Haup was the residence of the famous Metacomet, or King Philip, as he was called, the last Sachem of the Wampanoug Indians; and some of the Rhode Island antiquaries have hazarded the supposition that the name may have been transmitted to the Indians by the decendants of the Northmen who had settled in the place, and were gradually merged in the tribe of the Wampanougs. But if it were even a well established *fact*, instead of a *mere conjecture*, that the Hóp of the Northmen was the Haup of the old Indian Sachem, still this coincidence, like that of many other homonymous words belonging to different languages, which have so often led etymologists on a wild goose chase, might be quite fortuitous.

(15.) Although it may be difficult to fix the precise locality of each particular place mentioned in the narrative, there can be but little doubt that Massachusetts was the country known to the Northmen under the name of Vinland. When the English settlers first arrived in this part of America they found *vines growing wild on the hills, and Indian corn on the plains*, the rivers teeming with fish, and the islands covered with innumerable wild fowl, precisely as we are told the Northmen did several centuries previously. A modern writer, speaking of Massachusetts, says, "*La vigne sauvage grimpe de tous cotés sur les arbres*," and adds that, of some of the species, "*les fruits sont très estimés à cause de leur salubrité et de leur delicatesse.*"* A number of other passages from recent works might be quoted in corroboration of the descriptions given in the sagas and the old Icelandic geographical treatises of Vinland the Good; but we think no impartial person who takes the trouble to examine the evidence brought forward by Mr. Rafn will hesitate a moment in placing it, in what Mr. Warden, in the work above quoted, terms "*le paradis de l'Amérique.*" The supposition that such a country could have been situated on the bleak and barren coast of Labrador is too absurd to merit a refutation.

(16.) From this description, and their being called Skrællings, they were manifestly Esquimaux. Some recent writers, there-

* Warden's Description des Etats Unis. Paris, 1820.—See also Antiq. Am. p. 439 and 441.

fore, contend that we ought to place the Vinland of the Northmen on the coast of Labrador, and they treat the supposition of the Northern Antiquaries, that the Esquimaux race formerly extended much farther south than at present, as perfectly gratuitous. It requires, however, but a very superficial knowledge of ethnological history to be aware of the fact that whenever two races of men have come into contact, the one that was the inferior in physical or intellectual endowments has necessarily given way to the other. It was thus that the Finns retired before the Scandinavian and Slavonic races; the Slavonians of ancient Pannonia before the Magyars; the Celtic race of the British Isles before the Teutonic; the Britons before the Germanic (Anglo-Saxon); the Gaels before the Scandinavian branch: and we have in our own times seen how the Red men of the New World have gradually been obliged to recede before the Spaniards and Anglo-Americans. Though unsupported by historical evidence, we may therefore reasonably conclude that the Esquimaux were driven, in like manner, to the Polar regions by the superior race of Red Indians.

CHAPTER II.

ON THE LAWS AND INSTITUTIONS OF THE ICELANDIC COMMONWEALTH.

THE preceding chapters will have made the reader acquainted with the religious doctrines, manners and customs of the ancient Scandinavians. It will remain for us to give a succinct account of their literature; but as almost all the old Norse poems and sagas that have been handed down to us were either collected or written by Icelanders, we shall previously enter into a few details respecting the social institutions of these Norwegian colonists, in order to show what peculiar circumstances enabled them to acquire such a literary pre-eminence over their fellow-countrymen in Norway, Sweden, and Denmark, who, it must be borne in mind, spoke, at that period, precisely the same language.

We have elsewhere observed * that Scandinavian history does not reach beyond the middle of the ninth century. The person-

* See page 84.

ages who figure in the legendary accounts of events that happened, or that are said to have happened, before that period, belong to the *heroic age*, in which, among all nations, it is next to impossible to draw a line of demarcation between facts and fiction. Events that may have taken place, and which probably actually did take place—as Ragnar Lodbrok's famous expedition to Northumbria, for instance,—are so blended with what is purely imaginative, that any arguments founded on them must necessarily be inconclusive. It is, therefore, a fortunate circumstance that the colonization of Iceland falls within the *historical period*, which, for Norway, may be said to begin with Halfdan the Black, and more especially with his son Harald Hárfagra.

At this period Norway was divided into a number of independent states, each under its chieftain or king, whose authority, however, was far from being unlimited, all public affairs being discussed and decided at the *Things*, or general assemblies of the freemen, who gave their assent to a measure by striking their shields with their drawn swords. These freemen, or *thingsmen*, as they were called, were the landed proprietors of the country, and their sons and kindred. The tenure of land in Norway was then, as we believe it still continues to be, strictly allodial. The odalsman (ódalsma͡ðr) or *dominus allodialis*, whether he held extensive domains or only a few acres, could not alienate the land. At his death it was equally divided amongst his children, or next of kin, and at a later and more civilized period, when legal right became better defined, any one who could establish his relationship with the original proprietor, might evict a person who had acquired an estate once belonging to the family, without having any allodial claim to it. It would lead us too far to point out the advantages and evils resulting from this kind of tenure, which also prevails in Hungary, where it is regarded at the present day as one of the greatest obstacles to social improvement *. Its obvious tendency is to to fritter away

---

* Some of the Hungarian domains, those of Prince Esterházy, for instance, are entailed and inherited according to the law of primogeniture, but the tenure that generally prevails is such as we have described. Every manor in Hungary was originally bestowed by the crown, and, at the death of the last legitimate descendant of the person to whom it was granted, becomes again crown property. According to the strict letter of the law, a manor

the estates of a family by continual subdivisions, though they will at times become concentrated in the hands of two or three individuals, who have been lucky enough to survive their relatives. There was, however, no great fear in the turbulent ages we are speaking of, when a Scandinavian never quitted his arms *, and scarcely passed a day without exposing himself to danger, that an estate would have to be parcelled out among a too numerous progeny. We thus find that the chiefs of a powerful family continued to maintain their dignity for several generations, a circumstance which in more peaceable times would have been of rare occurrence.

A chieftain throughout Scandinavia generally presided over the *herad* †, or district, in which his allodial possessions were situated, in the triple capacity of chieftain, or military commander, pontiff, and judge. In Norway, the herad frequently formed an independent state, and its chief, when the territory was tolerably extensive, bore the title of *Fylkis-Kóngr* ‡.

that has devolved to the crown, is merely held in trust for the purpose of being again bestowed as a reward for services rendered to the state, but in point of fact is always sold to the highest bidder; a proceeding, however, which the Diet never fails to protest against. It might naturally be supposed that this law of *Aviticity*, as it is very appropriately termed, would prevent a person from selling an estate, for, by virtue of its provisions, any of the descendants of the original donee might make use of his right, either of pre-emption or re-emption. In the latter case, he would, however, have to refund any sums that might have been laid out in improvements, and, as a clever lawyer generally hits upon some expedient for evading a bad law, the Hungarian gentlemen of the long-robe have introduced the practice of inserting in the deed of conveyance double the sum actually given for an estate, and thus effectually deterring those who enjoy the right of re-emption from making use of it. The last Diet appointed a committee to inquire into the aviticity laws, and the next Diet will probably entirely abolish them, or at least render their operation less pernicious.

* This continued to be the case for centuries after the introduction of Christianity. The Norwegians only quitted their arms when they entered a church, when they hung them up in the porch; hence to this day, in the rural districts of Norway, the porch of a church is called a weapon-house— *Vaabenhuus.*

† Herad, properly speaking, means a tribe—the word being derived from *her*, an army, an armed multitude—a host.

‡ Folk's-King. *Fylki* signifies a district, and is derived from *fólk*, a word which has the same meaning as in English. The Old Norse name for king is konúngr, kongr; Swed., konung; Dan., konge, from *konr*, a man of noble birth, or simply a man; and *úngr* (young), a termination, signifying a son or descendant, and equivalent to the Ang.-Sax. and English *ing*. Hence the Ang.-

However, whether independent or not, the union of the sacerdotal and magisterial functions must necessarily have given him much the same kind of influence over the smaller landed proprietors, as a Roman patrician exercised over his clients. An attentive perusal of the Sagas will, in fact, convince any one whose judgment is not biassed by some favourite theory of Scandinavian optimism, that the boasted independence of the humbler class of thingsmen was more apparent than real. They, no doubt, made a great clatter with their shields, and bawled out most lustily for the adoption or rejection of the measure under discussion; but although a sagaman is not exactly a Horace Walpole, he often lets us sufficiently behind the curtain to become aware of the fact, that, even in that rude age, a man who possessed his hundreds of acres, was never at a loss how to influence the vote of his humble neighbour, who, although in the enjoyment of the same political rights, possessed but a score *. All odalsmen were, however, regarded

Sax., cyning; Eng., king; Dutch, koning; in German, könig. Kings were formerly as plentiful in Scandinavia as dukes are at the present day at Naples, the son of a king, though without territories, bearing the same title as his father. In the Drontheim district alone, Harald Hárfagra, according to Snorri, defeated and slew no less than eight kings.—See Heimsk. iii. 7.

* There is a striking coincidence between the civil institutions of the Hungarians (Magyars) and those of the ancient Scandinavians, and this coincidence, which we believe has never been pointed out, is the more remarkable from there not existing the slightest or remotest analogy between the Magyar and the Old Norse languages; and although it is by no means ascertained whether the Magyars belong to the Tshudic, Tatar, or Turkish races, they are unquestionably not a tribe of any of the so-called Indo-European races, and therefore differ in every respect, physiologically as well as psychologically, from the Scandinavians. Nevertheless, each of the fifty-five districts or counties into which Hungary is divided, has its *Thing* (county congregation), at which public affairs are discussed, as in ancient Scandinavia, by all the *odalsmen* or *thingsmen* of the district; a man possessing but a single rood of allodial land having the same vote and the same rights and privileges as the proprietor of the most extensive domains. But those who may have an opportunity, as we have frequently had, of being present at one of these stormy meetings, will not fail to remark what a powerful influence the possessors of such domains, or *full-spurred nobles*, exercise over the *half-spurred nobles*, as the petty allodial landowners are contemptuously termed, and, perhaps arrive at the conclusion that, in a multitudinous assembly of freemen, sound lungs are more requisite than a sound judgment. Although the Hungarian *Althing*, or *Diet*, has become in modern times a bi-cameral legislative body, it differs materially from the British Parliament. Every bill must originate in the lower house, the members of which are the

as freemen, and constituted a privileged class. Another class was that of the so called *unfree*, under which negative denomination were included cottiers, labourers, artizans, and others, who enjoyed personal freedom, but had no political rights; that is to say, were not thingsmen. They were, however, entitled to bear arms, and most of the opulent landowners or allodial lords, the real nobility of the country, had a number of them in their service as armed retainers. After these came the freedmen, or manumitted slaves, and, last of all, the slaves themselves, or thralls, to whom the law afforded no protection whatsoever. Their masters might dispose of them as they thought proper, and even kill them with impunity. These thralls were generally captives taken in war, who, if not ransomed by their friends, were sold in regular slave markets.

In the year 863, Harald Hárfagra inherited Westfold and one or two other petty states, and, before the close of the century, had made himself master of the whole country, and become, *de facto*, king of Norway. One of his first measures was to introduce a kind of feudal system. He accordingly made it known that all the allodial property in the country belonged to the crown, and that those who wished to retain possession of their estates would thenceforward have to pay a land-tax. In order to render the royal authority paramount, he placed over each of the petty states and districts he had conquered one of his own followers, with the title of *jarl* (earl), who was charged with the administration of justice, and the collection of the royal revenue derived from fines, and the newly imposed land-tax. A jarl was bound to keep sixty men-at-arms ready for the king's service, but was allowed to retain

mere delegates of the district Things, or county congregations, appointed by the majority of the Thingsmen, and are liable to be recalled at a moment's notice, so that, in point of fact, all legislative measures are decided by the fifty-five district Things, the table of magnates and the king having merely a veto, which, however, is, on most occasions, very adroitly made use of, though often in a manner the expediency of which it is foreign to our purpose to inquire into. The reader will find a graphic description of Hungarian public life in "The Village Notary," of Baron Joseph Eötvös, a work which has been translated into German, and which places its talented author—who has shown by his political writings and his eloquent speeches in the chamber of magnates, that a brilliant imagination may be happily combined with a correct judgment, and the most practical views of social amelioration—among the first-rate novelists of the present age.

one-third of the revenue collected. Each jarl had under him four *hersirs* *, each of whom received a salary of twenty marks, and was bound to furnish twenty men-at-arms. When the system was fully established, Harald did not scruple to augment the land-tax, and it soon became evident that his jarls possessed much greater power, and had much larger incomes than the petty kings they had replaced, a circumstance that induced several of the fallen chieftains to solicit the lucrative employment †. Those who preferred independence, or, more properly speaking, the exercise of authority, to submission, became sea-rovers, and infested the coasts of France and the British islands, or sought refuge in the Shetland, Orkney, and Færoe Isles, and especially in Iceland, which, as it was stated in a preceding chapter, had been recently discovered ‡. None but Northmen, inured from their infancy to a rude climate and the perils of a seafaring life, would have thought of settling in such a country, which is thus described by a modern writer § :—

" The opinion that Iceland owes its formation to the operation of submarine volcanoes, is not only confirmed by analogical reasonings, deduced from the appearances presented by other islands which are confessedly of volcanic origin, but gains ground in proportion to the progress of a closer and more accurate investigation of the geological phenomena which every part of it exhibits. In no quarter of the globe do we find crowded within the same extent of surface such a number of ignivomous mountains, so many boiling springs, or such immense tracts of lava, as here arrest the attention of the traveller. *The general aspect of the country is the most rugged and dreary imaginable.* On every side appear marks of confusion and devastation, or the tremendous sources of those evils in the yawning craters of huge and menacing volcanoes. Nor is the mind of a spectator relieved from the disagreeable emotions arising from reflection on the subterraneous fires

---

* The word hersir has the same root as herad, and might—though not very appropriately—be rendered by baron.

† Heimsk. iii. 6.

‡ See page 187.

§ Henderson, in his work entitled " Iceland ; or the Journal of a Residence in that Island during the years 1814 and 1815." We have somewhat abridged Mr. Henderson's description of this singular country.

which are raging beneath him, by a temporary survey of the
huge mountains of perpetual ice by which he is surrounded.
These very masses, which naturally exclude the most distant
ideas of heat, contain in their bosom the fuel of conflagration,
and are frequently seen to emit smoke and flames, and pour
down upon the plains immense floods of boiling mud and
water, or red-hot torrents of devouring lava.

" There are no less than thirty principal volcanoes in the
island, and besides these an immense number of smaller cones
and craters, from which streams of melted substances have
been poured forth over the surrounding regions. Tracts of
lava traverse the island in every direction. The most extensive fields are those in the volcanic region around the lake of
Myvatn. The vicinity of the sulphur mines of Fremri also consists of lava, and from the mountains around which these mines
lie, as far as the eye can reach, nothing is seen but one interminable region of desolation. The dismal gloom of this tract
is barely relieved by the columns of smoke that are constantly
ascending into the atmosphere through apertures and fissures
in various parts of the surface. Here the *odáda hraun*,
or horrible lava, begins and extends to a great distance toward the south and west. It is described as the wildest and
most hideous tract in the whole island. The surface is extremely rugged, consisting of broken and pointed rocks, between which are fissures and chasms of a tremendous size,
that throw insuperable barriers in the way of any traveller
who might wish to penetrate beyond them. In the south of
Iceland lie the extensive tracts of melted rock about Thingvalla, where scarcely any thing appears but one scene of universal desolation. The lavas about Mount Hekla are well
known ; and the whole plain, between that volcano and the
sea, is filled with the same substance till within a few feet of
the surface of the ground.

" Another proof of the universality of volcanic agency and of
the continued existence of subterraneous fires in Iceland, is
the multiplicity of hot springs in which it abounds. Many of
these springs throw up large columns of boiling water, accompanied by immense volumes of steam, to an almost incredible
height, and present to the eye of the traveller some of the
grandest scenes to be met with on the face of the globe.

" Celebrated as the island has been for its volcanoes and hot

springs, it is scarcely less remarkable on account of the enormous ice-mountains which occupy a vast portion of its surface.
To these mountains the natives give the name of Yökuls,
which signify large masses of ice.   They have generally ter-
reous and rocky mountains for their bases, and in many places
exhibit magnificent glaciers, which commence at a great height,
and run down with a very rapid descent into the plains.   The
most extensive of all the Icelandic yökuls is called the Klofa
Yökul, in the eastern quarter of the island.   It lies behind
the yökuls and other mountains which line the south-east
coast, and forms, with little or no interruption, a vast chain of
ice and snow-mountains, which are supposed to fill a space of
not less than three thousand square miles.   Five of these
yökuls are volcanic.   Though covered with coats of ice of immense thickness, when the internal parts of the mountains
become ignited, the mass of ice, or indurated snow, is cracked
and rent by the explosion which ensues ; a great quantity of
it is melted by the flames or by the exundations of hot water;
and whole fields of ice are sometimes deposited on the neighbouring plains.

"Numerous ridges of rugged and irregular mountains stretch
across the interior, and from these other inferior mountains
branch out toward the coast, and, in many instances, terminate
in high and steep promontories.   Between these ridges, in
the vicinity of the coast, *are rich and beautiful valleys*, in which
the inhabitants have erected their dwellings ; and many of the
low mountains are covered with coarse grass, which afford
summer pasturage to the cattle.   The most extensive tract
of low country is that between the districts of Myrdal and
Öræfa, where the traveller pursues his journey for the period
of four days without seeing any thing like a mountain in the
immediate vicinity.   The whole of the interior, as far as it has
been explored, consists of a vast inhospitable desert, traversed
in various directions by barren mountains, between which are
immense tracks of lava and volcanic sand, with here and there
a small spot scantily covered with vegetation."

Such was the country that afforded the discontented Norwegian chieftains a secure retreat from what they were pleased
to term the tyranny of Harald.   The colonization commenced
in the year 874, and in little more than half a century the
whole coast of the island had been taken possession of.   Expe-

ditions to Iceland were necessarily attended with considerable expense, for the emigrants had to take every thing with them, provisions, winter stores, live stock, and even the timber for the construction of their dwellings. They were, therefore, generally fitted out by the pontiff-chieftains; a circumstance which naturally increased the authority already exercised by these sacerdotal magistrates over the less wealthy landowners whom they permitted to accompany them.

Previous to embarking the pontiff chieftain held a *blót-veitsla* *, or sacrificial banquet, in the temple over which he presided. A Scandinavian temple was in fact nothing more than a large wooden banqueting hall, with a small recess at one end that formed a kind of sanctuary. In winter a fire was kindled on a hearth placed exactly in the centre of the hall, the smoke finding its way out through apertures in the roof, which also served for windows, and appear to have been furnished with shutters. On the southern side of the hall, opposite the fire hearth, was the *öndvegi*, or high seat, a kind of throne raised on steps, and placed between two wooden columns called the *öndvegissulur* †, which were generally carved

---

* *Blót*, a sacrifice, from the verb *blóta*, to sacrifice; *veitsla*, a banquet, from the verb *veitna*, to supply, to make ready. A curious instance of the different meaning attached to the same word in different ages is furnished by the Old Norse verb *blóta* which, in Pagan times, meant to sacrifice, to consecrate; but after the introduction of Christianity, quite the reverse, viz., *to curse*. The monks having transformed Odin into Satan, it was but reasonable that *blóta* should undergo a similar transformation. The northern philologists generally derive *blót* from *blód*, blood; but Grimm has shown that this derivation is ungrammatical, observing, at the same time, that the real derivation of the word is unknown to him, an admission which, coming from the greatest philologist of the present age, ought to be a caution to those who indulge so freely in mere *conjectural etymology*. Grimm further remarks, that the Anglo-Saxon verb *blótan* is used by Cædmon, for the sacrifices of the Hebrews, and cites, among other instances, *blótan sunu* (filium sacrificare). From this verb he derives the verb *blétsian*, more recently *blessian*, whence the English verb to bless.—See Grimm's Deutsche Mythologie, 2nd edit., page 32.

† This word may be rendered by sacred columns; *súlur* being the plural of *súla*, a column; Germ., *seule*. There are numerous etymologies of the word *öndvegi*, but as none of them appear to us to be satisfactory, not even that given by Grimm in his Deutsche Grammatik. ii. 715, we will not fatigue the reader by their enumeration. That the öndvegi seat was placed *opposite* the morning sun, consequently on the south side of the hall, is certain, and this circumstance would seem to indicate a very remote Asiatic origin; but whether the first syllable of the word be derived from *and*, op-

with Runic inscriptions, and ornamented with images of Odinic divinities. This was the seat occupied by the chieftain, his most distinguished guest being placed on another öndvegi seat, probably not quite so high, and without columns, on the northern side of the hall, the fire blazing between them *. The other guests and the retainers and dependents of the chieftain were ranged with their backs to the wall, on benches to the right and left of these öndvegi seats, the other side of the tables placed before them being unoccupied. The flesh of the sacrificed animals, after being boiled in a large kettle over the fire, was served up to these rude banqueters, who frequently amused themselves by throwing the bones at one another, the manner in which they were placed on the opposite sides of the hall being very convenient for indulging in this elegant pastime †. After they had finished eating their boiled horse flesh ‡, they generally sat swilling their ale out of capacious drinking-horns and listening to the lay of a Skald or the

posite, or from *aund, önd,* soul, spirit, Danish *aand,* we will not pretend to determine.

* Southey, in one of his notes to " Madoc," cites from Bede, lib. ii. 13, an argument made use of by a follower of Edwin of Northumbria to advise that king respecting his intended conversion to Christianity which we cannot refrain from borrowing, as it not only alludes to *the fire blazing in the centre of the hall,* but contains a highly poetical comparison. One of the chieftains having finished his discourse, another arose and addressed Edwin as follows:— " The present life of man upon the earth, when compared with the future, has appeared to me, O king ! like as when thou and thy chieftains and thy servants have been seated in winter time at supper ; the hearth blazing in the centre and the viands smoking, while without it is storm, or rain, or snow ; and a sparrow flies through the hall, entering at one door and passing out at another ; while he is within, in that brief moment of time, he does not feel the weather, but after that instant of calm, he returns to winter, as from winter he came, and is gone. Such and so transitory is the life of man, and what follows it or what precedes it is totally unknown to us. Wherefore if this new doctrine should bring any thing more certain, it well deserves to be adopted."

† In the year 1011, Elphege, Archbishop of Canterbury, was killed by the Danes throwing bones at him, as he was labouring to convert them to Christianity, a kind of martyrdom which we may readily account for, by supposing these rude warriors seated in a hall in the manner described, and the archbishop standing between the tables.

‡ The eating of horse flesh was common to all the tribes of the Teutonic race previous to their conversion to Christianity, and was, no doubt, a use they had learned on the steppes of Asia. At such banquets as we have described, beef, mutton and pork were also served up, and although the fare was coarse, it appears to have been very abundant.

tale of a Sagaman, until they were most of them in that happy state of mind, when, according to Dr. Johnson, man is alone capable of enjoying the passing moment of his fleeting existence *.

When this noisy festival, which sometimes lasted several days, was over, the chieftain embarked with his friends and retainers, carrying with him his *öndvegissulur*, and frequently also the earth on which had stood the image of his tutelar deity. On approaching the coast of Iceland the *sacred columns* were thrown into the sea, and the place where they were washed ashore was chosen by the chieftain for his new residence. The columns were sometimes carried out of sight, which was regarded as a bad omen. This happened to Ingolf, the first colonist †, who, after a fruitless search for them, landed on a promontory at the *south-eastern* extremity of Iceland, at a place called to this day Ingólfshöfdi. Three years afterwards some of his followers having been sent out to explore the country, found the sacred columns cast ashore near the *south-western* point of the island. Although the place where he had first settled was agreeable and fertile, and that where the columns had been washed ashore remarkable for its sterility, Ingolf, on learning the auspicious event, instantly removed thither with his family and retainers. This place afterwards became the town of Reykjavik, the capital of Iceland. The guidance of the sacred columns was, however, sometimes disregarded. We are told, for instance, that when Kraku-Hreidar approached the coast, he said, that he considered it very foolish to follow a floating piece of wood wherever it might be carried to, and that for his part he would ask Thor—in what manner we are not informed—to point out a landing-place, and if he found that the land was already occupied, he would challenge its possessor to single combat, and thus ascertain by wager of battle whether he had not the best right to it. Hreidar was, however, shipwrecked, notwithstanding which he persisted in his resolution, and finding that Sæmund had already formed a settlement on that part of the coast on which his vessel had been stranded, instantly

* Johnson being asked " whether a man was not sometimes happy in the moment that was present," answered, " Never but when he is drunk."—Boswell, viii. 271 ; edit. of 1819.

† See page 188.

sent him the intended challenge. Havord, with whom Sæmund had passed the first winter as guest, at last persuaded
Hreidar to consult Eiri, the chief of the district. To Eiri he
accordingly went, who told him that there was plenty of waste
land in the island, and that he himself would cede to him
the whole promontory below Skalamyra, and that this was the
very place which Thor had pointed out to him, for when he
invoked that deity the prow of his vessel must have been
turned towards it. Hreidar was perfectly satisfied with this
conclusive argument, and established himself on the promontory *. Another immigrant, named Kvölld-Ulf, having fallen
dangerously ill on the passage, ordered that when he died his
body should be placed in a coffin—or probably on a shield—
and thrown into the sea, and that his son should settle on
that part of the coast on which it was washed †.

The first colonists seem to have made the ridges of hills,
the banks of rivers, and other natural boundaries, the limits
of their respective settlements. The usual manner of taking
possession was by lighting fires. Helgi, for instance, lighted
fires at the mouths of all the streams running into the frith
bounded by the promontories of Siglunes and Reynesnes, and
thus took possession of the whole district. Shooting a fiery
arrow over a river was also regarded as equivalent to taking
possession of the land on the other side from the place where
the arrow fell to the mouth of the stream. Örmund the Wise,
for instance, had occupied that part of a valley lying eastward
of the rivulet that ran through it, but having heard that Eirek
wished to occupy the western part, he hastened to take possession of it by shooting a fiery arrow over the rivulet ‡.

The ceremony of taking possession by lighting fires on the
boundaries, appears to have been regarded as a consecration
of the land to tutelar deities, and to have only been practised by pontiff-chieftains. Several of these chieftains having
appropriated in this manner very extensive territories, it was
made an established rule that no one should occupy a larger
district than what he and his followers were able to inclose
and dedicate by fires, lighted at sunrise, and kept burning till
sunset, the distance between the fires not to be greater than
would enable a man placed at one to discern the smoke of the
other by day, and its flame by night.

* Landnámab. iii. 7.   † Landnámab. i. 18.   ‡ Landnámab. iii. 8.

It would appear that if the leader of the settlers was a woman, another manner of proceeding was observed. Asbjörn, for instance, having died on the passage to Iceland, the duty of leading the settlers devolved to his widow, Thorgerda, who, according to established usage, could only take possession of as much land as she was able, on a summer's day from sunrise to sunset, to drive a two-year old cow, or a young bull, round *. However, if this was a rule, an exception was made to it in favour of ladies who had plenty of money, or its equivalent, at their command; for we are told that when Aud the Rich arrived, she took as much land as she pleased and divided it among her followers, several of whom were her manumitted slaves.

Immigrants, who arrived in a district after all the land had been occupied, had the alternative of purchasing an estate, or gaining one by wager of battle. They generally preferred the latter, for it was considered more honourable to acquire land by the sword than by purchase. The victory in a wager of battle was awarded by the gods, and the victor might boast that he had received his land from Thor himself as a reward for his valour. There are many instances on record of an immigrant requiring a previous settler either to cede to him his land, or to do wager of battle for it. We have already mentioned one that ended without bloodshed, but it would appear that this was an exceptionable case, and that more frequently the question at issue was decided with sword and battle-axe by a *holmgang*. It was in this way that Thorolf Bægifót acquired the estate of an old man named Ulfar†. Another immigrant named Gudlaug Audgi, perceiving that the land on which Thorir had settled was the best in the district—in which it would appear waste land was still to be had—went to Thorir and gave him the usual choice of a cession or a combat. Thorir's son Thorfinn did not hesitate a moment in preferring a holmgang to dishonour. To work they accordingly went; both combatants were grievously wounded: Thurida, the fair daughter of Tungu-Oddi, healed their wounds, and, while she was performing this good office, persuaded them to enter into an amicable arrangement ‡.

* Landnámab. iv. 10.
† See Walter Scott's abstract of the Eyrbyggja Saga.
‡ Landnámab. ii. 6.

Instances also occur of a man already in possession of an estate offering to exchange it for another, leaving its possessor the choice of accepting his offer or having recourse to a holmgang. Hrolleif, for instance, having remained several years in the place where he had settled, proposed to his neighbour, Eyvind, that they should exchange their possessions, intimating, at the same time, that if Eyvind was not willing to do this, he was ready to meet him in single combat. Eyvind preferred making the exchange, though he was no doubt a loser by the transaction *. This, it must be confessed, was a very convenient way of acquiring land for those who were skilful in the use of the battle-axe; mention, however, is frequently made of immigrants purchasing a part of the ample domains of the early settlers.

When a chieftain had taken possession of a district, he allotted to each of the freemen who accompanied him a certain portion of land, erected a temple (hof), and became, as he had been in Norway, the chief, the pontiff, and the judge of the herad. Such a chieftain was called a *godi* or *hofgodi* †, and all to whom he had allotted land were bound to accompany him on his journeys, and to pay a tax for the support of the temple. We thus find these sacerdotal magistrates appearing at the public assemblies with a number of armed followers, not retainers, but odal-born freemen. When they went on their private affairs, they were generally accompanied by their retainers and guests, and we rarely meet with an instance either of a godi or a wealthy landowner going out alone. The whole frame of society in Iceland was, in fact, essentially aristocratic. The laws only recognised four classes, as in Norway; freemen, unfree, freedmen, and thralls, but among the freemen themselves a distinction was made betwen the *godar* or pontiff chieftains, and the opulent landed proprietors called *stormenn* ‡, or magnates, who had also taken possession of extensive territories, and allotted land to their followers, and a still greater distinction between these and the

* Landnámab, v. 13.
† Godi, properly Goði, literally a God, plural, Godar, properly Goðar, gods; the priests being designated by the same epithet as the deities they worshipped.
‡ Great men, from *stor* great, and *maðr*, a man.

less wealthy freeholders to whom, generally speaking, land had been allotted.

A number of independent chieftains being thus located on the coasts of Iceland without any general law or central authority to control their actions, were continually embroiled in petty feuds and dissensions. The evil consequences resulting from this state of things became at length so great that, in the year 925, Ulfliot was charged with the task of devising a remedy for the ever increasing dissensions of the infant colony. Ulfliot, in order to prepare himself for the duties of a legislator, went to Norway, where he remained three years with Thorleif the Wise, justly renowned for his knowledge of the laws and usages of the parent country. When Ulfliot returned he convoked a general assembly of the people, in which all his proposed enactments were adopted, and a republican form of government finally constituted.

The island, in conformity with its physical features, was divided into four provinces or quarters—*Fjórðúngar*, called respectively the east, west, north and south *Fjórðúngr*,—and each quarter into three districts. A few years later, however, one of the districts of the northern quarter was divided for the convenience of the inhabitants, thus making, in all, thirteen districts, which were subdivided into *hrepps*, or parishes, as they might not inappropriately be termed. A *hrepp* was to be a tract of country that should not contain less than twenty landholders, five of whom were to be elected by the inhabitants for the management of the affairs of the locality, and especially—as we shall presently show—for the due administration of the *Poor Laws*. They were empowered to convene a public meeting whenever they might deem it necessary to submit any measures to the discussion of the ratepayers.

Each of the thirteen districts had its temple (*höfud-hof*, chief temple) and its Thing, over which presided three godar,—hence called *samgodar* *—who were to be chosen from amongst those the most distinguished for their wisdom and love of justice. It would appear, however, that although these godar must necessarily have been elected or appointed in the first

---

* *Sam*, from *saman*, together.

instance, the dignity afterwards became hereditary; for it is expressly stated in the Grágás how a female, inheriting such a sacerdotal magistracy, is to appoint a deputy *. Frequent mention is also made of a godi selling his office, or *godord* †, as it was termed, when, according to express law, it was to devolve to the heirs of the purchaser ‡. The godord was, in fact, regarded as a possession that might be sold, and bequeathed, and inherited, but not entailed. A district Thing, called a *Varthing*, was held annually in spring, and attended by all the freemen of the district, with a crowd of retainers. It was not to last more than seven, nor less than four days. The Thingstead was always near the temple, in which one of the sacerdotal magistrates performed a sacrifice and sprinkled the walls of the edifice, as well as the bystanders, with the blood of the victims; holding in his hand, on this as on every other solemn occasion, a massive silver ring, with which the altar of every temple was furnished. The Things were held in the open air, and served both for the discussion of public affairs and the administration of justice. For the latter purpose a circle called the doom-ring, *dómhringr*, was formed with hazel twigs or with upright stones, to which were attached cords called *vebönd* §. Within this circle sat the judges, the people standing on the outside, and in the midde stood the *blótsteinn*, a huge stone with a sharp ridge, on which the backs of criminals condemned to death were broken ‖. Each of the three godar summoned twelve assessors or doomsmen (*dóms-menn*), to sit

* Grágás, iii. 61. We frequently read of females holding this office. Thus, in the tenth century, Steinvora entered an action against Thorleif, who having been baptized during his residence abroad, had refused, on his return to Iceland, to pay the accustomed tribute to the temple over which she presided.—See Müller, Sagabib, i. 99.

† Properly goðorð, literally *god-word*—orð, word, authority.

‡ " Ef maðr hefir keypt goðorð eðr var hanom gefit ok skal that at erfðom fara." Grágás, iii. 61.

§ Vebönd—the consecrated or sacred cords—*bönd* the plural of *band*, a band or cord. In the glossary to the second volume of the Edda several significations of the word *ve* are given—religion, peace, justice, right &c., and it seems to be cognate with the Mœso-gothic, *veihan*, Germ. *weihen*, to consecrate; the Pehlvi *veh*, pure, and the Persian *veh*, excellent, &c.

‖ *Sacrificial stone*, human victims being sometimes offered on it, as an expiatory sacrifice, to appease the offended deities. Such sacrifices were very common in Sweden, but do not appear ever to have taken place in Iceland.

with him within the forensic circle which thus formed a court
of justice composed—if we may apply modern terms to ancient
institutions—of three judges and thirty-six jurymen. Any
doomsman, to whom either plaintiff or defendant might object,
was to be instantly replaced by the godi, who had nominated
him *. The altar-ring we previously made mention of was
used for the administration of oaths. Every one engaged in
a lawsuit, whether as plaintiff or defendant, as witness, or com-
purgator, or doomsman, was obliged to swear on this ring,
" in the name of Frey, Njörd, and the Almighty God," † that
he would fulfil the duty imposed on him—to give evidence,
or plead, or judge as the case might be—conscientiously, and
to the best of his abilities.

A few miles to the north-east of Reykjavik is a lake, formerly called Olvus-vatn, into which flows the river Öxerá.
The surrounding country has been convulsed and torn to pieces
by earthquakes and volcanic eruptions. To the north of the
lake stretches an arid plain, bounded by rugged mountains, in-
tersected by indurated volcanic streams, and rent into fissures
and yawning chasms, presenting, with their jagged acclivities
and piled up masses of disrupted lava, an ever varied scenery
of the most awful sublimity ‡. It was on this wild and deso-

---

* We have evidently here the trial by jury, for which we are probably more
indebted to our Scandinavian than to our Saxon ancestors. In Eigil's Saga
there is a graphic description of a Norwegian Thing—also with thirty-six
doomsmen, twelve from each district, seated in a doom-ring, formed with
hazel-twigs, in the middle of a wide plain. At this Thing, Queen Gunhilda,
fearing that the verdict would be pronounced in favour of Eigil, caused one
of her followers to cut the sacred cords (vebönd), and thereby put a stop to
the proceedings : cutting the cords being regarded as a profanation of the
forensic circle, and as a crime that merited the severest punishment.—See
Eigil's Saga, and Müller's Sagabib, i. 115.

† By "the Almighty God" the Icelanders and Norwegians meant Thor,
the Swedes and Danes, Odin.

‡ The reader may form some idea of this terrific scenery, by the following abridged extract from Henderson's "Iceland : "—"The track we
followed," says this traveller, "led us all at once to the brink of a
frightful chasm, where the solid masses of burnt rock have been disrupted
so as to form a fissure or gap not less than 180 feet deep ; in many
places nearly of the same width, and about three miles in length. On the
west side of the rent it is met by another opening, partially filled with large
masses of broken rock, down which the traveller must resolve to proceed.
To the north-west of Thingvalla church, (situated near the ancient Law-
mount,) we entered on a long and narrow track of solid lava, completely

late spot, amidst the elemental strife of nature, that the Ice-landers held their *Al-thing*, or national assembly. On the banks of a frightful precipice stood the Law-mount, (Lögberg,) with a mystic doom-ring of huge volcanic stones fixed in the earth, so as to withstand the storms of centuries.

The Al-thing * was held annually in summer, and lasted sixteen days, and it was regarded as disreputable for a free-man not to attend it. People of all classes, in fact, pitched their tents, and erected their booths on the Thingvalla plain on such occasions. The chieftains were accompanied by their retainers, the litigants by their witnesses and compurgators †. Tradesmen came from Norway and Denmark, and at a later period also from England, to exchange their goods for the produce of the country, and there appears to have been no lack of stalls for the sale of provisions. This multitudinous assem-bly was kept in good order by a police magistrate, called the *Allsherjar-godi* ‡, specially appointed for the purpose. The

separated from the rocks on both sides by two parallel fissures, which, in many places, are upwards of forty fathoms in depth, and in some places no bottom can be found at all. They are filled with the most beautiful pellucid water till within about 60 feet of the brink on which we stood."

* *Al*, all. The word *Thing*, Ang. Sax. *Thing*, Germ. *Ding*, requires, for the English reader, no explanation in the sense in which it is usually taken ; but it also signifies a colloquy, a conference, from the Old Norse, *thinga*, to de-liberate on, Ang. Sax. *thingean* to say ; hence the word *thing* became an ap-pellative denoting a deliberative assembly ; *völlr* is the Old Norse for a field, or plain, *Thingvöllr* the field or place in which a Thing is held. Several places show by the names they still bear that they were originally Thingsteads, as Thingvalla in Iceland ; Tingvold in Norway ; Tingwall in the Shetland Isles ; Dingwall in the county of Ross ; Tynwald in Dumfries ; Tynwald in the Isle of Man, and Dingsted in the Duchy of Oldenburg, which has still its doom-ring of upright stones, with the *blótsteinn* in the centre.

† The magistrates and doomsmen had their expenses defrayed by a tax called the Thingfararkaup, *Thing-faring-tax—farar* from the verb *fara*, to fare, to go ; *kaup* from *kaupa* to buy—levied on the inhabitants of their respective districts, and it would appear more particularly on the class of the unfree.—See Grágás, viii. c. 25. A *Thing-faring-tax* is also levied in Hungary, but exclusively on the class of the unfree or peasantry ; and as the Hungarian Al-thing frequently lasts upwards of a year, and each delegate receives 12*s.* a day, and 3*s.* a day for his amanuensis, the expenses are pretty considerable. The nobility, however, defrayed the expenses of the last Diet by levying a con-tribution on themselves, having at length become aware of the injustice of saddling the burden on the poorest class of the community.

‡ That is, magistrate of all the assembled people—literally *All-hosts'-god*. The Scandinavian and Magyar institutions offer a remarkable coincidence,

Al-thing itself was presided over by the supreme magistrate of the Republic, called the *Lögsögumadr**, or Promulgator of the Law, who was elected for life, and, according to received notions, by the free suffrage of his fellow-citizens ; that is to say, in plain language, by the free suffrage of the few, who adroitly disposed, either by justifiable or unjustifiable means, of the votes of the many ; the only kind of free suffrage which we fear was ever enjoyed in any age, or in any country on the face of the earth, by a popular assembly. Within the doom-ring were three rows of stone seats. On the middle row sat the godar, twelve from each of the four quarters of the island †, and on the front and back rows their assessors, or doomsmen, each of these sacerdotal-magistrates being accompanied by two men whom—it was supposed at least—he had chosen for their knowledge of the laws and usages of the country. This forensic assembly consisted, therefore, of 144 persons, besides the Lögsögumadr who presided over it, and must have had a very imposing appearance ‡.

We find it stated in several works that an appeal lay from a district Thing to the Al-thing. This, however, was not the case, as the writers would have found had they consulted the Grágás, or read Schlegel's commentary on that intricate code §. It was, however, optional for parties to bring their suits either before the Thing of their district, or before the Al-thing, and even when proceedings had commenced before the former,

not only in their general features, but even in their details ; thus the Hungarian Al-thing has also its *Allsherjargodi*, or police magistrate, specially appointed for the occasion—an office which was held at the last Diet by Count Feri Zichy.

* Properly Lögsögumaðr, literally *Laws'-narrations'-man*, or, *Law-saying-man ; lög*, nom. plural of *lag*, law, from *leggja*, to lay, to lay down ; *sögur*, plural of *saga*, a narration, a say, from *segja*, to say ; and *maðr*, man.

† The north quarter had, as we before observed, four districts, and consequently twelve godar : the south, east and west quarters, only three districts and nine godar each. In order to render the number from each quarter the same, the three godar of each of these districts were empowered to appoint a fourth godi to accompany them to the Al-thing.

‡ After the introduction of Christianity, the two bishops of the island sat with the supreme magistrate, and appear to have exercised a considerable influence on public affairs.

§ Grágás, 2 v. 4to, Copenh. 1829, with the original Icelandic text, a Latin translation, and an admirable " Commentatio Historica et Critica," by W. Schlegel.

either the plaintiff or defendant might put a stop to them and bring the case before the latter, but when judgment had been pronounced no appeal lay to a superior tribunal. A suit brought before the Al-thing was heard and decided by the twelve godar, and twenty-four doomsmen of the province, or quarter, to which the litigants belonged ; the forensic circle of the Al-thing being formed for judicial proceedings into four sections, or tribunals, corresponding to the four quarters into which the island was divided. Each of these quarters had also its Thing, but these provincial Things are seldom mentioned, and appear to have only been occasionally held for the convenience of suitors whose cases could not be terminated at the Al-thing, and their forensic circles to have been composed of the same godar and doomsmen, who had represented the province at that national assembly.

The suits at the Al-thing, were conducted in the same manner as at a district Thing, oaths being administered to all the parties concerned, facts elicited by witnesses, and the corroboration of compurgators, and the verdict pronounced by a simple majority of the court ; the Lögsögumadr having, it would appear, in all the four courts the casting vote. Until the end of the eleventh century every one went armed to the Al-thing, the chieftains being generally accompanied by very numerous retinues. Many a sanguinary scene was the natural result ; and we read of men being slaughtered within the doom-ring itself, and of parties preventing the promulgation of an act, or verdict, by occupying with an armed force the Law-mount. In order to remedy these evils, it was at length decreed that all who were present at an Al-thing should lay aside their arms, and not resume them until the assembly broke up *, and that no suitor should be accompanied by more than thirty men, only three of whom should be admitted at the same time within the doom-ring.

Less than a century's experience seems to have shown the Icelanders the necessity of having a court of appeal or revi-

---

* Hence the word *vopnatak*—resumption of arms, (*weapons'-take*)—was used to denote the termination of an Al-thing. The Hungarians still retain their weapons, and their magnates may still be seen leading on, sword in hand, like the Icelandic chieftains of the olden time, a crowd of dependent Thingsmen, ready at their nod to decide a question under discussion, or carry the election of a magistrate *vi et armis*.

sion. They accordingly instituted, in the year 1004, at the suggestion of Njáll,—whom we shall have occasion to make mention of in the next chapter—a fifth court, *Fimtardómr*, composed of the sacerdotal magistrates of the Al-thing. But as the litigants had the right to exclude twelve of them, the court actually consisted of thirty-six of these magistrates, nine from each quarter of the island. The sittings were held in the same place as the Al-thing; but this tribunal could only annul a decision of the other courts on the ground of informality, arising from the non-observance of prescribed usages, false evidence, subornation of witnesses, forcible detention of any one engaged in the suit, &c. It was invested, in fact, with much the same kind of authority as the French *Cour de Cassation;* and it is a very remarkable fact, as Schlegel observes, that a tribunal similar to that which the French legislators of the present age so justly pride themselves in having established, should have existed in this remote island in the beginning of the eleventh century. About the same period an act was also passed to empower the godar of each district to hold a court called a *Leidar-thing* *, fourteen days after the termination of an Al-thing, for the purpose of promulgating the laws that had been passed in that assembly, fixing the day on which the district Thing was to be held, making known any change that had taken place in the magistracy, and other matters concerning the administration of the Republic.

It will be seen from the sketch we have given of the civil institutions of the Icelanders, that the form of government was strictly aristocratic, the administration of affairs being, in a great measure, in the hands of hereditary sacerdotal magistrates. The Lögsögumadr himself chiefly exercised his authority at the Al-thing: out of that assembly he seems to have possessed little or no power. The office was, however, regarded as the highest dignity in the state, and from the year 930, when the Republic was finally consti-

---

* *Leidar,* from the verb *leita,* to inquire into, according to Thorkelin, but more probably from *liða,* to go. Schlegel has shown that although the English word *leet* is cognate with the old Norse *leið,* Thorkelin was wrong in supposing that the English court-leet corresponded to the Icelandic Leidar-thing.—See Comm. de Grágás, note, p. 92.

tuted, until the year 1264*, was held by thirty-nine individuals, the periods at which they respectively exercised this magistracy forming so many distinct epochs in the national annals. Ulfliot, who had been so instrumental in founding the Republic, was made its first Lögsögumadr, by the same national assembly that adopted his legislation. We have already given an account of the political and administrative measures introduced by this Icelandic Solon; but it is impossible to ascertain, at the present day, what were the precise laws he submitted for the approval of his countrymen; for they were handed down by oral tradition for nearly two centuries, during which period, the title of *Law-saying-man*, borne by the supreme magistrate of the republic, was a very appropriate one, for he had to recite and expound the laws to the assembled people at every Al-thing. When a case had been decided he had also to announce the decision, which was regarded as a precedent equivalent to a formal law on the subject. In the year 1117 these laws and precedents were first committed to writing, and after being thoroughly revised by the most experienced jurisconsults, underwent a public discussion at the following Al-thing, when those that had been approved of by a majority of the Thingsmen were digested into a regular code, into which subsequent laws and precedents were, from time to time, incorporated until the final extinction of the Republic. This code, known under the name of the Grágás†, is unquestionably one of the most remark-

* The north, south, and west quarters became tributary to Norway in the year 1261, and the east quarter in 1264. But in becoming the subjects of the Norwegian kings the Icelanders expressly stipulated that they should retain their own laws and customs, and be exempt from taxation, and, although they subsequently adopted several Norwegian laws, the spirit of their ancient code continued to prevail for centuries. The Al-thing also continued to be held annually on the Thingvalla plain—though, in modern times, more as a judicial than a legislative assembly—until the year 1800, when the frequent earthquakes were made a pretext for removing the courts to Reykjavik.

† The name of Grágás, *grey goose*, was first applied to it in the seventeenth century by Björn of Skardsa, some say because grey goose quills were generally used for writing Icelandic manuscripts; others, because the manuscript copy of the Grágás was bound in a grey goose skin; but Schlegel is of opinion that the name was given because a grey goose was formerly supposed to live for ages. The two vellum MSS., which Schlegel has made use of for his admirable edition of this ancient code, are supposed to have

able documents of the kind in existence. What strikes us the
most in perusing it are the legal formularies with which it is
overloaded. Every judicial proceeding has its prescribed
form, the manner in which the accusation and defence are to
be conducted, witnesses summoned, evidence given, verdict
pronounced, &c., are detailed with the greatest minuteness,
and the omission of a single phrase in any one of these formularies sufficed to render the judgment invalid *.

We have frequently observed that subtilty was a leading
trait in the character of the ancient Scandinavians; should
any one doubt this he has only to read the Grágás and Njálssaga, which is the best commentary on it, and he will find that
the Icelanders have surpassed all other nations, ancient or
modern, in legal chicanery. Jurisprudence was the favourite
study of the rich. A wealthy Icelander was always ambitious
to plead a cause before the Al-thing, and the greater pro-
ficiency he showed in the art of prolonging, or involving it by
having recourse to legal quibbles, the greater was his celebrity.
A man, in fact, gained as much reputation for defeating his
adversary in a lawsuit as for killing him in a duel †. The
Icelandic legislators were, in some respects, like those Catholic
divines who indite manuals for the confessional, in which
every conceivable sin a poor mortal could by any possibility
ever fall into is duly registered; for we find in the Grágás
every imaginable combination of circumstances that might in
any way tend to attenuate or increase the criminality of an

been written towards the end of the thirteenth or beginning of the fourteenth
century, consequently about half a century after the fall of the Republic. The
code is divided into ten sections; the first as well as the second of these sections
only contains one law or chapter, relating to the political division and administration of the country. Section iii. has 72 chapters relating to judiciary proceedings. Section iv., 25 chapters on the inheritance of property. Section v.,
poor laws, 35 chapters. Section vi. contains 59 chapters relating to marriage,
divorce, conjugal rights, &c. Section vii., commercial laws, laws of debtor
and creditor, &c., 85 chapters. Section viii., criminal laws, 121 chapters.
Section ix., laws relating to property, 72 chapters. Section x., navigation
laws, 4 chapters.

* A number of these formularies, which are only referred to in the Grágás
as the "accustomed manner of proceeding," have been preserved in Njálssaga,
which is filled with them.

† These gentlemen were, however, by no means averse to taking a fee,
for mention is frequently made of milch cows, and a certain number of ells
of wadmal being given as a con-si-der-a-tion for their services.

act, and the punishment graduated accordingly. The endless distinctions and quiddities of the scholastic disputants of the middle ages are here embodied into law. It is thus enacted, to cite one instance among a hundred, that " If a man holds his weapons in a peaceable manner, as a person ordinarily does when he is not going to use them, and when they are in this position another man runs against them and wounds himself, he who held the weapons is liable to the punishment of banishment if competent witnesses can prove that he held them in this apparently quiet manner, in order that the other might run against them and be wounded thereby."*

The punishment of death seems only to have been inflicted for witchcraft and magic, and in order to prevent the ghosts of those who were executed for these imaginary crimes from revisiting " the glimpses of the moon " the bodies were either burnt or cast into the sea. The punishments for most other crimes and misdemeanors were the so called *Fjörbaugsgarðr* and *Skóggángr* †. Both these terms imply outlawry, but the former may be rendered by *exclusion*, i. e. from society, and the latter by *exile*. Exclusion was the ordinary punishment for what would be deemed in modern times very trifling offences, and generally lasted three years, during which period the condemned person had to remain within doors, three houses being assigned in which he might dwell at his option, and the road indicated by which he might go, at stated times, from the one to the other, or to a place of embarkation if he preferred leaving the island. Any one who found him at any other time out of these houses, or off these roads, might kill him with impunity. This punishment might, however, be remitted at the discretion of the court on the offender paying a fine of three marks ‡. If this had not been the case, most

---

* Grágás, viii. 34.

† Schlegel derives Fjörbaugs, or as he will have it Fjörbeygsgarðr, from *þiör*, vital energy, life ; *beygr*, fear ; and *garðr*, a fence ; and the word would therefore express that a man condemned to such a punishment would always be in fear of his life. Skóggángr from *skógr*, a forest, and *gánga*, to gang, to go.

‡ A mark was divided into eight ounces. Pecuniary transactions were, however, adjusted in Iceland, not by the medium of a metallic currency, but by the coarse woollen cloth of the country, called wadmal, *vadmal ;* mark and ounce are therefore only used as designations for so many ells of wadmal.

people in those days would have had to pass the greater part of their lives within doors. For graver crimes, such as homicide and arson, and, as we shall presently show, even for several minor offences, the punishment was twenty years' exile, (*Skóggángr*,) at the expiration of which period the exile might return, and, provided he could effect a reconciliation with the kindred of the party he had injured, might live unmolested. During the period of his banishment he was, in the most rigorous acceptation of the term, an outlawed man. Any one holding communication with him was liable to be prosecuted, a price was set on his head, and he might be killed with impunity, not only in Iceland but also in a foreign country. The spirit of revenge was even carried so far that a man who had passed some years in exile might expiate his offence and return to Iceland by killing another who had been recently banished. The property of an exile was generally confiscated, a portion reserved for the maintenance of his family, and the rest equally divided between the accuser and the community *.

In no code of the middle ages do we find such rigorous enactments for the protection of person and property, nor such detailed police regulations, as in the Grágás. Yet notwithstanding this legal terrorism there was probably no country in Europe, during that turbulent epoch, where acts of violence were more frequently committed than in Iceland. The want of a central administration will, in some measure, account for this seeming anomaly, and police regulations, however excellent, would naturally be infringed in a country without a police to enforce their due observance; but it was, no doubt,

---

The Grágás, viii. 3, defines a *legal ounce* to be 6 ells of wadmal, 2 ells wide. A fine of 3 marks would consequently be equivalent to 144 ells. We often find in the Sagas a large hundred, or 6 score ells of this cloth, made equivalent in value to a cow or to 6 sheep.

   * A child born in exile of legitimate parents, even when only one of them was exiled, could not inherit property. Here again the Icelanders drew one of their scholastic distinctions. If the father was exiled and not the mother, the child was called *an Exile's drop*, Vargdropi; from *vargr*, a wolf, also an exile—an outlawed man being regarded as a wolf—and *dropi*, a drop; in the contrary case, the mother being exiled and the father not culpable, the name of *Cavern-child* (Bæsingr) was bestowed on it, as it was supposed that a man would only hold communication with his outlawed wife in a cavern.

chiefly owing to the system that prevailed, not only in Iceland, but in most of the other European states at that period, of leaving it to the option of an injured person either to prosecute those who had injured him, or receive a pecuniary compensation for the injury sustained. When a man had been killed, for instance, his son or next of kin, as the case might be, had three courses open to him. He might in his turn kill the person who had, whether in self-defence or not, deprived his father of life; he might enter an action at law against him, or he might receive a compensatory fine, in which case no further notice was taken of the transaction.

The facility thus afforded for expiating an offence by the payment of a fine will account for the severity of several enactments in the Grágás. A man, for instance, was liable to the punishment of *exile*, and all its terrible consequences, for merely throwing dirt at another, or striking him with his fist, or attempting to throw him into the mire, though he might not actually fall therein *. We find these compensatory or expiatory fines accurately specified in all the codes of those barbarous ages, but the Grágás offers in this respect many striking peculiarities. Thus a whole chapter is devoted to show how the amount of a fine is to be apportioned among the kindred of a person who has either to pay or receive it. The fourth cousin of one party, for instance, would have to pay the same portion of the fine as the fourth cousin of the other party would have to receive, but this portion would be less than a third cousin and more than a fifth cousin would have to pay or receive, the amount decreasing with the degree of consanguinity †. In the Germanic codes each limb has its tax, and a man knew beforehand how much he would have to pay for lopping off another man's ear, or rendering him for life a cripple. There is nothing of the kind in the Grágás. The Icelanders were, in this respect, greatly in advance of their contemporaries. They enter, it is true, into endless distinctions to appreciate the extent of a bodily injury, and the manner in which, and the circumstances under which, it might be inflicted, whether by stabbing, sticking, cutting, hewing

---

* Grágás, viii. 90, 91.
† Grágás. Baugatal. viii. 114.

&c., but the punishment awarded is, according to the gravity of the case, either *exile* or *exclusion*.

A master could, of course, kill his slave with impunity: but if a slave killed his master, or any of his master's near relatives, he became, on conviction, an outlawed exile. It would appear, that exiled slaves generally sought refuge in the uninhabited parts of the island, though their lives were continually in danger, for among other remorseless enactments in the Grágás there is one which states that, when an exiled slave is found in a district, he shall be taken to the person at whose suit he had been exiled, and this person shall lead him to a cross road, and there cut off his legs, and afterwards kill him in whatever manner he may take a fancy to: a refusal to comply with this regulation rendered him liable to the punishment of *exclusion*, and those who brought the slave to him might for that purpose enter an action at law against him *.

A singular distinction is made between murder and manslaughter. If a man killed another and kept the deed secret, or concealed the body of the person he had killed, he was guilty of murder; but if he publicly avowed the deed on the same day that it was committed, and did not conceal the body further than by covering it sufficiently to protect it from birds and beasts of prey, only of manslaughter.

The Icelanders were famous throughout the north for their *nithing-verses*, or pasquinades †, which were, however, generally speaking, of the coarsest description. Scandal, slander, ill-natured remarks on neighbours, and abusive language, were indulged in at their social meetings to an extent that called for legislative interference. Hence we find in the Grágás the most stringent enactments for the punishment of such kind of offences. Composers of nithing-verses, or writers of foul and scandalous libels, as our gentlemen of the long robe would term them, are as rigorously dealt with in the Grágás as in a modern act of parliament. The Icelandic definition of a libel is also much the same as our own. Verses composed and repeated before another, or written and circulated for the purpose of holding any one up to ridicule, or casting a slur on

* Grágás, viii. 111.
† For the explanation of the word nithing, see the note p. 155.

his character, are declared to be libellous, irrespective of the truth or falsehood of the allegations they contain *. Expressions made use of for the same purpose are placed in the same category. We should be inclined to conclude, from several chapters of the Grágás, that the coarse wit of the Icelandic poetasters was principally directed against the sacerdotal magistrates and other leading men of the commonwealth; for these gentlemen, who were the *bona fide* legislators of the country, the crowd of Thingsmen being no doubt completely under their influence, appear to have had a peculiar dislike to verse-making in all its stages. Thus, in the chapter entitled "*Um Skaldskap*†, it is enacted that no one shall compose verses even in praise of another," "neither in a man's praise nor dispraise," *lof ne löst*—are the words made use of; and, in conformity with that pettifogging spirit that pervades the whole code, some curious distinctions are drawn to show the precise degree of criminality that is to be attached to each kind of verse, and to each individual concerned in its composition. The composer of a half strophe (four short lines) that contains no satirical expression is liable to a fine of three marks; of a whole strophe, to the punishment of *exclusion*. But if the half strophe contains any satirical expression against another person, the punishment of *exile* is to be awarded. If, in the latter case, the half strophe has been composed by two or even by four individuals, or the whole strophe by eight individuals, each of them is liable to the same punishment as well as those convicted of reciting it. If no allusion is made in the strophe to a particular individual, any one may apply it to himself, and enter an action against its composer or composers. Even love ditties were not exempt from this general proscription of versification; and if a young lady, to whom such effusions were addressed, was hard-hearted enough to render the amatory wight who composed them liable to the punishment of banishment or its pecuniary equivalent, she had only to enter an action against him; or, if a

---

* In Norway, and the other Scandinavian states, truth might be told even in satirical verse, and it was only false allegations that were regarded as libellous.

† *On Poetry*—on doggrel would have been a more appropriate term, for most of these nithing-verses are as arrant doggrel as ever was cudgelled out of the brain of a poetaster.

minor, persuade her parents or guardians to do so in her name and behalf,—a proceeding which we will presume, for the honour of the Icelandic fair sex, was not often resorted to*.

One of the most remarkable sections of the Grágás is that of the Poor-laws, which we have no hesitation in saying might be studied even at the present day with advantage. It is laid down, as a maxim, that when a person is unable through age, or infirmity, or misfortune, to maintain himself, those who are his nearest of kin, and possess sufficient means, are bound to maintain him. Hence many fine distinctions are drawn respecting the legal claim that persons in such a situation may have on their relations; a claim regulated both according to the degree of consanguinity in which the individuals on whom it was made might stand to the claimant, and the value of the property they might respectively be in possession of. Every one, say the Icelandic legislators, is bound to maintain his mother, if his circumstances admit, also his father, then his children; in the third degree, his brothers and sisters, and so on according to the means he may have at his disposal. Consequently, when a person was unable to maintain himself, the parish (hrepp) authorities were empowered to ascertain on which of his relations he had a legal alimentary claim, and compel that relation to take charge of him; or, supposing for instance, that a widower with four children, and aged and infirm parents, could satisfactorily show that he was only able to maintain himself and his mother, the parish authorities were then bound to see that his father and children were duly provided for. If no legal claim could be made out, that is to say, if all the relations of a destitute person were equally destitute, the charge of supporting him devolved on the parish. It was one of the chief duties of the five administrators of the affairs of a parish †, to allot to each rate-payer a number of paupers proportionate to the value of his property, whom he was bound to supply with the necessaries of life in the manner prescribed by law. A dépôt of provisions for the poor was also established in each parish. If a poor man's house was burnt down, the parish rebuilt it for him. In short, the most praiseworthy care

* Grágás, viii. 106.

† The hrepps, see page 290, after the introduction of Christianity, generally became parishes, though the terms were not synonymous.

seems to have been taken that no citizen of the common-wealth should perish by starvation.   Hence the reciprocal duties of *alimentor* and *alimentee* are defined with the usual minuteness.   An alimentee who was ill treated, or ill fed, might seek redress from the parish authorities, or bring his case before the district Thing.   An alimentor who quitted his parish for the purpose of evading his duties, was liable to the punishment of *exclusion*.   No alimentor was allowed to leave the island until he had given his alimentees into the charge of a competent individual, and placed at his disposal sufficient funds to provide, during three years, for their maintenance.   We thus find that, in respect to the poor, an Icelandic parish was, to say the least, equally as well managed as an English one.   The Icelanders, however, did not charge themselves with the support of their poor without taking especial care to keep the number of paupers within due limits ; a care which we have grossly neglected, and are now enduring the fearful consequences of our want of foresight. Hence it was enacted that no one who had not sufficient pro-perty to maintain a family should be allowed to marry *, and that when a person manumitted a thrall, he should allot him a piece of land sufficient for the maintenance of a family, failing to do which, he and his heirs should be regarded as the legally bound alimentors of the freedmen and his pos-terity †.   Very stringent regulations were also passed to keep the poor within their respective parishes.   Clothes and shoes

---

* The minimum is fixed, Sec. viii. 12, at six score legal ounces, that is to say, a property equivalent in value to 720 ells of wadmal, besides clothes and other necessaries. A man whose property was under this legal minimum rendered himself, by marrying, liable to the punishment of *exclusion*, " except his wife should be barren," an exception quite in accordance with the whole tenor of Icelandic legislation.

† The land was not given unconditionally, certain services being required from the donee, at whose death, provided he left no children, it reverted to the donor ; otherwise the children inherited, and many hypothetical cases are laid down to show when the heirs of the donor may, in default of issue of the descendants of the donee, again enter into possession of it. This enactment offers a very favourable contrast to a Norwegian law (in the Gulathing code) of the same period, which ordains that the destitute orphans of a manumitted thrall shall be placed in a grave dug for the purpose in the parish churchyard—Norway, was, at this period, a *Christian* country—and only the child that remained alive the longest be entitled to claim support from his father's former master.

might be given to a pauper of another parish, but any parish-
ioner who furnished such a pauper with victuals, except he
was merely passing through the parish to go to his own,
rendered himself liable to the punishment of *exclusion*. The
Icelanders also took care to make able bodied paupers work
for their living. An able-bodied pauper found begging was
liable to be punished with *exile*, which, for such a man, was
tantamount to death, as he would have no means of leaving
the island, and might, consequently, after conviction, be
killed with impunity. Begging was not tolerated, especially
at the Al-thing. If a beggar entered a booth on the Thingvalla plain, the booth-man might forcibly eject him, and every
one who furnished such a beggar with meat, was liable to be
punished with exclusion. All persons who wandered about
the country for fifteen days and upwards were to be regarded
as vagabonds, or *ganging-men* (göngomenn), as they are
termed in the Grágás, and punished accordingly. Besides
other punishments to which they were liable, any one who
thought proper might mutilate them in the manner practised
in the East to qualify a man for the service of the seraglio *.

The Icelandic rural code, as well as the laws for the protection of property, the laws of inheritance, mortgages, and
debtor and creditor, are also well deserving of attention, but
our limits will only allow us to notice a few of the enactments on these subjects. The legal rate of interest was ten
per cent. Insolvent debtors appear to have been very mildly
treated,—a circumstance that reflects the more credit on the
Icelanders from the contrast it affords to the barbarity that
prevailed in this respect in Norway, where a debtor was not
only obliged to work for his creditor, but if his friends would
not liquidate his debts the creditor might lead him to the
Thingstead, and there, in the presence of the assembled
Thingsmen, "hew off any part of his body, either above or
below," that he might think proper, or, in other words, an insolvent debtor whom no one would redeem from thraldom
might be legally cut to pieces.

The age for attaining to majority was fixed, for males, at

---

* Rett er at gelda göngomenn, or as the clause is rendered in Latin—though
we should be inclined to substitute *vagabundos* for *mendicos*—" Mendicos
castrare fas est, nec delicti in leges commissi pœna quis tenetur, etiamsi inde
vel plagam vel mortem retulerint."—Grágás v. 35.

sixteen, and for females at eighteen, but a boy when twelve years old was a competent witness, and might enter an action against a person who had killed his father. A person who had arrived at the good old age of fourscore was not allowed to sell his estate, except it was deeply mortgaged, and if he married, any children his wife might have were to be regarded as illegitimate*. Very good regulations were also framed to prevent a person from suffering his land to lie waste. If, after due notice had been given, he refused to cultivate it, or to let it to another willing to do so, his neighbours might make use of it as a common pasture. A person was only allowed to fish or to kill game on his own estate, but he might kill wolves, bears, eagles, and crows anywhere.

The Icelanders did not follow the whale fishery, though they sometimes harpooned a whale that approached the shore, and when one of these leviathans of the deep was stranded or entangled in the ice off the coast, the whole population of the district was in movement, and it was seldom that such an event occurred without giving rise to lawsuits and sanguinary contests. Hence we find in the Grágás no less than eighteen chapters (Sec. ix. ch. 55—72) to define in what manner a legal claim is, in such cases, to be established, and what portion of the spoil has to fall to each of the claimants—to the owner of the land on which the whale was stranded, to the person who first descried it, &c., &c.

At the early period of the commonwealth, when a man was suspected of theft, a kind of tribunal composed of twelve persons named by him, and twelve by the person whose goods had been stolen, was instituted before the door of his dwelling, and hence called a *door-doom* (duradómr); but as this manner of proceeding generally ended in bloodshed, it was abolished, and an act passed authorizing the suffering party to summon thirty of his neighbours to accompany him for the purpose of making domiciliary visits in search of the stolen property; any one refusing to go, to be fined three marks, and those who would not allow a search to be made on their premises, to be liable to the punishment of *exile*. This

---

* Grágás, iv. 18. The *godord* also came within the provisions of this law, which is another proof that it was regarded as real property that might be disposed of whenever the holder thought proper.

act * contains as usual numerous regulations respecting the
manner in which the search is to be made, and mutual
pledges, in the presence of competent witnesses, are to be given
that no bodily injury should be inflicted by any of the parties
concerned.   Highway robbers or brigands might not only be
killed with impunity, but those who killed them were entitled to a recompense.

These and numerous other enactments, in the Grágás, as
well as the incidents related in the Sagas, show that a man's
property was more secure in Iceland than his person.   In an
age, in fact, when every one went armed, when it was regarded as an act of cowardice to brook the slightest insult,
and when a pecuniary compensation might be offered and received without dishonour for a bodily injury, a man's life
must have been in daily jeopardy.   The same causes would
also, in a great measure, have rendered property equally insecure.   Hence, although the Icelandic laws both for the protection and inheritance of property are much superior to those
of the mother-country, and the Germanic states of the same
period, a person skilful in the use of his weapons would, no
doubt, frequently have braved their stringent regulations with
impunity.   This was particularly the case during the times of
Paganism, but in the eleventh century legal right appears to
have been much more respected.   We think, however, that
it would be erroneous to suppose, with some writers, that a
sudden change of public opinion had been effected by the introduction of Christianity.   A change there certainly was, but
we should attribute it more to the knowledge of jurisprudence,
and especially of judicial forms, which the Icelanders had acquired in the forensic circle of the Al-thing.   An influential
person had been taught by experience that he might crush his
adversary more effectually, and with less bodily risk, by
having recourse to legal chicanery, and underhand practices,
than by meeting him with sword and battle-axe at a holmgang.   In the tenth century a prudent man in Iceland was,
no doubt, often deterred from enforcing a legal claim by reflecting on the personal risk he would necessarily incur, and
the probability that any step he might take would only be the

* Grágás, viii. 118.

commencement of one of those hereditary feuds that were the cause of so much bloodshed.   In the eleventh, and especially in the twelfth and in the thirteenth century, he would be equally deterred by the certain prospect of involving himself and his family in a ruinous and interminable lawsuit.   At the early period of the commonwealth the Icelanders acted on the principle—a principle which, as worshippers of Thor, was quite in accordance with their religious tenets—that might constituted right; but the proceedings in their forensic circles gradually effected a great change in their sentiments, and they appear to have finally arrived at the conviction that rights could only be maintained or enforced by legal astuteness.

CHAPTER III.

MANNERS AND CUSTOMS OF THE ICELANDERS.

IN our remarks on the Grágás, we purposely abstained from noticing the laws that define conjugal rights and regulate the intercourse between the sexes, it being our intention to give a brief outline of them in the present chapter, together with a few anecdotes from the Sagas, which will serve as their best commentary, and at the same time enable the reader to form a more correct idea of the state of society in Iceland during the earlier period of the commonwealth than any observations we could make on the subject.   We should certainly be inclined to doubt whether some of the incidents related in these narratives actually occurred; but the same doubt exists when we read the chronicles of the middle ages or any of the numerous French memoirs of the last three centuries.   Yet, where is the age of chivalry portrayed with such vivid colours as in the graphic pages of Froissart?   Who presents us with a more truthful picture of the turbulent freedom of a mediæval Italian republic than Giovanni Villani?   And do not the memoirs of Saint Simon, and the letters of Sévigné, throw a greater light on the social state of France during the reign of Louis XIV. than the most elaborate history?   Such kind of works should not be subjected to too severe a criticism.   We should be satisfied when the author's statements and opinions,

taken as a whole, are sufficiently trustworthy to enable us to
mark the principal traits in the national character of a people
—the action of their civil and religious institutions on their
social condition—the reaction resulting from the conflict of
opposing interests by which these institutions are modified—
the gradual development of principles destined to exercise a
beneficent or baneful influence on future generations—to follow the statesman from the tribune to the council board—the
brawling patriot from the clamorous arena of popular agita-
tion to the confidential interview—the humble citizen from
his daily avocations to the privacy of the domestic circle, and
thus seize a few of the evanescent and ever-blending shades
that diversify the chequered woof of human existence. The
manners of a semi-barbarous people are certainly not so attractive as the polished refinement of modern civilization ; but
they show, at least, that man, in whatever circumstances he
may be placed, is invariably guided by the same motives, and
that, however the forms which his passions assume may differ
in appearance, they will be found on closer examination to be
essentially identic. Under this point of view, a sketch of
Icelandic life in the olden time, while the deities, that ancient
lore had symbolized into being from nature's varied phenomena, were still the objects of public worship *, will not be
devoid of interest. In giving this sketch, we shall let the
Sagas speak for themselves. These Sagas, it is true, were
committed to writing upwards of a century, in some cases two
or three centuries, after the events narrated are said to have
taken place. Yet, notwithstanding this untoward circumstance,
they bear internal evidence of being trustworthy records of
the periods to which they severally refer. Each of the leading families or septs of Iceland had its Saga, and when we
take into consideration the state of society at that period, we
may readily admit that a family history might have been
handed down by oral tradition for three or four generations
without undergoing any material alteration. The statements
of one Saga are also frequently corroborated by those of

* Christianity was embraced by the Icelanders at the Al-thing of the year
1000, but they stipulated that the former religion should be tolerated, and
the eating of horseflesh and the exposition of infants permitted. When the
Al-thing broke up, the assembled multitudes went to the hot baths to be baptized, preferring for this rite hot water to cold.

another, and the Danish literati of the present day who have subjected these ancient documents to a critical examination, regard upwards of a hundred of them to be fully entitled to the claim of historical authenticity.   Although we are inclined to suspect that the *amor patriæ* of these gentlemen has led them, on this occasion, as it usually does, rather too far, we should have no hesitation ourselves to admit that a few of the best authenticated Sagas, Njáls and Kormaks for instance, were fully equal in point of veracity to most of the memoirs that French vanity ever indited, an admission which certainly does not preclude a considerable degree of scepticism from prevailing in their perusal.   However, such as they are, they furnish the best information that can be rendered available for our present purpose, and, we repeat, on the whole, give a faithful picture of the state of society during the most turbulent period of Scandinavian history.

The manners and customs of the ancient Scandinavians and Germans—people belonging to the same Teutonic race, and placed in much the same circumstances—could not have offered any very striking difference, and, although these customs must necessarily have undergone a considerable change during the lapse of centuries, several modern writers, as the reader will have remarked in the preceding chapters, have not scrupled to apply the glowing description which Tacitus has given of those Germanic tribes, that the Romans, in his time, were acquainted with, to all the nations of Teutonic origin, whether Germanic or Scandinavian, and that, too, from the earliest period of their history to their conversion to Christianity.   The Germans of the second century, according to Tacitus, possessed all the virtues that adorn humanity.   The men were distinguished for their courage and love of justice, the women for their chastity and conjugal affection.   The golden age of primæval innocence still existed in the forests of Germania.   This primitive simplicity continued to prevail in Scandinavia, according to M. Mallet, so late as the tenth century.   The Icelandic laws, he tells us, " not only denounced very severe punishments against rapes and adulteries, but proceeded farther, expressly prohibiting even kissing or secret embraces."*   Now all this

* See page 205.

is amazingly fine and very consolatory, but, unfortunately, only applicable to a state of society that never existed, and which we fear was never destined, at least not in this wicked world of ours, to be the lot of humanity. At all events, the reader will find that the customs of the Scandinavians of the tenth century, as they are depicted in the Sagas, were far less primitive than those which Tacitus thought proper to attribute to their Germanic brethren of the age of the first Cæsars. And this could not be otherwise. The Sagaman relates the actions of his fellow-citizens without attempting to draw a single conclusion from the facts stated. Tacitus, from hearsay and the few personal observations he was enabled to make among a people whose language was totally unknown to him, constructed a brilliant theory of primæval virtue as a contrast to the vices which civilization had necessarily introduced among the Romans. The Sagaman, in a word, dealt with every-day facts, with sober reality; Tacitus with theoretical fiction. We shall, therefore, proceed to lay before the reader the homely truths of the Norse chroniclers, and leave those who still imagine that a barbarous people can combine primitive simplicity of character with the refinement of civilization, to peruse the classic pages of Tacitus.

Polygamy may perhaps have prevailed in Scandinavia, at least among the wealthy, at a very early period, but in the ninth and tenth centuries it seems, if it had really ever been a general custom—which we very much doubt—to have fallen into disuse. At all events no mention is made in any of the Sagas relating to Iceland of polygamy. We only read of the *mater familias*, the house-wife, *húsfreyja*, and the husband, *húsbóndi*, though frequent instances occur of a man keeping, with the knowledge and sometimes consent of his wife, a *frilla* or concubine *. These *frillas* were frequently the cause of domestic quarrels. Thus, in the Laxdæla-Saga, we are informed

---

* Húsbóndi, *pater familias*, our husband, means literally *house-dweller;* *hús*, house, and *bóndi*, contracted from *bóandi*, *búandi*, the participle of the verb *búa*, to dwell, to inhabit. Húsfreyja, *mater familias*, house-wife. The Old Norse word *frú*, Dan. *frue*, Germ. *frau*, Dutch, *vrouw*, is used both for woman and wife. In the Prose Edda, ch. 24, the word is derived from Freyja the name of the goddess of love, but in the glossary to the Poetical Edda, from *fríðr*, handsome, whence fridla, frilla, a concubine. Another derivation is given from the verb *fría*, Mæso-Gothic, *frijón*, to love, but all these words appear to be cognate.—See the word Freyr in our glossary to the Prose Edda.

that Höskuld having gone to Norway, in the middle of the tenth century, to purchase timber, fell in with a Russian trader, who, amongst other merchandise, had a dozen very pretty girls on sale. Höskuld was particularly struck by the fine features and symmetrical proportions of one of these lovely captives, and did not hesitate to pay three marks of silver for her, although the Russian told him that she had one great defect, that of being deaf and dumb,—a circumstance which Höskuld may have probably regarded as no very great blemish in a woman. On his return home, his wife, Jorunna, eyed the fair slave with a very scrutinizing glance, and asked her husband who in the world he had brought with him. Höskuld told her without much circumlocution that she was a slave he had purchased, and made his *frilla*, and begged that she might not only be allowed to remain in the house, but also be treated with due consideration. Jorunna, with the proper pride of an Icelandic matron, said she should not think of quarrelling with a woman of that description ; but was not at all dissatisfied to find that the girl was deaf and dumb. Höskuld was very much pleased with his wife's conduct, and appears to have lived very lovingly with her during the winter, and to have somewhat neglected his beautiful *frilla*, who, however, in the spring, became the mother of a very fine boy, Höskuld acknowledging his paternity by the usual ceremony of taking the new-born babe in his arms, and sprinkling it with water, while he gave it the name of Olaf *. In the summer Jorunna told her husband that if he did not choose to let his favourite do the work of a maid-servant, he must send her somewhere else, as she was determined that, in a house over which she presided, no idle woman should remain. Höskuld did not hesitate to intimate by signs to Olaf's mother that she must thenceforward wait on Jorunna, and do whatever menial services might be required of her. Some time after this, Höskuld, to his great surprise, found his favourite talking to her son. Seeing she could no longer conceal her secret, she told him that her name was Melkorka, and that she was the daughter of the Irish king Mirkjartan, (Murcatoc,) and had been taken captive when she was eleven years old.

---

* We had occasion to speak of this pagan baptism in the note, page 206, to which we refer the reader.

After this discovery Jorunna began to be rather jealous, and, as Melkorka could now make use of her tongue, Höskuld had no very easy life of it. One evening as Melkorka was undressing her mistress she happened to let her stockings fall, on seeing which Jorunna not only gave her a good scolding, but taking up the stockings struck her on the head with them,—a proceeding which Melkorka responded to in the true Irish fashion, by dealing a blow with her fist which sent Jorunna reeling with a bloody nose to the other end of the apartment. After this scene, Höskuld deemed it advisable to send Melkorka and her son to one of his estates higher up the valley, on which he assigned her a house, and supplied her with every thing she might stand in need of *.

Frequent mention is made of a marriage being contracted to save a young lady's reputation; thus Uni, a Danish trader, during a winter he passed in Iceland, was the guest of Leidolf-Kappa, with whose daughter, Thorunna, he contracted a very intimate acquaintance, insomuch so, in fact, that when Uni had left in spring, to get his vessel ready for the home voyage, Leidolf discovered that Thorunna would ere long present him with a grandchild. He accordingly went with his retainers to the Danish vessel; an altercation ensued, ending, as was usually the case, in a combat, in which several of the Danes lost their lives. Uni was obliged to return with Leidolf, who told him that provided he would marry Thorunna, and remain in Iceland, he should inherit the family estates. Uni tacitly consented to this proposal, but shortly afterwards left his bride

* Müller, Sagabib. i. 198. The reader will find extracts from this Saga, in the original Norse, with an English translation by Thorkelin, in vol. vi. of the Bib. Topog. Britannica. Thorkelin's translation was, no doubt, highly appreciated in the last century; but at the present day one much more conformable both to the sense and the spirit of the original would be required. The Norse text in the work referred to is far from being correctly printed.

The Laxdæla-Saga further informs us that, when Olaf was grown up, his mother sent him to Ireland to make himself known to his grandfather, king Murcatoc, and gives an account of his subsequent adventures, which, though somewhat romantic, are by no means improbable. In fact, at a period when the coasts of Ireland were infested by Scandinavian sea-rovers, there is nothing more likely than that one of them should have snapped up the daughter of a petty Irish king, and sold her, with his other booty, to a Russian trader. Such events, in those ages, must have been of daily occurrence.

to bewail her fate, and made off for the coast.   Leidolf pursued him in hot haste, and in the skirmish that ensued Uni and his Danish followers fell under the battle-axes of the enraged Icelanders *.

The due observance of judicial formalities was required to constitute a legal marriage contract.   When a person had obtained the consent of the *legal guardian* † of the maiden he wished to marry, a day was fixed for the betrothal.   The betrother had then to take the hand of the guardian, and, in the presence of competent witnesses, promise, within a year and a day, to marry the ward, at the same time time paying him a stipulated sum, called the *mundr* ‡, the guardian on his part promising to make over, when the nuptials were celebrated, to his ward or to the betrother, or conjointly to both, as the case might be, the stipulated *heimanfylgja* §, or marriage portion.   If the marriage did not take place within the time prescribed, the parties were relieved from the contract, and if its non-fulfilment had been owing to the betrother he could not recover the *mundr*.   The marriage itself appears to have been celebrated without any kind of religious ceremony ||. We only read of banquets being given to the friends and relatives of the parties, the feasting at the marriage of a wealthy person being kept up for several days, and frequently ending by some of the guests quarrelling over their ale, and hewing each other to pieces with their battle-axes.

* Landnámabók, iv. 4.

† A widow or a maiden who had attained her majority might marry without the consent of her legal guardian.   The Grágás defines the *legal guardian* of a maiden to be, in the first place, her father; at his death, her brother; then her mother; and so on, according to the proximity of relationship.

‡ From *mund*, hand, so much in hand—a sponsal gift, or *brida ransom*, as it might appropriately be termed ; for the *mundr* appears to have been regarded as the symbolical juridical ceremony of ransoming or freeing the bride from the authority of her legal guardian, and whether she brought her husband a large property, or a small one, or none at all, the *mundr* had always to be paid.   The legal guardian generally gave the *mundr* to the bride as a present on the day of her marriage.

§ *Heiman*, at home, *fylgja*, to follow ; *i. e.* the marriage portion to follow the bride to her new home—a home-following.

|| All the observances relating to the marriage ceremony, are detailed in the Grágás ; but although this code, in the form we have it, was drawn up two centuries after Christianity had become the established religion of Iceland, no mention is made of a priestly benediction being required.

The rights of woman are in no code more clearly acknowledged and defined than in the Grágás. A married woman
might dispose of her personal property, and a considerable
portion of her real (landed) property, as she thought proper.
Her husband had, in this respect, no control over her actions,
except it had been expressly stipulated at the betrothal, in
the presence of competent witnesses. that the goods, chattels,
and estates of the husband and wife should be held conjointly,
in which case the husband had the administration of the
property, but the wife and her heirs, or next of kin, had a
legal claim to one third of it. When no such stipulation
had been made, it would appear that, to a certain extent,
a married woman had not the absolute disposal of her property, for we find it stated in the Grágás, sec. vi. 21,
" That a married woman cannot legally sell the half of her
landed property, nor her *godord*, if she be in possession of one,
nor any sailing vessel that may belong to her, without the advice of her legal guardian," which implies that she might
dispose of one half of what would be termed in English law her
real property, and all her personal property without restriction.
When a divorce took place the wife of course retained the
property held in her own name, and if the divorce had been
legally constituted by the decision of a competent tribunal,
she might claim one third of any property held conjointly by
her and her husband. If the divorce was owing to the loose
conduct of the wife, the husband might reclaim the *mundr* he
had paid at the betrothal.

The Icelandic legislators seem to have been particularly
anxious to prevent the abuse of marital authority,—a proof that
female influence was as predominant in the forensic circle of
the Al-thing as in the family mansion. We are aware that
some passages might be cited from the Sagas to prove the contrary—of men exchanging their wives, for instance ; but they
are by no means conclusive. Thus Illugi the Red exchanges
with Holm Starri estate, live-stock, and wife. Illugi, by this
transaction, obtains Jorunna, with whom he appears to
have had a *liaison*, but Sigrida, his wife, is so outraged at
his proceedings that she goes in the temple and hangs her-
self*. This, however, was a very exceptional case, and, in-

* Landnámabók, i. 21.

stead of Sigrida hanging herself, she might have entered an action at law against her husband, which would have been a much wiser proceeding.

The women not only enjoyed much the same rights as the men, but appear to have asserted them with becoming spirit,—a circumstance that rendered divorces of very frequent occurrence. A wife, in fact, had only to tell her husband that from that day they ceased to be man and wife, and the marriage was *de facto*, and in pagan times also *de jure*, dissolved. A woman who had any claim to joint property would, of course, prefer suing for a divorce before a competent tribunal. She might do this on the most frivolous pretexts, and even when Christianity became the established religion a wife might sue for a divorce, if her husband had secretly disposed of any part of her property, had attempted to take her out of the island against her will, or had been absent from home for the space of three years *.

The following story, from the Laxdæla-Saga, will serve to show in what light marriage was regarded in Iceland, and in what a very equivocal manner a *mater familias* sometimes exercised her authority. Olaf, the son of Höskuld and Melkorka, previously mentioned, was accompanied, we are told, on his return from Norway, where he had been to purchase timber, by one of his old sea-roving friends named Geirmund, at whose house he had passed the winter. Geirmund, in his turn, became the winter guest of Olaf in Iceland, and soon fell in love with that chieftain's daughter, the beautiful Thurida. Olaf, although he was very fond of his Norwegian friend, would not hear talk of a marriage. Geirmund, seeing that he had no chance of succeeding with the young lady's father, began to flatter her mother Thorgerda, and, by dint of entreaties and *costly presents*, at length obtained her consent. The marriage was celebrated with great pomp, Olaf inviting his numerous friends and dependants to a sumptuous feast, in a large banqueting hall he had recently erected, the walls

---

* Grágás, vi. When Christianity was fully established, the consent of the bishop was necessary to constitute a divorce, but in the above instances the law appears to have been imperative. The clergy, however they might disapprove of a judicial sentence, were often obliged to sanction it, although they of course strove to render the marriage tie indissoluble by merely admitting a separation *à mensâ et thoro*, which in pagan times was unknown.

of which were hung with tapestry representing the story of Baldur and the prowess of Thor *. When Geirmund had passed three years in the marriage state, he began to get tired of his wife, and Thorgerda was at length obliged to tell her husband that she had ascertained that their son-in-law intended to return to Norway, leaving Thurida and her daughter Groa behind him without making any provision for their support. Olaf said the marriage was her doing, not his, and, instead of showing any sign of displeasure, he was more friendly than usual with Geirmund, and even made him a present of a fine trading vessel, being probably very glad to get rid of him. Geirmund went on board this vessel, and was only waiting for a favourable wind, when one morning, at break of day, Thurida entered the cabin when he was asleep, placed her child in his bed, and taking a splendid sword, which she knew he set a great value on, got into her boat, and told her men to row off again. Geirmund awoke at the moment, and, becoming aware of what had happened, called on his wife to come back and take Groa and return him his sword, for which he offered to give her any sum she might think proper to demand. Thurida told him that she would do no such thing, that he had acted dishonourably towards her, and that they were no longer man and wife, and accordingly returned home, and gave Geirmund's sword to her cousin Belli. Thurida, after this proceeding, could, of course, re-marry, and we presume that in those days the want of maternal affection she had evinced, by exchanging her only child for a sword, would not have prevented her from finding a second husband.

Liberty, as is well known, cannot be enjoyed without being abused. Liberty of speech, in a public assembly, will often be mere scurrility; liberty of the press, licentiousness and sedition; people who live under a constitutional form of government are inclined to kick up a row now and then, under an autocratic despotism they will remain as noiseless as the earth they tread on; and so it is with the fair sex. Ladies who, when shut up in an oriental seraglio, become very harmless beings, are apt, when allowed such liberty as in Iceland,

---

* A fragment of a poem on this tapestry, composed by Ulf Uggison, has been preserved in the Skalda. Ulf received a valuable consideration from Olaf for this poetical effusion, the Skalds being always well paid for stringing together their far-fetched metaphors.

to let their passions get the upper hand, and lead them into scrapes which they sometimes have occasion to repent of. The Icelanders seem, in general, to have regarded the freaks of their wives with tolerable equanimity. Asmund, for instance, has the misfortune to have a wife much younger than himself; the usual consequences ensue. Asmund wishes to lead a quiet life, Thora is fond of flirtation. Tired of her conduct, Asmund at length leaves her, and passes his old age on another of his estates. After his death, Thora opens a kind of inn on the roadside, seats herself before the door, and invites those she takes a fancy to to enter and regale themselves. Ladies who were divorced, or widows, and fond of a gay life, and had the means at their disposal, appear to have frequently amused themselves by keeping such hostelries, in which meat and drink, and lodging, and every thing else—the fair hostess included—were to be had *gratis*.

Some husbands were, however, as full of " the green-eyed monster " jealousy as Othello himself, and sometimes gave vent to it much in the same fashion. Thus Hallbjörn, having married Hallgerda, passed the first winter at the house of her parents. Notwithstanding their recent marriage, Hallbjörn began to suspect that Hallgerda had a *liaison* with her uncle Snæbjörn, and being as fully averse as the Moor

> " To keep a corner in the thing he loved
>   For others' uses,"

hastened the construction of the dwelling they were to inhabit, and early in the spring made preparations for their departure. One morning Hallbjörn goes and tells his wife that the horses are at the door and every thing ready for setting out; she refuses to leave the room; Hallbjörn, regarding this conduct as a proof that his suspicions were well founded, draws his sword, tells his wife she has been false to him, and severs her head from her shoulders, and then mounts his horse and rides off. Snæbjörn pursues him, they fight, and Hallbjörn falls pierced by the sword of his adversary *.

The loose conduct of the Icelandic women will account in some degree for the exposure of infants. In poor families this cruel custom was, no doubt, often resorted to from neces-

* Landnámabók, ii. 30.

sity, though no necessity, however great, can justify or even
extenuate it; but in wealthy families other motives must have
prevailed. It must be borne in mind that when the husband
took the new-born babe in his arms, or offered it milk and
honey, or sprinkled it with water and gave it a name *, he
thereby acknowledged his paternity. If a man suspected his
wife, whether justly or unjustly, of infidelity, he would, of
course, refuse to perform this ceremony of legitimation, and
the child was then carried out and generally placed under a
tree, and protected with stones from beasts of prey. If the
mother had really carried on a criminal intercourse, and still
retained any influence over her seducer, she would not fail to
apprize him of what had happened, and enjoin him to rescue
her babe and have it duly provided for. This right of legitimation which a husband possessed was probably, like all other
rights, frequently abused; but, on the whole, it must have had
much the same effect in restraining the indulgence of a criminal passion as the fear of being involved in a *crim. con.* proceeding has in this country.

Among other curious enactments in the Grágás, we find
that a man was liable to *exile* for taking an unmarried woman
without her consent, or a married woman either with or without
her consent, out of the island, or even out of her own *fjórdúngr,*
or province ; and for a similar elopement with an unmarried
woman, she consenting, to *exclusion*. All persons found guilty
of aiding or abetting him, to be condemned to the same punish-
ment†. For kissing another man's wife, with or without her
consent, the punishment of *exclusion* or its pecuniary equivalent was awarded. A man was also liable to the same punishment for kissing an unmarried woman under legal guardianship without her consent, and, even if she consented, the law
required that every kiss should be atoned for by a fine of three
marks ‡, equivalent to one hundred and forty-four ells of
wadmal, a quantity sufficient to furnish a whole ship's crew
with pilot jackets.

These anti-kissing laws have been frequently cited by modern
writers as a proof that the fair dames of the north, in the olden
time, were remarkable for their chastity and propriety of conduct. One hundred and forty-four ells of cloth for a kiss! Why,

---

* See the note, page 206.   † Grágás, vi. 29, 38.   ‡ Grágás, vi. 24.

the Puritans themselves would have visited such a breach of decorum with greater leniency! We fear, however, that the anecdotes previously given, and the abstracts of two or three of the most trustworthy Sagas, which we shall now proceed to lay before the reader, will by no means warrant the conclusions that have been drawn from these singular enactments of the Grágás. We shall begin by Kormak's Saga *, the heroine of the story having been regarded by her contemporaries as a model of female perfection—coquetry, we presume, forming in their opinion an essential ingredient of the female character. Kormak, we must premise, was one of the most celebrated Skalds of the tenth century, though his compositions, if we may judge by the sixty or seventy strophes that are attributed to him, were equally as devoid of true poetic genius as those of the other *verse-smithiers*—we can use no better epithet to designate the generality of these northern Skalds—who, in that rude age, hammered out their rhapsodical ideas into the form of alliterative metre.

The Saga commences by stating that one of the earlier settlers in Iceland was Skeggi, a celebrated sea-rover, who took possession of the country around the Midfjörd, in the northern part of the island. Shortly after the death of Harald Hárfagra, another sea-rover, named Ögmund, cast anch or in this frith, into which his sacred columns had been driven, and established himself on an estate called Mel, which Skeggi is said to have gratuitously ceded to him. This estate at Ögmund's death passed to his two sons Kormak and Thorgils, who continued to reside in the paternal mansion with their mother Dalla. Kormak is represented as a very handsome young man, with fine dark eyes, black hair, and a fair complexion. He was of a very enterprising character, and soon acquired the reputation of being a good Skald and a skilful swordsman. His brother, who appears to have been very much attached to him, was, unlike the generality of his countrymen, of a mild and taciturn disposition.

* Kormak's Saga, 1 vol. 8vo., Hafniæ, 1832.—Professor Müller, who has given a very meagre abstract of this Saga in his Sagabib. i. 140, judging from the intrinsic evidence of the style, supposes that it was written in the twelfth century. The MS. from which the Saga was printed is, however, of the fourteenth century. The events narrated fall within the latter half of the tenth century.

Not far from Mel lay Gnupsdale, where Steingerda, the
beautiful daughter of Thorkell of Túnga, then resided with
her foster-parents. From the first moment that Kormak
beheld this fair maiden he fell violently in love with her, and
did not fail to make known his passion in plaintive ditties,
which the young lady appears to have listened to with great
complacency. When Thorkell became aware of what was
going forward he took his daughter home, and, although
he could not well refuse to let Kormak see her, he strove
to render his visits to Túnga as disagreeable as possible by
encouraging Oddur and Gudmund, the sons of a famous sorceress named Thorveiga, who were frequently his guests,
to jeer him when present, and cast aspersions on his character
the moment he had left the house. Kormak bore this annoyance for some time with exemplary patience, only indulging
himself now and then by composing satirical verses on his
adversaries. One day the two brothers lay in wait for Kormak
as he returned home from Túnga. Thorkell, who was privy
to their design, when he heard the clash of arms, seized his
battle-axe, and would have gone to aid them had not Steingerda who perceived his intention, prevailed upon him, while
she held his hands with no feminine grasp, to await the issue
of the combat. The issue was not long doubtful; Kormak
slew both his antagonists, and then went to Thorveiga and
told her that she must instantly remove to another part
of the country, for he would no longer suffer such a vile sorceress to remain in the neighbourhood. Thorveiga was
obliged to comply with this injunction, but avenged herself by
prophesying that he who had killed her sons would never
become the husband of Thorkell's daughter. Although not
entirely free from the superstition of the age respecting sorcery, Kormak continued his visits to Túnga, and, having at
length obtained the reluctant consent of Thorkell, was formally betrothed to Steingerda, and a day fixed for their nuptials. Kormak, however, let the day pass by, and the sponsal
contract was consequently broken. What his motives were
for this strange proceeding it is difficult to divine; he may
have been dissatisfied with the pecuniary arrangements that
his friends had entered into with Thorkell respecting the fair
bride's dowry, or began to dread the ominous words of Thorveiga, or, like most poets, have been somewhat crotchety; at

all events, his conduct gave great offence to Thorkell's relatives, and was regarded as a gross insult offered to the family.

At Saurbær, in the western province of the island, dwelt a wealthy and valiant gentleman named Bersi, generally called, from his pugnacious propensities, Holmgang, or Duelling Bersi. At the death of his wife the care of his household, and of his infant son Asmund, devolved on his sister Helga, a young lady distinguished for her beauty and accomplishments. Shortly after the events narrated a family council was held at Túnga to consider what steps ought to be taken in consequence of Kormak's proceedings. Thorkell's sons said that the only way of settling the business was by making the young Skald feel the weight of their battle-axes; but Narfi, a retainer of the family, told them they would inflict a greater punishment on him by marrying Steingerda without delay to a man of acknowledged influence and reputation, and that in his humble opinion the rich widower Bersi, of Saurbær, was just the kind of person that would suit her. This advice having been unanimously approved of, they mounted their horses and rode to Saurbær on pretext of paying Bersi a friendly visit, taking care, however, as they emptied their drinking-horns, to say a great deal in praise of Steingerda, Narfi artfully insinuating that no one who feared encountering Kormak need demand her in marriage. Bersi, who knew how to kill his man in a duel as well as most people, on hearing these words resolved to make Steingerda his wife. He accordingly went to work in a very business-like manner, not paying much attention to the fair damsel herself, but negotiating with her father respecting her dowry. These arrangements having been concluded to the mutual satisfaction of the contracting parties, the betrothal took place with the usual formalities, and a very early day was fixed for the nuptials. Steingerda saw this day approaching with ever increasing anxiety. She had given her tacit though reluctant consent to the marriage with the hope that ere it took place Kormak would own his fault and become reconciled with the family. "But if he allow Bersi to become my husband!" said Steingerda, as she braided her long silken tresses. "Well, I will then strive to forget that Kormak was once my lover, and he will one day repent him of his conduct. And, after all, Bersi

Y 2

is not much amiss; Is n't he acknowledged to be the most
valiant man in his district! Who can wield a battle-axe like
Holmgang-Bersi!" These consolatory reflections did not,
however, prevent her from sending to apprize Kormak of
what had happened, but the messenger was detained by
Bersi's cousin Vigi, who kept strict watch and ward around
the premises, and would suffer no one to pass without knowing his errand.

On the day appointed Bersi came with a splendid cavalcade
to conduct his fair bride from the paternal mansion to his
own dwelling. Piqued at Kormak's apparent neglect, Steingerda packed up her trinkets, bade adieu to her relatives,
and, mounting her horse with a joyous mien, rode off with her
husband. Steingerda's message was now delivered to Kormak, with the unpleasant addition that the lady was passing
the first night of her marriage at Múli, the residence of
Bersi's friend, Thord Arndisarson. Kormak, on learning these
fatal tidings, mounted his horse, and, accompanied by his brother Thorgils, rode in hot haste to Múli to demand satisfaction for the insult which he deemed had been offered to him.
Bersi, who appears on the whole to have been a good kind
of fellow, though somewhat too pugnacious, said he really
could not see what Kormak had to complain of. Kormak had
been betrothed to Steingerda, but from some motive or other
had thought proper to break the sponsal contract. He, Bersi,
had been betrothed to the same lady, but, unlike Kormak,
had fulfilled his engagement. This cogent argument was not
much relished by Kormak, who contended that he had been
fraudulently deprived of Steingerda, and that she must be
restored to him. Bersi said that was quite out of the question, that Steingerda was now his wife and his wife should
remain. "But to show," he added, "that I am willing to
effect a reconciliation, I shall have no objection to offer
to Kormak the hand of my sister Helga,—an offer, methinks,
which is not to be slighted;" and so saying left Kormak to his
own meditations. Thorgils strongly advised his brother to
accept this advantageous proposal, for Helga, in addition
to her personal charms, was possessed of broad lands and
numerous flocks and herds—things which, though not essentially conducive to conjugal felicity, render at least the marriage state exceedingly comfortable.

At this moment Thordisa of Spákonufell*, a woman noted for her skill in magic, entered the room, and began to insinuate that Helga, with all her wealth and beauty, had no mind—was, in fact, quite a simpleton, and not at all fit to be the wife of Kormak. Thord declared this to be a vile calumny, and told the sorceress to be gone about her business. Kormak observed that, whether the words were true or false, he should not accept the offer that had been made to him, and ended the colloquy by challenging Bersi to meet him that day fortnight in a holmgang, a challenge which Bersi of course willingly accepted. Kormak before he left managed to see Steingerda, whom he reproached for marrying another after she had plighted her troth to him. She told him that he would do better to reproach himself for his own unaccountable conduct, which had forced her to act in a manner repugnant to her feelings.

On the day appointed Bersi and Kormak met on a small island, since called Battle Isle, to decide their quarrel in the presence of numerous spectators. Bersi had a famous sword called Hviting, to match which Kormak had persuaded his father's friend Skeggi to lend him Hrolf Kraki's sword Sköfnúng, which that old sea-rover had in one of his expeditions taken from the Danish king's barrow†. Bersi, as an experienced duellist, thought proper before they commenced to explain the difference between a *holmgang* and an *einvigi*‡, and said that, although Kormak had challenged him to the former, he would allow him, as this was the first affair of the kind he had been engaged in, to choose the latter, which was attended with less danger. Kormak, however, refused to avail himself of this generous offer, and Bersi then laid down the laws of the holmgang with great precision. The person

---

* The Rock of the Sorceress. Scoticè, the Spae wife's fell.

† It was reckoned a daring exploit to break into the barrow of a celebrated warrior and carry away his sword. We must observe, however, that Hrolf Kraki is one of those problematic personages of the *heroic period* whose very existence may be called in question, though there are reasonable grounds for supposing that Hrolf himself was not a mere creation of the fancy, but actually reigned, and performed some valorous deeds towards the middle of the sixth century.

‡ Holmgang—literally *isle-gang*, such duels generally taking place in a small island; einvigi, *single combat*. Both terms were, however, used to designate a single combat, the difference being in the manner in which the combatants were to use their weapons.

challenged, he said, had the right to strike the first blow; when his opponent was wounded so that his blood stained the ground, the seconds * might interfere, and put an end to the combat. He that was the first wounded had to pay the customary holmgang fine of three marks. The validity of these laws having been acknowledged by Kormak, the combatants went to work and displayed great skill in the use of their weapons. After each party had had three shields cloven in twain, Kormak received a slash from Bersi's sword across the hand, and as blood flowed from the wound in profusion, the seconds declared the duel to be honourably terminated. Bersi then demanded the fine from Kormak, who promised that it should be punctually acquitted.

Kormak, on leaving the field, went to his uncle Steinar—a man of a very turbulent disposition—and told him that he intended to go abroad, begging, at the same time, that he would pay the fine for him. "Thou dost things in too great a hurry," said Steinar; "however, if the fine must be paid, I will pay it." A few days afterwards, as Kormak was riding home, accompanied by his uncle, he met Bersi, who greeted him very amicably, and asked him how his wound was going on. "Not very well," replied Kormak. "Well," said Bersi, "as I gave it thee, if thou wilt, I will also heal it." Kormak very coldly refused to accept any service from his rival, intimating, at the same time, that hostilities had not ceased between them. To which Bersi, who was a bit of a Skald, replied by extemporizing a strophe in allusion to the recent duel, and then rode off with the numerous friends and retainers who accompanied him. Kormak, on his return home, consoled himself, whilst his mother healed his wound, by hammering out a due quantity of Skaldic lays, in which he attributed the unfavourable issue of the duel more to his adversary possessing a charmed sword than to his skill in using it.

Shortly after this, Bersi's son, Asmund, happened to hurt one of Thord's children while they were playing together, which so vexed Thord's wife that she gave her husband no peace until he demanded a pecuniary compensation from Bersi for the slight injury which the child had sustained. Bersi

---

* Each combatant was attended by a second, who had to protect him with a shield.

laughed at his friend for making such a demand, but a coolness arose in consequence between the two families. Bersi
and Thord had always been accustomed to ride together to the
Thorsnes Thing. When the time fixed for holding the Thing
arrived, Bersi went as usual to Múli to call for Thord, but
found that he had already set out. "What change has come
over him," said Bersi; "why did he not wait for me as he was
wont to do?" "Thou art the cause of the change," replied
Thord's wife; "and this will be but a slight revenge, if
a greater do not follow." Bersi then rode off, and, as he was
the Thingsman of Olaf Pá, went, on his arrival at the place of
assembly, to that chieftain's booth *. The booth was so
crowded with Olaf's Thingsmen and retainers that Bersi could
scarcely make his way through them. On the seat usually
occupied by Thord he found a man of athletic frame, who was
wrapped up in a bear-skin cloak, and had altogether the appearance of one who, like a Scotch Knight of the Thistle, cannot be touched with impunity.

"What's thy name?" demanded Bersi.

"Glum or Skum, or what thou wilt," growled the stranger,
as he drew his cloak tighter about him.

"Nay," said Bersi, "thou need'st not muffle thyself up in
thy bear-skin, for I see plainly thou art Steinar."

"Ay," replied the stranger, "I am Steinar, and am come
to pay thee my nephew's fine, but before I pay it I challenge
thee to meet me in a holmgang."

"As thou wilt," answered Bersi; and the day and place of
meeting were fixed with the usual formalities.

The next day Bersi and Steinar had a swimming match,
when Steinar perceiving that his competitor wore an amulet
—called a life-stone—round his neck, swam up to him, and
tearing it off threw it into the sea. It was however found at
ebb tide by Thord, who, being now at enmity with Bersi, kept
possession of it.

On the day appointed for the duel Bersi went to the place
of meeting accompanied by several of Olaf Pá's retainers.

---

* We have here an example of a wealthy and influential landed proprietor being, in some measure, dependent on a powerful chieftain,—a circumstance that will serve to strengthen the arguments we made use of in the
beginning of the preceding chapter. Olaf Pá was the son of Höskuld and
Melkorka previously mentioned.

Kormak was his uncle's second or shield-holder. The combatants, with the assistance of their shield-holders, warded off each other's blows for some time with great dexterity; but Steinar at length succeeded in giving his adversary a terrible wound across the hip joint which completely disabled him.

"There," said Steinar, "thou hast now received full payment for my nephew's fine."

Stung by these words Bersi sprang up, clove Steinar's shield in twain, and slightly wounded him in the breast, and then fell exhausted with loss of blood, and was borne from the field by his retainers, and conveyed to his own mansion. Thord, on learning the dangerous state of his wound, went to Saurbær and gave Bersi his amulet, and, being well skilled in the healing art, never quitted him until a perfect cure had been effected. It is needless to add that the two friends were now reconciled, and remained ever afterwards on terms of the greatest intimacy.

One day, while Bersi was still confined to his bed, Steingerda entered the room, and after giving her husband a surname descriptive of his wound, and far more emphatic than elegant, formally announced her intention of being divorced from him. So saying, she left him to his own reflections, packed up her trinkets, mounted her horse, and rode off to her father's residence. Here she passed the winter, and managed at length to persuade her brother Thorkell to go and reclaim her marriage portion from Bersi, a mission not unattended with danger. Thorkell, on his arrival at Saurbær, was received by Bersi with due courtesy, who would not, however, listen to his demand, Steingerda he contended having no legal claim upon him. Thorkell intimated that if he persisted in that opinion they would have to meet in Battle Isle, near Tjaldnes, and decide the question at issue by single combat.

"Be it so," said Bersi, "I promise thee thou shalt not have to await my coming."

On the day appointed Thorkell went, with his friend Vali for shield-holder, to Battle Isle, where they found Bersi and Thord awaiting them. Thorkell objected to Bersi's sword being longer than the laws of duelling allowed, but this objection appears to have been overruled by the seconds. They accordingly began the combat, and after two shields had been rendered useless, Thorkell fell mortally wounded at the feet of his adversary, who very coolly extemporized a Skaldic verse as he regarded him. Vali, after bearing off his dying friend, re-entered the lists and challenged Bersi to fight with him on the spot. Bersi, placing himself in an attitude of defence, said he had never any objections to fighting; but as they were going to begin the combat, Thord stepped between them, declaring that it was a pity two such valiant fellows should kill each other to no purpose, and that they would do better to leave the quarrel to his arbitration. On their consenting to this proposal, he said the best way for effecting a reconciliation would be for Bersi to marry Vali's sister Thordisa. Bersi expressed his willingness to become the young lady's husband provided Vali would give her, for her marriage portion, the estate of Brekkuland. Vali having promised that it should be hers the parties left the field, and rode off mutually satisfied with the arrangement. The marriage took place shortly afterwards, and Bersi, strange to say, led for several years a very quiet life, occupying himself in improving his estates, and enlarging his family mansion.

Not far from Saurbær dwelt Oddur, who had a very pretty daughter, Steinvöra, surnamed from her delicate proportions Mjóbeina (*slender-bones*). Another of Bersi's neighbours was Thorarin, who had in his time been a celebrated navigator and sea-rover, but now resided on his estate of Thambardal with his three sons, Alf, Loptur, and Skopti. One evening, as Oddur and his friend Glum sat drinking their ale by the fireside, they began to exercise their wits at the favourite Icelandic pastime of instituting comparisons between the leading men of the district. Glum, after enumerating all the good qualities of Thorarin, contended that he was justly entitled to pre-eminence. Oddur, however, was loud in his praise of Bersi. Each of the disputants sought of course to strengthen his arguments by detracting from the merits of his opponent's hero, until at length Oddur, as he emptied his drinking-horn, swore by Thor and Odin that it was quite preposterous to compare the knavery of Thorarin with the valiantness of Bersi. Glum did not fail to tell Thorarin what Oddur had said of him. "I will soon teach him better manners!" exclaimed Thorarin, and mounting his horse, rode with his retainers to Oddur's dwelling and carried off Steinvöra, intimating to her father that if he made any complaint his life would be in danger. Oddur, however, notwithstanding this threat, went to Bersi and begged that he would assist him to recover his daughter. Bersi having armed himself from head to heel, and buckled on his famous sword, *hviting*, rode over to Thambardal and knocked late in the evening at Thorarin's door, which was at that moment opened by a man named Thorleif, who was leaving the dwelling. Thorarin hearing a noise at the door went to see what was the matter, when Bersi ran him through the body and left him weltering in his gore on the threshold. He then mounted his horse, placed Stein-vöra before him, and galloped off with her to a neighbouring forest*. Telling her to remain here with his horse until he returned, he went with three javelins in his hand towards Thambardal, being determined that Thorarin's sons should share the same fate as their father. He found them on the road already in pursuit of him, Thorleif having informed them when they came and found their father lying dead on the threshold who it was that had slain him. Bersi, before they were aware of his presence, hurled one of his javelins, which brought Alf to the ground: he then attacked Loptur and Skopti, who soon lay beside their brother. Having thus had the satisfaction of killing the whole family, Bersi re-turned to the forest and took Steinvöra with him to Saurbær, where they arrived before the servants were yet stirring. Oddur was very glad to see his daughter again, and on his asking how she had been rescued, Bersi extemporized a strophe, in which he awarded due praise to himself for the sanguinary deeds he had committed. Oddur then went home, leaving his daughter in the care of Bersi, a proceeding which Thordisa did not by any means relish†. Steinvöra, however, continued to reside at Saurbær in spite of the good lady's re-monstrances, and appears to have lived with Bersi on terms of the strictest intimacy. Some time after these events Bersi perceiving that he was growing old, and having lost his only

---

* In the Sagas relating to Iceland frequent mention is made of forests, but the Icelanders probably applied the word forest to designate a tract of country covered with brushwood, and in some places, perhaps, with stunted birch trees. See page 189.

† "Thetta likar Thórdisi illa," that liked Thordisa ill, quaintly observes the Sagaman.

child, made Haldor, the son of Höskuld, his adopted son and heir. Thordisa had farmed out her estate of Brekkuland to her brother Vali, and appears, by so doing, to have mightily offended young Haldor and Steinvöra, for the last mention made of Bersi is, that he went at the instigation of the slender-boned lady and waylaid, and, with the assistance of Haldor, then in his twelfth year, killed his brother-in-law Vali, and boasted of the deed as a proof that in his old age his valour had not deserted him.

It is now time to return to Steingerda, who, it is natural to suppose, left Bersi in order to become the wife of Kormak. Such, however, does not appear to have been that capricious lady's intention, for we find her the following summer giving her hand to Thorvald, a wealthy man, and a very good poet, and it would appear from his surname of Tintein, (Tinfounder,) equally as expert in fusing metals as in casting far fetched metaphors into the stiff forms of Skaldic metre. Thorvald, or Tintein, as he was generally called, notwithstanding the many very useful and very amiable qualities he possessed, had the defect of being rather chicken-hearted, a circumstance, which, in that age of the sword and battle-axe, often placed him in a very embarrassing position. Kormak, when the marriage took place, was fitting out a vessel for a trading voyage to Norway. Feigning not to be aware of what had happened, he went to Steingerda and begged her to make him a shirt. Steingerda told him very coolly that she was now the wife of Tintein, and that his visit was very inopportune, and would not be tolerated either by her husband or his relations. Kormak replied by extemporising a satirical strophe on Tintein, whom he designated as the stanniferous Skald. Steingerda was highly incensed at his conduct, and declared she would repeat the verse to her husband. Kormak then extemporised a very gallant strophe in praise of her beauty and accomplishments, which somewhat appeased the fair lady. They parted, however, as the Sagaman quaintly remarks, " without any blithesomeness having passed between them."

Kormak then sailed with his brother, A.D. 962, to Norway, and met with a good reception from King Hakon, the Good. He afterwards entered into a sea-roving partnership with a German named Sigurd, and on his return to Norway found Harald Greyskin on the throne. Kormak accompanied this

king on his expedition to Ireland, and gained great renown
both as a warrior and a Skald, the favourite theme of his lays
still continuing to be the charms of Steingerda.   Being, however, unable to support any longer his absence from the fair
charmer, he set sail for Iceland.   On approaching the coast he
descried a woman on horseback, and recognised at the first
glance—lovers have a very keen vision—that it was she whom
he adored; rowing, therefore, to shore in the ship's boat, he
borrowed a horse, and soon overtook her.   Dismounting from
his steed, he very gallantly assisted Steingerda to alight from
hers, and then led her to a verdant sunny bank beside a mur-
muring stream, where they sat down, and, while she

> " With a greedy ear
> Devoured up his discourse,"

he told her of all " the moving accidents, by flood and field,"
that had befallen him.   The hours thus glided away unheeded,
and still they sat

> " Linked in the inwoven charm
> Of converse, and caresses sweet and deep,"

until the shades of evening began to creep over the mountains, when Steingerda bethought her that it was high time
they should look for their horses.   The horses, however, were
no where to be found; the lovers were therefore obliged to
seek shelter in a neighbouring cottage, when Steingerda, retired with the house-wife to her apartment.   The next morning she told Kormak that it would be better if they did not
meet, adding, with a sigh, that he would perhaps find another
more worthy of his affection.   " Nay," said Kormak,

> " Till the rock on the river
>   Shall float like the plume,
> Till the firm oak shall quiver
>   And earth meet its doom ;
> Till the sky-cleaving mountain
>   Be whelmed in the main,
> To contend with Steingerda
>   In beauty, were vain."

A strophe that was amply rewarded by the fair lady telling
the young Skald, with one of her archest smiles, that he was
too great a flatterer.

When lovers meet after a long absence they are loath to quit each other. Kormak and Steingerda, therefore, passed four or five days very agreeably in their rural retreat; Steingerda retiring every evening with the house-wife, leaving her lover to complain in Skaldic verse, that, although, under the same roof he was still separated from her, whose embrace would consummate his fondest wish, by an envious wainscot; a most provoking impediment certainly, which Steingerda, however, told him, as he repeated his longing stanzas to her during their morning's walk, should on no consideration be removed. Kormak's verses becoming every day more ardent, it at length occurred to the fair dame that she had a husband who might probably be uneasy at her absence, and as her horse had been caught, she told her lover they must part. Kormak, as he placed her on the saddle, attempted to put a gold ring on her finger, but she told him, somewhat petulantly, that he might keep it himself, and whipping her horse galloped off, not in the best of humours, to her loving spouse, who, good-natured soul that he was, after a short lecture that made no great impression, pardoned his wife's *escapade*, though he begged it might not be repeated.

During the winter Kormak frequently visited Steingerda in her own house, but, although Tintein could overlook an *escapade* he had not been an eyewitness to, his equanimity became somewhat ruffled when he saw his wife listening, with great complacency, to the amatory lays of a brother Skald, who had, moreover, the advantage of being able to recount the feats he had performed as a sea-rover. Tintein was, however, too peaceable a man to make known his displeasure, further than by putting himself in a very ill-humour, and giving Steingerda a curtain lecture now and then for carrying on such a provoking flirtation. In this conjuncture, Tintein received a visit from his brother Thorvard who, on becoming aware how matters stood, declared that the family would be dishonoured if Kormak's visits were any longer tolerated. Tintein vowed that he wished Kormak were in Valhalla, though that would be too good a place for him; but how was he to rid himself of the annoyance. Thorvald who knew that his brother was sadly deficient in courage, and that he could not supply him with it, not having himself much to part with, suggested that they should get Narfi to indite a satirical stanza on Steingerda, and pay a wandering minstrel to sing it in her presence, and say that it was the composition of Kormak. Tintein highly approved of the plan, declaring that any thing would be better than a holmgang, and the stratagem had the desired result. Steingerda, when the minstrel sung the lay, flew into such a violent passion that the poor fellow thought himself fortunate in making his escape, and she not only refused to see Kormak, but would not even hear his name mentioned. It was in vain that he sent to supplicate the enraged beauty to admit him to her presence, or at least to let him know what crime he had committed. She continued for a long time inexorable. At length, by dint of entreaties, Kormak obtained an interview, when Steingerda told him that the shameful verse he had composed on her was in every one's mouth, there was not a social meeting held in the whole district where it was not repeated amidst the jeers of the guests, and the coarse laughter of their retainers. Kormak strenuously denied having any knowledge of it, but promised her that its authors, whoever they might be, should not go unpunished He, accordingly, went in quest of the wandering minstrel from whom he elicited the desired information. He then rode to Túnga, and slew Narfi, and would have slain Tintein too, whom he had dragged from his hiding place, had not the servants separated them.

These proceedings caused a great noise, and every one said that the brothers would be disgraced if they put up with such an insult. Having no other alternative, Thorvard at length sent one of his friends to challenge Kormak to a holmgang. On the appointed day, Kormak went to the place of meeting, but waited in vain for his antagonist, who being of Falstaff's opinion that " the better part of valour is discretion," remained quietly at home with Tintein. Kormak now thought himself justified in showing up the two brothers in a nithing-verse *, which, among the scandal-loving Icelanders, soon obtained an extensive circulation. When Tintein and Thorvard heard this satirical strophe, they signified their intention, if due compensation were not offered, to bring an action at law against its author for defamation. Kormak would not allow his relations to compromise the matter, contending that, as

* See page 155.

Thorvard had shown himself to be a coward, he had a right to call him one. When the suit was pleaded before the district Thing, Thorvard, perceiving from the raillery of his friends that he would gain no reputation, even if he brought it to a successful issue, screwed up what little courage he possessed and challenged Kormak a second time. The doughty gentleman made preparations for his duel, by going to the sorceress of Spákonufell, and inducing her, for a due consideration, to impart to his sword a magical efficacy. Kormak, more in compliance with his mother's entreaties, than from any faith he had in sorcery, also went to Spákonufell, but after he had witnessed Thordisa's manner of working a spell told her, in a Skaldic strophe, that her art was sheer nonsense *.

Thorvard, relying on the efficacy of his sword, duly kept his appointment. Kormak, as he prepared for action, descried Steingerda among the spectators, and greeted her in a very gallant verse, purporting that she was the fair cause of the combat. After a few blows had been exchanged, Kormak, although he did not wound his adversary so as to draw blood, managed to break two of his ribs, which put an end to the duel; Thorvard, as the wounded person, being obliged to give his antagonist a gold ring equivalent to the legal fine of three marks, which he did with great reluctance. Kormak, seeing a

---

* Sorcery must have been a lucrative profession in Scandinavia, for the belief in it was pretty general, though frequent instances are to be found in the Sagas of men, who, like Kormak, treated it as a mere delusion. It would be superfluous to remark, that the marvels related of witchcraft and magic, merely show the popular belief of the age, and by no means warrant the conclusion that because they are evidently false, the whole Saga must be devoid of veracity. The Sagaman states what he believed to be true, in the same manner as the learned Sir Thomas Brown, at a trial for witchcraft in the year 1664, gave evidence against two poor women, and professed his firm belief in the absurd prodigies attributed to them. And it was on such groundless evidence that, in that comparatively enlightened age, Sir Matthew Hale did not hesitate to condemn the supposed criminals to be burned at the stake. See " Memoirs of Extraordinary Popular Delusions," by Mr. Mackay, who calculates that in the seventeenth century no less than 40,000 persons were burned in England alone, for the imaginary crime of witchcraft. It would have been a fortunate circumstance if parliament at that period had adopted a law of the Hungarian king Kaloman, (A.D. 1095—1114,) which simply declares, that as witches do not exist, there can be no question about them : " De strigis vero, quæ non sunt, nulla quæstio fiat." Colomani regis decret. lib. i. c. 57, in the Corpus Juris Hungarici.

bull grazing in an adjoining field, went up and slew it, observing that the duel should not be entirely bloodless. The day being very hot, he then took off his helm, and wiped his forehead with the hem of Steingerda's kirtle, extemporizing, at the same time, a due quantity of Skaldic verse, in praise of her beauty. He used all his eloquence to persuade her to make another *escapade* with him, but she told him that she had something else to do, and must go home and look after the house, and so saying left him somewhat piqued that his amatory lays had made no greater impression. Steingerda then went to Thorvard and bound up his broken ribs, but before she left the ground, Kormak managed to have a little more chat with her. Thorvard, when his wound was healed, rode over to Mel, and challenged Kormak to another holmgang, having previously paid Thordisa a good round sum to render him, by her incantations, invulnerable. He soon found, however, that his money had been thrown away, for Kormak dealt him a blow that fractured his shoulder bone, and laid him sprawling on the earth in utter helplessness. This wound effectually damped Thorvard's nascent courage, and as he had to part with another gold ring, he began to find that duelling was not only a dangerous, but also an expensive amusement.

Kormak, before he set sail for Norway, paid a farewell visit to Steingerda, and on taking leave could not refrain from giving her two kisses, which the Sagaman, being we presume of opinion that the intensity of a kiss ought to be measured by its duration, takes care to inform us were by no means *short ones*. This proceeding of the enamoured young Skald was more than even Tintein's good nature could tolerate, but being puzzled how to act, he turned to his brother, who declared that Kormak ought to pay the legal fine for his audacity.

"What do ye demand?" asked Kormak.

"The two rings, replied Thorvard, which I had to give thee in virtue of the holmgang regulations."

"Be it so." said Kormak, and in giving him the rings extemporized a strophe, which, divested of its far-fetched metaphors, would run somewhat as follows :—

> For two kisses, impressed,
>   With glowing desire,
> On woman's sweet lips
>   Two gold rings ye require.

The gems shall be yours,
    Though methinks 'tis not meet
To tax a poor wight
    For so luscious a treat.

Not long after Kormak's departure, Steingerda told her husband that he must fit out a vessel, for she was determined to go and see what kind of a country Norway was. Tintein, who knew by experience that his wife would have her own way, in spite of any thing he could do to oppose her caprices, resigned himself to his fate, and soon got one of his ships in sailing order. On their voyage to Norway, Steingerda and Tintein fell into the hands of sea-rovers. Kormak, on being apprized of their disaster, set sail and rescued them and took them in his vessel to Dronthem, where they met with a very gracious reception from King Harald, with whom Kormak was in high favour. Kormak walking one day in the court yard of the palace, saw that Steingerda was alone in her apartment, he accordingly went in and sat down beside her, and this time gave her four kisses, which we presume—the Sagaman being unfortunately silent on this important point—were also of tolerable duration, for while his lips still clung to those of Steingerda, Tintein rushed in, sword in hand, followed by the maidservants, whose screams brought King Harald himself to ascertain the cause of the uproar. Harald told the disputants to put up their swords, and let him be their arbitrator. Tintein said he would acquiesce in whatever the king in his wisdom should decide.

"Well then," said Harald, addressing himself to the irritated husband, "one kiss shall go for Kormak having saved thee from the sea-rovers, one for his having saved Steingerda, and for the two others he shall pay two ounces of gold." A truly royal decision this of a kissing case.

Some days afterwards, the king was again alarmed by a noise in Steingerda's apartment, but this time it was the fair lady herself who was crying out for assistance. On entering the room, Harald in fact found her struggling with Kormak, who was attempting to carry her off by main force, for which uncourteous proceeding the king gave him a good scolding. All parties were however soon reconciled, and appear to have passed the winter very merrily at the court of the Norwegian sovereign.

z

In the spring Harald set sail on an expedition to Bjarmaland, and was accompanied by Kormak and Tintein, each having the command of a galley. One day, as they were sailing in company, Kormak took out the tiller of his vessel, and hurled it at Tintein, who fell down senseless. Steingerda, who was sitting near her husband, instantly took his place at the helm, and, bidding her men ply their oars, steered her vessel with such dexterity that she ran down Kormak's before the rudder could again be rendered serviceable. Having thus taught her lover better manners, she went, while her men were saving the crew of the sinking vessel, to console her husband, who was, however, less hurt than frightened.

Tintein, on the return of the expedition, sailed to Denmark, whither Kormak followed him, and found the poor gentleman on a small island in a very pitiable condition. Thorstein, a famous old sea-rover, having plundered him of all he possessed and carried off Steingerda. Kormak instantly set sail in quest of Thorstein, and the following night descried his vessel at anchor in an island creek with the crew carousing on shore, round a blazing fire, heedless of danger. Every thing being thus favourable for his design, Kormak left his vessel concealed from view by a sheltering rock, and went with his brother, in a skiff to that of Thorstein. On entering the cabin, they found Steingerda fast asleep in the arms of a sea-rover. After killing this poor fellow while he was yet dreaming of the *faveurs enivrantes* that had been granted him, they swam to shore with Steingerda, and brought her in safety to her husband. When Tintein heard how her deliverance had been effected, he said that Kormak was a very good fellow, and that as he had twice rescued Steingerda he might now take her. Overjoyed at this unexpected offer, Kormak was going to clasp the fair lady in his arms, but she told him with great composure, that she had no inclination to change her condition, that she was the wife of Tintein, and the wife of Tintein would remain. " Thou art right," replied Kormak, " Go with thy husband—the envious fates have decreed that thou shalt never be mine."

After taking a tender leave of the enamoured Skald, Stein·gerda returned with her good-natured spouse to Iceland : Kormak and Thorgils then sailed to the Orkneys, and for several years exercised their old trade of sea-roving on the coasts of the British islands, Kormak still attuning his northern lyre, amidst the tempest's howl, and the din of battle, to her, who, through life, had been the object of his fond affections.   After various exploits and adventures, Kormak at length fell in a single combat with a gigantic Scotchman, and expired in the arms of his brother, reciting, with his dying breath, a strophe in praise of Steingerda.

Such is the eventful story of this northern Skald, whom we should not hesitate to call the Scandinavian Petrarca. It would certainly be almost a profanation to compare the rude lays of Kormak with the dulcet strains of the Italian poet; however, such as they are, they were no doubt equally as appreciated in the north, as were the voluptuous sonnets of the Florentine in the sunny clime of Italy.   Kormak, too, like Petrarca, was the lover of a married woman, and Steingerda appears to have been as great an adept in the art of coquetry as Laura herself; both ladies having managed for years to carry on a flirtation without any further impropriety of conduct than mere flirtation necessarily implies ; Laura, not having had a Sagaman at her elbow, even escaping, in this respect, somewhat more unscathed than the fair Scandinavian.

Kormak's Saga is, comparatively speaking, free from those sanguinary scenes that form such tragical episodes in the generality of the Icelandic Sagas.   The following abstract of Njálssaga * will, we fear, in this respect, not tend to efface any unfavourable impression which the perusal of Kormak's may have left on the mind of the reader.

The Sagaman begins his narrative by informing us that a powerful chieftain named Rút, after having been betrothed to a rich heiress, called Unna, went to Norway, where he passed a winter very agreeably at the court of Harald Greyskin, his recent betrothal not preventing him from forming a very tender *liaison* with Harald's mother, Queen Gunhilda.   On his return to Iceland his marriage with Unna was celebrated

---

* Njálssaga bears internal evidence of having been written towards the middle of the twelfth century at the latest. The events narrated extend from the middle of the tenth century to the year 1017.   The Saga may, consequently, have been first committed to writing by the grandson, or even by the son of a person who heard it from one of the chief actors mentioned in the story—from Kári or Flosi, for instance.—See Müller's Sagabib. i. 51.

with the usual festivities.   Not long afterwards Unna, having
accompanied her husband to the Al-thing, took an opportunity
of complaining to her father that the enjoyments of the marriage life were not such as she had anticipated, and therefore
requested him to bring about a legal divorce.   This was
easily effected, but it was a much more difficult matter to
make Rút return the discontented lady's dowry.   Female
charms can, however, work wonders even in the rudest age,
and Unna appears to have employed hers to soften the heart
of her cousin Gunnar, and induce him to enter an action
against Rút for the recovery of her dowry.   Gunnar, aided
by the counsel of his friend Njáll, brought the suit to a successful issue at the Al-thing, and afterwards went to Norway,
in order to recruit his finances by sea-roving.   On his return
he attended the Al-thing, where he became enamoured of
Hallgerda, who was generally regarded as the most beautiful
woman in Iceland, though her character by no means corresponded to her beauty, as she had been twice married, and
was strongly suspected of having caused the death of both her
husbands.   Gunnar was, however, too much in love to listen
to the prudent advice of his old friend and neighbour Njáll,
and he accordingly offered his hand to Hallgerda, which she
willingly accepted.   At the marriage festival a dispute respecting precedence took place between Hallgerda and Njáll's
wife Bergthora,—the Icelandic ladies being on such points
equally as punctilious as the patronesses at Almack's " when
George the Fourth was King."   Hallgerda, in order to cause
dissension between the two families, sent her people to
kill one of Njáll's men, a proceeding which Bergthora retaliated by inciting her sons to murder one of Gunnar's retainers.   This man's death was of course avenged by Hallgerda, and the two ladies went on murdering in this manner
for some time, their husbands paying the usual expiatory fines,
and remaining, to Hallgerda's great mortification, as good
friends as if nothing of the kind had happened.   Hallgerda,
however, soon involved Gunnar in quarrels with persons who
were not so well disposed towards him, and although he once
gave her a box on the ear for one of her misdeeds, he was
obliged to defend them both in the forensic circle and the
holmgang.   A protracted lawsuit her proceedings had given
rise to, terminated by Gunnar being condemned to three years'

banishment. As he was riding to the place of embarkation
he turned round to take a last look at his family mansion,
and, dismounting from his horse, exclaimed:

" Never did this spot appear to me so lovely! the streams
are so clear, the grass so green, the fields so well manured
—no—I cannot leave it, I must turn back whatever may be
the consequences."

Gunnar accordingly returned, and, in spite of the remonstrances of Njáll, remained a banished outlaw in his own
dwelling. His enemies, on becoming aware that he had not
left the island, surrounded his house one morning at break of
day, knowing that there was nobody with him except his wife
and mother, all the men having been sent to another farm to
make hay. Gunnar was awakened by the barking of his faithful dog, and seizing his bow and arrows prevented his adversaries from entering the premises. He had already wounded
eight of them, and though severely wounded himself, would
probably have succeeded in driving them off had not the string
of his bow snapped in twain. In this conjuncture he begged
his wife to cut off one of her long ringlets in order that his
mother might twist it into a bow-string for him.

" Dost thou absolutely require it?" asked Hallgerda.

" My life depends on it!" replied Gunnar.

" Therefore," said the fiery lady, " the time is come when
I can repay thee for the box on the ear thou gavest me, it is
quite indifferent to me whether thou art able to defend thyself
or not."

" Every one seeks honour after his own fashion," mildly
replied Gunnar, and contended with sword and shield against
his adversaries, who now rushed in, until he was at length
overpowered. His heroic defence became the theme of many
a Skaldic lay, and his death was amply avenged by Njáll's son,
Skarphedin.

Soon after this tragical event Skarphedin, and his brothers
Grim and Helgi, left Iceland, and after two years spent in a
wild adventurous sea-roving life on the coasts and islands of
Scotland, sailed with their friend Kári and a considerable
booty to Norway, and cast anchor in the frith of Drontheim.
Sometime previous to their arrival an Icelander named Hrapp
had sought refuge in Norway, and although a perfect stranger,
was treated with great hospitality by Gudbrand, one of Jarl

Hakon's courtiers, an hospitality which Hrapp repaid by se-
ducing Gudbrand's daughter, and killing one of his retainers.
Having been outlawed for these misdeeds, he plundered and
set fire to Jarl Hakon's chief temple, and then concealed himself on board one of the Icelandic ships lying in the harbour
and belonging to Thrain Sigfusson. The jarl suspecting that
Njáll's sons had aided Hrapp in effecting his escape, sent a
party of men to arrest them ; a deperate conflict ensued, which
ended in Skarphedin and his brothers being taken and thrown
into prison. Having, however, plenty of money at their command they managed, through the good offices of their friend
Kári, and the intercession of Jarl Eirek*, to regain their liberty.
Thrain, meanwhile, kept Hrapp concealed on board his vessel.
and conveyed him safely to Iceland.

In the year 998, Njáll's sons returned from their Viking
expedition, in which they had amassed a considerable booty,
bringing with them their friend Kári, to whom Njáll gave his
daughter in marriage. Njáll's sons then sought to establish a
legal claim for compensation from Thrain for all they had suffered on his account from Jarl Hakon, but before the suit was
decided Hallgerda and Hrapp, who had formed a most intimate *liaison*, exercised the baneful influence they had acquired
over Thrain by exciting him to apply to his adversaries one of
those satirical epithets which an Icelander regarded as the
greatest insult that could be offered to him. The natural
consequence of this proceeding was a combat, in which Thrain
was killed by Skarphedin. The peaceable old Njáll, who was
universally respected for his rectitude, not only paid the usual
expiatory fine, but took Thrain's son, Höskuld, under his
fosterage, and thus put an end to the quarrel.

Njáll, however, was not destined to end his days in peace.
Höskuld, when he grew up, fell in love with Hildigunna, one
of the most lovely, but, at the same time, most fiery and
freakish young ladies in the island, and of so haughty and ambitious a disposition that she had made a vow only to marry
a pontiff-chieftain. It unfortunately happened that at this
period none of these sacerdotal-magistracies† were to be disposed of; however Njáll at length succeeded in procuring one
for Höskuld and marrying him to Hildigunna. Mörd Val-

* The son of Jarl Hakon.—See page 147.
† See page 291.

gardson, one of the most influential persons of the district, but of a very bad character, being displeased at this proceeding, involved Höskuld in a quarrel with Njáll's sons, which he took care to embitter by all kinds of malicious insinuations.

Skarphedin and his brothers got rid of Höskuld in the usual Icelandic way, by entering his house when he was unprepared for defence, and killing him. Hildigunna conjured her uncle Flosi, as she cast over his shoulders her husband's blood-stained mantle, to avenge his death. Flosi deemed the best way of doing this would be by entering an action at law against the murderers. The case was brought before the Althing, and after due recourse had been had to the usual legal quibbles, it was finally decided that Njáll should pay on the spot a triple fine in atonement for the murder of the sacerdotal magistrate. It was a large sum, but Njáll managed to raise it. As he appeared to make the payment, Flosi let fall some injurious expressions against him, which were retaliated by Skarphedin. Flosi then declared that the reconciliation was at an end, and that no compensation could be accepted.

Shortly after this, Flosi, at the head of one hundred followers, appeared before Njáll's house, which he set fire to, but his proceedings, sanguinary though they were, present a few redeeming traits which are worth citing for their singularity. He not only allowed the servants, male and female, to escape, but when the house was in flames went to the door and begged Njáll to come out with his wife, saying, that he did not wish that the innocent should suffer with the guilty.

" I will not stir," cried Njáll, " for I am an old man incapable of avenging my sons, and with dishonour I will not live."

" And I," said Bergthora, " when a young woman, plighted my troth to Njáll that his fate should be mine, and that troth shall be kept unbroken."

She then said to Kári's son, " Thee shall they carry out, thou must not be burnt."

" Thou didst promise me, my dear grandmother," answered the child, " that we should never part so long as I wished to remain with thee, and methinks it is much better to die with thee and Njáll, than to live with those people."

Njáll and Bergthora then went to their bedroom, and laying themselves down with their grandson between them, calmly awaited the approach of the devouring element. Their son-in-law Kári was the only one of the family who escaped from the scene of devastation.

Kári for some time sought in vain to obtain redress for the injuries he had sustained, but at length succeeded in having his powerful enemies summoned before the Al-thing. The legal proceedings that took place on this occasion are the most curious that have been preserved in the Icelandic Sagas. Flosi took advantage of the endless formalities and distinctions which law and precedent had sanctioned to render the evidence of Kári's witnesses and compurgators unavailing. The pleadings were conducted on both sides with such acrimony that the parties at length came to blows, and blood was shed within the sacred precincts of the doom-ring. The leading men of the commonwealth now interfered, and it was finally decided that Flosi and his associates should pay heavy expiatory fines for the murders they had committed. For Njáll, a triple fine; for Bergthora and her sons, Helgi and Grim, double fines; and for the other victims, single fines. The murder of Skarphedin was set against that of Höskuld, and the homicidal account thus balanced. Flosi was banished for three years, and most of his associates for life. Kári was, however, by no means satisfied with this verdict; he accordingly ranged the district in which his enemies dwelt, and managed in a short time to kill a round score of them *. Flosi, however, escaped, and sought refuge at the court of Sigurd, Jarl of the Orkney Islands. We are told that the jarl thought at first of punishing Flosi for killing Njáll's sons, two of whom had formerly been in his service, but he did not long persist in this laudable resolution, Flosi in a short time becoming his *hirdman*, or courtier, and one of his greatest favourites. One day, when a retainer of Flosi was relating the story of the burning of Njáll's house, in a manner which placed the conduct of his chief in the most favourable light, Kári, who had long been prowling about the coasts, rushed in, and with a stroke of his battle-axe felled to the ground the narrator. Sigurd ordered the audacious intruder to be seized, but when the jarl's followers recognised their old sea-roving friend Kári, they interfered in his behalf, and Sigurd allowed

---

* As they were outlawed, he could kill them with impunity. See page 300.

him to depart unmolested. Flosi accompanied Jarl Sigurd in his expedition to Ireland, and fought under his banner at Brian Boroimhe's celebrated battle of Clontarf, in which the Orkney jarl was killed. Flosi then sailed to Italy, and, after obtaining absolution for his crimes from the pope himself, returned in the year 1016 to Iceland. Kári also went to Rome and obtained absolution, we presume, much on the same terms as his opponent. On his return, he was shipwrecked on the coast, not far from Flosi's dwelling. Flosi went out with his people and rendered him every assistance, and in the evening placed him by his side in the high seat, when old quarrels, that had already been cancelled by the pope's absolution, were for ever obliterated by copious draughts from the drinking-horn. Shortly afterwards Kári married Höskuld's widow, Hildigunna, and thus became a member of Flosi's family.

We have already had occasion to speak of Höskuld and Melkorka, and of the visit which their son, Olaf, paid to his maternal grandfather, the Irish King Murcatoc, and shall now proceed to give an abstract of the latter part of the Laxdæla-Saga *, which principally relates to Olaf's son, Kjartan.

Olaf, who had obtained the surname of Pá †, from an old gentleman who made him his heir, on his return to Iceland married the lady whom we previously made mention of ‡, and being now in possession of great wealth, erected a stately mansion on his principal estate, called, from the numerous herds of cattle he kept on it, Herd-holt. It was Höskuld's wish that the family estates should devolve conjointly to his two legitimate sons and to Olaf, but as he could not induce his son Thorleik to consent to this arrangement, he made over, during his lifetime, personal property to Olaf to the amount of twelve ounces of gold §. At Höskuld's death Olaf offered to defray two-thirds of the expenses of the heirship-banquet ||, provided his brothers would let him have the

* The Laxdæla-Saga embraces a period extending from the middle of the ninth to the beginning of the eleventh century ; the principal events taking place in the latter half of the tenth century. The Saga itself does not appear to have been written before the thirteenth century.

† Pá, or páfugl, a peacock.

‡ See page 317.

§ Illegitimate children might succeed to real property when their father left no legitimate issue, and had neither brother nor sister.

|| See page 143.

management of it, and postpone it until the following year, the season being too far advanced for holding such a festival with becoming splendour. This offer having been accepted, Olaf at the next Al-thing ascended the Law-mount, and made known that ten weeks before winter he and his brothers would drink their heirship ale, and that for fourteen days open house would be kept at Herdholt, inviting first the sacerdotal magistrates, and then every one who chose to be his guest, to come and pledge a bumper to Höskuld's memory.

At the appointed time upwards of a thousand persons repaired to Olaf's mansion, and were feasted with a splendour seldom before witnessed in Iceland; the principal guests receiving at their departure presents of a more costly description than were usually given on such occasions*. When Olaf's house-steward began to reckon up the number of fat beeves slaughtered, gammons and flitches taken from the larder, barrels of ale tapped, and other such items required to keep up a fortnight's unbounded hospitality, Thorleik was quite astounded at the sum total, and, although he had only to pay one-sixth of it, declared that Olaf intended to ruin him. The son of Melkorka, who liked to do things *en grand seigneur*, told him, however, that he need not put himself to any inconvenience respecting the payment, offering at the same time to take his son Bolli in fosterage, an offer which Thorleik very gladly accepted. Olaf appears to have lived on very good terms with his wife, Thorgerda, though the lady, as we have seen, was fond of having her own way now and then†. Their eldest son, named Kjartan, after his royal grandfather, is represented as one of the handsomest and most accomplished young men of the age. Few could compete with him in manly sports and exercises, and his engaging manners rendered him a general favourite with the fair sex. Kjartan, and his cousin and foster-brother Bolli, were sworn friends and inseparable companions.

At a short distance from Herdholt dwelt a wealthy gentleman, named Osvif, whose daughter, Gudruna, was the most lovely maiden in the whole island, *agaçante, espiègle, et très*

---

* The two greatest heirship-festivals which the Sagas relating to Iceland make mention of, are those of Olaf and one given by the sons of Hjalti to upwards of fourteen hundred persons.

† See page 317.

comme il faut, as our lively neighbours would say; but, where-withal, like most young ladies of surpassing beauty, somewhat whimsical and freakish. When Gudruna had reached her fif-teenth year, Osvif gave her in marriage to Thorvald Haldor-son, a gentleman amply provided with every thing that tends to render life comfortable, stipulating that she should have the management of her own property, and, that whenever a legal divorce took place, should retain a fair moiety of it, and should, moreover, wear the most costly apparel that could be procured in Iceland. Although Gudruna had no great incli-nation for Thorvald, these favourable conditions induced her to give her tacit consent to the marriage, which was celebrated with the usual boisterous festivity.

Gudruna, as a married woman, was by no means of opinion that beauty is "when unadorned, adorned the most;" for she was continually teazing her loving spouse to purchase her rings and necklaces, and fur-lined kirtles and other costly articles, which fair ladies have in every age regarded as necessary acces-sories to their loveliness. Thorvald, as long as the honey-moon lasted, willingly complied with his young wife's caprices, but deemed at length that it was high time to put a stop to her extravagance, his resolution in this respect being probably strengthened by a very provoking flirtation she was carrying on with an intimate friend of his, named Thord Ingunnarson, who resided in the neighbourhood. Thorvald at first mildly remonstrated with her on the impropriety of her conduct, but had the mortification of finding that his words produced no effect. Gudruna was fully determined to dress and to flirt as she thought proper; a woman of her beauty and accomplish ments was made to be admired, and her husband ought to think himself fortunate in possessing a wife who was the ob-ject of universal admiration. Acting on these principles, she received Thord's assiduous homage with renewed affability, the more so, as she was well aware that it caused the greatest annoyance to his wife, Audura. Matters went on in this manner for some time, until Thorvald began to suspect that his wife's flirtation with Thord had grown into a regular *liaison*, and as remonstrances were unavailing, he one day let the fair lady feel the weight of his hand by giving her a smart box on the ear, which she, no doubt, had richly merited. Gudruna, however, regarded this uncourteous proceeding as an insult not to be put up with, and accordingly consulted her lover respecting the means she might employ in order to obtain a legal divorce. Thord advised her to make Thorvald a shirt with very wide sleeves, so that it might come under the designation of a shift *, and then she might sue for a divorce at the Al-thing on the plea that her husband had worn female apparel †. Gudruna lost no time in having recourse to this expedient, which was attended with the wished for result. Thord, meanwhile, obtained a divorce from Audura on an equally frivolous pretext, and the two lovers shortly afterwards became man and wife, their marriage being celebrated with the usual festivities. A few months after these auspicious nuptials Thord was drowned at sea, and Gudruna, now a blooming widow of eighteen, went to live with her father in Sælingsdale.

Sælingsdale was celebrated for its warm baths, which Kjartan and Bolli often frequented. Kjartan was naturally very fond of Gudruna's company, and many a fair damsel soon learned with regret that the *agaçante* young widow was going to make him her third husband. Olaf, who had by no means approved of his son's frequent visits to Sælingsdale, on becoming aware how matters stood, began to make a right use of his paternal authority by striving to convince Kjartan that a marriage with Osvif's daughter, though unobjectionable in point of rank and fortune, was not likely to insure either his future happiness or welfare. Kjartan listened very unwillingly to this prudent advice; but Olaf at length persuaded him to take a share in a trading vessel ready to sail for Norway, flattering himself that absence and change of scene would soon restore him to his sober senses. In a few days Olaf had made the necessary preparations for the projected voyage, and Kjartan was at length obliged to communicate

---

* We ought to have said *chemise*, the homely old English word shift having, for ears polite, long since become obsolete.

† It would appear that, in the tenth century, one sex wearing the garments of the other, constituted, according to Icelandic notions, a ground for divorce. No mention is made of such a plea in the sections of the Grágás relating to marriage; but that code enacts that women wearing male, or men female apparel, from a motive of frivolity, render themselves liable to the punishment of exclusion or its pecuniary equivalent.—See Grágás, vol. i. p. 111, and Note 4, page 338.

the fatal tidings to Gudruna.   The young lady at first flew into a violent passion, and had then recourse to tears and tender expostulations, but as Kjartan still persisted in his resolution of going to Norway, she finally declared that she would accompany him.   Kjartan was, however, ungallant enough to refuse this kind offer, telling her that she would do much better to remain with her father in Sælingsdale, but if she would plight him her troth to wait for three years, he would, before the expiration of that term, return to Iceland and marry her.   " Nay," said Gudruna, "that is more than I can promise thee or any one else;" thinking, probably, that in three years she had already had two husbands; so the lovers parted not in the best of humours with each other.

Kjartan and Bolli arrived in the harbour of Drontheim on a fine autumnal day, when a number of people were displaying their dexterity in the art of swimming.   Kjartan, who was passionately fond of manly exercises, soon joined the party, and making up to one of the most dexterous swimmers, ducked him under the water.   The Norwegian on rising managed in his turn, after a short struggle, to duck Kjartan, and they thus continued to display their strength and agility, amidst the cheers of the spectators, until they found that they were fully a match for each other.   When they came to land, the Norwegian asked Kjartan who he was, and whether he was as expert in other feats as he had shown himself to be in swimming.

" If people in Iceland did not rate my other qualities higher than my swimming," coldly replied Kjartan, " I should not have much to boast of."

" That depends on whom thou hast for a competitor," said the Norwegian; " and methinks thou mightst condescend to inquire the name of the person that thou hast now been contending with."

" It is a matter of perfect indifference to me," replied Kjartan, " what thy name may be."

" By my troth, 'tis a hardy fellow I have to deal with ! " exclaimed the Norwegian; " but although thou art too proud to ask, I will tell thee my name—know, then, that it is Olaf Tryggvason thou hast been swimming with."

Kjartan, without making any reply, went in his swimming attire towards his vessel; but King Olaf called him back, saying, as he took off his rich scarlet mantle, and placed it on Kjartan's shoulders. "There, as thou hast now no occasion to fear taking cold, thou needst not be in such a hurry to leave me!"

When Kjartan returned on board his ship, his republican countrymen blamed him for accepting the king's mantle, which they said was tantamount to his acknowledging himself in the royal service. The Icelanders were, in fact, at this time highly displeased at the Norwegian king, for placing an embargo on three of their vessels lying in the harbour on account of their crews having refused to embrace Christianity. Olaf, then in the third year of his reign *, had already converted his courtiers, and at a Thing held shortly after Kjartan's arrival, managed to persuade most of the inhabitants of the Drontheim district to receive the rite of baptism, giving the Icelanders, at the same time, plainly to understand that they should not set sail, ere the same rite had been administered to them. Seeing that the king's resolution was not to be shaken, the Icelanders held a meeting in the hostlery they frequented to consult what steps they ought to take in this emergency. Bolli declared that, for his part, he had no great inclination to embrace such effeminate doctrines as those of Christianity appeared to be.

" And I, said Kjartan, am of opinion that instead of sitting here to be taken like sheep in a fold, and compelled, as these poor Norwegians have been, to kneel before a kirtled monk, we should do better to fall on King Olaf, and burn him in his palace.

This plan, though highly approved of, was deemed too hazardous to be put in execution, and, after a long discussion, the meeting broke up without any resolution having been adopted. The following day, Olaf, who had been duly informed of their proceedings by his spies †, summoned the Icelanders to his presence, and told them that he was fully determined to make them Christians before they left Drontheim, adding that he was well aware that one of them had proposed to burn him to death in his palace. Kjartan unhesitatingly avowed that it was he who had made the proposal.

---

* He reigned A. D. 995—1000.

† This is not the only instance of spies we meet with in the Sagas; in fact, *espionage* has been in every age the necessary accompaniment of despotism.

"Well, this time I will not punish thee," said the king, "and, as ye are averse to the doctrines of Christianity, ye may depart in peace, for the God we worship does not wish that any one should be brought to him by compulsion." *

"In this manner," replied Kjartan, "I may be induced to become a Christian; and at all events will promise that next winter, in Iceland, Thor shall not often be worshipped by me."

"Methinks," said Olaf, smiling, "thou art one of those that put their trust in their own might and main, and care very little either for Thor or Odin."†

When Christmas came, Kjartan and the Icelanders having attended the midnight mass, and heard the king himself preach a very edifying sermon, declared their willingness to be baptized—a resolution which the king no doubt ascribed to the impression made by his homily, and the monks to the pompous ceremonies of the mass; but which was probably as much owing to a due regard for their trading interests, as to any motives of religion. Kjartan, in fact, now began to fit out his vessel for a trading voyage to England, having heard that Scandinavians who had renounced heathenism were well received in that country, and found a ready sale for their merchandise. Olaf told him that he would have preferred his going to Iceland to preach Christianity, but that at all events he would do better to remain at his court, which was a more fitting place for a man of his valour and abilities than the deck of a trading vessel. This was of course too flattering an invitation for Kjartan to refuse, and he soon became one of the king's greatest favourites, receiving, among other costly presents, a splendid suit of clothes from the royal wardrobe,

* Strange words these for Olaf Tryggvason to make use of; for it was by sheer compulsion that he made the Norwegians embrace Christianity. His short reign was in fact entirely devoted to the propagation of the new faith, by means the most revolting to humanity. His general practice was to enter a district at the head of a formidable force, summon a Thing, and give the people the alternative of fighting with him, or of being baptized. Most of them of course preferred baptism to the risk of a battle with an adversary so well prepared for combat; and the recusants were tortured to death with fiend-like ferocity, and their estates confiscated.—See Heimsk. vi., 59—100, and the note *, page 180.

† See pages 120 and 148. Most of the incidents respecting Kjartan and King Olaf are also related, with very slight variations, in Olaf Tryggvason's Saga, which forms the sixth book of the Heimskringla.

which, as Olaf was about his own size, fitted him admirably. The Norwegian king, in the mean time, sent his court chaplain, Thangbrand, to convert the Icelanders, but his mission was unsuccessful; the skalds or poetasters of the island (the terms are generally synonymous) having turned his proceedings into ridicule by lampoons of the coarsest description. On Thangbrand's return, Olaf again laid an embargo on the Icelandic vessels, and the following summer (A. D. 1000) sent two Icelandic exiles, named Hjalti and Gissur, to convert their countrymen, keeping Kjartan and three other Icelanders at his court as hostages for their safety. Kjartan appears to have been a very willing hostage, for the charms of the king's sister, the fair Ingjibjörg, rendered his sojourn in the palace exceedingly agreeable. Bolli, in fact, seeing that he was always in her company, returned to Iceland, declaring that his foster-brother was too deeply in love to stand in need of a companion.

When King Olaf received the welcome tidings that the Icelanders had embraced Christianity at the Al-thing *, he took off the embargo, and released the hostages, telling Kjartan that if he wished to return home, he would fit out his vessel in a manner that his countrymen should see how he was esteemed in Norway, intimating, at the same time, that it would be more agreeable for him, if he remained in his service. Kjartan, however, preferred home to the enjoyments of a court, graced though it was with the enrapturing presence of such a beauteous being as Ingjibjörg. When the vessel was

---

* The sudden conversion of the Icelanders to Christianity is generally ascribed to the conclusive arguments made use of by Gissur, Hjalti, and Snorri before the assembled people at the Al-thing (See Henderson's Iceland, p. 29, and a note to Walter Scott's abstract of the Eyrbyggjasaga); but we think this embargo was more calculated to bring about so desirable a result than any proceedings which are said to have taken place on the occasion. Without a foreign trade Iceland would soon perish. On the breaking out of the war between Great Britain and Denmark, in the year 1807, the Icelanders were apprehensive of absolute starvation, and would probably have been decimated by famine and pestilence had not Sir Joseph Banks induced the British Cabinet to grant licences to Danish vessels to trade with Iceland, on condition of their touching at Leith both on their outward and homeward bound passage. And in the year 1810 an order in Council was issued, prohibiting all acts of hostility against Iceland and the other Danish colonies in the Arctic Seas, and taking the inhabitants and their property under the special protection of Great Britain.—See Henderson's Iceland, p. 403.

ready to set sail, Kjartan, as he entered the lovely princess's apartment, regretted having taken such a rash resolution. Ingjibjörg received him with her accustomed affability, and, placing him by her side, said that she trusted no one had forced him to leave Norway, adding, with a sigh, "No! thou art not forced, it is thy own inclination that leads thee to Iceland."

A long silence ensued, Kjartan not venturing to make a reply, or even to cast a look at the disconsolate fair one. Ingjibjörg at length arose, and opening her wardrobe, took out a splendid white and gold brocaded head dress, saying, as she placed it in Kjartan's hands,

"This will become Gudruna, the daughter of Osvif; give it her as a bridal present; the ladies of Iceland shall see that the maiden thou wert acquainted with in Norway was not of ignoble lineage. Go—return to thy home—I cannot, I must not accompany thee; may every happiness be thine."

Kjartan, we are told, summoned all his fortitude to stammer out a last farewell, and leave a place endeared to him by such fond recollections *.

Long before Kjartan set sail, Bolli had arrived in Iceland, and on his first visit to Sælingsdale had described his foster-brother as living in the greatest splendour at the court of the Norwegian monarch. Gudruna hesitatingly inquired whether any other motive than King Olaf's friendship kept him at the court.

"Why, I must needs tell thee," said Bolli, "that Kjartan is greatly beloved by the Lady Ingjibjörg, and it is generally supposed that sooner than part with him the king will give him his sister in marriage."

"Good tidings thou bringest me," replied Gudruna, with affected indifference, "for such a marriage will but be the just reward of Kjartan's merits;" and so saying, left the room in

---

* The Lady Ingjibjörg was afterwards married to Earl Rögnvald of Gothland. Snorri, in speaking of her, says, "She was of a beauteous appearance, mild and condescending with the common people, firm and manly in her purpose, and of a most graceful and winning demeanour. She was very fond of the Icelanders who were there, (at the court,) but Kjartan Olafsson was her greatest favourite, for he had been with the king longer than the others, and it was often his delight to converse with her, for she was both wise and clever in her discourse."—Heimsk. vi. 113, Schöning's Edit.

order to conceal the violent emotion which she had tried in vain to stifle. Bolli, after the first burst of passion was over, frequently visited Gudruna, and finding her one day in her usual flow of spirits, ventured to ask her what she would say if he solicited her hand in marriage

"Thy suit would be in vain," replied the fair widow; "never will I contract another marriage whilst I know that Kjartan is still in existence."

"If thou still thinkest of Kjartan," said Bolli, "thou wilt have to wait long enough for a husband, for if he had cared any thing about thee, he would have made me the bearer of a message to thee, instead of letting me depart without even mentioning thy name."

Shortly after this Bolli, accompanied by Olaf's sons—Olaf himself having declined to interfere in the business—rode to Sælingsdale and formally demanded from Osvif the hand of his daughter in marriage. Osvif said that Gudruna, being a widow, might act as she thought proper, but promised to use his influence in Bolli's behalf. Gudruna at first would not listen to the proposal, but was at length persuaded to give her hand to Bolli. The marriage festival was, however, scarcely over when Kjartan unexpectedly returned. Gudruna now reproached her husband with having intentionally deceived her; Bolli declared that he had merely stated facts which no one at the court of the Norwegian king would think of calling in question. Gudruna remained silent, and never afterwards made the least allusion to the subject, though Bolli did not fail to remark that Kjartan was still the object of her affections.

Kjartan, on learning that Gudruna had become the wife of his sworn friend and foster-brother, was plunged in the deepest melancholy: studiously avoiding company and being now a zealous Christian, he kept Lent with the greatest strictness, and people flocked to Herdholt to behold the singular spectacle of a man fasting, wondering how it was possible for any one to keep body and soul together without tasting flesh meat: The year after his arrival, Olaf's family were invited to hold the autumnal festival * at Sælingsdale. Kjartan wished to

---

* This festival, called *haustboth* (autumn-invitation), was held toward the autumnal equinox, when the Icelanders were accustomed to kill all their

remain at home ; but his father at length persuaded him to join the party, and Gudruna had the satisfaction of seeing him arrive, dressed in the splendid suit of clothes and scarlet mantle that King Olaf had made him a present of, with a helmet and sword richly studded with ornaments of burnished gold, and bearing a shield on which a golden cross was conspicuously emblazoned, his suite consisting of thirteen armed retainers, sumptuously apparelled. Bolli received his foster-brother with great cordiality, and at his departure offered him, as guest-gift *, a fine white and bay mottled stallion and three mares of the same colour, which Kjartan refused to accept, wishing to show Bolli that after what had taken place, a renewal of their former friendship was not to be expected.

Kjartan still continued a prey to melancholy; but the following year was induced by his sister to marry a friend of hers, named Hrefna, the daughter of one of the wealthiest gentlemen of the district. Kjartan made his fair bride a present of the splendid head-dress which Ingjibjörg had destined for Gudruna, and at the marriage festival recovered his wonted

cattle in good condition, and lay in a store of provision for the winter, and was, like the winter or Yule—*Jól*—festival, attended with religious ceremonies. No mention is made in the Sagas relating to Iceland of a midsummer festival ; but the Icelanders, like most other heathen nations, had probably a festival at each of the four astronomical periods of the year—at the vernal as well as the autumnal equinox, and at the summer as well as the winter solstice ; festivals which, after the introduction of Christianity, were replaced by Lady-day and Easter—by Midsummer (St. John's-day), Michaelmas (in honour of Michael the Archangel), and Christmas. The reader will find some curious details respecting the coincidence of Christian and heathen festivals in Finn Magnusen's " Specimen Calendarii Gentilis," in the 3rd vol. of the Edda.

* At these festivals the principal guests received presents—generally horses, swords, battle-axes, and gold rings—at their departure. The Icelanders were passionately fond of horses and horse-racing ; and money, or its equivalent, wadmal, appears to have changed hands at their races much in the same manner as at Epsom and Newmarket. Thus, Thorir Dufunef, to cite one instance among a hundred, when riding through Hrinverja dale on his famous mare Fluga, (Fly, or, in modern turf language, Highflyer,) was met by Örn, who was mounted on a mare equally celebrated for her racing qualities. Örn bet Thorir two marks and a half (one hundred and twenty ells of wadmal) that his mare would beat Fluga. When the race *came off* Örn was, however, completely *distanced*, which had such an effect on his mind that he shortly afterward committed suicide. (Landnámab. iii. 8.) Bowls, quoits, wrestling and swimming, were also favourite amusements, bets being taken as at horse-racing.

gaiety, and related—to the great delight of his numerous friends,
what they had so long been desirous of hearing,—his adventures
at the court of King Olaf, suppressing, we presume, the most
tender parts of the story, in consideration of his fair lady, who,
notwithstanding her gorgeous head-dress, would scarcely have
listened to them with becoming matronly decorum.

The next autumnal festival was held at Herdholt. When
the guests were going to take their seats, a lady asked for
whom the high seat was reserved. "For Hrefna!" exclaimed
Kjartan, "for as long as I live she shall be the most honoured." Gudruna, who had always occupied the high seat
on these festive occasions, looked at Kjartan and turned
deadly pale, but placed herself at the table without uttering a
syllable. The next day Gudruna told Hrefna that she ought
to put on the Lady Ingjibjörg's head-dress, in order that people might see the most costly article of the kind that had yet
been worn in Iceland; but Kjartan objected to Hrefna wearing it, observing, that it was far more agreeable for him that
his wife should possess a treasure than that the public should
feast their eyes on it *. Gudruna, however, was determined
to see the head-dress, and, as ladies are very fond of displaying their finery, she had no great difficulty in persuading
Hrefna to show it her; but what effect it produced Hrefna
could not divine, Gudruna, after turning it about in her hands
and examining it minutely, giving it her back without making
a single observation. When the festival was over, a splendid
sword that had been presented to Kjartan by King Olaf was
missing. This sword was afterwards found, very much da-
maged, in a morass, into which Kjartan ascertained that it had
been thrown by one of Gudruna's brothers.

The winter festival was held at Osvif's mansion, Olaf, sadly
against Kjartan's inclination, repairing thither with his family.

---

* The Lady Ingjibjörg's head-dress, which caused so much
mischief, was probably one of those high-peaked caps much
in the same style as those worn in Iceland at the present day.
The annexed wood-cut, copied from "Henderson's Iceland,"
represents an Icelandic female (of the nineteenth century)
in her bridal attire; the high-peaked cap, or *falldr*, as it is
called, being of fine linen or muslin, with a fillet ornamented
with gold lace.

Hrefna was easily persuaded by her mother-in-law, Thorgerda, to take her splendid head-dress with her, which, on her arrival, she gave to one of Gudruna's waiting-maids to take care of. The next day, when she was going to dress for the banquet, it was nowhere to be found. The scene that ensued may easily be imagined—Hrefna in tears, Thorgerda giving due vent to her passion, Kjartan chafing with rage, and Olaf striving in vain to pacify them. Kjartan vowed by all that he held sacred that he would make Bolli restore the lost treasure. Bolli, in his turn, felt himself insulted in being accused of theft, declaring that he knew nothing about the head-dress, and that Kjartan ought to be aware that he was not the man to do the mean action attributed to him. In the midst of this confusion, Gudruna very coolly observed, that if any one in the house had taken the head-dress, it must be some one who wished it to come into the possession of its rightful owner. Olaf's family and retainers then mounted their horses and rode home, Kjartan declaring that after what had passed a reconciliation was out of the question.

Shortly after this event, Kjartan, with sixty retainers, surrounded Osvif's mansion, and kept it for three days and nights in a state of the strictest blockade. On his return home, Olaf blamed him for having had recourse to such a proceeding, but Thorgerda declared that he had acted with becoming spirit, Osvif's family having deserved a much greater insult. Hrefna asked him whether he had not spoken to any of the family.

" I exchanged a few words with Bolli," replied Kjartan, in a tone of affected indifference.

" Nay," said Hrefna, " I have been told for a certainty that thou didst converse with Gudruna, who wore the Lady Ingjibjörg's head-dress, which became her amazingly."

" I have not seen what thou chatterest about," answered Kjartan, reddening with anger, " and let me tell thee that Gudruna has no need to deck herself out with a head-dress to be the most lovely of her sex."

Some time afterward Kjartan, having heard that Bolli had bargained for an estate but had not yet paid the purchase-money, went to the proprietor and induced him to let him have it on the same terms. Gudruna incited her brothers to avenge this insult in the Icelandic manner, namely, to waylay

Kjartan and murder him, and by dint of jeering him for what
she was pleased to term his cowardice, at length induced her
husband to acompany them.   Kjartan had been warned not to
go out without a numerous retinue, but he daily visited his
new estate accompanied only by two retainers, observing, that
he cared not for Osvif's sons, and as for Bolli he was sure
that his foster-brother would never lift his sword against him.
One day, as he was returning home, he found himself waylaid
by nine armed men, among whom he descried Osvif's sons and
Bolli.   His two retainers were soon despatched, but Kjartan
defended himself with his usual dexterity, and managed to
kill several of his opponents without receiving the slightest
injury.   Bolli having remained at a short distance without
taking any part in the sanguinary action, Kjartan called out
to him to come amongst them, saying, " Cousin Bolli, why
didst thou leave thy home to stand there the idle spectator of
a combat, thou wouldst do better, methinks, to side with one
of us."   Bolli, however, pretended not to hear either Kjartan
or his brothers-in-law, who jeered him for his inaction.   Provoked at length by their sarcasms, he rushed sword in hand
against Kjartan.

" Thou art now going to do a nithing-work *, friend Bolli,"
said Kjartan, " and it will be better that I receive my death
wound from thee, than for me to give thee thine ; " and so
saying, he threw down his sword and shield and refused any
longer to defend himself.   Bolli, unmoved by this noble conduct, ran Kjartan through the body with the sword which
Thurida had given him †.   With feelings of bitter compunc-
tion for the rash act he had committed, Bolli then raised
Kjartan from the ground, who expired without uttering a
single word of reproach in the arms of his foster-brother.
Olaf would not let his sons avenge their brother's death on
Bolli himself, but allowed them to kill several of that chieftain's retainers.   He then summoned Osvif's sons to appear
before the Al-thing, but could not be induced to include Bolli
in the summons.   Bolli, however, paid the usual expiatory
fine, and Osvif's sons having been found guilty in the forensic
circle of the Al-thing, were condemned to the punishment of
exile.   Hrefna, inconsolable for the loss of Kjartan, to whom
she appears to have been tenderly attached, died shortly after-

* See page 155.   † See page 318.

wards of a broken heart, and before three years had elapsed, Olaf Pá expired, (A.D. 1006,) with Christian resignation, in his family mansion of Herdholt.

Thorgerda, after her husband's death, told her sons that they ought now to take ample vengeance on Bolli. They accordingly, in compliance with the old lady's wishes, went to Sælingsdale with several of their friends and retainers, and Bolli, being unprepared for an effectual resistance, fell under the battle-axe of Helgi Hardbeinson. Gudruna, who had been out with her maidens bleaching linen, on entering the house found her husband weltering in his gore at the feet of Helgi, who very coolly wiped his battle-axe with the hem of her kirtle. Gudruna regarded him with a significant smile of derision, and Helgi, on being reproached by Olaf's sons for his inhuman conduct, said, " Ye need not reproach me, for I have a presentiment that under that kirtle lies my bane." Gudruna, in fact, a few months afterwards gave birth to a son, who received in baptism the name that had been borne by his father.

When Bolli Bollison was twelve years old, a valiant, though somewhat foolish fellow, named Thorgils Holluson, fell in love with Gudruna, who promised him in the presence of witnesses that if he would join her sons in taking ample vengeance on Helgi, she would not marry any one else in the district. Helgi was accordingly attacked in the usual Icelandic manner and killed, as he had predicted, by Bolli Bollison. When Thorgils reminded Gudruna of the solemn promise she had made to give him her hand as a reward for the service he had rendered, she told him very coolly that she was on the point of marrying Thorkell Eyjulfson.

" How is this ! " exclaimed Thorgils, " thou hast deceived me."

" Nay," said Gudruna, " there is no deception. Thou knowest that I promised not to marry any one else *in the district* but thee. Now although Thorkell *does reside in the district,* he was in Norway when I made the promise. Thou seest, therefore, that thou hast nothing to reproach me with."

We are not informed what impression this scholastic distinction made on Thorgils ; but if the Jesuits had in that age darkened the earth with their ambiguous presence, we think Gudruna might have become a very useful member of their *worthy* community.

Gudruna's fourth marriage was celebrated with the greatest splendour imaginable. A short time previously she had taken under her protection a Norwegian, named Gunnar, who had killed a young Icelander of rank, and was hotly pursued by his relatives. At the marriage festival, Thorkell, after eyeing this gentleman for some time with great suspicion, ordered him to be arrested. Gudruna, however, instantly sprung from her seat and flew to his rescue, commanding her retainers to draw their swords and defend him, telling her husband, at the same time, that if he did not desist from his purpose, she would there and then be divorced from him. Thorkell, not knowing how to manage such a fiery lady, let her have her own way, and cooled his anger by emptying, at a draught, the capacious drinking horn placed before him. Gudruna afterwards persuaded her indulgent husband to make Gunnar a present of a fine trading vessel, in which she packed him off to his own country.

Some years afterwards Thorkell went to Norway, and was well received by King Olaf II.*, who gave him 100 marks of silver, and sufficient timber to erect a large church in Iceland. Not long after his return home, Thorkell was drowned in the Breidafjörd. Gudruna being again a widow, became very devout, and was the first woman in Iceland that learned psalm singing. She was also the first who became a nun, having in her old age entered the first convent established in the island. Bolli Bollison passed several years abroad, and served with distinction in the famous Varangian body-guard of the Byzantine emperors. On his return to Iceland, he frequently visited his mother in her solitude, and one day had the curiosity to ask her for which of her wooers she had entertained the greatest affection. Gudruna replied by saying something in praise of each of her husbands ; but on Bolli reiterating his question, she exclaimed, with a sigh, " He to whom I was the most evil disposed was the most beloved by me ! "

These abstracts of three of the most interesting Sagas that relate to Iceland will render any further details respecting

---

* Olaf II. reigned from 1015—1028, when Norway was subdued by Canute. Olaf attempted to recover his crown, but was slain in a battle fought near Drontheim, A.D. 1030, and, after being duly canonized, became the patron saint of Norway, or, in other words, the successor of Thor : patron saint and tutelary deity being in those days pretty nearly synonymous.

the manners and customs of the Icelanders superfluous. The reader has seen them at their drinking-bouts *, their festivals, their legislative and forensic assemblies, and obtained a good insight both of their public and private intercourse, and he will probaby coincide with us in opinion that the graphic sketches which they have themselves given of their social existence, produce, on the whole, an unfavourable impression. The worst traits of the ancient Scandinavian character—craftiness, remorseless cruelty, a spirit of sanguinary revenge, perfidy, malice, slander, recklessness regarding the lives and property of others—are, in fact, every where but too conspicuous; though we also find the Scandinavian energy, valour, enterprise, love of independence, and a few other redeeming traits, that render the picture somewhat less sombre. And if a strict comparison were instituted between the social condition of Iceland and that of other countries, we should probably be induced to place it, notwithstanding its viciousness, rather above than below the average standard of civilization that prevailed in Europe during those barbarous ages. That an aristocratic republic should have flourished for four centuries on a comparatively barren island, placed amidst the wild waves of the Arctic Ocean, and that the leading men of this republic should have framed a code of laws, which, whatever may be its defects, secured at least an ample provision for the poorest member of the community, and suffered no one to perish from starvation, are facts which will always render Iceland peculiarly interesting to all who make human nature—or the development of humanity on earth, in its multifarious and ever varying aspects—the object of their

* Antiquaries have not been able to ascertain whether the Icelanders brewed their beer from oats, rye, or barley. Previous to the eleventh century bread and wine were unknown in Iceland. The standing dish of an Icelandic family was oatmeal porridge; they had also plenty of butter and cheese, and, on festive occasions, their tables were abundantly supplied with beef, mutton, veal, pork, and horseflesh, and with fresh and dried fish. They appear to have been equally as fond of steaks as the people of this country; in fact, the Old Norse word for cook, is *steaker*, (steikari,) though *meat swain*, (mat-sveinn,) is also used to designate that indispensable household functionary. Our word steak is evidently derived from the Old Norse *steik*, which, however, was not restricted to beef; the term being applied by an Icelandic *steaker* to any slice of flesh meat that he had to prepare for the table. Horse steaks were probably as much in request at an Icelandic convivial meeting, as rump steaks are in a London tavern at the present day.

special attention. It is also a very remarkable fact, that, notwithstanding its rude climate, the Icelanders should have evinced, in every age, an ardent attachment for their native island. To leave it, and lead for a few years an adventurous life in foreign countries, was considered, in the olden time, as the necessary complement of a youth's education. "*Heimskr er heimalid barn.*" Inexperienced is he who remains in his native land—literally, *homely is the home-bred child*—was a favourite Icelandic maxim. But whatever might be his career—whether he acquired wealth and renown as a daring sea-rover, or served with distinction in the Varangian body-guard of the Byzantine emperors; whether he pursued the more peaceful avocations of a Skald or a Sagaman, and became a welcome guest at every court his wandering disposition induced him to visit, the Icelander was sure to return and pass at least his old age amidst the volcanic fires and eternal snows of his own cherished island. And even at the present day, when an Icelander hears tell of the genial climes of the south, he exclaims, while he views with a happy contentment the bleak scenery around him, "After all, Iceland is the best land that the sun shines upon! *Island er hinn besta land sem solinn skinnar uppá.*"

CHAPTER IV.

ICELANDIC LITERATURE.

OUR limits only allow us to give a mere sketch of the literature of Iceland in the olden time. We shall regard it as naturally falling into the three divisions of Eddaic, Skaldic, and Saga literature, and say a few words respecting each:

EDDAIC LITERATURE.

There are two works which bear the title of Edda, the one in verse, the other in prose. The Poetic, or Elder Edda *,

---

* Various derivations have been given of the word Edda, which in Old Norse signifies simply, *great grandmother*, in which sense it is used in the Rígs-mál. In M. Gothic *atta* is used for father, and *aithei* for mother. Sæmund's Edda was quite unknown to the learned world until the seventeenth century, when the celebrated Torfæus received a MS. containing

consists of thirty nine poems, which were collected by Sæmund Sigfusson, (n. 1057. ob. 1131,) surnamed the Learned, towards the latter end of the eleventh or the beginning of the twelfth century. Sæmund, after pursuing his classical and theological studies in the universities of France and Germany, became, on his return to Iceland, the parish priest of Oddi, a village situated at the foot of Mount Hekla, and which had belonged to his family from the time of the first colonization of the island, and where he seems to have devoted himself with great zeal to the cultivation of letters and the education of youth. Some writers maintain, though without being able to adduce the slightest evidence in support of their arguments, that Sæmund merely transcribed the Eddaic poems from Runic manuscripts, or Runic staves; but the most probable conjecture seems to be that he collected them from oral tradition, though he may possibly have found some of the most important amongst them in manuscripts written in Roman characters, shortly after the introduction of Christianity.

The Eddaic poems may be classified as follows:—1. The Mythic-cosmogonic. 2. The Mythic-ethnologic. 3. The Ethic. 4. The Mythological. 5. The Mythic-heroic. 6. The Miscellaneous. One of them—the Sólar-ljód—was probably composed by Sæmund himself, as it is the only one that contains the least allusion to Christianity *. All the others, especially the Mythic-cosmogonic poems, bear internal evidence that entitles them to the claim of a much higher antiquity than the eleventh century.

The Mythic-cosmogonic poems are the *Völuspá*, the *Vafthrúdnis-mál*, and the *Grímnis-mál*. The *Völu*, or *Völo-spá*— a compound word, signifying *The Song of the Prophetess* †,—

---

it from Iceland. Resenius gave two of the poems in the first edition of the Prose Edda, published in 1665, but we have now a complete edition of all the poems, with notes and glossaries, in 3 volumes, 4to., published by the Arni-Magnæan Commission at Copenhagen, the 1st volume in 1787, the 2nd in 1818, and the 3rd, which is provided with an excellent " Lexicon Mythologicum " by Finn Magnusen, in 1828.

* With the exception of a couplet in the thirteenth strophe of the *Grougaldur*, in which mention is made of the (magical) evil to be apprehended from the dead body of a Christian woman, "*kristin daud kona*," and perhaps also one or two obscure allusions in the mythic-heroic poems.

† *Scoticè* Vala's spae.—See the Glossary to the Prose Edda. All the Teutonic nations appear to have had their Valas or prophetesses; Cæsar remarks, i. 50, that " apud Germanos ea consuetudo esset, ut matres familias

appears to be the oldest as it is the most interesting of the Eddaic poems. It is a kind of Sybilline lay, supposed—though we think without any adequate grounds—to have been recited before the assembled people at the religious festival of the summer solstice, and contains the whole system of Scandinavian mythology—the creation, the origin of man, how evil and death were brought into the world, and concludes by a prediction of the destruction and renovation of the universe, and a description of the future abodes of bliss and misery. As numerous extracts from this poem are given in the Prose Edda, of which it in fact forms the groundwork, any further details respecting it would be superfluous.

The *Vafthrúdnismál* * contains the same system of cosmogonic mythology in the form of a dramatic dialogue between Odin and the giant Vafthrúdnir. The poem commences by Odin telling his wife, Frigga, that he intends to visit Vafthrúdnir in order to ascertain the extent of his knowledge of sacred lore. Frigga fearing that Odin—to whose fate that of gods and men was indissolubly linked—might be vanquished in an intellectual encounter with a giant so renowned for his omniscience, advises him to desist from his purpose. Odin, however, proceeds on his journey, and enters the halls of Vafthrúdnir as a mere mortal under the name of Gangrad. The giant finding, after he had asked the stranger a few questions, that he had a worthy antagonist, invites him to take a seat, and expresses his willingness to enter into a disputation with him on the condition that the vanquished party—the one unable to answer a question put to him by the other—should forfeit his head. They accordingly discuss by question and answer the principal topics of Scandinavian mythology; but the pretended Gangrad at length asks his adversary what

eorum sortibus et vaticinationibus declararent, utrum prœlium committi ex usu esset, nec ne;" and Tacitus in giving an account of *Veleda*, the prophetic virgin of the Bructeri, says, Hist. 4. 61, " Ea virgo nationis Bructeræ, late imperitabat, vetere apud Germanos more, quo plerasque feminarum fatidicas, et augescente superstitione arbitrantur deas." He afterwards speaks of Veleda giving her oracular responses from the tower in which she dwelt. The classic writers also make mention of *Ganna* and *Aurinia* (probably a Latin corruption of *Alirúna*) as Germanic prophetesses.

* *Mál*, song, discourse, speech, a word cognate with the Ang. Sax. *mal*, *mæ'*, the Gr. μίλος, &c. For an explanation of the proper names that occur in this chapter, see the Glossary to the Prose Edda.

Odin whispered in the ear of his son Baldur before he had him placed on the funeral pile,—a question by which the astonished giant becomes aware that his antagonist is Odin himself, who was alone capable of answering it, and therefore acknowledges himself vanquished. Although the limits of the present work only allow us to give a mere summary of these ancient myths, we cannot refrain from remarking that most of them admit of a satisfactory explanation. The dispute between Odin and Vafthrúdnir, for instance, is the symbolical expression of the strife between summer and winter —between light and darkness; the earth, (Frigga,) naturally awaiting with anxiety the issue of a combat on which her fate depends. As darkness was also supposed to conceal some profound mystery, some primordial knowledge which could only be revealed by the rays of light dissipating the enshrouding gloom, the disputation of Odin and Vafthrúdnir may typify, not only the elemental antagonism of light and darkness, but also the strife between intellectuality and obscurantism—a strife coeval with man, and which we fear will only end when time shall be no more; although it were certainly much to be wished that obscurantism should become like Vafthrúdnir, a headless monster; or, in other words, that the rays of science should at length dissipate that deadening and soul-withering gloom in which the human understanding is still unfortunately enshrouded.

The *Grímnis-mál* (Grimnir's lay) contains, among other matters, a description of twelve habitations of celestial deities, which were possibly meant (for we will not venture to speak so dogmatically on the subject as Finn Magnusen, and other interpreters of Eddaic esoteric doctrines,) for the twelve signs of the zodiac. Should this be the true interpretation, Grimnir's lay may be regarded as a mythic-uranographic poem, under which point of view it is well deserving of attention.

The Mythic-ethnologic class contains only one poem, the *Rigs-mál*, which explains, in an allegorical manner, the origin of the different races, or, more properly speaking, castes, located in Scandinavia at the period it was composed. Heimdall—who, as the warder of heaven, is here a symbol of the sun—wanders, under the name of Rígr, over the earth, then but thinly peopled, probably, according to the notions of the

Skald, only with the immediate offspring of Ask and Embla *
Heimdall is received and entertained with great hospitality,
first by Ai (Great Grandfather) and Edda (Great Grandmother),
dwelling in a lowly hut; then by Afi (Grandfather) and Amma
(Grandmother), located in a more comfortable habitation; and
lastly by Faðir (Father) and Móðir (Mother), who possess a
splendid mansion. The deity, by his beneficent presence,
infuses a vital energy into his hosts, and nine months after
his departure Edda, Amma, and Moðir respectively give
birth to a son. The children are sprinkled with water at the
moment of their birth †; Edda's son is called Thræll (Thrall);
Amma's, Karl (Churl); and Moðir's, Jarl (Noble); and Thrall,
Churl, and Noble have each of them a numerous offspring. We
have thus an aristocratic explanation of the three castes that
appear, at a very early period, to have formed the framework
of Scandinavian society. The thralls or slaves, the churls
or free peasants—bœndur or odalsmen, as they were afterwards called—and the nobles. The Skald describes the
thralls as having black hair, an unsightly countenance, an
uncouth appearance, and as being of a low and deformed
stature; physiological traits, characteristic of the Lapps, who
were probably reduced to a state of vassalage by their Scandinavian conquerors. The destiny of the thralls is, of course,
to toil incessantly, in order that by their labour, the churls
may obtain sufficient produce from the earth to enable the
nobles to live with becoming splendour. The Skald shows
his contempt for this caste by giving Thræll's sons such names
as Frousy, Stumpy, Plumpy, Sootyface, Slowpace, Home-
spun, &c., and calling his daughters Lazybody, Cranefoot,
Smokynose, Tearclout, &c. The churls are described as
having red hair and a florid complexion; and among the sons
of Karl, the progenitor of the caste, we find Stiffbeard, Hus-
bandman, Holder (of land), and Smith ‡, the daughters being

* See the Prose Edda, ch. 9.
† See note, page 206, and pages 313 and 320.
‡ We trust that all who bear the ubiquitous homonyme of Smith, be they
Smiths, or Smyths, or Smithsons, or Goldsmiths, or Smythes, *par excellence*,
will duly acknowledge the sturdy Scandinavian yeoman, Smiðr, son of Churl,
son of the jovial old fellow, Grandfather, who had the honour of pledging a
bumper with a celestial deity, as their common ancestor.

designated by such names as Prettyface, Swanlike, Blithespeech, Chatterbox, &c. But the Skald reserves all his eloquence for the nobles, who, he tells us, "have fair hair, a clear complexion and fine piercing eyes, their sole avocations being to wield the sword, dart the javelin, rein the fiery steed, chase the deer, and other elegant amusements, which Jarl's descendants still delight to astonish the churls with. The Skald marries, Jarl to Erna (Lively), the daughter of Hersir (Baron), but only gives us the names of their sons, which generally denote relationship, as Cousin, Nephew, &c. The *Rigs-mál* furnishes a striking proof of the aristocratic spirit that prevailed in Scandinavia at a very early period of its history, and we should recommend its attentive perusal to those writers who, allowing a tolerable free scope to their imaginative faculties, expatiate on the marvels which, according to their notions, have been wrought by the influence of a Scandinavian democratic element, transfused into the veins of the phlegmatic Saxon. For our own part we are inclined to regard an aristocratic feeling as one of the inherent psychological traits of the Teutonic race, and this trait was unquestionably, in the olden time, more conspicuous among the nations forming the Scandinavian branch of this race, than among those constituting its Germanic branch.

There is only one Eddaic poem, the *Háva-mál* *, that can be placed in the Ethic class; but it forms of itself a tolerable complete code of Odinic morality, though the reader will find by the following extracts, translated by Bishop Percy †, that several of its precepts would be "more honoured in the breach than the observance."

1. "Consider and examine well all your doors before you venture to stir abroad: for he is exposed to continual danger, whose enemies lie in ambush concealed in his court."

3. "To the guest, who enters your dwelling with frozen

* Háva-mál signifies the discourse or canticle of the sublime; *i. e.* deity. The canticle of canticles,—Odin himself being supposed to have given these precepts of wisdom to mankind.

† Bishop Percy remarks that he made his translation from Mallet's French translation, occasionally consulting a manuscript copy of Resenius's Latin version. We have numbered the verses as in the original, omitting some, unimportant in themselves, which offered too great a discrepancy with the original Norse text published in the third volume of the Edda.

knees, give the warmth of your fire: he who hath travelled over the mountains hath need of food, and well-dried garments."

4. " Offer water to him who sits down at your table; for he hath occasion to cleanse his hands: and entertain him honourably and kindly, if you would win from him friendly words, and a grateful return."

5. " He who travelleth hath need of wisdom. One may do at home whatsoever one will; but he who is ignorant of good manners, will only draw contempt upon himself, when he comes to sit down with men well instructed."

7. " He who goes to a feast, where he is not expected, either speaks with a lowly voice, or is silent; he listens with his ears, and is attentive with his eyes: by this he acquires knowledge and wisdom."

8. " Happy he, who draws upon himself the applause and benevolence of men! for whatever depends upon the will of others, is hazardous and uncertain."

10. " A man can carry with him no better provision for his journey than the strength of understanding. In a foreign country this will be of more use to him than treasures; and will introduce him to the table of strangers."

12-13. " A man cannot carry a worse custom with him to a banquet than that of drinking too much; the more the drunkard swallows, the less is his wisdom, till he loses his reason. The bird of oblivion sings before those who inebriate themselves, and steals away their souls."

16. " A coward thinks he shall live for ever, if he can but keep out of the reach of arms; but though he should escape every weapon, old age, that spares none, will give him no quarter."

17. " The gluttonous man, if he is not upon his guard, eats his own death: and the gluttony of a fool makes the wise man laugh."

21. " The flocks know when to return to the fold, and to quit the pasture: but the worthless and slothful know not how to restrain their gluttony."

22. " The lewd and dissolute man makes a mock of every thing: not considering how much he himself is the object of derision. No one ought to laugh at another, until he is free from faults himself."

23. " A man void of sense ponders all night long, and his mind wanders without ceasing : but when he is weary at the point of day, he is nothing wiser than he was over-night."

32. " Many are thought to be knit in the ties of sincere kindness : but when it comes to the proof, how much are they deceived. Slander is the common vice of the age. Even the host backbites his guest."

37. " One's own home is the best home, though never so small *. Every thing one eats at home is sweet. He who lives at another man's table is often obliged to wrong his palate."

39. " I have never yet found a man so generous and munificent, as that to receive at his house was not to receive : nor any so free and liberal of his gifts, as to reject a present when it was returned to him."

41. " Let friends pleasure each other reciprocally by presents of arms and habits. Those who give and those who receive, continue a long time friends, and often give feasts to each other."

43. " Love both your friends, and your friends' friends : but do not favour the friend of your enemies."

47. " When I was young I wandered about alone : I thought myself rich if I chanced to light upon a companion. A man gives pleasure to another man."

51. " Peace, among the perfidious, continues for five nights to shine bright as a flame ; but when the sixth night approaches, the flame waxes dim, and is quite extinguished : then all their amity turns to hatred."

55. " Let not a man be over wise, neither let him be more curious than he ought. Let him not seek to know his destiny, if he would sleep secure and quiet."

58. " He who seeks to destroy the flock, or to take the life of another, must rise early. The sleeping wolf gains not the prey ; neither the drowsy man the victory."

67. " They invite me up and down to feasts, if I have only need of a slight breakfast : my faithful friend is he who will give me one loaf when he has but two."

70. " Whilst we live, let us live well : for be a man never

---

* This is like our English proverb, " Home is home, be it never so homely."—P.

so rich, when he lights his fire, death may perhaps enter his door before it be burnt out."

72. "It is better to have a son late than never. One seldom sees sepulchral stones raised over the graves of the dead by any other hands but those of their own offspring."

77. "Riches pass away like the twinkling of an eye: of all friends they are the most inconstant. Flocks perish; relations die; friends are not immortal; you will die yourself; but I know one thing alone that is out of the reach of fate: and that is the judgment which is passed upon the dead."

81. "Praise the fineness of the day when it is ended; praise a woman when she is buried; a sword when you have proved it; a maiden after she is married; the ice when once you have crossed it *; and the liquor after it is drunk."

84. "Trust not to the words of a girl; neither to those which a woman utters; for their hearts have been made like the wheel that turns round; levity was put into their bosoms."

86, 7, &c. "Trust not to the ice of one day's freezing; neither to the serpent who lies asleep; nor to the caresses of her you are going to marry; nor to a sword that is cracked or broken; nor to the son of a powerful man; nor to a field that is newly sown."

90. "Peace between malicious women is compared to a horse who is made to walk over the ice not properly shod; or to a vessel in a storm without a rudder; or to a lame man who should attempt to follow the mountain goats with a young foal or yearling mule."

92. "He who would make himself beloved by a maiden, must entertain her with fine discourses, and offer her engaging presents: he must also incessantly praise her beauty. It requires good sense to be a skilful lover."

95. "The heart alone knows what passes within the heart: and that which betrays the soul is the soul itself. There is no malady or sickness more severe than not to be content with one's lot."

117. "Seek not to seduce another's wife with the alluring charms of Runic incantations."

* This is not unlike the English proverb, " Praise the bridge that carries you safe over."

119. "Never discover your uneasiness to an evil person, for he will afford you no comfort."

121. "Know, that if you have a friend, you ought to visit him often. The road is grown over with grass, the bushes quickly spread over it, if it is not constantly travelled."

123. "Be not the first to break with your friend. Sorrow gnaws the heart of him who hath no one to advise with but himself."

130. "I advise you be circumspect, but not too much: be so, however, when you have drunk to excess; when you are near the wife of another; and when you find yourself among robbers.

131. "Do not accustom yourself to mocking; neither laugh at your guest nor a stranger: they who remain at home often know not who the stranger is that cometh to their gate."

135. "Where is there to be found a virtuous man without some failing? or one so wicked as to have no good quality?

136. "Laugh not at the gray-headed declaimer, nor at thy aged grandsire. There often come forth from the wrinkles of the skin words full of wisdom."

140. "The fire drives away diseases; the oak expels the stranguary: straws dissolve enchantments *: Runic characters destroy the effect of imprecations: the earth swallows up inundations; and death extinguishes hatred and quarrels."

THE RUNIC CHAPTER †.

149. "I am possessed of songs: such as neither the spouse of a king, nor any son of man can repeat; one of them is called the Helper: it will help thee at thy need, in sickness, grief, and all adversities.

150. "I know a song, which the sons of men ought to sing, if they would become skilful physicians.

151. "I know a song, by which I soften and enchant the arms of my enemies; and render their weapons of no effect!

---

* Hence probably is derived the custom of laying two straws crosswise in the path where a witch is expected to come.

† This chapter does not appear to have originally formed part of the Háva-mál. At all events, the learned editors of the Edda will not allow it to be attributed to Odin; that is to say, to the same high sacerdotal dignitary or dignitaries who dictated the preceding precepts.—ED.

152. "I know a song, which I need only to sing when men have loaded me with bonds; for the moment I sing it, my chains fall in pieces, and I walk forth at liberty."

156. "I know a song, useful to all mankind; for as soon as hatred inflames the sons of men, the moment I sing it they are appeased.

157. "I know a song of such virtue, that were I caught in a storm, I can hush the winds, and render the air perfectly calm.

158. "When I see magicians travelling through the air, I disconcert them by a single look, and force them to abandon their enterprise.

159. "If I see a man dead and hanging aloft on a tree, I engrave Runic characters so wonderful, that the man immediately descends and converses with me."

161. "If I will that a man should neither fall in battle, nor perish by the sword, I sprinkle him over with water at the instant of his birth.

162. "If I will, I can explain the nature of all the different species of men, of genii, and of gods. None but the wise can know all their differences."

164. "If I aspire to the love and the favour of the chastest virgin, I can bend the mind of the snowy-armed maiden, and make her yield wholly to my desires."

166. "But I know one which I will never impart to any female, except my own sister, or to her whom I hold in my arms. Whatever is known only to one's self, is always of very great value."

The following verse, which neither M. Mallet nor Bishop Percy thought proper to give, is too Scandinavian to be omitted.

45. "Hast thou a friend whom thou canst not well trust, but wouldst make him useful to thee, speak to him with bland words, but think craftily, and thus render him levity for lies."

The poems conclude with the following verse.

167. "Now have sublime strains been sung, in halls sublime. Useful are they to the sons of men; useless to the sons of giants! Hail to him who hath sung them! Hail to him who hath understood them! may they profit him who hath retained them! Hail to those who have lent an ear to them!"

The poems we have given this summary account of, may be regarded as forming a logical sequence, and constituting a system of heathen doctrine complete in all its parts ; for the three mythic-cosmogonic poems explain the mysteries of creation ; the Rigs-mál shows the origin, and points out the duties of the castes into which society was then divided ; and the Háva-mál lays down precepts, of a somewhat dubious morality, for the better regulation of this society. Our notice of the remaining poems, which appear to be of a more recent date than the preceding ones, must necessarily be very brief.

The Mythological class contains six poems. 1. *Vegtams-kviða* (The Wanderer's lay)*. The Prose Edda informs us that Baldur, " having been tormented with terrible dreams, indicating that his life was in great peril, communicated them to the assembled gods, who resolved to conjure all things, to avert from him the threatened danger." † Odin, however, being aware that the fate of the gods depended on that of Baldur, has still his doubts whether these precautions would avert the dreaded evil. He accordingly mounts his horse, Sleipnir ‡, and rides to the abodes of death, in order to evoke the spirit of a deceased Vala, or Prophetess, with Runic incantations, and learn Baldur's fate. It is this descent of Odin to the regions of Hela, that forms the subject of the Vegtams-kviða, which has been so beautifully paraphrased by Gray, in his ode beginning—

> " Up rose the king of men with speed,
> And saddled straight his coal-black steed.'

Odin, under the name of Vegtam, evokes the sybil from her tomb §, who reveals to him how Baldur will fall by the hand of Hödur, in the manner related in the 49th chapter of the Prose Edda, to which we refer the reader.

2. *För Skirnis* (The journey of Skirnir). A very beautiful

* The lay of one accustomed to the road—literally, *Waytamer's-quoth.* Kviða, (formerly written, as in the edition of the Edda, quida,) from the verb *kveðja*, to say ; cognate with the English *quote, quoth.* Vegtam, from *vegr*, way, and *tamr*, accustomed ; cognate with the Germ., *zahm*, and the English *tame.*

† See the Prose Edda, chap. 49.

‡ See the Prose Edda, chap. 42.

§ This is the only instance of a tomb being mentioned in the regions of Hela.

poem, giving, in a dramatic dialogue, the story of Frey and Gerda, which the reader will find in the 37th chapter of the Prose Edda *.

3. *Hárbards-ljód* †, is a dialogue between Thor and Hárbard, a ferryman, who refuses to convey the Thunderer across a frith, which furnishes them with an occasion to relate the valorous exploits they have respectively been engaged in. The esoteric doctrine concealed by the Skald under this popular form, is probably that of the elemental antagonism of light and darkness, represented at a period when darkness— Hárbard, or the Demon of Winter—is in the ascendant.

4. *Thryms-kviða eðr Hamarsheimt*, (Thrym's lay, or the Recovery of the Mallet,) is, irrespective of its signification, one of the most amusing poems of the Eddaic collection. Thor's

---

* The reader will find very beautiful poetical versions of the *För Skirnis,* and other Eddaic poems, in the works of the late Hon. William Herbert, Dean of Manchester. Mr. Herbert's translations are generally correct, and always elegant, though somewhat too ornate; but the most ludicrous bombast ever published is the so-called translation of, "The Edda of Sæmund, into English verse," by Amos Cottle, of Bristol. A luckless wight was the said Amos Cottle; for just as he was sinking, with his rhapsodical effusions, into the charitable void of utter oblivion, Byron caught him up, and, with his

> "Oh! Amos Cottle! for a moment think
> What meagre profits spring from pen and ink,"

has preserved him, like a fly in amber, for future generations to wonder at. As poor Amos has thus become a literary curiosity, we subjoin a specimen of his *translation.*

> "Chief of lineage divine !—
> Long may thy princely virtues shine—
> Tell me, for I wish to know,
> The story of thy bitter woe;
> Say, why you shun the field and grove,
> And lonely thus your chambers rove.
> Should you my boldness disapprove,
> Forgive me— 'tis the crime of love."

The *literal* translation of the original text of this Cottlized Eddaic strophe, the third of the För Skirnis, would be—

"Say thou to me, (tell me,) Frey, Leader of Gods ! what I wish to know ; why my chief (or my lord—*minn drottinn*) sittest thou, the whole day, in the hall alone?"

Mr. Herbert renders the passage by—

> "Prince of the gods, and first in fight,
> Speak, honour'd Freyr, and tell me right !
> Why speeds my lord the tedious day
> In this lone hall, to grief a prey ?"

† *Ljód*, properly *ljóð*; German, *lied ;* Ang.-Sax., *leoth ;* English, *a lay.*

mallet has fallen into the possession of the giant Thrym, and lies buried eight miles beneath the gelid rocks of Jötunheim, or, in other words, to speak physically, summer is in the power of winter, light has succumbed to darkness, or, metaphysically, obscurantism has overshadowed intellectuality. Loki is sent to negotiate with Thrym, who vows that the formidable weapon shall only be restored when Freyja will consent to become his bride. Loki returns to Asgard; but the Goddess of Love is of course quite horrified at the idea of bestowing her charms on the King of the Frost-giants. In this emergency Loki persuades Thor to dress himself in Freyja's clothes, and accompany him to Jötunheim. Thrym receives his veiled bride with due courtesy, but is greatly astonished at seeing her eat for her supper eight salmons and a full-grown ox, besides other delicacies, washing the whole down with three tuns of mead. Loki, however, assures him that she has not tasted any thing for eight long nights, so great is her desire of sharing the nuptial couch with the renowned ruler of Jötunheim. Thrym has at length the curiosity to peep under his bride's veil, but starts back in affright, and demands why Freyja's eye-balls glisten with fire. "Because, replied Loki, she has not slept for eight nights, so ardently does she long to become thy spouse!" Thrym then orders the mallet to be brought in, and "laid on the fair maiden's lap." But Thor now throws off his disguise, grasps his redoubted weapon, (his thunder-bolt,) and slaughters Thrym and all his followers. "And thus" concludes the poem, "did the son of Odin recover his mallet."

5. The *Hymis-kviða*, also relates to Thor's exploits. Ægir, the ocean deity, entertains all the gods of Asgard at the festival of the autumnal equinox, but although he gives them plenty to eat, Thor finds, to his great regret, that drink is sadly wanting to give a due zest to the banquet, and it at last turns out that Ægir has not a cauldron sufficiently capacious to brew ale for such a numerous company. Thor having heard that the giant Hymir is the owner of a famous cauldron, sets out with Tyr to Jötunheim, in order, either by force or fraud, to obtain possession of it. Various adventures are then related; amongst others, Thor's fishing for the Midgard serpent, an account of which is given in the 48th chapter of the Prose Edda. Thor at length succeeds in bearing off the cauldron, and is followed by the giants, whom he kills with his redoubted mallet.

6. The *Ægis-drekka*, (Ægir's banquet, or drinking-bout,) forms, in some measure, the sequel of the preceding poem. Ægir, having now a capacious cauldron, is able to brew as much ale as his guests require. They accordingly sit down to a regular drinking-bout, but Loki kills one of Ægir's servants, for which the gods expel him, and drive him into a forest. Loki, however, shortly afterwards returns, and persuades Odin to let him take his place at the table again—a favour which he repays by calumniating every one present.

In the Mythic-heroic class we have—1st, the *Völundar-kviða* narrating the tragical adventures of Völundr, the Northern Dædalus *; and, 2nd, *a cyclus of twenty heroic lays*, forming a complete epos—a grand epic poem, in fact, in twenty cantos, containing the same tragical story of the Volsungians and Niflungians as the German Nibelungen-lied—Sigurdr (Siegfried) and his fatal treasure—his liberation of Brynhildr (Brunhild) from her magic sleep; his marriage with Gudrun (Chrimhilt); Brynhilda's marriage with Gunnar (Günther); Sigurd's murder, Gudrun's marriage with Atli (Etzel, Attila); and all the terrible scenes that result from it. The Scandinavian Epos is, however, of a much earlier date than the German, the personages are more mythological, the style more simple; and the whole has a certain grandeur and sublimity which place it far above the Nibelungen †.

The Miscellaneous Poems are—1. *Hrafna-galdur Odins* (Odin's Raven-song); an obscure poem, which one of the learned editors of the Edda, after devoting four months to the study of it, declares his inability to explain. 2. *Fjöl-svinns mál*, another obscure poem, in the form of a dramatic dialogue. 3. The *Hyndlu-ljóð*, fragmentary and obscure, containing the genealogies of the Ynglingians, Skjöldungians, and other mythic and mythic-heroic dynasties. 4. *Grou-galdur* (Groá's

---

* The Norse Völundr is the Ang.-Saxon Wealand.—See the word in the Glossary to the Prose Edda. We may remark, that the Wayland Smith, in "Kenilworth," is no other than the Northern Völundr, though our great novelist does not appear to have been aware of the homonymy.

† Professor Müller (in his Sagabib, vol. ii. p. 129 and 139) has ably refuted the supposition of Weber, (in the ",Illustrations of Northern Antiquities," 1. vol. Edinb. 1814,) that this Eddaic Epos was derived from German sources, and has shown by the most satisfactory and conclusive arguments that most of the poems must have been composed prior to the reign of Harald Hárfagra, and in all probability at a much earlier period.

magic lay); a collection of magical terms and incantations. 5. The *Alvis-mál*, a mere collection of synonymes.   The dwarf Alvis has been promised Thor's daughter in marriage, but when he goes to fetch his bride, Thor cunningly detains him all night, by asking him questions concerning the regions, or worlds, he had visited.   Alvis answers by giving the names of the various objects of nature in the respective languages of gods, men, giants, dwarfs and elves; until the morning at length dawns, when the dwarf, being one of those genii who shun the light of day, is obliged to depart without the fair bride whom he expected would have accompanied him.   6. The *Sólar-ljód* (Solar lay); which was obviously written by a Christian, the Trinity being invoked, and a future state being described partly in accordance with Christian doctrines.   This poem, in fact, is generally ascribed to Sæmund himself, who may probably have written it to show that, notwithstanding his love of Heathen literature, he was a very good Christian.   It is, however, a most fortunate circumstance that the sacerdotal proprietor of an Icelandic village was sufficiently enlightened to rescue from approaching oblivion the interesting remains of antiquity which we have given this summary account of.

The Prose, or Younger Edda, is generally ascribed to the celebrated Snorri Sturlason, who was born of a distinguished Icelandic family, in the year 1178, and after leading a turbulent and ambitious life, and being twice the supreme magistrate of the Republic, was killed A. D. 1241 *.   When Snorri

---

* Snorri, at the death of John Loptson, (A. D. 1197,) does not appear to have possessed any property whatever, though he afterwards became the wealthiest man in Iceland.   His rise in the world was chiefly owing to his marriage with Herdisa, the daughter of a priest called Bersi the Rich,—a very enviable surname, which no doubt enabled the Rev. gentleman to brave the decrees of Popes and Councils, and take to himself a wife—who brought him a very considerable fortune.   If we may judge from Snorri's biography, Christianity appears to have effected very little change in the character of the Icelanders.   We have the same turbulent and sanguinary scenes, the same loose conduct of the women, and perfidy, and remorseless cruelty of the men, as in the Pagan times.   Snorri, for instance, after living twenty-five years with Herdisa, obtained a divorce, married a rich heiress, quarrelled with the son and daughter of his first wife respecting pecuniary matters, had a number of illegitimate, or rather adulterine, children, and was finally murdered by three of his sons-in-law and a step-son.   Three of his illegitimate daughters were

was three years old, John Loptson of Oddi, the grandson of
Sæmund the Wise, took him into fosterage. Snorri resided
at Oddi until his twentieth year, and appears to have received
an excellent education from his foster father, who was one of
the most learned men of that period. How far he may have
made use of the manuscripts of Sæmund and Ari, which were
preserved at Oddi, it is impossible to say, neither do we know
the precise contents of these manuscripts; but it is highly
probable that the most important parts of the work, now known
under the title of "The Prose Edda," formed a part of them,
and that Snorri—who may be regarded as the Scandinavian,
Euhemerus—merely added a few chapters, in order to render
the mythology more conformable to the erroneous notions he
appears to have entertained respecting its signification. Be
this as it may, the Prose Edda, in its present form, dates from
the thirteenth century, and consists of—1. *Formáli* (Fore
discourse); or the prologue.. 2. *Gylfa-ginning* (The de-
luding of Gylfi). 3. *Braga-rœður*, (Conversations of Bragi).
4. *Eptirmáli*; (After discourse); or Epilogue. The Prologue
and Epilogue were probably written by Snorri himself, and are
nothing more than an absurd syncretism of Hebrew, Greek,
Roman, and Scandinavian myths and legends, in which Noah,
Priam, Odin, Hector, Thor, Æneas, &c., are jumbled together
much in the same manner as in the romances of the Middle
Ages. These dissertations, utterly worthless in themselves, have
obviously nothing in common with the so-called "Prose Edda,"
the first part of which, containing fifty-three chapters, forms a
complete synopsis of Scandinavian mythology, derived principally from the Poetical Edda, as we shall have occasion to
show in our remarks on the work, to which we refer the
reader *.

married to men of rank, who were, however, obliged to get rid of them, by suing
for legal divorces, on account of their loose conduct. Ingjibjörg. one of these
ladies, married a second time, but was again divorced, and became notorious,
even in Iceland, for her debauchery.—See the Sturlunga-Saga.

* "The Prose Edda" was first published by Resenius, in 1665, but the original Norse text is very inaccurately printed, and the Latin and Danish
translations are, at the present day, quite undeserving of attention. The same
may be said of the Latin version published by Goranson in 1754. In the year
1818, Rask published a very correct edition of the original text, together
with the "Skalda," under the title "Snorra-Edda, ásamt Skáldu og
tharmeð fylgjandi Ritgjörðum."

SKALDIC LITERATURE.

The account which M. Mallet has given of the Skalds *, and the occasional mention we have made of them in the preceding chapters, will render any further remarks superfluous. We shall, therefore, merely observe, that of the 230 Skalds whose names have been preserved, there are probably not half a dozen whose compositions are worth perusing; and even the best of these Skaldic lays are greatly inferior to the Eddaic poems, which are, generally speaking, remarkable for their grandeur of conception, and their noble simplicity of language. Hence we have drawn a broad distinction between *Eddaic* and *Skaldic* literature. The Eddaic poems are the compositions of Sages and Poets; whereas the productions of the Skalds who flourished during the historical period can only be regarded, with a few striking exceptions, the more striking for their rarity, as the mechanical handywork of *verse-smiths;* the term by which these would-be-poets were not inappropriately designated †. One of the latest and most celebrated Skalds was Snorri Sturlason's nephew, Olaf Thordson, surnamed Hvitaskald. It is principally to Olaf that we are indebted for the " Skalda," which is a kind of *ars poetica,* containing—1. A collection of the epithets and far-fetched metaphors employed by the Skalds, illustrated by numerous specimens of their compositions, as well as by a poem written by Snorri, in upwards of a hundred different metres. 2. Various treatises on grammatical and rhetorical figures—on the Roman characters, &c. The " Skalda " has been confounded by most writers with the " Prose Edda," with which

---

* See page 237.

† *Ljóðasmiðir,* literally *Lay-smiths* or *verse-smiths;* though we are perfectly aware that this was a common expression, and not by any means a term of reproach; *smith* being, in fact, used to designate any one who exercised an art, whether merely mechanical or intellectual. An architect, for instance, is still called, in Icelandic, a *House-smith,* (húsasmiðr). But in the tenth and eleventh centuries the Skaldic art was as much a handywork as that of the blacksmith; the latter, however, being of far greater utility. The sturdy blacksmith hammered out iron into horseshoes and ploughshares, the mercenary Skald, in like manner, hammered out far-fetched metaphors into a jingling rhapsody in praise of any one who would amply reward him for his mechanical labour.

it has no further connection than the adventitious one of having been found in the same manuscript. The one is a treatise on Prosody, Rhetoric, &c., the other a Synopsis of Odinic Mythology.

Rask, we believe, had the merit of being the first who clearly showed that the versification of the Anglo-Saxons and ancient Germans was regulated on the same principles as that of the Scandinavians, or in other words, that the same rules of prosody are applicable to all the ancient Teutonic languages. A short account of the structure of Scandinavian (Icelandic) verse may, therefore, not be uninteresting to the English reader; in giving which we shall take Rask for our guide, no one having thrown a greater light on the subject than that truly learned philologist [*].

The chief characteristic of Icelandic versification is its *alliteration*, for which either consonants or vowels may be made use of. All the Icelandic poems are divided into regular strophes. A strophe (*erendi; visa* [†]) has generally eight lines, two of which form a quarter strophe (*visufjórðúngr*) or couplet. Alliteration with consonants requires that three words or accentuated syllables in a couplet have the same initial letters, and that two of these words be placed in the first, and the other in the second line. The initial letter of the latter is called the *höfuðstafr* (headstaff) or *cardinal letter*, the initials of the words placed in the first line being termed *studlar* (props or stays) from their supporting or giving force to the *cardinal letter* on which they are dependant, and of which they may be regarded as the *auxiliaries;* for instance :—

> Farvel fagnaðar
> Fold og heilla [‡].

When the cardinal word begins with a double consonant, as

[*] We have chiefly taken this account from his Icelandic Grammar, Danish edition, Copenhagen, 1811; his Anglo-Saxon Grammar, English edition, by Mr. Thorpe, Copenhagen, 1830; and his Icelandic Prosody, German edition, by Mohnike, Berlin, 1830.

[†] *Erendi, eyrendi*, derived from *ár* a messenger, originally signified a message, a speech delivered; and was afterwards applied to designate a strophe. The English word *errand* is obviously derived from the same source; *visa*, like the German *weise* means the manner, or *wise* of doing a thing; this wise—otherwise.

[‡] Literally, " Farewell joyful land, and blissful" (land).

sp, st, sk, bl, &c., the auxiliary words or syllables must begin in the same manner.

The rule for alliteration with vowels is quite the reverse of the preceding; for although each of the three words must begin with a vowel or diphthong, these vowels, if possible, must not be the same.

The alliterative letters, whether vowels or consonants, "must always be found in those words which have the stress or tone on the syllable that begins with them; but a word may commence with a toneless derivative syllable without disturbing the alliteration. It is, moreover, a rule that, in the two connected lines, there must not be more than three words beginning in this manner; though a toneless prefix or a toneless particle is not considered as any infringement. The *cardinal letter* does not necessarily stand first in the second line, but is often preceded by one or more short words, yet not by such as require the tone or emphasis in reading. These short precursory words, which, though independent of the structure of the verse, are necessary to the completion of the sense, constitute what may be called the *complement*,"* or what is termed in Icelandic the *verse-filling* (mál-fylling).

The most ancient Icelandic (Norse) poetry has only *alliteration*, though at a very early period *Line-rhyme* and *Final-rhyme* were also made use of. *Line-rhyme* is either *consonant* or *assonant*. Consonant or perfect line-rhyme is when two syllables, in the same line, have the vowels and the consonants immediately following them alike; as *sum-ir* and *gum-ar*, *merk-i* and *sterk-a*. Assonant or demi line-rhyme is when the vowels differ, but are followed by the same consonants; as *stird-un* and *nord-an*. Both are generally made use of in the same couplet, the *assonant* for the first, and the *consonant* for the second line; for instance:—

> Fastorðr skyli fírða
> Fengsæll vera thengill †.

Final rhyme is sufficiently known as a characteristic of

---

* Rask's Ang.-Sax. Gram. p. 136. Rask has shown that these rules are equally applicable to Icelandic and Anglo-Saxon versification.

† The king who wishes to keep warriors in his service should perform what he promises. Literally, "word fast should be (that) warriors keep will, the king."

modern versification. In Icelandic poetry it is either mono-
syllabic or dissyllabic; and previous to the sixteenth century
we only find consecutive lines rhymed in this manner, and
never the first line rhyming with the third, and the second
with the fourth, which is frequently the case in modern Icelandic poetry.

The Skalds distinguished upwards of a hundred kinds of
verse, which Rask very properly refers to three principal
classes, termed by him *Narrative verse, Heroic verse*, and
Popular verse. Narrative verse (*fornyðalag*)*, which has
only alliteration, is the oldest, and also the most unrestricted
in its metre, having the greatest *complement*, and frequently
only one *auxiliary letter*. There are several varieties; the
most regular kind is when each line has only two, or when the
second line of a couplet has two, and the first line three long
syllables, each of which, however, " may be followed by one,
two, or even more syllables, provided the natural intonation
in the reading admits of their being pronounced short; but
these long and short syllables do not appear to be arranged
according to other rules than those prescribed by the ear," and
as they have nothing to do with the structure of the verse
" are to be passed over as lightly as possible."† All the
Eddaic poems are in *narrative verse*, twelve of them have
eight-lined strophes, seven are in six-lined strophes, and the
others are in this respect irregular, some of the strophes containing ten and twelve lines; strophes of six and eight lines,
though used in the same poem, being, however, the predominant. In a six-lined strophe, the first and second, and fourth
and fifth lines form regular *couplets*, the third and sixth being
unconnected, and exceeding, in the number of their long syllables, the common measure.

---

* *Forn-yrði*, an old word, an archaism, hence applied to designate the
oldest kind of verse.

† Rask's Ang.-Sax. Gram. p. 146. All the Anglo-Saxon poetry which
has been preserved appears to be in *narrative verse*. The " Vision of Peirce
Plowman," written by Robert Langland in 1359, offers a very regular old
English specimen of this kind of versification; for instance :—

> " I Looked on my Left halfe,
>   as the Lady me taught,
>   and was Ware of a Woman
>   Worthlyith clothed."

Heroic verse (dróttkvæði *) has *alliteration* and *line-rhyme* and a stricter metre, not admitting of a *complement*. It was generally used by the Skalds who flourished after the ninth century for the honorary and encomiastic poems which they composed to celebrate the deeds of the valorous kings and jarls whose courts they frequented, in full expectation, however, of being amply repaid for their effusions.

Popular verse (rúnhende †) has *alliteration* and *final-rhyme* without line-rhyme. It is more regular in its metre than *narrative*, but less restricted than *heroic verse*. It is always in eight-lined strophes, the lines being generally of the same metrical length, and is subdivided into numerous varieties according to the number of accentuated syllables, generally two, three, or four, in each line.

We have refrained from filling our pages with specimens of the different kinds of verse, fearing that the reader would have found them, especially when unaccompanied by alliterative metrical translations, which we had no great inclination to hammer out, totally devoid of interest. A single specimen will probably more than suffice to satisfy his curiosity in this respect. We have selected for this purpose the first and second strophes of Ragnar Lodbrok's famous Death Song, and attempted to render them line for line in the same metre, and with the same alliterative letters ‡ as the original, in order that any of our readers unacquainted with the Old Norse language may form some idea of the rude strains that were jingled on the Skaldic lyre. We must premise that Ragnar Lodbrok was a Danish king of the heroic period, and, consequently, a somewhat problematical personage. In one of his numerous predatory expeditions to the shores of these islands, he is said to have been taken prisoner by Ella, a Northumbrian prince §,

---

* From *drótt*, people, or *drottinn*, chief, hero, lord ; *kvæði*, or kviða, a song.

† From *rune*, which, among its other significations, also means a poem ; poets being sometimes called *Runemen*.

‡ See page 381, for the rule respecting the alliteration of vowels and diphthongs.

§ The northern antiquaries have been very much puzzled to reconcile the *legend* of Ragnar Lodbrok with the *facts* of history. According to the Anglo-Saxon chronicles, Ella usurped the throne of Northumbria in the year 862, whereas Ragnar's death is placed by Suhm—who has brought it down to the latest possible epoch—in 794, and by other writers at a much earlier period.

thrown into a dungeon, and condemned to die by the bite of
vipers. This death song * is alleged to have been composed
by him during his torments, but is probably the composition
of a Skald of the ninth century †. In the first strophe Ragnar relates his expedition to Gothland. Thora, the daughter
of a chieftain of that country, was detained in captivity by an
enormous serpent, and was to become the reward of the daring
champion who should deliver her. Ragnar undertook the task ;
and in order to protect himself from the serpent's venom, put
on shaggy trousers, from which circumstance he was afterwards called Lodbrok (*Shaggy-brogues*) ‡. The poem is in
the *heroic verse*, though not of the most regular description.

Hjuggum vér með Hjörvi !	Hew'd we with the Hanger !
Hitt var ei fyrir laungu,	Hard upon the time 't was,

Scandinavian *history*, as we before observed, only dates from the middle of the
ninth century, prior to which period it is quite useless attempting to discriminate between facts and fiction. We are told, for instance, that Ragnar's
second wife was a lady named Kráka, who, after she had become the mother
of four sons, told her husband that her real name was Aslauga, and that she
was the daughter of Sigurd Fafnisbana ; that is to say, of one of the mythic
heroes of the great Eddaic Epos ! !

* It is called in Norse Lodbrokarkviða (the Song of Lodbrok), and also
Krákumál (the Song of Kráka), the lady of mythic descent mentioned in the
preceding note. Several writers have confounded the Krákumál with the
Bjarkamál, which is a war song, said to have been composed to excite the
courage of Hrolf Kraki's warriors, and attributed to the Skald Bragi the Old.
Be this as it may, the Bjarkamál was no doubt composed prior to the reign
of Harald Hárfagra. Fragments of it have been preserved in the Heimskringla, and the Skalda, and Saxo-Grammaticus has given a Latin paraphrase
of it in his history.

† Professor Rafn—in his excellent critical edition of the Krákumál, published
in 1826—does not hesitate to ascribe part of the poem to Ragnar himself ; but
as our scepticism respecting *heroic history* leads us to question even the
existence of such a personage, we must persist, until we are furnished with
much more conclusive evidence to the contrary than that adduced by the
learned Danish Professor, in regarding it as the rhapsody of a Skald of the
ninth century.

‡ Writers who strive to reconcile fiction with facts, observe that as *Ormr*,
the Norse word for serpent, is also a proper name, the Skald who composed
the poem may have simply designated a chieftain of the name of Ormr under
the allegory of a serpent ; but the manner in which the story is related in
the first chapter of Ragnar Lodbrok's Saga—the serpent gradually growing,
with the gold placed under it, until it at length encircles Thora's virgin
bower as the Midgard serpent the earth—will not admit of this explanation.

er á Gautlandi Gengum
at Grafvitnis * morði;
THá fengum vér THóru,
THaðan hétu mik fyrðar,
thá er Lýngál † um Lagða'k,
Lodbrok : at thví vígi
STakk ek á STorðar-lykkju ‡
STáli bjartra mála.

when in Gothlandia Going
to Give death to the serpent;
THen obtained we THora,
THence have warriors called me,
the Ling-eel since I Laid low,
Lodbrok : at that carnage
STuck I the STealthy monster
with STeel of finest temper.

Hjuggum vér með Hjörvi !
Heldr var ek úngr, thá er skifðum
AUstr í EYrasundi §
Undurn frekum vargi,
ok Fótgulum Fugli;
Fengum vér thar, er súngu
við Háseymda Hjálma
Hörð járn, mikils verðar;
Allr var Ægir sollinn;
Oð hrafn í valblóði.

Hew'd we with the Hanger !
it Hap'd that when I young was
EAst in EYra's channel
OUtpoured we blood for grim wolves,
and golden-Footed Fray birds;
there Found we them, while sung loud
on Highseamed Helmets
Hard iron, food in plenty;
All was Ocean swollen
through OOzed blood went the raven

Finn Magnusen first pointed out the striking resemblance between the ancient Icelandic narrative verse and the hexameter, which is acknowledged to be the oldest national verse of the Hellenic nations; and Rask observes, that " the hexameter seems to be merely a somewhat, though very little, restricted variety of the freer, rougher, and probably elder form exhibited in the narrative verse," and arranges Greek and Latin hexameters chosen at random, according to the rules of narrative verse; for instance, the beginning of the Æneid:—

Arma virumque
cano, Trojæ
qui primus ab oris
Italiam,
fato profugus,
Lavinaque venit
littora; multum
ille et terris
jactatus et alto,

vi superûm,
sævæ memorem
Junonis ob iram
multa quoque
et bello passus,
dum conderet urbem,
inferretque
deos Latio,
genus unde Latinum.

* See the word Grafvitnir in our Glossary to the Prose Edda. The word is used here metaphorically for a serpent.

† Ling-eel, or heath adder ; i. e. serpent.

‡ Storð, the earth ; lykkja, a clasp, lock, buckle ; hence a clasp or ring of the earth, and, figuratively, a serpent.—See the account of the Midgard Serpent in the Prose Edda, chap. 34.

§ The Eyra Sound, or, as we call it, The Sound.

" This decomposition," he observes, "produces neither Pindaric nor Adonic verse, but the Teutonic narrative verse so completely, that in these eighteen verses of Virgil there is not a single deviation from, or fault against, the rules of narrative verse, but the whole reads just as fluently when arranged according to the Icelandic metre, as according to the laws of hexameter. Thus we have in every verse two long syllables or pauses for the voice, each of which is usually followed by one and sometimes two short ones, all the rest of the arrangement is as flowing *fornyrðalag* as any part of the Edda, though the Latin metre is totally subverted. The reverse of the process does not hold good, for narrative verse cannot, by any means, be so easily turned into hexameter; the reason of which is, that the hexameter is subjected to greater restriction, yet it often falls in pretty exactly." As in the Háva-mál, st. 22,

Vesæll | maður ok | illur | skapi | hlær at hvi | vetna *,

"which is a tolerable hexameter; but the alliteration is destroyed by this transformation, as the metre is by the decomposition of the hexameter. Notwithstanding, then, that each of these races (the Teutonic and the so-called Greco-Romanic) has changed this species of verse, according to its own fancy, it nevertheless seems evident that the original idea was the same, and, consequently, that the groundwork of the poetry, no less than of the language itself, was in the beginning common to both." †

SAGA LITERATURE.

We have already had occasion to state in what light we view the Icelandic Sagas ‡, and cannot do better than give the reader a few extracts from Professor Müller's Introduction to his " Sagabibliothek," § which will fully show the importance of these interesting documents.

" The Sagas," says the learned Professor, " present a picture of the public and private life, the feuds and trading

---

* A pitiful and ill-minded man laughs at everything.

† Rask's Anglo-Saxon Grammar, p. 154.

‡ See page 309.

§ We have taken these extracts from the original Danish edition of Professor Müller's admirable work, published in three volumes, Copenhagen, 1820, omitting a few passages which would be uninteresting to the English reader, but giving a full translation of those we have retained.

voyages of the Icelanders, and offer at the same time a sphere
of action that embraces their whole social state, while the
number of these biographies that have been preserved, renders it possible for us to form a perfect notion of Icelandic history from the first colonization of the island down to the present time.   What is derived from such a source may certainly
appear to be of very little utility to other nations.   The active
population of the country did not, in the most flourishing period, amount to more than 3800 men, and the total number of
inhabitants can scarcely ever have reached 100,000.   Separated from the rest of the world by the Northern Ocean, the
Icelanders must, upon the whole, have been prevented from
taking a part in the great events of history.   The island itself,
that has little else to offer than fire and ice, would appear to
other nations to be of importance only as a place of banishment.   But this island possessed in the ninth and tenth centuries two inestimable treasures—civil liberty and security *.
The boldest Northmen were thus induced to seek refuge there,
and for four hundred years it flourished as a free state.   Its
history, in fact, during this period, may in so far be said to
present the image of a perfect commonwealth, that the island
was never subject to attacks from without, but everything,
both the good—the deep-rooted constitution—and the evil—
which at length laid it waste—sprung up within its own limits.

  " In a free state, a concern for the common welfare would
naturally direct public attention to the conduct of each individual chieftain ; hence the curiosity to have an account of each
separate action, the desire to relate such an action, and the endeavour to relate it well.   The art of narration, which at the
frequent Folkmotes and solemn banquets served as a means
of social entertainment, was continually looking out for
fresh materials.   It was in the recollections of the olden time
which the lays of their forefathers had faithfully preserved,
and in the events that took place in the other Northern States—
events which must necessarily have been well known to their
numerous travellers—that the Icelanders sought for these
materials.   The Sagaman was in this manner the narrator of
everything that happened in the north, and as soon as Christianity made him acquainted with the literature of other

* That is to say, when compared with other countries, at the same period.

countrics he became an historian. It is therefore not merely
as a free state, it is as the foster-mother of northern history,
that the Icelandic Republic is of importance to us. Consequently, inasmuch as the investigators of this history bestow
attention on the domestic occurrences of Iceland, will they
not only requite the care with which the early inhabitants of the
island received and preserved so many Sagas relating to the
period of northern heathenism, but will also be rendered more
capable of availing themselves of these documents. It is only
by knowing how these ancient songs and tales became tra-
ditional in the island that we can be fully aware of their possible authenticity. By comparing the numerous narratives concerning Iceland itself with those that relate to the other
Northern States, it will be easier to fix the degree of validity
that may be assigned to the latter. As, moreover, the Sagas
respecting Iceland are not only numerous, but also offer numerous characteristic traits in common, they may be the more
easily compared, their age, both on intrinsic and extrinsic
grounds, decided upon, and the result, thus obtained, applied to
similar memorials.

" But it is in a more immediate manner than this that the
Sagas relating to Iceland will serve to elucidate the history of
the other Northern States ; not merely by the casual connections which Icelandic travellers formed with northern princes,
but more especially by the light which these narratives throw
on the social life of the north in the olden time. Climate
and civil institutions, religion and a maritime life, and, above
all, a common language, united, in heathen times, the various
consanguineous Scandinavian tribes, from the frontiers of
Finmark to those of Holstein, from the Northern Ocean to
the Gulf of Bothnia. We shall consequently find that the
manners and customs of the Norwegian emigrants who first
colonized Iceland were, at that period, common to all the
Scandinavian nations ; but these institutions and customs
were retained in Iceland after they had, in the other states,
undergone considerable changes, caused by the arbitrary power
of the Norwegian kings, and the beneficent influence of Christianity. Temples, in which the gods of Valhalla were worshipped, arose in every part of the island ; the memory of the
heroic races lived in the songs of the Icelandic Skalds, while
the actions of the Danish and Norwegian kings constantly

furnished subjects for poetic imagery. The proceedings of
the Icelandic Things were conducted as of old; the place
where the doom's-men sat was inclosed with the same sacred
cords, the ancient forms were strictly observed, and the Norwegian legislature served as a model for the Icelandic. An
Icelandic chieftain was not much less powerful at a Thing
than a Norwegian sub-king; he lived like a Norwegian herse,
or petty jarl. In Iceland, the whole household dwelt in the
long smoky hall, and the three annual religious festivals and
the public games afforded, as in Norway, the best opportunities
for social intercourse. We may, therefore, often acquire from
these numerous narratives, that lead us, as it were, into the
domestic circle of the old Icelander, and offer the minutest
details respecting the civil institutions of the country, a more
intimate knowledge of northern heathenism than could be obtained from the traditions of the period itself. Fixed points
of comparison may consequently be established which will
enable us to judge, on intrinsic grounds, whether a Saga bears
the stamp of northern antiquity, or is the romantic offspring
of a later age. But if the Sagas that relate to the domestic
occurrences of Iceland serve to elucidate the history of northern heathenism, and to show its predominating spirit, they
will, for the same reason, acquire an importance, not only for
Britons, in whose veins there flows so much Scandinavian
blood, but also for most of the other European nations.
Cimbri and Teutons, Franks and Lombards, Germans and
Goths *, were allied not only in blood, but in bodily and
mental qualities, in manners and customs, in language, and,

---

* It would seem, from this confused and anomalous juxtaposition of Teutonic
tribes, that Professor Müller regarded the Cimbri, Lombards, and Goths, as
belonging to the Scandinavian, and the Teutons, Franks, and Germans to
the Germanic branch of the Teutonic race. Now, in strict language, the term
" Teutons " ought to be applied to all the tribes of the Teutonic race, and the
term " Germans " to all the tribes of the Germanic branch of this race. We
know too little of the Cimbri to say with certainty even to what race, much less
to what branch of a race they belonged, and the Franks, Lombards, and Goths
were tribes of the Alemannic sub-branch of the Teutonic race (see page 30),
though at the period when Professor Müller wrote his work, it was a favourite
theory of Danish and Swedish writers to identify the Mœso-Goths, Ostro-
Goths, Visi-Goths and Lombards with the so-called Goths of Sweden, that
is to say, with the Gothlanders : a theory which at the present day they
would not, even with all their praiseworthy *amor patriæ,* think of main-

without doubt, also in origin, as much so, in fact, as the Do-
rians were with the Ionians. Much of what relates to the
north is therefore applicable to the destroyers of the Roman
Empire, and we shall consequently find that the disputes at
the Icelandic Al-thing will serve to elucidate many of the old
laws and institutions of the states of modern Europe."

After these excellent remarks of the learned Danish Professor, it will only remain for us to point out the different
kinds of Sagas, which we shall venture to classify, as we have
done the Eddaic poems, according to our own notions on the
subject. We think, therefore, that the Sagas are susceptible
of being arranged, as follows :—1. The Mythic-heroic. 2. The
Heroic. 3. The Historical. 4. The Romantic Sagas.

The *Mythic-heroic class* comprises—1. The Volsunga Saga,
Norna Gests Saga, and the Vilkina Saga, in which we have
the same tragical story of the Volsungians and Niflungians,
though in a less mythical form than in the Eddaic Epos.
The Vilkina Saga, being taken from German sources, is more
in accordance with the Nibelungen, and if it stood alone might
be placed in the Romantic class. 2. Fundin Noraegur, relating
to the Fornjòtr or primordial giant dynasty of Norway *.
3. The former part—chapters 1 to 45 inclusive—of the Yng
linga Saga †.

In the *Heroic class* we should place the latter part—chapters
46 to 55 inclusive—of the Ynglinga Saga, and Halfs, Frithiofs
Ragnar Lodbroks, Hrolf Krakis, and Bodvar Bjarkis Sagas,
the personages who figure in them having, in all probability,
actually existed, and performed most of the valorous deeds
attributed to them, but at a period (previous to the middle of
the ninth century) which renders it impossible to discriminate
between facts and fiction.

3. *Historical Sagas.* In this class modern Danish writers
place upwards of 100 Sagas and *Thættir* ‡. It is obvious,
however, that some of these documents are more historical—
more entitled to be regarded as authentic accounts of the

taining. If Professor Müller had merely said Scandinavians and Germans
were allied not only in blood," &c., his observations would have been perfectly correct.

* See the note page 183.

† See page 84.

‡ The plural of *thâttr*, a part, a section ; a term applied to denote a short
memoir, generally taken from a Saga.

transactions recorded than others, though we must not forget
that, with two or three exceptions, the best of them are *Sagas*
and not *Histories*, having been committed to writing from oral
tradition, frequently two, and even three and four centuries
after the events narrated are said to have taken place ; a circumstance which, as we observed in the preceding chapter,
naturally induces us to peruse them with a certain degree of
scepticism.   Considered under this point of view we shall
venture to form two classes or sub-divisions of historical Sagas,
placing in the one what may be termed the *corroborated Sagas*,
or Sagas that, in so far as regards the principal events narrated
in them, can be corroborated by collateral evidence ; and in the
other, the Historical Sagas which only partially admit of this
corroboration, or, in which the few facts recorded are too at-
tenuated with romantic stories to be of any great value.   In
the class of *Corroborated Historical Sagas*, we should be inclined
to place, 1st., from twenty to thirty Sagas relating to Iceland,
the most interesting of which—taken chronologically, not in
respect to the events narrated, but according to the dates when
they were first committed to writing—are the Heidarviga-
saga, Njáls, Eigils, and Kormaks Sagas, the Færeyinga,
Eyrbyggja, Laxdæla, Sturlunga, and Kristni Sagas, and Bishop
Arni's Saga.   The most voluminous of these documents is the
Sturlunga-saga, or story of the Sturla Family (the Sturlungians),
of which Snorri may be regarded as the real founder ; and as the
Saga was written towards the close of the thirteenth century,
and the events brought down to the subversion of the commonwealth in the year 1264, it has a greater claim to historical authenticity than the generality of Icelandic family
memoirs.   The Kristni-saga gives an account of the conversion of the Icelanders to Christianity, and Bishop Arni's Saga
—the biograghy of Arni, Bishop of Skalholt, A. D. 1269–98—
written by a contemporary, probably by one of his chaplains,
contains some interesting details respecting ecclesiastical
affairs.   To these may be added Ari Frodi's *Schedæ* and the
Landnámabók.   The former, which is supposed to be the
earliest document *written* (A. D. 1120) in the Norse language,
is a succinct account, drawn up by Ari hinn Fródi *, of the

---

* *Hinn Fródi* was a title given to men who devoted their lives to study,
especially to the study of history, and means the wise, the learned, the much-
knowing.

principal events that happened in the island, as well as in
Norway, from its first colonization to his own time; the latter,
written towards the close of the thirteenth or the beginning
of the fourteenth century, is a kind of Icelandic doom's-day
book, containing a detailed account of how *the land was taken
possession of* by the first settlers, with the names of 3000 persons and 1400 places.

2nd. The Sagas relating to Greenland and Vinland, which
furnished the materials for our first supplementary chapter.

3rd. Two Sagas, with a few fragments, and Thættir relating
to Denmark; viz., the Jómsvikinga-saga or the story of
Palnatoki's celebrated band of sea-rovers *, and the Knytlinga-
saga, which is a chronicle of the kings who reigned in Denmark from the middle of the tenth to the close of the
thirteenth century.

4th. From twenty-five to thirty Sagas and several *Thættir*
relating to Norway. The most important of these, and indeed
of the whole collection of Icelandic Sagas, are the eighteen
Sagas comprised under the title of "Chronicles of the Kings
of Norway," † which form a consecutive history of the Norwegian sovereigns from the year 841 to the year 1264. The
reign of Hákon Hákonson, the last of the series, (A.D. 1217–
63,) was written by Sturla Thordson, a Sturlungian, and a
celebrated Skald, between the years 1264 and 1271, and as
he had every opportunity afforded him for collecting materials
during his residence at the Norwegian court, his work is fully
entitled to the rank of history. The chronicle of the period
from 1177 to 1217 is the composition of several writers, and,
comparatively speaking, of no great merit. The chronicle of
the kings who reigned from 841 to 1177 inclusive, forms,

---

* See page 139.

† *Noregs Konunga-sögur*, 6 vols. folio. The first and second volumes,
published in 1777 and 1778, were edited by Schöning; the third, published in 1783, which completes the portion known as the *Heimskringla*, was
edited by Skulius Thorlacius; the fourth which appeared in 1813, and the
fifth in 1818, contain the remaining Sagas; and the sixth, published in 1826,
is devoted to explanatory remarks and dissertations. The two last volumes,
and a part of the fourth, were edited by Werlauff and Birgerus Thorlacius.
Since the year 1825, the Royal Society of Northern Antiquaries has published several collections of Sagas—Icelandic, Danish, and Latin editions,
each in twelve volumes octavo, of Sagas recording events that took place out
of Iceland; an edition of the Sagas relating to Iceland, two volumes, octavo;
another of the mythic-heroic Sagas, 3 vols. 8vo., &c.

with the Ynglinga-saga and an introductory chapter, the work known under the name of the "Heimskringla," * which is generally attributed to Snorri Sturlason, though he was probably more its editor than its author, and may have written himself the Ynglinga-saga, which is much on a par with the prologue and epilogue of the Prose Edda, from materials supplied by the Ynglinga-tal, and the Sagas founded on similar Skaldic effusions.

As M. Mallet has devoted a chapter to this part of Snorri's work, and as several of our own writers still imagine that the Icelandic historian had at least a trustworthy tradition for his legend, it may not be irrelevant to remark, in addition to our former observations on the subject †, that the Ynglinga-tal was composed by Thiodolf of Hvina, a celebrated Skald of the ninth century, in honour of Rögnvald, the son of Olaf Geirstad, and his successor to the petty state which fell to Olaf's share on the division of the kingdom of Westfold between him and his brother Halfdan the Black. In this poem Thiodolf, who was no doubt amply rewarded for his ingenuity, did not fail to give his patron a long line of royal ancestors ending in Odinic deities. And it is on such authority as this, on the encomiastic effusions of a mercenary Skald, that the Ynglinga-saga is chiefly founded—a circumstance that will enable the reader to appreciate the value of the erudite dissertations and similar literary rubbish which this Saga has given rise to. The learned, truly learned editors of the "Noregs Konunga-sögur," in their "Disquisitio de Snorronis fontibus et auctoritate," contend that the whole story of the so-called *historical Odin* ‡ was the invention of Snorri himself. The Christian historian, they say, could not represent the celestial beings worshipped by his forefathers as gods, and it being repugnant to his feelings to make them devils, as the monks had done, he transformed them into men endowed with many marvellous qualities, and adopting some of the geographical fables of Jornandes and Paulus Diaconus, whose

---

* Snorri's work obtained the singular title of Heimskringla, the World's Circle, on account of the Ynglinga-saga, which forms the first book, and immediately follows the introductory chapter, beginning with the words, "Sva er sagt at *kringla heimsins,*" it is said that *the circle of the world*——
† See page 84.
‡ Vol. vi. p. 247.

works were *probably* known to him, led his anthropomorphized deities from the Tanaquisl to Scandinavia. They chiefly ground this assumption on the fact that Snorri does not cite a single verse from the Ynglinga-tal in the first thirteen chapters of the Ynglinga-saga, although most of the other chapters rest on the authority of that poem. This argument of the learned editors is, however, by no means conclusive; for Snorri begins to corroborate his statements by quotations from Thiodolf's rhapsody in his fourteenth chapter, in which he relates the death of Fjölnir, the son of Yngvi-Frey, that is to say, of the anthropomorphized sun-god, Frey. These and other quotations from the Ynglinga-tal show, as we before observed, that Thiodolf traced up his patron's ancestors to the Odinic deities In what light he may have regarded these deities it is utterly impossible to say, neither is it worth while hazarding a conjecture on the subject; for, when the whole story of the *historical Odin* is admitted to be mere fiction, it is of very little consequence whether we ascribe this fiction to an ambitious Icelandic chieftain of the thirteenth century, or to a mercenary Skald of the ninth.

In respect to the *historical Sagas* of the Heimskringla, we should not be inclined to go so far as Professor Müller, who contends that Snorri did not even collect the materials for them, but found these materials already collected by his predecessors; nor did he arrange the events chronologically, that having been done by Ari Fródi, to whose chronology he refers; nor narrate them in a more elegant style, for "he narrates events as they had been narrated before his time, without introducing any reflections of his own, nor does his style differ from that of his contemporaries."* Be this as it may, Snorri must have been too much occupied with public affairs and the pursuits of ambition, and too much involved in family feuds, to find time for writing such a voluminous work as the Heimskringla. He probably collected the Sagas, and, after subjecting them to a thorough revision, had them copied by his amanuenses. This might be implied by the expressions "*cause to be written, have written*," which he more than once

* Sagabib. vol. iii. p. 403. Professor Müller also observes, in corroboration of his views, that the title of the Learned (hinn Fródi) was not given to Snorri, although every one who in those ages, and even at a later period, distinguished himself by his historical studies obtained it.

makes use of. At the end of the eighty-seventh chapter of Olaf Tryggvason's Saga, he says, for instance, " what I shall next *have written* will be respecting the Icelanders." * However, in whatever manner he proceeded, Snorri will always be deservedly regarded as the Herodotus of northern history.

Under the head *Uncorroborated* or *partially corroborated Historical Sagas*, we should place from thirty to forty Sagas relating to Iceland, and several Thættir concerning Norwegians.

4th. *Romantic Sagas.* This class comprises about twenty-five Sagas, of which the Hervarar-saga, and Hedin and Hognis-saga, are very good specimens. It may not be irrelevant to observe, that the distinction between a mythic-heroic and a romantic Saga is, that although both may place their heroes in connection with the Odinic deities, the former speaks of these deities as they are represented in the Eddaic Poems whilst the latter mixes them up with the fables and legends of the Middle Ages. These Sagas are, in fact, mediæval romances, and as such, in an historical or ethnological point of view, quite undeserving of attention. The writers of the last century, who were, generally speaking, not aware of this distinction, frequently grounded the most inconclusive arguments on their authority, and still more frequently included all the Icelandic Sagas under some sweeping denunciation, which modern criticism has shown would only be strictly applicable to the romantic class.

We may remark, in conclusion, that Professor Müller has given a list of 119 Icelandic Mediæval Romances which have been translated from foreign languages, French, German, Dutch, Latin, &c., or for which foreign romances supplied the materials. As, for instance, a translation of Gualteri's " Alexandriad," made by Bishop Brand Johnson at the request of King Hákon Hákonson; the story of Virgil (translated from the Dutch), the said Virgil marrying a daughter of the Soldan of Babylon, founding Naples, &c. † With these worthless productions the old Icelandic literature may be said to have reached its term. Its dawn was announced by the significant myths and heroic lays which oral tradition had transmitted

---

* *Næst rita láta,* next let write, cause to be written, are the words he makes use of.

† Sagabib. vol. iii. p. 480.

through the long night of barbarous ages. Developed by the genial influence of that peculiar constitutional freedom which the discussions at the Al-thing gave rise to, it attained its full maturity in the graphic Saga, flourished with the freedom that imparted to it its originality, and with this freedom decayed : the Al-thing degenerating into a Norwegian tribunal, the Saga into a mediæval romance.

With the Reformation began a new epoch—that of modern Icelandic or *Islenzka* literature, which, although it possesses no great claim to originality, has nevertheless produced several writers of considerable eminence. John Vidalin, Bishop of Skalholt, for instance, who died A.D. 1720, has been called the Icelandic Cicero, his sermons being, it is said— for we never had the curiosity to look at them—as remarkable for their elegance of diction, as they are for their learning and Christian piety. And in the present century Espolin has written a very good continuation of the Sturlunga Saga, and Sigurd Pétursson, and John Thorláksson have acquired a deserved celebrity as poets of no ordinary talents; the former, for his original compositions, and the latter, for his elegant translations of Klopstock's " Messiah," Pope's " Essay on Man," and Milton's " Paradise Lost." Modern Icelandic poetry being still a curiosity in this country, we subjoin, as a specimen, a very smooth flowing verse from one of Pétursson's poems, with an accompanying translation, in which we have attempted, though at the risk of making it more like Icelandic than correct English, to preserve the metre, and, as much as possible, also the alliteration of the original.

> " Thá eymdir striða á sorgfullt sinn,
> Og svipur mótgángs um vánga riða,
>   Og bakivendir thér veröldin,
> Og vellyst brosir að thinum kviða :
>   Theink, allt er hnöttótt, og hverfast lætr,
>   Sá hló í dag er á morgun grætr;
>   Alt jafnar sig."

> " When grief oppresses the mournful mind,
> And misery's scourges the pale cheeks furrow,
>   And back the world on thee wends unkind,
> And wanton joyaunce derides thy sorrow;
>   Think, all is round, and will turn anew,
>   Who laughs to-day may to-morrow rue;
>   All 's equalized."

THE PROSE EDDA.

PRELIMINARY OBSERVATIONS BY THE EDITOR.

It was our intention to have merely revised the translation of the "Prose Edda" given in Bishop Percy's edition of M. Mallet's Work, but, on comparing it with the Old Norse text, we found that a number of important passages had been omitted, and others rendered not only quite contrary to the spirit, but also to the sense of the original. In fact this could not be otherwise, for Mallet appears to have made his translation from the erroneous Latin version published by Resenius in the year 1665, and Bishop Percy expressly states that he merely turned Mallet's French translation into English, occasionally consulting Goranson's Latin version, which is not much better than that of Resenius. Under these untoward circumstances, it is a wonder that the English translation was not more incorrect than we found it to be. We have, however, naturally been obliged to subject it to a thorough revision, in fact, to retranslate the work ; a diligent comparison of Bishop Percy's text, with the Old Norse text of Rask's edition *, only allowing us to retain here and there passages conveying the true meaning of the original. We have also inserted the passages omitted, and given most of the extracts from the Elder Edda in a metre resembling the *narrative verse*, in which all the Eddaic poems are composed †, though without attempting to preserve the alliteration. Neither Mallet nor Bishop Percy deemed the Prologue and Epilogue worth translating, and, as we fully agree with them in this respect ‡, we have not disfigured our pages by reproducing these absurd productions, which, it is needless to say, throw not the least light on the subject they were intended to elucidate.

Each editor and translator of the Prose Edda having divided the work into chapters with suitable titles conformable to his own views, we have also taken the same liberty. In Rask's edition of the original text the chapters are without titles, and follow each other as paragraphs, the work being in fact divided into two chapters (parts), one containing fifty-three and the other four paragraphs, but as references to the Prose Edda are now generally made according to the enumeration of the chapters or paragraphs of Rask's edition, we have retained this enumeration, and not numbered our own divisions.

To each of the chapters into which he divided the work, M. Mallet added numerous "Notes," which were, however, but too frequently grounded on the most erroneous notions respecting Scandinavian mythology, owing, in some measure, to the ingenious author having adopted the crude theories of Cluverius and Pelloutier, on the origin of the Teutonic and Celtic nations §. Such of these Notes that are still of any value will be given after our "Critical Examination of the Leading Doctrines of the Scandinavian System of Mythology," and referred to in the text by letters in brackets. Many of them reflect great credit on M. Mallet's judgment, especially when we consider the period when they were written.

* Published at Stockholm in 1818.—See page 378.   † See page 382.
‡ See page 378.   § See Bishop Percy's Preface.

PART THE FIRST,

THE DELUDING OF GYLFI.

(GYLFA-GINNING.)

GEFJON'S PLOUGHING. *

1. KING GYLFI ruled over the land which is now called Svithiod
(Sweden). It is related of him that he once gave a wayfaring
woman, as a recompense for her having diverted him, as much
land in his realm as she could plough with four oxen in a day
and a night. This woman was, however, of the race of the
Æsir, and was called Gefjon. She took four oxen from the
north, out of Jötunheim, (but they were the sons she had had
with a giant,) and set them before a plough. Now the plough
made such deep furrows that it tore up the land, which the
oxen drew westward out to sea until they came to a sound.
There Gefjon fixed the land, and called it Sælund. And the
place where the land had stood became water, and formed a
lake which is now called "The Water" (Laugur), and the
inlets of this lake correspond exactly with the headlands of
Sealund. As Skald Bragi the Old saith:—

> "Gefjon drew from Gylfi,
> Rich in stored up treasure,
> The land she joined to Denmark.
> Four heads and eight eyes bearing,
> While hot sweat trickled down them,
> The oxen dragged the reft mass
> That formed this winsome island."

---

* This chapter is probably the interpolation of an early copyist, for it has
evidently no connection with the following one, and is not found in the
Upsal MS. of the Prose Edda, which is supposed to be the oldest extant.
Gefjon's ploughing is obviously a mythic way of accounting for some convulsion of nature, perhaps the convulsion that produced the Sound, and thus
effected a junction between the Baltic and the Northern Ocean.

GYLFI'S JOURNEY TO ASGARD.

2. King Gylfi was renowned for his wisdom and skill in magic [A]. He beheld with astonishment that whatever the Æsir willed took place; and was at a loss whether to attribute their success to the superiority of their natural abilities, or to a power imparted to them by the mighty gods whom they worshipped. To be satisfied in this particular, he resolved to go to Asgard, and, taking upon himself the likeness of an old man, set out on his journey. But the Æsir, being too well skilled in divination not to foresee his design, prepared to receive him with various illusions. On entering the city Gylfi saw a very lofty mansion, the roof of which, as far as his eye could reach, was covered with golden shields. Thiodolf of Hvina thus alludes to Valhalla being roofed with shields.

> " Warriors all care-worn,
> (Stones had poured upon them),
> On their backs let glisten
> Valhalla's golden shingles."

At the entrance of the mansion Gylfi saw a man who amused himself by tossing seven small-swords in the air, and catching them as they fell, one after the other. This person having asked his name, Gylfi said that he was called Gangler, and that he came from a long journey, and begged for a night's lodging. He asked, in his turn, to whom this mansion belonged. The other told him that it belonged to their king, and added, " But I will lead thee to him, and thou shalt thyself ask him his name." So saying, he entered the hall, and as Gylfi followed the door banged to behind him. He there saw many stately rooms crowded with people, some playing, some drinking, and others fighting with various weapons. Gangler, seeing a multitude of things, the meaning of which he could not comprehend, softly pronounced the following verse (from the Háva-mál, st. i.):—

> " Scan every gate
> Ere thou go on,
> With greatest caution;
> For hard to say 'tis
> Where foes are sitting
> In this fair mansion."

He afterwards beheld three thrones raised one above another, with a man sitting on each of them [B]. Upon his asking what the names of these lords might be, his guide answered: " He who sitteth on the lowest throne is a king; his name is Har (the High or Lofty One); the second is Jafnhar (*i. e.* equal to the High); but he who sitteth on the highest throne is called Thridi (the Third)." Har, perceiving the stranger, asked him what his errand was, adding that he should be welcome to eat and drink without cost, as were all those who remained in Háva Hall. Gangler said he desired first to ascertain whether there was any person present renowned for his wisdom.

" If thou art not the most knowing," replied Har, " I fear thou wilt hardly return safe. But go, stand there below, and propose thy questions, here sits one who will be able to answer them."

OF THE SUPREME DEITY.

3. Gangler thus began his discourse :—" Who is the first, or eldest of the gods?"

" In our language," replied Har, " he is called Alfadir (All-Father, or the Father of All); but in the old Asgard he had twelve names."*

" Where is this God?" said Gangler; " what is his power? and what hath he done to display his glory?" [C]

" He liveth," replied Har, " from all ages, he governeth all realms, and swayeth all things great and small."

" He hath formed," added Jafnhar, " heaven and earth, and the air, and all things thereunto belonging."

" And what is more," continued Thridi, " he hath made man, and given him a soul which shall live and never perish though the body shall have mouldered away, or have been burnt to ashes. And all that are righteous shall dwell with him in the place called Gimli, or Vingólf; but the wicked

---

As lists of names are frequently given in the Edda, and only serve to interrupt the text, we shall place them in notes, and refer the reader to the Glossary for their signification. The names here enumerated are :—1. Alfadir. 2. Herjan. 3. Hnikar, or Nikar. 4. Nikuz, or Hnikudr. 5. Fjölnir. 6. Oski. 7. Omi. 8. Biflindi. 9. Svidr. 10. Svidrir. 11. Vidrir. 12. Jálk.

shall go to Hel, and thence to Niflhel, which is below, in the
ninth world."

"And where did this god remain before he made heaven
and earth?" asked Gangler.

"He was then," replied Har, "with the Hrimthursar." *

OF THE PRIMORDIAL STATE OF THE UNIVERSE.

4. "But with what did he begin, or what was the beginning
of things?" demanded Gangler.

"Hear," replied Har, "what is said in the Völuspá.

> " ' 'Twas time's first dawn,
> When nought yet was,
> Nor sand nor sea,
> Nor cooling wave;
> Earth was not there,
> Nor heaven above.
> Nought save a void
> And yawning gulf.
> But verdure none.' "

"Many ages before the earth was made," added Jafnhar,
"was Niflheim formed, in the middle of which lies the spring
called Hvergelmir, from which flow twelve rivers †, Gjöll
being the nearest to the gate of the abode of death."

"But, first of all," continued Thridi, "there was in the
southern region (sphere) the world called Muspell. It is a
world too luminous and glowing to be entered by those who
are not indigenous there ‡. He who sitteth on its borders
(or the land's-end) to guard it is named Surtur. In his hand
he beareth a flaming falchion, and at the end of the world
shall issue forth to combat, and shall vanquish all the gods,
and consume the universe with fire. As it is said in the
Völuspa—

---

* Rime Giants, or Giants of the Frost.

† Viz., Svaul, Gunnthrá, Fjörm, Fimbul, Thulr, Slith, Hrith, Sylgr,
Ylgr, Vith, Leiptur and Gjöll.

‡ Literally, "It is light and hot, insomuch so that it is flaming and
burning, and it is impervious to those who are outlandish (foreign), and not
indigenous there" (or who have no home or heritage therein).

> " ' Surtur from the south wends
>   With seething fire
>   The falchion of the mighty one,
>   A sun-light flameth *.
>   Mountains together dash,
>   Giants headlong rush,
>   Men tread the paths to Hel,
>   And Heaven in twain is rent.' "

ORIGIN OF THE HRIMTHURSAR, OR FROST-GIANTS.

5. " Tell me," said Gangler, " what was the state of things ere the races mingled, and nations came into being."

" When the rivers that are called Elivagar had flowed far from their sources," replied Har, " the venom which they rolled along hardened, as does dross that runs from a furnace, and became ice. When the rivers flowed no longer, and the ice stood still, the vapour arising from the venom gathered over it, and froze to rime, and in this manner were formed, in Ginnungagap, many layers of congealed vapour, piled one over the other."

" That part of Ginnungagap," added Jafnhar, " that lies towards the north was thus filled with heavy masses of gelid vapour and ice, whilst everywhere within were whirlwinds and fleeting mists. But the southern part of Ginnungagap was lighted by the sparks and flakes that flew into it from Muspellheim."

" Thus," continued Thridi, " whilst freezing cold and gathering gloom proceeded from Niflheim, that part of Ginnungagap looking towards Muspellheim was filled with glowing radiancy, the intervening space remaining calm and light as wind-still air. And when the heated blast met the gelid

---

* The sense of this half-strophe is very obscure. Finn Magnusen renders it by, " *Surtur e meridie procedit advehens flagrantem flammam, sol resplendet e gladio cœlestis Dei.*" Jacob Grimm, (Deut. Mythol. p. 770,) by " *Surtus tendit ab austro cum vimine gigas, splendet e gladio (ejus) sol deorum,*" and concludes that Surtur is here expressly called a giant. As neither of these interpretations appears to us quite clear, and as that of Grimm would completely upset a very elaborate theory, we have purposely abstained from calling Surtur either giant or god—*mighty one,* being applicable to both, appearing to us, so long as the question is *sub judice,* the best designation.

vapour it melted it into drops, and, by the might of him who sent the heat [D], these drops quickened into life, and took a human semblance. The being thus formed was named Ymir, but the Frost-giants call him Örgelmir. From him descend the race of the Frost-giants (Hrimthursar), as it is said in the Völuspá, 'From Vidolf come all witches; from Vilmeith all wizards; from Svarthöfdi all poison-seethers; and all giants from Ymir.' And the giant Vafthrúdnir, when Gangrad asked, 'Whence came Örgelmir the first of the sons of giants?' answered, 'The Elivagar cast out drops of venom that quickened into a giant. From him spring all our race, and hence are we so strong and mighty.'"

"How did the race of Ymir spread itself?" said Gangler; "or dost thou believe that this giant was a god?"

"We are far from believing him to have been a god," replied Har, "for he was wicked as are all of his race, whom we call Frost-giants. And it is said that, when Ymir slept, he fell into a sweat, and from the pit of his left arm was born a man and a woman, and one of his feet engendered with the other a son, from whom descend the Frost-giants, and we therefore call Ymir the old Frost-giant" [E].

OF THE COW AUDHUMLA, AND THE BIRTH OF ODIN.

6. "Where dwelt Ymir, and on what did he live?" asked Gangler.

"Immediately after the gelid vapours had been resolved into drops," replied Har, "there was formed out of them the cow named Audhumla. Four streams of milk ran from her teats, and thus fed she Ymir."

"But on what did the cow feed?" said Gangler.

"The cow," answered Har, "supported herself by licking the stones that were covered with salt and hoar frost. The first day that she licked these stones there sprung from them, towards evening, the hairs of a man, the second day a head, and on the third an entire man, who was endowed with beauty, agility, and power [F]. He was called Bur, and was the father of Bör, who took for wife Besla, the daughter of the giant Bölthorn. And they had three sons, Odin, Vili, and Ve; and it is our belief that this Odin, with his brothers, ruleth both heaven and earth, and that Odin is his true name, and that he is the most mighty of all the gods " [G].

HOW THE SONS OF BÖR SLEW YMIR AND FROM HIS BODY MADE HEAVEN AND EARTH.

7 " Was there," asked Gangler, "any kind of equality, or any degree of good understanding between these two races?"

" Far from it," replied Har; " for the sons of Bör slew the giant Ymir, and when he fell there ran so much blood from his wounds, that the whole race of Frost-giants was drowned in it, except a single giant, who saved himself with his household. He is called by the giants Bergelmir. He escaped by going on board his bark, and with him went his wife, and from them are descended the Frost-giants. As it is said *—

> " ' Ages past counting
> Ere the earth was yet formed,
> Was born Bergelmir :
> Full well I remember,
> How this crafty giant
> Secure in his skiff lay.' "

8 " And what became of the sons of Bör, whom ye look upon as gods?" said Gangler.

" To relate this," replied Har, " is no trivial matter. They dragged the body of Ymir into the middle of Ginnungagap, and of it formed the earth. From Ymir's blood they made the seas and waters ; from his flesh the land ; from his bones the mountains; and his teeth and jaws, together with some bits of broken bones, served them to make the stones and pebbles."

" With the blood that ran from his wounds," added Jafnhar, " they made the vast ocean, in the midst of which they fixed the earth, the ocean encircling it as a ring, and hardy will he be who attempts to pass those waters " [H].

" From his skull," continued Thridi, " they formed the heavens, which they placed over the earth, and set a dwarf at the corner of each of the four quarters. These dwarfs are called East, West, North, and South. They afterwards took the wandering sparks and red hot flakes that had been cast out of Muspellheim, and placed them in the heavens, both above

* In Vafthrúdnis-mál, st. 35.

and below, to give light unto the world, and assigned to every other errant coruscation a prescribed locality and motion. Hence it is recorded in ancient lore that from this time were marked out the days, and nights, and seasons [I]. As is said in the Völuspá—

> " ' The sun that knew not
> Where was *her* home ;
> The moon that knew not
> What was *his* power ;
> The stars that knew not
> Their dwelling place.' *

" Such are the events that took place ere the earth obtained the form it now beareth."

" Truly great were the deeds ye tell me of ! " exclaimed Gangler ; " and wondrous in all its parts is the work thereby accomplished. But how is the earth fashioned ? "

" It is round without," replied Har, " and encircled by the deep ocean, the outward shores of which were assigned for a dwelling to the race of giants. But within, round about the earth, they (the sons of Bör) raised a bulwark against turbulent giants, employing for this structure Ymir's eyebrows [J]. To this bulwark they gave the name of Midgard †. They afterwards tossed Ymir's brains into the air, and they became the clouds, for thus we find it recorded ‡.

" Of Ymir's flesh was formed the earth ; of his sweat (blood), the seas ; of his bones, the mountains ; of his hair, the trees ; of his skull, the heavens ; but with his eyebrows the blithe gods built Midgard for the sons of men, whilst from his brains the lowering clouds were fashioned."

OF THE FORMATION OF THE FIRST MAN AND WOMAN.

9. " To make heaven and earth, to fix the sun and the moon in the firmament, and mark out the days and seasons, were, indeed, important labours," said Gangler ; " but whence came the men who at present dwell in the world ? "

" One day," replied Har, " as the sons of Bör were walking

---

* In the Norse, as in the German language, the sun is of the feminine, and the moon of the masculine gender.
† More properly speaking, to the earth which it encircled.
‡ In Grímnis-mál, s. 40.

along the sea-beach they found two stems of wood, out of which they shaped a man and a woman. The first (Odin) infused into them life and spirit; the second (Vili) endowed them with reason and the power of motion; the third (Ve) gave them speech and features, hearing and vision. The man they called Ask, and the woman, Embla. From these two descend the whole human race, whose assigned dwelling was within Midgard. Then the sons of Bör built in the middle of the universe the city called Asgard, where dwell the gods and their kindred, and from that abode work out so many wondrous things, both on the earth and in the heavens above it. There is in that city a place called Hlidskjálf, and when Odin is seated there on his lofty throne he sees over the whole world, discerns all the actions of men, and comprehends whatever he contemplates. His wife is Frigga, the daughter of Fjörgyn, and they and their offspring form the race that we call the Æsir, a race that dwells in Asgard the old, and the regions around it, and that we know to be entirely divine. Wherefore Odin may justly be called All-father, for he is verily the father of all, of gods as well as of men, and to his power all things owe their existence. Earth is his daughter and his wife, and with her he had his first-born son, Asa-Thor, who is endowed with strength and valour, and therefore quelleth he everything that hath life " [K].

OF NIGHT AND DAY.

10. " A giant called Njörvi," continued Har, " who dwelt in Jötunheim, had a daughter called Night (Nótt) who, like all her race, was of a dark and swarthy complexion. She was first wedded to a man called Naglfari, and had by him a son named Aud, and afterwards to another man called Annar, by whom she had a daughter called Earth (Jörd). She then espoused Delling, of the Æsir race, and their son was Day, (Dagr) a child light and beauteous like his father. Then took All-father, Night, and Day, her son, and gave them two horses and two cars, and set them up in the heavens that they might drive successively one after the other, each in twelve hours' time, round the world. Night rides first on her horse called Hrimfaxi, that every morn, as he ends his course, bedews the earth with the foam that falls from his bit. The

horse made use of by Day is named Skinfaxi, from whose mane is shed light over the earth and the heavens " [L].

OF THE SUN AND MOON.

11. " How doth All-father regulate the course of the sun and moon? " said Gangler.

" There was formerly a man," replied Har, "named Mundil-fari, who had two children so lovely and graceful, that he called the male, Máni (moon), and the female, Sól (sun), who espoused the man named Glenur.   But the gods being incensed at Mundilfari's presumption took his children and placed them in the heavens, and let Sól drive the horses that draw the car of the sun, which the gods had made to give light to the world out of the sparks that flew from Muspell-heim.   These horses are called Arvak and Alsvid, and under their withers the gods placed two skins filled with air to cool and refresh them, or, according to some ancient traditions, a refrigerant substance called *ísarnkul* *.   Máni was set to guide the moon in his course, and regulate his increasing and waning aspect.   One day he carried off from the earth two children, named Bil and Hjuki, as they were returning from the spring called Byrgir, carrying between them the bucket called Sægr, on the pole Simul.   Vidfinn was the father of these children, who always follow Máni (the moon), as we may easily observe even from the earth."

OF THE WOLVES THAT PURSUE THE SUN AND MOON.

12. " But the sun," said Gangler, " speeds at such a rate as if she feared that some one was pursuing her for her de-struction."

" And well she may," replied Har, "for he that seeks her is not far behind, and she has no way to escape than to run before him."

" But who is he," asked Gangler, " that causes her this anxiety? "

" There are two wolves," answered Har; " the one called Sköll pursues the sun, and it is he that she fears, for he shall one day overtake and devour her; the other, called Hati, the

* A ferreous or glacial refrigeration.

son of Hrodvitnir, runs before her, and as eagerly pursues the moon that will one day be caught by him " [M].

" Whence come these wolves ?" asked Gangler.

" A hag," replied Har, " dwells in a wood, to the eastward of Midgard, called Járnvid, (the Iron Wood,) which is the abode of a race of witches called Járnvidjur. This old hag is the mother of many gigantic sons, who are all of them shaped like wolves, two of whom are the wolves thou askest about. There is one of that race, who is said to be the most formidable of all, called Mánagarm : he will be filled with the life-blood of men who draw near their end, and will swallow up the moon, and stain the heavens and the earth with blood. Then shall the sun grow dim, and the winds howl tumultuously to and fro. As it is said in the Völuspá—

> " ' Eastward in the Iron-wood
> The old one sitteth,
> And there bringeth forth
> Fenrir's fell kindred.
> Of these, one, the mightiest,
> The moon's devourer,
> In form most fiend-like,
> And filled with the life-blood
> Of the dead and the dying,
> Reddens with ruddy gore
> The seats of the high gods.
> Then shall the sunshine
> Of summer be darkened,
> And fickle the weather.
> Conceive ye this or not ? ' "

OF THE WAY THAT LEADS TO HEAVEN.

13. " I must now ask," said Gangler, " which is the path leading from earth to heaven ?"

" That is a senseless question," replied Har, with a smile of derision. " Hast thou not been told that the gods made a bridge from earth to heaven, and called it Bifröst ? Thou must surely have seen it; but, perhaps, thou callest it the rainbow. It is of three hues, and is constructed with more art than any other work   But, strong though it be, it will be broken to pieces when the sons of Muspell, after having traversed great rivers, shall ride over it."

"Methinks," said Gangler, "the gods could not have been in earnest to erect a bridge so liable to be broken down, since it is in their power to make whatever they please."

"The gods," replied Har, "are not to be blamed on that account; Bifröst is of itself a very good bridge, but there is nothing in nature that can hope to make resistance when the sons of Muspell sally forth to the great combat."

THE GOLDEN AGE.

"What did All-father do after Asgard was made?" demanded Gangler.

"In the beginning," answered Har, "he appointed rulers, and bade them judge with him the fate of men, and regulate the government of the celestial city. They met for this purpose in a place called Idavöll, which is in the centre of the divine abode. Their first work was to erect a court or hall wherein are twelve seats for themselves, besides the throne which is occupied by All-father. This hall is the largest and most magnificent in the universe, being resplendent on all sides, both within and without, with the finest gold. Its name is Gladsheim. They also erected another hall for the sanctuary of the goddesses. It is a very fair structure, and called by men Vingólf. Lastly they built a smithy, and furnished it with hammers, tongs, and anvils, and with these made all the other requisite instruments, with which they worked in metal, stone and wood, and composed so large a quantity of the metal called gold that they made all their moveables of it. Hence that age was named the Golden Age. This was the age that lasted until the arrival of the women out of Jötunheim, who corrupted it."

ORIGIN OF THE DWARFS.

"Then the gods, seating themselves upon their thrones, distributed justice, and bethought them how the dwarfs had been bred in the mould of the earth, just as worms are in a dead body. It was, in fact, in Ymir's flesh that the dwarfs were engendered, and began to move and live. At first they were only maggots, but by the will of the gods they at length partook both of human shape and understanding, although they always dwell in rocks and caverns.

" Modsognir and Durin are the principal ones. As it is said in the Völuspá—

> " ' Then went the rulers there,
> All gods most holy,
> To their seats aloft,
> And counsel together took,
> Who should of dwarfs
> The race then fashion,
> From the livid bones
> And blood of the giant.
> Modsognir, chief
> Of the dwarfish race,
> And Durin too
> Were then created.
> And like to men
> Dwarfs in the earth
> Were formed in numbers
> As Durin ordered." ' *

OF THE ASH YGGDRASILL, MIMIR'S WELL, AND THE NORNS OR DESTINIES.

15. " Where," asked Gangler, " is the chief or holiest seat of the gods ? "

"It is under the ash Yggdrasill," replied Har, " where the gods assemble every day in council " [N].

* In order not to interrupt the text by a mere enumeration of names, we subjoin what follows.

The names of these dwarfs are—Nýi, and Nidi, Nordri and Sudri, Austri and Vestri, Althjófr, Dvalinn, Nár, Nain, Nipingr, Dáinn, Bivaur, Bavaur, Baumbur, Nori, An, Annar, Oinn, Mjödvitnir, Veigur, Gandálfr, Vindálfr, Thorinn, Fili, Kili, Fundinn, Náli, Thrór, Throinn, Thekkr, Litur, Vitur, Nýr, Nýrádr, Regin and Rádsvithr.

The above-mentioned dwarfs dwell in the earth, but the following in rocks.

Draupnir, Dólgthrasir, Hárr, Högstari, Hljódálfr, Glóinn, Dori, Ori, Dúfr, Anvari, Hepti, Fili, Hárr and Sjarr.

Others came from Svarin's Barrow (or rocky mountain) to Aurvánga in Joruvalla, and from them are the Lovar sprung, whose names are as follows :— Skirfir, Virfir, Skafidr, Ai, Alfr, Yngvi, Eikinskjalldi, Fjalar, Frosti, Fith, and Ginnar.

"What is there remarkable in regard to that place?" said Gangler.

"That ash," answered Jafnhar, "is the greatest and best of all trees. Its branches spread over the whole world, and even reach above heaven. It has three roots very wide asunder. One of them extends to the Æsir, another to the Frost-giants in that very place where was formerly Ginnungagap, and the third stands over Niflheim, and under this root, which is constantly gnawed by Nidhögg, is Hvergelmir But under the root that stretches out towards the Frost-giants there is Mimir's well, in which wisdom and wit lie hidden. The owner of this well is called Mimir. He is full of wisdom, because he drinks the waters of the well from the horn Gjöll every morning. One day All-father came and begged a draught of this water, which he obtained, but was obliged to leave one of his eyes as a pledge for it. As it is said in the Völuspá—

> " ' All know I, Odin!
> How thou hiddest thine eye
> In Mimir's well-spring
> Of limpid water.
> Mead quaffs Mimir
> Each morn from the pledge
> Valfadir left him.
> Conceive ye this or not?'

"The third root of the ash is in heaven, and under it is the holy Urdar-fount. 'Tis here that the gods sit in judgment. Every day they ride up hither on horseback over Bifröst, which is called the Æsir Bridge. These are the names of the horses of the Æsir. Sleipnir is the best of them; he has eight legs, and belongs to Odin. The others are Gladr, Gyllir, Glær, Skeidbrimir, Silfrintoppr, Sýnir, Gils, Falhófnir, Gulltoppr, and Léttfeti. Baldur's horse was burnt with his master's body. As for Thor, he goes on foot, and is obliged every day to wade the rivers called Körmt and Œrmt, and two others called Kérlaung.

"Through these shall Thor wade every day, as he fares to the doomstead under Yggdrasill's ash, else the Æsir Bridge would be in flames, and boiling hot would become the holy waters."*

" But tell me," said Gangler, " does fire burn over Bi-fröst ?"

" That," replied Har, " which thou seest red in the bow, is burning fire; for the Frost-giants and the Mountain-giants would go up to heaven by that bridge if it were easy for every one to walk over it. There are in heaven many goodly home-steads, and none without a celestial ward. Near the foun tain, which is under the ash, stands a very beauteous dwelling, out of which go three maidens, named Urd, Verdandi, and Skuld †. These maidens fix the lifetime of all men, and are called Norns. But there are, indeed, many other Norns, for, when a man is born, there is a Norn to determine his fate. Some are known to be of heavenly origin, but others belong to the races of the elves and dwarfs ; as it is said—

" 'Methinks the Norns were born far asunder, for they are not of the same race. Some belong to the Æsir, some to the Elves, and some are Dvalin's daughters.''

" But if these Norns dispense the destinies of men," said Gangler, " they are, methinks, very unequal in their distri-bution; for some men are fortunate and wealthy, others acquire neither riches nor honours, some live to a good old age, while others are cut off in their prime."

" The Norns," replied Har, " who are of a good origin, are good themselves, and dispense good destinies. But those men to whom misfortunes happen ought to ascribe them to the evil Norns."

16. " What more wonders hast thou to tell me," said Gangler, " concerning the ash ?"

" What I have further to say respecting it," replied Har, " is, that there is an eagle perched upon its branches who knows many things : between his eyes sits the hawk called Vedurfölnir. The squirrel named Ratatösk runs up and down the ash, and seeks to cause strife between the eagle and Nidhögg. Four harts run across the branches of the tree, and bite the buds. They are called Dáinn, Dvalinn,

---

* i. e. If Thor drove over Bifröst with his thunder chariot. The passage cited is the 29th s. of Grímnis-mál.

† i. e. Present, Past, and Future ; see these words in the Glossary.

Duneyr, and Durathrór. But there are so many snakes with Nidhögg in Hvergelmir that no tongue can recount them. As it is said *—

> " ' Yggdrasill's ash
> More hardship bears
> Than men imagine ;
> The hart bites above,
> At the sides it rots,
> Below gnaws Nidhögg.'

" And again—

> " ' More serpents lie
> Under Yggdrasill's ash
> Than simpletons think of ;
> Góinn and Móinn,
> The sons of Grafvitnir,
> Grábak and Gráfjöllud,
> Ofnir and Svafnir,
> Must for aye, methinks,
> Gnaw the roots of that tree.

" It is also said that the Norns who dwell by the Urdar-fount draw every day water from the spring, and with it and the clay that lies around the fount sprinkle the ash, in order that its branches may not rot and wither away. This water is so holy that everything placed in the spring becomes as white as the film within an egg-shell. As it is said in the Völuspá—

> " ' An Ash know I standing,
> Named Yggdrasill,
> A stately tree sprinkled
> With water the purest ;
> Thence come the dewdrops
> That fall in the dales ;
> Ever blooming, it stands
> O'er the Urdar-fountain.'

" The dew that falls thence on the earth men call honey-dew, and it is the food of the bees. Two fowls are fed in the Urdar-fount ; they are called swans, and from them are descended all the birds of this species."

* In Grímnis-mál, st. 34 and 35.

OF THE VARIOUS CELESTIAL REGIONS.

17. " Thou tellest me many wonderful things of heaven,"
said Gangler, " but what other homesteads are to be seen
there ? "

" There are many other fair homesteads there," replied
Har; " one of them is named Elf-home (Alfheim) [o], wherein
dwell the beings called the Elves of Light; but the Elves of
Darkness live under the earth, and differ from the others still
more in their actions than in their appearance. The Elves of
Light are fairer than the sun, but the Elves of Darkness blacker
than pitch. There is also a mansion called Breidablik, which
is not inferior to any other in beauty; and another named
Glitnir, the walls, columns and beams of which are of ruddy
gold, and the roof of silver. There is also the stead called
Himinbjörg, that stands on the borders where Bifröst touches
heaven, and the stately mansion belonging to Odin, called
Valaskjálf, which was built by the gods, and roofed with pure
silver, and in which is the throne called Hlidskjálf. When
All-father is seated on this throne, he can see over the whole
world. On the southern edge of heaven is the most beautiful
homestead of all, brighter than the sun itself. It is called
Gimli, and shall stand when both heaven and earth have
passed away, and good and righteous men shall dwell therein
for everlasting ages. It is thus spoken of in the Völuspá :—

> " ' A hall sees she standing,
> Than the sun fairer,
> With its glittering gold roof
> Aloft in Gimli.
> All men of worth
> Shall there abide,
> And bliss enjoy
> Through countless ages.' "

" But what will preserve this abode when Surtur's fire con
sumes heaven and earth ? " said Gangler.

" We are told," replied Har, " that towards the south there
is another heaven above this called Andláng, and again above
this a third heaven called Vidbláin. In this last, we think
Gimli must be seated, but we deem that the Elves of Light
abide in it now."

OF THE WIND AND THE SEASONS.

18. " Tell me," said Gangler, " whence comes the wind, which is so strong, that it moves the ocean and fans fire to flame, yet, strong though it be, no mortal eye can discern it? wonderfully, therefore, must it be shapen."

" I can tell thee all about it," answered Har; " thou must know that at the northern extremity of the heavens sits a giant called Hræsvelgur, clad with eagles' plumes. When he spreads out his wings for flight, the winds arise from under them. Thus is it said * :

> " ' Hræsvelgur's the giant,
> Who on heaven's edge sits
> In the guise of an eagle ;
> And the winds, it is said,
> Rush down on the earth
> From his outspreading pinions.' "

19. " Tell me further," said Gangler, " why the summer should be hot, and the winter cold."

" A wise man would not ask such a question, which every one could answer," replied Har ; " but, if thou hast been so dull as not to have heard the reason, I will rather forgive thee for once asking a foolish question than suffer thee to remain any longer in ignorance of what ought to have been known to thee. The father of Summer is called Svásuth, who is such a gentle and delicate being, that what is mild is from him called sweet. The father of Winter has two names, Vindloni and Vindsval. He is the son of Vásad, and, like all his race, has an icy breath, and is of a grim and gloomy aspect."

OF ODIN.

20. " I must now ask thee," said Gangler, " who are the gods that men are bound to believe in? "

" There are twelve gods," replied Har, " to whom divine honours ought to be rendered."

" Nor are the goddesses," added Jafnhar, " less divine and mighty."

" The first and eldest of the Æsir," continued Thridi, " is

* In Vafthrúdnis-mál, st. 37.

Odin. He governs all things, and, although the other deities are powerful, they all serve and obey him as children do their father [P]. Frigga is his wife. She foresees the destinies of men, but never reveals what is to come. For thus it is said that Odin himself told Loki, ' Senseless Loki, why wilt thou pry into futurity, Frigga alone knoweth the destinies of all, though she telleth them never?'

" Odin is named Alfadir (All-father), because he is the father of all the gods, and also Valfadir (Choosing Father), because he chooses for his sons all those who fall in combat. For their abode he has prepared Valhalla and Vingólf, where they are called Einherjar (Heroes or Champions). Odin is also called Hangagud, Haptagud, and Farmagud, and, besides these, was named in many ways when he went to King Geirraudr." *

" A great many names, indeed !" exclaimed Gangler ; " surely that man must be very wise who knows them all distinctly, and can tell on what occasions they were given."

" It requires, no doubt," replied Har, " a good memory to recollect readily all these names, but I will tell thee in a few words what principally contributed to confer them upon him. It was the great variety of languages ; for the various nations were obliged to translate his name into their respective tongues, in order that they might supplicate and worship him [Q]. Some of his names, however, have been owing to adventures that happened to him on his journeys, and which are related in old stories. Nor canst thou ever pass for a wise man if thou art not able to give an account of these wonderful adventures."

OF THOR.

21. " I now ask thee," said Gangler, " what are the names of the other gods. What are their functions, and what have they brought to pass?"

---

* Forty-nine names are here enumerated ; viz., Grimr, Gángrádr, Herjan, Hjálmberi, Thekkr, Thridi, Thudr, Udr Helblindi, Hárr, Sadr, Svipall, Sanngetall, Herteitr, Hnikarr, Bileygr, Báleygr, Baulverkr, Fjölnir, Grímnir, Glapsvidr, Fjölsvithr, Sidhöttr, Sidskégg, Sigfadir, Hnikudr, Alfadir, Atridr, Farmatýr, Oski, Omi, Jafnhár, Biflindi, Göndlir, Hárbardr, Svidr, Svidrir, Jálk, Kjalar, Vidur, Thrór, Ygg, Thundr, Vakr, Skiffingr, Vafudr, Hroptatýr, Gautr, and Veratýr.

" The mightiest of them," replied Har, " is Thor. He is called Asa-Thor and Auku-Thor, and is the strongest of gods and men [R]. His realm is named Thrúdváng, and his mansion Bilskirnir, in which are five hundred and forty halls. It is the largest house ever built. Thus it is called in the Grímnis-mál—

> " ' Five hundred halls
> And forty more,
> Methinketh, hath
> Bowed Bilskirnir.
> Of houses roofed
> There's none I know
> My son's surpassing.'

" Thor has a car drawn by two goats called Tanngnióst and Tanngrisnir. From his driving about in this car he is called Auku-Thor (Charioteer-Thor). He likewise possesses three very precious things. The first is a mallet called Mjölnir, which both the Frost and Mountain Giants know to their cost when they see it hurled against them in the air; and no wonder, for it has split many a skull of their fathers and kindred. The second rare thing he possesses is called the belt of strength or prowess (Megingjardir). When he girds it about him his divine might is doubly augmented; the third, also very precious, being his iron gauntlets, which he is obliged to put on whenever he would lay hold of the handle of his mallet. There is no one so wise as to be able to relate all Thor's marvellous exploits, yet I could tell thee so many myself, that hours would be whiled away ere all that I know had been recounted."

OF BALDUR.

22. " I would rather," said Gangler, "hear something about the other Æsir. "

" The second son of Odin," replied Har, " is Baldur, and it may be truly said of him that he is the best, and that all mankind are loud in his praise. So fair and dazzling is he in form and features, that rays of light seem to issue from him [S]; and thou mayst have some idea of the beauty of

E E

his hair, when I tell thee that the whitest of all plants is
called Baldur's brow *.   Baldur is the mildest, the wisest, and
the most eloquent of all the Æsir, yet such is his nature that
the judgment he has pronounced can never be altered.   He
dwells in the heavenly mansion called Breidablik, in which
nothing unclean can enter.   As it is said †—

> " ' 'Tis Breidablik called,
>   Where Baldur the Fair
>   Hath built him a bower,
>   In that land where I know
>   The least loathliness lieth.' "

OF NJÖRD.

23.   " The third god," continued Har, " is Njörd, who dwells
in the heavenly region called Noátún.   He rules over the
winds, and checks the fury of the sea and of fire, and is therefore invoked by sea-farers and fishermen [T].   He is so
wealthy that he can give possessions and treasures to those
who call on him for them.   Yet Njörd is not of the lineage of
the Æsir, for he was born and bred in Vanaheim.   But the
Vanir gave him as hostage to the Æsir, receiving from them in
his stead Hœnir.   By this means was peace re-established
between the Æsir and Vanir.   Njörd took to wife Skadi, the
daughter of the giant Thjassi.   She preferred dwelling in the
abode formerly belonging to her father, which is situated
among rocky mountains, in the region called Thrymheim, but
Njörd loved to reside near the sea.   They at last agreed that
they should pass together nine nights in Thrymheim, and
then three in Noátún.   One day, when Njörd came back from
the mountains to Noátún, he thus sang—

> " ' Of mountains I 'm weary,
>   Not long was I there,
>   Not more than nine nights;
>   But the howl of the wolf
>   Methought sounded ill
>   To the song of the swan-bird.'

* The *Anthemis Cotula,* still called *Balldursbrá,* Baldur's eyebrow, in
some parts of Sweden.
† In Grimnis-mál, st. 12.

"To which Skadi sang in reply—

> " 'Ne'er can I sleep
> In my couch on the strand,
> For the screams of the sea-fowl.
> The mew as he comes
> Every morn from the main
> Is sure to awake me.'

"Skadi then returned to the rocky mountains, and abode in Thrymheim. There, fastening on her snow-skates and taking her bow, she passes her time in the chase of savage beasts, and is called the Öndur goddess, or Öndurdís. As it is said—

> " 'Thrymheim's the land
> Where Thjassi abode
> That mightiest of giants.
> But snow-skating Skadi
> Now dwells there, I trow,
> In her father's old mansion.' "

OF THE GOD FREY, AND THE GODDESS FREYJA.

24. "Njörd had afterwards, at his residence at Nóatún, two children, a son named Frey, and a daughter called Freyja, both of them beauteous and mighty. Frey is one of the most celebrated of the gods. He presides over rain and sunshine, and all the fruits of the earth, and should be invoked in order to obtain good harvests, and also for peace. He, moreover, dispenses wealth among men. Freyja is the most propitious of the goddesses; her abode in heaven is called Fólkváng. To whatever field of battle she rides, she asserts her right to one half of the slain, the other half belonging to Odin. As it is said *—

> " ' Fólkváng 'tis called
> Where Freyja hath right
> To dispose of the hall seats.
> Every day, of the slain,
> She chooseth the half,
> And half leaves to Odin.'

* Grímnis-mál, 14.

"Her mansion, called Sessrúmnir, is large and magnificent; thence she sallies forth in a car drawn by two cats. She lends a very favourable ear to those who sue to her for assistance. It is from her name that women of birth and fortune are called in our language Freyjor*. She is very fond of love ditties, and all lovers would do well to invoke her."

OF TYR.

25. "All the gods appear to me," said Gangler, " to have great power, and I am not at all surprised that ye are able to perform so many great achievements, since ye are so well acquainted with the attributes and functions of each god, and know what is befitting to ask from each, in order to succeed. But are there any more of them besides those you have already mentioned?"

"Ay," answered Har, "there is Tyr, who is the most daring and intrepid of all the gods. 'Tis he who dispenses valour in war, hence warriors do well to invoke him. It has become proverbial to say of a man who surpasses all others in valour that he is *Tyr-strong*, or valiant as Tyr. A man noted for his wisdom is also said to be 'wise as Tyr.' Let me give thee a proof of his intrepidity. When the Æsir were trying to persuade the wolf, Fenrir, to let himself be bound up with the chain, Gleipnir, he, fearing that they would never afterwards unloose him, only consented on the condition that while they were chaining him he should keep Tyr's right hand between his jaws. Tyr did not hesitate to put his hand in the monster's mouth, but when Fenrir perceived that the Æsir had no intention to unchain him, he bit the hand off at that point, which has ever since been called the wolf's joint (úlflidr). From that time Tyr has had but one hand †. He is not regarded as a peacemaker among men."

OF THE OTHER GODS.

26. "There is another god," continued Har, "named Bragi, who is celebrated for his wisdom, and more especially for his eloquence and correct forms of speech. He is not only emi-

* See the note, page 312.
† See ch. 34.

nently skilled in poetry, but the art itself is called from
his name *Bragr*, which epithet is also applied to denote a
distinguished poet or poetess. His wife is named Iduna.
She keeps in a box the apples which the gods, when they feel
old age approaching, have only to taste of to become young
again. It is in this manner that they will be kept in renovated youth until Ragnarök."

"Methinks," interrupted Gangler, "the gods have committed a great treasure to the guardianship and good faith of
Iduna."

"And hence it happened," replied Har, smiling, "that they
once ran the greatest risk imaginable, as I shall have occasion
to tell thee when thou hast heard the names of the other
deities.

27. "One of them is Heimdall, called also the White God.
He is the son of nine virgins, who were sisters, and is a very
sacred and powerful deity. He also bears the appellation of
the Gold-toothed, on account of his teeth being of pure gold,
and also that of Hallinskithi. His horse is called Gulltopp, and
he dwells in Himinbjörg at the end of Bifröst. He is the
warder of the gods, and is therefore placed on the borders of
heaven, to prevent the giants from forcing their way over the
bridge. He requires less sleep than a bird, and sees by night,
as well as by day, a hundred miles around him. So acute is
his ear that no sound escapes him, for he can even hear the
grass growing on the earth. and the wool on a sheep's back.
He has a horn called the Gjallar-horn, which is heard throughout the universe. His sword is called Höfud (Head). Thus
it is said of him *—

> " ' 'Tis Himinbjörg called
> Where Heimdall they say
> Hath dwelling and rule.
> There the gods' warder drinks,
> In peaceful old halls
> Gladsome, the good mead.'

"And again he says of himself in Heimdall's lay—

> " ' Born was I of mothers nine,
> Son am I of sisters nine.'

* In Grímnis-mál, st. 13.

28. "Among the Æsir," continued Har, "we also reckon Hödur, who is blind, but extremely strong. Both gods and men would be very glad if they never had occasion to pronounce his name, for they will long have cause to remember the deed perpetrated by his hand *.

29. "Another god is Vidar, surnamed the Silent, who wears very thick shoes. He is almost as strong as Thor himself, and the gods place great reliance on him in all critical conjunctures.

30. "Vali, another god, is the son of Odin and Rinda, he is bold in war, and an excellent archer.

31. "Another is called Ullur, who is the son of Sif, and stepson of Thor. He is so well skilled in the use of the bow, and can go so fast on his snow-skates, that in these arts no one can contend with him. He is also very handsome in his person, and possesses every quality of a warrior, wherefore it is befitting to invoke him in single combats.

22. "The name of another god is Forseti, who is the son of Baldur and Nanna, the daughter of Nef. He possesses the heavenly mansion called Glitnir, and all disputants at law who bring their cases before him go away perfectly reconciled.

"His tribunal is the best that is to be found among gods or men. As it is said †—

> "' Glitnir's a mansion
> Upraised on gold columns,
> And roofed o'er with silver.
> There Forseti his days
> In peace ever passeth,
> And stilleth all law strife.'"

OF LOKI AND HIS PROGENY.

33. "There is another deity," continued Har, "reckoned in the number of the Æsir, whom some call the calumniator of the gods, the contriver of all fraud and mischief, and the disgrace of gods and men. His name is Loki or Loptur. He is the son of the giant Farbauti. His mother is Laufey or Nál; his brothers are Byleist and Helblindi. Loki is

---

* Namely, his having killed Baldur in the manner stated in ch. 49.
† In Grímnis-mál, st. 15.

handsome and well made, but of a very fickle mood, and most evil disposition. He surpasses all beings in those arts called Cunning and Perfidy. Many a time has he exposed the gods to very great perils, and often extricated them again by his artifices [U]. His wife is called Siguna, and their son Nari.

34. " Loki," continued Har, " has likewise had three children by Angurbodi, a giantess of Jötunheim. The first is the wolf Fenrir; the second Jörmungand, the Midgard serpent; the third Hela (Death). The gods were not long ignorant that these monsters continued to be bred up in Jötunheim, and, having had recourse to divination, became aware of all the evils they would have to suffer from them; their being sprung from such a mother was a bad presage, and from such a sire. one still worse. All-father therefore deemed it advisable to send one of the gods to bring them to him. When they came he threw the serpent into that deep ocean by which the earth is engirdled. But the monster has grown to such an enormous size that, holding his tail in his mouth, he encircles the whole earth. Hela he cast into Niflheim, and gave her power over nine worlds (regions), into which she distributes those who are sent to her, that is to say, all who die through sickness or old age. Here she possesses a habitation protected by exceedingly high walls and strongly barred gates. Her hall is called Elvidnir; Hunger is her table; Starvation, her knife; Delay, her man; Slowness, her maid; Precipice, her threshold; Care, her bed; and Burning Anguish forms the hangings of her apartments. The one half of her body is livid, the other half the colour of human flesh. She may therefore easily be recognised; the more so, as she has a dreadfully stern and grim countenance [V].

" The wolf Fenrir was bred up among the gods; but Tyr alone had the daring to go and feed him. Nevertheless, when the gods perceived that he every day increased prodigiously in size, and that the oracles warned them that he would one day become fatal to them, they determined to make a very strong iron fetter for him, which they called Læding. Taking this fetter to the wolf, they bade him try his strength on it. Fenrir. perceiving that the enterprise would not be very difficult for him, let them do what they pleased, and then, by great muscular exertion, burst the chain and set himself at liberty. The gods,

having seen this, made another fetter, half as strong again as
the former, which they called Drómi, and prevailed on the
wolf to put it on, assuring him that, by breaking this, he would
give an undeniable proof of his vigour.

" The wolf saw well enough that it would not be so easy to
break this fetter, but, finding at the same time that his strength
had increased since he broke Læding, and thinking that he could
never become famous without running some risk, voluntarily
submitted to be chained. When the gods told him that they
had finished their task, Fenrir shook himself violently,
stretched his limbs, rolled on the ground, and at last burst
his chains, which flew in pieces all around him. He thus
freed himself from Drómi, which gave rise to the proverb ' at
lɀysa or læðingi eˀða at drepa or dróma,' (to get loose out of
Læding, or to dash out of Drómi,) when anything is to be accomplished by strong efforts.

" After this, the gods despaired of ever being able to bind
the wolf; wherefore Al-father sent Skirnir, the messenger of
Frey, into the country of the Dark Elves (Svartálfaheim) to
engage certain dwarfs to make the fetter called Gleipnir. It
was fashioned out of six things; to wit, the noise made by the
footfall of a cat; the beards of women; the roots of stones;
the sinews of bears; the breath of fish; and the spittle of
birds. Though thou mayest not have heard of these things
before, thou mayest easily convince thyself that we have not
been telling thee lies. .Thou must have seen that women
have no beards, that cats make no noise when they run, and
that there are no roots under stones. Now I know what has
been told thee to be equally true, although there may be some
things thou art not able to furnish a proof of."

" I believe what thou hast told me to be true," replied
Gangler, " for what thou hast adduced in corroboration of thy
statement is conceivable. But how was the fetter smithied?"

" This can I tell thee," replied Har, " that the fetter was
as smooth and soft as a silken string, and yet, as thou wilt
presently hear, of very great strength. When it was brought
to the gods, they were profuse in their thanks to the messenger for the trouble he had given himself; and taking the
wolf with them to the island called Lyngvi, in the Lake
Amsvartnir, they showed him the cord, and expressed their
wish that he would try to break it, assuring him at the same

time that it was somewhat stronger than its thinness would warrant a person in supposing it to be. They took it themselves, one after another, in their hands, and after attempting in vain to break it, said, ' Thou alone, Fenrir, art able to accomplish such a feat.'

" ' Methinks,' replied the wolf, ' that I shall acquire no fame in breaking such a slender cord; but if any artifice has been employed in making it, slender though it seems, it shall never come on my feet.'

" The gods assured him that he would easily break a limber silken cord, since he had already burst asunder iron fetters of the most solid construction. ' But if thou shouldst not succeed in breaking it,' they added, ' thou wilt show that thou art too weak to cause the gods any fear, and we will not hesitate to set thee at liberty without delay.'

" ' I fear me much,' replied the wolf, ' that if ye once bind me so fast that I shall be unable to free myself by my own efforts, ye will be in no haste to unloose me. Loath am I, therefore, to have this cord wound round me; but in order that ye may not doubt my courage, I will consent, provided one of you put his hand into my mouth as a pledge that ye intend me no deceit.'

" The gods wistfully looked at each other, and found that they had only the choice of two evils, until Tyr stepped forward and intrepidly put his right hand between the monster's jaws. Hereupon the gods, having tied up the wolf, he forcibly stretched himself as he had formerly done, and used all his might to disengage himself, but the more efforts he made the tighter became the cord, until all the gods, except Tyr, who lost his hand, burst into laughter at the sight.

" When the gods saw that the wolf was effectually bound, they took the chain called Gelgja, which was fixed to the fetter, and drew it through the middle of a large rock named Gjöll, which they sank very deep into the earth; afterwards, to make it still more secure, they fastened the end of the cord to a massive stone called Thviti, which they sank still deeper. The wolf made in vain the most violent efforts to break loose, and, opening his tremendous jaws, endeavoured to bite them. The gods seeing this, thrust a sword into his mouth, which pierced his under-jaw up to the hilt, so that the point touched the palate. He then began to howl horribly, and since that time

the foam flows continually from his mouth in such abundance
that it forms the river called Von. There will he remain
until Ragnarök."

"Verily," said Gangler, "an evil progeny is that of Loki,
yet most mighty and powerful; but since the gods have so
much to fear from the wolf, why did they not slay him?"

"The gods have so much respect for the sanctity of their
peace-steads," replied Har, "that they would not stain them
with the blood of the wolf, although prophecy had intimated
to them that he must one day become the bane of Odin."

OF THE GODDESSES.

35. "Tell me now," said Gangler, "which are the goddesses?"

"The first," replied Har, "is Frigga, who has a magnificent mansion called Fensalir. The second is Saga, who
dwells at Sökkvabekk, a very large and stately abode. The
third is Eir, the best of all in the healing art [w]. The fourth,
named Gefjon, is a maid, and all those who die maids become
her hand-maidens. The fifth is Fulla, who is also a maid, and
goes about with her hair flowing over her shoulders, and her
head adorned with a gold ribbon. She is entrusted with the
toilette and slippers of Frigga, and admitted into the most
important secrets of that goddess. Freyja is ranked next to
Frigga: she is wedded to a person called Odur, and their
daughter, named Hnossa, is so very handsome that whatever is
beautiful and precious is called by her name (*hnosir*). But Odur
left his wife in order to travel into very remote countries. Since
that time Freyja continually weeps, and her tears are drops of
pure gold. She has a great variety of names, for having gone
over many countries in search of her husband, each people gave
her a different name. She is thus called Mardöll, Horn,
Gefn, and Syr, and also Vanadís. She possesses the neck-
lace Brísíng. The seventh goddess is Sjöfna, who delights
in turning men's hearts and thoughts to love : hence a wooer
is called, from her name, *Sjafni*. The eighth, named Lofna,
is so mild and gracious to those who invoke her, that by a
peculiar privilege which either All-Father himself or Frigga has
given her, she can remove every obstacle that may prevent
the union of lovers sincerely attached to each other. Hence
her name is applied to denote love, and whatever is beloved

by men. Vöra, the ninth goddess, listens to the oaths that men take, and particularly to the troth plighted between man and woman, and punishes those who keep not their promises. She is wise and prudent, and so penetrating that nothing remains hidden from her. Syn, the tenth, keeps the door in the hall, and shuts it against those who ought not to enter. She presides at trials when any thing is to be denied on oath, whence the proverb, ' Syn (negation) is set against it,' when ought is denied. Hlina, the eleventh, has the care of those whom Frigga intends to deliver from peril. Snotra, the twelfth, is wise and courteous, and men and women who possess these qualities have her name applied to them. Gná, the thirteenth, is the messenger that Frigga sends into the various worlds on her errands. She has a horse that can run through air and water, called Hófvarpnir [x]. Once, as she drove out, certain Vanir saw her car in the air, when one of them exclaimed,

> " ' What flieth there?
>   What goeth there?
>   In the air aloft what glideth?

" She answered,

> " ' I fly not though I go,
>   And glide through the air
>   On Hófvarpnir,
>   Whose sire's Hamskerpir,
>   And dam Gardrofa.'

" Sól and Bil are also reckoned among the goddesses, but their nature has already been explained to thee.

36. " There are besides these a great many other goddesses, whose duty it is to serve in Valhalla; to bear in the drink and take care of the drinking-horns and whatever belongs to the table. They are named in Grímnis-mál *, and are called Valkyrjor. Odin sends them to every field of battle, to make choice of those who are to be slain, and to sway the victory. Gudur, Rota, and the youngest of the Norns, Skuld, also ride forth to choose the slain and turn the combat. Jörd (earth), the

---

* Viz., Hrist, Mist, Skéggöld, Skögul, Hildur, Thrúdur, Hlökk, Herfjötur, Göll, Geirölul, Randgrid, Rádgrid, and Reginleif.

mother of Thor, and Rinda, the mother of Vali, are also
reckoned amongst the goddesses "

OF FREY AND GERDA

37. " There was a man," continued Har, " named Gymir,
who had for wife Aurboda, of the race of the Mountain-giants.
Their daughter is Gerda, who is the most beautiful of all
women. One day Frey having placed himself in Hlidskjálf *,
to take a view of the whole universe, perceived, as he looked
towards the north, a large and stately mansion which a woman
was going to enter, and as she lifted up the latch of the door
so great a radiancy was thrown from her hand that the air
and waters, and all worlds were illumined by it. At this
sight, Frey, as a just punishment for his audacity in mounting on that sacred throne, was struck with sudden sadness,
insomuch so, that on his return home he could neither speak,
nor sleep, nor drink, nor did any one dare to inquire the cause
of his affliction; but Njörd, at last, sent for Skirnir, the messenger of Frey, and charged him to demand of his master
why he thus refused to speak to any one. Skirnir promised
to do this, though with great reluctance, fearing that all that
he had to expect was a severe reprimand. He, however,
went to Frey, and asked him boldly why he was so sad and
silent. Frey answered, that he had seen a maiden of such
surpassing beauty that if he could not possess her he should
not live much longer, and that this was what rendered him so
melancholy. ' Go, therefore,' he added, ' and ask her hand
for me, and bring her here whether her father be willing or
not, and I will amply reward thee. Skirnir undertook to perform the task, provided he might be previously put in possession of Frey's sword, which was of such an excellent quality
that it would of itself strew a field with carnage whenever the
owner ordered it. Frey, impatient of delay, immediately
made him a present of the sword, and Skirnir set out on his
journey and obtained the maiden's promise, that within nine
nights she would come to a place called Barey, and there wed
Frey. Skirnir having reported the success of his message,
Frey exclaimed,

* See ch. ix. and xvii.

" ' Long is one night,
Long are two nights,
But how shall I hold out three ?
Shorter hath seemed
A month to me oft
Than of this longing-time the half.'

"Frey having thus given away his sword, found himself without arms when he fought with Beli, and hence it was that he slew him with a stag's antlers."

"But it seems very astonishing," interrupted Gangler, "that such a brave hero as Frey should give away his sword without keeping another equally good for himself. He must have been in a very bad plight when he encountered Beli, and methinks must have mightily repented him of the gift."

"That combat," replied Har, "was a trifling affair. Frey could have killed Beli with a blow of his fist had he felt inclined : but the time will come when the sons of Muspell shall issue forth to the fight, and then, indeed, will Frey truly regret having parted with his falchion."

OF THE JOYS OF VALHALLA.

38. " If it be as thou hast told me," said Gangler, " that all men who have fallen in fight since the beginning of the world are gone to Odin, in Valhalla, what has he to give them to eat, for methinks there must be a great crowd there ?"

" What thou sayest is quite true," replied Har, " the crowd there is indeed great, but great though it be, it will still increase, and will be thought too little when the wolf cometh [y]. But however great the band of men in Valhalla may be, the flesh of the boar Sæhrimnir will more than suffice for their sustenance. For although this boar is sodden every morning he becomes whole again every night [z]. But there are few, methinks, who are wise enough to give thee, in this respect, a satisfactory answer to thy question. The cook is called Andhrimnir, and the kettle Eldhrimnir. As it is said *,—
' Andhrimnir cooks in Eldhrimnir. Sæhrimnir.' 'Tis the best

* In Grímnis-mál, st. 18.

of flesh, though few know how much is required for the Einherjar."

" But has Odin," said Gangler, " the same food as the heroes?"

" Odin," replied Har, "gives the meat that is set before him to two wolves, called Geri and Freki, for he himself stands in no need of food. Wine is for him both meat and drink. As it is said *,—

> " ' Geri and Freki
>   Feedeth the war-faring
>   Famed Father of hosts,
>   For 'tis with wine only
>   That Odin, in arms renowned,
>   Is nourished for aye.'

" Two ravens sit on Odin's shoulders and whisper in his ear the tidings and events they have heard and witnessed. They are called Hugin and Munin †. He sends them out at dawn of day to fly over the whole world, and they return at eve towards meal time. Hence it is that Odin knows so many things, and is called the Raven's God (Hrafnaguð). As it is said ‡,—

> " ' Hugin and Munin
>   Each dawn take their flight
>   Earth's fields over.
>   I fear me for Hugin,
>   Lest he come not back,
>   But much more for Munin.'

39. " What have the heroes to drink." said Gangler, " in sufficient quantity to correspond to their plentiful supply of meat: do they only drink water?"

" A very silly question is that," replied Har; "dost thou imagine that All-Father would invite kings and jarls and other great men and give them nothing to drink but water! In that case, methinks, many of those who had endured the greatest hardships, and received deadly wounds in order to

---

* In Grímnis-mál, st. 19.
† Mind or Thought, and Memory.
‡ In Grímnis-mál, st. 20.

obtain access to Valhalla, would find that they had paid too great a price for their water drink, and would indeed have reason to complain were they there to meet with no better en tertainment. But thou wilt see that the case is quite other-wise. For the she-goat, named Heidrun, stands above Val-halla, and feeds on the leaves of a very famous tree called Lærath, and from her teats flows mead in such great abund-ance that every day a stoop, large enough to hold more than would suffice for all the heroes, is filled with it." [AA.]

" Verily," said Gangler, 'a' mighty useful goat is this, and methinks the tree she feeds on must have very singular virtues."

" Still more wonderful," replied Har, " is what is told of the stag Eikthyrnir. This stag also stands over Valhalla and feeds upon the leaves of the same tree, and whilst he is feed-ing so many drops fall from his antlers down into Hvergelmir that they furnish sufficient water for the rivers that issuing thence flow through the celestial abodes."*

40. " Wondrous things are these which thou tellest me of," said Gangler, "and Valhalla must needs be an immense building, but methinks there must often be a great press at the door among such a number of people constantly thronging in and out ?"

" Why dost thou not ask," replied Har, " how many doors there are, and what are their dimensions; then wouldst thou be able to judge whether there is any difficulty in going in and out. Know, then, that there is no lack of either seats or doors. As it is said in Grímnis-mál :—

    " ' Five hundred doors
      And forty more
    Methinks are in Valhalla.
    Eight hundred heroes through each door
      Shall issue forth
    Against the wolf to combat.'

44. " A mighty band of men must be in Valhalla," said

---

* As usual these rivers are enumerated as follows :—Sid, Vid, Sækinn, Ekinn, Svöl, Gunnthró, Fjörm, Fimbulthul, Gipul, Göpul, Gömul and Geir-vimul. Mention is also made of the rivers Thyn, Vin, Thöll, Böll, Grád, Gunnthrainn, Nýt, Naut, Nönn, Hrönn, Vina, Vegsvinn and Thjódnuma.

Gangler, "and methinks Odin must be a great chieftain to command such a numerous host. But how do the heroes pass their time when they are not drinking?"

"Every day," replied Har, " as soon as they have dressed themselves they ride out into the court (or field), and there fight until they cut each other in pieces. This is their pastime, but when meal-tide approaches they remount their steeds and return to drink in Valhalla [BB]. As it is said * :—

> " ' The Einherjar all
>   On Odin's plain
> Hew daily each other,
> While chosen the slain are.
> From the fray they then ride,
> And drink ale with the Æsir.'

" Thou hast thus reason to say that Odin is great and mighty, for there are many proofs of this. As it is said in the very words of the Æsir † :—

> " ' The ash Yggdrasill
>   Is the first of trees,
> As Skidbladnir of ships,
> Odin of Æsir,
> Sleipnir of steeds,
> Bifröst of bridges,
> Bragi of bards,
> Hábrók of hawks,
> And Garm of hounds is.' "

OF THE HORSE SLEIPNIR.

42. " Thou mad'st mention," said Gangler, " of the horse Sleipnir. To whom does he belong, and what is there to say respecting him? "

" Thou seemest to know nothing either about Sleipnir or his origin," replied Har, " but thou wilt no doubt find what thou wilt hear worthy of thy notice. Once on a time when the gods were constructing their abodes, and had already

---

* In Vafthrúdnis-mál, st. 41.
† In Grímnis-mál, st. 43.

finished Midgard and Valhalla, a certain artificer came and offered to build them, in the space of three half years, a residence so well fortified that they should be perfectly safe from the incursion of the Frost-giants, and the giants of the mountains, even although they should have penetrated within Midgard.   But he demanded for his reward the goddess Freyja, together with the sun and moon.   After long deliberation the Æsir agreed to his terms, provided he would finish the whole work himself without any one's assistance, and all within the space of one winter, but if anything remained unfinished on the first day of summer, he should forfeit the recompense agreed on.   On being told these terms, the artificer stipulated that he should be allowed the use of his horse, called Svadilfari, and this, by the advice of Loki, was granted to him.   He accordingly set to work on the first day of winter, and during the night let his horse draw stone for the building.   The enormous size of the stones struck the Æsir with astonishment, and they saw clearly that the horse did one half more of the toilsome work than his master.   Their bargain, however, had been concluded in the presence of witnesses, and confirmed by solemn oaths, for without these precautions a giant would not have thought himself safe among the Æsir, especially when Thor returned from an expedition he had then undertaken towards the east against evil demons.

" As the winter drew to a close the building was far advanced, and the bulwarks were sufficiently high and massive to render this residence impregnable.   In short, when it wanted but three days to summer the only part that remained to be finished was the gateway.   Then sat the gods on their seats of justice and entered into consultation, inquiring of one another who among them could have advised to give Freyja away to Jötunheim, or to plunge the heavens in darkness by permitting the giant to carry away the sun and moon.   They all agreed that no one but Loki, the son of Laufey, and the author of so many evil deeds, could have given such bad counsel, and that he should be put to a cruel death if he did not contrive some way or other to prevent the artificer from completing his task and obtaining the stipulated recompense. They immediately proceeded to lay hands on Loki, who, in his fright, promised upon oath that let it cost him what it

F F

would, he would so manage matters that the man should lose his reward. That very night, when the artificer went with Svadilfari for building stone, a mare suddenly ran out of a forest and began to neigh. The horse being thus excited, broke loose and ran after the mare into the forest, which obliged the man also to run after his horse, and thus between one and the other the whole night was lost, so that at dawn the work had not made the usual progress. The man seeing that he had no other means of completing his task, resumed his own gigantic stature, and the gods now clearly perceived that it was in reality a Mountain-giant who had come amongst them. No longer regarding their oaths, they, therefore, called on Thor, who immediately ran to their assistance, and lifting up his mallet Mjölnir paid the workman his wages, not with the sun and moon, and not even by sending him back to Jötun-heim, for with the first blow he shattered the giant's skull to pieces, and hurled him headlong into Niflhel. But Loki had run such a race with Svadilfari that shortly after he bore a grey foal with eight legs. This is the horse Sleipnir, which excels all horses ever possessed by gods or men. It is thus said in the Völuspá,—

" ' Then went the rulers there,
All gods most holy,
To their seats aloft,
And counsel together took,
Who all the winsome air
With guile had blended,
Or to the giant race
Oð's maiden given *.
Then Thor, who too was there,
Arose in wrathful mood,
For seldom sits he still
When such things he heareth.
Annulled were now all oaths,
And words of promise fair,
And faith, not long before
In council plighted.' "

* Viz., Freyja, the wife of Odur. See ch. 35, and the word Odur, Oð, in the Glossary.

OF THE SHIP SKIDBLADNIR.

43. "What hast thou to say," demanded Gangler, "of Skidbladnir, which thou toldst me was the best of ships? Is there no other ship as good or as large?"

"Skidbladnir," replied Har, "is without doubt the best and most artfully constructed of any, but the ship Naglfar is of larger size. They were dwarfs, the sons of Ivaldi, who built Skidbladnir, and made a present of her to Frey. She is so large that all the Æsir with their weapons and war stores find room on board her. As soon as the sails are set a favourable breeze arises and carries her to her place of destination, and she is made of so many pieces, and with so much skill, that when she is not wanted for a voyage Frey may fold her together like a piece of cloth, and put her in his pocket."

44. "A good ship truly, is Skidbladnir," said Gangler, "and many cunning contrivances and spells must, no doubt, have been used in her construction."

THOR'S ADVENTURES ON HIS JOURNEY TO THE LAND OF THE GIANTS.

"But tell me," he (Gangler) continued, "did it ever happen to Thor in his expeditions to be overcome either by spells or by downright force?"

"Few can take upon them to affirm this," replied Har, "and yet it has often fared hard enough with him; but had he in reality been worsted in any rencounter there would be no need to make mention of it, since all are bound to believe that nothing can resist his power."

"It would, therefore, appear," said Gangler, "that I have asked you of things that none of you are able to tell me of."

"There are, indeed, some such rumours current among us," answered Jafnhar, "but they are hardly credible; however, there is one sitting here can impart them to thee, and thou shouldst the rather believe him, for never having yet uttered an untruth, he will not now begin to deceive thee with false stories."

"Here then will I stand," said Gangler, "and listen to what ye have to say, but if ye cannot answer my question satisfactorily I shall look upon you as vanquished."

Then spake Thirdi and said, "We can easily conceive

that thou art desirous of knowing these tidings, but it behoves thee to guard a becoming silence respecting them. The
story I have to relate is this :—

"One day the God Thor set out in his car drawn by two
he-goats, and accompanied by Loki, on a journey. Night
coming on, they put up at a peasant's cottage, when Thor
killed his goats, and after flaying them, put them in the
kettle. When the flesh was sodden, he sat down with his
fellow-traveller to supper, and invited the peasant and his
family to partake of the repast. The peasant's son was named
Thjalfi, and his daughter Röska. Thor bade them throw all
the bones into the goats' skins which were spread out near
the fire-place, but young Thjalfi broke one of the shank bones
with his knife to come at the marrow. Thor having passed
the night in the cottage, rose at the dawn of day, and when
he was dressed took his mallet Mjölnir, and lifting it up, consecrated the goats' skins, which he had no sooner done than
the two goats re-assumed their wonted form, only that one of
them now limped on one of its hind legs. Thor perceiving
this, said that the peasant, or one of his family, had handled
the shank bone of this goat too roughly, for he saw clearly
that it was broken. It may readily be imagined how frightened the peasant was when he saw Thor knit his brows, and
grasp the handle of his mallet with such force that the joints
of his fingers became white from the exertion. Fearing to be
struck down by the very looks of the god, the peasant and
his family made joint suit for pardon, offering whatever they
possessed as an atonement for the offence committed. Thor,
seeing their fear, desisted from his wrath, and became more
placable, and finally contented himself by requiring the
peasant's children, Thjalfi and Röska, who became his bond-
servants, and have followed him ever since.

45. " Leaving his goats with the peasant, Thor proceeded
eastward on the road to Jötunheim, until he came to the
shores of a vast and deep sea, which having passed over he
penetrated into a strange country along with his companions,
Loki, Thjalfi, and Röska. They had not gone far before they
saw before them an immense forest, through which they
wandered all day. Thjalfi was of all men the swiftest of
foot. He bore Thor's wallet, but the forest was a bad place
for finding anything eatable to stow in it. When it became

dark, they searched on all sides for a place where they might pass the night, and at last came to a very large hall with an entrance that took up the whole breadth of one of the ends of the building. Here they chose them a place to sleep in; but towards midnight were alarmed by an earthquake which shook the whole edifice. Thor, rising up, called on his companions to seek with him a place of safety. On the right they found an adjoining chamber, into which they entered, but while the others, trembling with fear, crept into the furthest corner of this retreat, Thor remained at the doorway with his mallet in his hand, prepared to defend himself, whatever might happen. A terrible groaning was heard during the night, and at dawn of day, Thor went out and observed lying near him a man of enormous bulk, who slept and snored pretty loudly. Thor could now account for the noise they had heard over night, and girding on his Belt of Prowess, increased that divine strength which he now stood in need of. The giant awakening, rose up, and it is said that for once in his life Thor was afraid to make use of his mallet, and contented himself by simply asking the giant his name.

" ' My name is Skrymir,' said the other, ' but I need not ask thy name, for I know thou art the God Thor. But what hast thou done with my glove ?' And stretching out his hand Skrymir picked up his glove, which Thor then perceived was what they had taken over night for a hall, the chamber where they had sought refuge being the thumb. Skrymir then asked whether they would have his fellowship, and Thor consenting, the giant opened his wallet and began to eat his breakfast. Thor and his companions having also taken their morning repast, though in another place, Skrymir proposed that they should lay their provisions together, which Thor also assented to. The giant then put all the meat into one wallet, which he slung on his back and went before them, taking tremendous strides, the whole day, and at dusk sought out for them a place where they might pass the night under a large oak tree. Skrymir then told them that he would lie down to sleep. ' But take ye the wallet,' he added, ' and prepare your supper.'

" Skrymir soon fell asleep, and began to snore strongly, but incredible though it may appear, it must nevertheless be told,

that when Thor came to open the wallet he could not untie a
single knot, nor render a single string looser than it was before.   Seeing that his labour was in vain, Thor became wroth,
and grasping his mallet with both hands while he advanced
a step forward, launched it at the giant's head.   Skrymir
awakening, merely asked whether a leaf had not fallen on his
head, and whether they had supped and were ready to go to
sleep.   Thor answered that they were just going to sleep,
and so saying, went and laid himself down under another
oak tree.   But sleep came not that night to Thor, and when
he remarked that Skrymir snored again so loud that the forest
re-echoed with the noise, he arose, and grasping his mallet,
launched it with such force that it sunk into the giant's skull
up to the handle.   Skrymir awakening, cried out—

  " 'What's the matter ? did an acorn fall on my head ? How
fares it with thee, Thor ? '

  " But Thor went away hastily, saying that he had just then
awoke, and that as it was only midnight there was still time
for sleep.   He however resolved that if he had an opportunity
of striking a third blow, it should settle all matters between
them.   A little before day-break he perceived that Skrymir
was again fast asleep, and again grasping his mallet,
dashed it with such violence that it forced its way into the
giant's cheek up to the handle.   But Skrymir sat up, and
stroking his cheek, said—

  " 'Are there any birds perched on this tree ? Methought
when I awoke some moss from the branches fell on my head.
What! Art thou awake, Thor ? Methinks it is time for
us to get up and dress ourselves ; but you have not now a long
way before you to the city called Utgard.   I have heard you
whispering to one another that I am not a man of
small dimensions ; but if you come into Utgard you will see
there many men much taller than myself.   Wherefore I advise
you, when you come there, not to make too much of yourselves,
for the followers of Utgard-Loki will not brook the boasting of
such mannikins as ye are [cc].   The best thing you could do
would probably be to turn back again, but if you persist in
going on, take the road that leads eastward, for mine now lies
northward to those rocks which you may see in the distance.'

  " Hereupon, he threw his wallet over his shoulders and

turned away from them into the forest, and I could never hear that Thor wished to meet with him a second time.

46. " Thor and his companions proceeded on their way, and towards noon descried a city standing in the middle of a plain. It was so lofty that they were obliged to bend their necks quite back on their shoulders ere they could see to the top of it.   On arriving at the walls they found the gateway closed with a gate of bars strongly locked and bolted.   Thor, after trying in vain to open it, crept with his companions through the bars, and thus succeeded in gaining admission into the city.   Seeing a large palace before them with the door wide open, they went in and found a number of men of prodigious stature sitting on benches in the hall.   Going further, they came before the king, Utgard-Loki, whom they saluted with great respect.   Their salutations were however returned by a contemptuous look from the king, who, after regarding them for some time, said with a scornful smile—

" ' It is tedious to ask for tidings of a long journey, yet if I do not mistake me, that stripling there must be Aku-Thor. Perhaps,' he added, addressing himself to Thor, ' thou mayst be taller than thou appearest to be.   But what are the feats that thou and thy fellows deem yourselves skilled in, for no one is permitted to remain here who does not, in some feat or other, excel all other men.'

" ' The feat I know,' replied Loki, ' is to eat quicker than any one else, and in this I am ready to give a proof against any one here who may choose to compete with me.'

" ' That will indeed be a feat,' said Utgard-Loki, ' if thou performest what thou promisest, and it shall be tried forthwith.'

" He then ordered one of his men, who was sitting at the further end of the bench, and whose name was Logi *, to come forward and try his skill with Loki.   A trough filled with flesh meat having been set on the hall floor, Loki placed himself at one end, and Logi at the other, and each of them began to eat as fast as he could, until they met in the middle of the trough.   But it was found that Loki had only eaten the flesh, whereas his adversary had devoured both flesh and bone, and the trough to boot.   All the company therefore adjudged that Loki was vanquished.

* *i. e.* Devouring fiame.

" Utgard-Loki then asked what feat the young man who accompanied Thor could perform. Thjalfi answered that he would run a race with any one who might be matched against him. The king observed that skill in running was something to boast of, but that if the youth would win the match he must display great agility. He then arose and went with all who were present to a plain where there was good ground for running on, and calling a young man named Hugi *, bade him run a match with Thjalfi. In the first course Hugi so much outstripped his competitor that he turned back and met him not far from the starting-place.

" ' Thou must ply thy legs better, Thjalfi,' said Utgard-Loki, 'if thou wilt win the match, though I must needs say that there never came a man here swifter of foot than thou art.'

" In the second course, Thjalfi was a full bow-shot from the goal when Hugi arrived at it.

" ' Most bravely dost thou run, Thjalfi,' said Utgard-Loki, 'though thou wilt not, methinks, win the match. But the third course must decide.'

" They accordingly ran a third time, but Hugi had already reached the goal before Thjalfi had got half way. All who were present then cried out that there had been a sufficient trial of skill in this kind of exercise.

" Utgard-Loki then asked Thor in what feats he would choose to give proofs of that dexterity for which he was so famous. Thor replied, that he would begin a drinking match with any one. Utgard-Loki consented, and entering the palace, bade his cupbearer bring the large horn which his followers were obliged to drink out of when they had trespassed in any way against established usage [DD]. The cupbearer having presented it to Thor, Utgard-Loki said—

" ' Whoever is a good drinker will empty that horn at a single draught, though some men make two of it, but the most puny drinker of all can do it at three.'

" Thor looked at the horn, which seemed of no extraordinary size, though somewhat long ; however, as he was very thirsty, he set it to his lips, and without drawing breath pulled as long and as deeply as he could, that he might not be obliged to make a second draught of it ; but when he set the horn

* *i. e.* Spirit or Thought.

down and looked in, he could scarcely perceive that the liquor was diminished.

" ' 'Tis well drunken,' exclaimed Utgard-Loki, ' though nothing much to boast of; and I would not have believed had it been told me that Asa-Thor could not have taken a greater draught, but thou no doubt meanest to make amends at the second pull.'

" Thor, without answering, went to it again with all his might, but when he took the horn from his mouth it seemed to him as if he had drunk rather less than before, although the horn could now be carried without spilling.

" ' How now, Thor,' said Utgard-Loki; ' thou must not spare thyself more in performing a feat than befits thy skill; but if thou meanest to drain the horn at the third draught thou must pull deeply; and I must needs say that thou wilt not be called so mighty a man here as thou art among the Æsir, if thou showest no greater prowess in other feats than, methinks, will be shown in this.'

" Thor, full of wrath, again set the horn to his lips, and exerted himself to the utmost to empty it entirely, but on looking in found that the liquor was only a little lower, upon which he resolved to make no further attempt, but gave back the horn to the cupbearer.

" ' I now see plainly,' said Utgard-Loki, ' that thou art not quite so stout as we thought thee, but wilt thou try any other feat, though, methinks, thou art not likely to bear any prize away with thee hence.'

" ' I will try another feat,' replied Thor, ' and I am sure such draughts as I have been drinking would not have been reckoned small among the Æsir; but what new trial hast thou to propose ?'

" ' We have a very trifling game here,' answered Utgard-Loki, ' in which we exercise none but children. It consists in merely lifting my cat from the ground, nor should I have dared to mention such a feat to Asa-Thor if I had not already observed that thou art by no means what we took thee for.'

" As he finished speaking, a large grey cat sprung on the hall floor. Thor advancing put his hand under the cat's belly, and did his utmost to raise him from the floor, but the cat bending his back had, notwithstanding all Thor's efforts, only one of his feet lifted up, seeing which, Thor made no further attempt.

" ' This trial has turned out,' said Utgard-Loki, 'just as I imagined it would; the cat is large, but Thor is little in comparison to our men.'

" ' Little as ye call me,' answered Thor, 'let me see who amongst you will come hither now I am in wrath, and wrestle with me.'

" ' I see no one here,' said Utgard-Loki, looking at the men sitting on the benches, ' who would not think it beneath him to wrestle with thee : let somebody, however, call hither that old crone, my nurse Elli *, and let Thor wrestle with her if he will. She has thrown to the ground many a man not less strong and mighty than this Thor is.'

"A toothless old woman then entered the hall, and was told by Utgard-Loki to take hold of Thor. The tale is shortly told. The more Thor tightened his hold on the crone the firmer she stood. At length, after a very violent struggle, Thor began to lose his footing, and was finally brought down upon one knee. Utgard-Loki then told them to desist, adding that Thor had now no occasion to ask any one else in the hall to wrestle with him, and it was also getting late. He therefore showed Thor and his companions to their seats, and they passed the night there in good cheer.

47. " The next morning, at break of day, Thor and his companions dressed themselves and prepared for their departure. Utgard-Loki then came and ordered a table to be set for them, on which there was no lack either of victuals or drink. After the repast Utgard-Loki led them to the gate of the city, and, on parting, asked Thor how he thought his journey had turned out, and whether he had met with any men stronger than himself. Thor told him that he could not deny but that he had brought great shame on himself. ' And what grieves me most,' he added, ' is that ye will call me a man of little worth.'

" ' Nay,' said Utgard-Loki, 'it behoves me to tell thee the truth now thou art out of the city, which so long as I live, and have my way, thou shalt never re-enter. And by my troth, had

---

* i. e. Eld or Old Age.

I known beforehand that thou hadst so much strength in thee, and wouldst have brought me so near to a great mishap, I would not have suffered thee to enter this time. Know then that I have all along deceived thee by my illusions; first, in the forest, where I arrived before thee, and there thou wert not able to untie the wallet, because I had bound it with iron wire, in such a manner that thou couldst not discover how the knot ought to be loosened. After this, thou gavest me three blows with thy mallet; the first, though the least, would have ended my days had it fallen on me, but I brought a rocky mountain before me which thou didst not perceive, and in this mountain thou wilt find three glens, one of them remarkably deep. These are the dints made by thy mallet. I have made use of similar illusions in the contests ye have had with my followers. In the first, Loki, like hunger itself, devoured all that was set before him, but Logi was, in reality, nothing else than ardent fire, and therefore consumed not only the meat but the trough which held it. Hugi, with whom Thjalfi contended in running, was Thought, and it was impossible for Thjalfi to keep pace with that. When thou, in thy turn, didst try to empty the horn, thou didst perform, by my troth, a deed so marvellous, that had I not seen it myself I should never have believed it. For one end of that horn reached the sea, which thou wast not aware of, but when thou comest to the shore thou wilt perceive how much the sea has sunk by thy draughts, which have caused what is now called the ebb. Thou didst perform a feat no less wonderful by lifting up the cat, and to tell thee the truth, when we saw that one of his paws was off the floor, we were all of us terror-stricken, for what thou tookest for a cat was in reality the great Midgard serpent that encompasseth the whole earth, and he was then barely long enough to inclose it between his head and tail, so high had thy hand raised him up towards heaven. Thy wrestling with Elli was also a most astonishing feat, for there was never yet a man, nor ever shall be, whom Old Age, for such in fact was Elli, will not sooner or later lay low if he abide her coming. But now as we are going to part, let me tell thee that it will be better for both of us if thou never come near me again, for shouldst thou do so, I shall again defend myself by other illusions, so that thou wilt never prevail against me.'

" On hearing these words, Thor, in a rage, laid hold of his mallet and would have launched it at him, but Utgard-Loki had disappeared, and when Thor would have returned to the city to destroy it, he found nothing around him but a verdant plain. Proceeding, therefore, on his way, he returned without stopping to Thrúdváng. But he had already resolved to make that attack on the Midgard serpent which afterwards took place. I trust," concluded Thridi, " that thou wilt now acknowledge that no one can tell thee truer tidings than those thou hast heard respecting this journey of Thor to Jötunheim."

HOW THOR WENT TO FISH FOR THE MIDGARD SERPENT.

48. " I find by your account," said Gangler, " that Utgard-Loki possesses great might in himself, though he has recourse to spells and illusions; but his power may be seen by his followers being in every respect so skilful and dexterous. But tell me, did Thor ever avenge this affront? "

" It is not unknown," replied Har, " though nobody has talked of it, that Thor was determined to make amends for the journey just spoken of, and he had not been long at home ere he set out again so hastily that he had neither his car nor his goats, nor any followers with him. He went out of Midgard under the semblance of a young man, and came at dusk to the dwelling of a giant called Hymir. Here Thor passed the night, but at break of day, when he perceived that Hymir was making his boat ready for fishing, he arose and dressed himself, and begged the giant would let him row out to sea with him. Hymir answered, that a puny stripling like he was could be of no great use to him. ' Besides,' he added, ' thou wilt catch thy death of cold if I go so far out and remain so long as I am accustomed to do.' Thor said, that for all that, he would row as far from the land as Hymir had a mind, and was not sure which of them would be the first who might wish to row back again. At the same time he was so enraged that he felt sorely inclined to let his mallet ring on the giant's skull without further delay, but intending to try his strength elsewhere, he stifled his wrath, and asked Hymir what he meant to bait with. Hymir told him to look out for a bait himself. Thor instantly went up to a herd of oxen that belonged to the giant, and seizing the largest bull, that bore the name of Himinbrjót, wrung off his head, and returning with it to the boat, put out to sea with Hymir. Thor rowed aft with two oars, and with such force that Hymir, who rowed at the prow, saw, with surprise, how swiftly the boat was driven forward. He then observed that they were come to the place where he was wont to angle for flat fish, but Thor assured him that they had better go on a good way further. They accordingly continued to ply their oars, until Hymir cried out that if they did not stop they would be in danger from the great Midgard serpent. Notwithstanding this, Thor persisted in rowing further, and in spite of Hymir's remonstrances was a great while before he would lay down his oars. He then took out a fishing-line, extremely strong, furnished with an equally strong hook, on which he fixed the bull's head, and cast his line into the sea. The bait soon reached the bottom, and it may be truly said that Thor then deceived the Midgard serpent not a whit less than Utgard-Loki had deceived Thor when he obliged him to lift up the serpent in his hand : for the monster greedily caught at the bait, and the hook stuck fast in his palate. Stung with the pain, the serpent tugged at the hook so violently, that Thor was obliged to hold fast with both hands by the pegs that bear against the oars. But his wrath now waxed high, and assuming all his divine power, he pulled so hard at the line that his feet forced their way through the boat and went down to the bottom of the sea, whilst with his hands he drew up the serpent to the side of the vessel. It is impossible to express by words the dreadful scene that now took place. Thor, on one hand, darting looks of ire on the serpent, whilst the monster, rearing his head, spouted out floods of venom upon him. It is said that when the giant Hymir beheld the serpent, he turned pale and trembled with fright, and seeing, moreover, that the water was entering his boat on all sides, he took out his knife, just as Thor raised his mallet aloft, and cut the line, on which the serpent sunk again under water. Thor, however, launched his mallet at him, and there are some who say that it struck off the monster's head at the bottom of the sea, but one may assert with more certainty that he still lives and lies in the ocean [EE]. Thor then struck Hymir such a blow with his fist, nigh the ear, that the giant fell headlong into the water, and Thor, wading with rapid strides, soon came to the land again."

THE DEATH OF BALDUR THE GOOD.

49. " Verily," said Gangler, " it was a famous exploit which Thor performed on that journey, but did any other such events take place among the Æsir ? "

" Ay," replied Har, " I can tell thee of another event which the Æsir deemed of much greater importance. Thou must know, therefore, that Baldur the Good having been tormented with terrible dreams, indicating that his life was in great peril, communicated them to the assembled Æsir, who resolved to conjure all things to avert from him the threatened danger. Then Frigga exacted an oath from fire and water, from iron, and all other metals, as well as from stones, earths, diseases, beasts, birds, poisons, and creeping things, that none of them would do any harm to Baldur. When this was done, it became a favourite pastime of the Æsir, at their meetings, to get Baldur to stand up and serve them as a mark, some hurling darts at him, some stones, while others hewed at him with their swords and battle-axes, for do they what they would none of them could harm him, and this was regarded by all as a great honour shown to Baldur. But when Loki, the son of Laufey, beheld the scene, he was sorely vexed that Baldur was not hurt. Assuming, therefore, the shape of a woman, he went to Fensalir, the mansion of Frigga. That goddess, when she saw the pretended woman, inquired of her if she knew what the Æsir were doing at their meetings. She replied, that they were throwing darts and stones at Baldur without being able to hurt him.

" ' Ay,' said Frigga, ' neither metal nor wood can hurt Baldur, for I have exacted an oath from all of them.'

" ' What!' exclaimed the woman, ' have all things sworn to spare Baldur ?'

" ' All things,' replied Frigga, ' except one little shrub that grows on the eastern side of Valhalla, and is called Mistletoe, and which I thought too young and feeble to crave an oath from.'

" As soon as Loki heard this he went away, and, resuming his natural shape, cut off the mistletoe, and repaired to the place where the gods were assembled. There he found Hödur standing apart, without partaking of the sports, on account of his blindness, and going up to him, said, ' Why dost thou not also throw something at Baldur ?'

" ' Because I am blind,' answered Hödur, ' and see not where Baldur is, and have, moreover, nothing to throw with.'

" ' Come then,' said Loki, ' do like the rest, and show honour to Baldur by throwing this twig at him, and I will direct thy arm toward the place where he stands.'

" Hödur then took the mistletoe, and under the guidance of Loki, darted it at Baldur, who, pierced through and through, fell down lifeless. Surely never was there witnessed, either among gods or men, a more atrocious deed than this! When Baldur fell the Æsir were struck speechless with horror, and then they looked at each other, and all were of one mind to lay hands on him who had done the deed, but they were obliged to delay their vengeance out of respect for the sacred place (Peace-stead) where they were assembled. They at length gave vent to their grief by loud lamentations, though not one of them could find words to express the poignancy of his feelings. Odin, especially, was more sensible than the others of the loss they had suffered, for he foresaw what a detriment Baldur's death would be to the Æsir. When the gods came to themselves, Frigga asked who among them wished to gain all her love and good will; ' For this,' said she, ' shall he have who will ride to Hel and try to find Baldur, and offer Hela a ransom if she will let him return to Asgard;' whereupon Hermod, surnamed the Nimble, the son of Odin, offered to undertake the journey. Odin's horse Sleipnir was then led forth, on which Hermod mounted, and galloped away on his mission [FF].

" The Æsir then took the dead body and bore it to the sea-shore, where stood Baldur's ship Hringhorn, which passed for the largest in the world. But when they wanted to launch it in order to make Baldur's funeral pile on it, they were unable to make it stir. In this conjuncture they sent to Jötunheim for a certain giantess named Hyrrokin, who came mounted on a wolf, having twisted serpents for a bridle. As soon as she alighted, Odin ordered four Berserkir to hold her steed fast, who were, however, obliged to throw the animal on the ground ere they could effect their purpose. Hyrrokin then went to the ship, and with a single push set it afloat, but the motion was so violent that fire sparkled from the rollers, and the earth shook all around. Thor, enraged at the sight, grasped his mallet, and but for the interference of the Æsir would have broken the woman's skull. Baldur's body was then borne to the funeral pile on board the ship, and this ceremony had such an effect on Nanna, the daughter of Nep, that her heart broke with grief, and her body was burnt on the same pile with her husband's. Thor then stood up and hallowed the pile with Mjölnir, and during the ceremony kicked a dwarf named Litur, who was running before his feet, into the fire. There was a vast concourse of various kinds of people at Baldur's obsequies. First came Odin, accompanied by Frigga, the Valkyrjor and his ravens; then Frey in his car drawn by the boar named Gullinbursti or Slidrugtanni; Heimdall rode his horse called Gulltopp, and Freyja drove in her chariot drawn by cats. There were also a great many Frostgiants and giants of the mountains present. Odin laid on the pile the gold ring called Draupnir, which afterwards acquired the property of producing every ninth night eight rings of equal weight. Baldur's horse was led to the pile fully caparisoned, and consumed in the same flames on the body of his master.

"Meanwhile, Hermod was proceeding on his mission. For the space of nine days, and as many nights, he rode through deep glens so dark that he could not discern anything until he arrived at the river Gjöll, which he passed over on a bridge covered with glittering gold. Modgudur, the maiden who kept the bridge, asked him his name and lineage, telling him that the day before five bands of dead persons had ridden over the bridge, and did not shake it so much as he alone. 'But,' she added, 'thou hast not death's hue on thee, why then ridest thou here on the way to Hel?'

"'I ride to Hel,' answered Hermod, 'to seek Baldur. Hast thou perchance seen him pass this way?'

"'Baldur,' she replied, 'hath ridden over Gjöll's bridge, but there below, towards the north, lies the way to the abodes of death.'

"Hermod then pursued his journey until he came to the barred gates of Hel. Here he alighted, girthed his saddle tighter, and remounting, clapped both spurs to his horse, who cleared the gate by a tremendous leap without touching it. Hermod then rode on to the palace, where he found his brother Baldur occupying the most distinguished seat in the hall, and passed the night in his company. The next morning he besought Hela (Death) to let Baldur ride home with him, assuring her that nothing but lamentations were to be heard among the gods. Hela answered that it should now be tried whether Baldur was so beloved as he was said to be.

" ' If therefore,' she added, ' all things in the world, both living and lifeless, weep for him, then shall he return to the Æsir, but if any one thing speak against him or refuse to weep, he shall be kept in Hel.'

" Hermod then rose, and Baldur led him out of the hall and gave him the ring Draupnir, to present as a keepsake to Odin. Nanna also sent Frigga a linen cassock and other gifts, and to Fulla a gold finger-ring. Hermod then rode back to Asgard, and gave an account of all he had heard and witnessed.

" The gods upon this despatched messengers throughout the world, to beg everything to weep, in order that Baldur might be delivered from Hel. All things very willingly complied with this request, both men and every other living being, as well as earths and stones, and trees and metals, just as thou must have seen these things weep when they are brought from a cold place into a hot one. As the messengers were returning with the conviction that their mission had been quite successful, they found an old hag named Thaukt sitting in a cavern, and begged her to weep Baldur out of Hel. But she answered,

" ' Thaukt will wail
With arid tears
Baldur's bale fire.
Nought, quick or dead,
By man's son gain I,
Let Hela hold what's hers.'

It was strongly suspected that this hag was no other than Loki himself, who never ceased to work evil among the Æsir."

THE FLIGHT AND PUNISHMENT OF LOKI.

50. " Evil are the deeds of Loki truly," said Gangler; " first of all in his having caused Baldur to be slain, and then preventing him from being delivered out of Hel. But was he not punished for these crimes? "

"Ay," replied Har, "and in such a manner that he will long repent having committed them. When he perceived how exasperated the gods were, he fled and hid himself in the mountains. There he built him a dwelling with four doors, so that he could see everything that passed around him. Often in the daytime he assumed the likeness of a salmon, and concealed himself under the waters of a cascade called Fránán-gursfors, where he employed himself in divining and circum-venting whatever stratagems the Æsir might have recourse to in order to catch him. One day, as he sat in his dwelling, he took flax and yarn, and worked them into meshes in the manner that nets have since been made by fishermen. Odin, however, had descried his retreat out of Hlidskjálf, and Loki becoming aware that the gods were approaching, threw his net into the fire, and ran to conceal himself in the river. When the gods entered the house, Kvasir, who was the most distinguished among them all for his quickness and penetra-tion, traced out in the hot embers the vestiges of the net which had been burnt, and told Odin that it must be an in-vention to catch fish. Whereupon they set to work and wove a net after the model they saw imprinted in the ashes. This net, when finished, they threw into the river in which Loki had hidden himself. Thor held one end of the net, and all the other gods laid hold of the other end, thus jointly drawing it along the stream. Notwithstanding all their precautions the net passed over Loki, who had crept between two stones, and the gods only perceived that some living thing had touched the meshes. They therefore cast their net a second time, hanging so great a weight to it that it everywhere raked the bed of the river. But Loki, perceiving that he had but a short distance from the sea, swam onwards and leapt over the net into the waterfall. The Æsir instantly followed him, and divided themselves into two bands. Thor, wading along in mid-stream, followed the net, whilst the others dragged it along towards the sea. Loki then perceived that he had only two chances of escape, either to swim out to sea, or to leap again over the net. He chose the latter, but as he took a tremendous leap Thor caught him in his hand. Being, how-ever, extremely slippery, he would have escaped had not Thor held him fast by the tail, and this is the reason why salmons have had their tails ever since so fine and thin.

"The gods having thus captured Loki, dragged him without commiseration into a cavern, wherein they placed three sharp-pointed rocks, boring a hole through each of them. Having also seized Loki's children, Vali and Nari, they changed the former into a wolf, and in this likeness he tore his brother to pieces and devoured him. The gods then made cords of his intestines, with which they bound Loki on the points of the rocks, one cord passing under his shoulders, another under his loins, and a third under his hams, and afterwards transformed these cords into thongs of iron. Skadi then suspended a serpent over him in such a manner that the venom should fall on his face, drop by drop. But Siguna, his wife, stands by him and receives the drops as they fall in a cup, which she empties as often as it is filled. But while she is doing this, venom falls upon Loki, which makes him howl with horror, and twist his body about so violently that the whole earth shakes, and this produces what men call earthquakes. There will Loki lie until Ragnarök." [GG].

OF RAGNARÖK, OR THE TWILIGHT OF THE GODS, AND THE CONFLAGRATION OF THE UNIVERSE.

51. "I have not heard before of Ragnarök," said Gangler; "what hast thou to tell me about it?"

"There are many very notable circumstances concerning it," replied Har, "which I can inform thee of. In the first place will come the winter, called Fimbul-winter, during which snow will fall from the four corners of the world; the frosts will be very severe, the wind piercing, the weather tempestuous, and the sun impart no gladness. Three such winters shall pass away without being tempered by a single summer. Three other similar winters follow, during which war and discord will spread over the whole globe. Brethren for the sake of mere gain shall kill each other, and no one shall spare either his parents or his children. As it is said in the Völuspá—

> "'Then shall brethren be
> Each other's bane,
> And sisters' children rend
> The ties of kin.

Hard will be the age,
And harlotry prevail.
An axe-age, a sword-age,
Shields oft cleft in twain,
A storm-age, a wolf-age,
Ere earth shall meet its doom.'

" Then shall happen such things as may truly be accounted
great prodigies. The wolf shall devour the sun, and a severe
loss will that be for mankind. The other wolf will take the
moon, and this too will cause great mischief. Then the stars
shall be hurled from the heavens, and the earth so violently
shaken that trees will be torn up by the roots, the tottering
mountains tumble headlong from their foundations, and all
bonds and fetters be shivered in pieces. Fenrir then breaks
loose, and the sea rushes over the earth, on account of the
Midgard serpent turning with giant force, and gaining the
land. On the waters floats the ship Naglfar, which is constructed of the nails of dead men. For which reason great
care should be taken to die with pared nails, for he who dies
with his nails unpared, supplies materials for the building of
this vessel, which both gods and men wish may be finished as
late as possible. But in this flood shall Naglfar float, and the
giant Hrym be its steersman.

" The wolf Fenrir advancing, opens his enormous mouth ;
the lower jaw reaches to the earth, and the upper one to
heaven, and would in fact reach still farther were there space
to admit of it. Fire flashes from his eyes and nostrils. The
Midgard serpent, placing himself by the side of the wolf,
vomits forth floods of poison which overwhelm the air and the
waters. Amidst this devastation heaven is cleft in twain, and
the sons of Muspell ride through the breach. Surtur rides first ;
and both before and behind him flames burning fire. His
sword outshines the sun itself. Bifröst, as they ride over it,
breaks to pieces. Then they direct their course to the battle-
field called Vigrid. Thither also repair the wolf Fenrir and
the Midgard serpent, and also Loki, with all the followers of
Hel, and Hrym with all the Hrimthursar. But the sons of
Muspell keep their effulgent bands apart on the field of battle,
which is one hundred miles long on every side.

" Meanwhile Heimdall stands up, and with all his force

sounds the Gjallar-horn to arouse the gods, who assemble
without delay. Odin then rides to Mimir's well and con-
sults Mimir how he and his warriors ought to enter into
action. The ash Yggdrasill begins to shake, nor is there anything in heaven or earth exempt from fear at that terrible
hour. The Æsir and all the heroes of Valhalla arm themselves and speed forth to the field, led on by Odin, with his
golden helm and resplendent cuirass, and his spear called
Gungnir. Odin places himself against the wolf Fenrir; Thor
stands by his side, but can render him no assistance, having
himself to combat the Midgard serpent. Frey encounters
Surtur, and terrible blows are exchanged ere Frey falls; and
he owes his defeat to his not having that trusty sword he gave
to Skirnir. That day the dog Garm, who had been chained
in the Gnipa cave, breaks loose. He is the most fearful
monster of all, and attacks Tyr, and they kill each other.
Thor gains great renown for killing the Midgard serpent, but
at the same time, recoiling nine paces, falls dead upon the spot,
suffocated with the floods of venom which the dying serpent
vomits forth upon him. The wolf swallows Odin, but at that
instant Vidar advances, and setting his foot on the monster's
lower jaw, seizes the other with his hand, and thus tears and
rends him till he dies. Vidar is able to do this because he
wears those shoes for which stuff has been gathering in all
ages, namely, the shreds of leather which are cut off to form
the toes and heels of shoes, and it is on this account that
those who would render a service to the Æsir should take
care to throw such shreds away. Loki and Heimdall fight,
and mutually kill each other.

" After this, Surtur darts fire and flame over the earth, and
the whole universe is consumed [H H]. As it is said in the
Völuspá,—

> " ' High bloweth Heimdall
> His horn aloft.
> Odin consulteth
> Mimir's head.
> The old ash yet standing,
> Yggdrasill,
> To its summit is shaken,
> And loose breaks the giant.

'Hrym from the East comes,
Floods swell around him
Jörmungand * rolls
With giant rage,
And ocean smiteth.
With lurid beak screams
The corpse-pecking eagle;
While floats Naglfar.

'A keel from the East nears,—
Muspellheim's children
Come o'er the main—
And Loki it steereth.
All grim and gaunt monsters
Conjoin with the wolf,
And before them all goeth
The brother of Byleist †.

'How fare the Æsir?
How fare the Elves?
All Jötunheim's shaken,
The Æsir hold Thing.
Expert in rock dwellings
The dwarfs wailing stand
Before their cleft caverns.
Conceive ye this or not?

'Surtur from the South wends
With seething fire
The falchion of the mighty one ‡.
A sunlight flameth.
Mountains together dash,
Giants headlong rush,
Men tread the paths to Hel,
And heaven in twain is rent.

'O'er Hlina § then shall come
Another woe.

* The great Midgard serpent.
† Namely, Loki.
‡ See the note, page 402.
§ Hlina was one of the minor goddesses who had the care of those whom
Frigga intended to rescue from danger, (see chapter 35,) but she is here placed

' When Odin fares him forth
  The wolf to combat;
And he who Beli * slew
  'Gainst Surtur rideth;
Then shall fall the god
  To Frigga dearest †.

' Vidar, the mighty son
  Of victory's father,
With the ferocious beast
  To fight, then goeth.
And with firm grasp, his sword
  In the giant-born monster's heart
Deep planteth; thus
  His sire avenging.

' Then the renowned son
  Of Hlodyn ‡ cometh,
He, of Odin first born,
  Midgard's protecting ward
Bravely fights and slays
  The serpent monster.
Then shall all mankind
  The earth abandon.

' Dimm'd 's now the sun,
  In ocean earth sinks;
From the skies are cast
  The sparkling stars;
The fire-reek rageth
  Around Time's nurse §,
And flickering flames
  With heaven itself play.'

for **Frigga** herself. The former woe alluded to is the death of Baldur, the other woe the approaching death of Odin.

  * Namely, Frey.—See chapter 37.

  † Namely, Odin.

  ‡ Viz., Thor, the son of Frigga, here called Hlodyn—See this word in the Glossary.

  § Viz., the ash Yggdrasill.

" And it is moreover said *,

> " ' Vigrid is called the field
> Where Surtur and the mild gods
> Shall meet in combat.
> A hundred miles it hath
> On every side.
> For the gods 'tis marked out.' "

OF THE ABODES OF FUTURE BLISS AND MISERY.

52. " What will remain," said Gangler, "after heaven and earth and the whole universe shall be consumed, and after all the gods, and the heroes of Valhalla, and all mankind shall have perished? For ye have already told me that every one shall continue to exist in some world or other, throughout eternity."

" There will be many abodes," replied Thridi, "some good. others bad. The best place of all to be in will be Gimli. in heaven, and all who delight in quaffing good drink will find a great store in the hall called Brimir, which is also in heaven in the region Okolni. There is also a fair hall of ruddy gold called Sindri, which stands on the mountains of Nida, (Niŏa-fjöll). In those halls righteous and well-minded men shall abide. In Náströnd there is a vast and direful structure with doors that face the north. It is formed entirely of the backs of serpents, wattled together like wicker work. But the serpents' heads are turned towards the inside of the hall, and continually vomit forth floods of venom, in which wade all those who commit murder, or who forswear themselves. As it is said in the Völuspá (st. 34, 35)—

> " ' She saw a hall
> Far from the sun
> In Náströnd standing.
> Northward the doors look,
> And venom-drops
> Fall in through loopholes.
> Formed is that hall
> Of wreathed serpents.

> ' There saw she wade,
> Through heavy streams,

* In Vafthrúdnis-mál, st. 18.

Men forsworn,
And murderers.'

" Hvergelmir, however, is the worst.

" ' There Nidhögg quails
Of the dead, the bodies.' " *

THE RENOVATION OF THE UNIVERSE.

53. " Will any of the gods survive, and will there be any longer a heaven and an earth ? " demanded Gangler.

" There will arise out of the sea," replied Har, " another earth most lovely and verdant, with pleasant fields where the grain shall grow unsown. Vidar and Vali shall survive ; neither the flood nor Surtur's fire shall harm them. They shall dwell on the plain of Ida, where Asgard formerly stood. Thither shall come the sons of Thor, Modi and Magni, bringing with them their father's mallet Mjölnir. Baldur and Hödur shall also repair thither from the abode of death (Hel). There shall they sit and converse together, and call to mind their former knowledge and the perils they underwent, and the fight with the wolf Fenrir and the Midgard serpent. There too shall they find in the grass those golden tablets (orbs) which the Æsir once possessed. As it is said,—

" ' There dwell Vidar and Vali
In the gods' holy seats,

* The compiler of the Prose Edda has omitted two couplets of the thirty-fifth strophe, one of them very important, as it shows that the Skald destined Náströnd not only for murderers and perjurers, but also for adulterers (blandishers, seducers—literally, " they who murmur or whisper in the ears of others' wives.") If Snorri was the person who made the extract from the Völuspá, the omission may easily be accounted for—(see the note, page 377). The thirty-fifth strophe, when complete, is as follows :—

" There saw she wade,
Through heavy streams,
Men forsworn
And murderers,
And those who others' wives
Essayed to blandish.
There Nidhögg *sucked*
Of the dead the bodies ;
The wolf, too, tore them.
Conceive ye this, or not ? "

When slaked Surtur's fire is.
But Modi and Magni
Will Mjölnir possess,
And strife put an end to.'

"Thou must know, moreover, that during the conflagration caused by Surtur's fire, a woman named Lif (Life), and a man named Lifthrasir, lie concealed in Hodmimir's forest. They shall feed on morning dew, and their descendants shall soon spread over the whole earth. As it is said *,—

" ' But Lif and Lifthrasir
Shall keep themselves hid
In Hodmimir's forest;
The dew of the dawn
Shall serve them for food,
And from them spring the races.'

"But what thou wilt deem more wonderful is, that the sun shall have brought forth a daughter more lovely than herself, who shall go in the same track formerly trodden by her mother. As it is said †,—

" ' The radiant sun
A daughter bears,
Ere Fenrir takes her.
On her mother's course
Shall ride that maid,
When the gods have perished.'

"And now," continued Thridi, "if thou hast any further questions to ask, I know not who can answer thee, for I never heard tell of any one who could relate what will happen in the other ages of the world. Make, therefore, the best use thou canst of what has been imparted to thee."

Upon this Gangler heard a terrible noise all around him: he looked everywhere, but could see neither palace nor city, nor anything save a vast plain. He therefore set out on his return to his own kingdom, where he related all that he had seen and heard, and ever since that time these tidings have been handed down by oral tradition.

---

* In Vafthrúdnis-mál, st. 45.
† Ibid. st. 47.

PART THE SECOND,

COMMONLY CALLED

THE CONVERSATIONS OF BRAGI *.

(BRAGI-RŒÐUR.)

ÆGIR'S JOURNEY TO ASGARD.

1. Ægir, who was well skilled in magic, once went to Asgard, where he met with a very good reception. Supper time being come, the twelve mighty Æsir,—Odin, Thor, Njörd, Frey, Tyr, Heimdall, Bragi, Vidar, Vali, Ullur, Hœnir and Forseti, together with the Asynjor,—Frigga, Freyja, Gefjon, Iduna, Gerda, Siguna, Fulla and Nanna, seated themselves on their lofty doom seats, in a hall around which were ranged swords of such surpassing brilliancy that no other light was requisite. They continued long at table, drinking mead of a very superior quality. While they were emptying their capacious drinking horns, Ægir, who sat next to Bragi, requested him to relate something concerning the Æsir. Bragi instantly complied with his request, by informing him of what had happened to Iduna.

IDUNA AND HER APPLES.

2. "Once," he said, "when Odin, Loki, and Hœnir went on a journey, they came to a valley where a herd of oxen were grazing, and being sadly in want of provisions did not scruple to kill one for their supper. Vain, however, were their efforts to boil the flesh; they found it, every time they took off the lid of the kettle, as raw as when first put in. While they were endeavouring to account for this singular circumstance a noise was heard above them, and on looking up they beheld an enormous eagle perched on the branch of an oak tree.

* We have somewhat abridged the translation of this part, of which Mallet only gave a mere abstract.

If ye are willing to let me have my share of the flesh,' said the eagle, 'it shall soon be boiled;' and on their assenting to this proposal, it flew down and snatched up a leg and two shoulders of the ox—a proceeding which so incensed Loki, that he laid hold of a large stock, and made it fall pretty heavily on the eagle's back. It was, however, not an eagle that Loki struck, but the renowned giant Thjassi, clad in his eagle-plumage. Loki soon found this out to his cost, for while one end of the stock stuck fast to the eagle's back, he was unable to let go his hold of the other end, and was consequently trailed by the eagle-clad giant over rocks and forests, until he was almost torn to pieces. Loki in this predicament began to sue for peace, but Thjassi told him that he should never be released from his hold until he bound himself by a solemn oath to bring Iduna and her apples out of Asgard. Loki very willingly gave his oath to effect this object, and went back in a piteous plight to his companions

" On his return to Asgard, Loki told Iduna that, in a forest at a short distance from the celestial residence, he had found apples growing which he thought were of a much better quality than her own, and that at all events it was worth while making a comparison between them. Iduna, deceived by his words, took her apples, and went with him into the forest, but they had no sooner entered it than Thjassi, clad in his eagle-plumage, flew rapidly towards them, and catching up Iduna, carried her and her treasure off with him to Jötunheim. The gods being thus deprived of their renovating apples, soon became wrinkled and grey; old age was creeping fast upon them, when they discovered that Loki had been, as usual, the contriver of all the mischief that had befallen them. They therefore threatened him with condign punishment if he did not instantly hit upon some expedient for bringing back Iduna and her apples to Asgard. Loki having borrowed from Freyja her falcon-plumage, flew to Jötunheim, and finding that Thjassi was out at sea fishing, lost no time in changing Iduna into a sparrow and flying off with her; but when Thjassi returned and became aware of what had happened, he donned his eagle-plumage, and flew after them. When the Æsir saw Loki approach, holding Iduna transformed into a sparrow between his claws, and Thjassi with his outspread eagle wings ready to overtake him, they placed on the walls of Asgard bundles of chips, which they set fire to the instant that Loki had flown over them ; and as Thjassi could not stop his flight, the fire caught his plumage, and he thus fell into the power of the Æsir, who slew him within the portals of the celestial residence. When these tidings came to Thjassi's daughter, Skadi, she put on her armour and went to Asgard, fully determined to avenge her father's death ; but the Æsir having declared their willingness to atone for the deed, an amicable arrangement was entered into. Skadi was to choose a husband in Asgard, and the Æsir were to make her laugh, a feat which she flattered herself it would be impossible for any one to accomplish. Her choice of a husband was to be determined by a mere inspection of the feet of the gods, it being stipulated that the feet should be the only part of their persons visible until she had made known her determination. In inspecting the row of feet placed before her, Skadi took a fancy to a pair which she flattered herself, from their fine proportions, must be those of Baldur. They were however Njörd's and Njörd was accordingly given her for a husband *, and as Loki managed to make her laugh, by playing some diverting antics with a goat, the atonement was fully effected. It is even said that Odin did more than had been stipulated, by taking out Thjassi's eyes, and placing them to shine as stars in the firmament." †

THE ORIGIN OF POETRY.

3. Ægir having expressed a wish to know how poetry originated, Bragi informed him that the Æsir and Vanir having met to put an end to the war which had long been carried on between them, a treaty of peace was agreed to and ratified by each party spitting into a jar. As a lasting sign of the amity which was thenceforward to subsist between the contending parties, the gods formed out of this spittle a being to whom they gave the name of Kvásir, and whom they endowed with

---

* See Part I. chapter 23.

† Finn Magnusen's explanation of this myth is, that Iduna—the ever-renovating Spring—being in the possession of Thjassi—the desolating Winter—all nature languishes until she is delivered from her captivity. On this being effected, her presence again diffuses joy and gladness, and all things revive ; while her pursuer, Winter, with his icy breath, dissolves in the solar rays indicated by the fires lighted on the walls of Asgard.

such a high degree of intelligence that no one could ask him a question that he was unable to answer. Kvásir then traversed the whole world to teach men wisdom, but was at length treacherously murdered by the dwarfs, Fjalar and Galar, who, by mixing up his blood with honey, composed a liquor of such surpassing excellence that whoever drinks of it acquires the gift of song. When the Æsir inquired what had become of Kvásir, the dwarfs told them that he had been suffocated with his own wisdom, not being able to find any one who by proposing to him a sufficient number of learned questions might relieve him of its superabundance. Not long after this event, Fjalar and Galar managed to drown the giant Gilling and murder his wife, deeds which were avenged by their son Suttung taking the dwarfs out to sea, and placing them on a shoal which was flooded at high water. In this critical position they implored Suttung to spare their lives, and accept the verse-inspiring beverage which they possessed as an atonement for their having killed his parents. Suttung having agreed to these conditions, released the dwarfs, and carrying the mead home with him, committed it to the care of his daughter Gunnlauth. Hence poetry is indifferently called Kvásir's blood, Suttung's mead, the dwarf's ransom, &c.,

4. Ægir then asked how the gods obtained possession of so valuable a beverage, on which Bragi informed him that Odin being fully determined to acquire it, set out for Jötunheim, and after journeying for some time, came to a meadow in which nine thralls were mowing. Entering into conversation with them, Odin offered to whet their scythes, an offer which they gladly accepted, and finding that the whetstone he made use of had given the scythes an extraordinary sharpness, asked him whether he was willing to dispose of it. Odin, however, threw the whetstone in the air, and in attempting to catch it as it fell, each thrall brought his scythe to bear on the neck of one of his comrades, so that they were all killed in the scramble. Odin took up his night's lodging at the house of Suttung's brother, Baugi, who told him that he was sadly at a loss for labourers, his nine thralls having slain each other. Odin, who went under the name of Baulverk, said that for a draught of Suttung's mead he would do the work of nine men for him. The terms being agreed on, Odin worked for Baugi the whole summer, but Suttung

was deaf to his brother's entreaties, and would not part with a drop of the precious liquor, which was carefully preserved in a cavern under his daughter's custody. Into this cavern Odin was resolved to penetrate. He therefore persuaded Baugi to bore a hole through the rock, which he had no sooner done than Odin, transforming himself into a worm, crept through the crevice, and resuming his natural shape, won the heart of Gunnlauth. After having passed three nights with the fair maiden, he had no great difficulty in inducing her to let him take a draught out of each of the three jars, called Odhrœrir, Bodn, and Són, in which the mead was kept. But wishing to make the most of his advantage, he pulled so deep that not a drop was left in the vessels. Transforming himself into an eagle, he then flew off as fast as his wings could carry him, but Suttung becoming aware of the stratagem, also took upon himself an eagle's guise, and flew after him. The Æsir. on seeing him approach Asgard, set out in the yard all the jars they could lay their hands on, which Odin filled by discharging through his beak the wonder-working liquor he had drunken. He was, however, so near being caught by Suttung, that some of the liquor escaped him by an impurer vent, and as no care was taken of this it fell to the share of poetasters. But the liquor discharged in the jars was kept for the gods, and for those men who have sufficient wit to make a right use of it. Hence poetry is also called Odin's booty, Odin's gift, the beverage of the gods, &c., &c.

A CRITICAL EXAMINATION

OF THE

LEADING DOCTRINES

OF THE

SCANDINAVIAN SYSTEM OF MYTHOLOGY.

BY THE EDITOR.

It was our intention to have written a kind of commentary on the Prose Edda, in which we should have attempted to explain the myths contained in that work, and in the ancient poems of the Elder Edda, but having already exceeded our prescribed limits, we shall be obliged to conclude our editorial task by offering a few observations on a subject which, were it fully treated in all its details, would require a volume *.

We will not enter into the question whether the so-called primitive religion of mankind was monotheism or polytheism, such questions merely giving rise to idle speculations that cannot possibly lead to any satisfactory result. How, in fact, can we ascertain the primitive worship of mankind without knowing how mankind originated? And how are we to know this? Ask the Brahmin, and he will refer you to the Vedas, which he will assure you are the revelations of the Supreme Essence, and prove at least that *his myth* has priority of date in its favour. Ask the early Persian, and he will refer you to the Zendavesta. Ask the Israelite, and he will tell you that Jehovah revealed the work of creation to Moses. Inquire of modern science, and all that you will be able to learn is, that after the lapse of countless ages, in comparison to which the six thousand years of tradition and history are but as an infinitesimal fraction, the crust of this planet acquired its present form and consistency, and became a fitting abode for man.

* Finn Magnusen's *Eddalæren* fills, in fact, 4 volumes 12mo, containing altogether 1680 pages of letter-press, and his *Lexicon Mythologicum*, closely printed in double columns, takes up 850 quarto pages of the third volume of the Edda.

Guided by this science, you will also be able to perceive the
first faint glimmerings of intelligence that accompany the
rudimentary nervous system of the radiata, and to trace its
gradual development, along with this system, through the
collateral branches of molluscous and articulated animals to
the vertebrata, until it attains its full maturity in the highest
class of beings that has hitherto appeared on the earth: and
analogical reasoning will warrant you in drawing the conclusion that this intelligence is still in a state of development, and may, even on this planet, in ages far too remote for
human calculation, give rise to beings infinitely superior to
any that at present exist on its ever-changing surface. Vain
indeed must be the person who can imagine that Almighty
power has breathed into such an imperfect being as man all
the spiritual essence that mortality is capable of supporting *.

M. Mallet, in his inquiries respecting the religion of the
ancient Teutonic tribes, assumes that they originally worshipped
a sole, unique deity, and, as usual, gives extracts from Tacitus
in corroboration of his opinions. If our space allowed us, we
think we could show that the converse of all that he says on
this subject in the commencement of the fifth chapter of this
work would be much nearer the truth. If we follow the
Teutonic tribes to the plains of Asia, and thus remount far
beyond the bounds of authentic history and the times of
Tacitus, we may, in fact, with much greater reason suppose—
for in such inquiries anything that can be said will be little
better than mere conjecture—that their religion was essentially grounded on polytheism, for, like every other primitive
people, they were, no doubt, chiefly occupied in hunting and
in tending their flocks and herds. Now, when men are in this
rudimentary state of social existence, they will be forcibly
impressed by the varied phenomena of nature which they are
utterly unable to comprehend. They hear the thunder peal-
ing from the lurid clouds that veil the beneficent orb which
experience has taught them regulates the seasons. They behold the forked lightning darting athwart the jarring rack
winged with destruction. Trembling with fear, they naturally

* It may not be irrelevant to observe, that in a note to the second edition
of a pamphlet published in 1836, and entitled "A few Remarks on our
Foreign Policy," we had occasion to make use of a similar argument.

ascribe such terrible effects to a superhuman cause—to a wrathful deity, who rides the storm and launches his fiery bolts on the head of some devoted victim. Hence their firm belief in a God of Thunder—in a Thor, a Perun, a Perkunos, an Indra, a Jupiter Tonans. When located in a maritime district they venture in their frail barks to cross the seas that separate them from countries offering a rich spoil as the reward of their valour, and are suddenly assailed by a furious tempest that leaves little hope of safety, what can be more natural than their belief in a deity presiding over the ocean— a Njörd, a Neptune, an Ockopirn, a Varuna—who in this manner makes known his displeasure? All the great phenomena of nature are thus regarded as being under the guidance and control of elementary deities, and self-interest and self-preservation soon teach the most savage tribes to invoke these deities in order that their wrath may be averted, or their beneficent influence exercised for the good of the community.

At a much later period, when the tribes have acquired a certain degree of civilization, and have their priests or their pontiff chieftains, this rude form of public worship will be reduced into a system, and the most powerful of the elementary deities, generally the God of Thunder—Jupiter, Perun, Perkunos—will be regarded as the supreme divinity to whom all the others are subordinate. Temples will then be erected, and a public worship with sacrifices, sacrificial banquets and festivals instituted.

At a still later period, the chiefs, the priests and the poets, in a word, the most enlightened among the community, will form an esoteric doctrine,—will regard the deities to whom popular belief assigns a real superhuman existence, as the mere symbols of natural phenomena. The Bards, Skalds, Prophets, or by whatever name they may be designated, will draw up systems of cosmogony, theogony and mythology, susceptible both of an esoteric and an exoteric explanation. Some of these systems will be grounded on monotheism, some on pantheism, and others again on a dualistic monotheism, a system, in fact, which *apparently* offers the most rational explanation of the cause of evil in the world.

Tribes located in a sterile country, with a rigorous climate, have seldom passed beyond this stadium of intellectual development, which may be regarded as the transition period from systematic mythology to philosophy, from theology to free inquiry.   In the latter period the mind of man attains to the highest degree of intellectuality of which it is susceptible; but this culminating point of human intelligence presupposes several centuries of refinement and civilization, or, at least, a genial climate, a rich soil, wealth and prosperity; in short, a state of society in which men can find leisure to devote their lives exclusively to the study of the higher branches of human knowledge.   Such a state of society existed at a very remote period on the plains of the Ganges, and gave rise to various schools of philosophy, in which were taught the Mímánsá, Védánta, Nyáya, and Sánkhya systems, the prototypes of those of ancient Greece and of modern Germany, with this difference, that theological doctrines generally form the groundwork of Hindostanic speculations, whilst the Hellenic and German are entirely based on free inquiry.

Philosophy has assumed various forms, has been cast into various systems, has given rise to the wildest theories and speculations, and has, after all, arrived at no satisfactory result.   And how could it be otherwise?   The object in view was too vast for beings endowed with such limited faculties as we possess.   It was nothing less than to acquire the knowledge of things as they are in reality, and not as they appear to be.   In order to do this it was necessary to investigate the mysterious concatenation of cause and effect, and to answer the great questions—What is the universe? What is man? How came he here?   Whither will he go?   Is he mere matter superiorly organized, or is he a material being endowed with an immaterial spirit?   What is this spirit?   Is it an individual essence, or does it form but an infinitesimal portion of a general vivifying principle disseminated and undulating like light and heat throughout the universe?   What is this universe?   Is it a fortuitous combination of atoms, or is it the work of Infinite Wisdom?   May we suppose the Deity as a concentrated, and the universe as an extended immateriality, or must we acknowledge a personal Deity, an omnipotent, eternal, Supreme Essence, regulating matter at will, or subjecting it to unchangeable laws throughout eternity, and to whom time and space—those mysteries of mysteries—will be unknown?   Now, although it is self evident that such ques-

tions are quite beyond our comprehension, and that they
never have been, nor ever will be answered in a way to satisfy
a man of common sense and sound understanding, still it must
be admitted that philosophy has exercised a permanent, and,
on the whole, a highly beneficial influence on the most civilized portion of the human race.

The ancient Scandinavians were far from attaining to this
degree of intellectuality, for it was during what we have
termed the transition period of systematic mythology that the
Völuspá, and the other mythic poems of the Elder Edda—
which are the highest efforts of their genius—were composed *. The more, however, that we make ourselves acquainted with Saga literature, which enters into such minute
details respecting the social life of the Scandinavians, the more
we shall be convinced that the higher doctrines disclosed in
these poems must have been confined to a few Skalds and
Pontiff-chieftains, for they do not appear to have exercised the
slightest influence on the popular belief.

The faith professed by the great body of the people was
simply this, that all who died with arms in their hands, no
matter what had been their moral conduct throughout life,
would partake of the boisterous joys of Valhalla—would have
the pleasure of daily hewing each other to pieces, and then, to
use the words of the Edda, " sit down and drink ale with the
Æsir ; " whilst those who died a natural death would descend
to the cold and cheerless regions of Hela, which were, however, by no means regarded as a place of punishment †, the
sojourn in them being merely a negation of that rude kind
of celestial bliss reserved for the *chosen* heroes. It would
also appear to have been the popular belief that married
women after death would be comfortably lodged in Freyja's

---

* It is impossible to ascertain the precise date of their composition, but
the doctrines contained in them must at all events have been known prior to
the Scandinavian historical epoch, that is to say, previous to the middle of
the ninth century.

† Eating and drinking appear to have gone on in the hall of Hela much in
the same manner as in that of Odin. Hermod, for instance, finds Baldur
placed on the high-seat, and passes the evening very comfortably with him.
See the Prose Edda, ch. 49. In the Alvis-mál, st. 22 and 24, mention is
made of a kind of corn growing in the infernal regions, and it is stated that
the drink which men call *ale*, is known there under the name of *mead*. See
also Vegtams-kvida, st. 12.

mansion of Fólkváng, while the maidens were taken due care of by Gefjon *.

Several Danish and German writers have drawn a broad distinction between the worship of Thor and that of Odin, contending that this diversity gave rise to two principal sects, the Odinites and the Thorites, the former being the Catholics, and the latter the Protestants of Scandinavian Paganism, but we think their arguments are far from being conclusive. We will not deny that at a very remote period, when the Teutonic tribes were located on the plains of Asia, Thor may possibly have been regarded as their supreme deity, for, as we before observed, in most systems of mythology we find the God of Thunder represented as the chief of the celestial divinities ; but it is a well-ascertained fact that in more historical times all the *Germanic* tribes regarded Woden (Wodan, Odin) as the father of the gods, in which capacity he is invariably represented in the Eddaic Poems. It is certainly an equally well-established fact that the Norwegians and Icelanders were more devoted to the worship of Thor than the Danes and Swedes ; and the form of the Icelandic legal oath †, and several other circumstances, show that they regarded him as the most powerful of the Æsir. It was, in fact, quite natural that a nation of warriors should hold in peculiar reverence the deity who was continually engaged in combating giants and other typified principles of evil, but this does not appear by any means to have weakened their faith in Odin, for all the Icelandic Skalds send their heroes to Valhalla, and speak of Odin's Valkyrjor hovering over the field of battle ‡. Even Hakon the Good, notwithstanding his christianity §, is described, in the celebrated ode which Eyvind Skaldaspiller

* See the Prose Edda, ch. 35; Eigils-saga, c. 80, and Müller's Saga bib. i. 122.

† See page 292.

‡ In the dispute between Hárbard and Thor, the Skald makes the former say, "Odin has all the Jarls (the Freemen) who fall in battle, Thor all the Thralls."—See Hárbarz-ljód, st. 23.

§ Hakon (who reigned in Norway A.D. 940—63) was the son of Harald Hárfagra, who sent him to England, where he was fostered by King Athelstane, and instructed in the doctrines of Christianity. Hakon, however, when he became King of Norway, deemed it prudent not to interfere with the religious opinions of his subjects—hence Eyvind might justly regard him as one who respected, though he did not worship, the national deities.

composed on his death, as meeting with a splendid reception
in the hall of Odin.

When popular polytheism, which we must regard as the
primitive worship, has been refined into systematic mythology,
the esoteric doctrines engrafted on it will not long be limited
to a few individuals. The initiated will soon form a numerous
body, and the manner in which they cannot well refrain from
speaking of divinities in whom they no longer believe, will not
fail of exercising a considerable influence on the community *.
The popular faith will be gradually sapped to its foundations,
religious indifference and scepticism will prevail, and announce
that the reign of the ancient deities is drawing to a close.
The Scandinavians of the tenth century appear to have been
in this state of transition; hence the frequent instances of
warriors relying " on their own might and main," and others
openly contemning the national divinities †. Yet even during
this period the Eddaic doctrines of Ragnarök, of the destruction and renovation of the universe, and of a more refined
heaven than that of Odin—assuming, though by no means
taking for granted, that the latter doctrine is contained in the
Eddaic Poems—do not appear ever to have become popular.
The faith in the national deities was weakened without being
replaced. When men's minds are thus prepared for a change
any religious system that is a little more rational than the
ancient one will readily be adopted. Hence the Icelanders
were easily induced to embrace Christianity; not Christianity such as it is professed by the more enlightened classes,
in the present age, but monkish Christianity, with its legends
and miracles, and sainted divinities, ready to replace those of
Paganism; offering as a substitute for Thor, Michael the Archangel; for Freyja, the Virgin; for the god Vali, a St. Valentine
—probably manufactured for the occasion—and for every Pagan
festival a Christian one. The Norwegians clung more tenaciously
to the worship of their forefathers, and numbers of them died
real martyrs for their faith, after suffering the most cruel torments from their royal persecutor ‡; a proof that scepticism and

---

* The *Ægis-drekka* shows that the Scandinavians had their Lucian, like
most other nations when a national religion is in its wane.

† See pages 120 and 148.

‡ See the notes, pages 180 and 351.

religious indifference had made less progress amongst them than amongst the Icelanders, who, for a long time after their apparent conversion, appear to have had very little faith in either the old or the new doctrines.

If the view we have taken of the rise of mythological systems be correct, it will naturally follow that all such systems will offer striking coincidences. In all, we shall find a God of Thunder, a Sun-god, a Moon-goddess, in short, the same elementary deities under different names and attributes; and nothing, in our opinion, can be more illogical than to conclude from these coincidences between two or more mythological systems that they were derived from a common source; that is to say, from an historical or ethnological and not a physical source, natural phenomena being, in fact, the common source from which all of them originated. It is otherwise when we find the same spirit pervading two systems; for even if their respective deities have no great resemblance, still if the main doctrines engrafted on the popular belief offer a striking coincidence, we may be warranted at least in assuming that at some remote period they may either have had a common origin, or that the doctrines of the one may have been derived from those of the other, the more so, if this coincidence is between the mythologies of two cognate races whose languages are very nearly allied. Writers who ground more or less plausible theories on such coincidences, are, however, very apt to be led astray, and find analogy where none exists. Thus in the whole history of literature there is not, perhaps, an instance of a more signal failure than Finn Magnusen's elaborate attempt to identify Odinism and Buddhism. For our own part we cannot possibly conceive two religions so totally dissimilar. It is, however, unnecessary to enter into a discussion of the learned Icelander's hypothesis, as it has been amply and successfully refuted by Klaproth, A. W Schlegel, and other writers of acknowledged merit; but it is much to be regretted that a writer possessing such an intimate knowledge of northern antiquities as Finn Magnusen, should have rendered his *Eddalæren* and his *Lexicon Mythologicum* of much less utility than they otherwise would have been, did not this unfortunate theory appear under one form or other in almost every page. His comparison of the Scandinavian and Persian systems is more to the purpose. The coincidence between these systems has, in fact, been pointed out by several writers on the subject, and did not escape the penetration of M. Mallet *. It may, therefore, not be irrelevant to give a slight sketch of the doctrines attributed to Zoroaster, and contained in the Zendavesta, and show their analogy with those of the Scandinavian system as it is fully developed in the Eddaic Poems.

The doctrines of the early Persian or Iranite Magi are grounded on a system of dualistic monotheism. Ormuzd, the symbol of Light and Goodness, has for antagonist, Ahriman, the symbol of Darkness and Evil; but above this dualism which is finite—limited by a fixed period of time—is Zeruane Akherene (Illimited or Uncreated Time), the Infinite, Supreme Essence; or, if we regard the Persian system as a monotheism approaching very nearly to pantheism, *the Absolute* from which all things proceed and into which all things must return. Zeruane Akherene created Ormuzd by pronouncing the living word—the logos, Honover, (*enohe verihe,* i. e. I am, or be it). In Ormuzd are united the three primordial, ethereal elements, light, fire, and water. Ormuzd (Light, Goodness) has emanated from *Uncreated Time,* but as the Persian Sages could not admit that evil proceeded from such a pure source, and as they had nevertheless to account for the cause of evil in the world, they laid down the doctrine that Zeruane Akherene first created Light and Goodness, (Ormuzd,) and in order that a physical and moral antagonism—an ethical combat, might take place, without which there could in reality be no goodness, he permitted, *not allowed,* Darkness and Evil, (Ahriman,) but fixed a term of 12,000 years, at the expiration of which the strife should cease, and the antagonistic principles be united in Light and Love †

Ormuzd created the universe by pronouncing the living word Honover; first his own abode of light, Sakhter, and then the Genii, or deities of Light, in three classes. The first class consists of the seven Amshaspands, Ormuzd himself being included in the number; the others are Bahman, the

---

* See his note to the Prose Edda, [H H].

† According to these doctrines of the Magi all things originate through antagonism. When antagonism ceases, finite things also cease. Heraclitus and Empedocles appear to have derived several of their doctrines from this source.

genius of the region of light; Ardibehesht, the genius of ethereal fire; Shariver, the genius of metals; Sapandomad, the creatrix, or rather source, of fruitfulness; Khordad, the genius of time; and Amerdad, the tutelary genius of the vegetable world, and of flocks and herds. In the second class are the twenty-seven Izeds, male and female. These are the elementary deities, as Khorshid the sun; Mah the moon; Tashter the dog-star, also the deity of rain; Rapitan the deity of heat, &c.; and were probably those worshipped before the popular belief was not only thus reduced into a system like the Scandinavian, but refined to a high degree of intellectuality by the philosophical and ethical doctrines engrafted on it. The third class consists of the Fervers: these are the vivifying principles of nature, the ideal types of the material universe, corresponding in a great measure to the *ideas* of Plato. In heaven they keep watch against Ahriman and his host; on earth they combat against the Genii of evil. Every one, even Ormuzd himself, has his Ferver. An Iranite had thus constantly by his side his ideal type, or uncorrupted immaterial image, to guide him through life and preserve him from evil.

When Ahriman, by the permission, but not by the will of Zeruane Akherene, fell from Ormuzd—*i. e.* when darkness arose in opposition to light, evil in antagonism to goodness— he was bound down for the space of 3000 years in Duzakh (Hades—the Bottomless Pit) where he created the Devs; namely, six chief Devs, himself being the seventh, as the antagonists of the Amshaspands, and a number of inferior Devs —the typified principles of evil. Meanwhile Ormuzd went on with the creation of the material universe, making the sun, moon, stars, the earth, &c. The first living being was the ox Abudad, which was slain by Ahriman, but Ormuzd formed from its body the different species of beasts, birds and fishes, trees, plants, &c. When the ox expired, a being called Kajomorz sprung from its right leg. Kajomorz was killed by the Devs, but after the elementary particles that entered into the composition of his body had been purified in the light of the sun during forty years, they became the germ of the Ribas tree, out of which Ormuzd made the first man and woman, Meshia and Meshiane, infusing into them the breath of life and spirituality. He thus completed the work of creation in six periods, holding at the end of each the festival Gahanbar.

Ahriman soon contrived to seduce the first parents of mankind, by persuading them to eat of the forbidden fruit. Sin and death are now in the world; the principles of good and evil are in deadly strife; Ormuzd, however, predominates, but when he wishes to lead mankind against Ahriman, they join the Devs. Ormuzd then reveals to them his law through his prophet Zoroaster; the strife between the two principles continues, however, and will continue until the end of the predestined term. During the last 3000 years of the period Ahriman is predominant. The world now hastens to its doom; religion and virtue are nowhere to be found; mankind are plunged in sin and misery; but Sosiosh is born of a virgin and redeems them, subdues the Devs, awakes the dead, and holds the last judgment. A comet sets the world in flames; the Genii of Light combat against the Genii of Darkness, and cast them into Duzakh, where Ahriman and the Devs and the souls of the wicked are thoroughly cleansed and purified by fire. Ahriman then submits to Ormuzd; evil is absorbed into goodness; the unrighteous, thoroughly purified, are united with the righteous, and a new earth and a new heaven arise free from all evil, where peace and innocence will for ever dwell *.

That a certain analogy exists between the Persian and the Scandinavian systems cannot be denied. A decided dualism pervades both. Odin and the Æsir may be compared to Ormuzd and the Amshaspands; Loki, and his evil progeny, the wolf Fenrir and the Midgard serpent, together with the giants and monsters of Jötunheim and Hvergelmir, to Ahriman and the Devs. There is also a certain similarity in the cosmogonic myths—the ox Abudad answering to Ymir, and the creation of Meshia and Meshiane to that of Ask and Embla. The Persian system has also its Ragnarök: the Genii of Light and Darkness fight their last fight much in the same manner as the Æsir and their opponents, though the Æsir have to encounter not only Loki and his evil progeny, but also the sons of the empyreal region of Muspellheim; a myth which we shall presently have occasion to examine. Baldur,

* See Creuzer's Symbolik und Mythologie, 1 Th. 1 B. 3 Cap.

too, may in some measure be compared to the redeemer Sosiosh; yet notwithstanding these and other coincidences, and
notwithstanding the fact that the various tribes of the Iranic
and Teutonic races spoke languages strictly cognate, we should
not venture to conclude, as most writers on the subject have
done, that both systems were derived directly and immediately
from a common source, nor even—though this is more admissible—that the Scandinavian doctrines were borrowed from
the Persian.   The antagonism between light and darkness,
between good and evil, is a fact, and, in striving to account for
this fact, the sages and theologists of two primitive nations
may easily have fallen into the same train of reasoning, and
thus framed systems offering almost as striking coincidences
as if they had actually had a common origin.

It is unquestionably from India that we have derived, partly
through the Persians, but more especially through the Hellenic philosophers, most of our metaphysical and several of our
theological doctrines; and we will not deny that some of these
doctrines may have been handed down by oral tradition to the
Pontiff-chieftains of the Scandinavian tribes, and that the
Skalds who composed the mythic poems of the Elder Edda
may have had an obscure and imperfect knowledge of them.
Be this as it may, we must not forget that the higher doctrines of the Scandinavian system were confined to the few,
whereas those of the Zendavesta were the religious belief of
the whole nation; and so long as they continued uncorrupted
—for all religious doctrines become, in the course of time,
alloyed and perverted—must have exercised, and history at-
tests actually did exercise, a highly beneficial and humanizing
influence.   Iran was the land of Light and of the children of
Ormuzd; Turan (the steppes of Tartary), the land of Darkness and of the children of Ahriman, a notion grounded on
the feuds of rival races, which could only have produced
courage; but every thing that was good, every thing that was
of utility to mankind, also belonged to Ormuzd.   Hence it
was the duty of an Iranite to avoid crime, to lead a moral and
unblemished life, to show by the purity of his character that
he was a true Iranite and not a Turanite.   It was also his
duty to cultivate the soil, for its fruits were of the kingdom of
Ormuzd, and, consequently, to drain marshes, regulate the
course of rivers, destroy venomous reptiles, and, in a word, to

contend incessantly against both physical and moral evil, under whatever forms they might appear. If he had done this, he might after death fearlessly appear before Ormuzd and Bahman on the bridge Tshinevad, assured that the Izeds would conduct him in triumph to regions of celestial bliss; but if he had displayed throughout life the greatest valour in war, and had neglected to combat the principle of evil by restraining his own passions, he might justly fear being consigned to Ahriman and the Devs, waiting to seize his trembling spirit and plunge it into the tormenting, though cleansing, flames of Duzakh *.

This was a much more intellectual and refined faith than that of the Scandinavians, amongst whom valour was the one thing necessary, the only virtue, in fact, that claimed a future recompense. If a Northman died with arms in his hands stained with the blood of his adversaries, he was assured of enjoying a coarse and jovial kind of celestial happiness in Valhalla, even though his moral conduct had been far from irreproachable ; and if he died a natural death he would, at all events, swill his ale in the halls of Hela. The Persian system was calculated to form an energetic, intellectual, and highly moral people; the Scandinavian a semi-barbarous troop of crafty and remorseless warriors, whose energy would be solely displayed in deeds of slaughter, and the social intervals of their turbulent existence passed amidst scenes of the coarsest festivity. Yet such as they were these Scandinavians seem to have been destined by the inscrutable designs of Providence to invigorate at least one of the nations of which they were for centuries the scourge, in order, as we previously had occasion to observe †, that the genial blending of cognate tribes might form a people the most capable of carrying on the great work of civilization, which in some far distant age may finally render this world that abode of peace and intellectual enjoyment dimly shadowed forth in ancient myths as only to be found in a renovated and fresh emerging universe.

Although every system of mythology, when fully developed,

---

* Duzakh resembles the Purgatory of the Catholic Church ; the Persians, however, had a purgatory without a hell, being of opinion that the punishment, even for the greatest crimes, committed by a feeble being endowed with strong passions and propensities and a limited intelligence, could not last eternally.

† See page 44.

has its esoteric as well as its exoteric doctrines, we think that several eminent writers, in attempting to withdraw the veil and initiate us into the mysteries of the former, or, in other words, to show the true signification of a system, have frequently had recourse to the most unwarranted assumptions. They appear, in fact, to have altogether lost sight of the question it was intended to elucidate, to have forgotten that the main point of such inquiries is, not how a mythological system *may be explained*, but in what manner *it was actually explained or understood* by the most enlightened of the community professing to believe in its doctrines. It is thus that Finn Magnusen, with all the dogmatism of an ancient mystagogue, gives an astronomical explanation of the Scandinavian myths, without adducing the slightest historical evidence to show that the Pontiff-chieftains, from whom he himself claims descent, entertained such notions, or even that they possessed a sufficient knowledge of astronomy to warrant the conclusion that they were at least capable of entertaining them. Hence, notwithstanding the lucidity with which he invariably expresses his ideas, whether he makes use of the Danish or the Latin language, and notwithstanding the learning and erudition displayed in every page of his writings, we are reluctantly compelled to follow him as we should follow a guide, who professing to lead us out of a labyrinth, would only involve us, after fruitless circumgyrations, still deeper in its intricate mazes. We can, in fact, only regard but too many of the learned disquisitions in his " Eddalæren " and his Mythological Lexicon as plausible arguments in support of ingenious theories, that, generally speaking, will not stand the test of a rigorous criticism.

A mythology, when regarded irrespective of the manner in which it may have been understood by those who first reduced it into a system, is obviously susceptible of any interpretation that a writer may choose to give it. Hence we have historical, ethnological, astronomical, physical, and psychological or ethical explanations of most mythological systems.

Under the historical point of view the gods are mere deified mortals, either heroes who have been deified after their death, or Pontiff-chieftains who have passed themselves off for gods, and who, it is gratuitously supposed, found people stupid enough to believe in their pretended divinity. This was the manner in which Euhemerus explained the Greek mythology, and Snorri Sturlason the Scandinavian; but a method that presupposes an historical Odin, an historical Jupiter, an historical Osiris, &c., is, in our opinion, too absurd to merit the slightest attention, or at the present day to stand in need of a refutation.

Regarded ethnologically, myths are the mere allegorical accounts of the feuds and dissensions of rival races. The conflict of the Æsir and Vanir, for instance, which terminated in a lasting peace and the exchange of hostages, is a myth founded on the wars carried on between the Teutonic and Slavonic races; wars which were, however, so far from terminating in the manner described, that they continued for centuries after the extinction of Paganism; and even in the present comparatively enlightened age can scarcely be said to have subsided. Although the ethnological explanation is far more rational than the historical, and may possibly be the right manner of interpreting several myths, we must, nevertheless, regard it, in so far at least as it has been applied to Scandinavian mythology, to be equally undeserving of serious consideration.

It is otherwise with the astronomical, physical, and psychological methods. It is obvious, in fact, that when a myth was intended to convey an esoteric as well as an exoteric doctrine, the former would generally be grounded on the never ending strife of those antagonistic principles which pervade alike the material and the ideal universe, the realms of nature and the manifestations of human intelligence. Men who were sufficiently enlightened to reduce the popular belief in elementary deities into a rational system, would be forcibly struck by the antagonism between light and darkness, summer and winter, good and evil, virtue and vice; between barbarism and civilization, obscurantism and intellectuality. Hence we may safely assume that most myths contain both physical and psychological doctrines, a fact which for several of the Hindostanic, Iranic, Egyptian, and Hellenic myths can be fully proved by the testimony of ancient writers, and other direct historical evidence. It may also be taken for granted that the sages and philosophers of civilized nations, that are known to have possessed a competent knowledge of astronomy, clothed the truths of that science in popular myths, and that we are consequently warranted in making use of the *astronomical method* for the explanation of such myths, especially for those of the Egyptians, Phœnicians, Indians, and other Asiatic nations; and although we will not deny that several of the Scandinavian myths may have a remote Asiatic origin, and have been handed down to the Pontiff-chieftains by oral tradition, and may, therefore, contain astronomical truths, still we should not venture to attribute to these semi-barbarous sacerdotal warriors such a familiar acquaintance with the laws of nature as the astronomical explanation of their mythological system would necessarily imply. In proceeding to offer a few brief observations on the most interesting chapters of the Prose Edda, we shall, therefore, chiefly regard the myths under a physical and psychological point of view, occasionally giving some of Finn Magnusen's astronomical explanations, although our limits will not allow us to enter into any discussion respecting them.

CHAP. 2.—This chapter was probably written by Snorri, but although he commences by anthropomorphizing the Scandinavian deities, and making Gylfi take a journey to a terrestrial instead of a celestial Asgard, he concludes by placing him before the so-called Odinic Trinity, the High, the Equally High, and the Third.

The most ancient Trinitarian doctrine on record is that of the Brahmins. The eternal Supreme Essence—called Parabrahma, Brehm, Paratma—produced the universe by self-reflection, and first revealed himself as Brahma, the Creating Power; then as Vishnu, the Preserving Power; and lastly as Shiva, the Destroying and Renovating Power. According to the popular belief, Brahma, Vishnu and Shiva are three distinct deities, whereas the sages who framed the higher doctrines of the Vedas merely regarded them as the three modes in which the Supreme Essence reveals himself in the material universe. Payne Knight remarks that "this tri-form division of the personified attributes, or modes of action of one first cause, seems to have been the first departure from simple theism, and the foundation of religious mythology in every part of the earth."—"Hence, almost every nation of the world that has departed from the rude simplicity of primitive theism, has had its Trinity in Unity, which, when not limited and ascertained by divine revelation, branched out by the natural sub division of collective and indefinite ideas into the endless and intricate personifications of particular subordinate attributes, which have afforded such abundant materials for the elegant fictions both of poetry and art."* This is much the same kind of theory as that of M. Mallet, both assuming, we think quite gratuitously, that monotheism was the worship of every primitive race. That the Vedas are of a very high antiquity is unquestionable; but however remote we may place the period when they were written, we must necessarily presuppose that the Hindostanic race had already attained to a comparatively high degree of civilization, otherwise men capable of framing such doctrines could not have been found. Now, this state of civilization must necessarily have been preceded by several centuries of barbarism, during which we cannot possibly admit a more refined faith than the popular belief in elementary deities, a belief on which the metaphysical doctrines of the Vedas were, no doubt, subsequently engrafted. At all events, writers who maintain the contrary opinion will be reduced to the dilemma of admitting either that the ancient Indians were *ab origine* a civilized people, or that being still in a barbarous and unsettled state, they nevertheless possessed sages sufficiently enlightened to discuss the highest questions of metaphysical philosophy, and that, too, in one of the richest and most copious languages—we might perhaps even say in the richest and most copious language— ever spoken by man.

The monotheistic doctrines of the Vedas were subtilized in several Hindostanic schools of philosophy into an idealistic pantheism, Brehm or Paratma being regarded as a selfemanating and self-absorbing unity—as the All, the Absolute—as the Being of Beings in eternal repose, surrounded outwardly by Maja (illusion), that is to say, by the visible universe, which in respect to itself possesses reality, but in respect to Brehm,—to the Absolute, is a mere nullity. "By this universal expansion of the creative spirit," to use the words of Payne Knight, "every production of earth, water,

---

* "Inquiry into the Symbolical Language of Ancient Art and Mythology." Lond. 1818, § 229.

and air participates in its essence, which was continually emanating from and reverting back to its source in various modes and degrees of progression and regression."[*] A passage from the Puranas, cited by Colebrooke[†], speaks of one person in three divinities—a Unity in Trinity—*ékâ múrtis trayó dévás*. According to the Sánkhya doctrines, this unity, or great principle, is a mere modification of nature, and becomes distinctly known as three gods by the manifestation of three qualities ; 1st, *sattva*, goodness, or the presence of all that is good and the absence of all that is bad; 2nd, *radjas*, passion, *animi impetus*, a mixed quality, in which the passions and affections are the strongest, and give an occasional predominance to good and to bad; 3rd, *tamas*, obscurity, ignorance, or the presence of all that is bad and the absence of all that is good. In other Hindostanic systems we find the doctrine of an eternal dualism between mind and matter, between intellectual activity and material passivity[‡].

Finn Magnusen contends that the form of the legal oath administered in the names of the Almighty God, (i.e. Odin or Thor, see page 292,) Njörd and Frey, shows that in the latter ages of Paganism the Scandinavians worshipped "a holy Trinity;"[§] a conclusion which we deem perfectly unwarranted, the oath, in our opinion, merely implying that these gods were regarded as the most powerful of the elementary divinities, and therefore the most capable of punishing those guilty of perjury. We cannot but ascribe to a similar mania for theorizing the formation, by *modern writers*, of an Hellenic Trinity; the persons being Jupiter, Neptune, and Pluto, which we must also persist in regarding as three distinct deities, notwithstanding the fact, which these writers adduce in support of their hypothesis, that each of them was furnished with a *triform* symbol. Jupiter with the *tripartite*, or three-forked lightning; Neptune with the *trident*, and Pluto with the *tricephalic*, or three-headed dog, Cerberus. It is, how-

---

[*] Payne Knight's "Inquiry," &c., § 63.

[†] In his admirable dissertation "On the Philosophy of the Hindus," published in the 1st and 2nd vols. of the " Asiatic Researches."

[‡] See Pauthier's French translation of Colebrooke's Dissertation, with very interesting notes and remarks by the learned translator. See also Creuzer's Symb. und Mythol. 1 Th. 2 B. 2 Cap.

[§] Eddalæren, vol. i. p. 381.

ever, probable that the Scandinavian sages had a crude notion
of a Trinitarian doctrine, for in the present chapter of the
Prose Edda we have Har, Jafnhar and Thridi *, and in the
6th chapter Odin, Vili and Ve, who create Ask and Embla—
this creation being ascribed in the Völuspá, st. 16, to Odin,
Hœnir and Loð, beings which approach much nearer to the
metaphysical abstractions of the Brahmins than those invoked
in the oath administered within the Scandinavian doomrings.
It is also worthy of remark that Adam of Bremen describes
the statues of Odin (Wodan), Thor and Frey (Fricco), as being
placed in the temple of Upsal on three thrones, one above the
other, in the same manner as the High, the Equally High,
and the Third are represented in the Prose Edda†.

CHAP. 3.—M. Mallet was wrong in supposing that the doctrines in this chapter are "literally expressed" in the Völuspá‡.
There is nothing in that poem respecting an All-Father who
"liveth from all ages," or of a Supreme Being endowing man
with a soul "which shall live and never perish," &c. We should,
indeed, be inclined to attribute several passages in this chapter to a Christian writer of the thirteenth century. There is, in
fact, a palpable contradiction, for when Gangler asks where
this god, who, he had been told, "liveth from all ages,"
remained before he made heaven and earth, Har answers
"with the Frost-giants," consequently the god alluded to can
be no other than Odin, the son of the mythic-cosmogonic being
Bör. We may also observe that in this chapter Gimli and
Vingólf are synonymous terms, (Gimli or Vingólf,) whereas
in the 17th chap. Gimli is given as the name of the highest
heaven. In the 20th chap. Valhalla and Vingólf are described
as the place or places where the Einherjar dwell with Odin,
and in several of the compositions of the Skalds of the
historical period Vingólf is used for Valhalla. Add to this
Grimm's conjecture that the expression "in Gimli" means
simply in heaven, and it must be acknowledged that Gimli

* Trautwetter supposes that Har, Jafnhar and Thridi, are the three stars
of Orion's Belt! He also regards them as symbols of the Winter Solstice,
the (we presume both Vernal and Autumnal) Equinox, and the Summer
Solstice! an hypothesis which shows that the *Astronomical method* of ex-
plaining ancient myths is as apt to lead learned men on a wild-goose chase
as *conjectural etymology*. See *Eddal.* vol. i. p. 407.

† Adam Bremen. de situ Daniæ, c. 233.

‡ See his note to the Prose Edda (c).

does not form an over solid foundation for an elaborate theory.

Finn Magnusen and his followers have laboured very hard to show that the term All-Father is susceptible of a double signification, as one of the epithets of Odin, and as the designation of the One, eternal, Infinite, Supreme Being; but they have not, in our opinion, produced the slightest evidence to prove that the ancient Scandinavians understood it in this manner. In the Prose Edda, as the reader will have remarked, the term is invariably applied to designate Odin. In the Poetical Edda, the word *Alfadir* only occurs three times; in *Grímnis-mál*, st. 46, as one of the names of Odin; in a poem of the Eddaic Epos, *Helga-kvida Hundingsbana I*, st. 35, as the chief of the Valkyrjor and Einherjar, i.e. Odin, and in a somewhat obscure phrase in the 1st strophe of the *Raven-Song*, where it has, however, obviously the same signification. The Supreme Deity of the Scandinavians, and indeed of all the ancient Teutonic nations, was unquestionably Odin. A belief in a higher deity—in a real Supreme Being— may possibly have been entertained by a few enlightened Skalds and Pontiff-chieftains, but there is little or nothing to show that this belief was inculcated as a doctrine. The phrase "by the might of him who sent the heat," which occurs in the 6th chap. of the Prose Edda, and is noticed by Mallet, (note D,) is not found in any of the Eddaic poems, and may therefore be ascribed to Snorri, or to some other Christian writer of the thirteenth century. In the Elder Edda there are only two allusions to such an Omnipotent Being, and even these are very obscure, as the reader will find by the following literal translation of the strophes that contain them.

'Then cometh the Mighty One (*inn ríki*), to the divine judgment—the Potent from above who all (things) swayeth. He giveth judgment, putteth an end to strife and ordaineth laws (or a holy peace), which shall last for evermore."

Völuspá, st. 58.

"Another and a mightier one *, whom I venture not to name, will then come. Few there are who can look beyond the time when Odin will go against the wolf."

Hyndlu-ljóð, st. 41.

* Namely, than Thor.

We must remark that the strophe from the Völuspá is only found in paper MSS., and not in any vellum MS., though we think this is not a circumstance of sufficient importance to warrant the conclusion that several writers have drawn from it. We therefore do not hesitate to regard this strophe as having as great a claim to antiquity as any other in the poem; but the whole Völuspá is so unconnected and fragmentary, that the passage in question is equally as applicable to Odin as to a higher All-Father, and is at all events too obscure to serve as the basis of an elaborate theory. According to Finn Magnusen the "mightier one," alluded to in the strophe of the Hyndlu-ljóð is Surtur!! But why should Hyndla not venture to name this swarthy god or demon of Muspellheim, who is repeatedly mentioned in the other Eddaic poems? We will not, however, fatigue the reader by entering into a discussion of the learned Icelander's hypothesis, which has been ably refuted by writers who are much better acquainted with the subject than we can pretend to be *; and will merely observe in conclusion, that until much stronger evidence can be produced to the contrary, we must persist in regarding Odin as the only supreme deity *worshipped* or believed in by the ancient Scandinavians.

We had almost forgot to mention that Finn Magnusen, in conformity with his favourite *astronomical method*, takes for granted that the twelve names of Odin are the twelve signs of the zodiac; Alfadir being *Aries*, Herjan *Aquarius*, &c. † But how does it happen that these twelve names also occur in *Grímnis-mál*—not in the same order, but mixed up with thirty-two other names, there being in all forty-four epithets applied to designate Odin, of which Alfadir is the twenty-eighth, and Herjan the third?

CHAP. 4, 5, 6, 7, 8, 9.—The cosmogonic doctrines contained in

* See, for instance, Grundtvig's Nordens Mythologi, also a very clever work by Martin Hammerich, entitled "Om Ragnaroksmythen og dens Betydning i den oldnordiske Religion," Copenh. 1836. Although Mr. Hammerich has ably refuted Finn Magnusen's theories, we think that his own hypothesis of an Omnipotent Being called Fimbultyr will not by any means stand the test of criticism.

† Odin as Alfadir has thus undergone some curious transformations; in the olden time he was at least regarded as the lord of Valhalla and the father of gods and men; the monks changed him into the devil, but Finn Magnusen has again installed him in the heavens as the zodiacal ram!

these chapters are perfectly in accordance with those of the
Eddaic Poems, with the notable exception that the most important doctrine of all, implied in the phrase " by the might of him
who sent the heat," is, as we previously observed, nowhere to be
found in the latter, and must therefore be regarded as apocryphal, the myths and doctrines of the Prose Edda being only of
value when they can be corroborated by the authority of the
Elder Edda. It is certainly of very little consequence whether
several of the myths are susceptible of this corroboration or
not, for, although they may have been embellished, we may
take for granted that they were not invented by the compilers
of the Prose Edda. But it is otherwise with *words* and
phrases, which a compiler or even a mere copyist might have
inserted in a MS. at his pleasure. We therefore repeat that
a phrase in the Prose Edda, expressing a doctrine conformable to the precepts of Christianity, but quite at variance with
the cosmogonic system developed in the Elder Edda, must
be regarded as an interpolation, or at least of too doubtful a character to ground a theory on. We insist the more
on this point, as the arguments so frequently made use of by
M. Mallet*, and by several eminent writers since his time,
to prove that the Scandinavian theory of creation was founded
on the doctrine of an eternal Supreme Being, " placed above
the reach of all revolutions and changes," regulating primordial
matter, and producing the mundane deities to whom he entrusted the formation of the visible universe, rest entirely on
this apocryphal passage of the Prose Edda, and the two
obscure strophes of which we have given a translation.

If we take the cosmogonic system of the Scandinavians as it
is developed in the Elder Edda, and (with the exception of
the phrase in question) also in the Prose Edda, we shall
find that it is essentially based on materialism. Matter is
held to be, as it was in several of the Indian schools of philosophy, the plastic origin of all things, the gods themselves
being but a mere modification of it. Regarded in this point
of view, the Eddaic system, when divested of its allegorical
language, will be found to offer some curious coincidences
with the speculations of several eminent scientific men of the
present age.

* See especially his arguments in chap. v. and his notes to the Prose
Edda (D and F).

The Scandinavian sages being of the opinion of Lucretius and most of the ancient philosophers, that

" Nil posse creari
De nihilo, necque quod genitu 'st ad nil revocari,"

presupposed that, in the beginning, the coarser particles of matter were concentrated in a nebulous sphere (Niflheim), and the more etherealized particles in a luminous one (Muspell-heim), and that the latter by working on or vivifying the former, produced an incipient organic chaos; the more material parts of this chaos (typified as the gigantic being Ymir) being progressively developed by the influence of the more ethereal portion (the cow Audhumla nourishing Ymir by the four —elementary—streams that flowed from her teats), the finer particles of both (Audhumla licking the salt stones) finally bringing forth a higher organization (Bur and his offspring).

The view we have taken of the Eddaic system, up to this stage, does not materially differ from that of Finn Magnusen. But the question now arises—In what light ought we to regard Bur and his offspring? or, more properly speaking, in what manner may we *conjecture* that they were regarded by the Scandinavian cosmogonists? Now Finn Magnusen supposes that Odin, Vili, and Ve, are mere symbolical expressions for air, light, and fire, which by operating on the embryotic matter gradually produced the visible universe, and finally by acting on vegetable substances transformed them into animated beings (Ask and Embla) *. This is unquestionably a plausible hypothesis, but we think it savours too much of modern scientific speculations to be relied on, and, like too many of the learned Icelander's theories, becomes moreover in its details not only inconsequent but even somewhat ludicrous. He tells us for instance that " the cow licking the salt stones, by which a being more beauteous and noble than Ymir was produced, can mean nothing else than the emerging of a portion of land or a rock from the briny sea;" and after stating that this being was called Bur, and his son Bör, adds, " In my opinion it was intended to signify hereby the first mountain or mountain-chain, which it was deemed by the forefathers of our race had emerged from the waters in the same region where the first land made its appearance. This mountain

* Eddalæren, vol. ii. p. 63.

chain is probably the Caucasus, called by the Persians Borz
(the genitive of the Old Norse Borr). Bör's wife, Belsta or
Bestla, a daughter of the giant Bölthorn (*spina calamitosa*),
is possibly the *mass of ice* formed on the alpine summits." *
It will be needless to point out how inconsequent this theory
is. According to the Edda, "the seas and waters, and the
vast ocean," were made by *the sons of Bör* from the blood of
Ymir, consequently when Bur was produced no "briny sea"
existed for him to emerge from; and as Odin, Vili and Ve,
the sons of Bör and Besla †, are according to Finn Magnusen
Air, Light, and Fire, he must, in order to be consequent,
ascribe the origin of these elementary principles to the union
of an alpine rock and an alpine glacier! A somewhat too
frigid embrace we should imagine to bring forth *Light* and
Fire, not to mention the thorough deliquescence into which poor
Besla would have fallen in giving birth to such an offspring ‡.

Returning to our own views of the subject, such as they
are—for we are perfectly aware that *quot homines tot sententiæ*
is nowhere more applicable than to the explanations given of
ancient myths—we should be inclined to *conjecture* that the
Scandinavian cosmogonists may have regarded Odin as a real
mundane deity. The problem which they had to solve was
the origin of the universe. They might have had recourse
to the more pleasing, and at the same time far more rational

* Eddalæren, vol. i. p. 42.

† So the word is printed in Rask's edition of the Prose Edda.—Bestla
and Beyzla, we believe, are also found in MSS., but Finn Magnusen writes
the word Belsta, on what authority we know not, which may be derived from
belti, a belt, and thus signify the engirdling—i.e. the ocean engirdling the earth,
which suits his latter theory, stated in the note below, admirably. We have
so frequently expressed our opinion respecting *conjectural etymology*, that it
will be needless for us to observe that we cannot place the least value on any
inferences drawn from a supposed affinity between the Old Norse word Börr,
and the Persian Borz, or more properly Albordj.

‡ Finn Magnusen seems to have become aware of this himself, for in his
Lexicon Mythologicum, published four years after his *Eddalæren*, he converts Bör into the earth, and Besla into the *ocean*, adding, " Ex hocce terræ
et maris primo connubio prodeunt *Odinn* (spiritus mundi nostri ; terræ mag-
na anima, aëris et auræ numen) *Vili* sive *Hœnir* (lux, imprimis cœlestis)
et *Ve* sive *Lódur* (ignis, vel elementalis vel proprie sic dictus) qui Ymerum,
chaoticæ confusionis auctorem, interficientes ex ejus corpore, post magnum
illud diluvium, terram nostram formant, ea quidam specie quam jam retinet."
                                        Lex. Mythol. Edda, vol. iii. p. 314.

system that presupposes a Supreme Essence—a spirit moving, upon the face of the waters—whereas the one they adopted only recognizes matter which becomes at length sufficiently organized to produce Odin, Vili, and Ve. They may possibly have applied these names to designate three modes of action of one deity—Odin, or All-Father; but whether they regarded him as a corporeal being or as the *anima mundi*—the intelligent and co-ordinating principle of the universe—we think they ascribed to this being or this intelligence the further work of creation typified by the slaughter of Ymir, and the formation of the earth and the heavens from his body, as it lay extended in Ginnungagap.

CHAP. 15, 16.—The Yggdrasill myth, with its three arborescent roots, three fountains, and three destinies, is one of the most significant and poetical to be found in any system of mythology, but its explanation has, as usual, given rise to the most conflicting theories. Gräter and Finn Magnusen offer a physical, Trautwetter an astronomical, Mone an ethical explanation, and Grundtvig applies his favourite theory of "the heroic spirit of the north," (Nordens Kæmpe Aand)—pugnacious spirit would be a more appropriate designation—to this, as indeed to every other myth which he treats of in that most singular and rather too *crotchetty* work of his, entitled *Nordens Mythologi*,

According to Finn Magnusen, Yggdrasill is the symbol of universal nature. One of its *stems*, (so he terms the *roots*,) springs from the central primordial abyss—from the subterranean source of matter as it might be termed, (Hvergelmir,) runs up through the earth, which it supports, and issuing out of the celestial mountain in the world's centre, "called Asgard, Caucasus, Borz," * &c., spreads its branches over the entire universe. These wide-spreading branches are the ethereal or celestial regions; their leaves, the clouds; their buds or fruits, the stars; the four harts are the four cardinal winds; the eagle is a symbol of the air; the hawk, of the wind-still ether; and the squirrel signifies hailstones, snow

---

* These are the precise words he makes use of in his Mythological Lexicon, page 865; thus identifying, as usual, the Persian Albordj (Borz) with the Caucasus. If he had made the Hindu Kosh serve his purpose instead of the Caucasus, the theory would, at all events, have been somewhat more entitled to consideration; but we should really imagine that at the present day it would be quite superfluous to remark that the Persian Albordj, like the

flakes, vaporous agglomerations, and similar atmospherical phenomena. Another *stem* springs in the warm south over the ethereal Urdar-fountain, the swans swimming in which denote the sun and moon!! The third *stem* takes its rise in the cold and cheerless regions of the north, over the source of the ocean, typified by Mimir's well. The myth of Odin leaving his eye as a pledge to Mimir, signifies the descent of the sun every evening into the sea—to learn wisdom from Mimir during the night,—the mead quaffed by Mimir every morning being the ruddy dawn that spreading over the sky exhilarates all nature. Nidhögg, and the other monsters that gnaw the roots of the mundane tree, are " the volcanic and other violent torrents that are constantly striving to consume or destroy the earth's foundations." *

Although we agree with Finn Magnusen in regarding Yggdrasill as the symbol of universal nature, we think that, in attempting to explain the myth in all its details, he has let his imagination, as usual, get the better of his judgment, and lead him into the most palpable inconsistencies ; insomuch so, in fact, that when we begin to examine his theory we are almost tempted to exclaim, with Grundtvig, " one

Indian Meru, and the Riphæan mountains of the Greek mythology, is a mere mythic-cosmogonic symbol, and that the attempt to give it a geographical locality can only be ascribed to that theorizing mania which so frequently leads even the most learned men—and few possess greater learning than Finn Magnusen—into the most palpable errors. Not to fatigue the reader with numerous citations, we will merely refer to a small work—that happens to be at hand—by Arnold Hölty, entitled " Eine kritisch-historische Untersuchung über die beiden ersten Capitel des Vendidad," published at Hanover, 1829, with a preface by Heeren, in which the author takes the same view of the subject, and shows, moreover, that Albordj is only mentioned once in the Vendidad (in the twentieth Fargard), in a passage which he proves to be an interpolation, and that the account we have of it is exclusively derived from the Bundehesh.

The Grecian mythology has its Olympus ; the Persian, its Albordj ; the Indian, its Meru. Finn Magnusen was, therefore, determined to introduce a heaven-aspiring hill into the Scandinavian mythology. He accordingly places Asgard on the summit of a conical mountain, rising from the centre of the terrestrial disk, and gives us a pictorial representation of it in the plates of the *Eddalæren*. But where do we find a description of such a mountain, either in the Elder or Younger Edda? The only mention made of a celestial mount is that of Himinbjörg, the residence or mansion of Heimdall, which is placed on the edge of heaven, and which Finn Magnusen gives in his calendar as the zodiacal sign of the crab.

* See Lex. Myth. Edda III. p. 863, et sq., and Eddalæren, Bog. II.

would think it was meant for a joke." * Jacob Grimm—how refreshing it always is to turn to his admirable pages—very justly observes that the whole myth of Yggdrasill bears the stamp of a very high antiquity, but does not appear to be fully unfolded. "We learn," he says, "something respecting the enmity between the eagle and the snake, and that it is kept up by Ratatösk, but nothing as to the destination of the hawk and the four harts." † These remarks of Grimm are fully borne out by the very meagre account given of the Yggdrasill myth in the Völuspá, and the Grímnis-mál, the only Eddaic poems that make mention of it ‡. In order that the reader may be aware on what very slight foundations Finn Magnusen can construct an elaborate theory, we subjoin a literal translation of all the Eddaic strophes that relate to the myth, the words in brackets being inserted to render the obscure passages more intelligible.

From the Völuspá :—

St. 17. "An ash know I standing, called Yggdrasill. A high tree sprinkled with the purest water. Thence comes the dew that falls in the dales. It (the ash) stands evergreen over the Urdar-fountain."

18. "Thence come the much-knowing maidens—three from that lake (fountain) which is under the tree. One is called Urd, another Verdandi, and the third Skuld. They engraved (Runic inscriptions, i. e., recorded events) on tablets. They laid down laws ; they determined (determine) the life of the sons of men ; they tell (fix) the destinies (of men)." †

From Grímnis-mál :—

St. 29. "Körmt and Œrmt, and the two Kerlaugar—these (rivers) must Thor wade through every day as he fares to the doomstead, under Yggdrasill's ash, otherwise the Æsir-bridge would be in flames, and boiling hot would become the holy waters."

30. "(The horses), Gladr, Gyllir, Glær, Skeidbrimir, Silfrintoppr, Synir. Gisl, Falhófnir, Gulltoppr, and Léttfeti are ridden by the Æsir every day when they go to the doomstead under the ash Yggdrasill."

---

* See one of the somewhat too bilious pastor's diatribes against such physical explanations of Scandinavian myths, in fact, against every mythological doxy that does not happen to be *his doxy*, in his *Nordens Mythologi*, second edition, Copenh. 1822, page 230.

† Deut. Mythol. page 757.

‡ The Norns are mentioned, though in a very obscure manner, in the 49th st. of Vafthrúdnis-mál ; mention is also made of them in the poems of the Eddaic Epos, and in the 26th st. of the *Raven Song* an allusion is made to *a tree* under the roots of which are the giants.

§ This is all that we find in the Völuspá respecting the Yggdrasill myth, except the allusion to the mundane tree in the 51st strophe relating to the

31. " Three roots stand on three ways (extend to three regions) under the ash Yggdrasill.   Hela dwells under one ; (under) another (dwell) the Frost-Giants; (under) the third (dwell) mortal men " (*literally* human men).

32. " Ratatösk is called the squirrel that shall run (that runs) on the ash Yggdrasill. The eagle's words he shall bear (he bears) downwards, and shall tell (tells) them to Nidhögg below."

33. " There are also four harts that on the summit (of the ash), with bent necks, bite (the leaves), Dain, Dvalin, Duneyr and Durathrór are their names."

34 and 35 *.

We think that all that can be gathered from this account of the ash Yggdrasill, and that given in the Prose Edda, is, that the mundane tree is represented as embracing with its three roots the whole universe ; for one of these roots springs from Hvergelmir in Niflheim, another from Mimir's well, situated somewhere or other in the region of the Frost-Giants, and the third from the Urdar-fount, which is obviously placed in the celestial regions.   We have thus a super-terrestrial or supernal (the Urdar) root ; a terrestrial (the Mimir) root; and a sub-terrestrial or infernal (the Hvergelmir) root. That the fountain of the Norns was supposed to be in the ethereal regions, is unquestionable ; for we are told in Grímnis-mál that mankind dwell *under* it, and the Prose Edda expressly states that it is " in heaven," and it would appear *above* Asgard, for the Æsir are described as riding *up* to the doomstead beside the Urdar-fountain.   Finn Magnusen, as we have seen, places this fountain, and the root issuing from it, in the warm south.   In his *Eddalæren* he gives us, in fact, to understand that the fountain springs from a high and steep cliff at the *south pole*, though he admits, for once, that nothing respecting such a cliff is to be found in the Eddaic Poems ; the only authority he is able to adduce in support of this strange hypothesis being a figurative expression made use of by a Skald, in a poem written after his conversion to Christianity †.   Finn Magnusen is also of opinion that the pure water with which the tree is sprinkled by the Norns means " the snow agglomerated in the northern sky," and that " the

Ragnarök myth, a metrical translation of which has already been given, see page 455.   We have also given a translation of the strophe, (page 411,) relating to the myth of Odin and Mimir.

* A literal, though metrical, translation of these strophes has already been given, see page 413.   Also a translation of the 43rd strophe, (see page 432,) in which Yggdrasill is mentioned as " the first of trees."

† Eddalæren, vol. ii. p. 124.

dew that falls in the dales" signifies the ever-verdant aspect of the southern parts of the earth, as well as the clear azure sky by which this perennial verdure is canopied *. It is almost unnecessary for us to observe that this hypothesis would imply that the ancient Scändinavians were aware that the earth was a sphere ; the terms *south pole* and *northern sky* not being applicable, without a great perversion of language, to an earth represented, as it invariably is in the Eddaic Poems, as a disk in the middle of a vast ocean bounded by the mountainous region of the Frost-Giants †.

Mone regards the ash as the emblem of human life. Man is born of water, the swan is therefore the infantile soul that still swims on the water, but the eagle, the mature experienced mind that soars aloft; the hawk perched between the eagle's eyes being internal sensation. The snakes that gnaw the root of life are the vices and passions ; the squirrel, the double-tongued flatterer constantly running between these passions and the mind (the eagle) which has raised itself above their control. The harts denote the passions of the mind, folly, madness, terror and disquietude, and therefore feed on the healthy thoughts (the green leaves). But as man in his levity remarks not what enemies threaten his existence, the stem rots on the side, and many a one dies ere he attains to

---

* Eddalæren, vol. ii. p. 126.

† Finn Magnusen's pictorial representation of the Yggdrasill myth (copied from the *Eddalæren*, plate 1,) has been selected as a frontispiece to this volume. The central part of the plate representing the earth (Midgard) as a disk in the midst of the "vast ocean," and encircled by Jörmungand, the great Midgard Serpent, "holding his tail in his mouth" (see page 423) ; the outer shores of the ocean forming the mountainous region of Jötunheim, or Utgard, is perfectly in accordance with the descriptions given in the Eddas, with the exception of the conical hill, for which not the slightest authority can be adduced. The representation of the Mundane Tree itself is founded on a theory which we have attempted to show rests on the most unwarranted assumptions. It will, therefore, be merely necessary for us to observe that Yggdrasill is depicted with three *stems*, a main stem springing from Hvergelmir, and two secondary stems, the one branching out "towards the north," over Mimir's well ; the other, "towards the warm south," over the Urdar-fount. Bifröst (the rainbow) is made to extend from Asgard, placed on the summit of the hypothetical Scandinavian Olympus, to Jötunheim, and from Jötunheim to this fountain of the Norns which is, *apparently* at least, placed *under* the earth, but which we presume is intended to be located at the *south pole* of the terrestrial disk ; though its true locality, if we may assign a locality to such an ideal conception, would unquestionably be *above* Asgard in the highest ethereal regions.

wisdom, or figuratively before the bird of his soul (the eagle) is seated amidst the perennial verdure of the mundane tree.

Ling supposes Yggdrasill to be the symbol both of universal and human life, and its three roots to signify the physical, the intellectual, and the moral principles. Other writers cited by Finn Magnusen take these roots to have been meant for matter, organization and spirit, and the ash itself for the symbol of universal primordial vitality *.

We should be inclined ourselves to agree in the main with those who regard this mythic tree as the symbol of ever-enduring time, or rather of universal nature, ever-varying in its aspects, but subsisting throughout eternity †. The principles of evil and destruction (the monsters of Hvergelmir) are in constant operation, but the three Norns continually sprinkle the tree (the universe) with the renovating waters of life, and maintain it in everlasting verdure. We thus find that even when all things are consumed, and the gods themselves perish, Yggdrasill, " Time's hoary nurse," though " shaken to its summit," though " the fire reek rageth around it," still stands,

> " And ever blooming will stand
> O'er the Urdar-fountain."

The Ymerian and Yggdrasill systems, as Finn Magnusen terms them, may *possibly* have been held by opposite sects, though there is not the slightest evidence to show that such was the case. There are, in fact, *three* systems more or less fully developed in the Elder Edda—the Ymerian, the Yggdrasill, and the Ragnarök systems, the doctrines contained in which are, we think, far from being irreconcilable. We should, ourselves, regard these systems as having been framed at different periods, the Ymerian being the most ancient, and the Ragnarök the most recent of the three. We

---

* See Eddalæren, vol. ii. p. 146.

† The ash was the most appropriate tree that could have been chosen for such an emblem. Virgil describes it with its outspreading branches as enduring for centuries, and it is a singular coincidence that he should have represented it as a tree that reaches with its roots as far downwards as it does upwards with its branches.

> " Altior ac penitus terræ defigitur arbos ;
> Æsculus in primis: *quæ quantum vertice ad auras
> Æthereas, tantum radice in Tartara tendit.*

Georg. ii. 290.

We may here remark that the Maypole, and the German *Christbaum*, have a Pagan origin, the type of both being the ash Yggdrasill.

have shown that the Ymerian system is essentially grounded
on materialism; and in whatever light we may view the
Yggdrasill myth, whether it be explained physically or psychologically—a physico-psychological explanation would probably be
the true one—we shall find that its doctrines as essentially
rest on fatalism, as those of the Ymerian myth do on materialism.   The three Norns regulate the destinies of gods and
men; even Odin himself, who in the Ymerian myth is represented as the father of all, must submit to their decrees; which
means to say, in other words, that there is an inevitable succession of events in time; Uncreated Time, Time without beginning or end—the Zeruane Akherene of the Persians—personified in its three moments of the Past, the Present, and the
Future, as three maidens seated by the fountain of perennial
life, being the only deity recognised.   We shall now proceed
to examine the third system, and see whether it contain, as,
thanks to the *amor patriæ* of Finn Magnusen and other
northern writers, is generally supposed, more cheering and
consolatory doctrines.

    CHAP. 52 and 54.—In these chapters of the Prose Edda, as
well as in the strophes of the Eddaic Poems containing the Ragnarök myth, we can find nothing at variance with the doctrines of
materialism and fatalism laid down in the two preceding, and no
doubt more ancient systems. The world arose out of chaos, and,
after it has run its predestined course, into chaos will again
return.   And as the Ymerian system is based on the doctrine
of the indestructibility of matter, and the Yggdrasill system
on the more ideal conception of a necessary succession of
events in illimited time, we find that, in strict conformity with
these views, the Vala, or more properly speaking the ancient
Skald who composed the Völuspá, describes the conflagration
of the universe by the elemental fire of Muspellheim; that is
to say, the dissolution of all things into the primordial chaos.
But time (Yggdrasill) remains, and as matter is indestructible,
and contains, even in its most chaotic state, ethereal vivifying
principles, (the flakes of Muspellheim,) new organizations are
formed; the universe is renovated, or in the words of the
Völuspá, st. 52—

> " She sees arise,
> A second time,
> The earth from ocean,
> In verdant splendour.

> The waters fall *:
> O'er mountain tops
> The eagle flies,
> And preys on fishes."

We have here the earth arising from a pre-existing ocean, but there is nowhere the least allusion—not even a phrase that the most ingenious criticism could torture into a remote allusion—that it will arise by the fiat of an Omnipotent Being. We are not told in what manner this new world will be formed, nor any thing respecting the ocean from which it will emerge. We might even conclude by comparing the first couplet of the 51st strophe of the Völuspá—

> " Dimm'd 's now the sun,
> *In ocean earth sinks,*"

with the first and second couplets of the 52nd strophe previously cited—

> " She sees arise,
> A second time,
> *The earth from ocean,*
> In verdant splendour,"

that the framers of the Ragnarök myth supposed that the mere submersion of the earth under the waters of a primordial ocean would suffice for its renovation : a theory which, when divested of its allegorical language, would pretty nearly coincide with the facts established by modern geologists. At all events, it is evident that they regarded this new emerging earth as a mere re-arrangement of matter. They of course described it as a more lovely and a more innocent world than the old one—though, to judge from the fish-devouring eagle, it would appear that animals were still to prey on each other in it—as a world yielding an abundant produce without cultivation, and in which man—not created by a Supreme Being, but brought forth by the *vital energy* (Lif and Lifthrasir) that still subsisted amidst the general wrack and dissolution—would again abide, though in what manner we are not informed, even Thridi himself professing his inability to pry any further into futurity.

It may possibly be objected that, in taking this view of the three Eddaic myths, we have not drawn a distinction between the mundane deities (Odin, Vili, Ve, &c.) and the Elves of Light dwelling in the empyreal region of Muspellheim. The

---

* *i. e.* Recede as the earth emerges.

former, it is admitted, are represented as a mere modification
of matter; but those who, like Finn Magnusen, neglect stubborn facts for brilliant theories, make use of arguments which,
if they mean any thing, would seem to imply that, as the origin
of Surtur and the Elves of Light is not given in the Eddaic
Poems, they must necessarily have been regarded as immaterial
spirits. To this objection, futile though it be, we should reply,
that neither have we any account of the origin of Nidhögg and
the other monsters of Hvergelmir, nor of the terrestrial Elves
of Light, nor of the Elves of Darkness, nor of the Vanir, nor
of a number of other mythological beings that even the writers in question would not venture to spiritualize as they have
implicitly—though few of them explicitly—spiritualized the
Elves of Muspellheim. Arguments founded on such negative
facts are, therefore, quite inconclusive. We must also remark, that in the Eddaic Poems there is no mention made of
Surtur and the Elves of Light existing in Muspellheim *previous* to the formation of Ymir, neither can their pre-existence
be inferred from the passage in the fourth chapter of the
Prose Edda, which merely speaks of Surtur being seated on
the borders of Muspellheim, evidently at the time—that is
to say, long after the formation of the universe—when Gylfi
is supposed to have had these doctrines revealed to him.
As it is moreover explicitly stated that the union of the material particles of Muspellheim and Niflheim produced first
Ymir and the Frost-Giants, and afterwards the more intelligent race of the Æsir, we should be justified in assuming
that Nidhögg and the monsters of Hvergelmir, as well as
Surtur and the other inmates of Muspellheim, were supposed
to have arisen in much the same manner : the former being
modifications of the most dense material particles, the latter
of the most ethereal ones ; a peculiar combination of both producing the beings endowed with the highest intelligence. In
strict conformity with the dualistic doctrines held by the Scandinavian cosmogonists, we have thus on one hand the Intelligent Powers (Odin, Vili, Ve, and the Æsir), by whose benign
influence the heavens and the earth and the whole visible
universe were fashioned out of chaos; and, on the other, the
Material or Chaotic Powers, represented not only by the Frost-
Giants and the monsters of Hvergelmir, but also by Surtur and
the Elves of Muspellheim. Hence, on the last day, all these
powers fight against the Æsir, and the very fact that Surtur

is invariably described as the being who is to lead the Muspellheim bands against " the mild Gods," shows that he was
regarded as one of the chaotic demons. We must, therefore,
repeat, that throughout these myths we can trace no other
doctrines than those founded on materialism and fatalism.
All the mythological beings typify matter—some of them
matter in a chaotic state, the others a material vivifying
principle by which this chaotic matter becomes organized;
each of the antagonistic principles alternately prevailing, and
the universe being in consequence alternately destroyed and
renovated by an inevitable succession of events in never-end-
ing time—an evolution and devolution of matter in the in-
finitude of eternity.

CHAP. 53.—When—some fifteen years ago—we first read this
chapter of the Prose Edda, we rather too hastily concluded that
the Scandinavian doctrines respecting a future state were much
the same as those of Christianity. We were confirmed in
this opinion by the perusal of Finn Magnusen's *Eddalæren*,
in which we found it expressly stated that the ancient Scandinavians believed that an Omnipotent, though nameless
Being, would at the last day descend from his abode of ethereal radiancy to judge the human race; would condemn the
wicked to the torments prepared for them in the profoundest
abyss, and assign to the righteous an eternity of beatitude in
the empyreal region of the Elves of Light, " in highest
Gimli." * From the dogmatical tone assumed by the learned
Icelander throughout his work, we took it for granted that he
was able to corroborate his statements by the most undeniable and trustworthy evidence collected from the Eddaic
Poems. The reader may, therefore, judge of our surprise
when, after carefully looking ever these poems—which contain upwards of 1500 strophes—we found that the only allusions made to this nameless God were in the two obscure
strophes of which we gave a literal translation in our remarks
on the third chapter (see page 483); one of these strophes
merely alluding to the coming of " a mightier one " than Thor;
and the other to " a mighty one " coming to a judgment, but
not to the kind of judgment described in such glowing colours
in the *Eddalæren*. This discovery completely destroyed our

* See Eddalæren, iv. 102, and a number of similar passages throughout
the work.

confidence in Finn Magnusen's statements, and we were really
at a loss to imagine how a man of his learning could venture
to construct a brilliant theory—and support that theory, too,
by the most dogmatical assumptions—on such a very flimsy
foundation. We shall now proceed to examine the fifty-third
chapter of the Prose Edda and the Eddaic strophes on which
it is grounded, and see whether they really do contain the
doctrines that have been so unhesitatingly deduced from them.

The expressions made use of in the Prose Edda would imply that, after the dissolution of the universe, there will be a
place of punishment for certain crimes, and several abodes of
celestial bliss for " righteous and well-minded men," one of
which, at least, will be as plentifully provided with drink as
Valhalla. We previously observed that the statements in the
Prose Edda are of little or no value, unless they can be corroborated by the authority of the Elder Edda. Now the
reader will no doubt be surprised to learn, that the only authority that can be adduced in support of the assumption that
the Scandinavians believed that the wicked would be condemned to a place of eternal punishment, is a *single strophe*
of the Völuspá*, a faithful translation of which we gave in the
note, page 457. Several writers, no doubt with the laudable
intention of supporting a favourite theory—have rendered the
penultimate couplet of this strophe by " There Nidhögg
quails the dead for evermore—for eternity—throughout everlasting ages," &c. In the original it is—

> " Thar saug Niðhögg
> Nái framgengna,"

literally, " There sucked Nidhögg the corpses of the dead." †
There is, consequently, nothing in this strophe to warrant the
conclusion that the punishment is to last *eternally*. It must
also be borne in mind that the strophe occurs *previous* to the

---

* Náströnd is mentioned—though in a very indefinite manner—in the
20th strophe of *Gunnars Slagr*, a poem which, in respect to its subject,
belongs to the Eddaic Epos—but the editors of the Edda themselves regard
this poem as apocryphal, and have, therefore, printed it separately, as an
Appendix to their second volume.

† Both *saug*, sucked, and *sug*, sucks, are found in the MSS. The editors
of the Edda have adopted the latter reading, and, therefore, render the
passage by "Illic sugit Nidhöggus cadavera emortua," but we prefer the
former, for the verb in the following line is in the past tense in, we believe,
all the MSS.—the wolf *tore*, which the editors render by " dilaniavit fera

account given of the dissolution of the universe. Náströnd is described in the 34th and 35th strophes, and the sinking of the earth into the sea, and "the fire reek raging around Time's nurse," in the 51st strophe ; and as there is positively not a word, either in the 35th strophe or in the whole poem, that could be made to imply the designation of a place of eternal punishment after the conflagration of the universe, the only logical conclusion that can be drawn from the passage in ques- tion is, that the Skald who composed the Völuspá was of opi- nion that murderers *, perjurers, and adulterers, even though they died on the field of battle, would be deprived of the joys of Valhalla, and punished in the manner described, until the final dissolution of all things into the primordial chaos.

In respect to the abodes of celestial bliss, we find that, in the 33rd strophe of the Völuspá, Sindri is described as an habitation of the dwarfs, and Brimir as a drinking-hall (bjórsalr, *beer-saloon*) of the giants, without the least allusion to a future state. On the contrary, the employ of the past tense *stood*, " A hall of gold *stood* on the Nida moun- tains," " Another hall, Brimir, *stood* in Okolni," does not by any means indicate that the Vala, in repeating this strophe, had her prophetic vision directed towards futurity. Not- withstanding these facts, Finn Magnusen, as usual, does not hesitate to say that, " by comparing the passages of the Prose Edda with the Völuspá, we shall find that after the dissolu-

(lupus)." The learned editors conjecture that the wolf alluded to may be Fenrir, condemned *after the dissolution of the universe* to this place of punish- ment (see Edda III. p. 43, note 58)—but the word *vargr* means either a wolf or any ferocious beast—*fera* as they have rendered it—and may proba- bly have been meant for one of the monsters of Hvergelmir. Náströnd, in fact, is evidently placed by the Skald in Hvergelmir. We may also remark, that the Prose Edda has *qvelr*, quails—" There Nidhögg *quails* the bodies of the dead."

* It is difficult to say what the ancient Scandinavians understood by murder. In the modern acceptation of the term, there were few men in those turbulent ages that had not committed a murder. We have seen the curious distinction drawn in the Grágás between murder and manslaughter (page 302), and it would appear that, when a man killed another in a trea- cherous or cowardly manner, he was regarded as a murderer—as one who had done a *nithing-work*. Still, even in this signification of the word, the anecdotes we have given from the Sagas show that murder was thought very lightly of. It is a singular circumstance that murder, perjury, and adultery, which the Skald regards as the only crimes that merit a future punishment, should be precisely those which the Icelanders were the most addicted to.

tion of the universe three distinct paradises or blissful habi-
tations are destined for three classes of beings, namely,
Gimli, for righteous men; Brimir, for righteous giants; and
Sindri, for righteous dwarfs!"*

As our inquiries only concern the future state of man, we
will leave the *righteous* giants to guzzle down their ale in
Brimir, and the *righteous* dwarfs to ply their smithy tools in
Sindri, and see whether any better evidence can be adduced
in support of the Gimli *theory*. At first view there would
appear to be no doubt on the question, for Gimli is expressly
described in the 57th strophe of the Völuspá as a place of
eternal beatitude. The literal translation of this strophe (a
metrical translation of which has already been given, see
page 414, is as follows:—

> " A hall sees she standing, fairer than the sun, roofed with gold, in Gimli.
> There shall men of worth abide, and through all days (ages) enjoy bliss."

This, at least, is sufficiently explicit. We must remark,
however, that this strophe occurs *after* the description given of a
new world emerging from the ocean (which is in the 52nd
strophe), and we might therefore infer that the heaven described was intended to be for the inhabitants of the new world
what Valhalla had been for those of the old one; a more refined race of men naturally requiring a more refined heaven.
We say that such an inference *might* be drawn, which shows,
at least, that even this strophe—owing to the place it occupies
in the poem—is not free from obscurity. Admitting, however,
that the two last couplets—

> " All men of worth
> Shall there abide,
> And bliss enjoy
> Through countless ages,"

---

* Lex. Mythol. Edda III. p. 696. Finn Magnusen, like most theorists,
never fails to cite the authority of an ancient work in support of any of his
assumptions, but, when he is aware that these assumptions are at variance
with such an authority, observes a discreet silence. Now a single passage of
he Prose Edda — and for Finn Magnusen the Prose Edda is an authority
which he frequently refers to—will suffice to upset this theory of *righteous*
giants,—beings whose skulls Thor was continually splitting with his mallet,
and hurling their bodies, at times, into the abyss of Niflhel (see page 434),
— for it is expressly stated in the 5th chapter that Ymir and all his race,
that is to say, all giants without distinction, are wicked.

mean that all who lead an unblemished life in this world will have, at its dissolution, this place of eternal bliss assigned them for an habitation, the question arises whether we ought to regard these four lines as dating from the times of Paganism, or as being the interpolation of a Christian writer? The Northern writers of course deny both the *possibility* and *probability* of a single strophe of the Völuspá having been composed after the extinction of Paganism. We shall, therefore, examine the question under both these points of view; and first as to the *possibility*. Now we think that an impartial person, in reading the Völuspá, would find that the two last couplets of the 57th strophe differ even in style from the rest of the poem; however, as the Northern philologists have declared that they can perceive no difference in this respect, we must submit to their judgment. But it does not by any means follow that because the style of the 57th strophe does not differ from that of the other strophes, which it is admitted must have been composed previous to the reign of Harald Hárfagra, the authenticity of this strophe cannot be called in question. We will readily grant that no Skald of the *historical period* could have composed a whole poem in the simple and antique style of the Völuspá, and most of the other Eddaic lays; but it would be going too far to pretend that in the eleventh, twelfth and thirteenth centuries no Icelander could be found capable of inditing four short lines (which in the original Norse only contain ten words) in a style undistinguishable from that of a much earlier period. We say, in the eleventh, twelfth and thirteenth centuries, for the oldest manuscript of the Völuspá extant—the one made use of by the editors of the Edda—dates from the *fourteenth* century, that is to say, upwards of three centuries after the Icelanders had embraced Christianity. Several writers contend that the Völuspá and other Eddaic poems were preserved by being cut on tablets or staves in Runic characters during the times of Paganism, but they are unable to adduce the slightest evidence in support of this hypothesis. There is, in fact, every reason for supposing that these poems were handed down by oral tradition, and first committed to writing by the learned priest of Oddi upwards of a century after the introduction of Christianity. We admit that it is very unlikely that Sæmund inserted a strophe of his own composition in the Völuspá, but it must be borne in mind that the oldest manuscript extant, of this poem, was written two centuries after his time. And during the lapse of two centuries the poem may have been frequently copied by less conscientious persons, some of them sufficiently talented to arrange ten words into two metrical couplets offering not the slightest difficulty of construction. We think, therefore, that the *possibility* of these couplets having been composed by a Christian writer is undeniable, and, in our opinion, the *probability* of their having proceeded from such a source is equally incontestable. 1st, Because the doctrine inculcated is quite conformable to the precepts of Christianity, but quite at variance with the cosmogonic systems developed in the same poem, which, as we have attempted to show, are essentially grounded on materialism and fatalism; and 2nd, Because, although the Eddaic Poems contain upwards of 1500 strophes, this is the only one in which mention is made of a place of eternal bliss after the dissolution of the universe. In no other strophe do we find even the most obscure or most distant allusion to such an abode of beatitude—in fact, no mention made of any other heaven than that of Odin, predestined, like Odin himself, to perish in the general wreck of nature.

Several writers contend that as the Eddaic Poems—especially those of the mythic-cosmogonic class—are more or less fragmentary, the lost strophes may have contained a more definite account of a future state and a Supreme Being. This is, of course, a mere conjecture, and therefore not entitled to much consideration. And we should be more warranted in assuming that strophes containing such doctrines are precisely those the most likely to have been preserved, for the Christian priest who first committed the Eddaic Poems to writing would no doubt have been too delighted to find that his Pagan ancestors professed a belief in a higher deity than Odin, and a higher heaven than Valhalla, not to have assiduously collected any strophes inculcating such doctrines from those to whom they had been transmitted by oral tradition. It is, moreover, highly improbable that such strophes were ever composed, as they would have been quite at variance with the cosmogonic systems so fully developed in the Ymerian and Yggdrasill myths, with which the Ragnarök myth—if it be admitted that the two last couplets of the 57th strophe of the Völuspá are apocryphal—fully coincides.

If the view we have taken of Scandinavian mythology be correct, it will naturally follow that M. Mallet's assumption that this mythology " expressly distinguishes two different abodes for the happy, and as many for the culpable; " *—a Valhalla and a Helheim destined to perish, and a Gimli and a Náströnd that are to endure throughout eternity—is totally unfounded, as well as all the conclusions that Finn Magnusen and a host of modern writers have drawn from it. At all events this assumption rests entirely on the dubious authority of two strophes of an Eddaic poem, of which the oldest manuscript extant dates from the fourteenth century.

We must remark in conclusion, that the instances cited by M. Mallet † of men professing to believe in a more exalted deity than Odin, only prove that even in the most barbarous ages a few individuals may be found more enlightened than the generality of their contemporaries. We should have entered into these inquiries with much greater satisfaction if we could have shown that the opinions of these enlightened men had been embodied into a system, and been held, at least as esoteric doctrines, by a privileged class ; but we prefer *facts* to *theories*, and the only conclusion that we can draw from the facts stated is that the more refined, and probably esoteric, doctrines inculcated in the Eddaic Poems are essentially grounded on materialism and fatalism, as the popular belief was on polytheism: the highest deity, according to this popular belief, being Odin ; the highest heaven, Valhalla ; and the highest celestial bliss, a daily fight, a daily banquet, and a daily drinking-bout.

CHAP. 17.—The twelve (or it may be thirteen) celestial mansions described in the Grímnis-mál, some of which are mentioned in this chapter of the Prose Edda, are regarded by Finn Magnusen—who has a marked predilection for the *astronomical method* —as the twelve signs of the zodiac, and arranged as follows ‡ :—

Celestial Mansions.	Tutelary Deities.	Corresponding to the Sign of the Zodiac.	In which the Sun enters.
1. Ydalir	Ullur	Sagittarius	Nov. 23. §
2. Alfheimr	Frey	Capricornus	Dec. 23.
3. Valaskjálf	Vali	Aquarius	Jan. 22. ‖

* See page 104.   † See page 121.
‡ See his " Specimen Calendarii Gentilis," in the third volume of the Edda.
§ In 1827.   ‖ In 1828.

Celestial Mansions.	Tutelary Deities.	Corresponding to the Sign of the Zodiac.	In which the Sun enters.
4. Sökkvabekkr	Saga	Pisces	Feb. 21.
5. Gladsheimr	Odin	Aries	March 23.
6. Thrymheimr	Skadi	Taurus	April 22.
7. Breidablik	Baldur	Gemini	May 22.
8. Himinbjörg	Heimdall	Cancer	June 21.
9. Fólkvángr	Freyja	Leo	July 25.
10. Glitnir	Forseti	Virgo	Aug. 24.
11. Nóatún	Njörd	Libra	Sept. 23
12. Landvidi	Vidar	Scorpio	Oct. 23.

The Grímnis-mál positively designates Valaskjálf as the third mansion, Sökkvabekk as the fourth, &c., in the order that Finn Magnusen has arranged them, though we doubt whether he be strictly warranted in making Ydalir the first, and Alfheim the second mansion. The fourth, fifth, and sixth strophes of the Grimnis-mál are, literally, as follows :—

4. The land that I see lying (before me) near the Æsir and Elves is holy. But in Thrúdheim shall Thor remain until the Gods perish.

5. Ydalir it is called, where Ullur hath built him a hall. In the beginning (of the world) the Gods gave Alfheim to Frey when he was cutting his teeth.

6. The third habitation is that where the blithe Gods roofed the halls with silver : it is called Valaskjálf, which was chosen by the God (Ás) in the beginning (of the world).

7. The fourth is called Sökkvabekk, &c.

Several passages in the Eddas and the Skaldic poems show that Valaskjálf is here meant for Valhalla ; the god who chose it (for his abode) can therefore be no other than Odin. Finn Magnusen, however, assigns Valaskjálf to Odin's son Vali *. He also makes Ydalir the first mansion, and Alfheim the second, though we might obviously *conjecture* with much the the same degree of plausibility that Thrúdheim is designated as the first habitation, the second being either Ydalir or Alfheim, probably the former. At all events, by assigning the second mansion to Frey, Finn Magnusen makes the Sun-god correspond—and it must be confessed very appropriately—to the winter solstice, when the sun is, as it were, annually born, and may, therefore, be represented as an infant cutting its teeth. Forseti, who holds the scales of justice so perfectly *equipoised*, will also, by this arrangement, very appropriately

* We presume because *Valaskjálf* might be made to signify *Vali's shelf.*

correspond to the autumnal *equinox*, though we do not recollect that justice is any where typified in the Scandinavian, as it is in the Grecian mythology, as a being, either male or female, holding a pair of scales. Odin, who here figures as the zodiacal ram, corresponds to the vernal equinox, and Heimdall to the summer solstice, although other writers who have employed the *astronomical method* for the explanation of Scandinavian myths make Baldur correspond to it; his death being in their opinion evidently meant to typify the *wending* of the sun on the 21st of June. Hence the custom, still kept up in southern Germany and the Scotch Highlands, of lighting *bale fires* at Midsummer, on the day selected by the Catholic Church to celebrate the nativity of John the Baptist *.

In the third chapter of the Prose Edda Niflhel is represented as being " below in the *ninth world ;* " and in the thirty-fourth chapter we are told that Odin cast Hela into Niflheim, and " gave her power over *nine worlds.*" In the forty-fifth strophe of Vafthrúdnis-mál, the giant tells Gangrad that he has been *in nine worlds.* These allusions, it must be confessed, are both obscure and contradictory; nevertheless Finn Magnusen gives us a systematic classification of the *nine worlds* or regions which, according to his notions, were regarded by the Scandinavian mystagogues as constituting the universe. He in fact furnishes us both with a ternary and a nonary vertical division, as follows †.

I. THE SUPERIOR OR SUPERNAL WORLD.

1. Ljósálfaheim, in which he places Gimli, where righteous men, after Ragnarök, are to abide with Surtur, the Supreme Deity ‡ !! The heaven Vidblainn separates this region from,

2. Muspellheim, in which are the *Flame-spirits !!* or Muspell's sons, who are also under the immediate dominion of Surtur, both these regions being uncreated. The heaven Andláng separates Muspellheim from

3. Godheim, where the Æsir abide, and which is, " properly speaking, the ethereal or starry heavens."

---

* The reader will find the most ample information respecting such fires in the twentieth chapter of Jacob Grimm's *Deutsche Mythologie.*

† See his Eddalæren, vol. iii. pages 184 and 189.

‡ He does not inform us whether his *righteous* giants and *righteous* dwarfs will dwell in this region, though we presume that he would also place them in it.

II. THE MEDIAL WORLD.

4. Vanaheim or Vindheim—the abode of the Vanir, which he regards as the Spirits of Air; the region itself being the sky or the terrestrial atmosphere.

5. Mannheim; the earth; the abode of mankind.

6. Svartálfaheim; the subterraneous parts of the earth — holes, caverns, &c.; the abode of the Elves of Darkness.

III. THE INFERIOR OR INFERNAL WORLD.

7. Jötunheim; the abode of giants. In this region is also the great ocean with the Midgard serpent.

8. Helheim; the abode of death.

9. Niflheim; the deepest region also uncreated, in which are Hvergelmir and Náströnd.

If it be asked what authority the learned Icelander can adduce for this classification we must unhesitatingly answer, not the slightest. The distinction which he makes between Ljósálfaheim, and Muspellheim, placing in the former, along with the souls of righteous men, the Elves of Light—or rather leading us to infer that it was originally or will be their abode ; and in the latter beings which he is pleased to term *Flame-spirits*, is totally unwarranted. That the Vanir are the Spirits of Air dwelling in the atmosphere (Vanaheim) is a mere *conjecture*, a plausible one, perhaps, but still a *conjecture*, and it will be needless for us to point out the inconsistency of placing Jötunheim and "the earth-encircling ocean" *under* the earth, Finn Magnusen himself, when he follows the horizontal instead of the vertical division, ranging them on the same plane with it *. In short, this classification rests on the most groundless assumptions imaginable, and can only be ascribed to that theorizing mania, which it is much to be regretted that a writer of Finn Magnusen's learning should be so apt to indulge in.

We think, ourselves, that the only admissible division would be a ternary one, viz. :—

1. The Super-terrestrial Region, or the heavens—the abode of the mundane deities.

2. The Terrestrial Region, which was regarded as an horizontal circular plane. In the middle lay the earth (Midgard)

---

* See the Frontispiece to this volume.

the abode of mankind: the Elves of Darkness and the Dwarfs—
probably two designations of the same mythological beings—
dwelling beneath its surface in caverns and other subterraneous
places. The earth, we are expressly told, was encircled by
the vast ocean, the outer shores of which formed the cold,
cheerless, and mountainous region of Jötunheim, the abode of
the Frost and Mountain Giants, and other typified principles
of evil.

3. The Sub-terrestrial Region, or Helheim, the abode of
Hela, or Death *.

Muspellheim and Niflheim lay *without* the organized universe, and were obviously regarded as the primordial spheres
or material regions of light and darkness, of an active and a
passive principle—both mere modifications of matter—the
antagonism of which produced this universe, with the Æsir,
Vanir, Giants, Dwarfs, and other mythic beings that were
popularly supposed to be located in its various regions, though
they were no doubt regarded by the initiated as the mere
symbols of antagonistic elements †.

---

* Yggdrasill's three roots perfectly correspond to this ternary division.
One taking its rise in the Super-terrestrial Region, another at the outer part of
the Terrestrial Region, and the third in Helheim; Hela, according to the
Grímnis-mál (see page 491) dwelling *under* it.

† Our limits precluding us from entering into any further examination of
the Eddaic myths, we will merely observe that one of the most significant
amongst them is that relating to the death of Baldur (chap. 49). Baldur is
killed by Hœdur through the machinations of Loki, but his son Forseti sur-
vives, who

> "his days
> In peace ever passeth
> And stilleth all law strife."

that is to say, in other words, that when virtue succumbs to vice—
when innocence quits the world, justice remains, or, as Ovid so beautifully
expresses the same idea,

> "Victa jacet Pietas : et Virgo cæde madentes,
>   Ultima cœlestum, terras Astræa reliquit." *Metam.* i. 149.

NOTES TO THE PROSE EDDA.

BY

M. MALLET AND BISHOP PERCY*.

[A] Snorri informs us, in the beginning of the *Heimskringla*, that Gylfi was a prince, who governed Sweden before the arrival of Odin and his followers, and was obliged to yield to the supernatural power which those intruders employed against him, and to resign his kingdom up to them. This gave rise to the supposition that Gylfi was willing to make trial himself of the skill and sagacity of these new comers, by proposing to them a variety of captious questions.

[B] In the manuscript copy of the Edda, preserved at Upsal, there is a representation or drawing (very rudely done, as may be supposed) of these three thrones, and of the three persons sitting on them. They have crowns on their heads ; and Gangler is drawn in a suppliant posture before them.

[C] These are important questions; but the answers are still more remarkable. From their conformity with the Christian doctrines, one would be tempted to believe that Snorri had here embellished the religion of his Pagan ancestors, by bringing it as near as possible to the Gospel, if we did not find the same unfolded system literally expressed in the Völuspá, a poem of undoubted antiquity, and which was composed long before the name of Christianity was known in the north ; and also if the same system were not continually referred to in every other place of the Edda †.

[D] Here we have the pleasure to observe, that our philosophers saw the necessity of having recourse to the intervention of a deity in forming the world. The vivifying breath, here mentioned, seems to carry in it a strong affinity to the "Breath of Life" which God breathed into the nostrils of the first man ; according to the phrase of Scripture.—Gen. chap. ii. ver. 7 ‡.

[E] It has been a general opinion in the East that God began with creating genii, both good and bad, of very immense powers: who, for a long time before we existed, inhabited a world prior to this of ours. One may see in Herbelot what the Persians relate concerning the Dives, Nere, Peris, and their king Eblis.

[F] In all likelihood this legend is only an allegory. There is, however, a very important remark to be made here. A powerful being had with his breath animated the drops out of which the first giant was formed. This

---

* See page 397. Bishop Percy's notes are marked P.

† M. Mallet here falls into the same error as a number of eminent writers have done since his time ; an error which we have attempted to point out in our critical examination of the Eddaic doctrines. See page 482.—ED.

‡ See our remarks, page 485.—ED.

Being, whom the Edda affects not to name, was entirely distinct from Odin *, who had his birth long after the formation of Ymir. One may conjecture, therefore, that the hidden philosophy meant to inculcate that the supreme, eternal, invisible and incorruptible God, whom they durst not name out of fear and reverence, had appointed inferior divinities for the government of the world ; and that it was those divinities who, at the last day, were to yield to the efforts of powerful enemies, and be involved in the ruins of the universe : and that then the supreme god, ever existing, and placed above the reach of all revolution and change, would arise from his repose, to make a new world out of the ruins of the old, and begin a new period, which should, in its turn, give place to another; and so on through all eternity. The same was the system of the Stoics ; who, as well as the philosophers of the north, supposed that the world, after it had been consumed by flames, should be renewed ; and that the inferior deities should be destroyed at the same time. What confirms all this, is, that this god, superior to Odin himself, and of whom the vulgar among this people had scarce any idea, is represented in the Icelandic poems as making a second appearance, after the death of all the gods, in order to distribute justice, and establish a new order of things †.

[G] It is not undeserving of notice, that all the ancient nations of Europe describe their origin with the same circumstances. Tacitus says, that the Germans, in their verses, celebrated a god born of the earth, named Tuisco. This Tuisco had a son named Mannus, whose three sons were the orignal ancestors of the three principal nations of Germany ; namely, the Ingævones, Iscævones and Herminones. The Scythians, according to Herodotus, said that Targytaus, the founder of their nation, had three sons, Leipoxain, Anpoxain, and Kolaxain. A tradition received by the Romans, imported that the Cyclop Polyphemus had by Galatea three sons, named Celtus, Illyrius, and Gallus. Saturn, the father of Jupiter, Neptune, and Pluto, might very well come from the same source ; as well as the three sons whom Hesiod makes to spring from the marriage of Heaven and Earth, Coltus, Briareus, and Gyges. A tradition so ancient and so general must have certainly had its foundation in some real fact.

[H] Of all the ancient Theogonies, I find only that of the Chaldees which has any resemblance to this of the Edda. Berosus, cited by Syncellus, informs us that that people, one of the most ancient in the world, believed that in the beginning there was only water and darkness ; that this water and darkness contained in them divers monstrous animals, different in form and size, which were all represented in the temple of Bel ; that a female, named Omorca, was the mistress of the universe ; that the god Bel put to death all the monsters, destroyed Omorca herself, and, dividing her in two, formed of the one half of her the earth, and of the other the heavens : to which another tradition adds, that men were formed out of her head ; whence Berosus concludes, that this occasioned man to be endowed with intellectual powers.

[I] The matter of the sun and stars existed long before the formation of

---

* See our remarks, page 483.—ED.

† That is to say, an obscure allusion is made to such a deity in two strophes, the allusion in one of these strophes being applicable to Odin.—See page 483.—ED.

those bodies : this matter was the æther, the luminous world.   One cannot but remark in this fable the remains of the Mosaic doctrine ; according to which the creation of a luminous substance, in like manner, preceded that of the sun and moon.   And what indicates one common origin of both accounts, is what Moses adds in the same place.   " And God said, Let there be lights in the firmament of heaven, to divide the day from the night ; and let them be for signs of seasons, and of days, and of years," &c.—Gen. c. i. v. 14.

[J] The Persian mythology abounds with circumstances analogous to this. There are always giants, or mischievous genii, who wish ill to men, and hurt them whenever it is in their power. The heroes have no employment so dear and so glorious as that of making war upon those genii.   At this very day they are supposed to be banished among the rocks of Caucasus, or Imaus, ever since Tahmuras, surnamed Divbend (he who subdued the Dives), vanquished and put them to flight.   Mahometism has not been so severe as Christianity, in eradicating these ancient superstitions, and therefore the inhabitants of Persia are still very much infatuated with them.

[K] This fable proves that the ancient Skalds understood by the name Frigga, the spouse of the supreme god ; and that, at the same time, this Frigga was the earth.   This doctrine is of very great antiquity, and has been in general received by all the Teutonic nations. Their philosophers taught that the supreme god, Teut, or Woden, was the active principle, the soul of the world, which uniting itself with matter, had thereby put it into a condition to produce the intelligences or inferior gods, and men and all other crea- tures.   This is what the poets express figuratively, when they say that Odin espoused Frigga.   One cannot doubt, after having read this passage of the Edda, but it was this same goddess, to whom the Germans, according to Tacitus, consecrated one of the Danish islands, worshipping her under the name of Herthus, or the earth.   From this mystical marriage was born the god Thor.   He was the first born of the supreme God, and the greatest and most powerful of all the inferior divinities or intelligences that were born from the union of the two principles.

[L] We have here a specimen of the natural philosophy of the first ages. In attempting to explain things, the causes of which are obscure, men of all countries have gone in the same track ; and have represented what was un- known by the image of something they were well acquainted with.   This is doubtless the true origin of fable.   We perceive, at first sight, that it cannot be men who dispense rain and fine weather, who launch the lightning, &c. There was, therefore, a necessity for imagining there were beings of much superior powers, to produce these wonderful operations ; but none at all for assigning to them forms different from those of men and other animals. These solutions at once satisfied the curiosity and the imagination ; they were easy to be comprehended ; they interested the heart a thousand ways ; and must, therefore, succeed, and become lasting. In fact, they have every- where prevailed throughout the world.

[M] Here we have the cause of eclipses ; and it is upon this very ancient opinion that the general practice is founded of making noises at that time, to fright away the monsters, who would otherwise devour the two great lumi- naries.

[N] We see in the preceding, that the gods assemble together in the open air in a valley ; here is their principal residence under an ash-tree.   In this, as in other things, the gods are made to conform themselves to the manners of men. The ancient nations for a long time had no other place of rendez-vous than some tree remarkable for its size and age. The states of East Friesland, even so late as the thirteenth century, assembled under three large oaks which grew near Aurich; and it is not more than three centuries ago that most of the German princes held their conferences under trees.

[o] All the Teutonic nations have had these genii. The romances of chivalry are full of allusions to this imaginary system. The same opinions prevailed among the Persians. In many places of High Germany, the people have still a notion that these genii come by night, and lay themselves on those they find sleeping on their backs, and thus produce that kind of suffocation which we call the night-mare. In the same manner they accounted for those luxurious and immodest illusions so common in dreams; hence are de-rived the fables of Incubi and Sucubi; and that general opinion that there were genii or sylphs of both sexes, who did not disdain the embraces of mor-tals. The bad genii were particularly dreaded at the hour of noon; and in some places they still make it a point of duty to keep company at that hour with women in childbed, for fear the demon of noon should attack them if left alone. This superstition has prevailed no less in France than else-where, though it came from the East. St. Basil recommends us to pray to God some time before noon to avert this danger.

[p] I am obliged to return again to Odin. There is nothing in all Pagan antiquity more express than this passage, with regard to the supremacy of one God. The name of *As*, or Lord, is again ascribed to him in this place. It is to no purpose to object that the father of gods and men could not at the same time be called the father of combats, without manifest contradic-tion; for the Edda establishes this to be the fact too strongly to be disputed. Besides, contradictions do not always hinder an opinion from being received. Various modifications and distinctions are found out to clear up the difficulty. But there was no great need of any here, for the Teutonic nations regarded war as a very sacred occupation. It furnished, according to them, opportu-nities for displaying courage, and of fulfilling the views of Providence; which was to place us here as in a field of battle; and only to grant its favours as the peculiar rewards of fortitude and valour.

[q] This reasoning upon the names of Odin may contain something of truth in it. It is certain that almost all the names ascribed to the Supreme Deity, are either epithets taken from the qualities attributed to him, or the places where he was worshipped, or from the actions he had performed, &c.

[r] The reader will recollect here what I have previously said concern-ing this divinity of the northern nations. The function ascribed to him of launching the thunder, made him pass for the most warlike and formidable of all the gods. It was also Thor who reigned in the air, distributed the seasons, and raised or allayed tempests. The mallet which he hurled against the giants, and with which he crushed their heads, is doubtless the thunder, which most frequently falls upon elevated places. He was regarded as a di-vinity favourable to mankind, as he who guarded them from the attacks of giants and wicked genii, whom he never ceased to encounter and pursue.

[s] Baldur corresponds to the Apollo of the Greeks and Romans, the sun considered as a benign and salutary constellation, who chased away maladies,

animated the spirits, and warmed the imagination, that fruitful mother of poetry and all the other arts.

[T] This god, or at least a god with these attributes, has been adored by all the ancient nations of Europe, as also by the Persians. They all of them assigned a genius or god to the waters, whether of the sea, or of rivers, or fountains. This god would not fail to be adored and loaded with presents. Indeed all the people of Europe have had a great veneration for this divinity, and nothing was more difficult than to bring them off from the worship they paid him; this furnished subject for the prohibitions of many a council. Even within the bosom of the Christian Church the people long continued to repair in crowds to certain fountains, in order to adore the beneficent genius, who, by an incomprehensible power, made the waters flow in equal and uninterrupted abundance.

[U] I should be inclined to call Loki the Momus of the northern deities, did not the tricks he plays them often exceed the bounds of raillery. Besides, the monsters he has engendered, and who are along with their father, in the latter ages, to make rude assaults upon the gods, plainly indicates a system little different from that of the evil principle. Notwithstanding what has been advanced by some learned men, this opinion was not unknown either to the Persians or Goths: perhaps, indeed, we ought thus far only to agree with them, that it did not belong to the ancient religion of either of these people. But the hazardous and labouring condition in which they believed all nature to be, and the assaults which it was to sustain at the last day, led them insensibly to imagine that there was a power who was at enmity with gods and men, and who wrought all the evils which desolate the universe. This was the occupation of Ahriman among the Persians, and of Loki among the Scandinavians. Loki produces the great serpent which entirely encircles the world. This serpent, by some of the characteristics of it in this same mythology, seems to have been intended as an emblem of corruption or sin. He also gives birth to Hela, or Death, that queen of the infernal regions, of whom the Edda gives us here so remarkable a portrait; and, lastly, to the wolf Fenrir, that monster who is to encounter the gods, and destroy the world. How could the evil principle have been more strongly characterized?

[V] It must be borne in mind that the infernal region here described, where a punishment, rather disagreeable than cruel, is reserved for those who have died without their arms in their hands, is not an eternal hell, but only an intermediate abode, or, if you will, a prison, whence those who are confined will come forth at the last day to be judged upon other principles; and to be condemned or absolved for more real virtues and vices. To this intermediate hell was opposed an elysium of the same duration, viz. Valhalla, of which we shall presently have ample mention. One sees with surprise, in attentively reading this mythology, that the whole is better connected and the parts more dependent on one another than in any other work of the same kind that has come to our knowledge. The inferior gods, created along with this world, and united to it by their nature, and the conformity of their destiny, had every thing to fear at the last day from the enemies of nature. In order, therefore, to be the better able to resist them, they called home to them all the warriors, who had given proof of their valour by shedding their blood in battle. These, thus received into the residence of the gods, were still exercised in all the operations of war, in order to keep them in breath, ready against the last great conflict. This was the great end to which all their pleasures and employments were directed. As to cowardly or inactive persons, what could the gods have done with them, when they were thus threatened with an attack as sudden as dangerous? They gave them up to the custody of Death, who was to punish their weakness with languor and pain. All this has nothing to do with that eternal hell and elysium which we shall see sketched out in the Edda with much more force and dignity; and where nothing will be regarded but fidelity, chastity, integrity and justice *.

[w] Tacitus informs us that the Germans had no other physicians but their women. They followed the armies to staunch and suck the wounds of their husbands. In like manner, all the histories and romances of the north always represent the females, and often princesses, charged with this care. The same thing may be observed of almost all nations in their infancy.

[x] The travels of goddesses and fairies through the air are very common in all the poems and fables of the ancient inhabitants of the north, and most of the nations in Europe have thought in this respect along with them. When in process of time Christianity became prevalent, what had been formerly looked upon as a precious gift and signal mark of divine favour was now regarded as the effect only of diabolic arts. The assemblies of ecclesiastics made very severe prohibitions, and denounced their anathemas against all those who should travel through the air in the night-time. In the ancient law of Norway, called " Gulathings Lagen," c. i., we find this regulation, " Let the king and the bishop, with all possible care, make inquiry after those who exercise Pagan superstitions ; who make use of magic arts ; who adore the genii of particular places, or of tombs, or rivers; and who, by a diabolic manner of travelling, are transported from place to place through the air," &c. A council held at Rouen contains a prohibition of the same nature.

[y] The Edda never loses sight of the destruction of the world. It was owing to this expectation that the inferior gods received with pleasure warriors of approved valour, and such as they could depend on at the last times.

[z] This description of the palace of Odin is a natural picture of the manners of the ancient Scandinavians and Germans. Prompted by the wants of their climate, and the impulse of their own temperament, they form to themselves a delicious paradise in their own way ; where they were to eat and drink, and fight. The women, to whom they assign a place there, are introduced for no other purpose but to fill their cups. One wild boar furnishes out the whole of this celestial banquet : for, not very nice, they were only solicitous about the quantity of their food. The flesh of this animal, as well as that of the hog, was formerly the favourite meat of all these nations. The ancient Franks were no less fond of it ; a herd of swine was, in their eyes, an affair of such importance that the second chapter of the Salic Law consisting of twenty articles, is wholly taken up in inflicting penalties on those who stole them. In Gregory of Tours, Queen Fredegond, in order to

---

* See our remarks on the 53rd chapter of the Prose Edda, page 497.—ED.

alienate the mind of the king from one Nectarius, blackens him with the crime of having stolen a great many gammons or hams from the place where King Chilperic laid up his provisions. The king did not consider this at all as a laughing matter, but took it in a very grave and serious light.

[AA] Wine was very scarce in those times, and almost unknown. Beer was, perhaps, a liquor too vulgar for the heroes; the Edda, therefore, makes them drink hydromel, or mead, a beverage in great esteem .among all the German nations. The ancient Franks made great use of it. Gregory of Tours, speaking of a certain lord who generally drank it, adds, *Ut mos barbarorum habet.*—Greg. Turon. L. 8. c. 3.

[BB] From this passage of the Edda we may form to ourselves an idea of the amusements of the ancient Teutonic nations. When they were not engaged in any real war, they endeavoured, by the representation of battles, to gratify that fierce disposition which made them fond of the profession of arms. To this custom we may ascribe the rise and establishment of joustings and tournaments.

[CC] To conceive the force of this raillery, the reader must remember that Thor is represented of gigantic size, and as the stoutest and strongest of the gods. The Hercules of the northern nations.—P.

[DD] Our modern bacchanals will here observe that punishing by a bumper is not an invention of these degenerate days. The ancient Scandinavians were great topers. The drinking vessels of the northern nations were the horns of animals, of their natural length, only tipped with silver, &c. In York minster is preserved one of these ancient drinking vessels, composed of a large elephant's tooth, of its natural dimensions, ornamented with sculpture.—P.

[EE] We see plainly in the above fable the origin of those vulgar opinions entertained in the north, and which Pontoppidan has recorded concerning the craken and that monstrous serpent described in his History of Norway.—P.

[FF] Baldur, not having the good fortune to be slain in battle, was obliged to go, like all those that died of diseases, to the abode of Death. Saxo Grammaticus relates the same adventure, with some different circumstances.]

[GG] Loki having at length tired out the patience of the gods, they seize and punish him. This idea, at the bottom, has prevailed among almost all the ancient nations; but they have each of them embellished it after their own manner. One cannot doubt but our Scandinavians brought with them from Asia this belief, which appears to have been very widely established there from the earliest antiquity. In the book of the pretended prophecy of Enoch, we find many particulars very much resembling these of the Edda. The rebel angels causing incessantly a thousand disorders, God commanded the archangel Raphael to bind hand and foot one of the principal among them, named *Azael*, and cast him into an obscure place in a desert, there to keep him bound upon sharp-pointed stones to the last day. One may also safely conjecture that the fables of *Prometheus, Typhon,* and *Enceladus* are derived from the same origin.

[HH] What we have been reading is, for the most part, nothing else but the doctrine of Zeno and the Stoics. This remarkable resemblance has never been properly considered, and highly deserves a discussion. The ancients universally assure us, that the Stoic philosophy established the existence of an eternal divinity, diffused through and pervading all nature ; and being as it were, the soul and primum mobile of matter. From this divinity proceeded, as emanations from his essence, together with the world, certain intelligences ordained to govern under his directions, and who were to undergo the same revolutions as the world itself until the day appointed for the renovation of this universe. The fires concealed in the veins of the earth never cease to dry up the moisure contained therein, and will, in the end, set it all on flames : " A time will come," says Seneca, " when the world, ripe for a renovation, shall be wrapt in flames ; when the opposite powers shall in conflict mutually destroy each other ; when the constellations shall dash together ; and when the whole universe, plunged in the same common fire, shall be consumed to ashes." (Senec. Consol. ad Marciam. cap. ult.) This general destruction was to be preceded by an inundation : and in this respect the Edda perfectly agrees with Zeno. Seneca treats this subject of a future deluge at large, in his Quæst. Natural. lib. iii. c. 29, which he asserts must contribute to purify and prepare the earth for a new race of inhabitants more innocent and virtuous than the present.

But the consummation of the world by fire was the point most strongly insisted on by the Stoics. These verses of Seneca's kinsman, Lucan, are well known :—

> " Hos populos si nunc non usserit Ignis,
> Uret cum terris, uret cum gurgite ponti ;
> Communis Mundo superest Rogus."

But the strongest proof of the agreement between these two systems is this, that the destruction of the world will involve in it that of the gods ; that is to say all those created, or inferior divinities. This is expressed by Seneca, the tragedian, in most clear and precise terms, in those remarkable verses :—

> " Jamjam legibus obrutis   Amisso trepidus polo,
> Mundo cum veniet dies :   Titan excutiet diem ;
> Australis polus obruet,   Cœli regia concidens
> Quidquid per Lybyam jacet . .   Ortus atque obitus trahet ;
> Et sparsus Garamas tenet ;   Atque *omnes pariter Deos*
> Arctous polus obruet,   *Perdet mors aliqua, et chaos.*"
> Quidquid subjacet axibus,   Hercul. Oet. v. 1103.
> Et siccus boreas ferit.

In another place Seneca explains what he means by this death of the gods. They were not to be absolutely annihilated ; but to be once more reunited, by dissolution, to the soul of the world ; being resolved and melted into that intelligence of fire, into that eternal and universal principle, from which they had originally been emanations. It was, without doubt, in this sense also that our northern philosophers understood the matter. We may, from analogy, supply this circumstance with the greater confidence, as the poets have been ever more attentive to adorn and embellish the received doctrines, than to deliver them with precision. But, lastly, what must render this parallel more complete and striking, is, that according to the school of Zeno, no less than in the Icelandic prophecies, this tremendous scene is succeeded by a new creation, evidently drawn in the same colours by both.

" The world," says Seneca, " being melted and re-entered into the bosom of Jupiter, this god continues for some time totally concentered in himself, and remains concealed, as it were, wholly immersed in the contemplation of his own ideas; afterwards we see a new world spring from him, perfect in all its parts; animals are produced anew; an innocent race of men are formed under more favourable auspices, in order to people this earth, the worthy abode of virtue. In short, the whole face of nature becomes more pleasing and lovely." (Senec. Epist. 9. and Quæst. Nat. L. 3. c. ult.)

The Edda gives us the same descriptions in other words. They likewise occur in the poem of the Völuspá above alluded to.

The distance between Scandinavia and those countries where the Stoic philosophy prevailed, is certainly great, and must have been greater still in former ages than the present, when commerce and books lend wings to opinions, and diffuse them in a short time through the world. On the other hand, the system now under consideration is not such as all men would arrive at by mere dint of reflection. It appears then probable that all those who adopted it must have had it from the same hands; namely, from the eastern philosophers, and more particularly from the Persians. And history affords a sanction to this conjecture. We know that the Scandinavians came from some country of Asia. Zeno, who was born in Cyprus, of Phœnician parents, borrowed, in all probability, the principal tenets of his doctrine from the philosophers of the East. This doctrine was, in many respects, the same with that of the Magi. Zoroaster had taught that the conflict between Ormuzd and Ahriman (i. e. Light and Darkness, the Good and Evil Principle) should continue till the last day : and that then the Good Principle should be reunited to the supreme God, from whom it had first issued : the Evil should be overcome and subdued; darkness should be destroyed, and the world, purified by a universal conflagration, should become a luminous and shining abode, into which Evil should never more be permitted to enter.

Some of the points of doctrine, which I have been displaying after the Edda, have been consecrated by revelation. See, for instance, 2 Pet. ch. 3, v. 7, 10, 13; Mat. ch. 24, v. 10, 12; Mark, ch. 13, v. 24, 25; Luke, ch. 21, v. 25, 26; Rev. ch. 6, v. 12, 13, 14; ch. 12, v. 1, 2, 4; ch. 21, v. 1, 4, 18, 23, 27.

In the new earth, which was to succeed that which we inhabit, there were to be again subaltern divinities to govern it; and men to people it. This, in general, is what the Edda means to tell us : although the circumstances of the relation are darkly and allegorically delivered : yet not so obscurely, but that one easily sees it was the idea of the northern philosophers, as well as of the Stoics, that the world was to be renovated, and spring forth again more perfect and more beautiful. This is what is expressed here with regard to the sun and moon. *Lif* signifies life ; which is a farther proof, that by the fable of these two human beings who are to survive the destruction of the world, these northern philosophers meant to say that there still existed in the earth a vivifying principle, and seed proper to repair the loss of the former inhabitants.

ABSTRACT

OF THE

EYRBYGGJA-SAGA;

BEING THE EARLY ANNALS OF THAT DISTRICT OF ICELAND LYING
AROUND THE PROMONTORY CALLED SNÆFELLS *.

BY SIR WALTER SCOTT.

OF the various records of Icelandic history and literature, there is none
more interesting than the Eyrbyggja-Saga, composed (as has been conjectured
by the learned Thorkelin) before the year 1264, when Iceland was still
subject to the dominion of Norway †. The name of the author is unknown,
but the simplicity of his annals seems a sufficient warrant for their fidelity.
They contain the history of a particular territory of the Island of Iceland,
lying around the promontory called Snæfells, from its first settlement by
emigrants from Norway: and the chronicle details, at great length, the feuds
which took place among the families by whom the land was occupied, the
advances which they made towards a more regular state of society, their
habits, their superstitions, and their domestic laws and customs. If the
events which are commemorated in these provincial annals are not in themselves of great importance, the reader may, in recompense, derive, from the
minuteness with which they are detailed, an acquaintance with the manners
of the northern nations, not to be acquired from the perusal of more general
history. It is, therefore, presumed, that an abstract of the more interesting
parts of the Eyrbyggja-Saga may be acceptable to the readers of the Northern
Antiquities. The learned Thorkelin published a correct edition of this
history in 1787, executed at the expense of Suhm, the illustrious and
munificent patron of northern literature. A Latin version, supplied by the
well-known accuracy of the editor, assists the difficulties of those who are
imperfectly acquainted with the original Icelandic.

In the year of God 883, a Norwegian nobleman, named Biorn, having
been declared an exile by Harold, King of Norway, had recourse to the

---

* This abstract of the Eyrbyggja Saga, is printed *verbatim* from the
"Illustrations of Northern Antiquities, 1 vol. 4to. Edinb. 1814.—ED.

† This must be a *lapsus calami* of our great novelist, for it was in
the year 1264 that Iceland *became* "subject to the dominion of Norway."
See page 297.—ED.

protection of Rolf, or Rollo, who united the qualities of a priest and a warrior, and kept the temple of Thor in the Island of Mestur. Biorn was
kindly received, and furnished with a vessel to pursue his fortune in the
spring. But finding that by this proceeding he had incurred the resentment
of Harold, Rolf, or, as he was called from his sacred office, Thorolf, (quasi
Thor's-Rolf,) resolved to abandon his habitation and to set sail for Iceland,
where, ten years before, a colony had been settled by Ingolf, the son of
Arne. Thorolf made an immense sacrifice to Thor preparatory to his
departure; and having received or fabricated an oracle authorizing his
change of residence, he set sail, carrying with him the earth upon which the
throne of Thor had been placed, the image of the Mace-Bearer itself, and
the wooden work of his temple. When the vessel of the adventurer
approached Iceland, Thorolf cast the columns of the idol's sanctuary into the
sea, and declared his purpose of establishing his new residence wherever they
should be thrown on shore. Chance, and the current of the tides, directed
the pillars to a promontory or peninsula, called from that circumstance
Thorsness*. Here, therefore, Thorolf established himself and his followers,
and, mindful of his tutelar deity, erected a temple for Thor, the ample scale
of which testified the zeal of his devotion. An inner sanctuary contained
the altar of the deity, on which was placed a silver ring, weighing two
ounces, which was used in the ministration of every solemn oath, and which
decorated the person of the priest of Thor upon all occasions of public meeting. Here also was deposited the vessel which contained the blood of the
sacrifices, and the sacred implement for sprinkling it upon the altar and the
worshippers. Idols, representing the various deities of Scandinavian mythology, were placed around the altar, and a tax was imposed upon all the
settlers for the maintenance of the solemn rites and sacrifices by which they
were to be propitiated; Thorolf reserving to himself the office of high-priest,
with the duty of maintaining the temple and superintending the ritual. A
series of curious ordinances marked the foundation and extent of his authority. The whole promontory of Thorsness was under the protection of the
deity, but a small eminence entitled Helgafels (*i. e.* the Holy Mount) was
so peculiarly sacred, that none of the settlers were to look upon it until they
had performed their morning ablutions, and each living creature which should
trespass upon its precincts was liable to be punished with death. To the
terrors of religion were added the solemnities of legal authority. Near the
Holy Mount was established the place of justice, where the popular assemblies were held†. This spot was also sacred, neither to be defiled by blood,

---

* Thorsness seems to have been that small peninsula, mentioned by Sir
George Mackenzie in his Survey of the Gold-bringe Syssell of Iceland, which
is itself a huge indented promontory on the south-western coast of that
island. Near the peninsula the travellers saw the Helgafels, on which
there is still a small hamlet, which, they observe, derives its name from the
superstitious usages with which it was anciently connected.—*Travels in Iceland*, p. 186, 7.

† Each little district of settlers had its provincial assembly, for the purpose of making laws, imposing punishments, and accommodating differences.
At a later period, general assemblies of the whole Icelandic people, called

nor polluted by any of the baser necessities of nature, for satisfying which a neighbouring rock was appointed. In these institutions we recognise the rude commencement of social order and public law. The infant settlement of Thorolf was strengthened by the arrival of Biorn, the fugitive upon whose account he had incurred the indignation of King Harold, and by that of other northern chiefs, whom the fate of war, or the love of adventure, had banished from their respective homes. Each chose his habitation according to his pleasure, and the settlement began to be divided into three districts, called Eyrarvert, Alpta-fiord, and Breida-wick, all of which acknowledged the authority of the Pontiff Thorolf, and the sanctity of his institutions.

The death of Thorolf, however, led the way to internal dissension. A patriarch, called from the number of his family Barna-Kiallak (rich in children), was tempted to dispute the sanctity of the territory of Thorsness, which had been sedulously stipulated. His tribe, confident in their numbers, openly disputed the power of Thorstein, who had succeeded his father Thorolf as pontiff, and announced that when occasion pressed they would pay no more respect to the soil of the sacred territory than to unconsecrated ground, nor would they take the trouble to secede to the rock appointed for such purposes. With this foul intent they marched towards Thorsness, and were met by Thorstein at the head of his tribe, servants, and allies, who, after a sharp skirmish, was fortunately able to prevent the intended profanation of the sacred soil. But, as neither party could boast decisive success, an armistice was agreed upon, and a congress opened under the mediation of an aged settler called Thordus. This ingenious referee at once removed the ostensible cause of dispute, by declaring that the territory, having been polluted by human blood shed in the conflict, had lost its sanctity in future, and, to take away the secret cause of contention, he declared that Thorgrim, one of the sons of Kiallak, should be conjoined with Thorstein in the charge of the temple of Thor, with an equal share in the duties and revenues of the office of pontiff, and in the charge of protecting from sacrilege a new place of justice, which was now to be established. It is described as a circular range of upright stones, within which one more eminent marked the stone of Thor, where human victims were immolated to the Thunderer, by breaking or crushing the spine. And this description may confute those antiquaries who are disposed to refer such circles exclusively to the Celtic tribes, and their priests the Druids.

Thorstein, son of Thorolf, perished by shipwreck. His grandson Snorro became the most distinguished support of his family, and the following commencement of his history marks the singular system of laws which already prevailed in Iceland, as well as the high honours in which the female sex was held in that early period of society. The tutelage of Snorro, whose father died young, had devolved upon Borko the Fat, his father's brother, who had married Thordisa, his mother, and was thus at once his uncle and father-in-law. At the age of fourteen, Snorro, with two companions, went abroad to visit his relations in Norway, and returned to Iceland after the lapse of a year. His companion Thorlef was splendid in dress, arms, and

Althing, were held at a place called Thingvalla, on the shores of a salt-water lake.—See *Mackenzie's Travels.*

equipment, being girded with a sword of exquisite workmanship, and bearing a shield painted blue, and exquisitely gilded, and a spear the handle of which was plated with gold. But Snorro was dressed in a dark garment, mounted upon a black mare, and his whole appearance intimated want and dejection. This assumed poverty rendered Snorro more acceptable at Helgafels, the abode of his uncle Borko. For, by the law of descent, Snorro was entitled to one-half of the possessions of his grandfather, now administered by Borko; and his appearance gave the latter ground to think that he would sell them in his necessity for an inconsiderable price. He was, therefore, not displeased to see his nephew return in a condition which did not seem to supply to him the means of escaping from his tutelage. A singular incident, however, interrupted their family concord. Shortly after Snorro had taken up his abode with his uncle, a party of twelve armed men, headed by Eyolf Gray, suddenly appeared at Helgafels, and their leader announced that he had slain a relative of Thordisa, the mother of Snorro. Borko, to whom the slaughter was indifferent, and who was connected with Eyolf, received him joyfully, and commanded his wife to make him good cheer. While she obeyed his commands with undisguised reluctance, Eyolf chanced to drop the spoon with which he was eating; as he stooped to recover it, the vindictive matron, unable to suppress her indignation, snatched his sword, and severely wounded him ere he could recover his erect posture. Borko, incensed at this attack upon his guest, struck his wife, and was about to repeat the blow, when Snorro, throwing himself between them, repelled his attack, and placing his mother by his side, announced haughtily his intention to protect her. Eyolf escaped with difficulty, and afterwards recovered from Borko a fine for the wound which he had sustained, and the uncle and nephew were obliged to have recourse to justice to arrange their mutual claims, which were rendered yet more inextricable by this brawl. When they appeared before the assembled patriarchs of the settlement, Borko admitted that his nephew, in right of his father deceased, was entitled to one-half of the territory of Helgafels, and he also agreed that they could not conveniently possess it in community. Wherefore he offered to purchase that property from Snorro, and to make payment of an adequate price. To this proposal Snorro replied, that his uncle ought first to fix the price to be given, and that he, as descended of the elder brother, should then have it in his option either to sell his own share in the property, or to purchase Borko's moiety at the price to be so named. Borko, confident in the supposed poverty of his nephew, estimated the half of the joint property at sixty ounces of silver, a sum far beneath the real value; when, to his astonishment, Snorro at once made payment of the stipulated sum, and obtained full possession of his paternal mansion and estate. Nor did the vexations of Borko end here. For, when he was about to depart from Helgafels, his wife Thordisa invoked witnesses to bear testimony that she solemnly divorced her husband Borko, alleging as a sufficient reason, that he had raised his hand against her person. And such were the rights of an Icelandic Mater-familias, that the divorce and division of goods immediately took place between her and her husband, although one would have presumed that the attempt to murder a guest in his own presence might have been admitted as a satisfactory apology for the violence of the husband. Snorro, having thus at an easy rate obtained possession of his whole paternal

inheritance of Helgafels, lost no time in assuming the sacred character
of priest of Thor, and continued, from his boldness, craft, and dexterity, to
act a conspicuous part in the various feuds which agitated the settlers in this
sterile and dreary country as fiercely as if they had been contending for
the mines of Peru, or the vineyards of Italy; so that the subsequent part of
this history may be considered as the annals of Snorro's pontificate.

Our annalist has not left the scene altogether unvaried. Wars and pro-
secutions before the assembly of the people are indeed the groundwork; but
such spells and supernatural incidents, as the superstition of the age believed
in, are introduced like the omens and miracles of classic history. Such
incidents, indeed, make an invariable part of the history of a rude age, and
the chronicles which do not afford these marks of human credulity may be
grievously suspected as deficient in authenticity. The following account of a
trial of skill between two celebrated sorceresses occupies several pages of the
Eyrbyggja-Saga.

"Tell me," said Katla, a handsome and lively widow, to Gunlaugar, an
accomplished and gallant young warrior, "tell me why thou goest so oft to
Mahfahlida?—Is it to caress an old woman?" "Thine own age, Katla,"
answered the youth inconsiderately, "might prevent thy making that of
Geirrida a subject of reproach."—"I little deemed," replied the offended
matron, "that we were on an equality in that particular—but thou, who
supposest that Geirrida is the sole source of knowledge, mayst find that
there are others who equal her in science." It happened in the course of
the following winter that Gunlaugar, in company with Oddo, the son of
Katla, had renewed one of those visits to Geirrida, with which Katla had
upbraided him. "Thou shalt not depart to-night," said the sage matron,
"evil spirits are abroad, and thy bad destiny predominates."—"We are
two in company," answered Gunlaugar, "and have therefore nothing to
fear."—"Oddo," replied Geirrida, "will be of no aid to thee; but go, since
thou wilt go, and pay the penalty of thy own rashness."—In their way they
visited the rival matron, and Gunlaugar was invited to remain in her house
that night. This he declined, and, passing forward alone, was next morning
found lying before the gate of his father Thorbiorn, severely wounded and
deprived of his judgment. Various causes were assigned for this disaster;
but Oddo, asserting that they had parted in anger that evening from Geirrida, insisted that his companion must have sustained the injury through her
sorcery. Geirrida was accordingly cited to the popular assembly, and
accused of witchcraft. But twelve witnesses, or compurgators, having
asserted upon their oath the innocence of the accused party, Geirrida was
honourably freed from the accusation brought against her [*]. Her acquittal

---

[*] This ceremony of compurgation formed, as is well known, the remote
origin of the trial by jury. The compurgators were at first a kind of witnesses, who, upon their general knowledge of the character of the accused,
gave evidence of his being incapable of committing the crime imputed, but
gradually obtained the character of judges, who formed their opinion upon
the evidence of others adduced in their presence [a].

---

[a] This, in so far as regards Iceland and the other Scandinavian states, was
far from being the case. The Icelandic compurgators remained compur-

did not terminate the rivalry between the two sorceresses, for, Geirrida belonging to the family of Kiliakan, and Katla to that of the pontiff Snorro, the animosity which still subsisted between these septs became awakened by the quarrel

It chanced that Thorbiorn, called Digri, (or the corpulent,) one of the family of Snorro, had some horses which fed in the mountain pastures, near to those of Thorarin, called the Black, the son of the enchantress Geirrida. But when autumn arrived, and the horses were to be withdrawn from the mountains, and housed for the winter, those of Thorbiorn could nowhere be found, and Oddo, the son of Katla, being sent to consult a wizard, brought back a dubious answer, which seemed to indicate that they had been stolen by Thorarin. Thorbiorn, with Oddo and a party of armed followers, immediately set forth for Mahfahlida, the dwelling of Geirrida and her son Thorarin. Arrived before the gate, they demanded permission to search for the horses which were missing. This Thorarin refused, alleging that neither was the search demanded duly authorized by law, nor were the proper witnesses cited to be present, nor did Thorbiorn offer any sufficient pledge of security when claiming the exercise of so hazardous a privilege. Thorbiorn replied, that as Thorarin declined to permit a search, he must be held as admitting his guilt; and constituting for that purpose a temporary court of justice, by choosing out six judges, he formally accused Thorarin of theft before the gate of his own house *. At this the patience of Geirrida forsook her. "Well," said she to her son Thorarin, "is it said of thee, that thou art more a woman than a man, or thou wouldst not bear these intolerable affronts." Thorarin, fired at the reproach, rushed forth with his servants and guests; a skirmish soon disturbed the legal process which had been instituted, and one or two of both parties were wounded and slain, before the wife of Thorarin and the female attendants could separate the fray by flinging their mantles over the weapons of the combatants. Thorbiorn and his party retreating, Thorarin proceeded to examine the field of battle. Alas! among the reliques of the fight was a bloody hand, too slight and fair to belong to any of the combatants. It was that of his wife Ada, who had met this misfortune in her attempts to separate the skirmish. Incensed to the uttermost, Thorarin threw aside his constitutional moderation, and, mounting on horseback, with his allies and followers pursued the hostile party, and overtook them in a hay-field, where they had halted to repose their horses, and to exult over the damage they had done to Thorarin. At this moment he assailed them with such fury, that he slew Thorbiorn upon the spot, and killed several of his attendants, although Oddo, the son of Katla, escaped free from wounds, having been dressed by his mother in an invulnerable garment. After this action, more bloody than usually happened in an Icelandic engagement, Thorarin returned to Mahfahlida, and, being questioned by his mother concerning the events of the skirmish,

---

gators and nothing more; the judges being the *Godar*, with their assessors or doom's-men, as we have shown in the second supplementary chapter. It is to these doom's-men that we may trace "the remote origin of the trial by jury," and not to the "ceremony of compurgation." See page 292.—ED.

* That is to say, a *door-doom* was held; for an explanation of which see page 307.—ED.

he answered in the improvisatory and enigmatical poetry of his age and country,—

> From me the foul reproach be far,
> With which a female waked the war,
> From me, who shunned not in the fray
> Through foemen fierce to hew my way;
> (Since meet it is the eagle's brood
> On the fresh corpse should find their food,)
> Then spared I not, in fighting field,
> With stalwart hand my sword to wield ;
> And well may claim at Odin's shrine
> The praise that waits this deed of mine.

To which effusion Geirrida answered, " Do these verses imp'r the death of Thorbiorn ?"—And Thorarin, alluding to the legal process which Thorbiorn had instituted against him, resumed his song,—

> Sharp bit the sword beneath the hood
> Of him whose zeal the cause pursued,
> And ruddy flowed the stream of death,
> Ere the grim brand resumed the sheath ;
> Now on the buckler of the slain
> The raven sits, his draught to drain,
> For gore-drenched is his visage bold,
> That hither came his courts to hold.

As the consequence of this slaughter was likely to be a prosecution at the instance of the pontiff Snorro, Thorarin had now recourse to his allies and kindred, of whom the most powerful were Arnkill, his maternal uncle, and Verimond, who readily promised their aid both in the field and in the Comitia, or popular meeting, in spring, before which it was to be presumed Snorro would indict Thorarin for the slaughter of his kinsman. Arnkill could not, however, forbear asking his nephew how he had so far lost his usual command of temper. He replied in verse,

> Till then, the master of my mood,
> Men called me gentle, mild and good ;
> But yon fierce dame's sharp tongue might wake
> In wintry den the frozen snake.

While Thorarin spent the winter with his uncle Arnkill, he received information from his mother Geirrida, that Oddo, son of her old rival Katla, was the person who had cut off the hand of his wife Ada, and that he gloried in the fact. Thorarin and Arnkill determined on instant vengeance, and, travelling rapidly, surprised the house of Katla. The undismayed sorceress, on hearing them approach, commanded her son to sit close beside her, and when the assailants entered they only beheld Katla, spinning coarse yarn from what seemed a large distaff, with her female domestics seated around her.—" Her son," she said, " was absent on a journey ;" and Thorarin and Arnkill, having searched the house in vain, were obliged to depart with this answer. They had not, however, gone far, before the well-known skill of Katla in optical delusion occurred to them, and they resolved on a second and stricter search. Upon their return they found Katla in the outer apartment, who seemed to be shearing the hair of a tame kid, but was in reality cutting the locks of her son Oddo. Entering the inner room, they found the large distaff flung carelessly upon a bench. They returned yet a third time, and a third delusion was prepared for them ; for Katla had given her son the appearance of a hog, which seemed to grovel upon the heap of ashes. Arnkill now seized and split the distaff which he had at first suspected, upon which Katla tauntingly observed, that if their visits had been frequent that evening, they could not be said to be altogether ineffectual, since they had destroyed a distaff. They were accordingly returning completely baffled, when Geirrida met them, and upbraided them with carelessness in searching for their enemy. "Return yet again," she said, "and I will accompany you."—Katla's maidens, still upon the watch, announced to her the return of the hostile party, their number augmented by one who wore a blue mantle. "Alas!" cried Katla, "it is the sorceress Geirrida, against whom spells will be of no avail." Immediately rising from the raised and boarded seat which she occupied, she concealed Oddo beneath it, and covered it with cushions as before, on which she stretched herself, complaining of indisposition. Upon the entrance of the hostile party, Geirrida, without speaking a word, flung aside her mantle, took out a piece of seal's-skin, in which she wrapped up Katla's head, and commanded that she should be held by some of the attendants, while the others broke open the boarded space, beneath which Oddo lay concealed, seized upon him, bound him, and led him away captive with his mother. Next morning Oddo was hanged, and Katla stoned to death ; but not until she had confessed that through her sorcery she had occasioned the disaster of Gunlaugar, which first led the way to these feuds. This execution is remarkable, because it seems to have taken place without any previous ceremony of judicial procedure, which, in general, we find the Icelanders considered as necessary preliminaries to the condemnation and execution of criminals. Spring now approached, and it became necessary for Thorarin to take some resolution ; for, although it seemed possible that the slaughter might be atoned by a pecuniary imposition, yet so many persons had been slain, that the usual fines corresponding to their rank was more than sufficient to exhaust his fortune : and, to hasten his determination, Snorro, accompanied by a band of eighty horsemen, appeared before the house of Arnkill, for the purpose of citing Thorarin to answer for the slaughter of Thorbiorn. This citation was performed in obedience to the Icelandic law, which permitted no accusation to be brought against any party, who had not been previously apprized of the charge by a summons, delivered to him personally or at his dwelling-place *. The ceremony being peaceably performed, Thorarin, observing the strong party in attendance upon Snorro, broke forth into a poetical rhapsody :

> No feeble force, no female hand,
> Compels me from my native land ;
> O'er-match'd in numbers and in might,
> By banded hosts in armour bright,
> In vain attesting laws and gods,
> A guiltless man, I yield to odds.

---

* This law of summons is often mentioned, and seems to have been regularly insisted upon. It was attended with some risk to the party who ventured to make the citation, and often ended in a skirmish.

Accordingly, ere the popular assembly met, Thorarin, with his relative Verimond, embarked in a vessel for Scandinavia. Of the former the history tells us no more ; but Verimond, who separated from him, and spent the subsequent winter at the court of Count Haco, son of Sigurd, then regent of Norway, continues to make a figure in the Eyrbyggja-Saga.

It seems that Haco had at his court two of those remarkable champions, called Berserkir-men who, by moral or physical excitation of some kind or other, were wont to work themselves into a state of frenzy, during which they achieved deeds passing human strength, and rushed, without sense of danger or feeling of pain, upon every species of danger that could be opposed to them. Verimond contracted a sort of friendship with these champions, who, unless when seized with their fits of fury, were not altogether discourteous or evil-disposed. But, as any contradiction was apt to excite their stormy passions, their company could not be called very safe or commodious. Verimond, however, who now desired to return to Iceland, conceived that, in the feuds to which he might be there exposed, the support of the two Berserkir would be of the greatest advantage to him. Acting upon this idea, when Haco at his departure offered him any reasonable boon which he might require, he prayed that he would permit these two champions to accompany him to his native country. The count assented, but not without showing him the danger of his request. "They are only accustomed," said Haco, "to submit to men of great power and high rank, and will be reluctant and disobedient stipendiaries to a person of a meaner station." Verimond, however, grasped at the permission of the count, though reluctantly granted, and was profuse in promises to Halli and Leikner, providing they would accompany him to Iceland. They frankly objected the poverty of the country, yet agreed to go thither, apprizing their conductor, at the same time, that their friendship would not endure long if he refused them any boon which was in his power to grant, and which they might choose to demand. Verimond again assured them of his anxious wish to gratify them in every particular, and transported them to Iceland, where he was not long of discovering that he had burthened himself with a very difficult task. Halli's first request was, that he should be provided with a spouse, rich, nobly born, and beautiful. But, as it was not easy to find a maiden so gifted, who would unite her fate with a foreigner of mean birth, who was besides a Berserkir, Verimond was compelled to elude the request of his champion. This was likely to occasion such enmity, that Verimond began to think of transferring his troublesome and ungovernable satellites to his brother Arngrim, a man of a stern, fierce, and active disposition, who had carried on numerous feuds, and in every case refused to make pecuniary compensation for the slaughters which he had committed. Thus he was usually called Styr, (i. e. the Stirring or Tumultuous,) as Verimond was termed Miöfii, or the Delicate. Styr, nevertheless, tumultuous as he was, could not be prevailed upon to accept of the patronage of the Berserkir. It was in vain that Verimond protested that he gifted him with two such champions as would enable him to become an easy victor in every quarrel he might engage in, and that he designed this present as a gage of their fraternal union. Styr, professing a sincere confidence in his brotherly affection, intimated, that he had heard enough of the disposition of these foreign warriors to satisfy him that they would be rather embarrassing than useful dependants, and was fully determined never to admit them within his family. Verimond was therefore obliged to change his tone, to acknowledge the dread in which he stood of the Berserkir, and request his brother's advice and assistance to rid him of them. "That," answered Styr, "is a different proposal. I could never have accepted them as a pledge of favour or friendship; but, to relieve thee from danger and difficulty, I am content to encumber myself with the charge of thy associates." The next point was to reconcile the Berserkir, (who might resent being transferred like bondsmen from the one brother to the other,) to this change of masters. The warlike and fierce disposition of Styr seemed, however, so much more suitable to their own than that of Verimond, that they speedily acquiesced, and, accompanying their new patron upon a nocturnal excursion, evinced their strength in breaking to pieces a strong wooden frame, or bed, in which his enemy had taken refuge, so that Styr had an opportunity of slaying him. The presumption of Halli, however, soon discomposed their union. The champion cast the eyes of affection on Asdisa, the daughter of his patron, a haughty, fiery, and robust damsel, well qualified to captivate the heart of a Berserkar. He formally announced to Styr that he demanded her hand in marriage, that a refusal would be a breach of their friendship, but that, if he would accept of his alliance, he and his brother would render him the most powerful man in Iceland. At this unexpected proposal Styr for a time remained silent, considering how best he might evade the presumptuous demand of this frantic champion, and at length observed, that the friends of his family must be consulted upon his daughter's establishment. "Three days' space," answered Halli, "will suffice for that purpose, and be mindful that our friendship depends on thine answer." Styr, in great doubt and trouble, journeyed to Helgafels, to consult the experience of the pontiff Snorro. When Snorro learned that he came to ask advice, "Let us ascend," he said, "the sacred mount, for such councils as are taken on that holy spot rarely prove unpropitious." They remained in deep conference on the mount of Thor until evening, nor did any one know the purpose which they agitated; but what followed sufficiently shows the nature of the councils suggested upon the holy ground. Styri, so soon as he returned home, announced to Halli his expectation, that since he could not redeem his bride by payment of a sum of money as was usual, he should substitute in lieu thereof, according to ancient right and custom, the performance of some unusual and difficult task. "And what shall that task be?" demanded the suitor. "Thou shalt form," said Styr, "a path through the rocks at Biarnarhaf, and a fence betwixt my property and that of my neighbours, also thou shalt construct a house for the reception of my flocks, and these tasks accomplished thou shalt have Asdisa to wife."—"Though unaccustomed to such servile toil," replied the Berserkar, "I accept of the terms thou hast offered." And by the assistance of his brother he accomplished the path required, a work of the greatest labour, and erected the bound-fence, of which vestiges remained in the days of our historian. The Berserkir were now labouring at the stable for the flocks, while the servants of Styr were employed in the construction of a subterranean bath, so contrived that it could on a sudden be deluged with boiling water, or heated to a suffocating degree. On the last day, when the brethren were labouring at the conclusion of their task, Asdisa, the daughter of Styr, passed by them splendidly arrayed. Then sung Halli,

Oh, whither dost thou bend thy way,
Fair maiden, in such rich array,

For never have I seen thee roam
So gaily dressed, so far from home?—

Then Leikner also sung,—

Till now that stole of purple rare
Full seldom did the maiden wear,
Why is she now attired so fair?
The cause, O maid, benign display,
Of that unwonted raiment gay,
Nor thus disdainful pass us by
With silent lip and scornful eye.

But Asdisa, disliking either the bard or the poetry, or both, passed on without making any answer. Evening now approached, and, the stipulated task being ended, the champions returned to the dwelling of Styr. They were extremely exhausted, as was common with persons of their condition, whose profuse expenditure of strength and spirits induced a proportional degree of relaxation after severe labour. They therefore gladly accepted Styr's proposal that they should occupy the newly constructed bath. When they had entered, their insidious patron caused the trap-door to be blockaded, and a newly stripped bullock's skin to be stretched before the entrance, and then proceeded to pour in scalding water through the aperture contrived for that purpose, and to heat the bath to an intolerable pitch. The unfortunate Berserkir endeavoured to break out, and Halli succeeded in forcing the door, but, his feet being entangled in the slippery hide, he was stabbed by Styr ere he could make any defence: his brother, attempting the entrance, was forced headlong back into the bath, and thus both perished. Styr caused their bodies to be interred in a narrow glen, of such depth that nothing but the sky was visible from its recesses. Then Styr composed this song concerning his exploit:—

These champions from beyond the main
Of Iceland's sons I deem'd the bane,
Nor fear'd I to endure the harm
And frantic fury of their arm,
But, conqueror, gave this valley's gloom
To be the grim Berserkir's tomb.

When the pontiff Snorro heard that the stratagem of Styr had proved successful, he paid him a visit, in which, after a day's consultation, Asdisa, the daughter of Styr, was betrothed to Snorro. The marriage was solemnized shortly afterwards, and the activity and intrepidity of Styr being aided by, and aiding in turn, the wisdom and experience of Snorro, the power of both was greatly extended and fortified by this alliance.

Passing some feuds of less interest, we come to the history of Thorolf Bægifot. This chief had in his youth defied to combat an aged champion called Ulfar, for the sake of acquiring his territory. Ulfar, though old and dim of sight, preferred death to dishonour, and met Thorolf in single combat. Ulfar fell, but Thorolf received a wound in the leg, on which he ever after halted, and thus acquired the name of Bægifot, or the Crook-footed. Thorolf had one son, the same Arnkill who figured in the history of Thorarin the Black, and two daughters, one of whom was the celebrated enchantress, Geirrida. As Thorolf waxed aged, he became of a cankered and savage disposition, and as crooked in his mind as in his limbs. Many causes of discord occurred betwixt him and his son Arnkill, until at length they were in a state of utter enmity. The nearest neighbour of Thorolf Bægifot was Ulfar, a freedman of Thorbrand, possessed of a fair property. It was said of this cultivator, that he understood the art of making hay better than any man in Iceland, and that his crop was never injured by the rain, or his cattle by the storms. Thorolf went to consult this sage upon the management of the hay-crop on a field which they possessed in common. "This week," said Ulfar, "will be rainy; let us use it in cutting the hay; it will be followed by a fortnight of dry weather, which we will employ in drying it." Thorolf, however, became impatient, and, dubious of a change of weather, ordered his hay to be carried to his yard, and ricked up, while that of Ulfar was yet lying in the swathe, and then, whether impelled by cupidity, caprice, or jealousy does not appear, he carried home also that part of the crop which belonged to the weather-wise Ulfar. The latter reclaimed his property; but, after some altercation, saw no means of redress so effectual as to appeal to the justice of Arnkill, the son of Thorolf. Arnkill, after vain applications for justice to his father, was at length contented to indemnify Ulfar by making payment to him of the value of the hay—a proposal to which his father had refused to accede, saying, in the plenitude of oppressive power, "That the churl was already too wealthy." Arnkill, however, indemnified himself of the price of the hay by driving off twelve fat oxen belonging to his father, which he alleged were compensated by the money thus advanced to Ulfar. It was now the feast of Jol, and Thorolf, who had drunk freely, and circulated much liquor among his bondsmen, was so incensed against Ulfar, that he offered liberty to any of his serfs who would burn his house, and consume him among the flames. Six of his bondsmen set out upon this neighbourly exploit; but the flames, as they began to rise, became visible to Arnkill, who hastened to the house of Ulfar, extinguished the fire, and made prisoners the incendiaries. These he transported to his own house, and hanged them next morning without ceremony, to the great increase of his father's discontent. Ulfar, on the other hand, rejoiced at having acquired so active and powerful a protector, chose Arnkill for his immediate patron, to the displeasure of the family of his original master, Thorbrand, who viewed with resentment the chance of losing the inheritance of their father's freedman. Meanwhile the wrath of Thorolf grew so high against his son, that he went to the pontiff Snorro, to prevail on him to prosecute Arnkill to the uttermost for the slaughter of his six bondsmen. Snorro, at first, declined to have any interference with the matter, alleging the good character of Arnkill, and the foul treason in which the serfs of Thorolf had been engaged when seized and executed. "I wot well the cause of thy regard for Arnkill," answered Thorolf; "thou thinkest he will pay for thy support in the assembly more freely than I. But hearken: I know thy desire to possess the fair woods of Krakaness, which pertain to me. I will bestow them on thee, if thou wilt prosecute the cause arising from the slaughter of my bondsmen with the utmost severity, without sparing, on account of Arnkill's relation to me, or his friendship to thyself." Snorro could not resist the prospect of gain thus artfully held out to him, and agreed to prosecute the cause to the uttermost. The pleadings were ingenious on both sides, and show some progress in the intricate punctilios of municipal jurisprudence. The death of the bondsmen was urged by Snorro. The accused defended himself upon the fact of their being apprehended in the act of burning Ulfar's habitation. It was replied, that though this might have justified their being slain on the spot, yet it gave those who seized them no right to execute them elsewhere after a day's interval. At length the matter was referred to the award of the two brethren, Styr and Verimond, who appointed Arnkill to pay a fine of twelve ounces of silver for the death of each domestic. Thorolf, incensed to the highest pitch at this lenient imposition, broke forth into complaints against Snorro, whom he considered as having betrayed his cause, and retired from the convention to meditate a bloody revenge against all his enemies. Ulfar, the most helpless and inoffensive, was the first to experience his resentment. He had been feasting with his patron Arnkill, and had departed loaded with presents, when he was waylaid and assassinated by Spagil, a villain whom Thorolf had hired to the deed by an ample bribe. Arnkill, who chanced to be abroad that evening, observed a man at a distance bearing the shield which he had so lately bestowed on Ulfar. "That buckler," said he, "Ulfar hath not parted from willingly; pursue the bearer of it, and if, as I dread, he has slain my client through my father's instigation, bring him not before my sight, but slay him instantly." A part of his followers instantly pursued Spagil, and having seized and compelled him to avow his crime, and confess by whom it was prompted, they killed him on the spot, and brought back to Thorolf the spoils of the unhappy Ulfar. The disputes concerning the inheritance of Ulfar now augmented the dissensions of the settlement. It was claimed by the family of Thorbrand, as Ulfar had been his freedman, and by Arnkill as his immediate patron and protector. The former, however, proved the weaker party, and, on having recourse to Snorro, received little encouragement to cope with Arnkill. "You share only," said the pontiff, "the general lot of the tribe, which, while Arnkill lives, must put up with such aggressions unavenged."—"Most truly spoken," replied the sons of Thorbrand, "nor can we complain of thee, Snorro, for refusing to advocate our cause, who art so tame and cold in asserting thine own." With these words of reproach, they left the assembly in great discontent.

Thorolf Bægifot began now to repent having bestowed upon Snorro the woods of Krakaness without obtaining the stipulated gratification of his resentment. He went to the pontiff and demanded restitution, alleging that he had transferred the woods in loan, not as a gift. But Snorro refused to listen to his request, and appealed to the testimony of those who witnessed the transaction, that he had received the woods in full property. In the warmth of passion, Thorolf now had recourse to his son, and proposed to him to renew their natural alliance, and that the pledge of their friendship should be the union of their forces, to recover from Snorro the woods of Krakaness. "It was not for love of me," said Arnkill, "that thou gavest Snorro possession of these woods; and, although I know he has no just title to them, I will not enter into feud with the pontiff to gratify thy resentment by our quarrels."—"Thy cowardice," said Thorolf, "rather than any other motive, causes thy affected moderation."—"Think on the matter what thou wilt," said Arnkill, "but I will not enter into feud with Snorro on that subject." Thus repulsed at every hand, and in all the agony of impotent fury, Thorolf Bægifot returned to his own house. He spoke to no one, partook not of the evening meal, but, sitting in silence at the highest part of the table, suffered his domestics to retire to rest without quitting his seat. In the morning he was found dead in the same place and posture. A message instantly conveyed to Arnkill the news of his father's death. When he came, the corpse remained seated in the posture in which Thorolf had expired, and the terrified family hinted that he had fallen by the mode of death of all others most dreaded by the Icelanders *. Arnkill entered the apartment, but in such a manner as to approach the body from behind, and he cautioned the attendants that no one should look upon the face of the corpse until the due propitiatory rites were performed. It was not without application of force that the corpse could be removed from the seat which it occupied; the face was then veiled, and the customary ceremonies paid to the dead body. This done, Arnkill commanded the wall of the apartment to be broken down behind the spot where Thorolf had died, and the corpse being raised up with difficulty, and transported through the breach †, was deposited in a grave strongly built. But these meet honours, and this grave, however fortified, could not appease the restless spirit of Thorolf Bægifot. He appeared in the district by night and day, slew men and cattle, and harrowed the country so much by his frequent apparition and mischievous exploits, that his son Arnkill, on the repeated complaints of the inhabitants, resolved to change his place of sepulture. Some opposition was threatened by the sons of Thorbrand, who refused to permit the corpse to be carried through their domains, until reminded by their father, that it was illegal to refuse passage to those who were travelling in discharge of a duty imposed by law, and such was the burial of the dead. The body of Thorolf was found on opening the tomb, but his aspect was fearful and grisly to a preternatural degree. He was placed on a bier between two strong oxen, which, nevertheless, were worn out by fatigue ere they had transported him many miles. Others were substituted in their room, but when they attained the summit of a hill, at some distance from the destined place of sepulture, they became frantic, and, breaking their yokes, rushed down the precipice and perished. The corpse, too, became of such ponderous weight, that it could by no means be transported any farther, so that Arnkill was fain to consign it to the earth on the ridge of the hill where it lay, and which took its name henceforward from that of Bægifot. Arnkill caused a mound of immense height to be piled above the grave, and Thorolf, during the lifetime of his son, remained quiet in his new abode ‡.

---

* Suicide seems to be indicated [a].

† It is still an article of popular superstition in Scotland, that the corpse of a suicide ought not to be carried out of the apartment by the door, but lowered through a window, or conveyed through a breach in the wall. Neglect of this observance is supposed to expose the house to be haunted.

‡ After the death of Arnkill, Bægifot became again troublesome, and walked forth from his tomb to the great terror and damage of the neighbourhood, slaying both herds and domestics, and driving the inhabitants from the

---

[a] Certainly not suicide, for the incidents related are said to have happened towards the close of the 10th century, when the Icelanders were still Pagans; consequently at a period when suicide was regarded as an honourable kind of death. See p. 150.—Ed.

After the death of Thorolf, Arnkill engaged in various disputes with the pontiff Snorro for the recovery of the woods of Krakaness, and with the sons of Thorbrand on account of their old feud. He had the better in many skirmishes, and in many debates before the national convention. Nor was Snorro for a length of time more successful in his various efforts to remove this powerful rival. For, although a priest, he was not in any respect nice in his choice of means on such occasions, and practised repeatedly against Arnkill's life by various attempts at assassination. At length, however, irritated to the highest pitch, by a conversation in which he heard strangers extol the power and courage of Arnkill above his own, he resolved to employ in his revenge the sons of Thorbrand. To Thorlef Kimbi, the strongest of these champions, he gave a choice war-axe, and, bidding him observe the length of the handle, added, "Yet it will not reach the head of Arnkill while making hay at the farm of Ulfar." It must be observed, that Arnkill durst not occupy the farm of Ulfar, which had been so fiercely disputed between him and the sons of Thorbrand, otherwise than by sending labourers there in the day, and withdrawing them before nightfall. In the hay-season, however, he also employed his wains by moonlight to transport the hay from these possessions to his own domain. The sons of Thorbrand, embracing the hint of the pontiff, now watched his motions, and, learning that one moon-light night Arnkill had himself accompanied three of his bondsmen for the above purpose, they despatched a messenger to inform Snorro, that "the old eagle had taken his flight towards Orligstad." The pontiff instantly rose, and, accompanied by nine armed followers, traversed the ice to Altifiord, where he joined the party of the sons of Thorbrand, sie in number. Arnkill, who descried his enemies advancing towards him, despatched his unarmed attendants to his dwelling, to summon his servants to his assistance. "I meantime," said he, "will defend myself on the heap of hay, nor will I afford an easy victory to my foemen." But of these messengers one perished in crossing a torrent, the other loitered by the way. Meantime Arnkill, after defending himself valiantly, was finally overpowered and slain. Of which sings the Skald Thormoda Ulfilson :—

> A noble meal the pontiff strewed
> For the wild eagle's hungry brood,
> A noble corpse hath filled the tomb,
> When valiant Arnkill met his doom.

Arnkill is regretted by the annalist as a model of the qualities most valued in an Icelandic chief. He excelled all in accurate observance of ancient rites and customs, was stout-hearted and brave in enterprize, and so prudent and eloquent, that he was always successful in the causes which he prosecuted in the popular assemblies—qualities which drew upon him the envy that occasioned his death. His sepulchral mound, raised upon the sea-shore

---

canton. It was, therefore, resolved to consume his carcase with fire; for, like the Hungarian Vampire, he, or some evil demon in his stead, made use of his mortal reliques as a vehicle during commission of these enormities. The body was found swollen to a huge size, and equalling in size the corpulence of an ox. It was transported to the sea-shore with difficulty, and there burned to ashes.' A cow, licking some part of these ashes, brought forth the bull Glæser, by whom Thorodd, his master, was slain.

was visible in the time of the historian. The property of Arnkill, and the charge of exacting vengeance for his blood, passed to females, and hence the duty was but indifferently discharged. Thorolf Kimbi, who had struck the deadly blow, was banished for three years from Iceland,—a poor atonement for the slaughter of such a champion. And hence, says the annalist, it was enacted that neither a woman, nor a youth under sixteen years, should prosecute in a cause for avenging of blood. Arnkill was slain in the year 993.

Omitting a desperate feud between the sons of Thorbrand and those of Thorlak, we shall only notice the accuracy with which the *compensatio injuriarum* was weighed in the Comitia of Helgafels, when the quarrel was accommodated. Every disaster which had been sustained by the one party was weighed against one of a similar nature inflicted upon the other. Life for life, wound for wound, eye for eye, and tooth for tooth, were adjusted with the utmost precision, and the balance arising in favour of one of the contending septs was valued and atoned for by a pecuniary mulct. This compact, which was followed by an internal peace of unusual duration, took place in the year 999.

In the year 1000, the Christian religion was introduced into Iceland by her apostles Gizur the White, and Hialto *. Snorro became a convert, and lent the greatest assistance in extending the new faith †. It is not easy to see what motive the priest of Thor could have for exchanging a worship, over which he himself presided, for a new religion, since the unprincipled cunning and selfish character of Snorro seem to deprive him of the credit of having acted upon conviction. He procured the erection, nevertheless, of a Christian church at Helgafels, upon the site of the temple dedicated to Thor, and acted in every other respect as a sincere convert. As this was the third attempt to preach Christianity in the island, it seems probable that the good sense of the Icelanders had already rejected in secret the superstitions of paganism, and that the worship of Thor had declined in the estimation of the people.

---

* Hialto was an Icelander by birth, but had been banished for composing a song in disparagement of the heathen deities, of which the following is a literal version :—

> I will not serve an idle log
> For one, I care not which,
> But either Odin is a dog,
> Or Freya is a bitch.
>
> *Historia Ecclesiastica Islandiæ*, vol. i. p. 57.

† We learn from another authority that the heathen priests and nobles held a public conference with the Christian missionaries in the general assembly of the tribes of Iceland. While the argument was yet in discussion, news arrived that an eruption of lava was laying waste a neighbouring district. " It is the effect of the wrath of our offended deities," exclaimed the worshippers of Odin and Thor. " And what excited their wrath," answered Snorro, the hero of the Eyrbyggja-Saga, though still himself a heathen—"what excited their wrath when these rocks of lava, which we ourselves tread, were themselves a glowing torrent?" This ready answer silenced the advocates of heathenism.—*Historia Ecclesiastica Islandiæ*, vol. i. p. 62.

The same year is assigned as the date of a very curious legend. A ship from Iceland chanced to winter in a haven near Helgafels. Among the passengers was a woman named Thorgunna, a native of the Hebrides, who was reported by the sailors to possess garments and household furniture of a fashion far surpassing those used in Iceland. Thurida, sister of the pontiff Snorro, and wife of Thorodd, a woman of a vain and covetous disposition, attracted by these reports, made a visit to the stranger, but could not prevail upon her to display her treasures. Persisting, however, in her inquiries, she pressed Thorgunna to take up her abode at the house of Thorodd. The Hebridean reluctantly assented, but added, that as she could labour at every usual kind of domestic industry, she trusted in that manner to discharge the obligation she might lie under to the family, without giving any part of her property, in recompense of her lodging. As Thurida continued to urge her request, Thorgunna accompanied her to Froda, the house of Thorodd, where the seamen deposited a huge chest and cabinet, containing the property of her new guest, which Thurida viewed with curious and covetous eyes. So soon as they had pointed out to Thorgunna the place assigned for her bed, she opened the chest, and took forth such an embroidered bed coverlid, and such a splendid and complete set of tapestry hangings, and bed furniture of English linen, interwoven with silk, as had never been seen in Iceland. "Sell to me," said the covetous matron, "this fair bed furniture."—"Believe me," answered Thorgunna, "I will not lie upon straw in order to feed thy pomp and vanity;" an answer which so greatly displeased Thurida that she never again repeated her request. Thorgunna, to whose character subsequent events added something of a mystical solemnity, is described as being a woman of a tall and stately appearance, of a dark complexion, and having a profusion of black hair. She was advanced in age; assiduous in the labours of the field and of the loom; a faithful attendant upon divine worship; grave, silent, and solemn in domestic society. She had little intercourse with the household of Thorodd, and showed particular dislike to two of its inmates. These were Thorer, who, having lost a leg in the skirmish between Thorbiorn and Thorarin the Black, was called Thorer-Widlegr (wooden-leg,) from the substitute he had adopted; and his wife, Thorgrima, called Galldra-Kinna (wicked sorceress), from her supposed skill in enchantments. Kiartan, the son of Thurida *, a boy of excellent promise, was the

---

* He also passed for the son of Thorodd, but this was not so certain. Biorn, a stranger, who had acquired the name of the Hero of Bradwick, was assiduous in his visits to Thurida in the year preceding the birth of Kiartan. The jealousy of the husband was awakened, and he employed a sorceress to raise a nocturnal tempest to destroy Biorn on his way to his mistress. This attempt proved in vain, as well as several others to take his life by violence. At length, while Snorro was about to surround Biorn with a body of horse, conceiving his own honour interested in that of his sister Thurida, the champion, perceiving their purpose, suddenly seized on the pontiff, and, holding a dagger to his throat, compelled him to a treaty, by which Snorro agreed to withdraw his followers; and Biorn, on his part, consented to remove all further stain upon Thurida's reputation by departing from Iceland. Biorn kept his word, and for a long time was not heard of. Many years afterwards, however, an Icelandic vessel, while on the western coast of Iceland,

only person of the household to whom Thorgunna showed much affection ; and she was much vexed at times when the childish petulance of the boy made an indifferent return to her kindness.

After this mysterious stranger had dwelt at Froda for some time, and while she was labouring in the hay-field with other members of the family, a sudden cloud from the northern mountain led Thorodd to anticipate a heavy shower. He instantly commanded the hay-workers to pile up in ricks the quantity which each had been engaged in turning to the wind. It was afterwards remembered that Thorgunna did not pile up her portion, but left it spread on the field. The cloud approached with great celerity, and sunk so heavily around the farm, that it was scarce possible to see beyond the limits of the field. A heavy shower next descended, and so soon as the clouds broke away, and the sun shone forth, it was observed that it had rained blood. That which fell upon the ricks of the other labourers soon dried up, but what Thorgunna had wrought upon remained wet with gore. The unfortunate Hebridean, appalled at the omen, betook herself to her bed, and was seized with a mortal illness. On the approach of death she summoned Thorodd, her landlord, and entrusted to him the disposition of her property and effects. " Let my body," said she, " be transported to Skalholt, for my mind presages that in that place shall be founded the most distinguished church in this island. Let my golden ring be given to the priests who shall celebrate my obsequies, and do thou indemnify thyself for the funeral charges

---

was surprised by a storm, which drove her far into the Atlantic Ocean. After sailing far to the west they reached an unknown land, occupied by a savage people, who immediately seized on the merchants and crew of the vessel, and began to dispute whether they should reduce them to a state of slavery or kill them on the spot. At this moment there came up a body of horsemen, headed by a leader of eminent stature and distinguished appearance, whom the assembled natives regarded as their chief. He addressed the merchants in the Norse language, and, learning that they came from Iceland, made many inquiries concerning the pontiff Snorro and his sister Thurida, but especially concerning her son Kiartan. Being satisfied on these points, he intimated his intention to set them at liberty, cautioning them never to return to that country, as the inhabitants were hostile to strangers. The merchants ventured to inquire the name of their benefactor. This he refused to communicate, lest his Icelandic friends, coming to seek him, should encounter the danger from which his present guests had been delivered, without his having the same power to protect them ; for in this region there were chiefs, he said, more powerful than he himself. When they were about to depart, he requested them to present, on his behalf, a sword to Kiartan, and a ring to Thurida, as coming from one who loved the sister of Snorro better than the pontiff himself. These words were supposed to indicate Biorn, the Hero of Bradwick ; and the whole story serves to show that the Icelanders had some obscure tradition, either founded on conjecture or accidental intercourse, concerning the existence of a continent to the westward of the Atlantic [a].

---

[a] That the tradition was far from being obscure will be seen by referring to the first supplementary chapter.—ED.

out of my remaining effects. To thy wife I bequeath my purple mantle, in order that, by this sacrifice to her avarice, I may secure the right of disposing of the rest of my effects at my own pleasure. But for my bed, with its coverings, hangings, and furniture, I entreat they may be all consigned to the flames. I do not desire this because I envy any one the possession of these things after my death, but because I wish those evils to be avoided which I plainly foresee will happen if my will be altered in the slightest particular." Thorodd promised faithfully to execute this extraordinary testament in the most pointed manner. Accordingly, so soon as Thorgunna was dead, her faithful executor prepared a pile for burning her splendid bed. Thurida entered, and learned with anger and astonishment the purpose of these preparations. To the remonstrances of her husband she answered that the menaces of future danger were only caused by Thorgunna's selfish envy, who did not wish any one should enjoy her treasures after her decease. Then, finding Thorodd inaccessible to argument, she had recourse to caresses and blandishments, and at length extorted permission to separate, from the rest of the bed-furniture, the tapestried curtains and coverlid ; the rest was consigned to the flames, in obedience to the will of the testator. The body of Thorgunna, being wrapped in new linen and placed in a coffin, was next to be transported through the precipices and morasses of Iceland to the distant district she had assigned for her place of sepulture. A remarkable incident occurred on the way. The transporters of the body arrived at evening late, weary, and drenched with rain, in a house called Nether-Ness, where the niggard hospitality of the proprietor only afforded them house-room, without any supply of food or fuel. But, so soon as they entered, an unwonted noise was heard in the kitchen of the mansion, and the figure of a woman, soon recognized to be the deceased Thorgunna, was seen busily employed in preparing victuals. Their inhospitable landlord, being made acquainted with this frightful circumstance, readily agreed to supply every refreshment which was necessary, on which the vision instantly disappeared. The apparition having become public, they had no reason to ask twice for hospitality, as they proceeded on their journey, and arrived safely at Skalholt, where Thorgunna, with all due ceremonies of religion, was deposited quietly in the grave. But the consequences of the breach of her testament were felt severely at Froda.

The author, for the better understanding of the prodigies which happened, describes the manner of living at Froda, a simple and patriarchal structure, built according to the fashion used by the wealthy among the Icelanders. The apartment was very large, and a part boarded off contained the beds of the family. On either side was a sort of store-room, one of which contained meal, the other dried fish. Every evening large fires were lighted in this apartment, for dressing the victuals; and the domestics of the family usually sat around them for a considerable time, until supper was prepared. On the night when the conductors of Thorgunna's funeral returned to Froda, there appeared, visible to all who were present, a meteor, or spectral appearance, resembling a half-moon, which glided around the boarded walls of the mansion in an opposite direction to the course of the sun *, and continued to

---

* This is an important circumstance. Whatever revolved with the sun was reckoned a fortunate movement. Thus, the highlanders, in making the

perform its revolutions until the domestics retired to rest. This apparition was renewed every night during a whole week, and was pronounced by Thorer with the wooden leg to presage pestilence or mortality. Shortly after a herdsman showed signs of mental alienation, and gave various indications of having sustained the persecution of evil demons. This man was found dead in his bed one morning, and then commenced a scene of ghost-seeing unheard of in the annals of superstition. The first victim was Thorer, who had presaged the calamity. Going out of doors one evening, he was grappled by the spectre of the deceased shepherd as he attempted to re-enter the house. His wooden leg stood him in poor stead in such an encounter; he was hurled to the earth, and so fearfully beaten, that he died in consequence of the bruises. Thorer was no sooner dead than his ghost associated itself to that of the herdsman, and joined him in pursuing and assaulting the inhabitants of Froda. Meantime an infectious disorder spread fast among them, and several of the bondsmen died one after the other. Strange portents were seen within doors, the meal was displaced and mingled, and the dried fish flung about in a most alarming manner, without any visible agent. At length, while the servants were forming their evening circle round the fire, a spectre, resembling the head of a seal-fish, was seen to emerge out of the pavement of the room, bending its round black eyes full on the tapestried bed-curtains of Thorgunna. Some of the domestics ventured to strike at this figure, but, far from giving way, it rather erected itself further from the floor, until Kiartan, who seemed to have a natural predominance over these supernatural prodigies, seizing a huge forge-hammer, struck the seal repeatedly on the head, and compelled it to disappear, forcing it down into the floor, as if he had driven a stake into the earth. This prodigy was found to intimate a new calamity. Thorodd, the master of the family, had some time before set forth on a voyage to bring home a cargo of dried fish; but, in crossing the river Enna, the skiff was lost, and he perished with the servants who attended him. A solemn funeral feast was held at Froda, in memory of the deceased, when, to the astonishment of the guests, the apparition of Thorodd and his followers seemed to enter the apartment dropping with water. Yet this vision excited less horror than might have been expected, for the Icelanders, though nominally Christians, retained, among other pagan superstitions, a belief that the spectres of such drowned persons as had been favourably received by the goddess Rana were wont to show themselves at their funeral feast. They saw, therefore, with some composure, Thorodd and his dripping attendants plant themselves by the fire, from which all mortal guests retreated to make room for them. It was supposed this apparition would not be renewed after conclusion of the festival. But so far were their hopes disappointed, that, so soon as the mourning guests had departed, the fires

---

deasil, a sort of benediction which they bestow in walking round the party to be propitiated, always observe the course of the sun. And witches, on the other hand, made their circles, *widdershins*, as Scottish dialect expresses it (*widder-sins*, Germ.), or in opposition to the course of the orb of light. The apparition of the half-moon reminds us of Hecate, of the mysteries of Isis in Apuleius, and of a passage in Lucian's "Lears," where the moon is forced down by magical invocation.

being lighted, Thorodd and his comrades marched in on one side, drenched as before with water; on the other entered Thorer, heading all those who had died in the pestilence, and who appeared covered with dust. Both parties seized the seats by the fire, while the half-frozen and terrified domestics spent the night without either light or warmth. The same phenomenon took place the next night, though the fires had been lighted in a separate house, and at length Kiartan was obliged to compound matters with the spectres by kindling a large fire for them in the principal apartment, and one for the family and domestics in a separate hut. This prodigy continued during the whole feast of Jol; other portents also happened to appal this devoted family, the contagious disease again broke forth, and when any one fell a sacrifice to it his spectre was sure to join the troop of persecutors, who had now almost full possession of the mansion of Froda. Thorgrima Galldrakinna, wife of Thorer, was one of these victims, and, in short, of thirty servants belonging to the household, eighteen died, and five fled for fear of the apparitions, so that only seven remained in the service of Kiartan.

Kiartan had now recourse to the advice of his maternal uncle Snorro, in consequence of whose counsel, what will perhaps appear surprising to the reader, judicial measures were instituted against the spectres. A Christian priest was, however, associated with Thordo Kausa, son of Snorro, and with Kiartan, to superintend and sanctify the proceedings. The inhabitants were regularly summoned to attend upon the inquest, as in a cause between man and man, and the assembly was constituted before the gate of the mansion; just as the spectres had assumed their wonted station by the fire. Kiartan boldly ventured to approach them, and, snatching a brand from the fire, he commanded the tapestry belonging to Thorgunna to be carried out of doors, set fire to it, and reduced it to ashes with all the other ornaments of her bed, which had been so inconsiderately preserved at the request of Thurida. A tribunal being then constituted with the usual legal solemnities[*], a charge was preferred by Kiartan against Thorer with the wooden leg, by Thordo Kausa against Thorodd, and by others chosen as accusers against the individual spectres present, accusing them of molesting the mansion, and introducing death and disease among its inhabitants. All the solemn rites of judicial procedure were observed on this singular occasion; evidence was adduced, charges given, and the cause formally decided. It does not appear that the ghosts put themselves on their defence, so that sentence of ejectment was pronounced against them individually in due and legal form. When Thorer heard the judgment, he arose, and saying, " I have sate while it was lawful for me to do so," left the apartment by the

---

[*] It does not appear that the judges in Iceland were a separate order. On the contrary, every tribunal appears to have been constituted by a selection, *ex astantibus*, and so far every court of justice resembled a jury chosen to decide a special cause, and dissolved when that task was performed[a].

---

[a] The reader will find by referring to the second supplementary chapter, that this opinion is quite unfounded. "The solemn rites of judicial procedure" were merely those observed at a so-called *door-doom*. See page 307.—ED.

door opposite to that at which the judicial assembly was constituted. Each of the spectres, as they heard their individual sentence, left the place, saying something which indicated their unwillingness to depart, until Thorodd himself was solemnly appointed to depart. "We have here no longer," said he, "a peaceful dwelling, therefore will we remove." Kiartan then entered the hall with his followers, and the priest, with holy water, and celebration of a solemn mass, completed the conquest over the goblins, which had been commenced by the power and authority of the Icelandic law. We have perhaps dwelt too long on this legend, but it is the only instance in which the ordinary administration of justice has been supposed to extend over the inhabitants of another world, and in which the business of exorcising spirits is transferred from the priest to the judge. Joined to the various instances in the Eyrbyggja-Saga of a certain regard to the forms of jurisprudence, even amid the wildest of their feuds, it seems to argue the extraordinary influence ascribed to municipal law by this singular people, even in the very earliest state of society.

Snorro, who upon the whole may be considered as the hero of the history, was led into fresh turmoils and litigation by the death of his brother-in-law, Styr, slain by the inhabitants of a neighbouring district, for which slaughter neither Snorro's eloquence in the popular assembly, nor his power in the field, were able to procure adequate vengeance. He came off with more credit in his feud with Ospakar.

This Ospakar, a man of huge stature and great personal strength, surrounded always by satellites of the same description, differed from the other Icelandic chiefs in the open disregard which he professed for the laws of property. He kept a stout vessel, always ready for piratical excursions, and surrounded his house with a mound so as to convert it into a kind of citadel. It happened that a whale had been cast ashore upon a part of the island, where the law assigned a part of it in property to the pontiff Snorro, and part to his neighbour Thorer. While, however, Thorer, and Alfar, called the Little, steward of the pontiff, were engaged in making the partition, Ospakar appeared at the head of his armed followers, and, after stunning Thorer with a blow of his war-axe, appropriated the whole whale to himself. Skirmish followed skirmish, and blood was spilled on both sides, until Snorro bestirred himself in invoking the justice of the Comitia against the lawless Ospakar, and obtained a sentence condemning him and his followers to banishment. They submitted to this doom for a time, and Snorro caused the effects of Ospakar to be divided amongst those who had sustained the greatest losses by his rapine, of which spoil Thorer and Alfar obtained the larger share. It was, however, a gift fatal to the former. Ospakar, who still followed his piratical profession, made a sudden descent on the coast, and, seizing Thorer, put him to death before his own door. Alfar, escaping with difficulty, fled to the protection of Snorro; and Ospakar, in defiance of the sentence pronounced against him, resumed possession of his fortified mansion, and furnished it with provisions to stand a siege. Snorro proceeded on this occasion with his characteristic caution. It has been seen that an ordinary haystack was accounted a strong post in Icelandic tactics, but a house surrounded with a bank of earth was a much more serious fortification; nor did Snorro deem it safe to attempt storming the pirate's stronghold till he had assembled his most chosen friends and satellites.

Amongst these was Thrandar, who, before assuming the Christian faith, had been a Berserkar, and although he had lost the supernatural strength exercised by such persons, which the author states to have been the usual consequence of baptism, he nevertheless retained his natural vigour and prowess, which were very formidable. On the slightest hint from Snorro's messenger, he attended the pontiff, armed as one who has a dangerous task in hand. Snorro's other allies being assembled, they made a hasty march to the fortress of Ospakar, and summoned him to surrender at discretion. The robber having refused compliance, the mound was valiantly assaulted on the one part, and stoutly defended on the other. Thrandar, by striking the steel of his battle-axe into the top of the rampart, actually scaled it, raising himself by the handle, and slew Rafen, a pirate of great fame, who assaulted him upon his ascent. Ospakar himself fell by a stroke of a lance, and his followers surrendered upon the sole condition of escaping with life and limb. On this conflict, the Skald Thormodar composed his poem called Rafn-maal, or the Death of Rafen.

> The birds of Odin found their prey,
> When slaughter raged in Bitra's bay;
> There lay extended on the vale
> The three fierce plunderers of the whale,
> And, all his toils of rapine past,
> Grim Rafen found repose at last.

The annals proceed to detail the remarkable legend concerning the death of Thorodd by the bull called Glæsir; and, finally, they inform us of the death of Snorro, during the winter after the death of St. Olave, leaving a powerful and flourishing family to support the fame which he had acquired. He was buried in the church at Tunga, which he himself had founded, but when it was removed his bones were transported to its new site. From these relics the celebrated Snorro seemed to have been a man of ordinary stature; nor, indeed, does it any where appear that he attained the ascendancy which he possessed in the island by personal strength, but rather by that subtlety of spirit which he displayed in conducting his enterprizes, and by his address and eloquence in the popular assembly. Although often engaged in feuds, his valour seems to have been duly mingled with discretion, and the deeds of war, for which he was celebrated in poetry, were usually achieved by the strong arm of some ally or satellite. He was so equal in his demeanour, that it was difficult to observe what pleased or displeased him; slow and cautious in taking revenge, but tenacious and implacable in pursuing it; an excellent counsellor to his friends, but skilful in inducing his enemies to take measures which afterwards proved fatal to them. In fine, as the ecclesiastical historian of Iceland sums up his attributes, if Snorro were not a good and pious man, he was to be esteemed wise, prudent, and sagacious, beyond the usual pitch of humanity. This pontiff, or prefect, is mentioned with great distinction in other Icelandic chronicles, as well as in the Eyrbyggja-Saga. In the Landnama Bok, part ii. chap. 13, many of the foregoing incidents are alluded to, and also in the Laxdæla-Saga, and the Saga of Oluf Tryggason.

That such a character, partaking more of the jurisconsult or statesman than of the warrior, should have risen so high in such an early period, argues the preference which the Icelanders already assigned to mental superiority over the rude attributes of strength and courage, and furnishes another proof of the early civilization of this extraordinary commonwealth. In other respects the character of Snorro was altogether unamiable, and blended with strong traits of the savage. Cunning and subtlety supplied the place of wisdom, and an earnest and uniform attention to his own interests often, as in the dispute between Arnkill and his father, superseded the ties of blood and friendship. Still, however, his selfish conduct seems to have been of more service to the settlement in which he swayed, than would have been that of a generous and high-spirited warrior who acted from the impulse of momentary passion. His ascendancy, though acquired by means equally unworthy of praise, seems, in his petty canton, to have had the effect produced by that of Augustus in the Roman Empire; although, more guiltless than the emperor of the world, the pontiff of Helgafels neither subverted the liberties of his country, nor bequeathed the domination he had acquired to a tyrannical successor. His sons succeeded to the paternal property, but not to the political power of their father, and, his possessions being equally divided amongst them, they founded several families, long respected in Iceland as descendants of the pontiff Snorro.

W. S.

ABBOTSFORD, OCTOBER, 1813.

GLOSSARY TO THE PROSE EDDA.

BY THE EDITOR.

WISHING to render this work as complete as possible, we undertook the laborious task of searching for the etymologies of all the proper names (upwards of 400) that occur in the Prose Edda. We intended at first to have copied the etymologies given in the Glossaries to the Poetical Edda, but we soon found that in numerous instances they could not be relied on, were in fact merely *conjectural*. We had, therefore, recourse to that truly admirable work, the "*Deutsche Mythologie*," * in which Jacob Grimm has shown, as he had previously done in his *Deutsche Grammatik*, such a profound knowledge of the Teutonic languages, that he may be safely followed as an unerring guide in such inquiries. Grimm, however, had not occasion to mention above half of the words whose etymology we were in search of; we therefore consulted, for the remaining ones, the Glossaries of the Poetical Edda †, as well as Finn Magnusen's *Lexicon Mythologicum*, and his *Eddalæren* ‡, and several glossaries appended to the editions of various Sagas, making our selection, however, with due precaution, omitting from forty to fifty names, the derivations given of which appeared to us to be quite undeserving of attention, and qualifying those of several others, regarded by the learned editors of the Edda as undoubted, with the words *perhaps* and *probably*, words which cannot be too frequently made use of, when etymology is not founded on scientific principles.

Conjectural etymology, that is to say, etymology grounded on mere similarity of sound, or of orthography, was formerly quite in vogue, and is in fact still indulged in by several of our own writers, as well as by Finn Magnusen, to a degree which often borders on the ludicrous. The philologists of the German school have however done away with this futile method; and at the pre-

---

* "Deutsche Mythologie von Jacob Grimm," *German*, or more properly speaking, *Teutonic* Mythology by Jacob Grimm, is the simple title of this excellent work;—we have made use of the second edition, published at Göttingen in 1844.

† The edition published by the Arni-Magnæan Commission, (see page 363,) of which Finn Magnusen's "Lexicon Mythologicum in vetusta septentrionalium carmina quæ in Edda Sæmundina continentur," fills nearly the whole of the third volume.

‡ "Eddalæren og dens Oprindelse," 4 vols. 12mo, Copenh. 1825.

sent day, when a Grimm and a Bopp wish to show that words are cognate, they trace them through all their grammatical variations, in order to arrive at their radical affinities.   This of course presupposes an intimate knowledge of languages, of the principles that regulate the permutation of consonants and vowels, of analogical glossology in a word, which few possess and which can only be acquired by years of intense study.   Derivations established in this manner may be regarded as demonstrated facts ; all others either as more or less plausible *conjectures*, or as amusing instances of learned aberration.

It may not be irrelevant here to say a few words respecting the orthography we have adopted for the proper names that occur in this work.   As it was our intention to give the *correct* orthography of these names in the following Glossary, we purposely abstained from accenting the vowels in several of them, and in most instances substituted *d* for ð *.   Not wishing to depart too much from established usage, we also retained the common orthography of names, such as Odin, Thor, &c., which have long been familiar to the public, taking care, however, to avoid falling into the error of giving the Danish terminations in *e* and *er* (as Loke, Brage, Diser, Niflunger, for instance), instead of the Old Norse in *i*, *ir*, and *ar* (Loki, Bragi, Dísir, Niflúngar).   We also omitted, as a matter of course, the final *r* which is frequently found in Norse proper names, this *r* being merely the sign of the nominative case sing. masculine, (Rask's second declension,) and as Leif, for instance, is pronounced the same, whether written Leif or Leifr, and as the latter would only be *strictly correct* when in the nominative case, the *r*, when such words are used in English, or any other language than Old Norse, is superfluous.   In order that the reader may form some idea of the Old Norse language in this respect, we give the declension of the masculine noun, brandr, (a brand, either a fire-brand, or poetically a sword,) and the feminine noun, strönd, strand, shore.

	SINGULAR.		PLURAL.	
Nom.	brandr	strönd	brandar	strandir.
Accus.	brand	strönd	branda	strandir.
Dat.	brandi	ströndu	bröndum	ströndum.
Gen.	brands	strandar	branda	stranda.

As Scandinavian words may not be familiar to the generality of our readers, it will be necessary to say something respecting their pronunciation.   Were we, however, to attempt to give the *correct* pronunciation of all the words that occur in this Glossary, we should have to write a treatise on the orthoepy of the Teutonic languages.   We shall therefore merely lay down a few *general* rules, which will enable the *English* reader to pronounce most of

---

* Or, more properly speaking, retained the d—this letter having been replaced by ð only in editions of recent date.

these words, if not quite accurately, at least in a manner that would render them intelligible, and which will, at the same time, show that cognate words frequently differ more in orthography than in pronunciation.

We may remark as a *general rule*—there being of course no rule without its exceptions *—that the reader will not greatly err by pronouncing the vowels in all the Indo-European languages—we might indeed say in almost every civilized language, except our own †, as follows :—

i	short,	as i in	bill,	pill.
i	long,	as ee in	peel,	feel.
e	short,	as e in	met,	get.
e	long, either as a in	paper, or as e in there.		
a	short, as the first a in	papa.		
a	long, as the second a in	papa.		
o	short,	as o in	not.	
o	long,	as o in	note.	
u	short,	as oo in	hood,	good.
u	long,	as oo in	rood,	food.

In some languages the long vowels are accented, as they ought to be in all.

It will be more difficult to give rules for the pronunciation of sounds that are foreign to the English language ; discarding, however, nice distinctions which can only be acquired by the ear, we may remark that the Old Norse and the Anglo-Saxon *y*, the German *ü*, and the French *u* have much the same sound. Thus the Old Norse and the Ang.-Sax. word *fýr*, fire, would be pronounced much in the same manner as the German word *für*, for, and the French word *fur* in the phrase *à fur et mesure*, or more correctly, *au fur et à mesure ;* and the Norse *dýr*, an animal, like the first syllable of the Gerariman *dür*-re, aridity, and the French *dure*, hard, solid. The Norse and Ang.-Sax. *y*, however, gradually lost this sound, and acquired that of *i*. The reader may therefore pronounce the *y* in words from these languages either as the French *u*, or as *i* ; when short *y*, as i in bill, when long *ý*, as ee in peel.

---

* The French *u*, for instance, would form an exception.

† It has long been remarked that our orthography stands in need of a thorough revision. It were indeed " a consummation devoutly to be wished " that a congress could be held, not to determine the fate of dynasties nor the partition of kingdoms, but, under the superintendence of some learned German philologist, to devise a uniform standard orthography for all the Teutonic languages. The task would in fact be far less difficult than might be supposed ; our own language would, no doubt, be found the most refractory to deal with, and would probably demand and obtain an exemption from some of the laws that might be framed for the better regulation of its cousins.

There are certain shades in the pronunciation of the Norse *œ, œ*, the Ang.-Sax. *œ* and the German, Swedish and Danish *ä*, which we will not attempt to indicate. Rask observes that the Ang.-Sax. *œ* " seems to have represented a peculiar, simple, and very open sound, approaching to *a*." * At all events the reader must avoid pronouncing *œ* and *ä*, like we (most barbarously) pronounce the *œ* in the word Cæsar †. The *a* in paper would be the nearest equivalent. For the sound of *ö* we have no equivalent in our language.

To these general rules we subjoin a few observations respecting the pronunciation of certain letters in the Old Norse, Anglo-Saxon, and German languages.

OLD NORSE.

ó, has a broad sound, much broader than the o in fore.

á, has a peculiar sound, something between au in aurora and oa in broad. Rask makes it equivalent to the Italian *au* in the word *aura* ‡ ; hence *hár*, hair, would be pronounced *haur* with a clear *a*. The reader, however, will not be far from the true pronunciation by giving the Old Norse *á* the Swedish *â*, and the Danish *aa*, the sound of oa in broad, or that of a in warm.

au, has much the same sound as ou in house.

ei, something like ei in weight, *never* like the German ei.

ey, approaches the German eu, that is to say, has a broader sound than that of the English word eye—is pronounced, in fact, much in the same manner as the pronoun I in several of our provincial dialects—in the North Staffordshire dialect for instance.

j, invariably like y in yard.

g, invariably its pure sound, as g either in go or in give, *never* as g in gem, gentle.

s, always hard, as ss in Miss.

z, (which is a mere etymological sign,) as s.

th, (which we have substituted for þ,) always hard, as in think.

Ð, ð, always soft, as th in this, father, bathe.

---

* In his Anglo-Saxon Gram., page 9.

† In this reforming age, when rotten boroughs, and corn laws, and *divi divi* have gone to the wall, it is to be hoped that ere long we may be induced to abandon our most barbarous pronunciation of the Latin vowels, owing to which any of the ancient Roman worthies, if they might quit the Elysian fields and visit our universities, would be as much puzzled as learned foreigners are, to understand the congratulatory Latin discourses addressed to them.

‡ In his " Vejledning til det oldnordiske Sprog," Copenh. 1832.

ANGLO-SAXON.

c and q, as k.

þ, (for which we have substituted th,) as in Old Norse.

ð, as in Old Norse.

g, always its pure sound, either as in go or in give. When it is between two of the letters æ, e, i, y, it has, however, the sound of y in yard. Thus *brægen*, brains, is pronounced *bræyen*.

According to Rask *, *e* was used before *a* and *o*, and *i* before *e* and *u*, to mark the same sound. Thus *Eorl*, Earl, was pronounced like the Old Norse *Jarl*, viz. Yarl, Yorl. *Eótaland*, Old Norse *Jótland*, Jutland, as Yótaland; *iett* as *yet*, of which it has the signification.—The Ang.-Sax. *iett* and the English *yet*, would therefore only differ in orthography.

GERMAN.

The German	is equivalent to the English.	as for instance	pronounced.
j	y	jung, *young,*	yoong.
w	v	warten, *to wait,*	varten.
v	f	vater, *father,*	fater.
th	t	muth, *courage,*	moot.
sch	sh	schild, *shield,*	shild.
z	ts	ziel, *scope, aim,*	tseel, *not* as the English word zeal.

In respect to the peculiar sounds in this language, besides those already mentioned, we may remark that

ch, should *never* be pronounced like ch in cheese, nor as k—but invariably as an aspirated k or kh, like the Greek χ.

g, has always its pure sound, either as in go or give.

ei, has the same sound as the English word eye, or as the pronoun I.

ai, a somewhat broader sound, or one in which the a is heard.

eu, a still broader sound, for which we have no equivalent, except in our provincial dialects.

au, as ou in house—the English word house and the German haus having the same sound and signification.

ie, as ee in peel—*viel*, many, for instance, being pronounced like the English word *feel*, and the name of the celebrated Liebig, *Leebig*.

The Germans, instead of accenting their long vowels, generally lengthen them by adding *h*, thus ih, eh, ah, oh, uh, are equivalent to the long i, e, a, o, u, and have the sounds indicated in the above table of vowels.

---

* Anglo-Saxon Gram., pages 10 and 11.

GLOSSARY.

ABBREVIATIONS THAT OCCUR IN THE GLOSSARY.

a. active. v. a. verb active.
adj. adjective.
Al. Alemannic.
Anc. Ancient.
A. S. Anglo-Saxon.
Celt. Celtic, i. e. one of the ancient Celtic languages.
conseq. consequently.
D. Danish.
Dt. Dutch.
dt. doubtful.
E. English.
E. E. Editors of the Edda.
Etr. Ancient Etruscan.
etym. etymology.
f. feminine.
F. French.
F. Mag. Finn Magnusen.
Fr. Frisic.
G. German.
gen. genitive.
Gr. Greek.
I. Icelandic.
Ind. E. Indo-European languages.
It. Italian.
L. Latin.
lang. language, languages.

lit. literally.
m. masculine.
M. G. Mœso-Gothic.
met. metaphorically.
N. Old Norse.
n. neuter.
nom. nominative.
obs. obsolete.
P. Persian.
part. participle.
ph. perhaps.
pl. plural.
prob. probably.
prop. properly or correctly.
Sem. Semitic languages.
sig. signifies, signified, signification.
sing. singular.
Sk. Sanskrit.
Sl. Slavonic languages.
sub. substantive.
Sw. Swedish.
Sx. Old Saxon.
syn. synonymous, synonymously.
sylb. syllable, syllables.
v. verb.
Z. Zend.

ÆGIR or ŒGIR. F. Mag. derives Ægir from the v. ægia, aga, to flow. Œgir is derived by Grimm from the root aga, óg; whence the M. G. agis, óg; Anc. G.; akiso, egiso; A. S. egesa, horror; and Anc. G. akí okí; A. S. ege, terror, N. œgja, *terrori esse.*

ÆSIR, sing. ÁS; God, Gods. ÁSYNJA, ÁSYNJOR; Goddess, Goddesses: cog. with words of the same sig. in several lang., as Celt. Es (Esus); Etr. Æs, Aís, Æsar; P. Ized, and ph. the Magyar, Isten. Grimm remarks that a cog. expression must have been used in all the ancient Teutonic lang.

In *M. G.* it would have been Ans, pl. Anseis; *A. S.* Ós, pl. És. The word is still preserved in proper names, as *M. G.* Ansila, *Anc. G.* Anso. Grimm further remarks, that the *Old Germ.* names of Anshelm, Anspald, Anshilt, Ansnót, have the same sig. as Cotahelm, Cotahilt; the *A. S.* Osweald, Osláf, Osdæg; the *N.* Ásgautr, Ásmundr, Asbjörn (the divine bear, *ursus divinus*), Áslaug, &c. See *Deut. Mythol.* p. 22.

ÁI, from á, a river.

ALFAÐIR, or ALFÖÐUR, All-Father, or the Father of All.

ÁLFR, Elf.

ALSVIÐR, All-scorching; sviðr from v. sviða, to scorch.

ALTHJÓFR, lit. All-thief, an accomplished rascal—thiófr; *D.* tyv; *M. G.* thiubs; *Anc. G.* diup; *G.* dieb; *A. S.* thyf; *E.* thief; *Dt.* dief.

ALVÍSS, All-wise. *See* Grafvitnir.

AMSVARTNIR : am, dt. etym. ph. from ami, grief : svartnir, from svart *G.* schwartz, black, gloomy, swart.

ANDHRÍMNIR : and prob. from aund, önd, soul, spirit, breath : hrimnir, from hrim, congealed vapour, *rime;* but the word also sig. *soot.*

ANDLÁNGR, from aund, spirit, breath; and lángr, long.

ANDVARI, prob. from aund, spirit; and varr, cautious, timid; cog. with *E.* wary.

ÁNGURBOÐI, Anguish-boding, announcing or presaging calamity. *See* Bodn.

ARVAKR, awaking early; ár, the dawn, Aurora. *See* Vakkr.

ÁS, ÁSA. *See* Æsir.

ASGARD, prop. ASGARÐR, lit. God's-ward, or the abode of the gods : gar, gard, garðr and cog. words originally signified in most of the *Ind. E.* languages an inclosure, a fence; hence the *E.* to gird, girth, garden, guard, ward, yard, court, and a number of cog. words in various languages. *See also* Midgard and Utgard.

ASKR, an ash-tree : *D.* ask; *G.* esche; *A. S.* æsc, the *Fraxinus excelsior.*

ASYNJOR. *See* Æsir.

AUÐHUMLA, or AUÐUMLA, a word of very dt. etym. It is also written Audhumbla. F. Mag. writes it Aud-húmla, and derives it from audr, void, vacuity, and hum, darkness, tenebrosity.

AUÐR, rich, wealthy.

AURBODA, prop. AURBOÐA : aur may ph. mean snow, rain, storm; but it is also a mere extensive particle; (*see* Örgelmir)—boða, from the v. boða, to announce, whence *D.* bebude, cog. with *E.* to bode, and with the *N.* sub. Boð; *D.* Bud; *G.* Bothe, a messenger; hence the *G.* Botschafter, an ambassador.

AURVÁNGR. *See* Aurboda and Fólkvángr.

AUSTRI, East, Oriental.

BALDUR, prop. BALDR or BALLDR. If the a is accented it may be derived from bál; *D.* baal; *Scotch* bale; fire, flame, and would ph. be cog.

with the *Sem.* Baal; *Sk.* Bali; *Celt.* Bel, Beal, Beles, Belenus; though this is mere *conjecture.* If the a is unaccented it may ph. be cog. with the *M. G.* balths; *E.* bold.

BÁLEYGR, Bale-eyed, *i. e.* endowed with a clear, piercing vision: bál, *see* Baldur; eygr from auga; *Sw.* öga; *D.* öie; *M. G.* augo; *G.* auge; *A. S.* eáge; *E.* eye; *Dt.* oog, cog. with *L.* oculus.

BAREY, the Frondiferous-isle, as it may be derived from bar, lit. a bud, whence the *N.* ber; *D.* bær; *G.* beere; *A. S.* beria; *E.* berry: and ey, an island; *D.* ö.

BAULVERKR, or BÖLVERKR, Evil-worker; producing evil, calamity.

BAUMBURR, prob. cog. with bumbr, belly, cavity; cog. with *E.* bomb.

BELI, prob. from belja, to bellow.

BERGELMIR, when written Berggemlir, would mean Mountain-old, *i. e.* the old man of the mountain; but this is a transposition of syllables which we think quite unwarranted. *See* Örgelmir.

BIFLINDI, the Inconstant: from bif, motion; and lyndi, disposition, mind.

BIFRÖST, BIF-RAUST, the Tremulous-bridge or the Aerial-bridge, bif signifying also aerial: raust is cog. with *M. G.* röst; *Anc. G.* rasta, a certain space, a mile, a rest.

BIL, a moment, an interval, an interstice.

BILEYGR, endowed with fulminating eyes, from bilr, bylr, a tempest, especially a fulminating tempest or thunder-storm; and auga, eye. *See* Báleygr.

BILSKIRNIR, from bilr, storm; and skir, serene: it may therefore sig. sometimes stormy, and sometimes serene; which, as Thor's mansion prob. denotes the atmosphere, would be a very appropriate term; or storm-stilling, *i. e.* imparting serenity to the tempest; or simply serene, free from storms.

BIVAURR, BIVÓRR, or BIFUR, the Tremulous, from bif. *See* Biflindi.

BODN or BOÐN: very dt. etym. F. Mag. derives it, though we think very ungrammatically, from the v. boða, to announce. *See* Aurboda. From the *M. G.* v. biudan, to offer, Grimm derives biuds; *A. S.* beod, a table, a *board*, which is cog. with the *N.* bjoðr, *discus*, in so far as it originally signified an offer-table or altar. This *M. S.* verb is cog. with the *N.* sub. bodn, an oblation, though Bodn could not have been used in this sense as one of the jars in which the dwarfs' poetical beverage was kept.

BÖLL, same as Baul, the Calamitous.

BÖLTHORN, lit. Calamitous or Evil-thorn.

BÖR, prop. BÖRR, and BUR, prop. BURR or BURI, mean *born*, both words being derived from the v. bera, cog. with *M. G.* bairan; *A. S.* beran; *E.* to bear; whence also the *Old G.* barn, and the *Scotch, bairn,* a child.

BRAGI, the name of the God of Poetry, has exercised the ingenuity of etymologists; F. Mag. even strives to make it cog. with Brahma!! A prob. etym. is that from braga, to glisten, to shine, or from bragga, to adorn; ph. cog. with *G.* pracht, splendour; *F.* Mag. also mentions *Old G.* brage, (the brogue?) and *Modern G.* sprache. Grimm explains Bragr, by *vir facundus*, and mentions the *A. S.* brego, breogo, a king, a prince. Another appropriate etym. which he gives is *A. S.* brægen; *E.* brain; *Fr.* brein; *Low G.* bregen; prob. cog. with *Gr.* φρήν. Bragr, which in *N.* signified *poetry*, has become in *E. to brag*, and a Poet, *a Braggart*. From Bragi's bumper—the Bragafull, comes our word bragget, and prob. also the v. to brew, *N.* brugga; *D.* brygge; *G.* brauen; *F.* brasser.

BREIÐABLIK : lit. Broad-blink—latifulgent, wide-glancing, expanded splendour, from breiðr, broad, and v. blika, cog. with *G.* blinken, and blicken; *A. S.* blican; *E.* to blink.

BRÍMIR, prob. from brími, flame.

BRÍSÍNGR, may prob. mean flaming, and ph. cog. with *Gr.* βράζω; *F.* braize.

BUR, prop. BURR or BURI. *See* Bör.

BYLEISTR, from byr, a dwelling, a town; and v. lesta, to destroy, to break to pieces.

BYRGIR, prob. from v. byrgja, to conceal; cog. with *G.* verbergen; *A. S.* birgean; *E.* to bury, whence barrow, a tumulus.

DÁINN, prob. the Soporiferous; from dá, a swoon, or complete repose.

DELLINGR : dt. etym., but *F.* Mag. and Grimm think it ought to be written Deglingr, which would mean a short day—*a day-ling*, and *F.* Mag. then explains it to be syn. with the dawn, daybreak.

DÍS, pl. DÍSIR. Grimm has shown that this word corresponds with the *Anc. G.* itis, pl. itisi; *A. S.* ides, pl. idesa; and that it originally sig. a female, but was afterwards used in the sense of Nymph and Goddess. It enters into the composition of several female names, as Thórdís, Frey-dís, Vegdís, &c.

DÓLGTHRASIR : dólgr, a warrior: thrasir, from thrá, contentious, obstinate, persisting, from the v. thrasa, to litigate, to quarrel.

DRAUPNIR, from the v. drúpa, to droop, or the v. drjupa, to drip, cog. with to drop; *A. S.* driopan, dripan; *G.* tropfen.

DRÓMI, strongly binding.

DÚFR, ph. from djúp, cog. with *A. S.* dypa; *E.* deep; *G.* tiefe.

DUNEYRR, prob. from dynr, a hollow sound, from the v. dynja, to sound, to resound; cog. with the *E.* din: and eyra; *D.* öre; *G.* ohr; *A. S.* eár; *E.* ear.

DURATHRÓR : dt. etym. The first sylb. may be derived either from dúr, a light sleep, or from dyr, a door; and the last, either from the v. threyja, to expect, to wait for; or from thróa, to increase, to enlarge.

DURINN, prob. from dúr, a light sleep, cog. with the v. dúsa, to fall asleep; whence prob. the *E.* to doze, and ph. also dusk.

DVALINN, from dvali, sleep.

EIKINSKJALDI, furnished with an oaken shield: from eik, the ilex or scarlet oak; and skjöldr, shield.

EIKTHYRNIR. Eik is the ilex or scarlet oak ; thyrnir, a thorn.   Therefore an iliceous or arboriferous thorn, used prob. metaphorically for a stag's antlers.

EINHERJAR, sing. **EINHERI,** *i. e.* einn, one, unique; and heri, a hero, conseq. select, chosen heroes.

EIR : dt. etym. ph. from v. eira, to befriend, to tranquillize.

ELDHRÍMNIR : eldr, elementary fire : hrim, congealed vapour, rime, also soot; hence (a kettle) sooty from fire.   *See* Andhrímnir.

ELIVÁGAR, stormy waves : el, more recent jel, a storm : vagr, the sea, an estuary ; cog. with *Sk.* vaya, water; *G.* woge; *E.* wave.

ELLI, old age.

ELVÍÐNIR, ph. from el, a storm; and víðr, wide.

EMBLA.   The etymologies of the name of the first woman given by the *E. E.* are merely *conjectural,* and therefore not worth repeating *.   Grimm says the word embla, emla, *Anc. G.* emila, signifies a busy woman, from amr, ambr, aml, ambl, assiduous labour ; and remarks that if it had been written Eskja, it would have corresponded to the mas. Askr, and the two words would then have had the same relation as Meshia and Meshiane, the ancient Persian names of the first man and woman, who were also formed from trees.

FALHÓFNIR : fal, either from falr, a nail, a lamina, or from faulr, pale : hófnir, from hófr, hoof.

FARMAGUÐ, the God of Carriers and Sea-farers : farmr, a load, a cargo ; from the v. fœra, to carry, to transport either by land or by water. *See* God.

FARMATÝR, the same sig. as the preceding word.   *See* Tyr.

FENRIR, *vulgariter,* **FENRIS-ÚLFR,** ph. also from fen, and may then mean dweller in an abyss, or the monster wolf.   The *N.* úlfr; *Sw.* ulf; *D.* ulv; is cog. with *M. G.* vulfs; *G.* wolf; *A. S.* wulf; *E.* wolf; also with *L.* vulpes; and prob. with the *N.* v. yla; *D.* hyle; *G.* heulen; *E.* to howl; *L.* ululare.

FENSALIR, lit. Fen-saloon, from fen, a fen, but which it would appear may also be made to sig. the watery deep, or the sea; and salr, a hall, mansion, saloon.   *See* Valhalla.

FIMBUL : dt. etym.   F. Mag. thinks it is cog. with *A. S.* fymble, a fable, but this is a mere *conjecture.*   Grimm regards it as an augmentative, like jörmun (irmin)—*see* Jörmungandr—as in the words fimbulfambi, fim-

---

* F. Mag. changes by metathesis the *Gr.* word *melia,* an ash-tree, into *emlia,* which he soon transforms into emla and Embla, and hence concludes that the ash furnished the materials for both man and woman.   It is obvious, however, that by proceeding in this manner we might conjure Embla out of a score of words, some of them probably as significant as the one on which the learned Icelander has exercised his ingenuity.   In fact, if it had not clashed with his Yggdrasill theory, he would perhaps have derived Embla by *metathesis* from the *N.* almr, an elm tree, which would have been a more appropriate derivation, though equally conjectural.

bulthul, fimbulvetr, fimbultýr, &c. From fimbulfambi comes the *E.* provincialism, to fimble-famble; and the *D.* famle, to stammer, to hesitate in speaking.

FIMBULTHUL. Thulr means an orator or reciter, from v. thylja, to recite, to speechify; but the etym. of thul is unknown.

FIMBULVETR : vetr, winter; conseq. according to Grimm's explanation of fimbul, *the Great Winter*.

FJALARR and FJÖLNIR. Multiform : from fjöld, in composition fjöl, many; cog. with *G.* viel.

FJÖLSVIÐR or FJÖLSVITHR. The last sylb. from v. sviða: *D.* svide, to scorch : or ph. from svithr, wise, powerful, cog. with *M. G.* svinths; *A. S.* swið, potent, strong.

FJÖRGYN : dt. etym. The E. E. derive it from fjör, life, and vinr, a friend, the g being interposed; but Grimm, we think, has satisfactorily shown that fjörg is the *G.* berg, a mountain.

FJÖRM, prob. either from fjör, life, or fjarr, far.

FOLKVÁNGR or FÓLKVÁNGAR, lit. the folk's field, or habitation : fólk; *A. S.* folc; *Sw., D.* and *E.* folk; *G.* volk: vángr, an inclosure, a field; cog. with *G.* wohnung, habitation.

FORSETI, lit. the Fore-seated, *i. e.* the Judge, corresponding lit. to the *G.* Vorgesetzte : seti, from the v. sitja, to sit.

FRÁNANGURS-FORS, prob. from fránn, glittering, and öngr, narrow; or the obs. ángr, a frith, a river: fors, a force, still used to sig. a waterfall in the North of England.

FREKI, from frekr; *G.* frech, froward : the word has also the sig. of voracious.

FREYR and FREYJA. F. Mag. explains Freyr (which he also writes Fræir), the name of the deity who was the symbol of the sun—to mean the Seminator, the Fructifier, from the *N.* frió, fræ; *Sw.* and *D.* frö, seed : and that of Freyja—the symbolical representation of the moon—to be the f. of it, and mean the Seminated, the Fructified; but these, like the greater part of F. Mag.'s etymologies, are far more *conjectural* than grammatical. Grimm, with his usual profound knowledge of the subject, traces the *grammatical* affinities of these words through all the Anc. Teutonic languages, and shows that the original sig. is that of glad, joyful, imparting gladness, beauteous, lovely. See his *Deut. Myth.* p. 191 and 279. See also the note page 312.

FRIGGA, prop. FRIGG. Grimm has shown that the root of this word is, if not strictly syn., at least very nearly allied with that of the word Freyja, and explains it to mean the Free, the Beauteous, the Winsome. *See Deut. Myth.* p. 276, et seq.

FROSTI, the *E.* frosty.

FULLA, abundance; from fullr, full.

FUNDINN, found; from v. finna, to find.

GANDÁLFR. Álfr, an elf: first sylb. of dt. etym., prob. sig. a wolf. a serpent.

GANGLER, prop. GÁNGLERI, the tired wanderer: gáng, from v. gánga, to go, to gang: leri, from v. lára, to debilitate, to tire.

GANGRAD, prop. GÁNGRÁÐR, indicates a person directing his steps: gángr, a step, a gang; ráðr, from v. ráða, to advise; cog. with *G*. rathen.

GARÐROFA, Fence-breaker: garðr, a guard or fence, (*see* Asgard): rofa, from the v. rofna, to break, to break through.

GARMR, ph. from gérr, voracious, a word prob. cog. with *L*. gurges; *A. S* gara; *E*. to gorge; *F*. gourmand.

GAUTR, ph. may sig. a keeper, from v. gæta, to keep.

GEFJON, prob. from the v. gefa, to give; hence *The Donatrix*. F. Mag., who writes the word Géfjón, is inclined to make gé cog. with the *Gr*. Γη; *A. S*. geard, the earth; and explains fjón to mean separation, disruption; but it is needless to add that this is a mere *conjecture*, to suit a particular theory.

GEFN, from the v. gefa, to give; hence *The Donatrix*.

GEIRÖLUL, l`t. Spear-alimentrix: geir, from geirr, a spear: ölul, from the v. ala, to aliment, to nourish.

GEIRRAUÐR, or GEIRRÖÐR, lit. spear-red; hence King Spear-rubifier.

GEIRVIMUL : vimul is ph. from the v. veifa, to vibrate; hence the sig. would be, a river rushing or vibrating like a spear or javelin.

GELGJA, from gálgi, a gallows.

GERDA, prop. GERÐUR, the nom. m. of which would be Gerðr, which has the same meaning as the *E*. word girth, being derived from the v. girða, to gird, which is cog. with garðr. *See* Asgard. Both gerd and gard are common terminations of female names, as Hildigard, Irminigard, Thorgerda, &c.

GERI, or GÉRI. Géri, may be derived from gérr, covetous, greedy; cog. with *G*. gierig, begehren; and with *E*. gear.

GIMLI. Grimm observes that, in the Edda, Gimli is the dative case, "á gimli," and he thinks that the nom. was gimill, and had the same sig. as himill, heaven. The E. E. derive it however from gímr, the original sig. of which may ph. have been fire, but afterwards a gem, as in the *N*. word gímsteinn; *Al*. gimme; *A. S*. gim, gymstan; *E*. gem; whence also our colloquial words, gim, gimmy (neat), and gimcrack.

GINNARR, Seducer; from v. ginna, to seduce.

GINNÚNGA-GAP may be rendered the gap of gaps; the yawning, gaping abyss. See Grimm's explanation of the word, (in his *Deut. Mythol.* 2nd edit. p. 525,) which we prefer to that of F. Mag. and the E. E.

GJALLAR (horn); from the v. gjalla, to resound, to clang; cog. with *A. S.* giellan; *E*. to yell.

GJÖLL, prob. from gjallr, sonorous, fulgid.

GLAÐR, glad ; from v. gleðja, to gladden.

GLAÐSHEIMR: lit. Glad's-home; the abode of gladness or bliss: glaðr; *D*. glad; *A. S*. glæd; *E*. glad: heimr has the sig. both of home and world, and in composition denotes abode, region. This word is common to all the Teutonic lang. *N.* heimr; *I.* heimi; *Sw.* hem; *D.* hiem; *M. G.* haim; *G.* heimath, in composition heim; *A. S.* hám; *E.* home.

GLÆR, from glær, clear, pellucid; cog. with *E.* glare.

GLEIPNIR, the Devouring; from the v. gleipa, to devour.

GLITNIR, the Glittering; from the v. glitra; cog. with *A. S.* glitenan; *E.* to glitter, and to glisten.

GLÓINN, the Glowing; from v. glóa, cog. with *A. S.* glowan; *E.* to glow; *G.* glühen.

GOD. The *Old N.* lang. has two words for God, viz. Goð and Guð; and it would appear that the n. goð was used for an idol, and the m. guð for a God. Björn Haldorsson, in his "Lexicon Islando-Latino-Danicum," renders the word God (prop. Goð) by *idolum*, and Gud (prop. Guð) by *Deus, summum et unicum numen.* Both words are, however, frequently applied to denote a celestial deity. Gyðja is used for Goddess and Priestess. The Scandinavian Pontiff-chieftains were called Goðar (in the sing. Goði). See the note page 289. The forms of the word God in the Teutonic lang. are, *M. G.* Guth; *Anc. G.* Cot; *G.* Gott; *Old Sx., Old Fr., A. S., E.,* and *Dt.* God; *N.* Goð and Guð; *Sw.* and *D.* Gud. Grimm says (*Deut. Mythol.* p. 12) that the radical signification of the word has not been ascertained, but he shows that there is a grammatical difference between the words in the Teutonic lang. sig. *God* and *good,* which will not admit of their being regarded as originally syn. Good is in *M. G.* góds; *Anc. G.* cuot; *Old G.* guot; *G.* gut; *A. S.* gód; *E.* good; *Dt.* goed; *N.* góðr; *Sw.* and *D.* god. He also remarks that the word Goth has still less affinity with the word God. The Goths called themselves Gutans; in *Anc. G.* Kuzun; *N.* Gotar; but observes that *if* the *P.* Khodá can be derived from the *Zend* qvadáta; *Sk.* svadáta, *a se datus, increatus,* a very appropriate etym. of the word God would be furnished.

GÖLL, the same etym. as Gjöll.

GÖMUL, prob. from gamall, old.

GÖPUL, prob. from v. gapa, to gape.

GRÁBAKR, Gray-back.

GRÁFJÖLLUÐR, Gray-skin: from the obs. fjall, cog. with *G.* fell, the skin of an animal.

GRAFVITNIR, from the v. grafa, to dig, to delve; cog. with *E.* grave : and the v. vita, to know; cog. with *M. G.* vitan; *A. S.* witan; *E.* to wit, wist, wot.

GRÍMAR, and GRÍMNIR. These words with the i accented may be derived from an obs. *N.* word gríma, a helmet, or any kind of a covering; without the accent from grimmr, the *E.* grim. The former would be a more appropriate derivation for the name of Odin, viz., The Helmeted: gríma is also used poetically for night, the sun being then veiled or covered.

GULLINBURSTI, Golden-bristles : gull, gold; bursti, cog. with *G.* borste, bristle.

GULLTOPPR, Golden-mane : toppr, apex, crest, the top of any thing, hence mane.

GUNNLAUTH or GUNNLÖÐ, from gunnr, *see* the following word, and lauth, ph. from the v. latha, to invite; *G.* einladen.

GUNNTHRÁ, GUNNTHRAINN, GUNNTHRÓ, and GUNNUR. The first sylb. of these words is from gunnr, war, a combat. The second sylb. of the three first words may be derived from the v. thróa, to increase, to enlarge; or from the v. thrá, threýja, to desire: thrá also sig. grief, calamity; and thró, a cavity, a fosse. From gunnr is derived the *N.* gunnfáni, a war-banner; *Barb. L.* gunnfanones; *It.* gonfalone; *F.* gonfanon: fána is cog. with *G.* fahne; *A. S.* fana; *E.* banner; and ph. also with the *E.* word fan.

GYLLIR, from gull, gold.

HÁBRÓK. The E. E. render this word by *Altipes*, from hár, high; and brók, lit. breeches, brogues, but which they assume may also sig. a bird's leg.

HALLINSKITHI, or HALLINSKIÐI; F. Mag. derives it from v. halla, to decline; and skeið, course, space; hence it would be an appropriate term for the post-meridian sun.

HAMSKERPIR, prob. from hams, hide; and the v. skérpa, to sharpen, also to dry, to indurate.

HANGAGUÐ, from v. hánga, to hang; and guð, *see* God.

HAPTAGUÐ, ph. from haupt, a nexus, a tie, a band; guð, *see* God.

HAR, prop. HÁR or HÁRR, may mean either *high* or *hairy*. As a designation of Odin it has undoubtedly the former signification *The High*; and is cog. with *D.* höj; *M. G.* hauhs; *G.* hoch; *A. S.* heáh; *E.* high. As the name of a dwarf, the latter sig. would be more appropriate.

HÁRBARÐR, Hairy-beard.

HATI, ph. contracted from hatandi, the part. of v. hata, to hate.

HEIDRUN, prop. HEIÐRÚN: dt., etym. ph. from heiðr, serene, etherial; or heið, cog. with *M. G.* haithja; *G.* heide; *A. S.* hæð; *E.* heath.

HEIMDALLR: heimr, home, the world; but of dall we have found no satisfactory explanation.

HELA, prop. HEL., gen. HELJAR, the Goddess of the Infernal Regions, used instead of Helheimr for those regions themselves. A word of dt. origin; the E. E. are of opinion that its primary sig. was intense cold, and that it is cog. with the *L.* gelu, and was afterwards employed to denote, 1st, the chill of death; and 2nd, a frigid region, the abode of the dead; but, as is usually the case, Grimm gives a much more probable derivation from a v. hilan, to conceal, in which sense it would sig. a subterraneous cavity, *a hole*, which is prob. a cog. word. Be this as it may, all the Teutonic nations on their conversion to Christianity applied this word to denote the place where, according to popular notions, the souls of the wicked are punished by *fire*. Thus, *M. G.* halja; *Old G.* hellia, hella; *G.* hölle; *A. S.* helle; *E.* hell; *I.* helviti (prop. the pains of hell); *D.* helvede, &c.

HELBLINDI: hel, see the preceding word; blindi, from blundr, slumber; ph. cog. with *E.* blunder and blunt; also cog. with *N.* blindr, *E.* blind.

HEPTI, prob. means impeding, constraining, from heptr, part. of v. hepta, more recent hefta; cog. with *M. G.* gahaftjan; *G.* haften; *A. S.* hæftan, to seize, to take by force, to adhere to; hence the *I.* hepti, hefti; *A. S.* and *D.* hæft; *G.* hefte; *E.* haft.

HERFJÖTUR, lit. Host's-fetter, *i. e.* having the power to impede or constrain an army at will: her, an army, a host, a multitude; *M. G.* harjis; *G.* heer. *Sk.* hara, a destroyer; *P.* herameh, a pillager. *Z.* Hereté; *I.* Hertogi; *D.* Hertug; *G.* Herzog, Duke. *I.* Herra; *D.* Herre; *G.* Herr, Mr. or Gentleman; cog. with *Gr.* and *L.* heros; *E.* hero. *N.* v. herja, to make war; cog. with *G.* verheeren; *A. S.* herian; *E.* to harrow. Fjöturr, *A. S.* fetor; *E.* fetter; *G.* fessel.

HERJANN, the leader of an army; from her.

HERMOD, prop. **HERMÓÐR** : her from her, (*see* Herfjötur) : moðr, courage, (*see* Modgudur.)

HERTEITR, gay amongst warriors, a jovial soldier : teitr, glad, joyful.

HILDUR (Hilda). Grimm has satisfactorily shown that hildr is an old word common to all the Teutonic lang. with the same sig. as gunnr, war, a combat. Hence we find it in a number of Teutonic prop. names both m. and f., as Hilderic, Childeric, Hildegrim (the Helm of War), Brynhildr (Brunhilda), Clothild (Clotilda), &c.

HIMINBJÖRG, the Heavenly-Mountains. *See* the note, page 42 : björg, pl. of bjarg; *G.* berg, a rock, a mountain. It is very singular, as Grimm remarks in his *Deut. Mythol.* p. 661, that whereas the word heaven is in *N.* himin; *M. G.* himins; *Anc. G.* himil, himmel; it should be in *Old Sx.* hëbhan, hëvan; *A. S.* heofon. He derives himin from a v. himan, to cover, to bedeck; and heofon from a lost Gothic word hiba, haf. which he compares with the *L.* capio; it consequently means the Comprehending, the All-embracing.

HIMINBRJÓTR, Heaven-breaking : from the v. brjóta, to break.

HJÁLMBERI, Helmet-bearing : hjalmr, a helmet; beri, from v. bera, to bear, to wear.

HJÚKI, ph. from v. hjúka, to keep warm, to nourish, to cherish.

HLIÐSKJALF, ph. from hlíð; *A. S.* hlíð, a slope, a declivity; or prob. from hlið, a gate; cog. with the *E.* lid, a cover : skjálf, ph. from the v. skjálfa; *A. S.* scylfan, to waver, to tremble; hence expressive of the ambient air. Grimm, however, derives the word from skjalf; *A. S.* scylfe; *E.* shelf.

HLINA, prop. **HLÍN**. Grimm derives this word from the root hláin, cog. with the *Gr.* κλίνω, *L.* clino; and explains it to mean the *support* on which a person leans, *i. e.* a tutelary deity.

HLJÓÐÁLFR, the Genius or Elf of Sound : hljóð; *D.* liud, lyd; *G.* laut; *A. S.* hlúd, a sound; hence *E.* loud.

HLÓÐYN, prop. **HLÓÐYN**, the name of Frigga, as the symbol of the earth. Grimm has shown that the primary sig. of hlóð is a hearth, or prop. a pile, ara, from v. hlathan, to pile up ; the sig. of the word is conseq. *Protectress of the hearth*—of the household. The Romans also worshipped a goddess of the earth and of fire under the cemmon name of Fornax, dea fornacalis. *See* Ovid. Fast. 2, 513. Grimm mentions a stone found at Cleves with the remarkable inscription—DEAE HLUDANAE SACRVM C. TIBERIVS VERVS, and remarks that Hludana was neither a Roman nor a Celtic goddess, and could be no other than Hlódyn, which shows the identity of the German and Scandinavian Mythology.

HLÖKK, or HLAUKK. F. Mag. derives this word from the v. hlakka, to exalt, to clang, to cry like an eagle, a v. which he thinks may be cog. with the v. hlægja; *M. G.* hlajan; *G.* lachen; *A. S.* hlehan; *E.* to laugh. But Grimm gives a more prob. derivation from hlökk; *Old G.* hlancha, a chain; hence it would have much the same sig. as Herfjötur.

HNIKARR, or NIKARR, NIKKARR, and HNIKUÐR, or NIKUZ. Of dt. origin. The E. E. compare these words with the *Gr.* Νικάτωρ, a victor, a conqueror. F. Mag. derives them from v. hnika, to move, to agitate; cog. with v. hnikkja, to thrust forward, to take by violence; and hnekkja, to repel, to impede; and thinks they may be cog. with *G.* knacken; *E.* knack, knock. Grimm has proved the identity of the *N.* Hnikar, Nikuz, with the *Old G.* Nichus; *G.* m. Nix, fem. Nixe, an aquatic genius. We may remark that the monks having transformed Odin into the devil, our designation of his Satanic Majesty, as *Old Nick* appears to be a mere corruption of these appellations of the Teutonic divinity.

HNOSSA, prop. HNOSS, ph. from hnoða, a ball of yarn, a clew of thread, a knot; *G.* knoten.

HÖDUR, prop. HÖÐR, HÖDUR : very dt. etym. Grimm thinks that the original signification may have been war, combat.

HÓFVARPNIR : hóf, hoof: varpnir, from v. varpna; *G.* werfen, to throw, *i. e.* a horse that plies well its hoofs, a good goer.

HORN, a horn, applied prob. to denote the impetuosity of a fluviatile current.

HRÆSVELGUR, lit. Raw-swallower, *i. e.* swallowing raw flesh like an eagle. *N.* hræ; *Al.* hreu; *A. S.* hræw, sig. a corpse; cog. with *A. S.* hreaw; *E.* raw: svelgur, from v. svelgja; cog. with *D.* svælge; *A. S.* swelgan; *E.* swill, swallow; *G.* schwelgen, &c.

HRAFNAGUÐ, the Ravens' god: hrafn; *G.* rabe; *E.* raven.

HRÍMFAXI : hrím, rime, or hoar frost; *G.* reif: fax, a crest, a mane. The *E.* prop. name Fairfax, means fair-haired.

HRÍMTHURSAR, the Rime or Frost Giants: thurs, a giant, is a word of very dt. origin.

HRÍNGHORN, lit. a ringed or annulated horn.

HRIST, from v. hrista, to shake, to agitate ; cog. with *D.* ryste; *G.* rütteln; and with *A. S.* hristlan; *E.* rustle.

HRYM, HRYMUR, prob. from hrím, rime—hoar frost.

HUGI, and HUGINN, from hugr, spirit, breath, thought, mind, reason.

HVERGELMIR, the roaring cauldron : hver, a cauldron, a spring of hot water; ph. cog. with *E.* whirl and wheel : for gelmir, *see* Ür-gelmir.

HYRROKIN, lit. Smoky-fire: hyr, fire: rokin, from rauk, utter darkness, also smoke; cog. with *G.* rauch.

IÐAVÖLLR : völlr, a field, a place, *see* note, p. 293. The etym. of iða is very doubtful, among the *conjectures* of F. Mag. the most prob. would be from the v. yda, to flow together; or from idja, to work; but to which he also attaches the sig. of to ramble, to take a pleasant walk ; but such etym. are like too many of F. Mag's., *quite conjectural.*

IDUNA, prop. IÐUNN or ITHUNN : dt. etym.   F. Mag. derives id, like ida, either from the v. idja, or the v. yda ; and the last sylb. is prob. from v. unna, to love ; and *in this manner*, Iduna may mean one who loves either the confluence of waters, or to work, or to take a pleasant ramble.

JAFNHÁR. *The Equally High;* lit. even so high (*see* Hár): jafn ; *D.* jævn; *G.* eben; *A. S.* efen; *E.* even.

JÁRNVIÐR, Iron-wood : járn; *D.* jern; *M. G.* eisarn; *G.* eisen; *E.* iron : viðr, wood, *see* Vidar.

JÖRÐ, JÖRTH, *M. G.* airtha; *Anc. G.* ërda; *A. S.* eorðe; *E.* the earth.

JÖRMUNGANDR.   Gandr sig. serpent, and more prop. wolf : jörmun is a word of uncertain origin, but appears in all the anc. Teutonic lang. to have expressed the idea of great, maximus, universal.   We have thus the famous Irminsúl or Irmansúl of the Saxons rendered in Latin by *universalis columna.* In *Anc. G.* irminthiod ; *A. S.* eormencyn, sig. mankind in general; in like manner the *A. S.* eormengrund ; *N.* jörmungrund, the whole earth. The word also enters into the composition of prop. names, as, for instance, in that of the celebrated Gothic King, called in Latin *Ermanricus,*—which in *M. G.* would be Airmanareiks ; in *N.* Jörmunrekr ; in *A. S.* Eormenric—and in the *Hermiones* and *Hermunduri* of the classic writers.   The Ermingestrete of the latter *A. Sx.* and *Old E.* writers (in pure *A. S.* Eormenesstræt), has the same etym. The reader will find much curious information on this subject in Grimm's admirable work, p. 104, 327, et seq.

JÖTUNHEIMR, lit. Giants'-home, the region of the Giants.   Grimm remarks that the *Old N.* for giant is iötunn (not jötunn), and is cog. with the *A. S.* eoten, eten; *Old E.* etin, ettin; *Scotch* ettyn, eyttyn; *Old Sx.* etan, eten ; and thinks it may be derived from the *N.* v. éta; *M. G.* ïtan; *A. S.* etan, to eat; and might therefore be rendered by Polyphagos.

KÉRLAUG : kér, any kind of vessel, cup, bowl, &c. ; also used to denote the bed of a river.   The root of laug, lögr, may be the *N.* lá, liquor, and it would appear also in its primary sig. the sea: hence *N.* v. laga, to flow; leka, to trickle.   To this root may be traced a number of cog. words in the *Ind. E.* lang., as *N.* laug; *G.* lauge; *A. S.* læg; *E.* lye; *L.* lixivium. *N.* v. lauga; *L.* lavare; *E.* to lave. *N.* lögr; *Al.* lug; *A. S.* lagu (water); *E.* lake; *L.* lacus; and the lough, loch, and llwch of the Celtic languages.

KJALARR, prob. from v. kjala, to transport, to convey; whence prob. kjöll ; *A. S.* ceol, a ship, *a keel.*

KVÁSIR. This word seems to be foreign to the Teutonic lang., and ph. may be cog. with the *Sl.* kvas, leaven; also used in the sense of *a drinking bout.*

LAUFEY, lit. Frondiferous-isle : lauf, cog. with *G.* laube ; *E.* leaf : ey, an island.

LÉTTFETI, Lightfoot : léttr, *D.* let; *G.* leicht; *A. S.* leoht; *E.* light : fótr, pl. fætur ; *D.* fod ; *M. G.* fotus ; *G.* fuss ; *A. S.* fót ; *E.* foot.

LÍFTHRASIR, vital energy, longevity : líf, life : thrasir, from thrár, pertinacious, *i. e.* enduring a long time.

LITUR, ph. from litr, colour, complexion, form; cog. with *D.* löd; *Sw.* let, colour ; *M. G.* vlits; *A. S.* lyt, form : *N.* andlit; *M. G.* andauleizns; *A. S.* andwlit; *G.* antlilz, the face.

LÓDURR, LÓÐR, LÓTHR, from the ob. *N.* lóð, fire.

LOFNA, prop. LOFN, appears allegorically to denote perennial and unchangeable love : the word is cog. with the *N.* v. lofa; *G.* loben, to praise, and with the *M. G.* liubs; *G.* liebe; *Dt.* liefde; *A. S.* lufu; *E.* love.

LOGI, Flame : a word cog. with *M. G.* v. liuhan, to shine, and liuhath ; *G.* licht; *A. S.* leoht; *E.* light : also with the *D.* lue; *G.* lohe, a smothered flame, and ph. with the *E.* log, *i. e.* a log of wood burnt or to be burnt.

LOKI, has prob. the same etym. as Logi, though it may also be derived from v. loka and lúka ; *M. G.* lúkan ; *A. S.* lúcan, to shut; whence the *E.* lock. The *N.* lúka also sig. to finish.

LOPTUR, the Aerial, the Sublime : from lopt; *M. G.* luftus; *G.* and *D.* luft : *A. S.* lyft, the air ; whence the *E.* lofty and aloft, also a (hay) loft.

LÝNGVI, from lýng or líng, the sweet broom, heath or ling.

MAGNI, the Potent, the Powerful ; from magn, force, energy; cog. with *M. G.* mahts; *G.* 'nacht; *A. S.* miht; *E.* might; also with the *L.* magnus; *Sk.* maha, mahima.

MÁNAGARMR, lit. the moon's wolf : garmr, a monster wolf or dog, prob. from gérr, voracious. *See* Géri and Máni.

MÁNI. *Sw.* måne; *D.* maane; *M. G.* ména; *Al.* máno; *G.* mond; *A. S.* mona ; *E.* moon; *Dt.* maan; *Sk.* masi; *P.* mah, mai, mank. In all the Ancient Teutonic languages moon is of the *masculine,* and sun of the *feminine* gender. In the Slavonic languages moon is *mas.,* star *fem.,* and sun *neuter.* Until a very late period the people in some parts of Germany were fond of showing a proper respect to the sun and moon, by calling them *Frau Sonne* and *Herr Mond;* for instance, a popular expression cited by Grimm (page 664), *"Frauw Sonne geht zu rast und gnaden;"* (Mrs. Sun goes to rest and grace;) and he adds, that near Salzach, *"Hér Mán,"* (Mr. Moon,) is quite a common expression.

MARDÖLL, Sea-nymph : from mar; *M. G.* marei; *Sl.* more ; *A. S.* mere, the sea; whence our word mere, as Windermere, Buttermere, &c. : döll, a nymph; poetically a woman ; ph. cog. with the *E.* word, doll.

MEGINGJARDIR, the Girdle of Might, the Belt of Prowess : megin, might, prob. from v. megna, to be able, cog. with *A. S.* mægen, power, miracle, &c.; *E.* main, as the mainland (*I.* meginland); *P.* mih, mihin, great, powerful: gjardir, from the v. girda. *See* Gerda and Asgard.

MIDGARD, prop. MIÐGARÐR, answers to the *M. G.* midjungards; *Anc. G.* mittiligart; *A. S.* middangeard (Cædm. and Beow.) and midde-weard, the middleward; *see* Asgard. The *N.* miðr is cog. with *M. G.* midums, midia; *G.* mitte, mittel; *A. S.* midd, midlen; *E.* middle, mid-dling, mean; *Sk.* madhyam, medhi; *Z.* meiao; *P.* mijan; *Gr.* μισος, &c.

MÍMIR, or MIMER: dt. etym. Grimm thinks that written with a short i, it may be cog. with *A. S.* mimor, gemïmor, mimerian (to keep in memory); mimeren (to be fanciful); and with the *L.* memor (mindful); and the *Gr.* μιμέομαι.

MIST, prob. from the same root and the same sig. as the *I.* mistr; *A. S.* myst, mist; *E.* mist, a fog.

MJÖÐVITNIR, lit. knowing in mead: mjöð; *G.* meth; *A. S.* meodu, medu; *E.* mead (hydromel), prob. cog. with *Gr.* μιδυ; *P.* mei, wine; *Sk.* madja, palm-wine: vitnir, *see* Grafvitnir.

MJÖLNIR, or MJÖLLNIR, prob. from v. melja, to pound, or v. mala, to grind; both cog. also cog. with the *G.* mahlen (to grind), and *G.* mühle; *E.* mill, and prob. with *L.* malleus, a mallet; and ph. with the *Sl.* molnija and munja (lightning .

MODGUDUR, prop. MOÐGÚÐUR, a valiant female warrior, *animosa bel-lona:* móð, from móðr; *G.* muth, courage; *G.* gemüth, mind; cog. with *A. S.* mód; *E.* mood; *Sk.* anmodo; *G.* anmuth, gracefulness, delec-tation; '*Sk.* unmadoh; *G.* unmuth, ill humour: gúður, from gúðr, which has the same sig. as gunnr. *See* Gunnthrá.

MÓDI, prop. MÓÐI, from móðr. *See* Móðguður.

MODSOGNIR, lit. sucking in courage or vigour: from móðr, and v. sjúga; *G.* saugen; *A. S.* súcan; *E.* to suck.

MÓINN, ph. from mói; *I.* mór, a moor, *i. e.* dwelling on a moor.

MUNINN, from munr, cog. with *M. G.* gamund; *A. S.* mynd, gemynd; *E.* mind; *L.* mens; *Gr.* μινος, whence μινοινη, *impetus animi*; *Sk.* manah; *Z.* manó; *P.* menish, manish: *N.* minni; *D.* minde, *memory*, recollec-tion; *G.* minne, love *

---

* Although we have hitherto never felt the least inclination to indulge in *conjectural etymology,* having been too frequently warned from treading its slippery paths by the amusing vagaries of those who ride some favourite hobby or other roughshod along them, still we cannot refrain for once from noticing the curious coincidence between the names of Odin's ravens, Hugin and Munin—Mind and Memory—and those of two personages who figure so often in our comic literature, as Messrs. Huggins and Muggins. *Huggins,* like *Hugh,* appears to have the same root as *Hugin,* viz. *hugr,* mind, spirit; and as Mr. Muggins is as invariably associated with Mr. Huggins as one of Odin's ravens was with the other (as Mind is with Memory), the name may originally have been written *Munnins,* and *nn* changed into *gg* for

MUSPELLHEIMR, or **MUSPELLSHEIMR**, the Muspell region, or Muspell's region or home. The word muspell is evidently used in the sense of elemental or empyreal fire; but its etym. is quite unknown, for we cannot accept even Grimm's conjectural derivation of the word, given in the *Deut. Mythol.* p. 769.

NAGLFAR and **NAGLFARI**. F. Mag. derives nagl, from nagli, a nail (clavus), but it is more prob. from nagl, a human nail (unguis), being, according to the Prose Edda, c. 51, "constructed of the nails of dead men :" far, from v. fara; *M. G.* and *A. S.* faran; *G.* fahren; *E.* to fare, in the sig. of going—as a sea-faring man.

NAL. *G.* nadel; *A. S.* nædl; *E.* a needle.

NÁLI, ph. the same sig. as Nál.

NANNA. Grimm derives this word from the v. nenna, to dare, *audere*, and observes that in *M. G.* the form would have been Nanthó, from the v. nanthjan, and in *Anc. G.* Nandá, from the v. ginendan. F. Mag. is also inclined to derive it from the v. nenna, which he renders, however, by *favere, amare, indulgere.*

NAR, a corpse.

NÁSTRÖND. Both ná and nár, sig. a corpse: strönd (pl. strandir), a strand; hence The Strand of the Dead.

NAUÐUR, NAUTHR, necessity: cog. with *M. G.* nauths; *G.* noth; *A. S.* neód; *E.* need.

NAUT, ph. from the v. njóta, to make use of; cog. with *M. G.* niutan; *G.* nutzen and geniessen; *A. S.* noten.

NIÐAFJÖLL, from niðr, downwards, and fjall; *D.* fjæld; *G.* fels, a rock, a mountain.

NIDHÖGG, prop. **NIÐHÖGGR**: niðr, downwards: *ný ok nið* is a phrase used to indicate the new and the waning moon ; nið might thus be met. used for darkness: höggr, from the v. höggva; *A. S.* heawen; *E.* to hew; *G.* hauen; cog. with *N.* hakka; *G.* hacken; *E.* to hack and to hackle: hence Nidhögg may be rendered by the Tenebrous Hewer or Gnawer.

NIÐI, from niðr, downwards.

NIFLHEIMR, lit. Nebulous-home—the shadowy region of death. *See* Muspellheimr. Nifl, cog. with *G.* nebel; *L.* nebula; *Gr.* νεφέλη.

NIFLHEL, from nifl and hel. *See* the latter word.

NIFLÚNGAR; *G.* Nibelunge and Nibelungen. The mythic-heroic sept of the Niflungians would be the descendants of a *N.* hero, Næfill or Nefill, and a *G.* Nebel—ghosts of the shadowy realms of death. *See* Grimm, p. 760. Úngar sig. a progeny, the pl. of úngr; *D.* ung; *G.* and *A. S.* jung; *E.* young; cog. with *L.* junior; ob. *L.* junis; *Sk.* juva, juvana. *See* note, p. 278.

---

the sake of euphony. Should this *conjecture*, for it is nothing else, be well founded, one of the most poetical ideas in the whole range of mythology would in this plodding, practical, spinning-jenny age of ours, have thus undergone a most singular metamorphosis.

NIPINGR, ph. from nipr, handsome; or from v. hnippa, hneppa, to contract, to curve.

NJÖRD, prop. NJÖRÐR: very dt. etym. Grimm seems inclined to derive it from norðr, north; Mone from v. næra; *G.* nähren, to nourish. The goddess Nerthus that Tacitus mentions is no doubt identic with Njörd; the *M. G.* form Nairthus, would indicate both m. and f. gender. The E. E. mention the Greek and Roman deity Nereus, and F. Mag. remarks that the word may ph. be cog. with the *Gr.* νηρος, humid; *Sk.* nar, nir, water; *P.* nere, a wave; and Neriman, an aquatic man.

NORÐRI, from norðr, north.

NORN, pl. NORNIR. Etym. quite unknown.

NÓTT; *D.* nat; *M. G.* naht; *G.* nacht; *A. S.* niht; *E.* night.

NÝI, from ný, new. *See* Niði. It would appear from their names that these dwarfs were in some way or other symbolical of the new and the waning moon.

NÝR, from ný, new.

NÝRÁÐR, from ný, and v. ráða. *See* Gangrad.

NÝT, ph. from v. njóta. *See* Naut.

ODIN. According to Grimm the name of this supreme deity in the Teutonic languages is *N.* Óðinn; *M. G.* Vódans; *Anc. G.* Wuotan (which would of course be pronounced Vuotan). The *Longobardi* wrote Wódan and Guódan; the *Old Saxons* Wuodan, Wódan; the *Westphalian Saxons* Guódan and Gudan. In *A. S.* we have Wóden; *Fr.* Wéda; *Færoic* Ouvin. Grimm derives the word from the *Anc. G.* v. watan, wuot; *N.* vaða, óð, which has precisely the same sig. as the *L.* vadere, and sig. *meare, transmeare, cum impetu ferri,* cog. with the *E.* to *wade* through, consequently the Omnipotent Being that *permeates all things,* "qui omnia permeat—est quodcunque vides, quocunque moveris," as Lucan says of Jupiter. The *Anc. G.* sub. wuot; *N.* óðr, sig. mind, sense—*mens, ingenium;* but the *N.* adj. óðr, means rabid, furious, insane. The *Anc. G.* sub. wuot, like the *A. S.* wód, also sig. rage; whence the *G.* wuth. We may remark that several places still retain the name of Odin, as Odensberg, Odenskirka, &c., in Sweden; the Odenwald, in Germany; Wednesbury, in Staffordshire, &c.

ODUR, prop. ÓÐR, or ph. ÓDR: if the former, the name of Freyja's husband may be derived either from the sub. or adj. óðr. *See* Odin. Grimm remarks that the name of this vessel or kettle would have been in *Anc. G.* lang. renders etymological deductions uncertain. In *A. S.* wód. sig. rage, and wóð, poetry. Odur might, therefore, like Kvasir, be the personification of poetry.

ÓÐHRŒRIR, Mind-exciting; from óðr; (*see* Odin and Oður) and the v. hrœra; *Anc. G.* hruoran; *Old G.* rüeren; *G.* rühren, to stir. Grimm remarks that the name of this vessel or kettle would have been in *Anc. G.* Wuodhruori; and in *A. S.* Wóðhrére.

OFNIR, ph. from the v. vefa (óf, ofinn); *D.* væve; *M. G.* vaibjan; *G.* weben; *A. S.* wefan; *E.* to weave. The word would thus sig. the textile or creating power of Odin.

ÓMI, from ómr, a sound, a crash; a name given to Odin, when, like the Brahminic Indra, he rattles aloft during a battle, or at daybreak.

ÖNDURDÍS: öndur, snow skates, a word prob. derived from the v. andra, to go, cog. with *D.* vandre; *G.* wandern; *A. S.* wandrian; *E.* to wander; *It.* andare: dís, a nymph, a goddess. *See* Dís.

ÖRGELMIR: ör, or, aur, are extensive particles. F. Mag. transposes gelmir into gemlir, and it may then be derived from gamall, old; and Örgelmir would then sig. very old—*pervetustus, grandævus*—the Primordial Giant. But Grimm, without having recourse to such a metathesis, derives gelmir from v. gjalla, to roar, to howl, to clang, to resound; cog. with *A. S.* giellan; *E.* to yell.

ÓRI, ph. from órr, insane, delirious (with love), Óri being prob. one of the Erotic Genii : órr is cog. with the *A. S.* yrre, wrath; and *G.* irre, astray, from the v. irren; *L.* errare; *E.* to err.

ÓSKI, from ósk; *D.* önske; *G.* wunsch; *E.* wish : hence one who listens to the wishes of mankind. Grimm, with his usual erudition, has shown how the German *Minnesängern* of the 13th century personified the word wish. *See Deut. Mythol.* p. 126.

RÁDGRID, prop. RÁDGRID, lit. seeking power with avidity: ráð, power, empire council; from the v. ráða: *see* Gangrad: grið, *æstus animi.*

RÁDSVITHR, or RÁÐSVIÐR: ráð, *see* Gangrad: svithr, wise, powerful. *See* Fjölsviðr.

RAGNARÖKR. The etym. of this word has exercised the ingenuity of philologists, but we think that Grimm has given a very satisfactory explanation of it. At the very earliest period of the German lang. he observes, the n. ragin signified *rath*, council, the pl. of which, regin, is used in the Eddaic Poems for the gods, "bliö regin," the blithe gods; "uppregin, ginregin," the powers above; that is to say, the consulting, deliberating deities. He explains rök, rökr, to mean darkness; and contends that it cannot be derived from *N.* reykr; *G.* rauch, smoke. It answers in fact fully to the *E.* word *rack*, indicating atmospheric nebulosity ; hence Ragnarök is very approp. rendered by "The Twilight of the Gods," *Crepuscula deorum.*

R N, the Spoliatrix; from the v. ræna, to plunder, to snatch from; her spoil being those who were drowned at sea.

RANDGRÍD: rand, from rönd, a shield: grid, *see* Rádgrid.

RATATÖSKR, very dt. etym. Rata, according to Grimm, is evidently from the v. rata; *M. G.* vratón, to permeate; and he *conjectures* that the last sylb. may be derived from taska, pl. töskur; *G.* tasche, a pocket or pouch; hence *peram permeans?* the Permeating Pouch ?

REGIN. The explanation of this word will be found under Ragnarökr. It is often used in the sense of vast, immense ; as regnihaf, the vast sea ; regindjúp, the immense deep.

REGINLEIF, dear to the gods, *see* Regin : leifr, dear, cog. with *G.* lieb ; *E.* love.

RÍGR : dt. etym. F. Mag. makes it syn. with the *N.* Regin; *L.* Rex; *Sk.* Raja, Rajah, a king.

RINDA, prop. RINDUR, sig. symbolically, according to Grimm, the crust of the earth, being cog. with the *Anc. G.* rinta; *G.* rinde; *A. S.* and *E.* rind, *cortex,* the bark or *crust* of a tree.

RÖSKA, ph. from adj. röskr, f. rausk, quick, lively, active; cog. with *Sw.* and *D.* rask; *G.* rasch; *E.* rash.

SADR, SATHR, or SÁDR, SÁTHR. Without the accent it is syn. with sannr, which means just, true; *Sw.* sann; *D.* sand; *M. G.* sunjeins; *A. S.* sóð; *E.* sooth; *A. S.* sóðlice, in sooth, verily. With the accent its derivation would be from sád; *D.* sæd; *G.* saat; *A. S.* sed; *E.* seed : hence Sádr would correspond to the *L.* Sator; and F. Mag. *conjectures* may be cog. with Saturnus.

SÆGR, ph. syn. with sárr, a large vessel of any kind. The word was used by the Skalds metaphorically for the sea.

SÆHRÍMNIR, or SERIMNIR : very dt. etym.

SÆKINN, ph. from v. sækja; *Sw.* söka; *D.* söge; *M. G.* sokjan; *G.* suchen; *A. S.* sécan; *E.* to seek.

SAGA. The personified saga or narration, from the v. segja, imp. sagda, to say : cog. words are found in most of the *Ind. E.* lang., as *M. G.* sagath; *G.* sage; *L.* Saga, a sorceress; sagax, sagacious; præsagire, to foretel; *P.* sachen, &c.

SANNGETALL, inquiring after; lit. getting at, or guessing at truth : from sub. sannr, truth (*see* Sadr, under which the words cog. with the adj. sannr, true, are given), and v. geta, which sig. both to guess and to get.

SESSRÚMNIR, lit. Seat-roomy, *i. e.* having room for plenty of seats : sess, a seat; *G.* sitze : rúm; *G.* raum; *A. S.* rúm; *E.* room.

SÍD, declining, hanging, tending downward.

SIDHÖTTR, lit. Hanging-hat or hood. *N.* höttr; *I.* hattr; *Sw.* hatt; *D.* hat; *G.* hut; *A. S.* hæt; *E.* hat and hood.

SÍDSKÉGGR, lit. Hanging-beard: skégg; *Sw.* skägg; *D.* skjæg, beard, cog. with *E.* shag and shaggy.

SIF. Grimm supposes that from the *M. G.* sibja; *Anc. G.* sippia; *A. S.* sib; signifying peace, friendship, relationship, these nations had respectively a goddess, Sibja, Sippia, and Sib, corresponding to the *N.* Sif, gen. Sifjar.

SIGFADIR, or SIGFÖDUR, the Father of Victory: sigr; *Sw.* seger; *D.* sejer; *Al.* sigor; *G.* sieg; *A. S.* sige, victory; *Sk.* sigi, a victor: faðir; *D.* fader; *G.* vater; *A. S.* fæder; *E.* father; *Sk.* pider; *Gr.* and *L.* pater.

SIGUNA, prop. SIGYN : very dt. etym.*

---

* The etym. must in fact be more than doubtful, when Finn Magnusen, who is never at a loss to catch up a word as he flies on his favourite hobby in search of etymological spoil from Scandinavia to India, is obliged to admit

SILFRINTOPPR, Silver-mane: silfr; *Sw.* silfvor; *D.* sölv; *M. G.* silubr; *G.* silber; *A. S.* sylfor; *E.* silver: toppr, *see* Gulltoppr.

SINDRI, either scintillating or producing dross: from sindr; *Sw.* sinder; *D.* sinner; *G.* sinter, dross of iron; cog. with *A. S.* sinder; *E.* cinder.

SJÖFNA, prop. SJÖFN: very dt. etym. F. Mag. derives it from the v. sjá, to see.

SKADI, prop. SKAÐI: dt. etym. It would appear that the magpie received its name from this goddess as it is called in *N.* skaði; *Sw.* skata; *D.* skade*. The *N.* v. skaða; *D.* skade; *G.* schaden, sig. to injure, and is cog. with the *E.* word scath.

SKAFIÐR, shaving, scraping: from the v. skafa; *D.* skave; *G.* schaben; *A. S.* scafen; *E.* to shave.

SKÉGGÖLD, lit. Old-beard; *see* Sidskégg: but it appears that skégg also denoted a particular kind of battle-axe.

SKEIÐBRÍMIR may mean rapidly running fire, from skeið, a course, any space of time that is elapsing; and brími, fire, flame.

SKÍÐBLAÐNIR, from skíð, which sig. 1st, a chip, lath, shingle, billet of wood, and in this sense is cog. with *G.* scheit; *L.* schidium; *Gr.* σχιδαξ; and 2nd, a sheath; cog. with *D.* skede; *G.* scheide; *A. S.* sceath; *E.* sheath: blað; *G.* blatt, a leaf; cog. with *E.* blade, a blade or *leaf* of grass.

SKILFÍNGR, prob. from v. skélfa, to shake, to shatter.

SKINFAXI, Shining-mane: skin, splendour, light; from v. skina; *D.* skinne; *G.* scheinen; *A. S.* scinan; *E.* to shine; whence sheen. *See* Hrimfaxi.

SKÍRNIR. "Vox skírnir ætherem ipsum sine ullâ allegoria denotat," says F. Mag. Be this as it may, the word may be derived from skírr, serene, pure, clear; cog. with *A. S.* scir; E. sheer, which had formerly the same meaning.

SKÖGUL, prob. from v. skaga, to jut out; whence skagi, a promontory.

SKÖLL, ph. from v. skolla, to stick to, to adhere; or v. skélla, to strike, to smite.

SKULD. *See* Urd.

SLEIPNIR: dt. etym. F. Mag. derives it from sleipr, cog. with, and the same sig. as the *Sw.* slipprig; *D.* slibrig; *G.* schlüpfrig; *E.* slippery.

SLIDRUGTANNI: tanni, from tönn; *D.* tand; *G.* zahne; *E.* tooth: slidrig of dt. etym., ph. from a word cog. with *M. G.* sleidja, cruel, fierce, savage.

---

that "Etyma nominis hujus incerta sunt et id igitur variis modis, *quæ meras tantum conjecturas admittunt,* explicari potest."—*Mythol.* p. 695.

* The reader will find some curious details of popular superstitions respecting magpies, cuckoos, &c., in Grimm's *Deut. Mythol.* p. 639, et seq.

SNOTRA, from snotr; *M. G.* snutrs; *A. S.* snoter, prudent, polite, *neat, tidy.* Grimm says prop. *emunctæ naris;* hence it would be equivalent to the vulgar *E.* cog. word snot; *A. S.* snote, which is cog. with the *N.* v. snýta; *G.* schnäutzen; *A. S.* snytan; *E.* to snite, *i. e.* to blow the nose; a person, even a goddess, being much more *tidy* when the nostrils are thoroughly *emunctated.* A number of verbs beginning with *sn* denote a nasal function, or are in some way indicative of the nose, as to snuff, sneeze, snore, snarl, snuffle, snaffle, snivel, snub, sneer, &c.: to snuff is cog. with the *N.* v. snáfa; *D.* snue; *G.* schnupfen : to snore, with the *N.* snörla and snarka; *D.* snorke; *G.* schnarchen : to snub with the *N.* snubba.

SÖKKVABEKKR, lit. Sinking-brook: sökkva, from the v. n. sökkva; *Sw.* sjunka; *D.* synke; *M. G.* siggvan; *G.* sinken; *A. S.* sincan; *E.* to sink: and v. a. sökkva; *Sw.* sänka; *D.* sænke; *G.* senken; *A. S.* sencan; *E.* to sink: bekkr, an estuary, a shore, a brook; *Sw.* bäck; *D.* bæk; *G.* bach. The Scandinavian origin of several names of places in Normandy is attested by the termination bec, as Caudebec, Beaubec, Robec, formerly Rodebec (*N.* Rauðbekkr, *i. e.* Redbrook), Briquebec, &c. ?

SÓL was the personified sunna (sun). There seems to have been a similar relation between the *M. G.* sáuil and sunnó.

SÓN, very dt. etym. Grimm remarks that it has a radical affinity with the *Anc. G.* suona, *emendatio.* F. Mag., who never hesitates to make a word taily with a favourite theory, explains it to mean sound, song, *sonus, cantus.*

SURTUR, prop. SURTR, gen. SURTAR. Grimm is decidedly of opinion that surtr is, if not exactly correlative, at least radically cog. with svartr; *Sw.* svart; *D.* sort; *M. G.* svarts; *G.* schwartz; *E.* swart, swarth [*].

SUTTÚNGR, may prob. be a corruption of súptúngr, sipping-tongue, from v. súpa; *Sw.* supa; *D.* suppe, sibe; *G.* saufen; *A. S.* supan; *E.* to sup, and to sip: túnga; *D.* tunge; *G.* zunge; *A. S.* tunge; *E.* tongue.

SVAÐILFARI: svaðil, ph. from svaði, lubricity, also slippery ice : fari, from the v. fara. *See* Naglfar.

SVAFNIR, prob. from v. svefa, to cast asleep; whence sub. svefn, svafn, sleep, quiet, repose; cog. with *D.* sövn; with obs. *L.* sopnus, and prob. with *Sk.* svapal.

---

[*] Finn Magnusen also admits this derivation, but as it clashes with his favourite theory, (see page 484,) he does not hesitate to explain swart to mean obscure, invisible; and invisible, unintelligible ! ! and thus, *malgré* his swarthiness, Surtur, according to Finn Magnusen's notions, the invisible, unintelligible being whom the ancient Scandinavians regarded as "the great First Cause least understood" of all things,

SVALINN, the Refrigerating· svalr, frigid; from the v. svala; *D.* svale, to cool, to refrigerate.

SVARTÁLFAHEIMR, lit. Black or Swart Elves' home, *i. e.* the region of the Elves of Darkness in contradistinction to that of the Elves of Light.

SVARTHÖFÐI, Black-head: svartr, black, swart: höfuð; *Sw.* hufvud; *D.* hoved; *M. G.* haubith; *G.* haupt; *A. S.* heáfod; *E.* head.

SVÁSUTHR, or SVÁSUÐR, Sweet-south: svá, from svás, blithe, jocund, dear; *M. G.* svés; *G.* süss; *A. S.* swæs (dear); *E.* sweet: suðr, suthr, south.

SVAUL, from svalr. *See* Svalinn.

SVIÐR and SVIÐRIR, from v. sviða, to scorch; or from sviðr, svithr, wise, powerful. *See* Fjölsvidr.

SVIPALL, prob. from v. svipa, to hasten, to vibrate; cog. with v. svifa; *D.* svæve; *G.* schweben, to wave, to hover; also with *E.* v. to sweep.

SVÖL, from svalr. *See* Svalinn.

SYLGR. As both the *N.* sub. sylgr and svelgr sig. a draught or deglutition, this word is prob. derived from v. svelgja; *Sw.* svälja; *D.* svælge; *A. S.* swolgen; *E.* to swallow, to swill; cog. with *G.* schwelgen, to guzzle, to feast.

SYN. The E. E. derive this from v. synja, to deny; but Grimm remarks that in *M. G.* a fine distinction was drawn between sunja, truth, and sunjó, defence, or proof of truth, *probatio veritatis*. This is also the case in *N.* sannr, signifying equity; syn. defence, excuse, negation, impediment, which has been personified into a judicial goddess, Syn.

SÝNIR, having a fine appearance; being prob. from sýn; *D.* syn; *G.* gesicht; *E.* sight; *N.* v. sjá; *D.* see; *M. G.* saihvan; *G.* sehen; *A. S.* seón; *E.* to see.

TANNGNIÓSTR, Gnashing-teeth: tann, from tönn, *see* Slidrugtanni: gnióstr, from v. gnísta, to bruise, crack, grind, gnash.

TANNGRISNIR, from tönn, *see* Slidrugtanni; and grisinn, rare, or at intervals.

THEKKR, prob. from the v. thekkja, to know; cog. with v. thenkja; *D.* tænke; *G.* denken; *A. S.* thencan; *E.* to think. The adj. thekkr means also amiable.

THJÓÐNUMA, from thjóð, pl. thjóðir, men, people, nations; *M. G.* thjuda; *A. S.* theód : and v. nema, to take; cog. with *G.* nehmen; *A. S.* numen.

THOR, prop. THÓRR : dt. etym., though Grimm thinks that it is a contraction of Thonar, a word which, as indicating a God who, like Thor, presided over *thunder* and atmospherical phenomena, would correspond to a *M. G.* Thunrs; *Old Sx.* Thunar; *A. S.* Thunor. *See* Thundr. Thór enters into the composition of a great number of Scandinavian proper names, both male and female, as Thórvaldr, Thór-finnr, Thórsteinn, Thorgerð (Thorgerda), Thóra, Thórdís (Thordisa), &c.*

THORINN, from thor, audacity; whence the v. thora; *Sw.* töras (torde); *D.* turde (tör); *M. G.* dauran; *G.* dürfen (darf); *A. S.* durron; *E.* to dare.

THRÁINN, the Pertinacious; from the v. thrá, to desire vehemently.

THRIDI, prop. THRIÐI, *The Third.*

THRÓR, ph. from v. thróa, to increase, to amplify.

THRÚÐGELMIR. *See* Thrúður and Aurgelmir.

THRÚÐUR. Thrúðr is an obsolete *N.* word signifying fortitude, firmness; but it appears to have originally had, in most of the Teutonic languages, the sig. of maiden, virgin; and hence enters into the composition of proper names, as Himildrúd, Mimidrúd, Gérdrúd (*Gertrude*), and was afterwards used in the sense of witch, sorceress; as in *D.* Drude, Drut; *G.* Trude, Drude.

THRÚÐVÁNGR, the Abode or Region of Fortitude. *See* Thrúður and Fólkvángr.

THRYM, very dt. etym. F. Mag., who delights in *conjectural* etym., says the word is *undoubtedly* derived from thruma, thunder.

THRYMHEIMR. *See* Thrym and Gladsheimr.

THULR. *See* Fimbulthul.

THUNDR, can be derived from thund, a breastplate, a coat of mail; or from the v. thenja, to spread out, cog. with *G.* dehnen; or from the obs. v. thynja; *A. S.* thunian, thundian; *E.* to thunder; whence the *I.* duna; *Sw.* tordön; *D.* torden; *G.* donner; *A. S.* thuner; *E.* thunder.

THYN, ph. from the obs. v. thynja, more recent dynja, to thunder, to make a thundering noise, as a rapid current does. The *E.* word din is cog. with this v., and ph. also the names of several rivers, as the Tyne in England, the Dvina in Russia, &c.

TYR, prop. TÝR. Grimm has satisfactorily shown that the *Sk.* Djaus, gen. Divas; *Gr.* Ζεύς, gen. Διός; *M. G.* Tius, gen. Tivis; *N.* Týr, gen. Týs; are cog. words signifying God; as well as the *L.* Jupiter, for which he assumes a nom. Ju or Juz, Jupiter—Jus pater.

ULLUR, or ULLR. F. Mag. thinks this word may be derived from ull; *D.* uld; *G.* wolle; *A. S.* wull; *E.* wool.

URD, VERDANDI, and SKULD, prop. URÐR (Urður), VERÐANDI, and SKULD; the Present, Past, and Future. The names of the Des-

---

* Not wishing to depart too much from established usage, and an accented vowel being, moreover, the *bête noire* of English printers, we did not venture to accent the *o* in these proper names which occur so frequently in our Supplementary Chapters. We must remind the reader, however, that the *o* in such words should be pronounced long, like *o* in more.

tinies of the Present and Past are derived from the verb verða (Part. Pres. verðandi; Part. Past orðinn); D. vorde; G. werden; A. S. weor-ðan, to become. Skuld has her name from the Part. Past, skuld, of the verb skula; Sw. skola; A. S. sculon : in the Pres. tense skal; Sw. skall; D. skal; A. S. sceal; E. shall : in the Past tense skyldi; Sw. skulle; D. skulde; A. S. sceolde; E. should. Grimm remarks that the names of the three Destinies would have been in M. G. Vaúrths, Vaírthandei, and Skulds; and in Anc. G. Wurt, Werdandi, and Scult. The A. S. Wyrð, is like Urd, a Fate or Destiny, the pl. Wyrðas corresponding to the N. Urðir, Norns, Parcœ, or Destinies; hence our word weird, and the "Weird Sisters" of Shakspeare *.

UTGARD, prop. UTGARÐR, lit. Outer-ward. See Midgard.

VAFTHRÚÐNIR : vaf, from the v. vefa, to involve, prop. to weave; hence cog. with D. væve; M. G. vaibjan; G. weben; A. S. wefan; E. to weave : thrúðnir, see Thrúður.

VAFUÐR, the Weaver, or the Constrainer. See the foregoing word.

VAKR, VAKUR, alert, lively, vigilant, corresponding in this sense to the D. vakker; G. wacker. The root is in the v. vaka; D. vaage; G. wachen; A. S. wacian; E. to watch; also A. S. weccan; E. to waken.

VALASKJALF : vala, prob. from val; D. valg; G. wahl, choice, elec-tion : skjálf, see Hliðskjálf.

VALFAÐIR, or VALFÖÐUR, lit. the Choosing Father : val, choice, see the preceding word : faðir, father.

VALHALLA, prop. VALHÖLL, lit. the Hall of the Chosen : val, choice, see Valfaðir : höll; M. G. hallus; Old G. halla; G. halle; A. S. heal, hæll; E. hall, originally sig. a temple, another word for which in the N., Old G., Old Sx., and A. S. languages, wàs hof. See page 289. The N. word salr; Anc. G. sal; Old Sx. seli; A. S. sele; may also have originally indicated a temple. See Fensalir.

VALKYRJOR, or VALKYRJUR, sing. VALKYRJA (in the old orthog. Valkyrior), lit. Choosers of the Slain. The N. valr; Anc. G. wal; A. S. wæl, denoted the slain in battle; whence the D. Valplads; G. Wahl-platz (lit. the place of the slain), a poetical word for a field of battle : kyrja, from the v. kjöra; A. S. curon; Anc. G. küren, to choose. From the Anc. G. v. küren is the mod. G. part. erkoren, chosen, elected; and kur, or chur, expressing the Electoral dignity, as Churfürst, lit. Elected Prince. It may be remarked that such L. words as Bellona, Alecto, &c., and even Parca and Venefica, were rendered in A. S. by Wælcyrge and

---

* The reader will find a great deal of curious information respecting Norns, Fairies, and the White Ladies of the Middle Ages, in the 16th chap-ter of Grimm's Deut. Mythol. Our word fairy is from the French fée, and Grimm observes that from the L. word fatum was formed the It. fata; Span. hada; Provençal, fada; and F. fée : fata and fée having the same analogy of derivation as nata and née, amata and aimée.

Wælcyrre. Grimm concludes that the *M. G.* form would have been Vala-kusjó.

VANADÍS, prop. a Goddess of the Vanir. *See* that word, and Dís.

VANAHEIMR. *See* Vanir and Gladsheimr.

VANIR, the sing. would be Vanr; a word of dt. origin: the E. E. think that it may be cog. with *N.* vænn, beautiful; with the *L.* venustus and Venus, and ph. with the *E. wench;* but this etym. is too *conjectural* to be of much value.

VARR, prob. sig. wary. *See* Andvari.

VASAÐR, from vás, moisture, a word cog. with the *E.* wet and wash.

VE. Grimm has shown that the *N.* ve was used in the m. sing. to express a particular god; that in the pl. it would be vear, gods, idols; and that the n. pl. ve indicated sacred places, *loca sacra.* He also shows that the word is cog. with the *Anc. G.* wih, a grove; *Old Sx.* wih, a temple; and expresses an idea fluctuating between nemus, templum, fanum, idolum, and numen. Its root must be sought in the *M. G.* veihan; *G.* weihen, to consecrate. *See* the note, page 291.

VEÐURFÖLNIR might be rendered Storm-stilling; vedur being derived from veðr; *D.* væir; *G.* wetter; *A. S.* weder; *E.* weather: and fölnir, prob. from v. fela, to cover, to conceal; hence concealing the weather, or causing serenity.

VEGSVINN, lit. Road-knowing: vegr; *D.* vej; *M. G.* vigs; *G.* and *A. S.* weg; *E.* way: svinn, from svinnr (svithr), wise, cog. with *M. G.* svinths. *See* Fjölsvidr.

VEGTAMR. *See* note, page 373.

VERATYR, lit. the Man-god: vera, from verr, a man, cog. with numerous words in the *Ind. E.* languages, as *M. G.* vair; *Sl.* vyras; *Sk.* viroh; *L.* vir, &c.: týr, *see* Týr.

VERDANDI. *See* Urd.

VESTRI, west, occidental.

VÍÐ, from viðr; *D.* vid; *G.* weit; *A. S.* wíd; *E.* wide.

VIDAR, prop. VIÐAR, ph. from viðr, a tree; cog. with *E.* wood; and prob. also with weed and withy.

VÍÐBLÁINN, expanded azure (lit. Wide-blue): víð, *see* VÍÐ: bláinn, from blár; *D.* blaa; *G.* blau; *A. S.* blæw; *E.* blue.

VÍÐFINNR, prob. from viðr, wide, vast; and finnr, from v. finna; *D.* finde; *M. G.* finthan; *G.* finden; *A. S.* findan; *E.* to find.

VIÐÓLFR, or VIÐÁLFR, lit. Sylvan Elf: vid, from viðr, a tree, *see* Vidar: álfr, an elf.

VIÐRIR, Moderator of the weather; from v. viðra, to still the weather; and this from veðr, weather. *See* Veðurfölnir.

VIGRID, prop. VÍGRÍÐ, from víg, a battle; *A. S.* wíg (whence wígcræft battle craft, the art of war): ríð, from v. ríða; *D.* ride; *G.* reiten; *A. S.* rídan; *E.* to ride.

VILI, Will. The *N.* vili, vilji, like the *Anc. G.* willo, expressed not only *voluntas,* but also *votum impetus* and *spiritus;* and Grimm remarks that the *M. G.* v. viljan, to will, is nearly related to the v. valjan, to choose, to elect. *See* Valkyrjor.

VILMEITHR, or VILMEIÐR, from vil, favour, cog. with vili: and meiðr, an old word for tree.

VIN, and VINA, prob. from vinr, a friend, cog. with v. unna, to love, to favour; *A. S.* unnan, to give, to bestow; and the *E.* winsome.

VINDÁLFR, Wind Elf: vindr; *D.* vind; *G., A. S.,* and *E.* wind.

VINDSVALR; vindr, wind: and svalr, cold, glacial.

VINGÓLF, lit. the Abode of Friends: vinr, a friend, *see* Vin: gólf means lit. a floor; *D.* gulv.

VITUR, VITR, from vit; *G.* witz; *E.* wit. *See* Grafvitnir.

VÖLUNDR. The *N.* Völundr is the Velint of the Vilkina-saga; the *G.* Wielant, Wieland; the *A. S.* Weland, Welond (Wayland). The root of the word is the *N.* vél, art, skill, craft, cunning; cog. with the *A. S.* wil; *E.* wile and guile. Grimm remarks that we must presuppose an *Old G.* v. wielan; *A. S.* welan, to fabricate, the part. of which would be wielant and weland. This would be a more grammatical derivation than that of Prof. Müller, who derives the word from vél, art; and lundr, mind. At all events the word denotes a skilful artificer, in which sense it is still used by the Icelanders, *hann er völundr à járn;* he is a famous workman—a Wayland—in iron; and they very appropriately term a labyrinth a Wayland-house—*Völundarhús. See* the note, page 376.

VÖLUSPÁ. The *Old N.* has two generic terms for a sybil or prophetess—Völva and Vala, gen. Völu, which Grimm remarks would correspond to an *Old G.* Walawa or Wala. The word vala is prob. cog. with val, choice. *See* Valfadir and Valkyrjor. The *N.* spá, is cog. with and has the same sig. as the Scotch spae. See the note, page 363.

VÖRA, prop. VÖR, gen. VARAR; prob. the same root as Varr.

YGGDRASILL, very dt. etym. F. Mag. is of opinion that it may be derived either from ý, cog. with úr, moisture, rain; whence yg, ygg, was afterwards formed, and drasill, from the v. draga, to carry (prob. cog. with the *G.* tragen, and the *E.* to drag) ; or from Ygg, one of Odin's names (*see* the following word), and drasill, bearing; hence, according to F. Mag., it would sig. bearing (producing) rain, or bearing Odin.

YGGR. This name of Odin is prob. from the v. yggja, which sig. to meditate, and also to fear; hence the word might be rendered by either the Meditating or the Terrible. Yggr, in the *N.* lang., means simply, terror.

ÝLG, the Howling; prob. from v. ýla; *D.* hyle; *G.* heulen; *E.* to howl.

YMIR: very dt. etym. ymr sig. a confused noise,. like the rustling of trees when shaken by the wind; also the clang of metals; but whether the proper orthog. be Ymir, Ýmir, Imir or Ímir, the etym. given by the E. E. are alike conjectural. Grimm is inclined to derive it from the v. ymja, umði which has the same sig. as the v. gjalla, to roar, to clang.

INDEX.

ERRATA.